Kirklees
COUNCIL

The Uncommon Reader

The Uncommon Reader

A Life of Edward Garnett

HELEN SMITH

JONATHAN CAPE
LONDON

1 3 5 7 9 10 8 6 4 2

Jonathan Cape, an imprint of Vintage Publishing,
20 Vauxhall Bridge Road,
London SW1V 2SA

Jonathan Cape is part of the Penguin Random House group of com panies whose
addresses can be found at global.penguinrandomhouse.com

First published by Jonathan Cape in 2017

penguin.co.uk/vintage

A CIP catalogue record for this book is available from the British Library

ISBN 9780224081818

Typeset in India by Integra Software Services Pvt. Ltd, Pondicherry

Printed and bound in Great Britain by Clays Ltd, St Ives PLC

Penguin Random House is committed to a sustainable future for
our business, our readers and our planet. This book is made
from Forest Stewardship Council® certified paper.

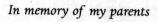

In memory of my parents

CONTENTS

I

A literary family

'For you into whose hands this document may come, I write these words, as a testimony from us who now lie dead & forgotten.'[1] The parchment containing these words (or some very similar) has yet to be read; since 1 September 1895 it has nestled in a carefully hollowed-out hole in a cornerstone of The Cearne, near Edenbridge in Kent, the house built by Edward and Constance Garnett, alongside 'various little articles which might be of antiquarian interest in centuries to come'.[2] Fortunately anyone curious to discover more about the founders of The Cearne will not have to wait for some calamitous event to reduce the house to a pile of rubble; a rough draft of the document in Edward Garnett's hand survives. In it he briefly details the building of The Cearne and the origin of its name ('the original name of the meadow, signifying, in Old French – a circle'), before going on to sketch its inhabitants, beginning with himself: 'in 1895 Edward Garnett was a little known writer & poet, a man of twenty seven, tall in height, of an idle temperament, careless of reputation, witty of speech, a real lover of the open air, literature & art, a scorner of trade [sic] industry.' While there is a touch of light-hearted self-deprecation in the portrait, Garnett revealingly selects the characteristics – and occupation – ('little known' was added as an afterthought) for which he would like to be remembered. At that time he had been 'reader' for the publisher T. Fisher Unwin for eight years and was currently greatly excited by one of Unwin's new authors, Joseph Conrad. Yet despite the lukewarm and in some cases hostile reviews of his own literary efforts, which then comprised two novels and a book of prose poems, in 1895 it was as a writer that Edward Garnett wished to make his name.

Given Garnett's firm belief in heredity ('that's the old Willoughby horse-thief strain coming out in her,' he reputedly announced, 'with all the gravity of Mr Shandy',[3] when a female house guest helped herself to a book), perhaps he would not be surprised to learn that, just like his father before him, he is principally remembered as one of literature's great enablers.

Richard Garnett was born on 27 February 1835 at Lichfield; his father, also named Richard, was a minor canon in the cathedral. The senior Richard Garnett (1789–1850) originally hailed from West Yorkshire, where his father William (1760–1832) managed the family paper mill on the river Wharfe near Otley. William's eleven offspring appear to have been a talented lot, and it soon became apparent that his eldest son Richard had a particular linguistic flair. After eight years in the paper mill, during which he studied languages in his spare time, Richard senior trained for the Church. His brother Jeremiah (1793–1870) was apprenticed to a printer in Barnsley and then worked on *Wheeler's Manchester Chronicle* before becoming the first printer, publisher and reporter on the fledgling *Manchester Guardian*. Initially his skills as a printer were much in evidence – he helped devise a machine that increased the rate of printing from 300 to 1,500 copies of the paper an hour – but in later years his interest became literary and editorial. In 1844 Jeremiah assumed the editorship of the paper for which his great-nephew Edward would eventually write.

In 1836 Richard senior moved with his second wife Jane (his first wife Margaret died in 1828) and their young son Richard to the living at Chebsey, a village near Stafford. A second son, William John, was born on 28 July that year. By this time Richard senior had established a reputation in the new field of philology and was keen to exercise his erudition in more promising intellectual pastures than Chebsey could offer. When in 1838 he was offered the post of Assistant Keeper of Printed Books at the British Museum he accepted with alacrity and resigned from the Church. The family moved to Burton Crescent just off the Euston Road in London and in 1840 Richard's final child Ellen Rayne was born. Ellen, who was referred to as 'Auntie Cuckoo' by her nephews and nieces, became a governess for a time. Her pupils included Osbert Sitwell's father Sir George and his sister Florence. Poor Ellen was remarkably plain: according to Osbert, her ugliness 'triumphed over the term and became raised to the level of a Chinese grotesque'.[4] Nevertheless she inspired affection in her charges and was invited to Christmas dinner with the elder Sitwells in Scarborough every year after her retirement. Ellen's brother William John, who was a lifelong practical joker and like his nephew Edward a great tease, drifted from job to job and country to country. Whether working as a consular agent in Egypt, a miner in Colorado or a music critic in Australia he was usually in pecuniary straits and a source of minor concern to his family. It was Richard who inherited his father's linguistic abilities and scholarly aptitude and it was he who would elevate the Garnett name in literary circles.

By 1850 Richard senior's health had deteriorated to the extent that he was granted leave of absence from the British Museum and returned to Otley with his family, enrolling young Richard and William John in Whalley Grammar School just months before he died in September. His family was left with £750, a reasonable sum, but it was clear that extra income would be required and so a university education was out of the question for either of the boys. Exactly who approached the Italian political exile Antonio Panizzi, Keeper of Printed Books at the Museum, about a possible post for the young Richard is unclear, but Richard senior had been aware of the gravity of his illness and may well have set the wheels in motion. Panizzi, who had a great regard for Richard senior, directed all his considerable powers of persuasion towards the Museum's trustees and just weeks after his sixteenth birthday young Richard joined the staff as an assistant in the department of Printed Books.

Richard Garnett junior never forgot Panizzi's act of kindness. 'One of my father's marked characteristics was lively gratitude,' his daughter Olive recalled years later. 'As an Italian exile, Antonio Panizzi, had befriended him, so, henceforth, he would likewise endeavour to assist political exiles.'[5] Richard stayed true to his resolution and a string of European political refugees, including Karl Marx, were to benefit from his assistance and generosity. In the years following his appointment to the British Museum, Richard read voraciously, contributed numerous articles to various journals and newspapers, continued to study languages, produced several translations and wrote poems, whilst at the same time working assiduously in the library. For the first ten years of his career he was a 'placer', allocating newly acquired books to the correct division of the library (which then had no complete subject catalogue). At the very least this required a swift perusal of each new volume, and Richard's memory was such that it was said he never forgot the contents or location of any book he had 'placed'. Richard's interest in Shelley scholarship led to his becoming a friend of Lady Shelley, the poet's daughter-in-law; unfortunately he also fell in with her attempts to sanitise Shelley in order to make him fit for Victorian consumption. This error of judgement apart, Richard became known among generations of library readers for his benevolence, helpfulness, prodigious memory and unrivalled knowledge of books.

Photographs of Richard Garnett reveal a square-faced young man with a high forehead, short nose and dark hair, cut in the rather unbecoming fashion of the day. He was tall and early developed a stoop. Later on he grew a beard and adopted round, gold-rimmed glasses. Careless of dress, he 'stuffed his pockets with books; badly folded newspapers, whole packets of letters: & remains of sandwich lunches'.[6] His hands were slim-fingered and as shapely as a woman's, an attribute he passed on to his son Edward. Richard's speech betrayed slight signs of his Yorkshire origins; 'he is the only man I ever knew,' wrote his obituarist, 'who really talked like a book. His sentences flowed on, unhesitatingly, in lengthy periods, all the commas and semi-colons almost visible to the eye.'[7] Garnett had an ironic and sarcastic turn of wit, but it was never directed against individuals; by midlife his mellowness had reached the point where it was reputed that the hardest thing he said of anybody was 'she doesn't like cats'[8] – a more serious indictment than first appears given Richard's passion for felines. His other great enthusiasm (perhaps not remarkable considering the late Victorians' interest in the occult and spiritualism, although it surprised many of his contemporaries in such an otherwise learned man) was astrology. Richard cast numerous horoscopes of the great and the good and penned astrological articles under the anagrammatic pseudonym A. G. Trent.

The British Museum offered many opportunities to gain an entrée into new social circles and Richard's network of friends rapidly expanded. By the time his career became fully established there were few people in literary London he did not know. The young men working at the Museum were seen as a useful fund of potential dancing partners when the ladies of the neighbourhood were organising dances for their daughters. It was in this capacity that Richard attended a dance in a house near Camden Square in 1859 where he became captivated by the daughter of his hostess's next-door neighbour, a young lady of seventeen whom he sat beside 'and talked [to] very fast, and in such low tones that I could hardly hear about poetry'.[9]

Olivia Narney Singleton was born in 1842 in County Waterford of an Anglo-Irish family. Her grandson David rather romantically describes Narney (as she was always known) as coming from a line of 'warm-hearted, passionate, lavish, open-handed libertines and duellists'.[10] Her father had suffered a mental breakdown and as a result her mother brought Narney and her younger brother Edward to England to continue their education. Like many Anglo-Irish boys, Edward was destined for the army, where he eventually attained the rank of major. Mrs Singleton, the two children and their nurse Christina Chapple, set up house near Camden Square. Narney was a girl of considerable wit and vivaciousness, and she clearly charmed the twenty-four-year-old Richard Garnett, who, on the occasion of their engagement three years later, wrote to his brother William John extolling her virtues:

She is rather tall and slender, with a corresponding contour of face, delicate complexion, brown eyes and hair, prominent forehead and an elegant profile approaching the retroussé ... Though not regularly handsome, she would, I think, be generally considered graceful and pleasing, but of course you will allow for a lover's partiality. Her manners are in general quiet and somewhat reserved, but she can summon up a good deal of Irish vivacity on occasion ... She is clever and well-educated, fond of reading and music; ... she speaks and writes French very well, and has more or less acquaintance with several other languages.[11]

After that first dance Richard escorted Narney home. The front door was opened by Chapple, who, on closing it, turned to her young charge and exclaimed delightedly, 'And is that himself, Miss Narney?'[12]

The relationship blossomed and on 11 April 1860 Richard proposed to Narney as they sat by the fire with her cat between them. 'Puss, does your mistress love me?' enquired the nervous suitor, to which the reply came, 'Puss, she does.'[13] Mrs Singleton, however, considered her daughter too young for any serious commitment and removed Narney to Geneva, where her brother was studying French and German. Eighteen months later mother and daughter returned to London to find Richard, undaunted, on the doorstep of some close friends enquiring as to their whereabouts. A second proposal this time met with maternal approval and the couple were married on 13 June 1863 at St Mark's Church, Regent's Park.

Richard and Narney rented a recently built four-storey brick house in St Edmund's Terrace on the north-west corner of Regent's Park, just across from London Zoo. Number 4 (it was later renumbered 3) faced fields and the West Middlesex waterworks. The Primrose Hill area in which it stood was popular with artists and literary figures, attracted by its relative tranquillity and the feeling that it was out of town. Ford Madox Brown, the Pre-Raphaelite painter, moved into 1 St Edmund's Terrace in 1887. Mrs Singleton lived at St Edmund's Terrace with Richard and Narney until her death in 1876, as did Chapple, who became Narney's maid and nurse to her six surviving children. May, the eldest, was named after the month of her birth in 1864; Robert followed in March 1866 and just under two years later, on 5 January 1868, came Edward William. Olivia Rayne, always known as Olive, was born in 1871 and another daughter, Lucy, arrived in 1875. In 1877 Narney gave birth to her third son, Richard Copley. He rapidly developed tuberculosis and died at the age of eight months in February 1878. Arthur, the much loved baby of the family, was born in 1881. At the age of six he developed a severe speech impediment, which he never lost, but inspired deep and lasting affection in all who knew him. 'All the Garnetts had a talent for friendship,' his niece later wrote. 'In Arthur it amounted to genius. He made and kept friends in every corner of the globe.'[14]

As it so happened, the temperamental traits of the Garnett children seemed to divide along lines of seniority. In a letter to John Galsworthy in which he sketches his family history, Edward dismisses his elder siblings, May and Robert, as 'sensible, practical, ordinary', but groups Olive, Lucy and Arthur altogether more approvingly under the headings 'independent' and 'critical'.[15] 'I look on Robert as a *very* good fellow, honest & not unintelligent, but lacking in all those finer subtler shades of perception – which in my view constitute "good judgment",' Edward later elaborated to Galsworthy. 'Robert looks on me as a most dangerous individual! Not to be relied on for one instant; well-meaning, but weak – with ability of a sort, but likely to plunge himself or others, any moment into hot water!'[16] Edward was closest to Olive as a child and retained that affection into adulthood, even though, despite her brother's urgings to the contrary, Olive became increasingly disinclined to challenge the conventionality that was so marked in pretty, pious May: 'Why I feel so passionate about Olive in rare moments is that I understand she has *eaten* fate, and has not had the colour of life, and has not *arrived* at the many things that have come to me,'[17] Edward once bemoaned. That impulse to challenge authority and custom may have been derived from his father's fierce (if the word can be used in association with such an essentially benign character) unworldliness and his positive discouragement of what society might term 'success'.

In some respects the Garnetts were quite a traditional Victorian family. Servants ensured domestic orderliness, and although Olive remembered there being 'no discipline in the ordinary sense'[18] a word from Richard at times of youthful over-exuberance produced 'instant and continuous silence'. Most of the time, however, 4 St Edmund's Terrace reverberated to the sound of heated arguments amongst the various siblings, with each disputant convinced he or she was in the right. Edward never lost that implacable confidence in his own opinion where literary matters were concerned – to the discomfort and occasional fury of many of his authors.

Every summer Narney would depart with her brood to seaside resorts such as Swanage or Southsea, where Richard would sometimes join them for the latter part of the holiday. Excursions to the nearby London Zoo were a regular feature of life at St Edmund's Terrace and fondly recalled by Olive, although she would have been too young to remember one autumn night of destruction in the city.

At five o'clock on the morning of Friday 2 October 1874 a barge carrying five tons of gunpowder exploded under the bridge by the North Gate of Regent's Park. The three barge crew and their horses were killed instantly and extensive damage was caused to property within the radius of a mile, including the animal houses at the zoo. Every window in 3 St Edmund's Terrace was blown in, with the exception of those in Narney's bedroom, but luckily none of the family was injured. The next morning the Garnett children were taken out by Chapple into the nut-strewn streets (a large quantity of Brazil nuts and almonds had been stored over the explosives) to view the devastation. The young Garnetts pocketed the spoils, oblivious to Chapple's repeated warnings about shards of glass. All over the weekend crowds of sightseers flocked to the park: 'the publicans and tobacconists would not be sorry to lose their windows on such terms every week,'[19] *The Times* remarked wryly. So momentous was the event that in the evening the children were allowed to come down after Richard's return from the Museum to listen as he read out accounts of the explosion from assorted newspapers.

Richard was a great reader of the press – he scoured the morning paper in the street as he walked to work, holding it out in front of him with one hand whilst clutching his ubiquitous umbrella and bag with the other – and he seems to have passed this enthusiasm on to Edward, who in October 1880 started the *Cats Newspaper*. This charming production announced itself as 'A Newspaper for Cats and for promotion of their welfare – Motto – *Cave Canem*', and declared itself to be 'of Moderate Liberal Politics'. Each week various topical news stories would be spun from a feline angle, occasionally accompanied by delightful illustrations by Uncle William John. Thus in the first edition of 20 October 1880 the 'Food' column carries the following report:

We are very sorry to hear that the Hull fishermen have struck. They are dissatisfied because they are in the winter compelled to remain at sea for longer periods than formally [*sic*] now that steam cutters have been established to carry the fish from the fishing grounds, without any extra pay. We are affraid [*sic*] that our cousins will miss their fish and pickings sadly.[20]

News from Ireland features particularly prominently; this partly reflects the extensive coverage surrounding the Home Rule debate in the national press, but it is also an early indication of Edward's lifelong interest in Ireland and his intense pride in his maternal Irish ancestry, evident in the edition of 5 November 1880:

> The Times considering the question 'What is to be done with Ireland' remarks that whatever may be the cause of the present agitation we have to face a state of things in Ireland which reasonable men, almost with unanimous voice declare to be intolerable. It is true the Editor of this paper is sorry for Ireland (his mother country he is partly descended (proud of it) in a direct line from Brian Baroo (who as our readers all know was one of the celebrated Irish kings). He feels this sort of thing <u>Cannot Go On.</u> "Think of the homeless cats, think of their murdered masters. Think of homeless families" think of wickedness and vice which is now coming for Ireland (O My Country) a dreadful name. And think above all of Charles Stuart Parnell. Think of this man, who even now may be stirring up the worst dregs of the Irish.
>
> <u>Notice</u>
>
> In consequence of the writer's feelings, he is not answerable for his writing or spelling in this article.[21]

The mature editor, who half a century later had a spat with Sean O'Faolain over what he considered to be the Irishman's overly negative portrayal of Parnell in an unpublished play, would have found his own youthful misspelling a lot easier to excuse than those last couple of sentences.

In another article, on 'Bad Literature', the editor deplores the 'weak trashy papers for boys', with the honourable exceptions of the *Boys' Own Paper* and the *Union Jack*. He then lays into the stories in the *Boys' World* in tones not dissimilar to those he would adopt in reader's reports for T. Fisher Unwin (the royal 'we' is already in evidence): 'a blood thirsty tale, with no apparent plot ... the tale is as badly written as it is absurd ... we do not know who Timothy Giggle may be, but we do not think much of his literary powers.'[22]

Each edition of the *Cats Newspaper* must have cost no small effort to produce: the contents were extensive and included 'Correspondence',

'Social Gleanings' and amusing feline 'Situations Vacant'. The last number
appeared on 27 June 1881. Perhaps Edward decided to cease production then because he wanted a good couple of months' holiday, for in
September he was off to a new school.

There is no record of Edward's education prior to his admittance to
the City of London School. Robert had been to St Marylebone and All
Souls Grammar School, at the corner of Cornwall Terrace and Regent's
Park, before graduating to the City of London School in September
1879, and Edward may have followed in his brother's footsteps. At that
time the school was housed in a 'crowded, ill-ventilated and insanitary'[23]
building in Milk Street in the centre of the City of London; it would
move to the Embankment in 1883. The headmaster, Dr Edwin Abbott,
was a Shakespearean scholar and a passionate advocate of English literature; various Old Citizens left glowing testimonials of his inspirational
teaching. However, Edward's scholastic record was unremarkable: he
was chiefly remembered by his contemporaries, including the future
Manchester Guardian journalist C. E. Montague and the illustrator Arthur
Rackham, for his spin bowling – 'bowls fairly at times; poor bat; too
loose and straggling in the field'[24] was the verdict of the school's cricket
correspondent – and his sharp tongue. Montague later described Edward
as 'the greatest teaze in the School'.[25] Three incidents remained in
Edward's memory long after he left the City of London: taking on and
beating the school bully, being set upon by his fellows in the athletics
team for not winning a race against another school, and having to give
up first prize on another occasion in favour of the prize-giver's son,
who had finished second. The injustice of this last incident rankled for
the rest of his life.

Edward's academic career was uninspiring, but his father's contribution
to the furtherance of knowledge received official scholarly recognition
in 1883 when Richard Garnett was made an Honorary Doctor of Laws
by Edinburgh University. Dr Richard, as he was henceforth known –
somewhat to his embarrassment – had been promoted to Superintendent
of the British Museum Reading Room eight years earlier. The guest
list for the 'At Home' evenings given by Narney on Thursdays featured
many readers who had sought Richard's assistance at the Museum and
subsequently become close friends, including Coventry Patmore, George
Meredith, Samuel Butler and the Pre-Raphaelite artist William Michael
Rossetti. The social circle of the young Garnetts centred on the children
and grandchildren of their parents' friends. Rossetti's daughters Helen

and Olive became great pals of the more junior Garnetts, and Ford Madox Brown's grandsons – the future novelist Ford Madox Hueffer (later Ford Madox Ford)* and his brother Oliver – were frequent visitors. Ford saw a great deal of the Garnett children while he was growing up and their friendship lasted well into adulthood. However, the relationship between the Garnett and Hueffer clans did not always run smoothly, as David Garnett recalls:

> There was a deep temperamental difference ... between the young Garnetts, who were sceptical, unworldly and over-critical, and the Hueffer boys, who were credulous, worldly (without being worldly-wise) and over-confident. The young Garnetts were inclined to regard the Hueffer boys as half egregious asses and half charlatans. The Hueffers, who originally respected the Garnetts, became more and more exasperated by their sceptical attitude and their strait-laced almost puritanical contempt for success and notoriety, which constituted the breath of romance for Ford and Oliver.[26]

In all probability the Garnett children inherited their scorn for worldly success from Richard, who Ford always revered as a near-mystical fount of learning. In this he was not alone. Richard was a well-known and universally popular figure and had attracted a devoted following of 'literary ladies', including the children's author Arabella Buckley, the German-born poet Mathilde Blind, whose brother had unsuccessfully attempted to assassinate Bismarck, and a woman named Frederika Macdonald, whom Olive Garnett was convinced exerted a strong influence over the teenage Edward. Frederika was in her early forties at the time; she had lived abroad extensively and was educated at the Pensionnat Héger in Brussels, where Charlotte Brontë had taught and fallen in love with the proprietor. Frederika Macdonald's husband John was a journalist on the *London Daily News* and, according to Olive, their fair-haired, blue-eyed daughter Katie became Edward's first love. Frederika wrote several books, ranging from novels to studies of Jean-Jacques Rousseau, of whose teachings she was an ardent disciple. In a letter to her nephew David, Olive

---

* Ford Madox Hueffer changed his surname to Ford in 1919. It has become usual to refer to him as Ford Madox Ford even when writing about him at the time when he was still known as Hueffer. This convention has been followed with the exception of those parts of the text that refer to D. H. Lawrence, who makes many references to him as Hueffer in his letters.

maintains that Frederika Macdonald 'imbued your father's opening mind with a thoroughgoing Rousseauism: which added to a cult for Shelley & Godwin led to intellectual indiscipline as a moral duty'.[27]

It was at this stage, Olive believed, that the temperamental differences between Edward and his two elder siblings became apparent and lasting. Robert had come under an opposing influence through his visits to his cousins, the Cumberlands, and he rapidly embarked on a steady career in the law, eventually becoming a partner in the solicitors' firm of Darley & Cumberland. However, when the seventeen-year-old Edward Garnett left the City of London School in July 1885 he had no such prospects on the horizon. In fact, he had nothing in view at all; both Edward and his father seemed blissfully unconcerned about his future. If one of Dr Richard's 'literary ladies' was culpable of fostering this disregard, then it was thanks to another that Edward stumbled onto his life's path.

Joining Unwin

Clementina Black was in her late twenties when she moved from the family home in Brighton, where she had been teaching and looking after her younger siblings, to join her sister Emma in London. For a brief time there were three Black sisters living at 26 Albany Street, near Regent's Park, when in 1882 eighteen-year-old Grace, the penultimate of the eight Black children, arrived in the capital to study art. Emma left to marry the Rev. James Dean Keriman Mahomed in September 1883, but less than a year later another Black sister, Constance Clara, came up to London from Cambridge, where she had spent a term lecturing in Classics at Newnham College, from which she had very recently graduated. Constance, then aged twenty-three, lodged in a room at Wrights Lane in Kensington, close to the home of Robert Owen White, a wealthy cement manufacturer whose daughters she was teaching. Shy and studious, Constance was fortunate to find that her sisters had already formed a network of friends eager to welcome her into their midst.

Clementina and Grace were frequent visitors to the British Museum: Clementina spent hours researching the historical novels she was writing, while Grace was often to be found there studying the Museum's art. The girls soon struck up a friendship with Richard Garnett and in the winter of 1885 or 1886[1] he asked Clementina to bring Constance over for Sunday tea at St Edmund's Terrace. Constance had already met May and Robert, but it was her initial encounter with Edward on that Sunday that remained sharply etched on her memory more than forty years later:

> To my surprise a very tall, very thin boy of eighteen walked in looking as though he had outgrown his clothes & his strength. With his very bright eyes, curly head, dimples & roguish expression, he was very charming. 'A kitten on the top of a maypole', was a happy description of him. He was at once shy & bold, & very amusing. I have never seen a face so full of mischief.[2]

The lanky eighteen-year-old was also noticeably struck, and lingered in the drawing room for the duration of the visit, a fact that did not pass unobserved: '"Edward hates visitors & always has tea in Chapple's room," the Black sisters were told.'[3] Soon afterwards Edward appeared at Constance's and Grace's new lodgings in Campden Hill, ostensibly with a message from his sister May. He stayed for hours, and afterwards the fair-haired, very beautiful Grace remarked to Constance, 'You say nobody looks at you when I am by, but there is someone with no eyes for anyone but you.'[4]

It is not difficult to understand why Edward was smitten. Like Grace, Constance was blue-eyed, fair-haired and 'tremendously attractive when happy'.[5] While Grace was the beauty of the family, Constance would probably have taken the prize for brains. She had won a scholarship to Newnham College and emerged with First Class Honours in the Classical Tripos. Since her arrival in London she had become interested in the newly formed Fabian Society and attended their meetings with George Bernard Shaw, whom she had met at 'The Club', to which she had been introduced by Clementina. Members of 'The Club' (founded in 1880 as The Men and Women's Club) met fortnightly; the meetings alternated between 'discussion', with various speakers often giving a paper, and 'social intercourse', usually musical evenings. This alternation between the convivial and the cerebral would have suited Constance, whose own moods were subject to similar oscillations. 'Connie had two sides to her character,' according to a close friend, '[either] she was very gay, almost frivolous & fond of dress, or else completely puritanical, which some days would come up so that there would be nothing else.'[6] That streak of austerity may have been inherited from her father David Black, a Brighton solicitor who exerted absolute authority over his children, all of whom were afraid of him. Constance attributed her 'frivolous' side to her maternal grandmother Lucy Patten, whose daughter Clara married David Black in 1849.

Constance was born on 19 December 1861, the sixth of a family of three boys and five girls. Her mother died when Constance was thirteen, by which time her father had been struck down by an illness that permanently deprived him of the use of his legs. Constance was devastated by Clara's death, and from thenceforth rejected religion. Life in the Black household without Clara became almost unremittingly depressing and Constance endured long periods of great unhappiness. The scholarship to Newnham College offered the seventeen-year-old Constance a tantalising chance of escape. She was the youngest girl in the college, but despite her extreme shyness and a chronic lack of money Constance made the most of the opportunities Cambridge offered her. She particularly revelled in the beauty of the buildings, and when she came to London began to gain a much stronger appreciation of literature and music, too. The narrow, constricted life of Brighton was a thing of the past, and although Constance was not enamoured of teaching, she was enjoying her independence in London and the assorted social, political and cultural activities opening up to her. The atmosphere and company of the St Edmund's Terrace drawing room that Sunday afternoon surely drew out the convivial side of her nature. The teenage Edward was entranced by this attractive, erudite, older woman who shared many of the Garnetts' intellectual interests. For her part, Constance found the roguish, witty, curly-headed boy a breath of fresh air; a delightful antidote to the oppressive, gloomy shadows that had dominated so much of her life.

That summer the three eldest Garnett children, together with the three youngest Black girls – Constance, Grace and Katie – as well as a young man called Beck, went for a walking tour of Sussex. Robert Garnett paired up with Katie, with whom he was at that time besotted; May attached herself to Beck, while Constance walked with Edward, leaving Grace to wander alone. The weather was beautiful, the countryside lovely and as Constance rather coyly phrased it in her memoir at the end of the five days 'Edward and I were great friends'.[7] Her original, but subsequently erased, comment – 'we were on much closer terms of friend[ship]' – may be more revealing.

The romance continued when the pair returned to London. Constance found Edward to be 'the most charming companion, amusing, fresh, original'.[8] They went for long rides on the tops of omnibuses together and in the evenings Constance persuaded Edward to accompany her to meetings of the Fabians and the Kelmscott House socialists. George Bernard Shaw, who once told David Garnett that he would have married Constance had his financial circumstances been better, enquired as to the identity of the 'pretty young man' who was now accompanying her to these meetings. Constance replied that he was 'a boy whose education I was undertaking'.[9] The boy, however, proved a somewhat recalcitrant pupil where political matters were concerned and refused to take subjects such as land nationalisation with anything like the seriousness Constance desired. He was far happier shifting furniture and decorating Constance's and Grace's new flat in Fitzroy Street (bedbugs had rapidly driven them out of Campden Hill) or whiling away the hours lounging with a book on the hearthrug in front of the fire at St Edmund's Terrace.

Edward's increasingly regular presence at 7 Fitzroy Street did not go unnoticed. According to Constance, Clementina became worried at her younger sister's growing absorption in Edward Garnett and felt it her duty to try and check it, despite her reluctance to interfere in affairs of the heart. May Garnett, however, had no such scruples, as Constance later recalled:

> She came to see me one day when I was unwell & in bed & went bluntly to the point at once. 'Of course, you would not dream of taking Edward's feeling for you seriously,' she began. 'Of course not,' I responded faintly. She proceeded to tell me that he was a hopeless character, 'he never says a prayer' & also 'he takes after Uncle William John & he'll never earn his living.' I was disinclined to look into the future; sure (as I thought) of the permanence of my own feelings, I could not think it possible that Edward's passion for me could last very long – & at that time had no thought of legal marriage. It seemed as though that would be 'taking advantage of him'.[10]

Richard Garnett, however, seemed quite unconcerned about the liaison between Constance and Edward – 'Any sensible father desires nothing better for a young man than a connection with an intelligent woman a little older,'[11] reasoned Constance – or about his son's nonchalant disregard for his own future. Edward had bestirred himself sufficiently to take evening classes in shorthand, but when Richard made a lukewarm suggestion that he might get a job on the *Manchester Guardian*, Edward promptly refused to leave Constance and go north to Manchester, and that was the end of the matter. However, May's casting of Edward in the same feckless mould as Uncle William John did have a galvanising effect: 'If it were true that [Edward] would never be self-supporting, obviously somebody would have to look after him,' reflected Constance, '& so why not I?'[12] That Richard finally arranged for Edward to enter the office of the publisher T. Fisher Unwin as a packer of books may owe more than a little to Constance's concern and subsequent promptings.

Edward's entry into the world of work was in every sense belated, as Constance later recalled:

> It happened that I was ill, & my sisters being away, Edward was staying at the flat looking after me when the day came on which he was to make his first appearance at the office in Paternoster Row. He

was to be there at nine – but to my consternation though I called him repeatedly, took him coffee in bed, & did all I could, it was impossible to get him off till long after that time. Finally I fetched a hansom – which seemed to me in those days a terrible extravagance – & with a sinking heart sent him off. It is quite possible, however, that this reckless unpunctuality was more diplomatic than a humble eagerness to please would have been. It probably gave Unwin the impression that Edward – though so young – was a person of consequence.[13]

It soon became apparent that the shapely fingers of Unwin's new employee, who joined the payroll in 1887 on 10/- a week, were hopelessly inept at packing books and tying parcels, and he rapidly slipped into the position of 'publisher's reader', which, as Constance rightly declared, was 'of all callings the one he was fitted for by character, tastes & habits'.[14]

The novelist Frank Swinnerton, who himself read for Chatto & Windus, once described his occupation as 'harmless necessary drudgery'.[15] Reading piles of manuscripts, solicited and otherwise, could be extremely tedious, but the number of well-known literary figures engaged in the task suggests the job was not entirely devoid of attractions. For novelists like George Meredith and John Buchan, who at different times in their careers read for Chapman & Hall and John Lane respectively, being a reader offered the opportunity to earn an income without the encumbrance of an inflexible office routine. This arrangement potentially left some time for other literary activities, although many readers found they had their work cut out just keeping up with the unceasing flow of manuscripts. As his tardy debut at Unwin's suggests, rigid working hours were anathema to Edward, who like most readers took manuscripts home and wrote his reports there, only going into the office to return them, collect the next batch and attend meetings in which decisions were taken on what to publish. Historically, the publisher's reader had received little recognition, remaining at best 'invisible behind his employer's arras'[16] or regarded more darkly as 'the author's unknown, unsuspected enemy, work[ing] to the sure discomfiture of all original ability'.[17] This hostility is reflected in Marie Corelli's 1895 novel *The Sorrows of Satan* in which an aspiring author castigates a publisher, telling him 'I know the kind of people who "read" for you – the gaunt unlovable spinster of 50 – the dyspeptic bookworm who is a "literary failure" and can find nothing else to do but scrawl growling comments on the manuscript of promising work'.[18] Happily, by the time Edward joined Unwin the qualities essential in a good reader were gradually being acknowledged. Frank Swinnerton explains:

> Now the professional reader of any quality takes no heed of the commercial vogue. His eyes are upon posterity, or at least upon the fashions of five or ten years ahead. He must be ready to see good in all styles; but he must never be deceived by the bad or what is called the *faux bon*. He has a duty to his employer, and a duty to literature; according to his fulfilment of those duties he will gain reputation [sic] as a critic or drop to the position of a hack.[19]

Unwin was soon to find out that young Garnett had not the slightest doubt where his allegiance lay: literature always came first, his employer a very distant second.

Edward's youth was matched by that of the firm he now worked for. Thomas Fisher Unwin had set up on his own account only five years earlier in 1882. His father Jacob, a printer, began a publishing dynasty: Edward Unwin, a son of Jacob's first marriage, became the father of Sir Stanley Unwin, one of the most illustrious publishers of his generation. Stanley's nephew Philip, who eventually joined his uncle on the board of Allen & Unwin, was the grandson of Jacob's eldest son George. Thomas Fisher, the son of Jacob's second marriage, was seven years old when his father died. He entered publishing as an apprentice to Jackson, Walford and Hodder, the predecessors of Hodder & Stoughton, where he learnt every aspect of the trade and eventually became one of their leading travellers. His trips to the Continent, and penchant for Paris in particular, established his reputation within the Unwin clan as a man of 'Continental sophistication and an international outlook'.[20] That internationalism would have appealed to Edward Garnett, but very little else did. He was not alone in finding 'TFU' (as T. Fisher Unwin was always known) chilly, humourless and mercenary. According to A. D. Marks, who became a director of the firm, Unwin 'could never understand how he antagonised people yet he was doing it all the time',[21] while Philip Unwin, who worked in the firm for a time, described his great uncle as 'tiresome, obstinate and capricious' in the office. Philip had no doubt that Unwin's 'difficulty in personal relations was the tragedy of [his] business life'.[22] Tall and rigidly upright, with a large head, very blue eyes and a beak-like nose flattened at the tip, Unwin had the disconcerting habit of wandering round the office tapping every desk he passed with a long pencil, singing 'yes' in a deep voice, immediately repeating it an octave higher until he came to a halt at the desk of some unfortunate, at which point he would lean over and mutter rapidly, 'Anything for me?'[23]

Unwin was not the only publisher to become established during the 1880s and 1890s. Heinemann, John Lane, Hutchinson and Dent were just some of the famous names who appeared during these decades, which saw considerable expansion and mounting competition in the publishing world. The demise of the three-volume novel constituted one of the biggest challenges for publishers and indeed for authors. Previously, both groups had had to bear in mind the tastes and sensibilities of the readers of the circulating libraries, which dominated the market. Chief of these was Mudie's Select Library ('Select' being the operative word – anything considered even remotely risqué was immediately banned) and to a lesser extent the bookseller and newsagent W. H. Smith. As the nineteenth century drew to a close, many more three-volume novels were being written, but demand for them in libraries was often short-lived, so that surplus stock was becoming a real problem. Often publishers had to decide whether to rush out a cheap, one-volume reprint based on the price libraries charged for second-hand copies of their three-deckers. The increase in the number of free public libraries, the cheap reprints and a growing demand for the latest fiction was making the three-volume novel uneconomic. In June 1894 Mudie's and W. H. Smith's announced that from the beginning of 1895 they would pay only 4/- per volume for novels; when the usual trade discount was applied this meant a price of 3/6 – a third of the list price of 10/6. They also demanded that no cheap reprints be issued until a year after a book's initial publication. Such was their power that this ultimatum sounded the death knell for the three-volume novel. The new single volumes were priced at 6/-, which put them within the financial reach of a far greater number of readers, who would previously have had to shell out 31/6 for a three-decker novel. Recently established, enterprising firms like T. Fisher Unwin saw an opportunity to take advantage of this change.

Some of the books Unwin published reflected his own interests: mountaineering, liberalism, free trade and the protection of minorities against persecution, but he was also willing to take a chance on young, unknown and often previously unpublished writers. His motives were far from altruistic and there undoubtedly was a mean streak in Unwin's dealings with authors (which frequently resulted in conflict with Edward, his new 'reader'). Yet as Stanley and Philip Unwin point out, TFU's willingness to invest in unproven writers initially lost the firm money. Certainly Unwin's profits at the turn of the century, when his list included such future luminaries as Conrad, Galsworthy and W. B. Yeats, were meagre.

Although Edward found Unwin at best uncongenial and their relationship was frequently tense, in many ways he could not have found a better place to launch his career. The discovery of a writer was always the greatest pleasure of Edward's professional life – David Garnett recalls that on such occasions his father was 'in the common phrase like a cat with kittens'[24] – and the job at a new, go-ahead firm eager to recruit fresh blood offered Edward a great opportunity to discover and exercise his flair for literary talent spotting. This was not the sole compensation for the irritations that seemed inevitably to beset those in Unwin's office: the publisher was also ready to take a punt on employees with literary aspirations, and in 1888 TFU produced Edward's first foray into authorship, a novel entitled *The Paradox Club*.

Reading the book now it is difficult not to conclude that Unwin must have been in an unusually generous mood when he agreed to publish it. The main protagonists are Patrick Weld, a young Irishman who shares several traits with his creator, and Nina Lindon, who, as Edward's grandson Richard observes, 'is Constance, but so idealised that were it not that the frontispiece, captioned "Nina Lindon" is clearly a drawing of Constance, one could hardly be certain of the identification'.[25] The story, such as it is, concerns the couple's tentative courtship, much of which is conducted at meetings of the Paradox Club, a debating society that is clearly modelled on 'The Club', and whose other members also bear a striking resemblance to the habitués at the fortnightly gatherings Constance attended, sometimes with Edward in tow. Large chunks of the novel consist of papers delivered by various members of the Paradox Club on the hot topics of the day, such as female emancipation, socialism, Irish Home Rule and land nationalisation. These run on laboriously for pages, followed by some rather clumsily constructed dialogue as the members debate the issues raised. Like Edward, Patrick is bewildered and ultimately amused by the earnest political rhetoric he encounters, although unlike his fictional alter ego Edward made little attempt to hide his amusement. The tone of the novel is satirical, but the satire is not particularly subtle, with a fair sprinkling of less than sparkling aphorisms such as Nina's comment: 'I always think ... that an unmarried woman is like an unthreaded needle; one is more struck by her sharpness than by her usefulness.'[26] Had Unwin himself read the novel attentively he would have been less than flattered by a discussion on the profession of publisher, in which one character proclaims that 'some authors affirm ... that the book that interests him most is his Cheque Book'.[27] Today the value of *The Paradox Club* lies in any light it may shed on the circles in which Edward and Constance were moving at the time; it has little literary merit of its own. Contemporary reviewers gave it a lukewarm reception. W. Wallace of the *Academy* got it just about right, discerning that 'the author of *The Paradox Club* is obviously a very young man, who has skimmed the surface of most of the leading controversies of the time. But his first effort supplies no data for judging whether he will or will not do anything important in literature.'[28]

At the end of *The Paradox Club* Patrick and Nina, their misunderstandings blissfully resolved, stroll, 'lost in one another',[29] westwards down the Mile End Road. As with Edward and Constance, their romance blossoms amongst the streets of the East End. The description of Wentworth Street in the novel reflects Edward's familiarity with the locality; Constance had moved there in 1887 following her acceptance of Walter Besant's offer of a job as librarian in the newly created library at the People's Palace in Mile End. 'A new interesting life that seemed intensely romantic began,' she later recalled. 'Whitechapel, with its numerous Jews and other foreigners, its broad picturesque highway and lively working-class manners is unlike all other parts of London. We found it full of charm.'[30] The uniqueness of the area clearly eclipsed other, considerably less captivating scenes that Edward and Constance must have come across – Whitechapel was at that time also one of the most poverty-stricken and squalid parts of the capital. Many of the Jews Constance mentions were Russians who had fled the merciless persecution that followed the assassination of Tsar Alexander II in 1881. Edward, steeped in the Garnett tradition of sympathy to political refugees, took a keen interest in his surroundings. His office in Paternoster Square was comparatively close by; the couple met for lunch whenever possible and Edward spent every weekend at Constance's tiny rooms in College Buildings, a routine which continued when Constance moved again, this time to Royal Mint Square in the autumn of 1888. Despite the charms of the East End, the couple harboured dreams of taking a cottage in the country, something that began to seem attainable when, in October 1888, Constance was promoted to Head Librarian and her salary was increased to £100 a year.

Nine months later the *Palace Journal* of 17 July 1889 expressed its sorrow at losing the services of Miss Black, who was leaving to get married. The wedding took place at Brighton Register Office on 31 August 1889. Edward was twenty-one, Constance twenty-seven. Three of her siblings, Ernest,

Grace and Kate, were witnesses along with Kate's husband Charles Clayton, an architect. The Garnett family hired a house on the Brighton seafront for the occasion.

The other notable event of the second half of 1889 was the publication of Edward's second novel, *Light and Shadow*, another Unwin production. It is a work of relentless gloom. The main protagonist Maurice Driscoll is orphaned at fifteen and comes down to London from Lancashire to take up employment as a clerk in his uncle's lace warehousing firm. He eventually inherits the business and makes an unhappy marriage with the beautiful Catherine Purchas. Maurice and Catherine rapidly grow to despise each other and Driscoll develops a strong, quasi-passionate friendship with a younger man, Francis Lester. Returning home unexpectedly one evening, he finds evidence that Francis is in the house, conceals himself and eavesdrops on his friend's seduction of Catherine. The rest of the novel, which constitutes more than half the book, is a detailed and tortuous exposition of Driscoll's state of mind as he lies in a depressing rented room in the East End, where he finally commits suicide. The East End features prominently in the book and Edward does not shirk from portraying the decidedly less salubrious side of the area, and the destitution and brutality of the lives of many of its inhabitants, which clearly disturbed him. The remark in the *Athenaeum*'s review that the book 'hardly answers the description of a "novel"' and 'grows into the likeness of the fantastic and almost subjective nightmare of a single mind [rather] than a story of action and incident'[31] is more than just. Shadow certainly overwhelms any light as far as subject matter goes, but the novel lacks any light and shadow in its execution, too. When Edward inflicted the book on John Galsworthy thirteen years later Galsworthy hit the nail on the head, remarking that Edward's 'technique was not the servant of your desires. You tried I think to give us the most inward emotion of a struggling foundering soul, and in the way you tried, you were attempting the impossible ... You beat too diligently, too strongly, too finely upon one note and you deafened your hearer's receptive power.'[32] What Richard Garnett, the novel's dedicatee, made of it can only be surmised: Edward confessed to his father that he had 'hoped the book to which I put your name would be more artistically perfect'.[33] A year later Edward admitted to Richard that his first two books were written 'to get money, and were plucked quite unripe'.[34] H. G. Wells, who read *Light and Shadow* in 1903, described it in a letter to Edward as 'a most interesting & curious book', and wondered 'Why afterwards you didn't go on? You must have been young enough when you did it, not to have thought it a final test.'[35] Edward started other fictions subsequently, including a historical novel about Ireland, but these were all abandoned and on the evidence of *Light and Shadow* it may have been just as well.

The letter in which Edward apologised to his father for the artistic shortcomings of *Light and Shadow* also contained a request that Richard postpone a pre-arranged visit to the newlyweds:

> We are going up to London to-day to see a doctor with whom we have an appointment. Nothing is really the matter, only a slight operation is required. I should not mention the fact, if it were not necessary to explain our departure – & it certainly need never be referred to again.[36]

Over twenty years later, when her son David was about to embark on a solo trip to Germany, Constance wrote him a letter as if from Edward, warning him of the perils of unprotected sex. In this letter she freely admits that she and Edward became lovers before their marriage.[37] Their grandson Richard Garnett, himself an editor and writer, speculates that this letter, coupled with the fact that Constance had left her job at the People's Palace unexpectedly, suggests that she became pregnant and had suffered a miscarriage which necessitated curettage.[38]

As it turned out, surgery was not required and Edward and Constance were able to settle down and fulfil their dream of a cottage in the country. They found the ideal place in Henhurst Cross, a small and attractive stone Victorian cottage on the edge of the Broome Hall estate near Beare Green, south of Dorking. With its fretted gable ends, lattice windows, small orchard, bluebell copse and stream at the bottom of the garden, Henhurst Cross was in many respects a country idyll. There was a single cottage across the road, but otherwise Edward and Constance could live in complete seclusion. Apart from the A29 now running past Henhurst Cross Lane, the landscape today remains remarkably unchanged, and it is easy to see why Olive Garnett, a frequent visitor, wrote so enthusiastically about the place in her diary. Yet for all its charm the cottage was also damp, draughty and infested with mice – on one occasion Edward and Constance came back from staying in Brighton to discover a mouse pickled in a jar of treacle, and the pantry was frequently in a state of disarray after nocturnal raiding by rodents. These were minor drawbacks, though, and Constance discovered a love of gardening that endured for the rest of her life. Edward, who, as his grandson attests, had an uncanny knack of choosing exactly the right present for any occasion, soon got into the habit of giving Constance special bulbs or rare plants for her birthday (when he managed to remember it), 'a gift she loved the best', as her niece recalled.[39]

Every Wednesday morning Edward walked the mile and a half to Holmwood Station and caught the London train. While he was away Constance sent a constant stream of affectionate, sometimes flirtatious letters, giving news of the garden, the cat and her own daily activities. Edward had retained rooms in College Buildings and stayed in the capital until Friday, returning home at about eight o'clock in the evening with a large bundle of manuscripts to read. The variety of manuscripts whose quality and commercial potential Edward was required to judge was vast. Novels published by Unwin ranged from works by the likes of George Moore and Mark Rutherford to popular fiction of considerably less literary merit. The firm's catalogue included biography, history, poetry, and such intriguing titles as the Rev. E. J. Hardy's opus *How to be Happy though Married* ('By a Graduate in the University of Matrimony') and *Birdsnesting and Bird-Skinning* by Edward Newman.

Reports were submitted on pre-printed forms marked 'Private' and resembled a school report, both visually and not infrequently in tone: 'We have read some very good work by Mr Gissing,' Edward declares in a report on *Sleeping Fires* (1895), 'but we have also read some very bad work by him (a story lately in the *English Illustrated* was simply shockingly poor) ... We feel that a strong effort ought to be made to get good work out of him.'[40] Manuscripts were read on average about ten days after submission; some arrived complete, others consisted of only a few chapters. 'The portion of the novel before us is certainly clever,' Edward pronounced after scrutinising part of George Moore's *Evelyn Innes*, which Unwin published in 1898, 'It is well written, composed with art[,] great care & a certain finesse. It is rather *affected* in tone, as perhaps the greater portion of Mr Moore's work is ... but it promises to be *artistically* the best thing in fiction that Mr Moore has done.'[41]

Edward was helped in his task of sifting through this mass of literary endeavour by W. H. Chesson and, from 1895, by a young G. K. Chesterton, who also read for Unwin. The advent of the irrepressible Chesterton lightened the atmosphere of the Paternoster Square office, not least on account of his duels with the cyclostyle duplicating machine, which invariably left his hands, hair and chin liberally doused with black ink. Both Chesson and Chesterton submitted their own manuscripts to Unwin; Edward reported favourably on Chesterton's projected volume of poetry

The Babe Unborn: 'Mr Chesterton has *temperament*, he has individuality, and *a new point of view*.'[42] However, Unwin was not impressed and did not publish the book. Originality was a quality Edward always prized highly: 'Yes, these stories are good,' he wrote of Edith Nesbit's *The Story of the Treasure Seekers*. 'They are written on a rather original idea, on a line off the common turn ... We think the stories are worth taking up, and worth publishing, for the stories are *individual*.'[43]

Edward took a dim view of the tastes of the British reading public, frequently bemoaning its insularity and the consistent demand that literature should 'entertain' and trumpet the attainment of moral growth and worldly success. His enthusiasm for the 'exquisite', understated writing of the American Sarah Orne Jewett was matched by his pessimism regarding its probable reception in England. '[T]he public will not understand her *deftness*[,] her *restraint*[,] the dignity of Miss Jewitt's [*sic*] simple and sober style,'[44] he prophesied. Despite this scorn of the public's literary appetite, Edward was well aware of what that audience wanted and of the commercial prospects of manuscripts. Reporting on John Buchan's first novel *Sir Quixote of the Moors* in 1895, he noted similarities with the work of the popular historical novelist Stanley Weyman: 'Between ourselves this Frenchman's character is an impossible one,' he observed of Buchan's hero, 'but 'twill serve in these days of historical novelettes.'[45] Buckram binding, a good frontispiece and a cover price of 5/- or 3/6 would, he predicted, ensure fairly good sales. A provocative sociological study, *Women and Economics*, the work of another American, Charlotte Perkins Stetson Gilman, was about as far removed from Buchan as possible, and Edward was convinced that 'old-fashioned people, the Conservatives & the popular Press will view the book with much disfavour'.[46] However, he advised Unwin to run a small edition, noting that the book 'is really a *sensible* one, if somewhat *one-sided* ... Miss Stetson deduces strong and *rational* argument for Woman's economic independence in the future.'[47] It is noticeable that, viewed retrospectively, the majority of eminent writers indebted to Edward's guidance were men. This was not because he cared little for women's writing, but because few of the female authors he supported have achieved literary longevity.

Nowhere is Edward's promotion of women's literary talent more apparent than in the Pseudonym Library, a series he inaugurated in 1890. It ran to more than fifty volumes, thirty-three of which were written by women. Fisher Unwin once declared that the Pseudonym Library was created because many manuscripts came to the firm 'which [were] too brief for the ordinary novel form, while at the same time [they] did not come under the heading of the short story'.[48] The fact that books could be advertised under the series title rather than individually, thus cutting publicity costs, doubtless appealed as well.

The American-born Pearl Craigie, writing as John Oliver Hobbes, launched her career when *Some Emotions and a Moral* was accepted by Unwin for the Pseudonym Library and she went on to contribute three other titles to the series. Olive Schreiner's *Dream Life and Real Life: A Little African Story* appeared in the Pseudonym Library in 1893 under the nom de plume Ralph Iron. When, four years later, the South African Schreiner submitted a projected book of political articles entitled *The Boer*, Edward was relieved to find the 'old charm of style' of her earlier novel *The Story of an African Farm* returning. 'In this series of articles, at least, there is practically none of that *posing, exaggeration and cheap sentimentality* which has spoiled Miss Schreiner's later writings,' he reported, admiring the way in which *The Boer* 'really brings *S. Africa and its people before us*, and is written in a free and lofty spirit'. However, a few caustic observations in the report – 'The authoress's good opinion of herself is of course too apparent' – suggest Edward's former reservations were not wholly dispelled.[49]

The Pseudonym Library was also notable for the number of translated works it contained. Nearly a third of the titles were translations from a variety of languages, including Danish, German, Greek, Italian and Russian. This reflected the cosmopolitan literary tastes of both Edward and his employer. T. Fisher Unwin was very keen on publishing series – he could boast of twenty-eight by 1917 – as, once hooked, enthusiastic readers were tempted to purchase subsequent volumes as they appeared in the series. Books in the Pseudonym Library were visually distinctive, being a non-standard, rectangular size ('Handy for the Pocket in Size and Shape' trumpeted one of Unwin's advertisements) with lemon-yellow paper covers and priced at 1/6; sturdier buff cloth-board editions cost 2 shillings. Edward persuaded Unwin's commercial travellers to target railway stalls in particular and the strategy proved highly effective, helping Edward achieve what Ford Madox Ford described as a 'meteoric publishing success'.[50] The 'little yellow-covered books ... spread all over England and the continent of Europe with a most astonishing rapidity,'[51] Ford later recalled.

Some of the volumes in the Pseudonym Library were reprints. One book that came under discussion for inclusion was George Bernard Shaw's early novel *Love Among the Artists* (1881). Edward was unconvinced of its suitability, arguing that it was 'a *clever reflection* of the strong minded pseudo-bohemian class ... whose lack of money is about as much responsible for their sharpened brains as a natural bias towards unconventionality. But who would understand the book outside of this class? Nobody ...'[52] He goes on to compare *Love Among the Artists* unfavourably with the work of a younger Irish writer for whom he confessed he had 'conceived an affection':[53] William Butler Yeats.

The dreamy, otherworldly side of Yeats rather appealed to Edward. When he invited the twenty-five-year-old Irishman to Henhurst Cross for the weekend, Yeats turned up with nothing but a toothbrush and a bit of soap. According to Edward, he then proceeded to beguile the severely rational Constance with his accounts of occultism.[54] Their meetings mostly took place in London, however, and for a short time Edward was a habitué of the Rhymers' Club, a circle of writers which met at the Cheshire Cheese public house in Fleet Street, described by Roy Foster as 'mainly "Celtic", with a strong Irish predominance'.[55] Yeats was a leading light, but Edward rapidly found the solemnity of the meetings insufferable and much preferred Yeats's company in less formal surroundings.

Sean O'Faolain remembered Edward telling him that 'when he was very young and they were both poor, in the days when W. B. used to have to black-up his heels so as to cover up the holes in his stockings ... they'd walk from his digs to Edward's digs and back again, all night long, absolutely forgetting everything in the most natural way.'[56] It is a romantic image, the dark-haired, impecunious poet and his tall, gangly companion traipsing London's nocturnal streets lost in conversation, not unlike a latter-day Richard Savage and Samuel Johnson. Like those eighteenth-century street-haunters, both Yeats and Edward considered themselves outsiders. Yeats's inability to feel at home in either Dublin or London was a peculiarly Anglo-Irish malaise, summed up by Elizabeth Bowen's remark that the only place the Anglo-Irish really felt at ease was on the crossing between Holyhead and Dun Laoghaire.[57] Edward once declared himself to be 'a bad fit'[58] in England and frequently flourished his claims to Irishness. It appears that his night walks with Yeats and their all-consuming conversations drew out that 'Irish' side of his temperament: 'More than most (and quite unlike the English) I am never myself till I can *lose* myself in what delights me and in everything I do,' he explained in a letter of 1898, 'and the reason I scorn myself is that daily life is such a half and half affair, such a temporising, and a frittering, such a cautious and compromising spirit. Perhaps it is my English half holds me back, and *that* my Irish half cannot bear.'[59]

Edward was irked at frequently having to bow to Unwin's preference for the 'English' virtues of caution and compromise. Nevertheless, he was able to persuade his employer to accept Yeats's novella *John Sherman*, as well as *Dhoya*, a story of Celtic mythography, for the Pseudonym Library (Yeats adopting the nom de plume Ganconagh). He also managed to secure Unwin's agreement to Yeats's scheme for a Library of Ireland series. Edward, who wholeheartedly shared Yeats' enthusiasm for the idea, advised on the practicalities before Unwin was approached. The plan was to publish one volume at two-monthly intervals, priced at a shilling. According to Yeats, Unwin's consent was dependent on Yeats assuming the editorship of the series. His declared aim was to promote books of high literary merit and 'sound national doctrine'[60] – which at that time in Yeats's life meant Parnellite and Fenian.

The whole project was closely linked with the newly formed Irish Literary Society of London under the presidency of Sir Charles Gavan Duffy. In his youth Duffy had been an active member of the Young Ireland movement, but by now his more moderate nationalism was at odds with that of Yeats. Duffy was to be a formidable opponent; he was an experienced politician, described by Yeats's biographer as 'gentlemanly, resourceful and devious'.[61] It turned out that Duffy had the year before proposed a similar library of reprints to John T. Kelly of the Southwark Irish Literary Club and he was not prepared meekly to give way to Yeats's schemes.

Duffy was not the only source of disquiet: many in Ireland's literary circles took a dim view of an Irish Literary Society based in London. Kelly returned to Dublin with the intention of setting up a similar society, but independent of the London one and lacking any neo-Fenian agenda. Yeats went back to Dublin and involved himself with the establishment of the 'National Literary Society' – but it was clear that Kelly had won the day and the Society was a long way from representing Yeats's aesthetic and political ideals. To make matters worse, Duffy soon appeared in Ireland and set himself up as head and effective editor of the National Publishing Company, which was now to produce books for the Library of Ireland. When the National Publishing Company failed, Duffy and T. W. Rolleston, secretary of the Irish Literary Society of London, contacted Unwin. Rolleston wrote to Edward, asking him to promote the idea to Unwin and informing him that Duffy was to control the whole scheme. Yeats felt that Rolleston and Duffy had poached his original idea and gone to Unwin behind his back. Livid, Yeats sent a letter to Edward requesting information as to what had gone on and appealing to him to 'do what you can to help me in this matter'.[62]

For once, Edward sought to bring the 'English' qualities of caution and compromise to this troublesome Irish affair. His letter in response to Yeats is a model of crafted, even crafty diplomacy. Sentences such as 'I know you well enough to know that *you* don't want the credit and honour and glory – you want the eternal things'[63] were calculated to assuage Yeats's wounded vanity, whilst clearing the way for Edward's reconciliatory aims. Assuring Yeats that 'my sympathies are all with you and the party you represent,' Edward still proposed that Yeats accept Duffy as the figurehead of the Irish literary schemes and most importantly effect a rapprochement with Rolleston, which he felt would lead to the eventual adoption of Yeats's ideas. 'Don't let loose the dogs of war against a Duffy Dictatorship when it could be turned into a Duffy Figureheadship,' counselled Edward, who ended the letter by warning Yeats that Unwin had definitely cast his lot with Duffy and that 'no English publisher would take up the rival scheme'.

His advice arrived too late: the dogs had already been unleashed by Yeats, who rashly talked of a split between London and Dublin and inferred that the Dublin Society supported him, a claim that was some way from the truth. As a result, Yeats lost any influence he might have had and the Library of Ireland was launched without him. That it enjoyed relatively little success may have come as some consolation: Edward later wrote that the series was 'killed after a couple of years by the books chosen by the editors'.[64] Four years later, Edward exacted a minor revenge when he reported on the manuscript of Duffy's autobiography. 'A weakness of the Volume is certainly the author's excessive *laudation of himself*,' he commented. 'The book adds little to anybody's knowledge and it may be described as the strong boom of a strong man of whom the public are tired.'[65] The shenanigans over the Library of Ireland was the first time Edward dipped his toe in the often turbulent waters of Irish literary affairs: it was not to be the last.

The friendship between Edward and Yeats fractured in 1903 when Edward wrote an article in the *Academy* comparing Eleanor Hull's translation of *The Cuchullin Saga* favourably with Lady Augusta Gregory's *Cuchulain of Muirthemne*. Gregory was one of Yeats's greatest friends and he had penned an overly effusive preface to her book, with which Edward took issue 'with a reverent and a humble firmness'.[66] When the two men later met at an eating-house the encounter was anything but reverential: 'How I wish I had been there to see when you and Mr Yeats were having it out at that restaurant,' lamented Miss Hull. 'It must have surprised the waitress a little.'[67] The rupture was not reflected in Edward's generous article in an *English Review* of 1909 in which he praised Yeats's 'verbal sorceries'[68] in the poems and plays, and vigorously rebutted politically inspired criticism from Ireland which denounced Yeats as unpatriotic for writing in English. Perhaps some nostalgic affection remained for those early days when Yeats was living at Bedford Park; the area certainly loomed large in Edward's life at that time, for just a couple of streets away from the Yeats residence stood 31 Blandford Road, the home of one of the Russian revolutionary exiles with whom the Garnetts were becoming increasingly involved.

3

'Quite a little Russian world'

On 4 November 1891 Olive Garnett travelled down from London to Holmwood Station, where she was met by Constance and another visitor to Henhurst Cross. 'I should have imagined he was a Russian,' Olive noted in her diary, 'something perhaps in the expressive brown eyes and thick straight falling hair.'[1] The stranger was Felix Vladimovich Volkhovsky, a political exile who had arrived in London via Vancouver and New York in July 1890 after escaping from Siberia the previous summer.

Volkhovsky was forty-four when he came to England. Arrest and detainment for alleged political subversion had been permanent features of his existence from the time he was a law student in Moscow. His skirmishes with the Russian authorities culminated in what became known as the Trial of the 193 in 1877–8 (770 activists were originally arrested, but only 193 stood trial). Volkhovsky was accused of distributing political propaganda and was sentenced to lifelong Siberian exile. Political protest came at great personal cost: in his last spell of imprisonment, Volkhovsky was kept in darkness for eighteen hours a day and was then moved to another prison where the noise and conditions were so terrible that he became deaf; his health was severely damaged and the hair remarked on by Olive turned white. His first wife, Mariya, died in Italy of tuberculosis in 1875 while Volkhovsky was in prison. Aleksandra, his second wife, committed suicide in Siberia and his youngest daughter Katia also perished in exile. Volkhovsky's eldest daughter, nine-year-old Vera, joined him in London in 1890, having been smuggled out of Russia disguised as a boy.

Shortly after his arrival, Volkhovsky began writing for *Free Russia*, the journal of the newly formed Society of Friends of Russian Freedom. This organisation had been founded seven months earlier by another Russian exile, Sergei Stepniak, and Robert Spence Watson, a radical lawyer from Newcastle, with the aim of alerting the British public to the prevailing despotism in Russia and countering Tsarist propaganda abroad. The Society was Anglo-Russian in composition: T. Fisher Unwin was one of its leading lights and a member of its managing subcommittee. In 1892 he published Volkhovsky's *A China Cup and Other Stories for Children*, and Edward may have first encountered the Russian at his employer's Paternoster Square office. Constance recalled Edward returning home from London one day in the summer of 1891 and telling her 'I have met a man after your heart – a Russian exile – and I have asked him down for a weekend.'[2] Volkhovsky rapidly became a great friend and, as he then had no permanent home, he made Henhurst Cross his headquarters. 'He was a curious mixture,' Constance later wrote:

> [O]n one side, a fanatical almost Puritanical revolutionary, pedantic and strict, ready to go to the stake rather than disown or disguise opinions really of no practical importance, scrupulous, – on the other hand, pleasure-loving, vain, rather intriguing, a tremendous 'ladies man' a first-rate actor, fond of dancing. One day he was a pathetic broken down old man – very sorry for himself – the next day he would look 20 years younger, put a rose in his buttonhole & lay himself out very successfully to please and entertain.[3]

When Olive met the mercurial Volkhovsky at the station in November 1891 he and Vera had been in residence at Henhurst Cross since July.

The previous months had brought about considerable change in the lives of the Garnetts. Edward had managed to persuade Unwin to raise his salary to £4 a week in return for reading a greater number of manuscripts. Amazingly, Edward reported that his usually parsimonious employer 'met my wishes in a kind and liberal spirit'.[4] In March Edward and Constance had moved their London residence from College Buildings to 'two very nice rooms'[5] at 24 John Street, near Holborn. That September Constance had written to her father-in-law 'to tell you what I hope will be a great pleasure to you – that I am hoping to bring you a little grandchild early in the Spring. It is a great happiness to us.'[6] Volkhovsky's presence during Constance's pregnancy proved to be fortuitous: she attributed her unusually good health to his insistence that she take long walks. More importantly, it was Volkhovsky who suggested that she learn Russian to while away the hours of enforced idleness, thus launching Constance's distinguished career as a translator of more than seventy volumes of Russian literature.

At the time of Olive's visit in November, Constance was immersed in her study of Russian and Olive herself took some lessons from Volkhovsky. Her diary records walks in the autumn countryside and debates in the evenings, when Edward came home from London, on false ideas of morality, in which Olive was ribbed as 'the representative of Mrs Grundy'.[7] Volkhovsky's company lent the cottage a distinctly exotic air: 'When Volkhovsky is here we live in quite a little Russian world,' Olive explained to her father. 'It is so curious to awake from Siberia to a Surrey lane.'[8]

The baby was expected in February, and as there was no doctor near Henhurst Cross, Constance went to her father's home in Brighton for the birth. Sitting by the pier, rather desultorily studying her Russian grammar, Constance pondered on the coming child and how she hoped he or she 'must grow up without any of the Black coldness, or the Northern Garnett obstinacy'.[9] Edward was absent, confined to London with a severe bout of flu. He recovered in time to be in Brighton when David Garnett eventually made his extremely tardy appearance in the early hours of 9 March 1892. Constance endured what she described as a 'terrible labour'[10] and a forceps delivery; she took a long time to recover from the ordeal and was unable to return to Henhurst Cross until a month after David's birth. On the journey back to the cottage she had to run for the train, 'and this was followed by troubles that caused me discomfort on and off for thirty years afterwards, and made it necessary for me to lie down almost all day for a long time'.[11] Her grandson Richard speculates that Constance suffered a prolapse of the uterus, something that is quite easily rectifiable today, but for which the treatment then was prolonged rest.

From the moment of his birth until the moment of her death, David was the centre of Constance's life. The arrival of a child inevitably alters the dynamics of a marriage and before she left Brighton, Constance had a conversation with her 'very sympathetic and nice' old doctor, who gloomily warned 'that I must now expect to feel middle-aged – that a certain spring of youth is always lost in childbirth – that one can never look at life in the same way again'.[12] Constance was thirty when David was born and Edward twenty-four; childbirth had blunted Constance's feelings of sexual desire, something which clearly caused her anxiety: 'it is very important to our happiness that I *should* get back a little of the keen edge of my old feelings again,' she told her husband, explaining

The only thing that I can do in which I really feel satisfied is in *doing* things – working at my translation – making Baby a frock etc. Of course you know I do get a great great [*sic*] happiness out of Baby and I never felt a tenderer love for you. But it is a passionless unegoistic love ... Dearest don't think me selfish and self absorbed. It is terrible to feel the stone wall going up – petrifaction beginning at thirty! and it will spoil your happiness as well as mine.[13]

Edward's side of the correspondence is absent and his feelings and response therefore unknown, but he was an involved and doting father. Although Constance was delighted to get away from Brighton, which she hated, life did not magically improve back at Henhurst Cross. Both the new parents were poor sleepers and, according to his mother, 'David drove us almost gibbering the first six months of his life'.[14] Edward's exhaustion was not helped by a prolonged summer drought, which necessitated his fetching pails of drinking water from a farm a mile distant after the well at Henhurst Cross ran dry. When he was still quite small David became enamoured of Caldecott's illustration of Baby Bunting in his rabbit skin and so was given a rabbit skin cap. The village boys immediately christened him 'Bunny', a name that stuck for the rest of his life.

Meanwhile, Constance's concern about the state of her physical relationship with Edward continued. 'I want to tell you how dear you are to me,' she wrote reassuringly, confessing that

I am frightened sometimes that because I am selfish about little things (I will try and I do try to be a better girl) and because one side of passion seems to have died away for a while in me, you may begin to doubt my love. Dear one, do believe that my heart is full of tenderness and love and gratitude to you; and no new interest – not even my little beebi – can ever make that less.[15]

When not absorbed by maternal preoccupations Constance was pursuing her other great new interest – Russian. Aided by Volkhovsky, she had painstakingly translated Ivan Goncharov's *A Common Story*, and in the summer of 1892 Volkhovsky took her to 31 Blandford Road, a small semi-detached house in Bedford Park, to meet one of his closest confederates, Sergei Mikhailovich Kravchinsky, more familiarly known as Sergius Stepniak. It was an outing Constance later described as 'one of the most important events in my life'.[16]

Stepniak arrived in London in July 1884 aged thirty-three. His life up to that point had certainly been as eventful as, if less traumatic than, Volkhovsky's. The son of an army doctor, he resigned his own commission as an artillery officer in 1871 to study forestry. This he also abandoned in order to promote the populist cause; he joined a secret socialist society, the Circle of Tchaikovsky, in St Petersburg and sought to distribute propaganda amongst the city's working classes. When he furthered his activities in the Tver and Tula provinces in 1873 he was arrested. Kravchinsky (he did not adopt his pseudonym until 1881) rapidly escaped from custody and evaded the pursuing authorities for a year; he then went abroad, turning up at various times in Brussels, London, Paris, Herzegovina (where he fought at the beginning of the Balkan crisis), Lugano and Geneva. He met the anarchist Mikhail Bakunin in Lugano, who convinced him to turn to political violence. After a brief time back in Russia, Kravchinsky headed for Sicily and took part in Errico Malatesta's Benevento uprising. Jailed by the Italians for nine months, he was able to return to Russia in 1878 thanks to the amnesty that followed the accession of Umberto I. On 1 August 1878 (OS) in St Petersburg Kravchinsky fatally stabbed Adjutant General Mezentsev, head of the 'third department' of the Tsar's secret police, and then made another dramatic escape to Geneva. After spells of living in Milan and Geneva once more he ended his peripatetic existence by settling in London with his wife, Fanny Markovna Lichkus, a former medical student he had met in 1878.

By the time he came to London Stepniak had moderated his views on violence and become convinced that political change could best be effected through the pen rather than the pistol. He had survived financially in Italy by translating Italian and Spanish fiction for the St Petersburg monthly *Delo*, and had written a weekly series of profiles of revolutionaries and sketches for an Italian newspaper, which were then collected and published as *La Russia Sotterranea*. A year later in 1883 this volume was translated into English as *Underground Russia*. It was well received by English radicals and acclaimed by the likes of William Morris, Mark Twain, Ivan Turgenev and Eleanor Marx, who wrote a long appreciation of it.[17] In 1889 Stepniak produced a novel, *The Career of a Nihilist*, which like *Underground Russia* contains much autobiographical material; that violent political activity is not entirely condemned in either book suggests that Stepniak may not have abandoned his former creed completely when in London. However, George Bernard Shaw – who first met him in 1884 at the great demonstration in Hyde Park against the House of Lords' rejection of the last Reform Bill, and who came to know Stepniak well – once remarked that both he and the Russian 'were politicians and reformers by force of circumstances, artists by natural disposition'.[18] Stepniak himself reportedly once proclaimed 'I am not an Anarchist, I am an artist.'[19] Given Stepniak's interest in literature and translation it is hardly surprising that he and the Garnetts swiftly struck up a rapport.

Stepniak made an immediate and lasting impression on those who met him. Though by no means conventionally handsome, he was extremely attractive to women and possessed tremendous personal magnetism, as Constance's description of him indicates:

> He was of medium height and burly with very broad shoulders, a dark beard, dark eyes, a big forehead and broad Russian nose. He was very strong and he had the gentleness, the quietness, which so often goes with great physical strength in men. He had also great warmth of heart, often found among Russians, and a genius for drawing out the best qualities in people around him, and this warmth of heart and interest in other people seemed as though they were part of his physical make-up. Just as his broad powerful hands seemed able to understand material without any trouble, so that he could make anything he wanted, of wood, or leather, or metal, so his warm heart enabled him to understand all kinds of people, and to set them on the road they should follow.[20]

In her unpublished memoir Constance declares that Stepniak was 'the most aesthetically sensitive and appreciative man I have known'.[21] True to character, he showed great interest in her Goncharov translation, offering to go through it with her and urging her to get it published. Soon she was going over to Bedford Park once a week to improve her Russian and falling deeper and deeper under Stepniak's spell.

Edward was also won over by the Russian. Like so many others he responded warmly to Stepniak's quick sympathy, but what particularly appealed was the fact that the émigré loved literature and that he was a Russian – an irresistible combination to Edward, who was increasingly preoccupied with the shortcomings of the Republic of Letters at home and was scanning the wider horizon in search of solutions.

Edward was not alone in deploring the intellectual and cultural insularity that shrouded Britain in the latter decades of the nineteenth century – these were years in which Henry Vizetelly was prosecuted for obscene libel after he published a translation of Zola's *La Terre* and public performances of Ibsen's plays were banned, his characters condemned as 'morally deranged' by the Examiner of Plays.[22] The deaths of William Makepeace Thackeray, Charles Dickens and George Eliot had left British fiction in a parlous state, neatly summarised by Matthew Arnold in his 1887 essay on Tolstoy, in which he lamented the fact that 'the famous English novelists have passed away, and have left no successors of like fame'.[23] Edward, whose job it was to ferret out likely candidates, had little doubt as to where such pretenders to the throne should turn for inspiration. By 1890 he had expanded his activities into the field of literary journalism, reviewing chiefly for the newly founded *Speaker* and the *Academy*. In his 1890 notice of *The Modern Novelists of Russia* by Charles Edward Turner, Edward proclaimed, 'It is time someone should estimate for us what the Russians have done in literature, should show clearly how they have successfully widened the whole scope and aim of the novel.'[24] This was a task he himself was to take up with unflagging enthusiasm for the rest of his life through his books, prefaces, critical columns and his espousal of the Russian example to his protégés. His job was made immeasurably easier by Constance's steady stream of translations, which made the works of the great Russian authors readily available and superseded often unsatisfactory translations made from French or German versions of the original Russian.

It is easy to forget that Edward's appeal for a new appreciation of the Russian novelists was made at a time when the novel was far from being considered the dominant and intellectually respectable literary form that it is today. Nine years later, in 1899, he still felt it necessary to champion the cause of the novel, pointing to the fact that

> Many men of letters to-day look on the novel as a mere story-book, as a series of light-coloured, amusing pictures for their 'idle hours,' and on memoirs, biographies, histories, criticism and poetry as the age's *serious* contribution to literature. Whereas the reverse is the case. The most serious and significant of all literary forms the modern world has evolved is the novel; and brought to its highest development, the novel shares with poetry to-day the honour of being the supreme instrument of the great artist's literary skill.[25]

This impassioned advocacy formed part of Edward's preface to Constance's translation of *The Jew and Other Stories* by Ivan Turgenev, the writer whom Edward confessed 'is dearer to me than any author'[26] and whose work he consistently held up as an example to anyone with literary aspirations.

Part of Russia's attraction lay in the importance that nation attached to literature: as one commentator has explained, the political, cultural and spiritual traditions of Russia made it 'unthinkable that the novel would become merely a source of entertainment; Russians have always been much too conscious of the symbolic value of the word'.[27] It would have been impossible for Edward to spend any length of time in Stepniak's company without becoming aware of this fact. The Russian was a frequent lecturer at venues all over the country; his subjects were just as likely to be literary as political. In July 1890, for example, he and a fellow exile, Peter Kropotkin – 'the Anarchist Prince', who also became a great friend of the Garnetts – gave a series of joint lectures in the Portman Rooms in Baker Street at which Stepniak spoke on 'Tolstoi, as Novelist and Social Reformer'.

Stepniak was spending increasing amounts of time with the Garnetts, both at Henhurst Cross – where he passed a fortnight in furious activity writing a novel whose hero was based on Edward (it was never published, but according to Richard Garnett the hero of Stepniak's short story 'Domik na Volge' ('The House on the Volga') bears some resemblance to his grandfather) – and at 24 John Street, where Olive Garnett was summoned by Edward to meet the Russian for the first time on 20 October 1892. Olive was soon severely smitten: by the end of the year she was confiding rather girlishly to her diary, 'I like Stepniak more and more, and in proportion as I like him I find him positively handsome.'[28] She was not alone in succumbing to the Russian's charms. Constance was captivated, too, but whereas Olive's passion for Stepniak remained entirely innocent, that of her sister-in-law in all probability did not. In his unpublished autobiography David Garnett states that 'undoubtedly Sergey Stepniak was the man for whom my mother felt the greatest love in her life',[29] but he was also convinced that although Constance did not censure married women who had affairs, 'She did not make such experiments herself.'[30] Suggestions to the contrary can be found in the notes and correspondence of the woman who was to be as central to Edward's life as Stepniak was to that of Constance: Ellen Maurice Heath.

Ellen (who was known as Nellie to everyone except her French friends) was born at Epsom on 13 June 1872, the fifth and last child of Richard Heath and his wife Anne, who died of cancer early in 1881, when Nellie was eight. The Heaths lost their eldest daughter Mary in the same year

Nellie was born. Richard had been apprenticed to a wood engraver at the age of fourteen and worked for a firm in the Strand who provided many of the illustrations for magazines and art journals. After his wife's death Richard took his young family across the Channel, initially to Normandy and then for two years to Paris, where he worked at the Bibliothèque nationale and inspired Nellie's interest in art. David Garnett remembered him as 'a small man, with silver hair and beard, blue eyes in which one was surprised to detect a twinkle of humour'.[31] Heath was a committed Christian Socialist; his son Carl described him as a man of great sensitivity, 'idealistic in temperament' and 'constitutionally incapable of "getting on"'[32] – which would immediately have endeared him to Edward.

Richard's fundamental interests in life were religion (of the nonconformist variety) and politics; he was particularly affected by the increasingly desperate plight of the agricultural worker. Amongst his body of writing was a series of articles on the English rural labourer which were later collected in a book entitled *The English Peasant*, published by Unwin in 1893. Carl Heath, who became a Quaker, inherited his father's social conscience and worked for a time amongst the destitute of Whitechapel; it was he who had found the rooms in College Buildings for Constance. Nellie, too, shared some of her father's characteristics: she had great compassion, remarkable unselfishness and was one of those truly rare spirits who inspire immediate and unshakeable affection in everyone they meet. Edward's niece Rayne declared that her love for Nellie 'has coloured my life as my love for no one else has done'[33] – sentiments that many of those who knew Nellie would recognise. 'The first impression,' writes David Garnett,

> was of extraordinary softness, a softness physically expressed at that time in velvet blouses and velveteen skirts; a softness of speech and a gentleness of manner and disposition which made it difficult and painful for her to disagree with, and impossible flatly to contradict, any statement made to her ... But under this softness was an iron will-power which has sometimes reminded me of Emily Brontë. She would not be driven; she refused, in spite of her extreme gentleness, to be coerced.[34]

Nellie trained as an artist, studying first with Frederick Brown, for many years Professor at the Slade School of Fine Art, and then with Walter Sickert, for whom she developed a powerful but unrequited passion. She painted mainly in oils, specialising in landscapes and portraiture.

It was in the autumn of 1892 that Nellie first stayed with Edward and Constance at Henhurst Cross. From that time she was gradually drawn further and further into their lives. Nellie was certainly aware of Constance's deepening relationship with Stepniak, whom she later described as 'a delightful person ... full of human love – and a very fine man,'[35] and she also observed Edward's reaction to the situation. 'Connie was very much in love with Stepniak,' Nellie recalled, 'and Edward took it very hard. In a way he showed his character, by being intensely sympathetic to Stepniak. It was the first real deepening in life for Edward, until then he had really been a boy.'[36]

Some further insight into the relationship between Constance and Stepniak and Edward's feelings about it can be found in a letter Edward wrote to Nellie. Like so much of their correspondence it is undated other than 'Sunday', but from the contents it was certainly written in the latter half of the 1890s and very probably in 1898.[37] While it does not offer incontrovertible proof that Constance and Stepniak were lovers it strongly suggests as much. In the letter Edward attempts to persuade Nellie of the spuriousness of the outside world's judgements, and argues that the private world of lovers is inviolable and 'annihilates' external opinion. 'When S & Connie were together,' Edward explains,

if I *regarded* the outside opinion I should be a coward. I knew that *I* knew, and that no one else but us three *could* know, could enter – that made outside opinion ridiculous dust or chaff to me. Yet just think what the outside opinion would have been of those nearest and dearest to me, of my friends, relations, the world at large?[38]

Later in the letter Edward returns to the relationship between Constance and Stepniak and his own belief in the primacy of love, constructing an imaginary dialogue between himself and the 'Religious Spirit':

The Religious Spirit would have said to me:
    RS "But this is *wrong*"
    EG "Why?"
    RS "Because she is married"
    EG "But she does not love me"
    RS "But she ought to"
    EG "Why?"
    RS "Because to indulge in passion is wicked"
    EG "Why?"

RS "Because to sacrifice herself for your good was her duty"
EG "But it wouldn't have been for my good"
RS "Why?"
EG "Because a living thing is greater than a dead thing"[39]

If this exchange reveals the sympathy in Edward that Nellie describes, the bleak devastation of the final line also gives some indication of the force with which the discovery hit him.

Tensions in the marriage were building through 1893 and the year commenced with an event so horrible that it was never spoken of thereafter, even amongst the most candid members of the family. On 19 January Edward wrote a hurried note to his father from Brighton informing him that Constance's eldest brother Arthur Black had killed his wife Jessie and his son Leslie aged fifteen months and had then put an end to himself. Edward declared that Arthur was 'undoubtedly insane at the time' and instructed his father that 'the matter had better not be discussed before strangers and servants and that the halfpenny papers be kept out of the house'.[40] The inquest jury concluded that Arthur had killed his wife and child and then committed suicide, but there were several curious and unresolved aspects to the case. Leslie had suffered a knife wound to the back of the neck and a broken skull, while Jessie was discovered with her head violently smashed in and a probable bullet wound in the neck. There was a trail of blood up the stairs to the couple's bedroom in which Arthur was found face down on the bed. He had been bleeding from the nose and had a bullet wound in his thigh which, according to medical opinion, could not have been self-inflicted. A revolver lay on a table by his bed – four bullets had been fired and two remained – alongside a bloodstained knife and a coal hammer. There were also medicine bottles on the table, some containing the chloroform Arthur had drunk to kill himself. A neighbour reported hearing two shots on the Tuesday morning, but another said she had seen Arthur at 6.30 on Wednesday evening, although the police surgeon believed he must already have been dead. Why had the neighbour heard only two shots when four had been fired? Whose blood was on the stairs? If it was from Arthur's thigh wound, had Jessie shot him? Had the neighbour really seen Arthur on the Wednesday? Jessie was reputed to be neurotic and also possibly an alcoholic. She allowed the house to become so chaotically disordered that Speedwell, her five-year-old daughter, was taken to live with her aunt Clementina, who subsequently brought her up. The Deputy Coroner for Brighton, who represented Arthur's family at the inquest, suggested that Jessie killed Leslie 'and the husband might then have taken her life'.[41] Edward wrote again to his father on 20 January, noting that 'the whole thing was so hastened through that several very curious features in the case were not gone into. It is better so.'[42]

Despite Edward's insistence that 'the matter must be dropped entirely', he almost certainly later related it to Joseph Conrad. In his introduction to Letters from Conrad, Edward recalls how he described to him 'a terrible family tragedy of which I had been an eye-witness'. Far from expressing sympathy or horror, Conrad 'became visibly ill-humoured and at last cried out with exasperation: "Nothing of the kind has ever come my way! I have spent half my life knocking about in ships, only getting ashore between voyages! I know nothing, nothing! except from the outside. I have to guess at everything!"'[43] Edward rather charitably attributes this predatory outburst to 'the artist's blind jealousy speaking, coveting the experiences he had not got', adding that Conrad 'certainly ... could have woven a literary masterpiece out of the threads I held, had he known the actors'.[44]

Although it was Edward who had rushed to Brighton and was present at the distressing official formalities, Constance was at the emotional centre of the tragedy. As an adult she had not seen a great deal of Arthur, but he had been very kind to her when she was a child and she had retained a great affection for him. The circumstances of his death precluded the habitual rites of mourning – 'Of course no friends are expected at the funeral, and no letters of sympathy must be written,'[45] Edward warned his father – leaving Constance to fall back on her considerable reserves of stoicism and inner strength as she sought to come to terms with her shock and grief. Part of her response was to immerse herself ever more deeply in her study of Russian, and with Stepniak's encouragement she began to translate Turgenev's Rudin.

Just before the appalling events at Brighton, plans had been made for Constance and Edward to spend May in Paris with Stepniak and his wife Fanny. For some reason the Stepniaks decided not to go in the end; perhaps Fanny had her suspicions about the blossoming relationship between Constance and her husband. David Garnett maintained that during Stepniak's life Fanny was 'violently jealous of every woman he met, including Constance',[46] but Olive's diaries, which contain many accounts of Fanny Stepniak, offer little or no evidence of this. Springtime in Paris did nothing to restore harmony to the Garnett marriage; Constance was disgusted by what she called the 'cynical materialism and indecency of the [Parisian] people'.[47] Olive reported that her sister-in-law 'saw a good deal of the students and their mistresses and thought the absence of idealism and commonplace immorality horrible ... Edward on the contrary was delighted and reproached her for behaving like a British matron.'[48] Constance's disagreements were not confined to arguments with Edward: the food upset her, too, and a wretched trip ended on receipt of a telegram summoning them home with the news of the death of Constance's father.

The miseries of the year continued. Constance was plagued again by her 'internal troubles' and the friction with Edward mounted inexorably. On 6 July Constance wrote a long, agonisingly frank letter to her husband, who was at their rooms in John Street. It was never posted, but Richard Garnett is certain his grandfather read it. Constance had been re-reading Tolstoy's *Boyhood, Adolescence and Youth*; one passage in particular gave her a jolt of painful recognition:

'She would sigh as if enjoying her grief and giving herself up to the contemplation of her misery. In consequence of this and sundry other instances of her always considering herself a victim a *kind of intermittent feeling of calm dislike* began to be noticeable in his treatment of his wife – *that restrained dislike for the once-loved being which betrays itself by an unconscious desire to say something disagreeable* to him & to her.'

That is just what I see so clearly in you just now. I see so generally a slightly sarcastic and contemptuous attitude to me. You can't help it of course but it is ridiculous to abuse me for my consequent want of warmth & initiative. I am tired of flogging a dead horse ...

The consequence of your critical attitude is to make me shrivel up and feel I must not stir hand or foot for fear of making things worse. Love certainly makes people better than they are without it; when it is withdrawn it is not only that the character is seen clearer, it also deteriorates yourself. At least I feel myself so soiled and spoiled, so degraded in my own eyes, and every hour is such a false position. I am constantly courting the love of a man who treats me with obvious contempt; I try to console my pride by thinking it is more for his sake than mine.

When you are away I can take interest in outside things and work and regain my self respect. When you are here, I am apt to alternate between trying to excuse your attitude to me by humiliating myself in my own eyes, and then at intervals simply hating you for it, which makes me much more miserable.

What I want is work and independence – to regain my self respect. If you would manage to let us see little of one another for some time, there might be a hope of getting into a new and better relation to one another. We are both too sore from too much friction to be able to be natural. If we could be more apart, and keep at a distance when we meet, we might come to realize what is precious in what is left to us and to forget a little some of the pain and desecration and want of mutual respect which is spoiling everything for us.[49]

It is a bleak portrait of the state of the marriage: Edward's periodic fits of irritability were mentioned by more than one member of the Garnett family and he had lost none of that verbal acerbity noted by his schoolfellows. The recurrence of Constance's internal problems, coupled with her reference to her 'want of warmth and initiative', suggest that the physical side of the relationship had not been fully restored either.

Stepniak was undoubtedly a complicating factor and Constance's misery may have been compounded by the fact that the Russian was paying increasing amounts of attention to Olive, who was seeking his advice on her writing. This is certainly the impression given by Olive's account of a tense evening at the Stepniaks' house in late July. She and her sister Lucy had been invited to meet Vladimir Korolenko, author of The Blind Musician, who was visiting London en route to Chicago and staying with Stepniak. A large Anglo-Russian party was assembled, including Edward and Constance. At one point in the proceedings Constance complained to Olive, '"I feel very sore, Stepniak doesn't think anything of me now. You are just in the hey-day, wait a bit and you will be in my position" ... She wasn't joking,'[50] noted a rather taken aback Olive. A further testy exchange took place later in the evening when Olive, whom Stepniak often referred to as his 'daughter', was sitting on a sofa between her hero and Fanny. 'You are quite a little family,' remarked Constance. 'I feel sore that you haven't asked me to belong. What am I, your daughter's brother's wife?' 'But S.S. did not ask her to belong,' observed Olive a touch triumphantly. 'In fact it struck me that he treated her quite severely, for in answer he said, "Oh, you must go to Russia" and that was all.'[51] This apparently casual remark was taken in deadly seriousness by Constance, who was on her way to Russia by the end of the year. Edward's frame of mind was no better than that of his wife:

Olive reported that he 'didn't seem to be specially friendly with anyone, he spoke only to men, and chaffed the ones he knew'.

The accumulating strain was in evidence three days later on 1 August when May Garnett married Guy Hall. According to Olive the bridegroom was 'pale and trembling, looking quite boneless and flabby as men always seem to do under the influence of strong emotion'.[52] Constance came to the house for a moment, but then rapidly disappeared with a bad headache; Edward looked 'very pale and nervous'.[53] He had done his best to ensure that May's four-year engagement ended at the altar – a prospect that had looked distinctly dubious at one time due to Guy's chronic shortage of funds. May had seen little of her fiancé during the engagement, a large part of which he had spent working for a bank in Rio de Janeiro in an attempt to make some money. Edward had written to his father in 1891 suggesting that 'the £12 you wish to give us for a future day would be better spent on May's happiness: indeed we could make it up to £20 now'[54] – a characteristically generous gesture prompted by Edward's conviction that if they married, 'May's nature would be ripened and softened by happiness and Guy's simplicity of heart would work towards a closer union.'[55] Sadly he turned out to be entirely mistaken. Guy, whom his niece described as 'a stupid man with a slow drawl then fashionable ... handsome with a straight back to his head like a Prussian officer, blue eyes and a fine golden moustache ... smell[ing] of cigars and wine',[56] proved constitutionally incapable of making or keeping money and was soon forced to return to Rio with May, despite a previous promise to come home for good. He later confided to Edward that he had contracted syphilis. May vainly attempted to keep her husband in order by making sure he had no cash; she had been desperate to become Mrs Hall and, as Olive remarked on the wedding day, 'now and henceforth that cannot be taken from her; she has had her cake, however it may taste in the eating'.[57] It turned out to taste very stale indeed.

Constance, meanwhile, pursued her belief in the restorative powers of work and independence. She was overjoyed when the newly established firm of William Heinemann agreed to publish her translation of Goncharov's *A Common Story*, and then commissioned her to translate *The Kingdom of God is Within You* by Tolstoy. Edward was polishing up a book of prose poems he had written and was 'very hot about a scheme for a complete edition of Tourgueneff [sic]'.[58] It was proposed that Stepniak would write a critical introduction and prefaces to each volume of these translations.

For a while this literary activity and their love for David dampened the chords of disharmony in the Garnett marriage, although when Edward suggested that Stepniak receive 5 per cent of the money Constance earned from the Turgenev as a fee for his contribution, she objected that this was not nearly enough. Eventually they settled on 20 per cent – four times Edward's figure. The Turgenev project was first offered to T. Fisher Unwin, who turned it down; it was taken up by the equally cosmopolitan William Heinemann, who then promptly took fright at the idea of prefaces carrying the name of the revolutionary Stepniak and proposed Henry James or the Norwegian writer Bjørnstjerne Bjørnson as alternatives. This did not meet with Constance's approval and neither did Edward's attempts at compromise. Olive recorded that

> Edward has made an overture that Stepniak's name shall merely appear at the end of the introductions, not be advertised at all. Of course as Connie says she will not have half the pleasure of translating if Stepniak has no share, the idea was his, and no one else can give the facts about these epoch making novels as he can. Other writers may write their critical introductions, they cannot write the critical-historical introductions that he can, which will make the edition unique.[59]

In the event the first two Turgenev volumes, *Rudin* and *A House of Gentlefolk*, appeared with prefaces by Stepniak, although his name did not appear on the covers. This was not the last argument about the project, which to some extent became a conduit for more personal tensions simmering below the surface.

As the year drew to a close Constance put the finishing touches to her preparations to go to Russia – a consequence of Stepniak's throwaway comment at the edgy evening with Korolenko. The trip would certainly be invaluable in improving her Russian, but her main reason for going may well have been personal rather than professional. As a lone lady traveller she was unlikely to be subjected to any great scrutiny by the Russian authorities and was therefore the ideal person to carry letters and books which would not have passed the mail censors in Russia. She may also have taken in funds raised by the Society of the Friends of Russian Freedom to aid political prisoners and for famine relief. All this she did for Stepniak and there was surely nobody else who could have persuaded her to embark on such a potentially hazardous journey or to leave her beloved son, then three months short of his second birthday, for nearly eight weeks – even if there was by then a resident nursemaid at Henhurst Cross. Edward apparently 'agree[d] unquestioningly that it was right'[60] that Constance should go. David Garnett claims his father gave his blessing in accordance with the Garnett tradition of supporting political exiles; he may also have realised that resistance was futile.

A few days before Constance's departure the Anglo-Russian fraternity in London was severely agitated by the appearance of an article in the *New Review* which, without actually naming him, left little doubt as to the identity of Adjutant General Mezentsev's assassin. The article was in two parts, each written by a pseudonymous author, 'Z' and 'Ivanoff' respectively. 'Ivanoff' has been identified as P. I. Rachkovsky, head of the Russian foreign secret service. His contribution, while abusing Kropotkin as a fanatic 'with a kink in his mind'[61] and denouncing the activities of foreign anarchists in London for 'shamefully misus[ing]' the 'ungrudging hospitality' of the British, contained little that would have really alarmed his targets. 'Z's' essay was a different matter entirely. The identity of 'Z' has never been confirmed, but the Anglo-Russian community was convinced that even if she was not the actual author, much of the information came from 'OK', the nom de plume of Olga Novikoff (née Kiréeff), a London-based champion of the Tsarist regime. The final pages of 'Z's' article set out to turn British public opinion against the revolutionary exiles by providing a detailed account of the infamous career of 'one who, under an assumed name, is one of the most notable refugees in London';[62] it ended with a highly coloured description of Mezentsev's murder.

The article cast a long shadow over the farewell party given by Edward and Constance at John Street on 29 December, two days prior to Constance's departure. This was a gathering of the Garnetts' closest friends – Nellie Heath, Gustaf Steffen, a Swede working in London as a political journalist, his wife Oscara, and Eustace Hartley, who was a great friend of Edward's. Like the Steffens, Hartley, a wholesale tea dealer, was a member of the Fabian Society; according to Olive he and his wife Margaret had 'a very "advanced" atmosphere about them, all the latest literary and social gossip, the newspapers, ... etc, it seems as if it were only by keeping himself in full swing, laughing, joking, talking etc that Mr Hartley can endure life, and as if *nothing* could take away his wife's grave patient smile.'[63] Olive, Lucy, Stepniak and his wife Fanny completed the party. The *New Review* article, unmentioned and unmentionable, hung heavy in the atmosphere which not even generous amounts of cham-pagne and plum pudding could lighten. Edward and Hartley made some heavy-handed and in Olive's view distasteful attempts at frivolity which Constance attempted to explain away to her sister-in-law the following day: 'She says after *all* Hartley *is* reliable in practical matters, and Edward is just a bundle of paradoxes whom *no one* can possibly understand.'[64] Constance also airily dismissed the significance of the *New Review* article 'because she had read the accusations in a book long ago, and everyone was supposed to know'.[65]

Late on the last night of what had been a difficult year, Edward saw Constance off at Holborn Viaduct, the first stage of her journey to St Petersburg. After the train had moved away, carrying Constance, 'a little, not much, excited',[66] towards her distant destination, Edward turned, left the station and walked back into the darkness.

4

'Why *not* write another?'

On 5 January 1894 – Edward's twenty-sixth birthday – Constance sat down in her large and airy rented room in St Petersburg to write her first letter home:

> It is your birthday today. I wish you were here. You would enjoy it so. I arrived at eleven yesterday. The journey was interesting but I felt very exhausted on the evening of each day … You would always be in the street – so picturesque and full of life – the queer little sledges about as big as goat chaises with rough shaggy ponies so prettily harnessed and everywhere the delicious sound of metal in the frost like the clink of skates. You must come some day – it seems a waste I should be here alone, you would gain so much and enjoy it so and you could describe it much better. And how nice you would look in a shuba and a big fur hat![1]

Despite her protestations to the contrary, Constance gives some very vivid impressions of the city and its inhabitants. She was being looked after by Zina Vengerov, whom she had met at the Stepniaks' in London, and was thrilled at the prospect of a trip to Moscow to meet Tolstoy. Yet amidst all the novelty and the flurry of activity her thoughts turned to Edward: 'Please write to me often. I am homesick in spite of all these excitements,' she confessed. 'Keep a warm place in your heart for me, dear one, don't dwell on our differences, but remember that I am the mother of Twee and that you are very dear to me.'[2] Letters from England generally took about three days to arrive. By 7 January Constance had heard from Richard Garnett, but had received nothing from Edward. His silence made her increasingly anxious that something was seriously amiss (particularly with David, who had been left at Henhurst Cross in the care of May) and she began to think that the geographical distance between them offered some perspective on their emotional remoteness.

'I think so much of you here and more and more clearly I see that you ought never to lose sight of the necessity of building up your nervous health,'[3] Constance wrote. She continued:

> You ought to make that an object always present to you and try to get over insomnia and nervous irritability now while it is still possible by putting yourself in the best conditions of fresh air, early hours etc. In a few years it would be too late, and you would have become a pessimist, a slave to your moods, dependent on stimulants for sleep and work. You will think I am terribly moral. It isn't morality, simply I want you to become healthy and happy and manly – instead of peevish and irritable and nervous. I could not bear you to become to Bunny what our father was to us, poor man, when we were children, through his nervous irritability. You know anyone who cannot be freely approached because of the possibility of throwing him into a bad temper or nervous agitation, becomes more and more isolated. Everyone has a tendency to avoid treating him openly and to try to get round him. If you are not careful that will happen to you. Already I am afraid it begins to be so.[4]

Throughout the letter Constance is at pains to point out that her reproaches are prompted only by her love and concern, and she finishes by assuring Edward 'my heart is full of tenderness for you, of true and unselfish love for you', and begs him to 'forgive me for all I did and said that last week to vex you'.

When ten days had passed since her departure and there was still no word from Edward she wrote once more, accusing him of 'cruel' neglect and signing herself, 'Yours, C Garnett'. Edward's side of their correspondence has not survived, but it is clear his letters were indeed far from frequent, partly because he was under the weather, seeking the doctor's advice and 'weak and low-spirited'.[5] Constance's often fragile health, however, held up remarkably well during her trip, which involved some long and arduous journeys, including two to Moscow. On the first of these she met Tolstoy, whose *The Kingdom of God Is Within You* she had just translated. 'He made a great impression on everybody who saw him for the first time,' she later recounted. 'His piercing eyes seemed to look right through one and to make anything but perfect candour out of the question; at the same time there was an extraordinary warmth and affection in them.'[6] Constance also went to Nizhny Novgorod, where she visited Vladimir Korolenko, gave him correspondence from Stepniak and took delivery of a long letter from Korolenko to his fellow Russian. This she later had to burn when she was briefly detained at the frontier on her way home; as Richard explained in a letter to William Michael Rossetti, 'the Russian police laid its paw upon her, but took it off again'.[7] Constance arrived back in England on 24 February, invigorated and elated by her experiences, her head full of plans for the future.

The day after Constance's return, she and Edward lunched with the Garnett family at the British Museum. Richard had moved into one of the Museum's official residences when he had been appointed Keeper of Printed Books in 1890 and Edward often dined there when he was staying up in London. Constance distributed the various gifts she had brought back, 'talked all the afternoon'[8] and asked the family to start looking out for a house in Hampstead immediately. This sudden announcement was prompted by the fact that the Stepniaks were planning to move to North London and Constance insisted that she must live close by on account of her translations. As it turned out, when the Stepniaks did move in the autumn they took a house in Woodstock Road, the street adjacent to their old quarters in Blandford Road. In less than a week the Hampstead plans had been altered; Gustaf Steffen had seen a house in Richmond and the new proposal was for the Garnetts and Steffens to share the property and the domestic staff. Very close to Kew Gardens and only a short walk from Richmond Station, 12 Lion Gate Gardens had a reasonable-sized garden and nine 'bright and airy' rooms; the 'paint and papers and fittings [were] charming',[9] according to Olive, who wondered 'what the Stepniaks will say'.[10] The move was fixed for 21 March.

The week before, Olive and Constance attended the third in a series of four lectures on Russian literature given by Stepniak at 11 Airlie Gardens, Campden Hill Road, the home of a Miss Chadwick. These were advertised as 'the first systematic course of Lectures upon the subject delivered in this country'.[11] Stepniak's delivery left much to be desired; on the occasion of the initial lecture, Olive reported that 'his face was crimson and for the first quarter of an hour he laboured very much in his speech'.[12] Things had not noticeably improved by the time he gave the third talk – 'he was not any more coherent, and laboured very much to explain his meaning'.[13] Immediately he had finished speaking a flustered Constance gave Olive a letter from Edward to read 'in which he said that he felt too ill and nervous to come up [from Henhurst Cross] this week. She must do the moving by herself.'[14] The day before the move Olive was at home when Connie came in very much agitated. Would Lucy and I go and keep house for Edward at the Cottage as soon as possible and persuade Fanny Stepniak or Stepniak to go? Edward has been advised to take an entire rest and Fisher Unwin has given him two months' holiday to go abroad in, if he likes. He has decided not to go with Hartley to Cornwall but simply to stay all the time at the Cottage, doing nothing as far as possible and in cheerful society. He thinks Lucy, Fanny and I will be nice quiet companions as Connie cannot leave the new house. Connie does not want him to be left alone. Jane [the nursemaid] is leaving and so Baby will have to be at Kew with the Steffans' [*sic*] servants and her.[15]

Constance had been right to fear for Edward's health in her letter from Russia: the emotional stresses of the past year had resulted in what would now be termed a nervous breakdown. Edward was someone who thrived in company, but was subject to what he called 'nerve crisis',[16] especially when alone. 'Last night I had one of my nerve crisis [*sic*],' he wrote to Nellie Heath a few years later, '"the pent-up rivers of myself" (in Whitman's phrasing) free themselves, apart from my will; and one wakes exhausted, grey and weak ...'[17] In another letter to Nellie, in which he may well be describing his breakdown of 1894, Edward talks about the terrible experience 'when you lose *feeling*':[18]

I went through that some years ago – and its [*sic*] horrible – it's a sort of continual leaden coffin inside yourself – a pressing heavy blasphemy in your soul which makes all life without significance at all.

Olive and Lucy responded to Constance's request and went down to Henhurst Cross (Fanny Stepniak was unable to go because of a drama with her domestic help). The spring weather and countryside were glorious, 'the bridal blossom of the blackthorn rising in fairy array amid the gray green foliage of willow and ash'.[19] 'Edward and I have long moral discussions,' Olive recorded in her diary. 'Edward all for spontaneity, nature, impulse, change; I for solidity, intellect, reliability, truth.'[20] Although he was supposed to be taking a complete rest, Olive reported that 'post time [is] a great excitement, so many letters and packets for Edward'.[21] In the afternoons the convalescent retired to the copse behind the cottage and sat hidden among the young trees reading the manuscripts brought by the postman. By 23 April Edward had recovered sufficiently to go up to London and Olive filed a summary report of her visit:

Edward has been away from London for six weeks now and is very much better, quite different ever since I have been here; his stay here has been most successful, I consider, and so has ours. We have discussed the universe all day and every day: only to make me more strong in my own convictions, and to modify his but temporarily I think ... I have seen Edward in his trying moods now, and I understand him much better and his affairs generally.[22]

Olive does not elaborate on either the trying moods or her improved comprehension of Edward's affairs; she may have gained some insight into the state of the Garnett marriage, but she almost certainly remained in ignorance about the role Stepniak played in it.

Edward completed his recuperation in Somerset, staying at an old farmhouse next to Tarr Steps. He returned to London in the first week of May, but his health was far from fully restored. A tooth abscess that had flared up during Olive's stay at Henhurst Cross grew steadily worse, the facial swelling and nagging pain wearing him down. This was not the summer's only aggravation; in July he was confronted with what Olive rightly described as a 'slashing'[23] review of his latest literary production, a book of prose poems entitled *An Imaged World*.

An Imaged World was published by J. M. Dent, who, twelve years later, in 1906, would establish the famous Everyman's Library series. He offered Edward £25 for the manuscript. For the past year or so Edward had been doing a bit of reading for Dent and had suggested him as a possible publisher to writers whose works were unsuited to Unwin's list. He had also introduced Dent to the writer Ernest Rhys, who was later employed as the first editor of the Everyman's series. Dent, who, according to the novelist Frank Swinnerton, published books 'not as drab dollops of culture, but as treasure for the eye and mind',[24] may have decided to publish *An Imaged World* because it contained five drawings by the artist William Hyde, who also provided illustrations for works by George Meredith, A. E. Housman and Hilaire Belloc amongst others. Black-bearded, impecunious and in the words of Ford Madox Ford, 'a ferocious, gipsy-like figure',[25] Hyde was a great friend and Edward did all he could to promote his career.

It seems that *An Imaged World* was a long time in the making. In 1891 Edward wrote to his father telling him he was sketching an outline for what he thought would be his third novel. 'My difficulty is not with the *idea* at the back of the book,' he explained, 'or with the psychology of character: that I find easy enough – but it is in the translating of the idea into modern surroundings and requirements which hampers me. When I succeed best, I find I am not writing a *novel*, but a sort of prose poem.'[26] The poetic voice in *An Imaged World* is that of a lover who, wherever he looks in the external world, discerns symbols of his own hopes or fears, whether he is in the deepest countryside or moving amidst the crowds of London. As with *Light and Shadow*, the emphasis is very much on the subjective mind. Like so many other writers at that time, Edward was attempting to find an effective literary form in which to represent individual consciousness, but he lacked the creative talent of the likes of Joseph Conrad, Virginia Woolf or Ford Madox Ford, as the over-strained and deliberately archaic language of *An Imaged World* makes only too clear. Reviewing the book in the *Academy*, Ernest Rhys described it as a 'puzzling experiment'[27] and pointed out that the reader gains little knowledge 'of things "as they really are", but [Garnett] makes it clear enough if sometimes by rather roundabout ways what Night – the "lawless old Night" – and Day, the Thorn-Blossom and the Storm-wind, signify to his own rather extravagant fancy.'[28]

The more effective parts of the book are those set in London with Edward – again, like his contemporaries – eager to explore the dehumanising power of the metropolis:

> Here where all this massed humanity splinters into irregular fragments of groups of people, where barriers, shutting off each from each, are erected by inviolable custom, here amid this formless grey Multitude struggling in the vortex of labour which each endures, goaded by the will-to-live, here not far from the centre of the great city circles the current of a little centre of life: a few dirty noisy streets, a few dark arches and grimy lanes, a network of decaying houses make up this little world, where, sitting at an open window in one of the large tenements, for a few intermittent hours, I snatch passages of the life passing below, of the people streaming from work back to their homes, streaming from their houses each morning, back to their real homes, the whirring wheels within the noisy factory walls.[29]

Rhys, whose notice was far from entirely negative, detected the possible influence of 'Celtic romancers' in Edward's use of adjectives, particularly in the sections set in the countryside. As a founding member of the Rhymers' Club, Rhys was doubtless aware of Edward's penchant for all things Celtic. *An Imaged World* was also reviewed by another Rhymer, W. B. Yeats, who astutely perceived the shadow of two other Garnett gods, Walt Whitman and Richard Jefferies, hovering over its pages. Yeats let his friend down as gently as he could, declaring that 'it is almost impossible to open [the book] without finding beauty, but in the midst of the most beautiful passages will come a word without precision or a phrase without music, and the impression of the whole is a little vapoury.'[30] The *Daily Chronicle*'s reviewer had no time for such diplomatic niceties and mounted a savage attack, ridiculing the use of archaic language and castigating Edward for 'bad prose, turgid, rhetorical, cumbrous in structure, affected in diction'.[31] Olive Garnett was convinced that the reviewer was Henry Norman, and that his vitriol was prompted by a desire for revenge, as Unwin had rejected his wife's manuscript on Edward's advice. If it was Norman, his thirst for vengeance was still not sated by the final paragraph in which he proclaimed, 'Before plunging into prose poetry Mr Garnett should have stopped (or stoppèd) to reflect whether he had mastered the art of plain prose.' Even Hyde's drawings, highly praised in other reviews, failed to attract a good word.

The *Chronicle*'s laudatory treatment of Constance's first Turgenev translation, *Rudin*, which appeared the day before the assault on *An Imaged World* could hardly have been more different, something Edward must have noticed. Two of the most favourable reports on Edward's book came from American papers: the *New York Critic* noted 'power as well as passion'[32] in some of the chapters, while the *Boston Literary World* considered that 'Mr Edward Garnett has written intensely beautiful descriptions of nature in his prose poems'.[33] Welcome crumbs of comfort after the *Daily Chronicle* mauling.

By August Edward's abscess and facial swelling had got so bad that he went to Brighton to consult Constance's brother Robert, a doctor at Brighton Hospital, about a possible operation, as well as to take the sea air. There was illness at Henhurst Cross, too: Constance was suffering from prolonged headaches and sleeplessness, while David had constant diarrhoea.

On top of all this, trouble was brewing over the prefaces to Constance's Turgenev translations. *Rudin* had been published with Stepniak's name appearing only at the end of his introduction, as Edward had suggested. Constance considered this 'shabby treatment'[34] – a view shared by Stepniak himself, who, after reluctantly writing a preface to *A House of Gentlefolk*, withdrew his labour because 'Heinemann had treated him so badly'.[35] Constance wanted the remaining Turgenev volumes to be issued without prefaces; Stepniak suggested asking George Moore or Edmund

Gosse to provide them, while Edward was all for writing them himself. The mention of Gosse's name in connection with the project would have infuriated Edward, who had a lifelong contempt for 'academic' critics in general and for Gosse in particular. Constance was opposed to Edward becoming involved and wrote to him, arguing that,

> To write something good on Turgenev you must either put the accepted views on him more beautifully and aptly than they have been in the past, or else take a new line about him. You could perhaps do either of these if you gave time and trouble. But you feel no impulse to do it from within, and I won't have you lose time and trouble on it. You want to keep all your energies for work you care for and really feel drawn to. I know if you did the work ever so slightly and quickly I should like it a great deal better than a preface by a fool like Gosse and his tribe. But I would rather have a foolish preface by Gosse than a slip-shod one by you, or a good one that cost you time and trouble.[36]

Whether Constance's objections were wholly based on her concern that Edward would find the work an uncongenial distraction it is difficult to say, but her assurance that she would prefer a 'slightly and quickly' written preface by Edward to anything by Gosse rings rather hollow in the light of her final sentence. She may well have seen Edward's involvement as a threat to her independence, as Richard Garnett suggests,[37] but she may also have resisted the idea of her husband invading her literary union with Stepniak. It seems that Edward did have the impulse to write the prefaces and as Heinemann wanted them, he got his way.

As might be expected, Edward's approach to Turgenev was very different from that of Stepniak, who read the novels from a socio-political perspective and presented Turgenev as a chronicler of intellectual and social dissent. Edward discussed the historical and social context of the novels at some length, but his emphasis is very much on Turgenev the literary artist. It is the Russian novelist's ability to suggest a wealth of meaning in the employment of a single detail, the poetic concision of his writing and his capacity to capture the essence of the general in the particular that earned Edward's unstinting admiration. Furthermore, he argued that Turgenev's fusion of the psychological and the external resulted in a higher form of literary 'reality' than that to be found in the novels of writers like Dickens and Balzac: 'At the precise point of psychological analysis,' Edward argues, 'Turgenev throws a ray of light from the outer to the inner world of man and the two worlds are revealed in the natural depths of their connection.'[38] It is this exploration of the life of the mind and Turgenev's uncanny ability to distinguish that enduring secret essence in a transitory world that made him the writer to whom Edward believed the aspiring artist should turn in an effort to capture modernity in all its dizzying complexity.

By 1900, when Turgenev's *The Jew and Other Stories* was published, Edward was openly using his prefaces as artistic manifestos for the novice author: 'In England alone, perhaps,' he writes, 'is it necessary to say to the young novelist that the novel can become anything, can be anything, according to the hands that use it ... If you would study [art] in its highest form, the form the greatest artist of our time has perfected – remember Turgenev.'[39] Edward's appreciation of the Russian novelist and his insistence on Turgenev's 'modernity' pre-empt many of the remarks made by Virginia Woolf in her essay 'The Novels of Turgenev' (1933).

Edward's efforts had an early effect on one young man on the brink of publishing his first novel. 'Your prefaces to the different novels contain some of the best criticism of fiction that I have ever come across,'[40] enthused Arnold Bennett in a letter of 1897. Bennett later paid public tribute to Edward's work, declaring that 'Mr Garnett's introductions constituted something new in English literary criticism; they cast a fresh light on the art of fiction, completing the fitful illuminations offered by the essays of Mr George Moore.'[41] As Bennett's remark suggests, Edward was not the only person extolling Turgenev's qualities – Henry James for one had written essays on the Russian prior to the appearance of the prefaces – but these introductions (which appeared over six years) helped to establish Edward's critical credentials, particularly as an authority on Russian literature, just when his own ambitions in the creative field seemed doomed to disappointment.

The relationship between criticism and creativity was something that had preoccupied Edward from an early stage in his career. In a letter written when he was twenty-two he explained to his father:

> Unless criticism be creative I am not drawn towards it, and most critics are created, not creative ... But I have had at the back of my brain for a long time that it is not impossible to put criticism into living form, or rather that it is one's duty to try and do so. Anyway I am convinced that genius with many is like a smouldering fire. Generally it gets choked up, or dies out, but a chance wind, another's hand ... may cause a burst of beautiful flame.[42]

At the time he wrote this Edward was struggling with what he then thought would be his third novel (it turned out to be *An Imaged World*) and harbouring thoughts of shaping some of his critical ideals into fictional form – a project Constance astutely diagnosed as being 'so difficult that he can hardly hope to be even moderately successful'.[43] Yet while the door appeared to be closing on this particular aspiration another was opening – one which offered a different kind of creative criticism from that originally envisaged by Edward. For what he unwittingly describes in the final sentence is nothing less than his future vocation: his was to be the hand that ignited the flame of genius in so many.

One of the first people to benefit from Edward's critical acuity was his old childhood friend Ford Madox Ford. Ford's grandfather, the Pre-Raphaelite artist Ford Madox Brown, had died in 1893 and Ford was to write his biography. The book had been planned during the summer of 1894 – an anxious time for Ford, who that spring had eloped with and subsequently secretly married Elsie Martindale, the eighteen-year-old daughter of an analytical chemist. The Garnett family had been involved in these cloak-and-dagger proceedings, which resulted in various court hearings over the summer, instigated by Elsie's irate father, who had made his daughter a Ward of Court before the wedding. A frantic Ford had sought the advice of Edward's solicitor brother Robert, who took Elsie to Gloucester to stay with the Garnetts' old nurse Chapple and her sister prior to the marriage, at which Chapple was a witness, and both bride and groom lied about their ages.

Ford was perhaps fortunate eventually to emerge a free and legally married man from the subsequent court hearings, which were attended with great interest by Olive Garnett. His anxieties on the amatory front finally alleviated, Ford turned his attention to his grandfather's life. Two publishers – Bell and Longmans – were interested in the book and Ford's uncle William Michael Rossetti, whose wife Lucy was Madox Brown's daughter, was willing to supply letters and other materials; the trouble was that Ford had little idea how to set about the task. One evening at the British Museum residence Elsie told Olive Garnett that 'Ford was worrying very much over the business.'[44]

> Fortunately Edward was dining with us and after dinner, we sat round the table and discussed pros and cons. Edward talked extremely well, brilliantly and gradually evolved something 'practical' out of the vagueness. He showed Ford what a valuable literary

property the Life was, one which any publisher would be glad to secure, provided he could have a glimpse at the materials etc and showed him how to approach the matter in his negotiations ... Ford of course has to think of how to live while he is preparing the book ... [Edward] is therefore going to try and induce Dent to take F's novel, "The Sowing of the Oats" ... which would provide the necessary for a while. Edward's exposition of Ford's position as holder of this literary property was most interesting and Ford became reassured and hopeful.[45]

This is an early example of Edward's ability to 'talk' a book into being, a skill he employed to some effect throughout his career, adapting his approach to the temperament of the protégé, reassuring the timid, cajoling the reluctant and bellowing at the bloody-minded. In the case of Ford, Edward (who was five years older) initially assumed the tones of sage authority: Olive reports a further 'hammering out' of the Madox Brown Life a few days later, during which, after 'much talk and some wrangling', a concrete conception evolved from the vague. 'Edward was excellent in the discussion,' Olive noted, 'I merely sympathetic, Ford struggling, Elsie passive.'[46] Edward counselled Ford both on practical matters – suggesting he should interview Madox Brown's friends in search of anecdotes – but also on finer aesthetic questions: 'In point of style your suggestions would be gratefully received,' Ford wrote, 'the work being new to me is perhaps not up to much and I am not able to judge so let me have your advice.'[47] Edward approved the style of the few chapters he had seen, but when in September 1895 Ford presented the complete manuscript he was reprimanded like an errant schoolboy. 'Edward criticised Ford's MSS severely' noted Olive:

German – cumbrous – slovenly – vague, will generalise about things of which he knows nothing etc etc – He took trouble trying to make it better, underlining bad English, crossing out useless things and so on. But I can't help feeling for Ford. Of course it is kind of Edward and good for Ford. But when one thinks of the immense labour he had taken, one feels weakly [?] sorry for the further necessity of ruthlessly amending.[48]

There is little doubt that in these early days Edward was apt to regard Ford as a sixth-former might a twelve year old; on one occasion when he was staying with Ford and Elsie at their home on Romney Marsh he teased his host, 'treating Ford like a well meaning baby. "Are you awake?" stroking his hair, patting him on the back etc'.[49] At this stage in their relationship Ford seems generally to have taken it in good part; he was certainly full of gratitude for Edward's efforts on his behalf with *Ford Madox Brown*, which received some very good reviews when it appeared. 'Thanks for all you've done – I don't know why you do it,'[50] he wrote – words oft repeated down the years.

Edward's daily job of ploughing through all the manuscripts submitted to Unwin by authors considerably less accomplished than Ford was generally a pretty thankless task, but just occasionally something was sent in which caused real excitement. Wilfred Chesson initially took charge of the manuscripts as they arrived at Unwin's office and then passed on a selection to Edward, who did most of his reading at Henhurst Cross. On 5 July 1894 Chesson received a manuscript submitted for consideration for the Pseudonym Library. The author's name on the typescript was 'Kamudi'– the Malay word for 'rudder'. This tale of a Dutch trader's disintegration in Borneo impressed Chesson, who dispatched it to Edward. The story contained many of the elements of standard exotic 'romances' of the time, including piracy, elopement and betrayal, but Edward immediately recognised that the narrative had qualities that set it apart from the usual run of Far Eastern potboilers. Indeed, the manuscript seemed to challenge many of the conventions of such books: there was a distinctly antiheroic aspect to its main protagonist, the portraits of the natives ran counter to prevailing stereotypes and the narrative's mordant undercurrent was entirely unlike superficially similar works. The sophistication of the narrative point of view and the evocation of the tropical atmosphere evident in the opening chapter arrested Edward's attention. He was captivated, too, by the figure of Babalatchi, an elderly, one-eyed statesman, and by a night scene at the river's edge between the Dutch trader's Malay wife and her daughter. Having read the manuscript, Edward firmly advised Unwin, 'Hold on to this.'[51] He was curious about the author, who he thought at first must have Eastern blood in his veins. 'I was told however that he was a Pole,' Edward later recalled, 'and this increased my interest, since my Nihilist friends, Stepniak and Volkhovksy, had always subtly decried the Poles when one sympathized with their position as "under dog".'[52] The Pole and the Russians: that early association in Edward's mind was something he could never entirely relinquish.

Accounts vary of when and where Edward first met the author of the admired manuscript, *Almayer's Folly*. It may have been in October 1894 at Unwin's offices, but when he wrote about the occasion over thirty years later, Edward stated that it took place in November, in the plush surroundings of the National Liberal Club in Whitehall Place, whence reader and author had been summoned by Unwin, a life member. Edward may have become a little hazy as to the exact circumstances, but his impressions of the author remained razor sharp:

> My memory is of seeing a dark-haired man, short but extremely graceful in his nervous gestures, with brilliant eyes, now narrowed and penetrating, now soft and warm, with a manner alert yet caressing, whose speech was ingratiating, guarded, and brusque by turn. I had never before seen a man so masculinely keen yet so femininely sensitive.[53]

Despite his relative youth (he was twenty-six at the time of the encounter) Edward had already established something of a reputation. Even the mercurial novice author, who later described his initial view of the London literary scene as 'as inviting as a peep into a brigand's cave and a good deal less reassuring',[54] was aware of the Garnett name. 'The first time I saw Edward,' he later recounted, 'I dare not open my mouth. I had gone to meet him to hear what he thought of *Almayer's Folly*. I saw a young man enter the room. "That cannot be Edward so young as that," I thought. He began to talk. Oh yes! It was Edward. I had no longer doubt.'[55]

The meeting between Edward Garnett and Józef Teodor Konrad Korzeniowski came at an opportune moment for both men. As far as Edward was concerned the year had been blighted by marital tension, mental and physical illness and the further disappointment of his literary ambitions. Korzeniowski, who nine years earlier had anglicised his surname to Conrad, had fared little better. Orphaned at the age of eleven, he had subsequently been brought up by his maternal uncle Tadeusz Bobrowski. Although he had seen relatively little of Bobrowski after 1874, when he embarked on a career with first the French and then the English merchant marine, Conrad remained close to his uncle, who effectively became his surrogate father. In February 1894 he received a telegram from Ukraine informing him of Bobrowski's sudden death. Conrad was in London at the time, where a month earlier he had signed off as second mate on the steamer *Adowa*. He retreated to his cramped quarters in Gillingham Street, which he shared with several other boarders, and unavailingly looked for work, while putting the finishing touches to *Almayer's Folly*, which he had begun in the autumn of 1889. A month after sending the manuscript to Unwin in July 1894 Conrad, by now in the grip of one of his not infrequent bouts of depression, went off for a water cure in Champel-les-Bains near Geneva. He returned to London on 6 September in low spirits, unemployed and relatively short of funds.

Although he was unaware of it at the time, Conrad's maritime career was at an end. Henceforth he would earn his living by his pen, writing in his third language; a daunting prospect for a man rising thirty-seven, with nothing published to his name and few contacts in the literary world. Fortuitous indeed, then, that one of the first people he met when he peeped into the 'brigand's cave' was Edward Garnett, with his impeccable literary background, knowledge of publishers and, perhaps most crucially, his sensitivity to Conrad's fluctuating moods and often agonising self-doubt. In contrast, Edward's employer's lack of this last quality was evident at the National Liberal Club meeting when Unwin's efforts to engage Conrad in conversation about politicians and some of the authors on his list were 'as successful as an attempt to thread an eyeless needle'.[56] Edward looked on during this stilted exchange, hypnotised by the flash of Conrad's pointed patent leather shoes as he continually shifted one foot over the other. Unwin's casual reference to 'your next book' put an end to all pretence at conversation: 'Conrad threw himself back on the broad leather lounge and in a tone that put a clear cold space between himself and his hearers, said: "I don't expect to write again. It is likely that I shall soon be going to sea."'[57] Unwin 'expressed some deprecatory ambiguities'[58] and then made off to more promising-looking friends in the far corner of the room.

In this seemingly unpropitious situation Edward's instinct took over: speech came to him in a rush as he sought to persuade Conrad that the life he had seen on sea and land would vanish if he did not record it in literature and, more importantly, that it was clear from *Almayer's Folly* that he had the power and talent to do so. 'Conrad listened attentively,' Edward recalled, 'searching my face, and demurring a little. It seemed to me afterwards that he had come to meet me that night partly out of curiosity and partly as an author who, deep down, desires to be encouraged to write.'[59] Conrad himself stated on several occasions that it was Edward's finely tuned eloquence that convinced him to take up authorship as a career. Towards the end of his life he reiterated this belief to Gertrude Bone, a minor novelist and mutual friend:

If [Edward] had said to me 'Why not go on writing?' I should have been paralysed. I could not have done it. But he said to me, 'You have written one book. It is very good. Why not *write another?*' Do you see what a difference that made? Another? Yes: I would do that. I *could* do that. Many others I could not. Another, I could. That is how Edward made me go on writing. That is what made me an author.[60]

A few weeks later the two men met again for dinner in Wilton Street, after which they went back to Conrad's rooms at 17 Gillingham Street. Seated in an easy chair in the small, firelit room, Edward noted a row of French novels in the bookcase, a photograph of an aristocratic-looking woman on the mantelshelf, alongside an engraving of a 'benevolent, imposing man',[61] and a small table containing a neat pile of manuscript sheets. As the evening wore on Edward alluded once again to the merits of *Almayer's Folly* at which Conrad suddenly picked up the manuscript papers on the table, thrust them into his guest's hands and then disappeared behind a screen in search of Bénédictine. By the time he returned, Edward was transported:

> They were a half-caste, lazy lot, and he saw them as they were – ragged, lean, unwashed, undersized men of various ages, shuffling about aimlessly in slippers; motionless old women who looked like monstrous bags of pink calico stuffed with shapeless lumps of fat, and deposited askew upon decaying rattan chairs in shady corners of dusty verandahs; young women, slim and yellow, big-eyed, long-haired, moving languidly amongst the dirt and rubbish of their dwellings as if every step they took was going to be their very last.[62]

Conrad's assertion that it was Edward who made him write another novel might be described as a spiritual rather than an actual truth; he had begun *An Outcast of the Islands* (originally entitled *Two Vagabonds*) in August – several weeks before their first meeting. Edward's expressions of delight at the description of the inhabitants of the outskirts of Makassar exhilarated Conrad, who animatedly outlined the plot and the decline of his main protagonist, Peter Willems. Even in this atmosphere of excitement, however, Edward was struck by the volatility of Conrad's moods. When he began expounding on the necessity for a writer to disregard public taste, Conrad retorted passionately, 'But I *won't* live in an attic! ... I'm past that, you understand? I *won't* live in an attic.'[63] It was obvious to Edward that reassurance was required, both about the prospects of *Almayer's Folly* and that garret starvation had hardly been the lot of the likes of Robert Louis Stevenson, Rudyard Kipling or Rider Haggard. Conrad, partially mollified, rose up again at the mention of Haggard's name: 'too horrible for words'.

If Conrad needed convincing that he should and could complete *An Outcast of the Islands*, that evening in Gillingham Street tipped the balance. With Edward at his elbow the task of producing a second novel – which notoriously often presents different and arguably greater difficulties than the first – looked a much less lonely and daunting prospect.

Now there was someone Conrad could turn to and rely on for literary advice, someone who had absolute confidence in his talent and could bolster his frequently faltering self-belief. As for Edward, he recognised in Conrad something of a kindred spirit. The two men were not unlike temperamentally, sharing a sceptical turn of mind, an underlying strain of melancholy and a bleak view of man's materialist tendencies. Conrad had constantly lived a life on the margins. As a child he had been affected by his parents' insurrectionist politics, which put them at odds with the ruling Russian Empire; as a sailor he had led a peripatetic existence, going everywhere, belonging nowhere, an observer, rarely a participant. As an obscure, fledgling author in London his position was similarly isolated. It was this marginality that so appealed to Edward, himself a 'congenital outsider',[64] coupled with his conviction that on the evidence of *Almayer's Folly*, Conrad potentially offered a new, distinctive and unsettling voice to English literature. Years later, when he looked back on those very early days of their friendship, Edward recalled 'an atmosphere of humble conspiracy *à deux* which enfolded us'.[65] It is a telling phrase, capturing a kind of romantic excitement as the two men met in small Soho restaurants, St Paul's churchyard and a Cheapside café to plot the progress of *An Outcast of the Islands* and Conrad's assault on the literary world.

5

Rescuing Conrad

The midnight chimes heralding the year 1895 sounded particularly sweet to Edward. With the exception of meeting Conrad, the previous twelve months had brought one set of troubles hot upon the heels of another. Finally things appeared to be looking up. Under a new arrangement with Unwin, Edward was guaranteed an income of not less than £350 a year and was only required to go into the office on Thursdays. Constance had recently inherited about £1,000 from her father and the money from her translations was also helping to swell the family coffers. Such comparative riches transformed the Garnetts' desire to build a house in the country from dream to reality.

The first job was to find a site. Edward and Constance conducted separate searches; Edward went down to Limpsfield Chart on the borders of Kent and Surrey to stay with Sydney Olivier, a long-standing Fabian friend with keen literary interests who worked in the Colonial Office. Olivier and his wife Margaret had four daughters around David's age and had converted two cottages into a house, The Champions, at Limpsfield Chart. Edward, mindful that David was an only child, thought it a good idea that he should grow up knowing the Olivier girls. The completion of the railway line from London to Edenbridge in 1888 had attracted others who wished to live in unspoilt countryside but needed easy access to the metropolis: people like Marjory Pease and her husband Edward, one of the founders of the Fabian Society and its Secretary from 1890 to 1913. The Peases had settled within walking distance of the Oliviers in Pastens Road, whilst another Fabian, Henry Salt – a former schoolmaster at Eton whom David Garnett once described as 'the leading humanitarian and vegetarian in England'[1] – was not far away at Crockham Hill. In those days Limpsfield Chart consisted of some scattered houses and a few cottages grouped together behind an ancient wooden windmill on the edge of a common. The fields to the south fell away sharply, affording magnificent views of three counties; the pine and beech woods of the

High Chart bordered the common. It was here on the southern edge of the High Chart, where the woodland rapidly descended to meet a line of pasture fields called Scearn Bank, that Edward discovered his ideal site. Constance had also been scouring the area and came across what she considered to be the perfect spot. Both were adamant that their choice should prevail and a major argument was only avoided when it turned out that they had selected the same location. Constance bought the half-acre field for £300 from the Leveson Gower estate.

Beautiful as it undoubtedly was, the topography of the plot presented difficulties; there was no water until a sixty-foot well was sunk and all building material had to be transported on tumbrils along a rough, woodland track down the steep hillside. A shaft-horse was killed when the wheel of one of the tumbrils went over the edge of the track and cart, horse and cargo careered down the precipitous slope. The ancient, uncivilised aspect of the place appealed greatly to Edward and Constance; their house would be remote, half a mile from any highroad and far removed from popular notions of idyllic village life, as David Garnett explains:

> There was no church within two miles, no rookery, no immemorial elms, no ancient red brick or mellowed ashlar walls, no water, no fertile soil.
>
> Instead there was a great horizon, solitude, and the encompassing forest which may have given these fields [Scearn Bank] their name – for they are encerned or encircled by the woods. [My parents] were indeed pioneers, who would not have been happy in a community, or on the outskirts of one. Their choice of site was due to an awareness that they did not belong, that they rejected and did not wish to fit into the Victorian social hierarchy.[2]

The house was to be designed by William Harrison (Harry) Cowlishaw. Already a member of the Garnetts' social circle, Cowlishaw was spending increasing amounts of time in the company of Lucy Garnett, to whom he became engaged in June 1895. Cowlishaw was a disciple of William Morris: he had been articled to architects in Leicester and London, but had never built a house before. Edward and Constance firmly rejected his first plan, which indulged Cowlishaw's penchant for the medieval, but ignored the prerequisites for practical living. His second submission met with his clients' approval: the drawings were declared 'delightful'[3] and, according to Cowlishaw, could 'be worked out at a cost of £700 only'.[4] The Morris influence was apparent – everything was to be made by hand, from the wrought-iron hinges and door-latches, which were fashioned in the on-site smithy, to the bare wooden window seats. The two-storeyed, four-bedroomed building was to be L-shaped, built of irregular, rough-hewn stone, with lead-paned windows. There was to be a study for Constance, while the long, narrow, south-west-facing porch became Edward's favourite perch. In clement weather he would recline here for hours in his long wicker chair, often far into the night, perusing manuscripts or conversing with visiting protégés as the bats flitted back and forth to roost in the roof above.

Edward and Constance were anxious to be close to the site while the building work was in progress and in March they left Henhurst Cross and rented a tiny cottage at Froghole, just over a mile away. Constance told Richard Garnett that she and Edward were delighted with their temporary home, but the cramped quarters soon became irksome and Froghole boasted an even greater rat population than Henhurst Cross. The cottage was so small it was impossible to have anyone to stay, so when Arthur Garnett, Olive and her friend Bertha King visited in May they had to sleep in a neighbouring cottage. On the evening of their arrival Edward took the little party

to *the* site, now a buttercup meadow, on a slope with a copse rising behind to north and east and the magnificent view spread out to the south and west with undulating hilly ground between. The cuckoo called and cows with tinkling cow bells were driven in for the night. We wandered from peg to peg, imagining the rooms, the verandah, the kitchen garden and the rest of it.[5]

The Garnetts were not the only new residents in the area. Stepniak and Fanny had recently rented an equally diminutive cottage in Pastens Lane and were soon chaffing Edward and Constance about their elevated status as 'landed proprietors'.[6] Constance's dearest wishes were being realised: her new home was shortly to rise from the buttercup meadow and Stepniak was close at hand, eager to assist with her translations.

'I see You have lighted Your camp fire in a new place,'[7] observed Joseph Conrad, writing to Edward from Champel-les-Bains, where he had retreated once more in an attempt to throw off an attack of paralysing melancholy. His poor mental state may not have been helped by his anxiety surrounding the publication of *Almayer's Folly*, which appeared on 29 April 1895. The reviews, however, were generally favourable and included a highly encouraging unsigned notice by H. G. Wells in the *Saturday Review*. When Edward had read the manuscript of Wells's *The Time Machine* a few months before he had been unable to offer similar encouragement: 'This is at all events an ingenious *idea*,' he concedes, before going on to lament the allegories and 'tiresome *hypnotism*' in the book. 'If it were a little better written, & published in a magazine like the *Idler* it might be read by uneducated people with great pleasure,' Edward continues loftily. 'It is however a poor performance, and we do not advise TFU to touch it.'⁸ Conrad once called Edward infallible, but *The Time Machine* has to be put on the admittedly short list of books that got away.

With *Almayer's Folly* off his hands, Conrad turned his attention to *An Outcast of the Islands*: he already trusted Edward's advice implicitly and was regularly seeking guidance and reassurance. Chapters of *An Outcast* arrived in batches in Edward's postbox: 'In chap. XII beginning with the words "And now they are – " are the two pars in the new style,' Conrad explained in an accompanying letter of 8 March. 'Please say in the margin what you think. One word will do. I am very much in doubt myself about it; but where is the thing, institution or principle which I do not doubt?!'⁹ The 'new style' involved a shift from the past to the present tense; evidently it did not meet with approval as Conrad reverted to the use of the past tense.

Edward was acutely aware that his dealings with Conrad involved a delicate balancing act: one wrong word, one hasty criticism could shatter his friend's ever fragile confidence and cause him to abandon *An Outcast of the Islands* and possibly a literary career altogether – Conrad was still actively seeking opportunities to return to sea. The 'strange atmosphere and poetic vision'¹⁰ of the novel enthralled Edward and gave him genuine grounds for high praise, but he later admitted that he was so intent on encouraging Conrad that it was not until the manuscript was nearly finished that he realised that the figure of Willems 'had to bear too great a burden of both feeling and commentary'.¹¹

Conrad sent the final chapters to Edward on 18 September; the response was swift and on 24 September he wrote again, replying to his mentor's comments. 'You gild the pill richly,' Conrad confessed, acknowledging Edward's diplomatic skills, 'but the fact remains that the last chapter is simply abominable.'¹² Edward's criticism centred on Conrad's handling of Willems's death, which he felt was too protracted and lacked psychological conviction. Conrad agreed to rewrite paragraphs

Edward had marked for remodelling, but unfortunately no record of them remains. Deep down, Conrad believed that the flaws in the final section of *An Outcast of the Islands* were not 'a matter of correction ... a matter of changed words – or lines or pages,'[13] as Edward had, perhaps tactfully, suggested, but rather that the whole conception was wrong. The prospect of completely recasting the offending chapters, however, was more than he could bear – or, as he put it to Edward, 'I lack the courage to set before myself the task of rewriting the thing.'[14] Conrad and Edward may have had their reservations about the ending of the novel, but Unwin paid Conrad £50 for it, plus 12.5 per cent royalties, a considerable improvement on the £20 he had received for *Almayer's Folly*.

The letter about the ending of *An Outcast of the Islands* is a good example of what Edward calls the 'chameleon-like quality'[15] of Conrad's private correspondence. He opens with fulsome expressions of gratitude – 'I want to tell you how much I appreciate your care, the sacrifice of your time, your evident desire to help me' – applauds the 'delicacy of feeling' of Edward's criticisms, with which he agrees, and says that he would like to 'scatter [the] ashes [of the final chapter] to the four winds of heaven'. After these remarks, which teeter on the brink of flattery, comes the 'confession' that he lacks the courage to undertake radical revision and that the situation is irredeemable, 'because all my work is produced unconsciously (so to speak) and I cannot meddle to any purpose with what is within myself ... It isn't in me to improve what has got itself written.' Although Conrad then declares that with Edward's help 'I may try', the promise rings rather hollow in the light of the previous statement, which has a warning note of recalcitrance about it. He then goes on to give a detailed explanation, effectively a defence, of his thought processes when writing the final chapter. The letter ends in self-abasement, with Conrad proclaiming it to be 'a confession of complete failure on my part. I simply could not express myself artistically.' Gratitude, flattery, dejection, defiance, self-deprecation – all can be found in this letter of shifting moods and rapidly changing tones. Edward soon discovered that it wasn't just Conrad's manuscripts that required careful and nuanced reading: his letters did, too. He had to learn to calculate Conrad's epistolary moods, to judge how seriously to take his declarations of despair and his cries for help.

Conrad's career was not the only thing occupying Edward through the summer and autumn of 1895. Nellie Heath was painting his portrait. Some of the sittings took place at 13 Robert Street, the studio of Nellie's past teacher Walter Sickert, who was in Venice at the time. As Nellie applied oils to canvas she and Edward talked of her work and Edward's literary ambitions (he was writing a series of London sketches, which were never published). Artist and subject were completely at ease in each other's company and their conversations became increasingly confiding: 'I said to you all the things I say to myself and you understand them all – that is real friendship,' wrote Nellie after one such occasion. 'You made me so glad on Friday – you cannot tell what it is like to trust someone absolutely.'[16] That sense of mutual confidence was particularly precious at a time when both were experiencing periods of emotional turbulence. Nellie was still in the throes of her passion for Sickert, while Edward remained very much conscious of Constance's feelings for Stepniak.

The finished portrait captures the atmosphere of informal ease which marked the studio sessions: Edward sits, leaning slightly forward with his left hand on his knee, a cigarette between the long, shapely fingers of his right; his head inclined slightly to one side as if considering his response to a recent remark. In the autumn of 1896 Sickert took to visiting Nellie in her own studio, in Endsleigh Terrace, off the Euston Road. George Bernard Shaw, whose portrait Nellie was painting at the time, described the studio as 'a little hole of a room',[17] but according to Sickert's biographer the place became 'a haven'[18] for the artist. It was a feeling Edward would have recognised from his own experience of sitting for Nellie the previous year.

Meanwhile work on the new house was advancing steadily, and on 'a crisp starlight night'[19] in the middle of November Edward and Constance visited the site with Olive, Ford and his wife Elsie. The little party took it in turns to swing the lantern over the heath, under the pine branches and through the copse:

> Then a stumble over builders' paraphernalia and the lantern held now to a window, a rafter, or a chimney nook, or a loose plank. No staircase as yet but we sat atop of a ladder and saw the stars shining serenely in the sky roof. Well might Connie and Edward be proud and we admiring and Cowlishaw admired.[20]

As building neared completion, Edward and Constance planned a great housewarming and Stepniak vowed to get a bear's ham from Russia for the party. It was a promise he was unable to fulfil.

In the autumn of 1895 the Stepniaks returned to their London house in Woodstock Road. On Monday 23 December Stepniak set off on foot from

there to go to Felix Volkhovsky's home in Rylett Crescent, Shepherd's
Bush, where he was to attend a meeting with Volkhovsky and a fellow
émigré, Egor Egorovich Lazarev, to discuss plans for a new monthly
journal. His route took him across the single track line of the North and
South Western Junction Railway. Stepniak crossed the stile over the fence
enclosing the track; the driver of the approaching 10.20 from Chiswick
to South Acton saw him get over the stile and blew his whistle. When
the train was about ten yards from the level crossing Stepniak rushed
from the stile into the path of the engine. The stoker shouted, the
driver continued to blow the whistle and frantically applied the vacuum
brakes. It was to no avail; the engine buffer caught Stepniak, who was
knocked down and dragged along the line. By the time the train came
to a halt his body was under the second carriage. One of a group of
builders who had been working close by and knew Stepniak rushed to
tell Fanny what had happened. She sent her maid to Rylett Crescent and
it was left to Lazarev to go to the scene and discover the badly mutilated
remains of his friend.

The inquest was held on Boxing Day. One of the workmen had seen
Stepniak pass by and noticed that he was walking with his head bowed
and seemed to pay no attention to where he was going. The Coroner
affirmed that he himself had often observed the Russian walking and that
he habitually did so 'with his chin on his breast'.[21] Nicholas Tchaykovsky,
another member of the Russian revolutionary circle who knew Stepniak
well, was the final witness. He pointed out that Stepniak had been
educated in a military school where there was always tremendous noise
and that he had developed the ability to shut himself off completely from
all external distraction and immerse himself in his own thoughts. This
tallies with an entry in Olive's diary in which she remarks that Stepniak
had 'the faculty of retiring into himself when bored and forgetting his
surroundings'. When questioned about this, Stepniak replied, 'How else
could I survive English dinner parties?'[22]

The circumstances of the death were perplexing: several hundred
yards of track were clearly visible from the stile crossing, the driver had
blown his whistle and the train was hardly hurtling down the line, but
travelling at a sedate twenty-eight miles an hour. Suicide, therefore, had
to be a possibility. However, Tchaykovsky told the inquest that Stepniak
'would never take his life; there was no reason for it. He had exceptionally brilliant prospects, and was particularly respected and loved by his
friends.'[23] Stepniak was forty-three when he died; he was in good health
and planning to develop his literary career. However, entries in Olive's

diary suggest that Stepniak's relationship with Fanny was certainly not free of tension – there is more than one reference to her being 'ill' and 'wretched' – and in May of that year Constance had talked to Olive 'about Stepniak being urged by Fanny to shut himself up to produce; how he wanted a new life, to elope with someone, not to be set down to work ... Why didn't Fanny translate if she wanted money etc.'[24] How much of this was serious intent on Stepniak's part, how much Constance's personal opinion (with whom did he wish to elope and start a new life?) it is impossible to say. Such speculation was not aired at the inquest and in his summing-up the Coroner declared that 'there was nothing in the evidence to show that the deceased had any intention of committing suicide'.[25] The jury accordingly brought in a verdict of accidental death.

The funeral took place on 28 December. It was arranged by John Burns, MP for Battersea and a future cabinet minister, and had the air of a state occasion. The hearse was accompanied on its journey from Woodstock Road to Waterloo Station by a distinguished following which included Prince Peter Kropotkin, William Morris, Keir Hardie and Eleanor Marx. Hundreds stood in the unrelenting drizzle at Waterloo and listened to an array of eminent speakers. Amongst those who paid tribute were the German socialist leader Eduard Bernstein, the Italian anarchist Errico Malatesta, Morris (who gave what turned out to be his final speech in the open air), Hardie, Burns and Eleanor Marx, who applauded Stepniak's understanding that 'there could be no emancipation for men except it went alongside of emancipation for women'.[26] When all the speeches were over the coffin was put on a special train, which departed for the cremation at Woking. There is no record in public reports or private correspondence that any of the Garnett family was present at Woodstock Road, Waterloo or Woking, although it would have been easy to pass unnoticed in the crowd at Waterloo. What is certain is that Stepniak's death was a source of terrible anguish to Constance and Olive. David Garnett recalled that 'it was a blow from which it took my mother long to recover';[27] while Olive, according to her niece, 'like primitive people in bitter grief cut off all her hair'.[28]

The move to the new house, which was to be called The Cearne, took place at the end of February 1896. Although it was hardly the joyous occasion Edward and Constance originally planned, moving into the house was the fulfilment of a long cherished dream and the space and accommodation were a delight after the inconveniences and confinement of the cottage at Froghole. Three steps led up to a great studded oak door with decorative hinges and a large twisted iron ring as a handle.

This opened the latch into a dining room with a deep brick inglenook fireplace the width of the room with wooden seats running each side of the inglenook. The room occupied the ground floor of the left wing of the house. To the right of the staircase was Constance's book-lined study, which also had an inglenook fireplace, although on a much smaller scale than the one in the dining room. The casement window ledge often contained pots of seedlings or tender plants Constance was nurturing. The kitchen and scullery were behind the staircase, with the privy – equipped with an ash bucket and a large, illustrated catalogue of the Civil Service Stores – just outside the back door. Edward's bedroom was at the far end of the west wing; Constance slept halfway down the south wing, which also contained the best bedroom with its magnificent view and Cowlishaw's plasterwork briar roses; the room was strictly reserved for guests.

The floors downstairs were either light oak blocks or red tiles; none of the woodwork was stained. The walls were painted white throughout to lighten the rooms with their leaded casement windows. The Broadwood piano and heavy, bevel-edged table, which stood in the dining room, were both purchases from the sale of Ford Madox Brown's furniture. The piano was purely decorative as, although both Edward and Constance loved music, neither played. Richard Garnett remembers the pictures as being 'more interesting than decorative'[29] and both he and Constance's niece Speedwell recall several perils ready to catch the inattentive guest – beams positioned far too low and stone corbels supporting the ends of the fireplaces, 'which threatened to brain any unwary visitor approaching the fire'.[30] Needless to say, the place was crammed with books which overflowed the fitted bookshelves in every room; others were piled up awaiting review alongside Edward's never-decreasing heap of manu-scripts. Speedwell later wrote that 'there was through the house an atmosphere of learning, mixed with an easy going, out of door life and on entering a warm look of oak wood, red bricks and white freshness met the eyes'.[31]

One of the first visitors to The Cearne was Joseph Conrad. He arrived on 16 March, accompanied by his fiancée Miss Jessie George. On the face of it this was a curious match. Jessie was sixteen years younger than Conrad and shared none of his intellectual or literary interests. She came from a large, lower-middle-class family in Camberwell with whom she was still living. The exact circumstances of her meeting Conrad are unclear, but when he first knew her she was working for a typewriter manufacturing company in the City. If we are to believe Jessie, Conrad proposed on the steps of the National Gallery, urging a swift wedding, as 'he hadn't very long to live and further there would be no family'.[32] Despite this last statement there has been much speculation as to whether Jessie became pregnant and Conrad felt duty-bound to marry her. The hasty nuptials and subsequent extended honeymoon in France – during which time Jessie suffered an unspecified illness, which might just possibly have been a miscarriage – give some credence to the theory. In Ford Madox Ford's roman-à-clef *The Simple Life Limited*, published in 1911 when Ford and Conrad had fallen out, Simeon Brandetski, the character based on Conrad, has to marry his secretary after she becomes his mistress and falls pregnant.

After the Cearne visit Edward apparently wrote to Conrad in an attempt to dissuade him from the match; years later he attributed his concern to a belief that 'Conrad's ultra-nervous organization appeared to make matrimony extremely hazardous',[33] but it is more likely that he considered Jessie incapable of understanding, let alone alleviating, the enormous strains that literary composition imposed upon Conrad – something of which Edward was already acutely aware. Conrad received the intervention with good grace – 'I am very glad you wrote to me the few lines I have just received. If you spoke as a friend I listened in the same manner – listened and was only a little, a very little dismayed'[34] – and ignored the advice. He and Jessie were married on 24 March and the unlikely pair set off to Brittany for their honeymoon.

Edward may have failed to influence Conrad in affairs of the heart, but he had successfully prevented him from committing a potentially damaging literary indiscretion. There is an unexplained gap in their correspondence between September 1895 and February 1896. According to Edward, Conrad took a break from writing when he had finished *An Outcast of the Islands*, but then started a new manuscript called 'The Sisters'. This marked a radical departure from the first two novels in both writing style and subject matter. Set in mainland Europe, the first chapters deal with the wanderings of a young Ruthenian artist who leaves his homeland 'in search of a creed' and ends up in Paris, where, it seems, he would eventually have met up with the novel's other protagonist, a Basque orphan sent by one uncle to go and live in Paris with another. Ford Madox Ford, who wrote an introduction to the fragment, published posthumously in 1928, remembers the manuscript being covered with 'Mr Garnett's profuse annotations ... Mr Garnett criticizes the work with a minuteness that must have cost him infinite pains.'[35] It must also have caused Edward considerable pain when reading it. In his attempt to convey the musings of the moody, introspective artist, Conrad comes up with such sentences as 'The sweetness of the voice intoxicated him with pure delight, but the message sounded as if delivered in declaration of incomprehensible things, with a reserve of final clearness, with an incompleteness of emotion that made him doubt the heavenly origin of that voice.'[36] In the letter sent in response to Edward's misgivings about his marriage – 'So much for trifles'[37] – Conrad announces the really important news that he is abandoning 'The Sisters' and tells Edward, 'You have killed my cherished aspiration.'[38] What this treasured ambition was is far from clear; according to Ford, who is not always the most reliable source, Conrad desired to become 'what I would call a "straight" writer, as opposed to the relatively exotic novelist of the sea and the lagoons which fate, the public and some of his friends forced him to become'.[39] Later in the same piece Ford names the editor of the *New Review*, W. E. Henley, and Edward as those friends who pushed an apparently unwilling Conrad 'in a marine direction'. Ford may well be right in saying that Conrad wished to become the type of writer who evoked comparison with his French idols Gustave Flaubert and Guy de Maupassant, rather than with Rudyard Kipling and Robert Louis Stevenson, but the fact of the matter is that 'The Sisters' is badly written, with Conrad attempting to do something to which his talents were ill suited. Given Edward's lifelong conviction that authors should write about what they know, it seems unlikely that Conrad ever discussed his plan to write 'The Sisters' with his mentor. A contrite Conrad finally had to concede that Edward had 'driven home the conviction' that 'The Sisters' was a doomed project and promised to 'write the sea-story – at once ... It will be on the lines indicated to you'.[40]

Just over a fortnight after his arrival in France Conrad dispatched the first twenty-four pages of the new novel, tentatively titled 'The Rescuer', desperate for advice as to whether he was on the right track. 'I am so afraid of myself, of my likes and dislikes, of my thought and of my expression, that I must fly to You for relief – or condemnation – for anything to kill doubt with,'[41] he explained. 'I am ready to cut, slash, erase, destroy; spit, trample, jump, wipe my feet on that MS at a word from You. Only say where, how, when.' When the eagerly awaited letter from The Cearne arrived it came not from Edward but Constance and contained the alarming news that her husband was very seriously ill with typhoid.

How Edward came to contract the disease, which is spread through infected food or water, remains a mystery. The drains at The Cearne were pronounced to be 'above reproach',[42] but at the time this was little consolation. Although the real crisis lasted only a few days, Edward's temperature fluctuated, sometimes dramatically, over several weeks and he suffered the debilitating weakness typical of the condition. Complete rest and absolute quiet were essential; as Constance told her father-in-law, 'He must see no letters, hear nothing but good news, and have no worries of any kind.'[43] Copious doses of quinine were administered, which made Edward temporarily deaf, and he was given a tablespoon of Spey Royal whisky at six-hourly intervals. As if Constance's anxieties were not enough, at the worst point of Edward's illness David also developed a high temperature, headache and stomach ache. 'You may fancy my terror,'[44] Constance wrote to Narney. Happily this proved nothing more serious than tonsillitis and a chill on the stomach.

Uncharacteristically, Edward began to fret about money; as Constance explained to Richard Garnett: 'As he is paid by the manuscript he will lose more than two-thirds of April's and also of May's salary – about £35 together ... We shall probably be receiving nothing but about £20 from Fisher Unwin till July 1.'[45] Richard Garnett duly came to the rescue. By early May Edward had improved sufficiently for his bed to be moved onto a platform which allowed him to see out of the window. 'This of course tends to raise his spirits,' Olive reported to her father, adding 'I fear that they will be deluged with visitors at the Cearne when it is known that E is better. Some means of protection will have to be devised.'[46]

Proof that Edward was finally on the road to recovery came in the shape of a flying bowl of tapioca pudding, which, in a fit of exasperation with the invalid's food he was being served, he flung at Mary Belcher, a friend who had supported Constance through the crisis. By early June Edward was able to report to his mother that he could 'hobble round the garden with a stick, of course very slowly and with difficulty. My legs are much swollen, but growing stronger each day ... I am beginning to read MSS again for Mr Unwin this week.'[47] However, he was unable to attend his brother Robert's wedding to Martha ('Matty') Roscoe on 26 June. Matty was the daughter of Richard Roscoe, formerly the senior partner in Sheen Roscoe, the firm for which Robert then worked. She had literary ambitions and eventually wrote four books, including a novel, *Amor Vincit*, about which she consulted closely with her brother-in-law.

Edward did not fully regain his strength until the autumn, but at least he had survived. Typhoid was then a disease from which many people

did not recover; it rarely lasted less than three weeks and the characteristic fluctuations in a patient's condition made it, in Constance's
words, the 'most treacherous of all illnesses'.⁴⁸ Edward was fortunate
to come through it as he did, but it left him with chronic circulatory
problems in his legs, which became increasingly troublesome in his
later years.

Towards the end of May Edward was well enough to tackle those
pages of 'The Rescuer' sent by Conrad. His response was enthusiastic:
'Excellent, oh Conrad. Excellent. I have read every word of *The Rescuer*
and think you have struck a new note.'⁴⁹ Edward's relief at finding the
chapter 'so strong, so *free* and so spontaneous' after the tortuous writing
in 'The Sisters' is almost palpable. Illness had not blunted his diplomatic
skills; after the praise came 'some hasty criticisms – mere whims of mine,
on *minute* points'. The opening page of the novel, however, presented
more serious problems:

> To the aspect of the narrow seas the rising sun gives a sudden and
> ethereal beauty flushed with the delicate light of the mass of violet
> tints, traversed by a bar of molten gold tinged as if with the blood
> of invisible victims; a bar that shines, ominous and splendid under
> the rapid darkening of the sky ... the rising moon sends a metallic
> dart of glittering light to pierce with its cold shaft the black heart,
> the heart pitiless and serene of the tropical night.⁵⁰

Edward's comment was a model of tactful restraint: 'the *description*,
the tone – seems not up to your level. The *feeling* – though poetical –
seems a little *forced* a little dragged out of you, a little over elaborated
...' Conrad's response stated the case more succinctly: 'It's perfectly
rotten, that paragraph, and when one touches it the putrid particles
stick to the fingers.'⁵¹ The opening was the only real aberration and the
early pages of 'The Rescuer' reinforced Edward's opinion that Conrad
had the potential to become a major new force in English fiction. His
description of the first mate Shaw, for example, earned the comment
'charming and admirable touch' from Edward:

> Shaw with his hand on his stomach had hooked himself with both
> elbows to the rail that supported him and gazed apparently at the
> deck between his feet but in reality he was contemplating a shabby
> little house with a front garden paraded by a lean and dirty cat,
> somewhere away in the distant desolation of Barking-town.⁵²

It is an arresting image: Shaw's vision of the house in Barking rises spontaneously from the depths of the deck and it was Conrad's ability to conjure up moments like this that later led Edward to draw comparisons with the great Russian writers. In 1900 Edward wrote an article on Tolstoy and Turgenev in which he maintained that Tolstoy impressed 'on the European mind, for the first time, an adequate recognition of the way human life builds itself up out of man's trivial thoughts and emotions'.[53] Conrad's description of the contemplative Shaw has just such a quality.

Yet for all the admirable touches, Conrad was still prone to adjectival excess, a common fault with relatively inexperienced writers and something of which Edward himself had been found guilty: 'too many adjectives'[54] commented Olive briskly on reading his prose poems. Conrad's failings in this direction might partly be explained by the fact that he was not writing in his first (or indeed his second) language and that English words did not stand for things in the same unquestioned way as they did in Polish. Edward was well aware that Conrad's distance from English was a source of both struggle and liberation: struggle as he attempted to capture the essence of what he sought to describe and liberation because he was free of the native speaker's linguistic preconceptions. He also realised that at times Conrad needed advice on English nuance. Conrad's analysis of Captain Lingard's disposition – 'No doubt, he, like most of us, would be uplifted at times by the lyricism of his heart in regions charming, empty and dangerous'[55] – prompted Edward to remark '? Too far fetched for Lingard's case – also *lyricism* not good in the *associations* the word awakens',[56] to which Conrad replied, 'I don't want the word. I want the idea. Could You help me to shape it in an unobjectionable form.'[57]

On 10 June Conrad sent all he had written of 'The Rescuer' along with a letter full of uncertainty as to its merit: 'I had some hazy idea that in the first part I would present to the reader the impression of the sea … But I doubt having conveyed anything but the picture of my own folly … Probably no more will be written till I hear from you.'[58] He need not have worried; Edward was thrilled by what he saw:

Just a line to say *you have never done better than in the part of 'The Rescuer'* which you sent me … all is in your best style – and rather a new style for you – so crisp, so admirably firm … It is really extraordinary how *real* how wonderfully *actual and vivid* your characters are in the midst of your poetry, your exquisite poetry … I think the public will be hit and brought down as well as the critics. Go on! Go on![59]

While Edward was far too honest to praise something he actually cared little for (his honesty could be devastating), his enthusiastic exhortations may have been prompted by the end of Conrad's letter, which contained some ominous references about his lack of progress on the novel: 'I dream for hours, hours! over a sentence and even then can't put it together so as to satisfy the cravings of my soul. I suspect that I am getting through a severe mental illness.'[60] The next letter from Brittany was blacker still. Over the course of eight days Conrad had written just one page and was fast succumbing to writer's block and its accompanying terrors. 'To be able to think and unable to express is a fine torture,'[61] he told Edward. 'Now I've got all my people together I don't know what to do with them ... I feel nothing clearly. And I am frightened when I remember that I have to drag it all out of myself ... I am exceedingly miserable'. In the final paragraph of the letter he thanked Edward 'with all my heart for the time, the care, the thoughts you give to me so generously. I am getting so used to your interest in my work that it has become now like a necessity – like a condition of existence.' Edward doubtless appreciated the gratitude, but Conrad's confession of dependence must sometimes have felt like an onerous responsibility.

Edward's role was not confined to cheering Conrad on and attempting to cheer him up; he was also hard at work trying to find outlets for Conrad's short stories. This was crucial for two reasons: short stories were potentially fertile sources of income, which could help finance the writing of a new novel, and they kept Conrad's name in the public eye. Money was very much on both men's minds in July 1896; after his brush with typhoid Edward was still worrying about 'Bills rolling in'[62] and Conrad had lost most of his capital when a South African mining venture in which he had invested collapsed. The number of magazines and periodicals had rapidly expanded in the latter decades of the century and the market for short stories was large and lucrative. Edward's contacts and his knowledge of the market proved invaluable. One of his significant introductions to Conrad was his great friend E. V. Lucas, who was working as a journalist at the time. Lucas mentioned Conrad to the editor of the prestigious *Cornhill Magazine*, who got in touch asking for short stories and offered to pay a guinea per 500 words – untold riches compared with the £20 Conrad had received for *Almayer's Folly*. When Arthur Symons wrote to Edward asking if Conrad had anything suitable for *The Savoy*, Conrad was able to sell his first short story 'The Idiots' to the magazine for £42. Given that the story ran to approximately 10,000 words, this was a sum that compared extremely favourably with his £50 advance for *An Outcast of the Islands*.

The arrival of an envelope from Brittany addressed in Conrad's writing was a charged moment for Edward: it might contain thrilling confirmation of his potential as a writer – as with the first part of 'The Rescuer' – but it was just as likely to convey what Conrad later called a 'howl of distress'[63] from the French coast:

> ... since I had Your last letter – I have been living in a little hell of my own; a place of torment so subtle and so cruel and so unavoidable that the prospect of theological damnation in the hereafter has no more terrors for me.
>
> It is all about the ghastly 'Rescuer' ... I am in desperation and have practically given up the book. Beyond what you have seen I cannot make a single step. There is 12 pages written and I sit before them every morning, day after day, for the last 2 months and can not add a sentence, add a word! ... When I face that fatal manuscript it seems to me that I have forgotten how to think – worse! how to write. It is as if something in my head had given way to let in a cold grey mist. I knock about blindly in it till I am positively, physically sick – and then I give up saying – tomorrow! And tomorrow comes – and brings only the renewed and futile agony. I ask myself whether I am breaking up mentally. I am afraid of it ... I hope You never felt as I feel now and I trust that you will never Know what I experience at this very moment. The darkness and the bitterness of it is beyond expression.[64]

Even given Conrad's propensity for epistolary exaggeration this was a disturbing account to receive, let alone to respond to. Unfortunately, like so many of his letters to Conrad, Edward's reply has not survived. He himself found writing a tortuous business and so could offer heartfelt sympathy, but rescuing Conrad from his creative doldrums was beyond Edward's or anybody else's power. All he could hope was that simply providing an outlet for Conrad's despair was of some help. 'Had I suspected the long Odyssey of acute distress and worry that Conrad was to undergo over "The Rescuer",' Edward wrote later, 'I would of course have persuaded him to abandon the book.'[65] Conrad worked sporadically on the novel up to 1898, but then laid it aside until 1916.

The Conrads returned from Brittany at the end of September and rented a semi-detached villa in Stanford-le-Hope, Essex: 'I feel better since I know myself near You,'[66] Conrad confessed. Just as he and Jessie left France, Nellie Heath was considering crossing the Channel in the

opposite direction. The death of her older sister Grace the previous year
had been a great blow and Nellie had not been well. Her family and
friends, including Edward, were urging a change of scene, partly in the
hope that the delights of Paris would break 'the spell of Sickert's personality'.[67] Sickert painted Nellie's portrait around this time and gave her
the finished result; the picture, which is now in Leeds City Art Gallery,
captures the serenity of the sitter, a quality often remarked upon by
those who knew her.

Nellie's letters to Edward suggest that he wished to advance their
friendship, but the prospect of a more intimate relationship alarmed her.
'I care about you in the same way I did two years ago,' she told him

> and that's a jolly healthy friendship and I wish you would not say
> I am afraid, for how could I be? I am only afraid when you won't
> talk sufficiently about our works or our ideas but will talk about
> ourselves. I don't want ever to talk about ourselves. It is an under-
> stood thing we are friends who care a great deal about one another.[68]

Despite Nellie's reluctance to 'talk about ourselves', her letters contain
some shrewd observations about Edward. His propensity to form rapid
and fixed judgements vexed her. 'You label a thing or a person and then
you stick to your own label and work from that,' she complained, 'like
a man labelling a bottle "vinegar" and long after it has ceased to be
vinegar, forcing all his friends to accept it as such.'[69] She was also very
conscious of a highly developed streak of self-analysis and self-criticism
in Edward:

> ... as I have *so* often said you are a little fond of pulling up your
> roots to see how you are growing. You know you are – you are
> too critical about yourself and everybody else – especially work
> and how can you prosper if you are not more sympathetic and
> indulgent to your work. You don't take a fatherly enough pride in
> your own productions and like delicate children they are afraid of
> your critical ways and won't sprout.[70]

Nellie puts her finger unerringly on the major problem Edward encountered whenever he tried to write: his critical faculty overwhelmed his
creative aspirations. That critical faculty was invaluable to those he
mentored, however, and if, as Nellie said, Edward lacked the paternal

pride essential to his own creativity, then it may have been because it was exhausted in the service of others. As Joseph Conrad explained at the end of another of his appeals for help, 'You are my "Father in Letters" and must bear the brunt of that position.'[71]

6

Sympathy, criticism and counsel

Once Edward had recovered from typhoid, the family was finally able to establish some sort of routine at The Cearne. Edward's insomnia meant that he was a very late riser, often not appearing for his meagre breakfast of coffee or china tea, a crust of bread and an apple or orange until eleven o'clock. He had a cold bath every day of the year, regardless of the season. The first indication of his rejoining the world was the sound of his 'heavy lunging tread'[1] as he made his way, naked, from his bedroom to the bathroom. Any visitor who happened to enter the house by the front door at the time of this daily excursion would be treated to the sight of Edward in a full state of undress, much to Constance's consternation. She, by contrast, rose early and by the time Edward put in an appearance had been round the garden, done some housework and called David in to start his lessons with her. On Thursdays Edward took the train from Oxted to London, returning again on Friday night; the rest of the week he spent reading manuscripts at home, usually in the long wicker chair in the porch. As darkness fell he lit a little copper lamp hanging from an iron tripod made by Stepniak which stood on a low stone wall beside him and carried on reading and writing into the night.

Conrad's affairs continued to occupy much of Edward's time. When Unwin offered what Conrad considered to be the unsatisfactory figure of £50 advance for *Tales of Unrest*, his first volume of short stories, he immediately turned to Edward, seeking reassurance as to his literary and commercial value: 'Ought I not to get more? I want £100 ... Can I honestly ask for it? Am I worth that advance? – I shall not write to him till I *hear from you.*'[2] Edward backed Conrad's valuation and drew up detailed suggestions for a financial agreement to put to Unwin, his own employer. Still more controversially, he suggested that Conrad might seek a new publisher and introduced him to Longman and to Sydney Pawling, a partner in the relatively recently established firm of William Heinemann. Edward also put Conrad in touch with another publisher,

Smith, Elder & Co., and coached him prior to his meeting with Reginald Smith. 'I kept your advice in mind during the interview,' Conrad reported, 'I was dignified and not abjectly modest.'[3]

The main subject of these negotiations was a story Conrad had begun whilst in Brittany. As with several of his novels, Conrad initially envisaged *The Nigger of the 'Narcissus'* as a short story, earmarked for inclusion in the forthcoming volume. By the time he finished it, however, it had grown to novella proportions. Conrad always regarded *The Nigger of the 'Narcissus'* with great affection, once describing it as 'the story by which, as creative artist, I stand or fall'.[4] His fondness for the book stemmed from several sources: it was written in tribute to the 'old chums'[5] with whom he had sailed; its serialisation in the *New Review* (thanks to Edward) established Conrad in the most select literary company, and it marked a significant moment in his emergence as a writer. When *The Nigger of the 'Narcissus'* first appeared in serial form in August 1897 Conrad's situation was anything but secure. He had published two novels – *Almayer's Folly* and *An Outcast of the Islands* – and three of his short stories had appeared in magazines. 'The Sisters' had been permanently abandoned and 'The Rescuer' was persistently becalmed. Conrad would be forty in December 1897 and Jessie was expecting their first child. Edward later summed up the position succinctly: 'had Conrad failed to "bring off" *The Nigger*,' he wrote, 'or had the novel missed fire, in the reviewers' eyes, as many a masterpiece has done, nothing more disheartening for Conrad and ominous for his future could be imagined.'[6]

Once again, the story of the *Narcissus*'s voyage home from Bombay to London, her crew's battle with a fierce storm and the illness and death of James Wait, came to Edward in batches. 'I think the pages just written won't dishonour the book,' Conrad told his mentor several weeks before he completed the manuscript, 'Your book which you try to coax into bloom with such devotion and care.'[7]

The Nigger of the 'Narcissus', dealing for the first time with an English subject, was quite unlike Conrad's earlier novels with their 'exotic' settings and adventure story plots. This was the book Edward had envisaged at that early meeting at the National Liberal Club when he sought to persuade Conrad to write about his experiences at sea. As he read the manuscript Edward became increasingly convinced that he had been doubly right: right to nudge Conrad towards a maritime subject and vindicated in his assessment of the ex-mariner's literary potential. Edward's marginal comments are nearly all delighted expressions of praise. At the end of Conrad's depiction of the onset of the ferocious storm, Edward notes,

'Of this section I enjoyed every word, every idea. A naïve testimony – but what affirmation of your power!'[8] He applauded Conrad's deployment of the small but significant detail, like the mug which remains unbroken in the clutch of a sailor thrown to the deck by the force of the storm and which is subsequently passed round the thirsty crew. Such heightening of detail or gesture was something Edward often discerned in what he considered to be great writing: in his later book on Turgenev he cites a moment in *Rudin* when Anna Pavlovna takes the rose offered her by the unctuous Pandelevsky and then lets it fall to the path.[9]

The Nigger of the 'Narcissus' is also a much more cinematic novel than its predecessors. Conrad creates many memorable scenes, not least the *Narcissus* docking in the Thames, which Edward singled out for commendation. Conrad's development of the 'scenic' method delighted Edward; it was a technique he often encouraged his protégés to adopt, occasionally at the cost of bringing him into conflict with those reluctant to employ it. The few critical suggestions Edward made on the manuscript nearly all involved directions to condense or delete, only some of which Conrad obeyed. One instance where he did as he was told came at the point when the malingering Donkin emerges from the cabin, following Wait's death:

> And the immortal sea stretched away, immense and hazy, like the image of life, with a glittering surface and lightless depths; exacting tears and toil; promising, empty, inspiring and terrible – ever changing and always the same. Donkin gave it a defiant glance and slunk off noiselessly as if judged and cast out by the august silence of its might.[10]

'Cut', demanded Edward and Conrad removed 'exacting tears and toil' and 'ever changing and always the same'; the effectiveness of the description is much improved as a result.

Conrad made one small but rather interesting alteration unprompted by Edward: originally the name of the venerable sailor who stands for the old, established traditions of the sea was Sullivan, but Conrad changed it to Singleton – the maiden name of Edward's mother, to whom he sent a copyright copy, which he inscribed, paying tribute to 'Your son and my friend whose sympathy criticism and counsel have encouraged and guided me ever since I took pen in hand ...'[11]

For some time Conrad had set his heart on his work appearing in the *New Review*, a prestigious monthly periodical which serialised fiction by the likes of Henry James, Robert Louis Stevenson, Rudyard Kipling and

H. G. Wells. The editor of the *New Review* was W. E. Henley, whose political views and advocacy of the British Empire abroad were anathema to Edward. Quite aside from its title, *The Nigger of the 'Narcissus'* has become a problematic work in Conrad's oeuvre, frequently condemned for what are perceived to be its racist overtones and ultra-conservative politics. It has been suggested that Conrad 'rigged' the text to meet with Henley's approval,[12] and it does seem ironic that the book of Conrad's most closely associated with the left-leaning, fiercely anti-imperialist Edward should be regarded now as the most politically troubling. In the last essay he ever wrote, Edward himself claimed that the 'true' subject of *The Nigger of the 'Narcissus'* was not the story of the subversive and disruptive Wait, but rather the account of the battle against the storm which incarnates 'the tough spirit of the British sailor',[13] to whom Conrad wished to pay an affectionate and lasting tribute.

If Conrad did 'rig' the text, his gamble paid off. Despite his dislike of Henley's politics, Edward asked Sydney Pawling to show him some pages of *The Nigger*; Henley's response – 'Tell Conrad that if the rest is up to the sample it shall certainly come out in the *New Review*'[14] – was immensely gratifying. 'I am as You may imagine exceedingly pleased with what Pawling writes,' Conrad told Edward. 'My dear fellow you are the making of me!'[15]

In August 1897 Conrad sent Edward a draft preface to the novel, imploring him 'not to be impatient with it' and to do his best to get it printed. 'Implicitly the Nigger is *Your* book,' he continued, 'and besides You know very well I daren't make any move without Your leave.'[16] Conrad's trepidation suggests he was well aware of Edward's hostility to anything that smacked of an aesthetic theory. As David Garnett explains, few things irritated his father more:

> [Edward] had little use for theory and could seldom bolster up his opinions by inventing one. He arrived at his opinions, especially his aesthetic ones, by instinct and by sympathy. He was intensely sceptical and never more so than when confronted by theories of aesthetics. He did not believe there were any rules and preferred that there should be none.[17]

On this occasion Edward suppressed any visceral antipathy he may have felt; indeed, the Preface, now regarded as a key document of literary modernism, may reflect some of the discussions the two men had about writing. Conrad's insistence on the importance and the enduring legacy of the artist is certainly something Edward would have recognised and he would have loved Conrad's remark about the 'temporary formulas' of art and the sly dig at the reader who may find amongst the 'encouragement, consolation, fear, charm' demanded from a novel, 'also that glimpse of truth for which you have forgotten to ask'.[18] Clearly Conrad wanted to define himself as a writer and the Preface gave him the opportunity to do so, but he still felt the need of Edward's guiding hand. When Edward suggested that he drop a paragraph which amounted to an apologia for writing a preface at all, Conrad did so, admitting, 'It is certainly much better as expurgated by you.'[19] When *The Nigger of the 'Narcissus'* was published in December 1897 Conrad paid public tribute to the part Edward had played in its genesis and execution by dedicating 'To Edward Garnett This Tale About My Friends of the Sea'.

Around the time he was finishing *The Nigger of the 'Narcissus'* Conrad talked to Edward about the work of a friend of his, an aspiring writer he had met on his way back from Australia in 1893, when he was first mate on the clipper *Torrens*. Edward promised to look out for the stories, which arrived at Unwin's office on 20 February 1897. His report on *From the Four Corners* was hardly effusive. 'The stories are all readable and two or three of them show the author has a faculty of observation,' Edward conceded. 'All are up to a good level of literary technique, but none of them show *strong or any particular talent*. The fact is the author is a man of action and *he is not artist enough* to score high success in literature ...'[20] Although he could not possibly have known it, the author of *From the Four Corners* did himself no favours by giving his address as the Junior Carlton Club, which raised Edward's hackles from the outset.

When just under a year later another manuscript, *Jocelyn*, arrived, the Junior Carlton still loomed large in Edward's mind:

> Truth to say Mr Galsworthy is an excellent fellow, a good Briton, and one neither stiff nor prejudiced. He visits foreign countries diligently and examines foreign manners intelligently, but he is always hopelessly *bored* and he sees things through the eyes of a Clubman who carries England with him wherever he goes. He sees 'life' as the phrase goes, but *he has not much inside him* to see it with. But he tries very hard.[21]

Unwin did publish John Galsworthy's tales under the revised title *From the Four Winds* (at the author's own expense); *Jocelyn* eventually appeared under the Duckworth imprint and Edward dismissed the Clubman from his thoughts.

While Galsworthy's manuscripts were the subject of mild disparagement, another author, a young medical student who had submitted his first novel a month before *From the Four Corners*, elicited a very different reaction. Edward pronounced *A Lambeth Idyll* 'a *clever, humorous study* of rather low life', and prophesied 'Mr Maugham has insight and humour, and will probably be heard of again ... If TFU does not publish "A Lambeth Idyll" somebody else certainly will.'[22]

This was not the first time Edward had encountered William Somerset Maugham's work: six months before he had reported on 'A Bad Example', one of two short stories Maugham had submitted to Unwin. Edward detected 'some ability in this, but not very *much*',[23] and advised the author to try the humbler magazines, adding that if Maugham attempted anything more important he should send it in to the firm. 'This was so great an encouragement,' Maugham later recalled 'that I immediately sat down and wrote one.'[24]

A Lambeth Idyll could, Edward believed, take advantage of the 'slowly growing' Arthur Morrison public, a reference to the author of *Tales of Mean Streets* (1894) and the recently published *A Child of the Jago* (1896), which also dealt with life in the London slums. In fact, when Maugham's book eventually appeared under its revised title *Liza of Lambeth*, a reviewer in the *Academy* actually accused him of plagiarising Morrison. Edward predicted the novel would be divisive, not on account of any alleged plagiarism, but because 'half the critics will call the book "brutal"', which indeed they did.

Despite the fact that Maugham's decision next to try his hand at a historical novel was influenced by an article by Edward's future adversary – the renowned man of letters Andrew Lang, who declared it the ideal form for a young writer – Edward greeted *The Making of a Saint* with enthusiasm: 'Mr Maugham is going *strong*,' he reported. 'The novel ... is decidedly interesting and shows Mr Maugham has plenty of talent left him to start on so new a tack.'[25] However, when Maugham submitted five short stories a year later, Edward was disappointed, finding them '*flat*, a little heavy ... We feel Mr Maugham's reputation will suffer if he publishes the present collection.'[26] The honourable exception was 'Daisy', a story Edward had read just prior to the poor quintet then before him. Although he felt 'Daisy' lacked subtlety, Edward praised its emotional force and commended Maugham for 'really writing of *life*: and that goes a long way'. Edward's reservations notwithstanding, Unwin published the stories under the title *Orientations* in 1899.

As soon as his three-book contract expired, Maugham left Unwin, convinced the publisher had done him down financially. When in 1902 Edward read the manuscript of Maugham's *Mrs Craddock*, a novel about illicit passion which had been turned down by several publishers on account of the frankness of both its depiction of female desire and its language, he was distinctly unimpressed. 'It is a very heavy, ponderous examination of the eternal *Marriage* question,' he complained. 'The story has probably been all round the trade, and some publishers don't think it proper, and others think it too clever, and others think it won't succeed. We think it isn't *good* enough – and it won't advance Mr M's reputation.'[27] In fact, when the book was eventually published under the Heinemann imprint it received several plaudits from the critics, their praise prefaced with a warning about its explicitness.

In general Edward took a gloomy view of the aptitude of his critical confrères and schooled his protégés to expect little from them: misapprehension the best-case scenario, open hostility the more likely. That the reviewer in the *Evening Standard* was able to appreciate the merits of *Liza of Lambeth* amazed Joseph Conrad (who did not much care for the novel himself): 'to think the *Standard* could see it', he marvelled to Edward. 'D'you think I will get my share of loaves and fishes. Eh?'[28] The object of his speculation, not to say anxiety was *The Nigger of the 'Narcissus'*, which he had completed at the beginning of 1897 to his own and Edward's satisfaction.

It seemed that the year had started well, but a dreadful blow fell in the spring. Edward's great friend Eustace Hartley had been suffering from debilitating sciatica for six months; he was in deep financial trouble and his wife Margaret was very probably having an affair.[29] On 24 March, exhausted by constant pain and lack of sleep and unable to endure the prospect of bankruptcy, Hartley retired to his rooms in Gray's Inn Square and took a cocktail of morphine, chloral and sulphonal. His death, at the age of thirty-seven, came as a terrible shock to his friends and to Edward in particular, who blamed himself for having neglected Hartley when he was ill in favour of his increasingly ardent but unfulfilled pursuit of Nellie Heath. 'Mr Hartley died very suddenly,' Narney told Olive, who had gone to live with a family in Russia for nine months. 'Edward was dreadfully cut up.'[30] Further evidence of Edward's distress and his feeling that he had been disloyal to his friend can be found in a series of notes he made for a projected novel based around Hartley's suicide. These also reveal that this latest tragedy resurrected memories of the earlier one involving Stepniak and led Edward to confront some uncomfortable truths concerning his reaction to it. In one of his notes he exhorts himself to 'Analyze your own indifference to SS's death mercilessly.'[31] Shortly after the terrible events surrounding Hartley, Edward went away to the New Forest in an attempt to recover. As a result he missed his sister Lucy's wedding to Harry Cowlishaw, but he was hardly in a mood to celebrate anyway.

National celebration was very much the order of the day, however, on the occasion of Queen Victoria's Diamond Jubilee. In the evening of 28 June 1897 a party consisting of Edward, Constance and David, Lucy and Harry, Arthur Garnett, Fanny Stepniak, Peter and Sophie Kropotkin and Lyndhurst Giblin, a young Australian cousin of Narney's, walked from Kent Hatch to the top of Crockham Hill. 'Here we saw a fine sight from the top of the common,' Constance reported to her father-in-law, 'No less than fifty-nine bonfires were visible all round the horizon.'[32] Edward gathered up glow worms and decorated the ladies' hats with them; the darkness was punctured by the 'bewitching green light'[33] given off by the beetles and the orange gleam of the distant bonfires. 'No country,' David Garnett observed, 'at the close of a day of patriotic rejoicing, can have retired to sleep so certain of the peacefulness and security of the world.'[34]

The situation at The Cearne was considerably less secure; by early summer a letter from the bank manager made it very clear that Edward and Constance could no longer carry on living in the manner to which they had become accustomed since moving there. Edward's illness had reduced his income and Constance had suffered badly with sick headaches and been unable to progress with her translations as quickly as she had hoped. As a result, when the home help Alice Martin left to get married she was not replaced; David's pony Shagpat was sold; and Bert Hedgecock, who looked after Shagpat and the garden, was dismissed.

The newest inhabitant of Oxted certainly knew all about living beyond one's means. His arrival in June caused a flutter amongst the locals, as Fanny Stepniak explained to Olive:

The wildest excitement in our neighbourhood is the advent and settlement at Oxted of Stephen Crane. Marjorie Pease called on the missus and found her attended by two greek men-servants. I suppose he, being a war correspondent during the Gr[aeco]-T[urkish] war, exported them – perhaps it was a present from King

George. Ed[ward] called on them too and liked him very much.
He invited him to come down to lunch any day last week, but up
to the present he did [sic] not yet appear.[35]

When Crane arrived in England from Greece in 1897 he was already
well known as the author of The Red Badge of Courage (1895), his
acclaimed novel about the American Civil War. Edward later described
Crane as 'the type of nervous, nimble-minded American, slight in figure,
shy and kind in manner, speaking little, with a great power of work, a
fine memory and an imagination of astonishing psychological insight'.[36]
'The missus' was Cora Stewart, a handsome, intelligent honey-blonde
six years Crane's senior. He had met her in Jacksonville, Florida, where
she was running the Hotel de Dream, which if not actually a brothel
was a house of highly dubious repute. Although she used Crane's
name, Cora was still married to her second husband Donald William
Stewart, the younger son of an English baronet, who refused to grant
her a divorce. It was probably through Harold Frederic, a compatriot
of Crane's and like him a novelist and journalist, that the new arrivals
rented a house in Oxted called Ravensbrook, a short distance from
The Cearne. By all accounts Ravensbrook was unpleasing to look
at and unpleasant to live in; Ford Madox Ford, whom Edward introduced to Crane, described it as 'a horrible place – in a bottom, damp,
and of the most sordidly pretentious type of suburban villa architecture'.[37] The dampness did Crane's already fragile health no good
and, to make matters worse, he and Cora had not been ensconced in
Ravensbrook many months before local tradesmen were banging at
the door demanding the settlement of bills.

There was much about Crane, man and writer, which appealed to
Edward, who was always attracted to those who lived unconventional
and colourful lives. The insatiably curious Crane, frequenter of New
York's notorious Bowery, war correspondent and detester of orthodox
opinion, scored on all counts. 'Crane's strange eyes, with their intensely
concentrated gaze, were those of a genius,' Edward later wrote,

and I recall how on his first visit to our house I was so struck by
the exquisite symmetry of his brow and temples, that I failed to
note, what a lady pointed out when he had left, the looseness of
his mouth. Yes, the intensity of genius burned in his eyes, and his
weak lips betrayed his unrestrained temperament.[38]

Although the burning eyes may have been as much a sign of illness as smouldering genius, Edward's conclusions about the American's physiognomy were not wholly fanciful. Crane, ably aided and abetted by Cora, knew no bounds when it came to largesse; as a result, he was under relentless pressure to write something, anything, to pay the bills. Yet Edward could see that that spontaneous element in Crane's make-up, in some ways so damaging to his art, was also a vital component of it. Crane was nothing if not an instinctive writer; the very idea of long conversations on aesthetic technique and the merits of Flaubert and Maupassant, which kept his friends Conrad and Ford happily occupied for so many hours, would have had him running for the hills. 'I told a seemingly sane man at Mrs Garnett's that I got my artistic education on the Bowery,' Crane told James Gibbons Huneker, the American music critic and writer,

> and he said 'Oh really? So they have a school of fine arts there?' ... Now I am going to wave the starry flag of freedom a little even if you contemn the practice in one who knows not Balzac and Dostoywhat'shisname ... For it has been proven to me fully and carefully the authority that all my books are stolen from the French. They stand me against walls with a teacup in my hand and tell me how I have stolen all my things from De Maupassant, Zola, Loti and the bloke who wrote – I forget the book.[39]

Edward did not entirely belong to the camp pushing the teacup into Crane's hand; he believed the American's writing smacked rather more of the samovar: 'On first reading *The Red Badge of Courage*,' he recalled, 'I concluded [Crane] had been influenced by the Russian masters, but I learned when I met him, that he had never read a line of them. Would that he had!'[40] Both Edward and the literary Francophiles were wrong in their assessment of Crane's 'influences', but this early skirmish between the champions of the French aesthetic example and Edward as a powerful advocate of the Russians was a foretaste of things to come.

It was just as well that Crane could regard the opinion of his literary peers with amused detachment, as his own aversion to aesthetic debate did not prevent others chewing over his work amongst themselves. On 1 December 1897 Conrad wrote Crane an effusive letter praising his short stories 'A Man and Some Others' and 'The Open Boat'. 'Garnett's right,' Conrad purred, '"A Man and Some Others" is immense ... The illusions of life come out of your hand without a flaw.'[41] Four days later, writing to Edward, he saluted Crane's 'strength ... rapidity of action' and 'amazing faculty of vision', but he also mentioned 'in confidence' that he considered Crane to be '*the only* impressionist and *only* an impressionist', and wondered 'why he disappoints me – why my enthusiasm withers as soon as I close the book'.[42] 'Impressionism' was a hot topic at the time as writers sought to discover whether literature could produce similar effects to those recently achieved by Impressionist artists. Conrad came to view literary impressionism more favourably as the years progressed – he is now considered by some to be an exponent of it himself – but aspects of his privately expressed doubts to Edward about Crane emerged a year later when Edward wrote an article on Crane for the *Academy*.

Creditors were not the only people beating a path to Ravensbrook. Crane's literary fame and Cora's rumoured infamy made them magnets for the curious, some camp-followers, others little more than parasites. The Cranes' bountiful hospitality was leaving Crane little opportunity to work. This state of affairs rapidly became intolerable and in November Edward told Crane about 'an ancient Sussex house, noble and grey with the passage of five hundred years'[43] which belonged to some friends of his who were looking to let it. As Edward put it, 'It was the lure of romance that always thrilled Crane's blood' and as soon as he heard about it 'nothing would satisfy [Crane] but that he must become the tenant of Brede Place'.[44] The dilapidated house was roughly eight miles from Hastings and thus 'less accessible'[45] from London. It was owned by Moreton Frewen and his wife Clara (née Jerome), whose sister Jennie was married to Randolph Churchill. Frewen was another colourful character, who at various times had been a cattle rancher in Wyoming, the inventor of a gold-crushing machine in Australia and financial adviser to a maharaja in India – all ventures which ended in disaster. Fortunately his wealthy father-in-law provided a town house in London where the Frewens took up residence. By March the situation at Ravensbrook was driving the Cranes to distraction and Cora wrote to Edward requesting further details of Brede Place. He sent a cutting and a map. 'No doubt a tip to the caretaker will give you admission to Brede Place, and information,' he advised Cora. 'Or Stephen's eloquence will move even a new tenant to vacate the house, and instal [sic] those who rightfully appreciate what they deserve. *But don't go with expectations* ... Heaven help and guide you!'[46]

As things turned out, neither Cora nor Crane went to view Brede Place that spring. On 25 April 1898 the United States formally declared war against Spain in support of Cuban independence. Crane was determined to witness the conflict and immediately boarded a ship bound for New York, leaving Cora to fend off the creditors at Ravensbrook as best she could. After spending some time with the Frederics in Ireland, Cora returned and went to see Brede Place. Edward had already been over it with Harry Cowlishaw, who had drawn up a report detailing the necessary repairs, the costs of which Edward suggested might be split between the Cranes and the Frewens, who were prepared to let Brede for a nominal rent. The romantic prospect of a Tudor manor house, steeped in history and complete with its own ghost, was considerably more than Cora could resist.

Meanwhile, Edward's exertions on behalf of the Cranes were not confined to securing them what he hoped would be cheaper accommodation and fewer unwelcome visitors (hopes that would be dashed on both fronts). In December 1898 he wrote an appreciation of Crane's work in the *Academy*. It was deemed 'admirable ... and masterly'[47] by Conrad and judged by Crane's biographer R. W. Stallman to be 'the best critical study published during Crane's lifetime'.[48] It is in this article that Edward declares Crane to be 'the chief impressionist of this age'.[49] Like the Impressionist artists, Crane's work is characterised by its economy and rapidity; he 'is undoubtedly such an interpreter of the significant surfaces of things that in a few strokes he gives us an amazing insight into what the individual life is'.[50] Edward maintains that it is Crane's unique ability to capture the fragmentary and episodic nature of modern life that sets him apart as a writer. A few words of revealing dialogue, the 'exquisite ... facility of exposing an individual scene by an odd simile ... a keen realising of the primitive emotions – that is Mr Crane's talent'. According to Edward, Crane was hatched into the world with that talent fully fledged and this accounts for his brilliant precocity, but it also explains his limitations. As it stands, Crane's work 'does not include the necessity for complex arrangements', it is perfect in its own way; but Crane's art is standing still. 'I do not think,' writes Edward, 'that Mr Crane will or can develop further.' Crane's work lacks narrative architecture (what Edward calls 'the building faculty') and his characters will never become beings possessed of a rich inner consciousness. The reader who believes that great art requires arrangements of intricate effects, 'striking contrasts, exquisite grouping of devices' (readers like Conrad, perhaps?) will be disappointed in Crane. Yet for all that, Edward insists that 'Mr Crane's talent is unique; nobody can question that. America may well be proud of him.' That America was not nearly as proud of him as she should have been was something that Edward was to express very forcibly in the future.

Crane eventually landed back in England on 11 January 1899 and a concerned Edward lost little time in going to visit. 'I am just off to see Crane,' he told Nellie Heath,

I hear he is back – very low, very ill and drinking whiskey all day. Their financial condition is desperate – bills all round and his future books mortgaged *ahead* to publishers! This is Mrs Pease's version. How I detest her silly tongue.[51]

Edward may not have liked what he heard, but Marjory Pease's report was not far off the truth. Crane had indeed returned exhausted and ill, having contracted malaria on his travels; he was also almost certainly suffering from the consumption which would end his life eighteen months later. As soon as he stepped through the door at Ravensbrook he was besieged by various creditors. The first thing that claimed his attention was not the pile of bills stacked up on his desk, but Edward's appraisal of his work in the *Academy*. What he thought of it is unrecorded, although Cora had written to Edward assuring him that – other than his comment that Crane might fail 'through using up the picturesque phases of the environment that nurtured him' (according to Cora 'The beautiful thoughts in Stephen's mind are simply endless!'[52]) – she liked the article 'very much indeed'.[53] With summonses flying at him from every direction, Crane lost little time in following up Edward's proposal to escape to Brede Place. 'We are going to move Heaven and Earth to get there,'[54] Cora announced, and sure enough a month later she was installed as the lady of Brede.

Crane and Cora may have got away from Ravensbrook, that 'suburban villa', but if they thought Brede's ancient massive oak door would protect them from their problems they were sorely mistaken. Edward looked on with mounting dismay as once again hordes of hangers-on descended, taking shameless advantage of Crane's rich but ruinous hospitality. The house itself was cold, damp and draughty, providing just about the worst possible conditions for a consumptive. Crane's study, a small red room over the front porch, was the coldest and draughtiest of all. Yet for all that Cora and Crane revelled in their new surroundings: Crane was able to ride in the mornings and rather relished playing the part of the lord of an English manor; the 'Indians', as Crane christened his unwelcome visitors, were certainly pestilential, but he and Cora loved hosting genuine literary friends such as Conrad, H. G. Wells and Edward himself.

It was just after a Christmas party attended by Conrad and Wells, amongst many others, that Crane fainted upon the shoulder of a guest and haemorrhaged from the lung. His condition deteriorated rapidly; by May 1900 a desperate Cora was making arrangements for him to travel to Badenweiler, a health resort in the Black Forest where another literary hero of Edward's, Anton Chekhov, saw out his final days four years later. Aware of the brevity and bleakness of his own future, Crane turned his attention to that of Conrad. On 14 May, in the last letter he ever wrote, Crane explained to Sanford Bennett

> I have Conrad on my mind just now. Garnett does not think it likely that his writing will ever be popular outside the ring of men who write. He is poor and a gentleman and proud. His wife is not strong and they have a kid. If Garnett should ask you to help pull wires for a place on the Civil List for Conrad please do me the last favour.[55]

Edward visited Crane the day before he left Brede. Two decades later he was still haunted by the memory of his friend's 'bloodless face and the burning intensity of his eyes'.[56] The pilgrimage to Germany was always going to be hopeless and in the early hours of 5 June Crane died at the Villa Eberhardt. He was twenty-eight. Four days later an obituary by Edward appeared in the *Academy*. Once again he praised Crane's 'swift and unerring characterisation', his 'vivid phrasing', and celebrated the American's 'rare gift' of knowing 'in a flash just what was essential to bring the picture vividly to the reader'.[57] Crane's 'brief, brilliant life'[58] was over and as the years passed Edward was saddened but unsurprised that his literary reputation looked as if it would be equally shortlived. 'Crane *was* a genius,' he declared in 1927 to H. E. Bates, one of several young protégés to whom he sent copies of Crane's work, 'and do you know since the day he died he has been shockingly "put on the back shelf". Nobody cares a damn . . .'[59] This Edward felt was particularly true of critics in Crane's homeland, whose recognition of 'the most original genius it has produced in story-telling' he considered to be 'grudging [and] inadequate'.[60]

Edward's fears for Crane's posthumous reputation proved to be unfounded – his stock rose in the 1950s and has been high ever since. His predictions regarding Conrad's future, of such touching concern to the mortally ill Crane, also turned out to be overly pessimistic. Conrad had to wait until the publication of *Chance* in 1914 before he enjoyed real commercial success, but reviews of his earlier novels were generally favourable and his work was certainly respected in 'the ring of men who write'. It is unlikely, however, that intimations of literary immortality lay behind Conrad's agreement to let Nellie Heath paint his portrait at The Cearne. This was accomplished in a single sitting of less than three hours in March 1898 and was by all accounts a pretty fraught affair. Conrad's presence at The Cearne always put Constance on edge, mostly on account of the fact that his demanding palate tested her very basic culinary skills to and beyond their limit. 'We have been having Mr Conrad here,' she reported to Richard Garnett. 'Poor man, he seems very nervous and exhausted.'[61] Fanny Stepniak's assessment of the distinguished guest was considerably less diplomatic:

Yesterday I went to the Cearne to see Mr Conrade [*sic*] ... and I saw him. I am glad I went, but (or perhaps because?) I shall never repeat such an experiment again. Best of all I liked Nellie Heath – there is no nonsense about her. She is painting the hero and a very good bit of work it will be. Now let me describe the man. First of all he is dark, dry, shapeless with a cruel smile in [*sic*] his face [,] he has nothing Polish neither in his appearance, nor in his manners. I took him for an Irishman at first glance. He is decidedly unsympathetic, his eyes have such a hard expression that you would never dream to see them veiled by a tear of tenderness or compassion. He has strong likes and dislikes, to be sure, judging by the few remarks he made on men of our time ... The great man had tea with us in the big room and very soon disappeared in the study, where he was kept all the time in undisturbed quiet, only Edward having free access to the room. Edward himself is very nice, much better than his idol, he is a dear warmhearted [*sic*] boy, only too easily influenced by others. But in what he cannot be influenced is his literary, artistic judgement ... Soon after six I left the house, the atmosphere of which was oppressing to me. Connie did not even put on her charming ways, I believe she was already exhausted by the hero worshipping exertions of the day before.[62]

Years later Edward also recalled that day in March, and how he tasked himself to entertain Conrad by relating anecdotes during the sitting. To his mind the painting captures 'the man I used to watch, nervously holding out, sardonically interrupting and listening to others while sitting huddled up in his chair.'[63] His one criticism of the portrait – that it 'does not ... convey the extraordinary soft warmth of Conrad's eyes'[64] – is in stark contrast with Fanny Stepniak's impression of the sitter. The tenseness of the occasion seems to have affected all those present, and the restless and irritable Conrad could not be prevailed upon to return for a further session. The finished portrait, which according to Borys Conrad bears a strong resemblance to his father, is now in the Leeds City Art Gallery.

The Nigger of the 'Narcissus' was the last book of Conrad's that Edward oversaw in its entirety. It was published to critical acclaim, bolstering Conrad's self-confidence as a writer, but he and Edward still met and corresponded regularly and Conrad continued to turn to Edward for advice and support. In September 1898 he was again in residence at The Cearne. Constance's trials in the kitchen were alleviated by the arrival of Sybil Rudall. 'Dark, with very black eyes and a gipsy look',[65] Sybil was an inspired cook and although Constance still found her mind 'chiefly occupied in providing a sufficiently refined and recherché menu every day for [Conrad's] artistic palate',[66] she also remarked that their guest was 'rather nice and quiet though, and I like him better than I usually do'.

The advent of Sybil may have contributed to Conrad's more emollient mood, but it probably had more to do with the fact that he was just emerging from another spell of depression, exacerbated if not caused by the never-ending saga of The Rescue. The North American serial rights of the novel had been sold to S. S. McClure in March, but as Conrad explained to Edward, 'this Rescue makes me miserable – frightens me',[67] and deadlines passed with little or no discernible progress. Edward recalls one warm night during Conrad's stay at The Cearne in September when they sat out in the lamp-lit porch, the moths fluttering into the glasses at their side, while they smoked and argued, as Edward tried to assuage Conrad's fears. It was long after midnight when the older man finally rose, exclaiming, '"It's indecent! I shall not forgive you for letting me unburden myself like this. Why didn't you stop me!" We were worn out,' Edward observed, 'I by his desperation, and he by my sympathy.'[68]

Edward was a great talker, witty and entertaining when in company, attentive and encouraging in private conversation with authors, but just as importantly he was also an extremely good listener. The knowledge that he was always there, ready to lend a receptive and sympathetic ear and instinctively understanding the various trials that can beset a writer was immensely reassuring to Conrad and numerous others over the years. It may have been during his September visit in 1898 that Conrad spent a morning with Edward, pacing up and down the long row of Scotch firs that leads to The Cearne, Edward silently enthralled as his companion delivered a full and detailed account of the novel he intended to write based on his experiences in the Congo. In December of that year Conrad started *Heart of Darkness*, his tale of the white man's disintegration in Africa. Edward was convinced that the trip to the Congo 'was the turning-point in [Conrad's] mental life and that its effects on him determined his transformation from a sailor to a writer'.[69] Edward had been instrumental in effecting that transformation, during which time he had come to appreciate the complexities of Conrad's temperament and had developed a deep affection for him. In a letter to Nellie Heath, probably written a couple of months after the portrait sitting at The Cearne, Edward mentions that he has been reading a book and 'come across a passage about the Polish character that exactly hits off Conrad':[70]

His character was indeed not easily understood. A thousand subtle shades, mingling, crossing, disguising, and contradicting each other rendered it almost undecipherable at first sight. His feelings were half hidden, half revealed. It would be naïve to interpret literally his courtesy full of compliment, his assumed humility. When they (the Poles) speak of themselves we may almost always be certain that they keep some concealment in reserve, which assures them the advantage in intellect and feeling. They suffer their interrogators to remain in ignorance of some circumstance[,] some mobile secret, through the unveiling of which they would be more admired, or less esteemed, and which they know well how to hide under the subtle smile of an almost imperceptible mockery – etc etc.

'That's Conrad!' Edward declared, 'and it explains why EG loves him.'

7

'Write it, *my dear Amigo*'

From the time that Nellie Heath painted Edward's portrait in 1896 his feelings for her had become increasingly strong. They frequently met on the days Edward was up in London, sometimes at an art gallery, sometimes at Nellie's studio; often they would walk the city's streets for miles, exhilarated by the vitality and variety of the metropolis, but at the same time disturbed by its power to crush and deaden. Both were drawn to London as a subject: Edward was still struggling with his prose sketches of the capital, while Nellie longed to capture the essence of the city in paint. Their reaction to what Nellie called 'the complex genius of London'[1] mirrors much writing of the period in which urban life is depicted with a mixture of fascination and foreboding.

While Nellie was only too willing to offer eager, if critically unschooled, encouragement to Edward when he sent her drafts of his London sketches, letters urging a deepening of their relationship met with a very different response. Although she could not deny that she had feelings for Edward, for at least two years Nellie fought them, and him, for all she was worth. Typically, her opposition was based on self-less grounds. Nellie's greatest concern was the distress that any liaison would cause her family; she was also very anxious about the potential effect on David, whom she adored. Constance, who might also have greatly troubled Nellie's conscience, let it be known that she would have no objections to any relationship – indeed, she positively encouraged it. On the face of it, this remarkable reaction suggests either extreme generosity of spirit or that the marriage had fallen into a state of abso-lute indifference. Such conclusions would fall somewhere wide of the mark. Constance knew that David forged a sacrosanct bond between her and Edward, with whom she also shared an intellectual intimacy that no third party could enter. Her own love for Edward had for some time been more maternal than conjugal in nature. Nellie thus represented no threat to those elements of her marriage that Constance really valued, added to which she was extremely fond of Nellie, who was about as far off being the 'scarlet woman' as it is possible to imagine.

In one of the numerous letters he wrote to Nellie in an attempt to steamroller her doubts and fears Edward declares 'I never loved anyone but you – I was a boy before.'[2] Whilst this may sound a glib dismissal of his previous emotional commitments, the fact remains that Edward was only twenty-one when he married Constance; he may well have been bowled over by the attentions of a formidably intelligent woman seven years his senior. Constance had been immediately attracted by the young Edward's effervescent wit and, although he admitted that he found it easy to amuse people, he told Nellie that in her company, 'I never find it necessary to mountebank around.'[3] Nellie gave Edward a sense of ease that Constance did not; when he was with her he felt no pressure to produce what he described as his 'surfacy' [sic] side.

Although Nellie's qualms centred on her fears for others, yielding to Edward's persuasion would place her in an awkward and in many respects unenviable position. If she became Edward's mistress there could be no children and her prospects of marrying somebody else in the future would be considerably lessened too. Any relationship with Edward could not be acknowledged publicly and would cause her father Richard Heath great pain – the one thing Nellie dreaded above all else. Edward was fully aware that Nellie was racked by the thought of being a source of grief to others, but he was relentless and at times quite ruthless in his determination to capture her, body and soul.

They sent each other countless letters during this time; most are undated, some written in the faintest pencil, the erratic and occasionally illegible handwriting suggesting they were often composed under conditions of high emotional stress. The tone of Edward's letters veers from tender to passionate, from gentle cajolement to an almost brutal forcefulness. In what appears to be a draft of one long letter, Edward accuses Nellie of being 'desperate and moody and capricious and obstinately *set* against me' and claims that her 'habit' of throwing back love makes it 'a thing you can call up at your caprice, and cut the poor thing's throat whenever your mood of discontent, or irresolution or faintheartedness begins'.[4] According to Edward, such reactions usually set in when Nellie did allow herself to acknowledge her feelings for him: 'Yesterday I felt joyous and confident for you,' he confesses. 'Today I feel cynical – because I feel *you aren't true to the love you felt*, you've got to learn to *close your ears to doubt* – must I drag you *every* inch of the way ...?'[5] To which Nellie responded rather superbly in the margin 'Must you? Should you?'

Nellie felt that she was being torn in two; that she had to decide between Edward and her father and what she believed to be the irreconcilable demands each was making. Edward tried to persuade her that 'what you can be in my world, and in your father's world are *different* things. You can plunge into one, and then into the other, and you needn't deny *either*, because you can't unite them.'[6]

However, Richard Heath was not the sole cause of Nellie's anguish. Her passion for Walter Sickert was strong, and despite Sickert's failure to reciprocate in any way, remarkably enduring. The shadow of the artist lingered for some time, notwithstanding Edward's attempt to explain Nellie's attachment away as

> [E]xalted, entirely-in-the heavens ... the purely romantic love of youth when everything conspires together (puberty and innocence and the freshest heart and hero worship) – to make life a dream and a song. It *isn't* based on realities, and when satisfied later on it's got to search for and find the *real realities* underneath the golden haze.[7]

In this instance, Edward may have been trying to convince himself as much as Nellie; later he admitted, 'I have known very well that if Sickert had lifted his finger idly, or accidentally, or through being bored, or through amusement, nothing would have kept you from saying practically "Good-by [sic] Edward. I shall never forget how much you've been to me. I shall always keep you in my heart – but *good-by*."'[8] Nellie's sister Marjory Pease was also perturbed by the persistence of Sickert's spell and in March 1898 she managed to ship Nellie off to Paris to further her artistic studies in an attempt to break it.

Edward followed Nellie to the French capital a month later and stayed with her for six days en route to a holiday in Italy. He travelled extensively for more than a month, visiting Pisa, Perugia, Orvieto, Genoa, Rome, Florence and Venice. He wrote to Nellie practically every day, lamenting the fact that she had refused to come with him, constantly declaring his love for her, and describing the people and places he encountered. Rome and his fellow English tourists were disappointing and disgusting, respectively; Pisa, Venice and the Italians were delightful – especially the women. In Florence, Edward stayed with his old friends the Steffens in their villa overlooking the Arno. Sitting on the veranda, he spied two peasant girls watching him from a nearby stable window, 'one of them ... ready to be most thoughtful, most kind'.[9] While staying in Pisa he made his way to the coast and bathed 'in a fine rolling stormy sea'[10] near the spot where Shelley's body was found. 'The coast was absolutely solitary – only sand, waste and loneliness and seagulls and pines in sight for miles,' he told Nellie. 'It was a good thing to die like that.'[11]

Edward returned home in May, the situation with Nellie still unresolved. Invigorated by his travels, he set to work on plans for a new series for Unwin. This was originally conceived of as the 'Colonial Series', but was eventually launched as the Overseas Library. Edward's prospectus left little doubt about the objectives or the political orientation of the new project:

[G]reat as is the growth of the Empire and the enterprise of its peoples, the new native-born literatures take years to germinate and generations to arrive. Thence comes it that often we do not understand the atmospheres of the new English-speaking peoples, and often misunderstand the problems, the ambitions, the attitudes, befitting them as new races. And while the British Empire grows richer daily in patriotic fervours, in speeches, in splendour, in cant, and in the oracular assurances of Statesmen, the English people seeks to understand its cousins by the interchange of cablegrams, by debates, and by all the ambiguities of official memoranda.

It is, however, the artist's work to bring the people of his nation and their atmosphere before the eyes of another. It is the artist alone, great or small, who, by revealing and interpreting the life around him, makes it living to the rest of the world ...

'The Over-Seas Library' makes no pretence at Imperial drum-beating, or putting English before Colonial opinion. It aims, instead, at getting the atmosphere and outlook of the new peoples recorded, if such is possible. It aims at being an Interchange between all parts of the Empire without favour, an Interchange of records of the life of the English-speaking peoples, and of the Englishmen beyond seas, however imperfect, fragmentary and modest such records or accounts may be.[12]

Edward did not merely rely on manuscripts submitted in response to the prospectus, but sought out likely sources himself. He had been particularly struck by an account of William Morris's funeral in 1896, and had kept a copy of the article in his pocketbook and a close eye on the writer, whose contributions to the *Saturday Review* had also impressed him. Edward considered some of these sketches to be *absolutely* the thing I want',[13] and to this end wrote to their author, Robert Bontine Cunninghame Graham. He sent the letter via Conrad, already a close friend of Graham's, who passed it on with the comment, 'I've heard all this said with greater warmth of appreciation, since You have been (in Your work) a subject of long discussions between us.'[14]

In *Thus to Revisit* (1921) Ford Madox Ford relates a story about Cunninghame Graham. Like many of Ford's accounts it may well be apocryphal, but equally typically it contrives to capture the essence of its subject:

Once, driving with Mr Graham to Roslyn Castle from Edinburgh I heard a politically minded lady say to him:

'You ought, Mr Graham, to be the first President of a British Republic.'

'I ought, madam, if I had my rights,' he answered sardonically, 'to be king of this country. And what a three weeks that would be!'[15]

Amongst the books in the library at Gartmore – the estate at Menteith near Stirling that Graham inherited in 1883 – were the volumes on heraldry from which he could claim to trace royal descent. Tall, lean, with abundant dark hair slightly tinged with red, a pointed beard, piercing black eyes and aristocratic bearing, Graham certainly looked the part, although his physical appearance suggested he might be more at home in the Escorial than at Holyrood. Graham's maternal grandmother was Spanish; from her he learned the language and inherited a love of all things Hispanic. In 1878 he eloped with the twenty-year-old Gabrielle de la Balmondière. She had reputedly been born in Chile, the daughter of a French merchant father and a Spanish mother. In reality, Gabrielle's background was somewhat less exotic. Her father was the eminently respectable Dr Henry Horsfall of Masham, North Yorkshire, who christened his bright but rebellious eldest daughter Caroline. Bored beyond endurance by both North Yorkshire and respectability, Caroline ran away from home twice and eventually ended up in London. The exact circumstances of her first meeting Graham three years after her arrival in the capital at the age of seventeen remain obscure, but one of Graham's biographers speculates that Gabrielle's fictitious history was invented by Graham's mother Anne Bontine, perhaps to obscure the fact that Graham had married outside his social class or possibly because his bride's means of earning a living in London prior to her wedding necessitated it.[16] Whatever the truth, Gabrielle's fabulous ancestry endured intact until the 1980s and the marriage, despite Mrs Bontine's unrelenting hostility, was a happy one.

When Edward first wrote to him, 'Don Roberto' was eight days off his forty-sixth birthday; the previous forty-five years had been nothing if not eventful. At various stages in his life Graham had been a gaucho in the Argentine, a rancher in Texas, Liberal MP for North West Lanark and an inmate of Pentonville Prison. His incarceration was the result of his participation in the Bloody Sunday riot of 1887, when he planned to address a crowd gathered in Trafalgar Square to protest against unemployment at home and British policy in Ireland. Sensing trouble, the government had banned political meetings in the Square and, as he attempted to make his way to it, Graham was felled by one of the numerous truncheon-wielding officers under orders to break up the demonstration. He was charged with unlawful assembly, riot and assaulting two policemen. A youthful Herbert Asquith acted as counsel for the defence; Graham and his co-defendant, the future cabinet minister John Burns, were found guilty of the first charge only and sentenced to six weeks in Pentonville. 'Sursum Corda', an essay on speech and silence, based on Graham's experience of what was effectively solitary confinement in prison, was published nine years later in the *Saturday Review*.

Graham was never happier than when on the move – Spain and Morocco were frequent destinations besides South America – and his party political allegiances were equally mobile. He rapidly became disillusioned with the Liberal leadership, in particular Gladstone's refusal to entertain the demand for an eight-hour working day, and in 1888, while still nominally a Liberal MP, became President of the newly formed Scottish Labour Party, whose secretary was his great friend Keir Hardie. When a year later in the House of Commons the President of the Board of Trade asked him accusingly whether he was advocating 'the tenets of pure unmitigated Socialism', Graham replied with characteristic nonchalance, 'Undoubtedly.'[17] In doing so he effectively declared himself the first Socialist member of the House. Later he would also grow disenchanted with the Labour Party; his final political resting place was with the Scottish National Party and in 1934 he was elected its President when it was founded in its modern form.

Graham was sixteen years older than Edward and thus much nearer the age of their mutual friend Conrad, who was only five years Graham's junior; however, in temperament and especially in their political views Graham was closer to the younger man. Cosmopolitan and irreverent, he and Edward also shared a sardonic wit coupled with a strong streak of melancholy, a fierce strain of anti-imperialism and a love of the underdog. One of Graham's biographers contends that Graham 'made failure into an aesthetic, even a moral virtue. He, for one, would not be cheering when the triumphal procession passed by.'[18] Sentiments endorsed by Edward, who, like Graham, 'observed Britain as a detached but easily angered stranger might have done'.[19] In his introduction to Graham's *Thirty Tales & Sketches*, Edward applauds the author's unflagging commitment to 'shiver ... a lance against the triple brass of British industrialism, commercialism and Imperialism'.[20] The image is not idly chosen: for all that Graham's political activities suggest a desire to shape the present and the future, he was also nostalgic for the past. As Edward suggests, there was a touch of the chivalric about Graham, in some respects a figure from a bygone age who mourned those worlds that were vanishing or had disappeared altogether. Edward, the congenital outsider, sympathised with this strong sense of spiritual and historical displacement: in one letter to Graham he maintains, 'I ought to be an Irishman of the 17th century system – Conrad in Poland – and you in the Scotland of the 14th or 15th centuries.'[21]

That mutual feeling of displacement and much else besides is revealed in the correspondence between Edward and Graham, much of which still survives. Spanning nearly four decades, it is a vast collection both in volume and scope and covers subjects ranging from the personal to the political, from Graham's stories of his travels to Edward's accounts of his skirmishes with publishers and magazine editors. Unsurprisingly the recurring theme is literature: there are frank exchanges about Graham's work (and about Edward's) and lively debates on other writers, past and present. Thus while Graham cannot share Edward's delight in Mary Mann's uncompromising tales of rural life in Norfolk – 'There is talent of course, but, to my mind, marred by the grossest affectation in almost every line'[22] – he enthusiastically endorses Edward's contention that although Kipling 'did create India to the Saxon world[,] that world of dullness that said it *owned* it!' he remains '*the* enemy. He is a creator; and he is *the genius of all we detest* ... I hate his essence.'[23] Amongst the acerbic outbursts are scattered concerned references to the travails of mutual literary friends: 'Just now Conrad seems in low health and worse spirits,' Edward reports in May 1898. 'No doubt as a friend you know this – anyway his friends ought to know it – as he is a very delicate instrument – and delicate instruments are easily broken.'[24]

At first glance Graham appeared to be made of more robust stuff than Conrad, but both lacked confidence in their abilities as writers. In Graham's case this may have been because the other demands on his time – politics, travel, estate management – precluded single-minded devotion to the literary art, a devotion which in all probability he would have been unwilling to give in any case. Yet when Edward approached Graham suggesting a list of sketches that might make up a volume for the Overseas Library he was writing to an author who already enjoyed a considerable reputation. Conrad had been overjoyed to receive the letter praising *An Outcast of the Islands* which ignited his friendship with Graham; in the late 1890s it was the Scot, not the ex-mariner, who was regarded as the more promising literary figure. Graham took up writing relatively late – in a letter to Edward he explains, 'I am, and have been a man of action all my life ... and writing came to me with grey hair'[25] – partly in an attempt to secure his future at Gartmore, which was encumbered with enormous debts. Graham never wrote a novel, but in addition to over a dozen volumes of sketches he produced a series of histories of South America, biographies and travel books, of which *Mogreb-el-Acksa* (1898), the account of his ultimately unsuccessful attempt in 1897 to reach, in disguise, the 'forbidden' Moroccan city of Taroudant, is the best known. Edward thought it showed Graham at his finest, praising the 'verve and brilliancy of tone' that in his opinion made it 'unique in English books of travel'.[26] That *Mogreb-el-Acksa* was considered 'too unorthodox and too witty for the serious British taste'[27] only added to its lustre in Edward's eyes. *Mogreb* consistently exhibited those qualities Edward detected in the best of Graham's work: a powerful evocation of atmosphere; clear, terse prose; and Graham's sharp eye for the telling detail, like the wicker birdcages carried by the emigrants en route to the River Plate in 'S S Atlas', one of the sketches included in *The Ipané* (1899). 'The bird-cages, those bird-cages show the hand of the cunning artist,' Edward enthused. 'It is the touch which makes the picture live ... those cages are a centre, a symbol amid the wealth and jumble of the steamer life you so well describe.'[28]

Graham's work had its flaws, however, and, according to David Garnett, Edward considered Graham 'a good, if not a great, writer'.[29] After praising those pieces he was suggesting for the projected Overseas Library volume, Edward mentions other sketches that 'with some strokes of the pen – an addition here, a deletion there'[30] – might also merit inclusion. 'The Evolution of a Village' was one such instance when 'a living figure ... or two ... might have the effect of art and not of argument'. Much as Edward delighted in the polemical slant of Graham's writing, he recognised that too often it lacked subtlety, blunting the edge of the piece both aesthetically and as argument. 'I think your account would be more likely to *live* if it had a little more wrist-play and a little less of battering blows: if its tone were quieter, more ironical, even congratulatory it would be more dangerous,'[31] he advised after reading 'Frundesia Magna'. Graham's tendency to digress was also something which Edward often sought to eradicate. Nearly all the sketches were drawn from personal experience and Graham was anything but a detached observer. The sardonic commentator on man's inhumanity to man and beast is never far away and frequently takes over the reins to the detriment of the aesthetic integrity of the piece. When Edward advised Graham to cut the opening digressive paragraphs of 'Heather Jock', an account of an ancient Scottish pedlar, Graham protested that it was 'impossible' to do so, because 'I am an essayist and impressionist, and secondly a story teller but have the story telling faculty very weakly. Therefore if you cut out my reflections, nothing remains.'[32]

Edward recognised the truth of this statement: 'You hit the whole thing when you say you are not a story teller, but an impressionist,'[33] he admitted when criticising 'Victory', a sketch which makes all too apparent Graham's feelings about the celebrations of Americans in Paris following their triumph over the Spanish in Cuba. Graham was present at the scene he describes and in a letter to Edward he confessed that he 'had to go into a quiet room, or I must have killed somebody'.[34] Edward felt that the numerous digressions in which Graham expresses his fury delayed the introduction of the elderly Spaniard and his daughter, whose dignified behaviour in effect gives them the 'victory' of the sketch's title and prevented them from becoming 'deep significant figures to the reader's consciousness'.[35] Once again, what Edward perceived as a flaw was the result of the deeply personal and subjective element of Graham's writing; the 'man of action', the disdainful witness gains the upper hand over the artist, despite Edward's attempt to persuade Graham that it '[is] the artist that is the most important now'.[36] However, when 'Victory' appeared in *Thirteen Stories* two years after its publication in the *Westminster Gazette* Edward confessed that 'my eyes were filled with sand when I criticized the structure of 'Victory' ... I admire, fully and deeply. Your method is so much your own.'[37] The author W. H. Hudson, who dedicated *El Ombú* to Graham, described him as a 'Singularisimo escritor ingles' and he is a singular writer in many ways. He was certainly a singular character and this presented Edward with something of a paradox; while he revelled in Graham as a personality, the dominance of that character on the page could make him frustrating to deal with as a writer.

However, there was another side to 'Don Roberto'. His letters to Edward reveal a contemplative, melancholic strain disclosed to few but his closest friends and rarely glimpsed in his published writing. In 1900 Graham finally gave up the struggle to hang on to Gartmore. Despite his protestations – 'I care nothing for mere possession, I have no family pride'[38] – he confessed that leaving the place was a 'bitter wrench'.[39] It affected him for a considerable time. Five years after the sale, he unpacked some cases of pictures from Gartmore which a friend had been keeping for him: 'As they came out one by one, it seemed that they were alive, and that I was buried,' he told Edward, before going on to describe a visit he had made to his old haunts a few months earlier:

> In the autumn, I went to the Lake of Menteith to get some things I left there, to look at the graves of many of my people in [sic] an island there. By the side of the lake, there lived two old sisters, ancient retainers of my family their people had been. The last had died not long ago. The cottage was shut and the garden deserted. I sat down on the doorstep in the evening, and smoked a cigarette. The tobacco was too bitter. I am trying to write about it, and cannot.[40]

Edward's response was swift:

> Your words about Gartmore, and that island burying place give me all that feeling of the things inside you which you find it so impossible to express ... *Write it*, my dear Amigo, in a journal, as though you were communing with yourself ... Cast it in that loose and fluid form, and write it, so that something beautiful and tender may live for others out of all this passing away and coming to nothingness ... You have a great deal in you which as yet you have not fully expressed. I mean – in your books. The most *personal* and in that sense most *preciously direct* from your life ... It is an instinct in you perhaps not to express those depths ... I want you to express yourself *fully* in literature ... I want you to think over what there is in yourself and life which you have shrunk from writing. Perhaps you don't see my meaning – but there are always deeper selves within us than we *know*.[41]

Despite this urging, Graham could not or would not introduce the tone Edward sought into his writing. 'I see I have not done what I feel,' he admitted, 'but that of course is impossible.'[42] Years later, when Edward sent him the letters about the loss of Gartmore and the death of Gabrielle to re-read, Graham told him, 'only to you and my mother did I ever write in that style'.[43]

A very different style was necessary when it came to conducting negotiations with T. Fisher Unwin, sardonically christened 'The Enlightened Patron of Letters' by Edward and Conrad. When Unwin sent Graham a letter regarding his proposed terms for *The Ipané*, the title of the volume destined for the Overseas Library, Graham forwarded it to The Cearne, where it 'tumbled out on the unastonished breakfast table'.[44] Had Unwin seen Edward's response it is likely that he would have sacked him on the spot. After paragraphs in which he mercilessly satirises the 'perilous work' of the publisher, Edward concludes, 'Let us not be harsh to [*sic*] the Patron's career! After all Mr Unwin is not *very* rich and when his memory conspicuously fails him it is merely that the exigencies of business manoeuvres prove too strong for the innate morality of a descendent of long lines of Scotch Salvagians and Essex Nonconformist traders.'[45] He returned Unwin's offending letter to Graham: 'My collection here is too rich in specimens for me to prize it.'

When the draft contract appeared it did not meet with Edward's approval either. He counselled Graham to insert a clause specifically nominating *The Ipané* as the first volume of the Overseas Library, as otherwise 'the "Sketches" *may not* reach the Colonials in the bombshell manner we planned'.[46] Graham was to demand a 15 per cent royalty for all copies sold in the colonies and Edward further advised him to retain the translation and dramatic rights, rather than relinquishing them to Unwin 'as any bloody fool might come along, and for a £5 note the Publisher might make you ridiculous'. Unwin's proposal that Graham receive half a dozen presentation copies of *The Ipané* was also given short shrift: '*Six* is very stingy. You will want twenty copies at least.'[47] In all this Edward was playing a role to which he was rapidly becoming accustomed – that of author's agent rather than publisher's reader. Exposing Unwin's mercenary tendencies gave him a certain mischievous pleasure: 'If you want to hear [Unwin's] praises sung you must go to Conrad,'[48] Edward chaffed in a letter to Graham.

Anyone wanting to hear Conrad's praises sung in 1898 needed to look no further than the 15 October edition of the *Academy*, which carried an enthusiastic appreciation by Edward. The article was important in several ways: it was the first general appraisal of the author to appear in the English press and set the tone for much subsequent writing on Conrad, both by Edward and other reviewers. It was also probably no coincidence that three months after the appreciation appeared Conrad

shared the *Academy's* award for promising writers and garnered a much
needed fifty guineas. 'I suppose Lucas [E. V. Lucas, the critic, journalist
and a close friend of Edward's] worked like a horse to get this awful,
awful job through,' Conrad concluded. 'I suppose you worked too – or
no – I won't suppose.'[49]

In the first half of the article Edward discusses the artist's mission,
which he defines as illuminating the darkness of human nature and that
of worlds both natural and psychological, hitherto unexplored. 'Wherever
the artists are absent,' Edward argues, 'human nature appears to the
imagination absolutely uncanny and ghost-like. But wherever the artist
has been ... the life of man appears suddenly natural and comprehen-
sible.'[50] Conrad's tales of the East and maritime life have given 'a new
world a voice'. He has enabled the reader to 'see', both imaginatively
and with understanding. Edward's argument and his vocabulary – the
insistent references to the 'artist' rather than the writer, for example –
resonate strongly with Conrad's preface to *The Nigger of the 'Narcissus'*
with its now famous declaration: 'My task which I am trying to achieve
is, by the power of the written word, to make you hear, to make you
feel – it is, before all, to make you *see*.'[51]

Conrad read this appreciation in proof and was delighted with
Edward's endorsement of his aesthetic ideals. There was one reference,
however, which may have tinged his pleasure with just a shade of trepidation. It appears in a passage in which Edward sets out to define the
quality of Conrad's art:

> This faculty of seeing man's life in relation to the seen and unseen
> forces of Nature it is that gives Mr Conrad's art its extreme delicacy
> and its great breadth of vision. It is pre-eminently the poet's gift
> and is very rarely conjoined with insight into human nature and a
> power of conceiving character. When the two gifts come together
> we have the poetic realism of the great Russian novels. Mr Conrad's
> art is truly realism of that high order.

To someone born a reluctant subject of the Russian Empire, whose
mother had died as a consequence of enforced political exile and whose
father had celebrated his child's birth by dedicating a poem 'To My Son
born in the 85th year of Muscovite Oppression',[52] this comparison was
hardly welcome. Conrad had a visceral and lifelong hatred of all things
Russian. Worse still, in his penultimate paragraph Edward announced
that Conrad's art 'seems to be on the line that divides East and West, to

spring naturally from the country that mingles some Eastern blood in the Slav's veins – the Ukraine'. If anything was guaranteed to make Conrad furious it was uttering his name in the same sentence as the word 'Slav', a description which he along with many others at the time took to be interchangeable with 'Russian'. However, the letter he sent Edward after reading the article in proof appeared to express only profound gratitude. 'It is magnificent,' Conrad declared:

> It is absorbingly interesting to me not as appreciation of myself but as disclosure of you. And I appear to myself wrapped in the glamour of Your intention – not of what has been done, but of what should be done, what should be tried for, what should be desired – what cannot be attained.[53]

Conrad was almost certainly genuinely touched by Edward's public affirmation of his talents, but the disclosure of his mentor's determination to present those qualities as an integral part of a 'Slavic' inheritance may have set the alarm bells ringing: if it didn't it should have done.

The 'Slavic' irritation aside, Conrad had every reason to feel grateful to Edward in the autumn of 1898. In early September he was staying with Edward again and, during the visit, his host took him to meet Ford, who was renting 'Grace's Cottage', two fields away from The Cearne. The cottage belonged to Constance's sister Grace, who bought the site in 1896 when she was home on leave from Ceylon, where her husband Hugh Human was the head of a technical college in Colombo. Grace's Cottage was another Cowlishaw construction, built of the same stone and in the same style as The Cearne, but rather oddly shaped. Family legend has it that Cowlishaw sent out a wax model to Ceylon for the Humans to approve, but that it melted in the Red Sea on the way home 'and was wrongly assembled by worried lascars and slavishly copied by ignorant workmen'.[54] The Fords took up the tenancy in March 1898 and Ford proceeded to play at being a smallholder, dressing up for the part in smock-frock and gaiters. The only livestock consisted of a few ducks, which Ford christened after the female members of the Black and Garnett families. 'Connie', 'Lucy', 'Katie' and the others were forced to form an orderly queue for a dip in the hip bath Ford had sunk in the garden in the absence of any pond.

Conrad soon reaped the benefits of the introduction to Ford, which turned out to be one of the most significant events of his literary life. As Edward had observed to Graham in May of that year, Conrad was at a low ebb, still struggling with *The Rescue*, which he had taken up

again in June, and being chased by editors for late work. The fact that
he felt exiled at Ivy Walls – the Elizabethan farmhouse he was renting
near Stanford-le-Hope, Essex – only added to his woes, so when Ford
offered to sublet Pent Farm at Postling near Hythe, Conrad jumped at the
chance. The neighbourhood was far more congenial, with Henry James,
H. G. Wells and Stephen Crane relatively close by. Valuable as the change
of surroundings was, it was not at the forefront of Edward's mind when
he brought Conrad and Ford together. He was well aware that Conrad
was desperately trying to catch up with missed deadlines and that he was
in dire need of money – money that was slow to appear given Conrad's
tortuous rate of composition and books, which, despite their artistic
merit, were unlikely to prove commercially attractive; fine writing, public
neglect and penury being inevitable bedfellows in Edward's opinion. Ford,
however, wrote with exceptional speed and facility and possessed what
Edward later described as a 'remarkable talent for romancing'.[55]

Ford and Conrad swiftly realised that their disparate literary strengths
might profitably be combined in collaborative authorship, something that
was not uncommon at the time. Whether or not Edward suggested this
in the hope that it would ease the emptiness of Conrad's wallet is unclear.
According to Ford's rather muddled account, Conrad intimated that he
consulted Edward, W. E. Henley and the novelist Marriott Watson about
the proposal, but from a letter Conrad wrote to Edward it seems that
his mentor had more than a few misgivings: 'I reckon Ford told you. I
reckon you disapprove. "I rebel! I said I would rebel". (d'you know the
quotation) I send you here Henley's letter over the matter.'[56] Edward
would certainly recognise the quote from *Fathers and Sons* by Turgenev,
as he had used it himself in his preface to Constance's translation of the
novel. Although the words are spoken by Bazarov's grief-stricken father
after his son's death, Conrad's allusion may be aimed more at the novel's
title, figuring himself as the rebellious 'son' acting against the advice of
the man he had come to regard as his literary father. As it turned out,
the results of the collaboration – *The Inheritors* (1901) – which includes
a flattering portrait of Edward as Lea, the publisher's reader – *Romance*
(1903) and *The Nature of a Crime* (1909) brought neither author the fame
and fortune they hoped for. Edward himself summed up his feelings about
the collaboration in 1936: 'Ford was in spirit a German romantic, and
Conrad a Slav realist in his psychological insight. And the two elements
could not mix, though this is by no means to say that the literary intercourse of the two men was unfruitful.'[57] This last remark was certainly
true: Conrad and Ford shared a deep interest in the craft of fiction, which

rapidly became the topic of hours of discussion and debate between them, to their mutual benefit. For several years Ford was a great help to Conrad, lending him money, acting as amanuensis, editor and even possibly writing an instalment of *Nostromo* when Conrad failed to meet a deadline. Ford for his part revelled in his association with the older, more prestigious writer, but his new friendship introduced an edginess into his relationship with Edward; an element of competition developed between them where Conrad was concerned, something Conrad was not above exploiting when it suited him. The meeting at Grace's Cottage that September not only sowed the seeds of a productive friendship, it also scattered those of future discord.

8

'I'm not such a fool as I seem'

The final year of the nineteenth century proved to be one of change for the Garnett family. On 20 March Richard Garnett officially retired as Keeper of Printed Books at the British Museum, and just over a month later he, Narney and Olive moved to 27 Tanza Road, Hampstead. Their new home overlooked Parliament Hill. It was described by Richard's granddaughter Rayne as a 'dark, narrow house of four storeys and a basement' with 'a small garden behind, chiefly productive of saxifrage and cats'.[1] Richard had left his post at the Museum a year early on account of Narney's health, which he believed was adversely affected by the smog and clamour of London, and his own deteriorating eyesight. Hampstead, which then had the reputation of being the healthiest place in London, seemed the ideal location for retirement. Edward still saw his parents fairly regularly, although Tanza Road was a good deal further from his office in Paternoster Square than the British Museum. He may have particularly looked forward to his weekly visits to the Museum during his father's final months at the residence as Constance had gone to Montpellier for three months in December, taking David with her. She had been advised to seek warmer climes in an effort to alleviate her sick headaches and the rheumatism that was beginning to afflict her in the winter.

Ford and Elsie were also on the move that spring. Towards the end of March they left Grace's Cottage and rented Stocks Hill at Aldington Knoll, on the edge of Romney Marsh. Olive went over to Grace's Cottage after Ford's departure and found it 'deserted save for three white pigeons who refused to be caught. An egg ... An ink pot, the bowl of a pipe and a piece of strap, a broken baby's bottle.'[2] The new tenant at the cottage was Nellie's father Richard Heath and to Edward's great delight it was not long before she returned from Paris to move in and look after him. Edward was gradually winning Nellie round, but her anguish at conducting an affair in secret and being forced to conceal the truth from those she loved remained. 'I've realized so intensely *your difficulties*,' Edward wrote reassuringly '... the feeling you have: "*I must live openly because I love them* and to give myself to you secretly means to lie, and to separate myself from other people" ... I shall leave you to find the way nearer to me. I shan't hurry or persecute you. I feel you will come naturally, by yourself.'[3] Nevertheless he was unable to resist instructing Nellie to 'Send everybody else to the devil, and take that for your motto.'[4]

Richard Heath's opposition to the liaison continued – he would refuse to talk to Nellie about Edward years after the relationship had become firmly established – but the arrival of Sydney Olivier hotfoot from the Colonial Office one summer's day with news of the Colonial Secretary Joseph Chamberlain's ultimatum to the Transvaal Colony provided a subject on which Edward and Heath were firmly united. David Garnett remembers his parents and Olivier setting off immediately to Grace's Cottage to deliver the tidings, and Heath 'standing short and resolute with blue eyes flashing as he heard the news and the sense of seething indignation in all the members of the little group'.[5]

The Boer War officially began on 11 October 1899; like many in the literary world, Edward and Constance were implacably opposed to it, which put them at odds with other members of the Garnett family. The war could not be mentioned in the hearing of either Richard (who published a sonnet vilifying President Kruger) or Edward's older brother Robert, both of whom firmly espoused the imperialist cause. To his later shame, David's games at the time involved the imaginary shooting of British soldiers, something he came to believe his parents should have stopped: 'For it was all very well Edward pretending to be Irish and a rebel, when he was in fact of mixed Yorkshire and Anglo-Irish blood, but I was English ... and I should have been encouraged to love and honour England.'[6] However, Edward and Constance always believed they owed their allegiance to the cause which came closest to their fiercely held principles, rather than to any national flag. As it was, David's pro-Boer sympathies became known in the village with the result that he and his friend Harold Hobson, son of the unorthodox economist J. A. Hobson, were frequently booed and stoned by other children when they ventured onto Limpsfield Common. When, at Hobson senior's invitation, Samuel Cron Cronwright, the husband of Olive Schreiner, came over from South Africa to speak at a series of pro-Boer meetings, Edward armed himself with an ash stick and acted as one of his bodyguards.

Luckily, Edward sustained no injury as a result of his activities, but conflict of another sort was brewing that autumn. 'I am sitting beside the fire in your room writing reports for Unwin,' Edward told Nellie. 'I rather think there is trouble ahead with that individual but I feel extremely indifferent.'[7] Edward had never got on with T. Fisher Unwin and increasingly came to despise him, as his letters to Cunninghame Graham make only too clear. Unwin certainly knew how to extract his pound of flesh – Edward calculated that he was reading and reporting on 700 manuscripts a year[8] – and apart from their internationalism and mutual sympathy for political refugees there was little else they agreed about. Edward's obstinacy, his certainty in his own judgement and his predilection for taking the author's side, even to the extent of recommending rival firms, did little to endear him to Unwin. The fact that his employer initially lost money on many of the writers Edward recommended didn't help either. By the autumn it was clear that his days at Paternoster Buildings were numbered and, as Edward later recalled, 'Mr Fisher Unwin dispensed with my services as his literary adviser at the end of 1899.'[9]

Constance greeted the news with relative equanimity: 'I have felt for such a long while that it was impossible Edward should remain at Fisher Unwin's' she explained to Richard Garnett, and added

the business seems to be going downhill in more ways than one. And it is so much better that such a crisis in our fortunes should come now when Edward is thirty than that he should have had to seek fresh openings a few years later, when he will be older and when too our expenses for the boy's education must necessarily be considerable. I do not myself feel apprehensive as to our future. I have complete confidence in Edward's energies and good sense. The only anxiety which troubles me is on the ground of his health. I doubt whether he is strong enough to stand a long strain of very hard work. His health is good as long as he leads a quiet life free from worry but if he should be forced to depend on journalistic work to any great degree, I am afraid the necessity of working against time and the uncertainty of the work would tell upon him.[10]

Edward had been steadily building up his contributions to journals and magazines, writing reviews and literary articles principally for the *Speaker* and the *Academy*, which was undergoing something of a renaissance under the editorship of C. Lewis Hind. Whenever he could, Edward took the opportunity to review the work of friends, such as Conrad, Crane and Cunninghame Graham, explaining their merits to a readership that in his opinion was in sore need of education. He also sought to bring some of the foremost contemporary European writers and thinkers to wider notice and appreciation. The insularity of the English and their attitude to writers they found unsettling or 'morbid' (in the sense of morally unhealthy) irritated Edward intensely. In an essay on Henrik Ibsen he asks whether English society has the ability to understand the Norwegian dramatist and concludes that 'the current of the national life sets too strongly in certain directions for Ibsen to be accorded genuinely more than a general lip-valuation'.[11] The problem with Ibsen is that he shows society its unflattering portrait and refuses to provide neat and, to the English mind, satisfactory solutions. According to Edward:

> The modern Englishman has almost come to be a well-paid share-holder in family life, political life, and remunerative opinion. He does not want to be unsettled, to be made uneasy in his convictions about life, he wants to be optimistic, to make things go better, to be made more *certain* ... He wants art to fit human life carefully into a special narrow ideal of how life *ought* to go, à l'Anglaise.[12]

Time and again in his critical writing, Edward maintains that the purpose of art is first and foremost to reveal; that the majority of readers determinedly averted their eyes from the resulting picture merely confirmed Edward's belief that the English were essentially antipathetic to fine writing. This did not stop him from trying to change attitudes, but he was frequently frustrated by the constraints of journalism and by the length of time it took him to produce copy. 'I have been working at my Nietzsche article all day,' he complained to Nellie. 'It's extraordinarily difficult to do partly because Nietzsche challenges all current valuations ... And to sum up such a man ... and to follow a line of criticism on his doctrine is quite impossible ... what can I ram into an article of 1500 words? ... moreover the English reader won't care to understand a word of Nietzsche!' 'Still,' he concludes, 'I like to try, because it brings back one's self respect to try and fail; and not to try is worst of all.'[13]

Constance's concern about the perils of Edward being forced to earn a living through journalism was not unfounded. Most reviewers were paid by the word and if Edward was to generate sufficient income from that source alone he was faced with the prospect of relentlessly having to churn out piece after piece to tight deadlines, day in, day out; a grim outlook for someone for whom 'even a sentence takes ... a ridiculous time'.[14] Happily help was at hand in the blond, athletic shape of Sydney

Pawling, reputedly the fastest bowler in England, Captain of Hampstead Cricket Club and a partner in the firm of William Heinemann. Edward had known Pawling for some time and their friendship had been instrumental in Heinemann publishing Conrad's *The Nigger of the 'Narcissus'*. The fact that the company published Constance's translations also brought the two men into contact, and in the second week of February Edward was able to report to his father that he had begun to read manuscripts for Pawling, although initially it was only a tentative arrangement.

Like T. Fisher Unwin, Heinemann was a relatively young firm which had already published novels by H. G. Wells, Israel Zangwill, the commercially popular Hall Caine and Ethel Voynich, whose tale of pre-revolutionary Italy, *The Gadfly* (1897), had the rare distinction of achieving critical acclaim and prodigious sales. William Heinemann himself was a cosmopolitan figure; short, dark and with a noticeable foreign accent, he was the complete opposite of Pawling, 'the handsome Saxon' as Edmund Gosse called him, both physically and in temperament. Heinemann had been raised in England but educated in Germany; he spoke German and French fluently and was widely read in European literature. A great lover of art and music, Heinemann considered the British to be philistines, a view with which his newest employee wholeheartedly agreed. If anything Edward worked even harder in his new job; as well as reading manuscripts he was asked to revise the work of incompetent translators whom Heinemann employed even though they had only a tenuous grasp of English – an arduous task when he had no knowledge of the source language. Despite this increased workload, Edward was paid only £3 to £3 10s a week; less than he had been earning at Unwin's. Nevertheless, he found the atmosphere at 21 Bedford Street in Covent Garden much more to his liking and thoroughly enjoyed working with the affable Pawling.

The reduction in income was hardly welcome, but as Constance suggested in her letter to Richard, it was not as serious as it might have been had David been older and the costs of his education higher. The 'thoroughgoing Rousseauism'[15] that Olive attributed to Frederika Macdonald's influence on the youthful Edward seemed to re-emerge in his attitude to David's early upbringing. Constance had been surprised when Edward, who felt children should develop skills in their own time, consented to David having a short, daily reading lesson, but from the age of about seven his son spent much of his time freely roaming the woods and hills round the Chart, which in his own words he soon 'learnt ... by heart'.[16] These excursions kindled a lifelong interest in the natural world and taught him a great deal about it. For a very short time David attended a school in Limpsfield, but it was not long before Constance went back to teaching him herself. Eventually he also had lessons with Nellie's brother Carl, who had previously taught in the slums of the East End. Constance reported to Richard that Heath found him 'a variable and uncertain pupil and tells me he is sure to be brilliant in some lines but will never be the steady good all-round pupil that schoolmasters prefer.' 'I am afraid he will be exceedingly opinionated,' she added, 'but perhaps considering the character of the two families from which he is sprung he is hardly to be blamed for that.'[17]

As an only child David took rather more notice of his parents' friends than he might have done had there been siblings to occupy his attention. Not unnaturally he tended to size his father's visitors up according to the amount of notice they took of him. Hence Conrad – who sat in a clothes basket, rigged up a sail with a clean sheet and issued orders to his young crew to take in or let out the sail – scored highly, as did W. H. Hudson, who used to accompany David on his woodland rambles, teaching him to identify birdsong and passing on invaluable snippets of country lore. David cared less for the flamboyant Cunninghame Graham, 'who impressed my imagination rather than won my heart',[18] perhaps on account of the fact that Graham did not put himself out to gain the boy's favour. However, the visitor who immediately inspired David's admiration and affection was the man whose initial contact with Edward had been so unfortunately soured by his use of Carlton Club headed paper.

One of John Galsworthy's early visits to The Cearne coincided with the arrival of a semi-feral cat and her kitten, which the Garnetts were looking after for the Peases, who were on holiday. When one of the Garnett dogs, Puppsie, bounded into the room and rushed up to the cat's bed, David grabbed the dog by the collar and was dragging him away when the cat sprang and clawed David's eyebrow, filling his eye with blood. Having seen off the intruders the mother cat stationed herself on the mantelpiece, hissing and spitting incessantly and attacking anyone who entered the room. Into this scene of chaos and carnage strode Galsworthy, who with great sangfroid trapped the ferocious feline in a wicker basket, where she yowled furiously and tore at the sides of her cell. David was tremendously impressed by this display of cool composure, which was soon repeated when Galsworthy was faced with a stinking, maggot-filled carcass that the incorrigible Puppsie had dragged into the Cearne hallway. Without turning a hair, Galsworthy fetched a shovel and wheelbarrow, buried the offensive object in the garden 'and then returned to wash his hands carefully and dust his knees with a handkerchief scented with a few drops of eau de Cologne'.[19] It was hard not to be struck by such nonchalance, but then, as Galsworthy had remarked to Edward with a gleam in his eye when they parted after their first actual meeting, 'I'm not such a fool as I seem.'[20]

It was Conrad who had initially brought Galsworthy to Edward's attention, and three years after Edward had spurned *From the Four Corners* he pleaded his friend's cause once more. Galsworthy and Conrad first met in 1893 when Galsworthy, who then had no plans for a literary career, was returning from a trip to Australia and the South Seas with his friend Ted Sanderson. Galsworthy and Sanderson had set out hoping to meet Robert Louis Stevenson in Samoa, a pilgrimage which came to naught when they were unable to get a boat to the island. In March the two set sail for home aboard the clipper *Torrens*. In a letter to his family Galsworthy describes the ship's first mate as 'a capital chap, though queer to look at; he is a man of travel and experience in many parts of the world, and has a fund of yarns on which I draw freely.'[21] The strange-looking spinner of tales was Joseph Conrad and by the time the *Torrens* docked in London that July he had established friendships with Galsworthy and Sanderson that would endure for the rest of his life. One summer morning in 1900 Conrad took Galsworthy over to The Cearne for lunch. 'Conrad that day was in his most silky, bantering mood,' Edward recalled, 'while Galsworthy sat listening to his lively exchanges, saying very little.'[22]

When Edward looked across the table at his taciturn guest he would have seen a fair, handsome man of thirty-three, less than six months his senior. Tall and slim, Galsworthy looked every inch the athlete he had been at Harrow; from his appearance, deportment and demeanour Edward might have concluded that his initial impression of Galsworthy as a basically amiable but to his mind typically representative example of the English upper-middle classes was not too far wide of the mark; however, there was a good deal more to Galsworthy than met the eye.

Arthur Waugh, father of Alec and Evelyn, was in Galsworthy's year at New College Oxford and noted that 'from the beginning he played the part of an observer, withdrawn, like Plato's philosopher, under the shadow of the wall, watching the crowd hurry past upon its headlong way'.[23] The role of observer is concomitant with that of outsider and Galsworthy had slowly developed a deep sense of unease within his own class. Little by little he had turned away from the shibboleths of his family – Conservative politics, hunting, shooting, a firm belief in the Empire (unlike the rest of his clan Galsworthy was deeply opposed to the Boer War) – and had rejected a fledgling career at the Bar in favour of writing, much to his father's disappointment. Gradually his vague feelings of disquiet had led Galsworthy into a sympathetic interest in those whose experiences were outside his own. This steady metamorphosis, especially on the literary side, had been encouraged and to some extent inspired by the woman with whom he had been conducting an affair for the past five years: Ada Cooper Galsworthy, the wife of his first cousin Arthur.

Such marital irregularities may have been unmentionable in the hearing of John Galsworthy senior, but Edward delighted in them and he found the attractive, dark-haired Ada, a pianist of near professional standard and a proficient translator, rather appealing. Divorce was out of the question as long as Galsworthy's father remained alive; the intractability of the situation troubled his son greatly, but it also fuelled his early work in which defiance of social mores is so often a prominent feature. Following the publication of *From the Four Winds* and *Jocelyn*, Galsworthy settled down to write some short stories and another novel, *Villa Rubein*. Having introduced his two friends, Conrad sent Edward the proofs of the novel and shortly afterwards dispatched one of the short stories, 'A Man of Devon'.

Appropriately enough, 'A Man of Devon' reached Edward when he, Constance and David were on holiday at Bantham near Kingsbridge. Edward was enjoying the beautiful Devon coastline and taking every opportunity to swim, but he was missing Nellie, to whom he sent passionate letters every day. 'I love you too much for even contemplation of it,'[24] he declared. In between bathing, writing to Nellie and 'socialistic talks' with a young local blacksmith – 'a splendid fellow, in a way Whitman would admire and Ed. Carpenter would sentimentalise over'[25] – Edward set down his thoughts about 'A Man of Devon'. Both he and Constance, who had also read the story, admired it and singled out Pasiance, the central female character, for particular praise. It was Galsworthy's presentation of Zachary Pearse – the feckless and swashbuckling son of a sea captain who captures Pasiance's heart – that failed entirely to convince. The problem, Edward believed, lay in Galsworthy's use of his narrator:

> ... one is left asking oneself whether the story would take higher rank if the objective method had suddenly vanished ... and if the hints and tokens of a fierce, unexplored subjectivity had expanded into a few pages of those flashes by which human nature suddenly goes off into tracks of intense individuality – individuality not to be challenged or contested, but only to be *seen*.[26]

When a month later Edward read what became the second story in the volume, 'A Knight', he detected a similar flaw in what he otherwise considered a fine piece. Again he explained to Galsworthy that 'in life the narrator's own exposition may be just what we can't quite stand, because it's complete.'[27] By this time the friendship between the two men was flourishing and they were regularly dining together to discuss Galsworthy's work and the state of the world in general. 'I must apologize ... for having over-laboured my "anti-war" diatribes the other night,'[28] Edward wrote in a letter chiefly concerned with Galsworthy's poem 'To the Spirit of Our Times'. 'The great thing in poetry I think,' he advised Galsworthy, 'is for the writer to throw out every line and every accessory idea which does not strengthen the whole. That needs more courage than most of us have.'[29]

If ever courage was needed it was required at The Cearne one February day in 1901. Bert Hedgecock, who had been released from his duties as Shagpat's groom and gardener in the economy drive of 1897, had an older brother, Bill, by all accounts a tricky individual who did not get on with his peers and had a volatile temper. Edward, the perennial champion of outcasts and outsiders, agreed to take him on to do odd jobs – much to Constance's annoyance and consternation. Edward gave an account of the resulting drama in a letter to Cunninghame Graham. After apologising for not having responded to a letter of Graham's, which 'arrived in the hours when I found myself living in a Dostoievsky novel', he goes on to explain:

A very interesting character, a young horse stealer, labourer, poacher and n'er-do-well, whom I was providing with food, work and shelter in a shed here, suddenly turned into a raving maniac and after wanderings to and fro with him in 'search of the Authorities', after twelve hours excitements was finally landed by me in the district Infirmary. The poor fellow is now in an Asylum.

I have been living inside this man's mind for days, and the final phase of deep sanity and insanity – though unforeseen – has left me more in sympathy with him than with any of the kind neighbours, friends, officials, doctors and police etc etc whom I have been forced to interview ...

My wife has been so upset by this madman episode – axes and pitchforks and knives were 'properties' on the scene of action – that I have had to take her away for a week or so, and have had less time than usual.[30]

This is a truncated and understated narrative of what actually took place. In 1935 David turned the incident into a novel, *Beany-Eye*, later claiming that 'every word in the book is as true as I could make it'.[31] As David's son Richard has pointed out, the accuracy of this statement is open to question. David later admitted that Beany-Eye, the Hedgecock character in the novel, has elements of another labourer he had known and David describes things in the novel he could not have seen or been aware of; so, given Edward's restraint and David's artistic licence, it is very difficult to say with any certainty exactly what happened. *Beany-Eye* is narrated by the only child of the house, obviously based on David. The Edward character is 'James', whilst the Constance figure is referred to only as 'my mother'.

According to the novel, the mother, who has been thoroughly scared by Beany-Eye's odd behaviour, tells James she will not spend another night in the house if he remains on the premises. James agrees to tell Beany-Eye to go, but feeling morally responsible, offers to set him up as a hawker with a pony and cart. In addition, James suggests that Beany-Eye take a large quantity of empty bottles that are lying around and would make a few pennies; he also asks Beany-Eye to tar the back of the stable before he leaves. While he is heating the tar Beany-Eye accidentally spills about half of it; this trivial incident sends him into a manic fury during which he smashes all the bottles he can see before departing. The next morning James realises that during the night Beany-Eye has broken back into the stable where he had previously been sleeping and goes to investigate. As soon as he opens the door Beany-Eye springs at him, wielding an axe, and chases his former employer to the front door of the house. James just manages to get in and shoot the bolt before Beany-Eye arrives and starts to hammer violently at the knocker. Having dispatched his wife and son out of harm's way through the back door, James then faces Beany-Eye and persuades him to hand over the axe, after which he wanders off. When James looks into the stable, he is horrified to see an arsenal of old knives, scythe-blades, billhooks and pitchforks neatly arranged in a semicircle with the blades pointing outwards – evidence that Beany-Eye has not been struck by a sudden fit of insanity, but has been mentally disturbed for some time whilst outwardly appearing sane. After further encounters with the dangerously unstable Beany-Eye, who is still carrying potentially offensive weapons, James eventually persuades him to accompany him to the nearest police station, where he is examined by a doctor who admits him to an infirmary. Beany-Eye then makes a murderous attack on the infirmary night-attendant and is committed to the local asylum.

Whether or not David's description of Beany-Eye flinging the two dogs – Nietzsche and the unfortunate Puppsie – sixteen feet into the air owes more to dramatic licence than fact is a matter of debate, but David later maintained that the novel's portrayal of 'Edward's courage, patience and humanity in dealing with Bill are not in the slightest degree exaggerated'. 'Edward was not the bravest man I have known,' David continues, 'but his behaviour on the morning when Bill went mad was the bravest I have witnessed.'[32] Edward's sole remark about the incident to his father – 'We have had a very annoying time with a workman here attacked by alcoholic mania'[33] – must rank as one of the finer examples of understatement.

William Hedgecock remained at Brookwood Asylum for the next three years; he wrote to Edward more than a few times, often in response to gifts of tobacco and books. Edward was keen to visit, but initially was told by the doctor that Hedgecock remained 'very incoherent and obscene – and not in a fit state to be visited'.[34] Five months after being admitted, Hedgecock sent Edward a letter describing his situation:

> Just a line hoping to find you quite well Mrs Garnett and son[.] Am getting on very fair but there is such a funey [sic] lot of people here that I cant sleep of a night so that I cant see the use of my stoping [sic] here and as for to get a little bit of tobbaco [sic] I have to go like a young horse I should be very thankful to you if you could send me some for I dont know which way to turn to get out of their way[.] I would sooner be out in the middle of some wood so that I did not know than stay here[.] Some of them are as sensible but others you cant make head nor tail of [,] it gets fair disheartening to stay here[.] I should be glad to hear from you or see you for some are as mad as march hare's [sic] and rough too[.] If you could get me away I should be very thankful. Yours truly
>
> W Hedgecock you know sir I havent done anything to be shut up here I do what I can to keep myself from mischief Yours sincerely WH[35]

This distressing plea for Edward's help to obtain a discharge was the first of several. In February 1904 Hedgecock was able to give news of his imminent release and asked if Edward could

> see to arrangements for my formal discharge ... As everything was left in your hands when you were last here[.] I am sorry to put you to so much trouble but I hope to be able to repay you after my

discharge by my intended Good Conduct and in following your advice regarding my future[.] I am deeply indebted to you in taking such a kindly interest in me during the period I have unfortunately been here and in doing so much for me on my discharge.[36]

Edward counselled Hedgecock to stay off alcohol and urged him to start a new life in Canada. There is little reason to suppose that the account in *Beany-Eye* in which the Edward character purchases Beany-Eye's ticket out and provides him with clothes and other useful items is any great departure from the truth. Hedgecock found jobs on various farms near Montreal; he continued to write to Edward and in 1906 married a widow from Essex. Many people over the years would confess a debt of gratitude to Edward, but few owed him more than Bill Hedgecock, and if Edward himself were asked whom over the course of his life he had derived most satisfaction from helping, it would be no surprise to find Hedgecock ranking above some of the great names of twentieth-century literature.

If the events of the winter of 1901 were dramatic, those of the summer were in their own way equally troubling. In August the previous year Constance had confessed to Richard that she was anxious about Edward, who was overworking. As he explained to his father, 'the amount of Reading, Editorial Assistance and Correcting that Heinemann requires for the sum of £3 10/- a week is ... exacting and continuous,'[37] and Edward appears to have approached William Heinemann about the prospect of better terms. The response was hardly what he hoped for. Heinemann informed him that he had decided to remodel the arrangements regarding reading, paragraphing and editing and in consequence 'we could I fear even less than in the past offer you what is so unquestionably your due, and we think therefore that it will be best if you at your own convenience and in your own time dispose of your work elsewhere'.[38] This was a considerable blow: Edward rated his chances of getting another position as Reader 'rather doubtful'[39] – such jobs were thin on the ground – and foresaw an increasing reliance on literary journalism, which he would have to do 'more quickly and on less difficult subjects than I have hitherto attempted'.[40] Edward himself attributed his dismissal to the fact that 'as Pawling's protégé I have, from the first, been looked on by Heinemann with some jealousy, and he has now taken the opportunity of putting his own man in my place.'[41] Business for publishers had not been brisk, partly because of the continuing Boer War, and as Edward remarked to his father, 'Nowadays, however good and clever Fiction may be if it is not carefully "boomed" and manoeuvred beforehand, it stands but little chance, and of course the Reader cannot arrange to "boom" or intrigue for the books he selects and helps bring into being.'[42] At least he had the consolation of knowing that Heinemann could not accuse him of lack of effort and his relations with Pawling remained excellent. Heinemann himself acknowledged the 'efficient, original and devoted manner'[43] in which Edward had conducted the firm's affairs: 'original' may be the key word here; Edward was never a biddable employee and was not afraid of speaking his mind when the occasion demanded. Fearlessness may have stood him in good stead when faced with the axe-wielding Hedgecock in February, but it may partly have contributed to him losing his job in July.

9

Joining Duckworth

Although William Heinemann had attempted to palliate his letter of dismissal by declaring that Edward should seek alternative employment at his own convenience and in his own time, it was clear that he did not expect his 'efficient, original and devoted' employee to be haunting 21 Bedford Street indefinitely. By September Edward had disposed of most of his work and it was on his last morning, as he was sorting through the final papers on his desk, that he heard the office boy suddenly announce 'Mr Hudson!' Looking through the window Edward spied a tall, dark figure standing outside his room. Realising that this was the author of *El Ombú*, a work Edward had tried to persuade his employer to publish – '"But we shan't sell it!" objected Mr William Heinemann in his nervous, excitable fashion'[1] – he approached William Henry Hudson and told him he had written a masterpiece. 'Hudson glared at me astonished, as though he wished to annihilate me and asked my name. I told him, adding, "It's my last day here. Where can I meet you?" Suddenly his face changed and he said, "Let's go and find a place to lunch."'[2]

Six years after Hudson's death, Edward confessed to Cunninghame Graham that he had 'never been so captured *wholly* by any man or writer as by Hudson'.[3] William Henry Hudson's literary work has now rather fallen into neglect,[4] but at the turn of the twentieth century and for some years afterwards he was regarded as a writer's writer, his pellucid, apparently effortless prose greatly admired by his peers. Ford's claim that 'there was no one – no writer – who did not acknowledge without question that [Hudson] was the greatest living writer of English'[5] may well be one of his less overblown statements.

Born near Buenos Aires in 1841 of American parents, Hudson came to London in 1874 and became a British citizen twenty-six years later. For some time after his arrival in England Hudson struggled to make ends meet and lived in London in conditions of genteel poverty with his wife Emily, a former professional singer he married in 1876. By the time

Edward met him he had published a picaresque novel, *The Purple Land that England Lost*, and a utopian romance – *The Crystal Age* – as well as books on the natural world, including the well-received *The Naturalist in La Plata*, which appeared in 1892. That same year he published another novel, *Fan*, under the pseudonym Henry Harford. It was a dismal failure and convinced Hudson that as far as writing was concerned his true metier was as an essayist rather than a novelist. However, in Hudson's eyes the whole literary business came a poor second to what he regarded as his true vocation – that of naturalist. Edward was enchanted not just by Hudson's writing, but by the man himself:

> Wherever he went, wherever he appeared in roads or fields, in cottages, inns, country houses, people succumbed quickly to the spell of his personality. His tall dark figure, his brusque, vivid talk, his magnetic eyes, his strength of manner, and the spice of mystery in his movements captivated his hearers. People were warmed by his rich vibrating feeling, by his picturesque aloofness, by his intimacy of tone, by something strange in his attitude, by his intense zest in the living fact. And by this power of vivifying his hearers and of stimulating their interests Hudson was a king in any company.[6]

The description conveys something of Hudson's complexity; aloof yet intimate, keen to engage with those he met, yet essentially an outsider, appearing, observing and moving on. People who encountered Hudson were unlikely to forget the lanky, slightly stooping figure, habitually decked out in a tweed tailcoat with pockets in the tails, matching trousers and waistcoat, stiff collar and tie. Hudson's abundant hair, short beard and untrimmed moustache had turned grey; the 'magnetic' eyes were brown, the prominent nose so irregularly shaped many suspected it had once been broken. Although not quite so strikingly Spanish-looking as his great friend Cunninghame Graham, Hudson could quite easily have passed as a native of that country. 'Charm' is not the right word to define Hudson's appeal; his letters to Edward show that he could be spiky, irascible and at times bitter – but then so could his correspondent. Both, however, were attentive listeners and had the ability to draw out those they met in conversation; both went their own way and revelled in others who did so too.

Although Edward did advise Hudson about his work – it was at Edward's suggestion that Hudson re-modelled the opening of *A Purple Land* when Duckworth republished it in 1904 for example – he did not mentor Hudson in the same way that he did writers like Conrad and Galsworthy. The different tenor of their relationship may have had something to do with age – Hudson was twenty-seven years Edward's senior – but a genuine affection existed in a relationship which also contained a distinctly combative element. This was partly due to the fact that their very firm views about literature by no means always coincided. Hudson was quick to take Edward to task over reviews he disagreed with: 'I fancy ... that you patted Miss Richardson a little too kindly on her back,' he remarked after reading Edward's enthusiastic appreciation of Dorothy Richardson's *Interim*. 'One gets rather sick and tired of her everlasting Marion [*sic*]. At any rate, *I* don't want to see all of a person's inside.'[7] He was equally unimpressed with Virginia Woolf's first novel, *The Voyage Out*, which Edward had admired. Hudson's verdict: the novel was clumsily constructed, 'there is not one real man', and 'all their talk – and God knows there's a lot of it – and all they think and do has no relation to the environment ... which only differs from an English background in having a sky of Rickett blue'.[8] Edward's commendation of Hudson's human portraits and his pleas that he should write more in this vein further irritated 'Old Huddy', who reckoned his passion and feeling for the natural world eclipsed any interest in mere human affairs. Neither man was above deliberately provoking the other for the fun of it; Hudson tended to admonish Edward for overpraising his work in reviews, but nevertheless he drew confidence from them. When Edward asked to see the manuscript of *Green Mansions*, which had been declined by one publisher on the grounds that it sent him to sleep, Hudson dug it out and, bolstered by Edward's advice and encouragement, set about editing and rewriting the narrative, which appeared in 1904 and is now probably the work for which he is best remembered.

At the time of that first meeting in Heinemann's office, the two men's respective stars appeared to be on very different trajectories: after long years of poverty and neglect Hudson's fortunes had quite literally begun to improve – he had just been awarded a Civil List pension of £150 a year in recognition of his work on Natural History – while Edward was about to fall into the ranks of the unemployed. Perhaps then it was Hudson who settled the lunch bill; if he did it would hardly have made an enormous dent in his pension. The Mont Blanc restaurant at 16 Gerrard Street to which Edward had taken his new acquaintance was known for its 'rustic' French cuisine and its cheapness. Already a popular meeting place among literary folk, the Mont Blanc soon became a regular rendezvous for Edward and Hudson, who lunched there nearly every

Tuesday at 1.30 p.m. Over time they were joined by other writers and the restaurant became renowned for these weekly lunchtime gatherings presided over by Edward, at which all the latest books and publishing gossip were chewed over with considerably more relish than the *navarin de mouton* on offer. R. H. Mottram, who was introduced to the Mont Blanc by Galsworthy in 1904, gives a vivid description of one such occasion:

> I was led through a rather dim ground floor full of the market porters of whom Albert Chevalier was then singing, to the first floor, where, between walls painted with romantic Swiss land-scapes, a long table was set, in true continental style, with piles of plates and carafes of rough red wine, on a coarse table-cloth. Here sat, at the head, Edward Garnett, something clerical in his garb belied by the fact that he was eating with his fork, holding a book which he was presumably scanning for review in the other hand, and controlling the conversation with a full mouth. On his left was Hilaire Belloc, bowler-hatted like myself, talking like a machine-gun between draughts of wine, Thomas Seccombe and Jack [Galsworthy] being opposite.[9]

The guest list altered over the years, but 'a small circle of habitués was formed, among them Thomas Seccombe, R. A. Scott-James, Stephen Reynolds, Edward Thomas, W. H. Davies, Hilaire Belloc, Muirhead Bone, Ford Hueffer, Perceval Gibbon, occasionally John Galsworthy, and rarely Joseph Conrad'.[10]

It was Conrad who introduced Edward to another Mont Blanc regular, Norman Douglas, who was for a time assistant editor of the *English Review*. Edward and Douglas shared a sardonic and sceptical turn of mind, a love of Rabelais and Voltaire and a belief that literature should broaden horizons and be unafraid to shine a light into some of the murkier corners of so-called civilisation. Douglas benefited from Edward's efforts to persuade reviewers of the merits of his work and from his advice on some of his manuscripts; he visited The Cearne, where he met the young David Garnett, who later recalled that his father would not leave him alone with Douglas for one minute. Whether this was true or written with the benefit of hindsight after Douglas was arrested for pederasty in 1916 it is impossible to say, but Edward kept in contact with Douglas after he skipped bail in January 1917 and fled to Capri. By then the Mont Blanc lunches were no more – the First World War effectively put paid to them, but for over a decade they were an important and influential strand in London's literary web, offering new and emerging authors the opportunity to make invaluable contacts and acting as a forum for literary debate.

Although the Mont Blanc menu was never wildly exciting, it at least offered a change from Edward's staple diet in the summer of 1901, which largely consisted of vegetables, Constance's home-baked bread and the mushrooms brought back by Edward from foraging expeditions in the Chart woods. Money was particularly tight in the Garnett household as the shadow of Edward's future unemployment loomed increasingly large. With this in mind, at the end of the summer Edward concentrated his efforts on finishing an essay on criticism he had been working on for some time. He had been encouraged in this venture by Conrad, who hoped to persuade William Blackwood to accept it for publication in his prestigious magazine. As ever, Edward struggled when it came to committing words to paper; Constance worried that the work 'seems such a terrible strain to him',[11] while Conrad found himself assuming the role usually occupied by Edward, assuring the self-doubting author that 'the authoritative attitude is the attitude for you. Every truth requires some pretence to make it live. Let this be your pretence, your pose. Speak magistrally [sic] no matter how you may feel.'[12] Despite a fulsome letter of recommendation from Conrad, Blackwood rejected the article out of hand with the brusque comment that he had 'little sympathy with articles of this kind, which to my mind are somewhat futile as nobody reads them'.[13]

Blackwood may not have been telling the whole truth when he dismissed 'The Contemporary Critic' entirely on the grounds of lack of interest. In the article Edward divides critics into two camps, the 'academic' and the 'contemporary', and censures the former for their unthinking condemnation of all new forms of writing. The man bearing the brunt of Edward's attacks is Andrew Lang, folklorist, anthropologist, historian, children's author, novelist and 'academic' critic par excellence. Lang's monthly column 'At the Sign of the Ship', which had appeared in *Longman's Magazine* since 1886, had become something of a national institution. The handsome, languid Lang, then aged fifty-seven, enjoyed great esteem as a man of letters and had written for *Blackwood's*. Despite Conrad's protestation that 'Mr Lang is by no means attacked ... On the contrary his utterances are used as the text of the argument because his position in the first rank is recognized as indisputable',[14] Blackwood may well have been reluctant to publish an article so openly hostile to such an eminent figure. Richard Garnett certainly thought so and lost no time in issuing an uncharacteristically stern parental rebuke:

> While at Clitheroe I heard that your essay had been declined by Blackwood, for which I was not unprepared, though I had hoped otherwise. Olive thinks that this may be partly owing to some reflections on Mr Andrew Lang contained in it. I know not how this might be, but I hope that in revising the essay for another trial you will be most particular to clear it of anything at which anybody could take personal offence. You have quite difficulties enough without needlessly adding to them, and of all persons in the world Mr Lang is the last with whom it is judicious to quarrel. It is of course impossible to illustrate principles without reference to persons, but by the exercise of a little tact it is generally possible to do so without giving annoyance.[15]

His words fell on deaf ears. Undaunted, Edward persevered, both with the attack on Lang and the attempt to place the essay. Fortunately, it was soon taken up by the *Monthly Review*, a relatively new but well regarded title, and, despite his father's fears, 'The Contemporary Critic' did much to establish Edward's critical reputation.

The essay is a clarion call for a reconsideration of the critic's role and ideals at the opening of the new century. Edward contends that the word 'critic' has come to be synonymous with that of fault-finder and that too often it is the critic himself who is the centre of attention rather than the book he is judging. Worse still, any work which is written in a new style or contains new ideas is doomed to immediate denunciation at the hands of the 'academic' critic, for whom only the long established, authorised forms of literature constitute true art. 'How', Edward wonders, 'have the "authorised" forms been attained ... if not through the uncouth beginnings, the ceaseless experiments of successive generations?'[16] Throughout his polemic are scattered various footnotes containing examples of the 'academic' critics' pronouncements on the evils of contemporary literature, with Lang's essay 'Literature in the Nineteenth Century' prominent amongst them. By contrast:

> The web of the contemporary critic's mind is otherwise woven. So complex and diverse are the worlds of modern tendency, which the critic's web must stretch to and embrace today, that one quality, receptivity, must be inherent in the fibre of the contemporary

critic's mind. The critic who ... is fond of waving various manifesta-
tions of contemporary literature aside, he who refuses to examine
certain aspects, and he who forbids life to manifest itself in this or
that fashion through literature, is in fact seeking to dictate to life
the new forces of its growth and the new horizons. A serious, an
invaluable academic critic he may be, but all the same a partisan
of the classics, priding himself on fencing out from his palisaded
enclosure that upheaving modern world which must evolve new
forms in art, new ideas, formulas, styles and jargons, or else drop
back into scholasticism, imitation, and conventionalism of form.[17]

The connection between literature and life is something that Edward
passionately believed in: 'all literature,' he claims 'is documentary
evidence on mind or life;'[18] it is the critic's job to detect and explain
that evidence to the reader. Like many of his contemporaries, Edward
was acutely aware of the complexity, fecundity and diversity of modern
life, a life that was 'being marvellously mirrored by the literature of our
time' – although he points out that by no means all of that literature
is of lasting value. The critic must be able to discriminate between
the 'comparatively small band of artists whose creative instincts shape
true works of art for us, and for posterity' and the popular writer who
merely reflects the 'common perishing valuations of our bustling and
self-important time' – popularity and posterity being in Edward's eyes
almost inevitably mutually exclusive. When in the final section of the
essay Edward talks about the necessity for a 'receptive spirit, which
hastens to recognize each writer's world, listens to his message whatever
it be, and responds to anything individual he is privileged to reveal to
us about which other men are dumb'[19] he is reciting the credo which
governed his working life. In the final analysis, Edward maintains that
the critic's chief duty is interpretation, that his 'aim will be to *account*
for authors, to explain them to their age, and their age through them'.[20]
Hudson for one was impressed: 'Your article in [*sic*] Contemporary
Criticism was excellent,'[21] he told Edward, 'and of course Andrew Lang
who is a good fighting cock will be having at you with his polished
spurs, probably in "At the Sign of the Ship".' Sure enough, the January
edition of *Longman's Magazine* contained a debonair riposte from Lang,
who confirms that he has little time for two of Edward's literary idols,
Ibsen – 'What I have read of Ibsen ... appears to me highly ludicrous'–
and Tolstoy – 'I do think that the "Kreutzer Sonata" is an unconsciously
comic production'[22] – and voices his objection to those contemporary

writers whose engagement with their times results in works which he
contends read more like social treatises than novels. Edward's enthusiasm
for writers like Conrad, Crane, the Australian Henry Lawson and Robert
Louis Stevenson, whose work brings previously remote corners of the
planet to attention and thus adds 'to the old world's realisation of its new
life',[23] is airily dismissed by Lang: 'the point is not to produce millions
of novels on all things mentionable and unmentionable, novels cast in
Cayagan Sulu or in the antarctic seas, but to produce *good* novels'.[24] Lang
graciously concedes that 'there are many meritorious authors' writing
after 1860 (the watershed between the literary greats and the modern
ruck, according to Lang), but insists that post-1860 'giants there are
not'.[25] He concludes his counter-attack with a glancing blow at Edward's
insistence on the central importance of receptivity to the critic: 'just
as there is natural creative genius, so there is natural receptive taste,
a gift to which some are born, a gift which can scarcely be imparted
by instruction.'[26] And with that the fighting cock struts off, back to his
palisaded enclosure.

Richard Garnett's fears that Edward's determination to ruffle Lang's
feathers would damage his job prospects turned out to be unfounded.
At the beginning of October Constance was able to report to her father-
in-law that Edward had got what promised to be permanent work as a
reader for Duckworth. 'I am very thankful,' she confessed, 'for Edward
has been exerting himself in all sorts of ways to a point where there
seemed to me great danger of his breaking down. And of course it is a
great piece of luck too. There are so few houses in which Edward could
possibly be employed that one could hardly expect him to find a vacancy
at once.'[27] Nothing could temper the relief that Edward had prospects
of settled employment, even though he joined Duckworth on the same
terms he had been on at Heinemann's.

Gerald de l'Etang Duckworth, half-brother to Virginia Woolf and
Vanessa Bell, founded the firm in 1898, when he was twenty-eight years
old. He had learned the business working at Dent's and set up on his
own account at 3 Henrietta Street, a four-storey brick Georgian terraced
house in Covent Garden. These were the days when Covent Garden
was the central market for flowers, fruit and vegetables in London and
Henrietta Street, home to a good number of publishing houses, was a
constant hive of activity. Horse-drawn vans delivered fresh supplies to the
market and porters rushed by with fruit and vegetables in wicker baskets
piled seven or eight high on their heads, often having to dodge groups
of fat, jolly women spilling out from the pavement on to the street as

they shelled peas at lightning speed into rapidly rising mountains. The smell, a delicate blend of horse dung and putrefying greengrocery, was all-pervasive and overpowering.

Small of eye and burly of stature, Duckworth was something of a gourmand; according to Virginia Woolf in later years he came increasingly to resemble 'a pampered overfed pug dog',[28] but then Woolf had little time for her half-brother, whom she accused of having sexually abused her when she was six. Others found Duckworth slightly pompous, conventional and as the years progressed, increasingly idle. On the whole Edward considered his new boss reasonably amiable, if at times pusillanimous when it came to committing to what Edward called 'subtle' pieces of work. 'I generally find it resolves itself into a question of will power,' he explained to Allan Monkhouse in 1912. 'D sometimes wearing me down, and vice versa.'[29] Duckworth entered publishing not through any great regard for books, but because he considered it a suitable occupation for gentlemen. Anthony Powell, who became the firm's literary editor in 1926, observed that as far as reading went Duckworth's interest 'was as slender as that of any man I have ever encountered'.[30] This might actually have been no bad thing as far as Edward was concerned, potentially leaving him greater scope for independence than otherwise.

The final decision on whether to publish remained with Duckworth, however, and despite his employer's apparent lack of enthusiasm for the task it was not uncommon for Edward to pass on borderline manuscripts for Duckworth's perusal and final arbitration. These were sometimes books that Edward disliked, but which he (often grudgingly) acknowledged might sell, such as 'The Eleventh Commandment' by Piers Hervy, described by Edward as so very bad that it might hit 'the 'orrible taste of the British public'.[31] Although he took a dim view of the marketplace, Edward was well versed in the tricks to exploit it and maximise a book's chances; a 'sensitive, delicate' talent like that of Margery Williams (later Bianco), which would all too easily escape attention, called for a concerted lobbying of reviewers; 'paragraphing' – writing short descriptions of forthcoming books for newspapers – and 'puffing' – originating and circulating praise for them – were also indispensable tools in getting a book noticed, as was a snappy, promotional one-liner. 'Duckworth must *boldly advertise and paragraph* [*Life in a Railway Factory*] as "A Book of National Interest",' Edward commanded, determined to leave no stone unturned in his quest to secure the railway forge-worker Alfred Williams ('the Hammerman Poet') the recognition his novel deserved: 'It will undoubtedly receive long notices in the Press ... but Duckworth had better send advance copies to men such as *W. L. Courtney, Robertson Nicoll,* [James] *Strachey,* the editor of *The Daily Chronicle* etc and any other editors Duckworth can get at.'³² A preface by a well-known name could also boost a book's chances. Greatly enthused by the French writer Gabriel Tarde's futuristic novel *Fragment d'histoire future* (1896), Edward advised Duckworth to publish a translation and to invite H. G. Wells to contribute a preface – Wells duly obliged. The title needed changing too in Edward's opinion; when the book was published in 1905 his original suggestion 'Subterranean Man' had become *Underground Man*. The importance of titles is a recurring theme of Edward's reports – either they should give a clear indication of the subject of a volume or else entice the reader with the promise of mystery or titillation. 'The Humour of Tipty' was hardly likely to lure readers into exploring George Bartram's rollicking historical novel of country life: 'If we were Duckworth, we would boldly call the novel "The Country Wenches", and see if Bartram's public cannot come to him through this roundabout channel: he wants running as *a masculine writer for men.*'³³

The great majority of manuscripts that arrived at 3 Henrietta Street were destined to be returned from whence they came, accompanied by a polite (and occasionally not so polite) letter. Rejection is rejection in whatever form it comes, but Edward got the nuance of refusal down to something of a fine art: depending on his mood, his stark instruction – 'Reject' – could be followed by 'with sweetness', 'kindly', 'with thanks', 'emphatically', 'and advise burial', 'sarcastically', 'as rubbish', and when his patience had been tried beyond endurance, 'insultingly'. Considering the number of manuscripts Edward read, the poor quality of much of the work and the tedium of ploughing through what were essentially the same hackneyed 'romance' plots again and again it is surprising there are not more reports as terse and exasperated as that for the unfortunate Shelland Bradley's *Coming of the Kings*: 'Trivial. Flat. Hurl away.'³⁴ Sometimes it was only Edward's sense of mischief that could alleviate the whole dreary business: 'We warmly sympathise with the hero, and we quite feel with the charm of the lovely Indian maiden (we wish indeed we had her here to talk to – at this moment).'³⁵

Generally it was work submitted by literary agencies rather than individuals which bore the brunt of his wrath: 'A. P. Watt's cheek is simply colossal!' Edward fulminated after perusing *Religion and the New Era* by Brenner. 'He chucks in his old rubbish – the very sweepings of his clientele's literary dustbin – with a magnificent air of favour.'³⁶ Publishers had greeted the rise of the literary agent with no little hostility, the more unscrupulous among them afraid that authors would now be put wise to any nefarious dealings. Edward's jaundiced view of agents stemmed rather from his irritation at having to read manuscripts that had already been touted round and rejected by every publisher in London, and by agents' propensity to submit work that clearly did not fit Duckworth's list. However, by the early twentieth century agents had become permanent and increasingly powerful figures in the literary landscape, thanks to expanding markets, changes in technology and the development of international copyright. Edward had no choice but to deal with them, frustrating as he found it at times. A. P. Watt is generally recognised as one of the first literary agents, but the man with whom Edward had most dealings was James Brand Pinker, who established his agency in Arundel Street, London in 1896. Described by Frank Swinnerton as a 'short, compact ... rosy-faced, clean-shaven, grey-haired sphinx with a protrusive under-lip',[37] Pinker's list of clients was every bit as impressive and extensive as Edward's roll-call of protégés, and inevitably many writers featured on both. Conrad, Galsworthy, D. H. Lawrence, Stephen Crane, Ford Madox Ford and Stephen Reynolds were all mentored by Edward and represented by Pinker. Edward was never close personal friends with the agent; their relationship remained purely professional and was by no means always harmonious, but Edward recognised Pinker's commercial usefulness to an author and even approached him himself when he was trying to get an American publisher for his book on Turgenev in 1917. Pinker certainly had his uses, but that didn't prevent Edward from getting infuriated with him at times: '[Pinker] ought to have his head knocked out with a copy of *The Golden Age of Classic Art* which is, we think, D's *heaviest* book' for sending in *The Maiden Aunts* – 'the worst novel D has had for over a twelve month',[38] he complained on one occasion.

One of the first things Edward did after his arrival at Duckworth was to convince his employer to publish *El Ombú*, the book of South American stories W. H. Hudson retrieved from Heinemann, who had refused to make a decision about publishing it. The volume was one of the early titles to appear in the Greenback Library, a new series inaugurated by Edward, designed for the 'Literary Public'[39] and with an emphasis on Continental fiction. This focus, however, did not prevent Edward from keeping a keen eye open for home-grown writers whose work he felt might enhance the Greenback list.

One such author was May Sinclair, whom Edward met in 1902 through his sister Olive. At the time Sinclair was living a rather solitary life in

Hampstead, following the recent death of her mother. She had already published two novels, poetry and some philosophical essays. 'I had a most amusing evening on Tuesday' Edward reported to Nellie:

> Olive had arranged for me to meet Miss Sinclair – the 'literary light' of Hampstead, the acknowledged 'literary queen'! She's a very clever woman in her <u>writing</u> – but a poor critic & Olive told me privately to 'go forth boldly & demolish her!' We quite broke through her defences, & generally worsted her! But when I came to read her <u>work</u> I saw how amusing the situation was. Because she is really very keen witted & very clever, & used to homage! Of course I am now pledged to give her 'advice'! Really my impudence almost equals Bernard Shaw's at times![40]

Edward had taken away with him a couple of Sinclair's stories and a novel she had published four years' earlier – *Mr and Mrs Nevill Tyson*. 'My view of your talent is that the more sternly you repress romanticism and *imagination* & the more you tell us exactly what you have observed in *others & in yourself* the better your work will be',[41] he told her after reading them. Sinclair acknowledged the criticism, describing it as 'excellent and just',[42] although she took issue with Edward's contention that 'in half [Neville Tyson's] being he is a woman's fine guesswork, an *unreal* hybrid'.[43] 'If I've failed to make you share my own simple faith in the reality of Mr Neville Tyson, I think that is due to my clumsiness in the portraiture and not to my idea of the man,'[44] she retorted. Edward never baulked at pointing out what he perceived to be the weaknesses in Sinclair's writing – in a review he described parts of *The Divine Fire* as 'laboured, dead, cold, brain-spun stuff, most carefully worked up, and most patently false'[45] – but they remained in friendly contact for years. In 1922 Sinclair published *The Life and Death of Harriett Frean*, the novel that is generally regarded as her masterpiece. Its elliptical, pared-down language is a long way removed from her much earlier work and it carries no trace of romanticism: Edward loved it.

Sinclair never did follow up Edward's suggestion that she write something for the Greenback Library, but he continued to trumpet its merits to other likely contributors. 'The Greenback L is started to supply the "real thing" and you would appear in very good company – in fact only in the *best* company,'[46] he told Arnold Bennett, whom he later described to Duckworth as 'a shrewd young man from the North of England with a great faculty for "getting on"', adding that Bennett had 'a very fair literary instinct' and that 'the most interesting thing about him is the strange amalgam he presents of *commercial* man pure and simple, and author.'[47] Bennett had sent his latest novel, *Anna of the Five Towns*, to Duckworth; Edward was 'much struck' with it and hoped to persuade Bennett of its suitability for the 'Greenback'. 'Your novel is so strongly conceived, and so well carried out; there is such a faithfulness of atmosphere, and so little straining after effect,'[48] he enthused. Edward did have one major reservation, however: he objected to the ending in which Willie Price, the man Anna Tellwright truly loves, throws himself down a pit-shaft after being forced to commit forgery. Anna, who has given Willie money to start a new life in Australia, is left in ignorance of his fate. Substituting a more prosaic denouement in which Anna knows Willie is alive and Willie himself continues 'to lead the everyday struggling life of us all, working, half forgetting and yet living' would, Edward argued, make the whole situation 'infinitely deeper'.[49] Bennett, however, felt unable – or was unwilling – to revise the end, despite a further letter from Edward on the subject. 'You shake me,' Bennett confessed after receiving the second missive. 'Yet I doubt if I *can* alter that ending. I quite see it is out of the picture, and of course its factual exactness is no excuse for it. But –.'[50] Edward was not alone in finding the conclusion of the novel unsatisfactory: H. G. Wells also expressed doubts about it, drawing a similarly defensive response from Bennett. Edward's only other criticism of the book, that Bennett should consider 'the pruning away of a little detail' and that 'occasionally there are detailed touches of a realism that is not needed, that *burdens* the book a little' anticipates Virginia Woolf's now celebrated attack on the 'materialist' Bennett in her essay 'Modern Fiction' (1919).

As it turned out, *Anna of the Five Towns* was published by Chatto & Windus, but Edward kept an eye on Bennett, believing that his true metier lay in writing about life in the Staffordshire Potteries where he had been brought up. Although he lauded Conrad, Hudson and Cunninghame Graham for bringing distant corners of the Earth to the attention of the reading public, Edward was concerned that there were large sections of life much closer to home that were slipping past unnoticed or deliberately disregarded by novelists and dramatists, who offered only 'perfunctory pictures, and practically no criticism of the national life'.[51] According to Edward there is 'not a single novelist of insight to-day who has analysed or mirrored the life of these great manufacturing centres, of the relations of the "classes" to the industrial population, from Birmingham to Newcastle.' This he attributed to the lack of any literary market in the provinces, which forced the aspiring writer to come to London to ply his or her trade in the 'shoals and shallows of metropolitan journalism', only to find 'their artistic talent is used up to satisfy the fourth-rate tastes of Philistia'.[52] As a result, Edward argued, such a writer loses touch with his or her roots, so often the source of artistic inspiration. 'Only the dreamer or the genius survives that depressing fight with the market-place which offers a starvation wage to a man who does not please the popular demand,' he concluded gloomily. Bennett, who had trodden that well-worn path from the provinces to the capital and served his time on the journalistic treadmill, had escaped it by 1900 and was pursuing a freelance career, turning out novels, short fiction, plays and assorted pieces of journalism with astonishing rapidity. Financially astute and a short while later extremely wealthy – by 1912 he was the proud possessor of a yacht – Bennett did not quite fit Edward's cautionary tale of the Provincial's Progress, but then neither did he quite measure up to the Garnett vision of the genius who one day would bring those industrial and provincial lives out of the shadows. That genius had yet to emerge.

In the meantime Edward had to content himself with promoting the cause of writers who did manage to reveal the lives of the obscure, albeit from further afield. One such was Henry Lawson, who arrived in England with his wife and two children in 1900. Edward had had his eye on Lawson for some time: 'Henry Lawson is *the* best native Australian writer we have come across,' he reported to Unwin in 1898. 'His work is original and brilliant ... The publisher should certainly bespeake [*sic*] any further work that Lawson does, or commission him.'[53] Lawson had published collections of short stories and verse in his native Australia, including what is now probably his best known work, *While the Billy Boils* (1896), which had received favourable reviews when it was published in England. Born in 1867, Lawson spent the first months of his life in a tent on a gold field in New South Wales, where his Norwegian father was working a claim. When he was fourteen Lawson became severely deaf and remained so for the rest of his life; already a solitary, unhappy child, his condition compounded pre-existing feelings of alienation. As an adult Lawson turned his hand to a variety of jobs, including journalism, but regular employment was always elusive. His deafness was certainly a drawback, but the periodic bouts of alcoholism which punctuated his life hardly enhanced his job prospects either. Nevertheless, by the time he came to England Lawson had established a literary reputation in Australia and was desperately keen to further it in London.

Much of Lawson's two-year residence in England was pretty miserable. He and his wife Bertha loathed the winters. Lawson was constantly short of money and in October 1900 it became apparent that Bertha was mentally unstable and suffering from hallucinations. During the time she was in England she was admitted to various mental hospitals, placing further strain on Lawson's already stretched finances. 'I respect and admire Lawson much,'[54] Edward told Nellie. He was aware of the Australian's difficult circumstances, and when Lawson moved to Duckworth Edward encouraged him to produce a volume for the Greenback series. Lawson stayed at The Cearne, where he rather scared the young David, who years later recalled 'a very tall man with large ears but almost totally deaf, who drank a good deal of whisky'.[55] Lawson may well have been at The Cearne to discuss the stories which Edward and E. V. Lucas eventually managed to persuade Methuen to publish under the title of *The Children of the Bush*. The Australian had taken Edward's advice and revised some of the stories, so that the character of Mitchell provided a link between them. When Lawson sent the redrafted manuscript to Edward, he liked what he saw, but the arrival of another packet of satirical sketches on the Australian and English literary scene set alarm bells ringing. Edward was immediately anxious, both about the content and the prospect of broaching the subject with the potentially truculent author: 'It is no good at all,' he reported to Nellie after reading the manuscript. 'I agree with every word he says but it is *journalism* and crude and I must not only try to get something else out of him, but also dissuade him from publishing this MSS at all. It is the story of his grievances. All true – but most inartistic ... I hope I shall be able to show him that I am on his side, and am not trying to "do" him.'[56]

If Lawson had any doubts on that score he had only to pick up the *Academy* of 8 March 1902; in an appreciation of his work, Edward maintains that Lawson's prose 'is that of a writer who represents a continent'.[57] Casual, at times sentimental his writing might be, Edward argues, yet nevertheless Lawson possesses that rare ability to convey a sense of a whole people's background, their struggles and cares, their humour and outlook through his 'racy language' and the observation of minute detail which reveals situation and character. What Edward really admires, though, is what he calls the 'democratic' tone in Lawson's work; his sketches ring absolutely true because he writes from the inside, unlike authors at home who nearly all 'have a middle-class bias or training, and so either write down to or write up to their subject when it leads them outside their own class, and accordingly their valuations thereof are in general falsified'.

Lawson was suitably grateful for the 'Appreciation', but the situation in London was becoming bleaker than ever. Bertha's mental state had deteriorated as her loathing of the capital had intensified; in May she and the children left for Sydney. Lawson, frantically worried about his son and daughter, swiftly followed her. He wrote to Edward several times on the voyage back to Australia, sending him proofs of *Children of the Bush* and carte blanche to alter them as he thought best. Lawson left London fully intending to return, however Edward never saw him again. When he got back to Australia Lawson attempted suicide; his wife obtained a separation and, although he continued to write, the quality of his work fell into irreversible decline as he once more took to the bottle, became subject to spells of insanity and more than once found himself in prison after failing to pay maintenance for his children. Edward never forgot Lawson or his work: the Australian was amongst the select band of writers whose stories were chosen by Edward for inclusion in *Capajon* (1933), a volume which in his opinion showcased the talents of some of the masters of the genre.

Lawson was not the only Australian writer on Edward's mind at this time, although Barbara Baynton's devastating portraits of outback life were very different from his, and to some extent written in retaliation against them. In 1902 Edward persuaded Duckworth to publish Baynton's *Bush Stories* in the Greenback Library. 'These stories of Australian Bush Life show quite exceptional power,' Edward reported to his employer. 'We are quite surprised by their remarkable force and real artistic skill ... "Squeaker's Mate" shows a sympathetic insight into the actual conditions of a woman's life in the Bush that is quite out of the common.'[58]

Barbara Baynton came over to England in 1902 with her second husband, a retired surgeon forty years her senior. The affluent circumstances of this second marriage were in stark contrast with her earlier life, during which Baynton had endured seven hard years living in the Australian bush with her first husband Alexander Frater, who ran off with a servant. Attractive, witty and vivacious, Baynton had tremendous force of personality and could more than hold her own in the face of Edward's teasing; she also appealed to him as an extremely talented writer: 'All day yesterday I was reading and annotating Mrs Baynton's Australian story,' he told Nellie, 'extraordinary piece of genius, "most revolting" people will say. Her MS is full of an instinctive understanding of life's *selfish* basis. She is a sort of Bush Maupassant – only wilder and fiercer.'[59] This 'most revolting' novel was *Human Toll*, published by Duckworth in 1907. It is a powerfully uncompromising account of bush life, which details the horrors suffered by women at the hands of brutal, selfish and stony-hearted men. Edward was right in thinking that *Human Toll* would prove to be too strong for English digestions; his review in the *Bookman* – in which he described the novel as 'a work of genius indisputably, disconcertingly sinister, extraordinarily actual'[60] – was the only substantial attention the book received and Baynton's work disappeared from view for the next fifty years, finally finding an appreciative audience among feminists in the 1980s.

While Edward searched in vain amongst the ranks of British writers for the genius who would bring the lives of the ordinary working man and woman to the reading public, he believed that such a talent had all too briefly existed in the field of art. This was Winnifred Matthews, a contemporary of Nellie Heath's at the Slade, who, like Nellie, had studied under Frederick Brown. Matthews had died in 1895 at the age of twenty, leaving sketchbooks full of drawings depicting London street life. Seven years later Edward's illustrated essay *The Art of Winnifred Matthews* was published in a limited edition by Duckworth. Edward had more than a passing interest in art – he wrote a monograph on Hogarth for Duckworth's Popular Library of Art in 1910 – but it was almost certainly Nellie who prompted him to write the book on Matthews, which contains a rare description of the sensations Edward experienced when he came across an unknown writer (or in this case artist) of singular promise. It was for moments like these that Edward toiled away as a publisher's reader for half a century, his enthusiasm undimmed into his seventieth year. Any of 'those weary ones, the busy tribe of examiners, indefatigable art critics, readers to publishers, literary editors,' he explains, would recognise

the keen shock of pleasure, the delighted flash of recognition, when, amid the mass of trivial, indifferent, or heavily conscientious efforts he lights once and awhile on a beginner's work showing that instinctive creative originality which we call *genius*. What hereafter may be fated in the development of this genius, to what point it may arrive or may never arrive, all this is hidden from him – it is enough for the discoverer in that happy moment to see there in the piece of work an individual talent bringing its special revelations, a talent which he knows cannot be reduplicated, however endless the chain of talents the world has in store.[61]

That tantalising but unknown future fired Edward's excitement; he relished nothing more than a fight against the odds – and in his opinion the odds against a truly talented writer gaining any sort of recognition were very long indeed. If the miracle happened, he almost invariably lost interest. Winnifred Matthews did not live long enough to get even the faintest whiff of success; her early death had in Edward's opinion robbed the world of a unique artist capable of illuminating 'that London life of the obscure multitudes'.

In 1902, the year that *Winnifred Matthews* was published, death also came to another whose life the wider world would consider to be amongst the obscure. Christina Chapple, Narney's maid and nanny to the Garnett children, died at Tanza Road on 14 April. Edward had always been very close to Chapple. '*Do* try and make Chapple happy, my dear mother,' he urged Narney two years previously. 'I do not feel at all easy about her in my mind. She is so very old, and she should be treated more as an invalid, & her last years made light.'[62] Although his plea might suggest that the Garnetts were inconsiderate and demanding employers, nothing was further from the truth. Olive nursed Chapple in her last illness, during which Edward, Robert and Lucy visited. Her death was a wrench to Edward; Chapple had been one of the pillars of his childhood, her passing a reminder of the increasing vulnerability of the world of his youth.

The following year that world was shattered. In June Narney, who that April had celebrated her sixty-second birthday, went to stay with Lucy and Harry at Four Elms. She became ill and was confined to bed with what was thought to be a severe attack of 'gastric catarrh'. Edward went over to see her and reported to Nellie that his mother was in 'the lowest of spirits and inclined to think herself in a dangerous state'.[63] Accustomed to Constance's frequent bouts of sickness, Edward was not unduly concerned by his mother's condition, believing that the attack would pass in a few days, although he did cycle into Westerham to get her some champagne. He visited again early on the Monday morning and then went off to London. On Tuesday Dr Maude, who was attending Narney and was also Constance's doctor, sent a telegram to Richard: 'Consider Mrs Garnett's state very grave, come this evening to Four Elms'.[64] According to family legend, Narney underwent an emergency operation performed on the kitchen table that evening. Early on Wednesday morning Olive received a telegram from her father: 'Matters most serious. Come with Edward if you think well.'[65] They arrived at Four Elms about 1 p.m., but it was too late; Narney had died four hours earlier. The death certificate gives the cause as a strangulated hernia.

Edward felt terrible guilt about his mother's death: 'I knew that *I* might have saved her,' he confessed to Nellie. He blamed himself for trusting Dr Maude, although it is not clear if he felt the doctor had been negligent in not realising the seriousness of the situation sooner or if he felt the operation had been botched. 'It was the ignorance of optimism,' he told Nellie, '*plus* something worse in my case. Do not attempt to persuade me otherwise. I *know* it – because I ... see now exactly where and why I was misled – partly through having so often seen Connie in her sick attacks, – and partly through my banishing a faint foreboding from my mind & going off to London lightheartedly.'[66]

Nellie was not the only woman to whom Edward unburdened his guilty conscience. 'Your reference to your mother's sad illness and death has touched me very much,' wrote Sarah Orne Jewett from her home in South Berwick, Maine. 'I know too well how such regrets doubles [*sic*] one's pain and that there is no such loss – one is a child as long as she lives and then we seem to front the world alone for the first time.'[67] Some years before Edward had advised Unwin to publish *The Country of the Pointed Firs*, admiring Jewett's 'exquisite, simple ... literary touch', although he doubted the English public capable of appreciating the 'deftness', 'restraint' and 'dignity' of her style.[68] In this instance his pessimism proved well founded, but having convinced Duckworth to issue an edition of *The King of Folly Island*, Edward wrote an article on Jewett which was eventually published by the *Academy* in its 'Books Too Little Known' column. Edward arranged for Duckworth to send a copy to Jewett, who could bask in the thought that her ability to indicate character in a few short, simple strokes was, in Edward's opinion 'the gift of the masters'.[69] Like Lawson, Conrad and all those writers whom Edward considered artists rather than mere writers, Jewett at her best manages to present a fleeting passage of a life or lives and suggest something greater and universal. When Jewett moves beyond her sketches of New England, however, as in her historical novel *A Tory Lover*, 'she has clearly stepped outside her own art, and her art has refused definitely to accompany her on this hasty excursion.' The failure of *A Tory Lover* convinced Edward that gifted as Jewett was, hers was a 'receptive but not constructive' talent. Jewett appeared to take this verdict with good grace and a year later assured Edward that she read 'everything you write of books and men with eager interest'.[70] Her comment was prompted by Edward's review of the American writer whose name glittered high in the sky of the British literary firmament, that of 'the Master' himself: Henry James.

'You have too good an eye'

One day, probably in 1901, Ford Madox Ford conducted Edward, Constance and David to Rye, East Sussex, to meet Henry James. David, who would have been nine at the time, later recalled how 'Ford, tall and fresh-coloured, smiling and showing his rabbit teeth, enjoyed himself, patronising my parents on one side and James on the other.'[1] By this time James had established himself as one of the most eminent figures in the literary world, venerated by his fellow authors; Conrad, for instance, sent him a presentation copy of *An Outcast of the Islands* with an inscription so effusive that even the Master's toes might have curled very slightly inside his embroidered *pantoufles*. Edward had little to do with James on a personal level, but he reviewed some of James's work and was by no means always ready to add his voice to the chorus of approval sung so loudly by others in his literary circle.

Other members of the Garnett family were wholehearted admirers of James. After reading *The Awkward Age* (1899), which Edward was reviewing, Constance told him it was 'a magnificent study of the vice of that mixture of gossip and psychological analysis, which spoils every natural impulse – and which by the way is *our* prevalent vice'.[2] Whether or not Edward recognised the vice, he was far from entirely convinced by the novel, which he reviewed in *Outlook*. Whilst James's drawing of the Brookenham household is 'beyond praise', with Mrs Brookenham the great success of the book, a suspicion was growing in Edward's mind that the characters' exclusive preoccupation with their own inter-relations is a device through which James advances 'a point in his *art*, that he is more of an *artist* and cares to be less pure realist'.[3] That preoccupation is reflected in the form of *The Awkward Age*, which is composed almost entirely of dialogue. Edward criticises James's portrayal of Nanda, the heroine, and dismisses Mitchy's marriage as a 'hastily erected piece of artistic mechanism'; but the 'diabolically clever' final pages of the book almost persuade him to sweep any reservations about it aside. However, his concluding line – 'And yet, and yet – is *The Awkward Age* simple enough in *form* to be great?' – confirmed his lingering doubts.

Ford sent James a copy of the unsigned review and told James Edward had written it. The Master found the article 'charming', adding '[it] gave me great pleasure and in fact greatly touches me'. Nevertheless, he maintained, 'There *is* a figure in the carpet of *The A.A.* which I think Mr G. hasn't quite made out.'[4] Edward's comments set James thinking, though; when a few months later he wrote to one of his close friends Henrietta Ruebell about the novel he specifically sought to explain and defend both its form and Mitchy's marriage. Nine years later, in the preface he wrote for the New York edition of his Collected Works, James was again at pains to insist that he had triumphantly created a 'really wrought work of art'[5] of form and substance.

Edward's review of *The Awkward Age* raised the politest of doubts about the direction that James's writing was taking; when he came to consider his next novel, *The Wings of the Dove* (1902), again under the cloak of anonymity, the gloves were well and truly off:

> The frequent failure of the man of letters to light the fire of inspiration from communion with actual life is strikingly seen in Mr Henry James' last novel, *The Wings of the Dove* ... Unfortunately the creator of 'Europe' and other masterpieces has for a time turned his back on his art, and is walking with his face averted from life. There are some isolated scenes and descriptions ... which show the subtlest workmanship; but as art, the whole novel is much like a heap of sand ... [W]hen an author abandons all probability, when his characters are no longer true types, but composite puppets, when their conversation is little but an interminably clairvoyant vivisection of their own motives, the remorseless analysis of artificial sentiment does not compensate for the absence of truth to nature.[6]

This assault was mounted in a column in the *Academy* in which Edward appraised 'Some Significant Books of the Year'. James's novel was significant for all the wrong reasons; those whose inclusion was entirely meritorious were Conrad (*Youth and Other Stories*, the other stories being *Heart of Darkness* and *The End of the Tether*) and Hudson's *El Ombú*. These in Edward's opinion are the beacons of light that show the way ahead to future writers, rather than the 'tenuous, tortured subtlety'[7] of James's late novels.

Edward may even have indulged in just a hint of gentle mockery in the reviews of *The Wings of the Dove* and then later of *The Ambassadors*. His reference to James walking with 'his face averted from life' suggests there may be a touch of the prissy old maid about the Master, a suspicion which his review of *The Ambassadors* – in which Edward likens James to an old apple woman dispensing fruit of variable quality to schoolboys – does little to dispel. Indeed, some of the language in the review – 'the actual flaring atmosphere of life',[8] 'the strange little gusts and eddies of forerunning changes' – sounds uncannily like a sly pastiche of James himself. Although considerably less vitriolic than his piece on *The Wings of the Dove*, there is still the concern that James's art is taking a deadly turn: Edward accuses James of 'insensibly practis[ing] his method more and more for its own sake, like a great specialist who is tempted to perform his favourite operation on all varying cases. Life so tied down indeed may be lost under the clever shredding knife, but the famous method flourishes.'

The models against whom Edward is silently and unfavourably comparing James are the Russians: in stark contrast with the Master's propensity to look the other way when confronted with the seamier side of existence, Russian writers 'from Gogol to Tchekov ... have aimed at writing life down as it appeared to be passing before their own eyes'.[9] According to Edward, the Russians 'are *instinctive* realists and carry the warmth of life into their pages'[10] – a far remove from the frigid, cerebral constructions of the author of *The Wings of the Dove*. James's stature was such that the appearance of a new work created considerable ripples amongst the literary intelligentsia; however, Edward was determined that aspiring writers should look to Russia rather than Rye in search of inspiration.

Russia loomed large in the mind of another Garnett in 1904. Constance had just finished translating Tolstoy's *War and Peace* – as far as the eye trouble which spasmodically plagued her would allow – and in May she and the twelve-year-old David set off from Hull to St Petersburg. There they planned to visit Madame Lavrov, an old friend from the Stepniak days. The idea was then to proceed to an estate in Tula province to stay with Sasha Yershov, whom Constance had met on her first trip to Russia, after which they would take up the invitation of a family called Ertel, friends of Peter Kropotkin, whose wife Sophie had made the arrangements.

A couple of days after Constance's and David's departure, Nellie set off for Paris to stay with Auguste Bréal, an artist she had met on a previous trip there, and his wife Louise. Nellie wrote enthusiastically about the city and her visit to an exhibition of Monet's London pictures, and Edward joined her there for the last week in May. By this time news had reached him that Constance's plans had been thrown into disarray. Sasha's daughter was ill with 'typhus' and Constance therefore decided to go to Moscow and then to the Ertels. 'Don't be anxious about us, my dear little Edward,' soothed Constance. 'If you knew how I feel the responsibility here every moment of the boy, you would not be afraid of my doing anything silly.'[11]

As before, Edward was a poor correspondent – 'What a wretch you are not to write ... You certainly don't deserve a letter'[12] – complained Constance, who nevertheless wrote assiduously herself, describing their activities at the Ertels', life on the estate and their hosts. Alexander Ivanovich Ertel and his common-law wife Marya Vasilievna had two daughters, seventeen-year-old Natalie (Natasha or Tata) and Elena (Lola) – 'a very jolly, plump good-tempered and amusing girl'[13] – who celebrated her fifteenth birthday during the Garnetts' visit. Natalie was home on holiday from studying in St Petersburg. 'She is such a very clever girl, so clever that she has always been treated as though intellectually grown up since she was about ten years old,'[14] reported Constance. David later described Natalie as having 'a keen, indeed brilliant, intellect, rather sphinx-like features and a considerable sense of humour – a very remarkable young woman'. Lola he considered to be 'of softer material than Natasha'.[15]

After a month Constance deemed it safe to go to Sasha Yershov's. The visit was not a success; Sasha's husband made his feelings about their stay quite evident from the outset by refusing to send a carriage to meet them. The food was covered with flies, the beds infested with bugs and to top it all Constance unwittingly drank kvass made from unboiled water and as a result suffered a severe bout of gastric enteritis. This did not strike until they had returned to the Ertel estate. Constance was seriously ill for a fortnight; Edward, stuck more than 1,500 miles away, could do nothing but fret and wait for Constance's letters with news of her progress. Her illness considerably delayed their return: 'Give my warmest love to dearest Nellie,' a by-now homesick Constance wrote to Edward. 'How I long to see her and you again and the dear Cearne and everybody. You can't think how fond one is of you all at this distance!'[16] Eventually they arrived back on 13 August after an overland journey via Warsaw.

Constance and David were away for more than three months, during which time Edward took the opportunity of making a couple of excursions himself. A hiker foolhardy enough to be ascending a fog-shrouded Carmarthen Fan one day in June might have stumbled across the curious sight of a tall, well-dressed man in his late thirties standing by the shore of one of the mountain lakes, 'fuming, watch in hand', as his companion sported blissfully (or was he obstinately oblivious?) in the water.[17] When eventually the fog dispersed, the swimmer regained land and the clock-watcher's temper improved, the two men began their descent, deep in a conversation in which the words Forsyte, Bosinney, Soames and Irene featured prominently. Carmarthen Fan was the unlikely backdrop against which an initially irritated John Galsworthy and a damp Edward (who as usual had been unable to resist the opportunity to plunge into the nearest stretch of water) discussed the manuscript of *The Man of Property*, Galsworthy's fourth novel and the first volume of *The Forsyte Saga*. The trek up the mountain, instigated by Edward against Galsworthy's better judgement, formed part of a fortnight's walking tour of South and Mid Wales, during which the two hikers visited Brecon, Llandeilo, Llandovery and Tregaron, finishing up at Rhayader.

The expedition points to an easing of the early tension in the relationship between Edward and Galsworthy. This had been brought about in part by their collaboration on Galsworthy's previous novel *The Island Pharisees* (1904), the first book Galsworthy published under his own name and also the first in which he openly attacked social inequality and the insularity and complacency of much of English society. Edward was enthused by the aim, but unconvinced by the method and told Galsworthy to rewrite the book. The narrator – a vagabond called Ferrand – was a failure, he maintained, because Galsworthy was attempting to draw a character whose world he knew little about. In response Galsworthy created the character of Shelton, like his creator, a man from the upper-middle class who is uncomfortable within his own caste. This gained Edward's qualified approval. However, he felt the novel still lacked subtlety and that Galsworthy was driving home the moral far too obviously: 'You will forgive these suggestions,' Edward reasoned at the end of a long letter, 'if you seize the main idea: viz. *naturalness*: one main idea to each chapter worked out through the chapter – throwing over all digressions which have to be pasted in and cemented artificially.'[18] He closed with words of encouragement, reassuring Galsworthy that he was suggesting 'nothing difficult or [that is] beyond your power'. Gamely, Galsworthy set to for a third time, producing a book Edward deemed 'very good, very cleverly done, and indeed brilliantly written'[19] – although he still listed a few areas of possible improvement, including the end, where he felt that 'the analysis of Antonia in Shelton's mind ought to be stronger. He ought to sympathize *with* her – see her position and yet let this position be more subtly damning.'

Edward tried to persuade his employer that 'On its literary merits alone, Duckworth ought to publish [*The Island Pharisees*], because it is original, and really does present and analyze aspects of modern life, and modern types of men with considerable skill and force.'[20] Duckworth, however, was wary, having lost money on *Jocelyn* and *A Man of Devon*. According to Edward, he took *The Island Pharisees* to his former colleague Sydney Pawling at Heinemann, who accepted it on condition that Galsworthy offered his next book to the firm. The novel was dedicated to Constance 'in gratitude for her translation of Turgenev's works'. Galsworthy saw *The Island Pharisees* as marking something of a rite of passage in his relationship with Edward, 'for in it I feel as if we had buried the hatchet of our many differences, and discovered something fundamentally in common'.[21]

The hatchet may have been buried, but tensions remained. Galsworthy had been working on *The Man of Property* for more than a year by the time he and Ada left for the Continent in January 1905. Galsworthy's father had died the month before, enabling Ada's divorce proceedings to get under way, and the couple departed for the Italian Riviera in order to escape any unpleasantness in England. Galsworthy did his best to persuade Edward to come out to Amalfi to visit and look over the manuscript – 'I *of course* providing the where withal';[22] an invitation Edward refused. He did not want to leave when Nellie had just returned from staying in Westbury, and as he explained to her, 'I don't want to be paid for, and I'm sure Mrs Galsworthy [*sic*] will be relieved at my declining.'[23] He may have been right in this last supposition: later that year Ada told Frances Mottram that although she liked Edward and Constance, she found The Cearne 'rather primeval, its owner too'.[24] In February Galsworthy informed Edward that he only had two and a half chapters of *The Man of Property* left to write, but he did not send it until the middle of May. Having done so, he then sat in a hotel in the Tyrol and fretted over the likelihood of it getting lost in the post and Edward's reaction to it if and when it did arrive.

A wire announcing the manuscript's safe delivery put Galsworthy's mind at rest; a letter from The Cearne two days later did the exact opposite. Although Edward hastened to assure Galsworthy that the manuscript contained 'splendid stuff, all on a high level' with two or three passages '*near to genius*',[25] he considered the end of the novel – in which Galsworthy had Bosinney commit suicide – to be *an artistic blot of a very grave order, psychologically false, and seriously shaking the illusion of the whole story* ... When I read it, I said "incredible", not in character'.[26] Edward then went on to enumerate his objections in detail: that in making Bosinney commit suicide, Galsworthy is perpetuating the popular stereotype of the artist figure as emotionally weak; that the suicide destroys the reader's sympathy for Bosinney; that having made love to Irene, Bosinney's feelings for her and his own fighting spirit would be strengthened, not diminished and that the prospect of financial ruin would not cause a man like Bosinney to take his own life. 'I don't think you have made a shadow of a case,' Edward continues. 'We open our mouths and stare.' He proposed two possible solutions: that Bosinney meet with an accident in a fog or that the lovers elope 'with £50 and *her* Jewels! ... leaving Soames and the jewel case, and all the Forsyte gang with their blasted hereditaments powerless behind them' – a case of Edward's own desire to see the eventual defeat of Forsyteism in England – which to Edward meant the middle classes' worship of property and propriety – overcoming his critical acumen.

Even after pages of remonstration, Edward cannot resist adding a postscript in which he accuses Galsworthy of having 'imported the attitude to life of the-man-who-has-always-had-a-bank-balance into the soul of a man-who-despises-a-bank-balance' and mixing the two up. Edward's passionate belief in his own literary instincts never waned – in his introduction to *Letters from Conrad* he confesses that what he said to Conrad 'with the fervency of youth would seem to me a little bizarre now, had I not caught myself the other day, thirty years later, addressing a young author with much the same accents and convictions'[27] – but even so, the vehemence of his letter is striking. Did Galsworthy's manuscript raise the ghost of Eustace Hartley and the trauma of his suicide in Edward's mind? David Garnett later maintained that Galsworthy modelled Bosinney on Edward; if true, Edward was unaware of it, but the possibility would give their altercation an added twist of irony. At the heart of Edward's letter is the old accusation that Galsworthy – independently wealthy and from a privileged background – is incapable of truly understanding and convincingly portraying a character whose outlook and experience is outside his own. Edward's insistence that Bosinney is an artist figure (actually he is an architect by profession) raises the suspicion that his underlying attitude might still have been 'it takes one to know one' as far as Galsworthy and artists were concerned.

Galsworthy's response – three letters in the space of two days – was swift and spirited. He agreed that financial stress would not induce Bosinney to commit suicide, but pointed out that his real motivation, which Galsworthy conceded he had not made sufficiently clear, was Bosinney's discovery that Soames had raped Irene. What really disturbed Galsworthy, however, was Edward's criticism of the end of the book and his suggestion that Irene and Bosinney should elope, leaving the Forsytes defeated. Galsworthy rightly reasoned that his denouement – in which the Forsytes achieve a 'victory' that is entirely hollow – was by far the most effective and that Edward's proposed ending threatened to destroy the book. By the time he wrote his third letter, Galsworthy was coming round to the idea of Bosinney meeting with an accident in the fog, with the question of suicide left vague. Edward approved the notion of a fatal collision with a cab, but regarded suicide 'through the shock of the rape, to be as incredible as suicide through financial worry'.[28] While partially acknowledging the justice of Galsworthy's comments on the novel's conclusion – 'It is an excellent end – though there might have been others' – Edward remained adamant that the ending was good, 'so long as B. *doesn't commit suicide*'. Eventually Galsworthy was unable to resist Edward's impassioned argument, which was endorsed by Constance who had also read the manuscript. 'I know you will rejoice to hear that I have thrown up the sponge,' Galsworthy reported to her. 'I am in a way delighted to give in, though still perhaps not quite convinced.'[29] To Edward he confessed that he had 'been re-reading your letters of criticism in the bulk and cold blood, and I am humbled and astonished at their clear justice. You have too good an eye.'[30]

Debate about the novel rumbled on into late July as Galsworthy rewrote bits of Part Three and sent them to Edward, who was still exhorting Galsworthy to redraft the final scenes and work up a more psychological climax, even after he had taken the retyped manuscript to Pawling, who accepted it on behalf of Heinemann. The exact extent to which Galsworthy heeded his mentor's advice is impossible to determine as he burnt the various manuscripts of the novel in a clear-out prior to moving house in 1913, but the precise circumstances of Bosinney's demise are never disclosed in the final version of the novel, with the possibility of suicide suggested and not entirely ruled out.

A moment in the dispute between Edward and Galsworthy was captured by Nellie, whose watercolour sketch 'A Letter to Jack' depicts Edward in the process of writing one of his heated epistles about the death of Bosinney. In a strange way the tenacity and occasional ferocity of their arguments seemed to draw the two men closer together; by the end of the correspondence the mode of address has changed from 'Dear Galsworthy' and 'Dear Garnett' to 'Dear Jack' and 'Dear Edward'. 'I think it is one of the very hardest thing to honestly criticize the work of those of whom we are fond,' Galsworthy told Constance as the letters flew back and forth across Europe, 'but it is what one expects and longs for from true friendship – and every time the courage is found makes the link stronger.'[31] *The Man of Property* was published on 23 March 1906 and was dedicated to Edward.

Further proof of Galsworthy's regard came in his willingness to lend Edward money – an offer that was made more than once, but never taken up. The Garnett finances were stretched in 1905; David was due to start at University College School in September and in June Edward and Constance rented a flat at 19 Grove Place, Hampstead, just off Christchurch Road. This became Constance's and David's residence during term time, as well as being a base for Edward when he was in London. 'The flat isn't half a bad little place,' he told Nellie, 'but there is the cursed London dead and aliveness about it.'[32]

David's school fees, the rent on Grove Place and the running expenses of The Cearne all had to be paid for and Edward was finding the reviewing which supplemented his income hard to come by. 'I have done exactly 3 reviews for [C. F. G.] Masterman and *The Daily News* after a lot of complimentary blather,' he complained to Galsworthy. '3 books since March! Every journal seems to be like [a] private business managed by a staff who keep *all* outsiders out except outsiders with big names.'[33] Despite the proliferation in the number of newspapers and journals that carried generous space for reviews, it could be difficult to break into the various cliques that existed between publishers and the owners and editors of newspapers and magazines. Changes in the ownership of these publications was not uncommon; Edward sniffed trouble in the air at the *Speaker* as early as 1905, and two years later the long expected change came about when the historian J. L. Hammond was replaced by Henry (H. W.) Massingham as editor and the paper was relaunched as the *Nation*. The *Speaker* – anti-imperialist and on the radical wing of the Liberal Party – had been a congenial pulpit for Edward, providing regular reviewing and the money that went with it. Edward was irked, not just at the prospect of losing income and having to try and find similar employment, but also because he realised that another paper was unlikely to give him the opportunity to 'slat[e] humbugs and advanc[e] friends'.[34] Luckily Cunninghame Graham rode to the rescue and put in a good word with Massingham, who contacted Edward and asked him to review fiction for the *Nation* on the same terms as the *Speaker*. Edward's relationship with the enigmatic Massingham was not always smooth; there are references in his letters to Nellie to 'uneasy talks' with the *Nation*'s editor, whom Edward describes as being 'so nervously strung that there is a sort of self conscious electricity playing about in every word we say'.[35] Massingham certainly was wary of some of Edward's more forthright criticism; he grew thoroughly alarmed when he read the copy of an article in which Edward openly expressed some 'advanced' views on sexual matters. 'Please be more careful in future,' Massingham admonished, ' ... good as your work is, just a little more care in tone might sometimes be useful. We write for serious people – mere flippancy discredits us.'[36] From the letter it appears the offending review was either revised by Massingham or omitted from the paper altogether. On another occasion Massingham castigated Edward for being 'rather militant as an anti-Puritan ... I certainly think that we ought not to dismiss them altogether as "rotters" and enemies of society.'[37] Edward's propensity to produce uncompromising reviews may have played a part in Massingham's decision to reduce his contributions to the paper in 1912.

Despite his complaints about the closed shop of reviewing, Edward was writing articles and reviews for a number of publications in the first decade of the twentieth century. He found outlets for 'slating humbugs and advancing friends' in the *Saturday Review, Tribune*, the *Daily News* and the *Fortnightly Review*, as well as the *Speaker* and later the *Nation*. Sometimes it was the review that sparked the friendship, rather than the other way round. This was the case with Charles Montagu Doughty, the explorer, travel writer and poet, whose monumental *Travels in Arabia Deserta*, published in two volumes in 1888, was the subject of one of Edward's 'Books Too Little Known' columns in the *Academy* in 1903. Describing how he had plunged into the middle of it ('a capital plan when you wish to taste an author's quality, and catch him off his defences'[38]), Edward proclaims the work to be a masterpiece and lauds the 'rich and racy' quality of Doughty's language. His enthusiasm for Doughty's highly individual prose, generously peppered with Old English, Arabic and Latin, was shared by other literary figures, including W. B. Yeats, Leonard Woolf and Henry Green. Others were less impressed: Cunninghame Graham conceded there was much that was splendid about it, but deplored the fact that Doughty wrote 'in that vile jargon'.[39] In the meantime Doughty had turned to writing poetry of equally marked linguistic idiosyncrasy and appeared one day at Duckworth's offices, clutching his epic poem

The Dawn in Britain in one hand and Edward's *Academy* article in the other. The meeting with Doughty stiffened Edward's resolve to take some practical steps to ensure *Arabia Deserta* became better known and appreciated. He persuaded Duckworth to issue a volume of extracts and offered to make the selection himself. Doughty announced that he was 'quite content to leave the series of Selections [*sic*] and their connecting links entirely to [Edward's] judgment',[40] and in 1908 *Wanderings in Arabia Deserta*, abridged by Edward, appeared to great acclaim, not only bringing Doughty's name to the public eye, but also igniting demand for *Arabia Deserta* itself.

Edward's admiration for Doughty's work extended to his poetry and to *The Dawn in Britain* in particular. Both Edward and Doughty were aware that the distinctive language of *The Dawn in Britain* would not be to everybody's taste: Doughty contended that hostile reviewers failed to see 'that epic language in any tongue cannot possibly be the decadent speech of the streets',[41] while in his review of the poem, Edward argued that Doughty's poetic diction conjured up the elemental and heroic subject matter of the poem in such a way that it became a style of 'epic greatness'.[42] Few at the time or later would agree. Doughty appreciated the review, both for what Edward said and that he wrote it during a time in his life 'when all such work must have been utter weariness'.[43]

Richard Garnett's health had been deteriorating for some time. He had become lame, his problems with his eyesight had worsened and he was growing gradually weaker. On 26 March 1906 Olive recorded that the blood vessels in her father's left eye had ruptured and he was unable to read. He had developed nephritis: 'My father is dying slowly,' Edward told Nellie just over a fortnight later. 'It may be hours or even days ... Last night I sat by his bed a good part of the night, holding his hand – but today he is nervous of people near him and orders them to go away.'[44] Richard died at 5.15 a.m. on Good Friday, 13 April, in the presence of Edward and the nurse. He was seventy-one. He was buried at Highgate East Cemetery in the grave of Narney's mother and his infant son, Richard Copley. A large number of mourners attended, including Hudson, Ford and a young woman eight days short of her thirty-fourth birthday: Violet Eveleen Neale.

Violet lived with her mother, grandmother and aunt at 89 Fellows Road, Hampstead, not far away from Tanza Road. A devotee of the poet P. B. Shelley, she had written to Richard in April 1903 with a query about his edition of Shelley's friend Edward Ellerker Williams's journal. At this time Violet and her mother were living in Ilfracombe and in June she sent Richard a sprig of myrtle allegedly picked from the cottage garden in Lynmouth, where Shelley and his first wife Harriet spent their honeymoon. It arrived on the day of Narney's funeral and was placed on his wife's coffin by Richard. Their friendship developed rapidly and they exchanged many letters on Shelley, religion, literature and art. When they met in July, Richard was not displeased to find that his correspondent was an attractive, brown-eyed brunette, sympathetic to his temperament and even sharing his interest in astrology. A year later they realised they were in love. According to Richard's biographer, he was 'desperately smitten'[45] and expressed his emotions in an anonymous volume of aphorisms on love, *De Flagello Myrteo* (1906), so called on account of the myrtle sprig Violet had sent him. Richard gave Violet the copyright to the book, which had quickly run into a second edition.

Both parties were anxious that their respective families should know little about the relationship: Violet because she was anxious to avoid parental disapproval, Richard because he was pretty sure his children would disapprove of their parent – Violet was after all only a year older than Lucy. From Olive's diary entry of 24 April – 'Edward and Robert dined here. We discussed VN and affairs'[46] – it is clear that the family were aware of Violet and bracing themselves for possible future difficulties. Richard died intestate leaving £2,734, which the children decided to divide equally between them. Edward and Robert gave Olive, who would now have to vacate Tanza Road, their shares for life.

It was not long before Violet contacted Olive about the copyright of *De Flagello Myrteo* and her letters to Richard were discovered in the house. The combination of events threw the Garnetts into a panic. They were appalled at the thought that Violet might make her relationship with Richard public and expose his memory to sly mockery. Just over a month after the funeral Edward interviewed Violet at Fellows Road, which, according to Olive, resulted in a 'very stormy scene', during which Edward told Violet the family had consulted Thomas E. Scrutton, KC, an expert in copyright law, who had assured them that the copyright was their property. 'Miss N appears to be a holy terror,'[47] Olive observed tartly. Constance probably had a point when she told Edward that Olive's 'cold and critical manner would make anyone hostile and suspicious'.[48] Edward, however, shared his sister's opinion of Miss Neale and made detailed notes about her letters to Richard, asserting that 'Miss VN shows herself throughout as possessed of an extraordinary tenacity of purpose, terrifying self-absorption, highly neurotic and hysterical ... and RG fails to grasp her character until it is too late.'[49] Edward was convinced Violet had been angling for marriage and that 'All RG's weaknesses – vanity, astrological superstitions, and absolute desire to shut his eyes to the character of a woman, so long as she "inspires him" – conjoin in a fatal manner with VN's weaknesses – vanity, womanly subterfuge and lack of clear intelligence.'

The whole episode, which could have come from the pages of one of the countless novels of 'romance' submitted to Duckworth, petered out when it became apparent that the much maligned Violet had no desire either to denigrate the memory of Richard or to antagonise his family by making details of the (probably platonic) relationship public. Edward's contribution to the advancement of Richard's posthumous reputation came in the shape of *The Life of W. J. Fox*, a biography of the orator and political writer, which Richard had started before his death and which Edward finished and published in 1910.

Amongst the generally favourable reviews of *De Flagello Myrteo* was one in the *Daily Chronicle* of 15 July 1905, which praised the book as 'altogether a lovely and unique monument of love'.[50] The name of the reviewer – like that of the author of *De Flagello Myrteo* – was undisclosed, although Richard believed it to be J. W. Mackail. He was mistaken, however; the appreciation was by another writer who had entered Edward's orbit only a few months earlier: Edward Thomas.

Turbulent times

As the first decade of the twentieth century recedes into historical distance the years before the First World War have become increasingly suffused with a golden aura. The reality, of course, was very different: the sun did not shine endlessly; you were as likely to hear raucous cries demanding votes for women as the sound of a sweetly struck forehand on a rectory lawn; and the land was far from flowing with milk and Grantchester honey, particularly if you happened to be labouring on it. Edward was the most unsentimental of men, his view of the world filtered through a grey rather than a rose-coloured lens, yet his account of a visit to Weald, near Sevenoaks, in September 1904 seems to fit the mythical mould.

The scene that remained so firmly etched in his memory sixteen years later centred on Elses Farm, a large, square farmhouse with a range of oast houses and outbuildings set back from the road amongst the fields. There, Edward was met by his host, a tall, lean, fair-haired man, and taken on a conducted tour of the farm and buildings. In one of the oast houses he was introduced to a woman in her late twenties, small, dark, plump and rather plain – the physical antithesis of her husband – and her two young children. The Thomas family – Edward, his wife Helen, their son Mervyn and daughter Bronwen – had just returned from the hop fields. 'That scene lingers in my memory as an idyll of gracious youth,' Edward recalled. 'The charm of Thomas in the freshness of his strength, of his beautiful eyes and hair which shone in the sunlight, brown bleached to fair gold, appeared at its best in the open air, recalling the people of the "Mabinogion", or some hero myth, such as that of the Argonauts.'[1] Such a reaction to Edward Thomas was not uncommon – the word that most frequently occurs when the men and women who met him describe him physically is not handsome, but beautiful.

The initial meeting between Thomas and Edward a few weeks earlier had not been auspicious. Thomas was brought over to The Cearne by an unidentified mutual friend and during the visit made 'some fastidious criticisms'[2] about Walt Whitman, provoking an onslaught from Edward in defence of the American poet. Strangely enough it was this friction that ignited a friendship that was to last until Thomas's death.

Thomas initially believed that Edward's hostility extended to his own work and even to him personally; that he was able to overcome this perceived antipathy only strengthened his eventual respect for Edward's opinion: 'I had something to break down before reaching him,' Thomas told his friend, the poet and dramatist Gordon Bottomley, five years later. 'And to succeed in that would always please my vanity ... The man who readily sympathises with my work and says he likes it I am with insistent cursedness, inclined to suspect, on the other hand.'[3] The early antagonism over Whitman was evidence of an impassioned commitment to literature on both sides; the mutual recognition of this swiftly brought the two men into an altogether more amicable relationship and they were soon corresponding regularly. Edward's reference to Thomas's 'fastidious' criticism and his own 'onslaught' by way of response suggests much about their differences in character. 'Fastidious' is a word that crops up repeatedly in Edward's descriptions of Thomas and his work, pointing to the refined, discriminating quality of Thomas's best writing and also, perhaps, hinting at the aloof, distant demeanour Thomas could quickly assume when in unfamiliar or uncongenial company, behaviour he himself attributed to chronic shyness. Thomas's attack on Whitman would have been pithy, elegant and delivered in a speaking voice noted for its beauty; Edward's riposte was likely to have been prolonged and heated.

Thomas was twenty-six at the time of that first meeting, ten years Edward's junior. Edward may have remembered the scene at Elses Farm near Sevenoaks as idyllic, but the reality of Thomas's situation at the time was far from it; his acute awareness of the financial needs of his family and his almost pathological fear of falling into debt demanded relentless employment as a reviewer, principally with the *Daily Chronicle*. Like Edward, Thomas could write some stinging reviews – the 'subtle destructive analysis'[4] Edward detected in Thomas's studies of Swinburne and Pater was equally true of some of his literary criticism – and both men possessed a streak of uncompromising sincerity that could at times be devastating. Like Edward, Thomas had been born in London of Celtic ancestry in which he took great pride; he and Edward shared a strong, some might say romanticised, attachment to their Celtic roots. *Oxford*, the book Thomas had lately published, and *Beautiful Wales*, the one he was shortly to begin, were commissions – textual descriptions of illustrations – written through gritted teeth out of sheer necessity. Thomas's diaries reveal a man hunted and haunted by figures. Numbers – of words written, of payments owed and received – dance down the pages. The physical strain of working fourteen- and fifteen-hour days and the accompanying nervous tension were taking their toll: Thomas was increasingly subject to severe bouts of depression. His work rate may have been heroic; his moods, particularly with his family, most certainly were not.

Edward had not met Thomas before his visit to The Cearne, but he had already encountered his work. In 1902 Duckworth had published *Horae Solitariae*, a book of essays which Edward later maintained marked Thomas's emergence from a stage of 'scholarly aestheticism'.[5] *Horae Solitariae* shared the fate of many of the books Thomas wrote because he wanted to rather than because he had to: good reviews, but unremarkable sales. It also, however, brought his name to Edward's attention and gained him a sympathetic 'reader' at Duckworth's. That Duckworth went on to publish Thomas's 'non-commercial' prose books – those he really cared about – was in no small measure due to Edward's support.

Thomas presented Edward with something of a conundrum, personally and professionally. Much has been made of Thomas's melancholy, the harrowing strain of churning out review after review and book after book, written solely to satisfy the demands of the market and his wallet, his feelings of entrapment in a marriage he had made too young. Yet as many who knew him testify, there was a lighter side to Thomas, the man who liked nothing better than to sing round a piano, who delighted in talk with close friends and who possessed a keen, dry sense of humour. As Edward himself remarked, Thomas 'when he wished ... could ... enjoy, none better, whatever [was] racily human'.[6] His conversations with Edward centred on books, mutual friends and contemporaries, and Thomas's experiences on his long rambles into the countryside. In many ways Thomas talked as frankly and openly as Edward, but when he came to write about his friend three years after Thomas's death, Edward wondered if 'he ever threw wholly aside his defensive armour'.[7] There was an elusiveness about Thomas, a certain quality Edward once described as an 'other-worldliness'[8] that could come across as cold, taciturn superiority: not an advantage when it came to currying favour with editors. Edward rapidly became aware of Thomas's need for income, but he also knew that the writing Thomas was being called on to produce by publishers went against the grain of his talent and that the realisation of this was a major contributory factor to Thomas's depression and the physical debilitation that frequently accompanied it. Thomas found it extraordinarily frustrating that the public did not seem to want to read the books he wanted to write: 'I seem to take what I write from the dictation of someone else,'⁹ he complained to Bottomley. Edward, of course, had been deploring the deficiencies in the reading public's taste for years: 'Never give the public what it wants – is a maxim we would gravely impress on every serious writer,'¹⁰ he wrote in his 1902 appreciation of W. H. Hudson – advice which was all very well if you could afford to take it, which Thomas could not.

Edward did all he could to open publishers' doors for Thomas. It was probably at his instigation that in 1906 his friend Ernest Rhys invited Thomas to write an introduction to George Borrow's *The Bible in Spain* for the Everyman Library, a commission that led to Thomas writing five similar pieces for Everyman over the next eight years, all much needed grist to the mill. That same year Dent, the publisher of the Everyman series, invited Thomas to write a book about the English countryside. *The Heart of England* appeared that autumn, taking the form of a series of essays, character sketches and short stories. Thomas had written some of the material, which he labelled 'ejaculations in prose', the year before and had shown it to Edward when he was staying with Thomas in September. Edward told Thomas the details were not always consistent and that he often failed to satisfy the reader's desire for a picture. 'Garnett quoted a good thing ... from Joubert,' Thomas explained to Bottomley, 'saying that it is possible to exaggerate the moral qualities of things, but impossible to exaggerate their physical qualities; & he quoted it against me ... ought I resolutely to leave out my "atmosphere" of fancy etc?'¹¹ Clearly Edward felt that in his desire to capture spiritual essence Thomas's writing tended to become nebulous; it was no coincidence that earlier that month he had introduced Thomas to the work of Conrad, whom he considered masterly at conjuring up scenes. This ability was something Edward cultivated in writers throughout his career. In 1924 another protégé, Liam O'Flaherty, relayed to Edward how, 'The other day a man paid me a great compliment. He said that the only two people who seemed to be able to get the Russian "picture" knack into their writing were Conrad and myself. Puffed up by such a combination of names, I said proudly: "Ah yes, but Conrad and myself studied under the same master."'¹²

The lack of structure and over-strained quality of some of Thomas's writing may be the reasons why *The Heart of England* has often been regarded as a failure, but parts of the book are very fine and it was these Edward singled out for congratulation. 'Garnett has been praising *The Heart of England*,' Thomas reported to Bottomley, '"The Brook",

"A Winter Morning", "First Daffodils", "Fox Hunt" etc & says I am a poet ..."[13] Another six years would pass before Thomas took the definitive turn to poetry, drawing on the earlier prose sketches as the basis for much of his verse.

The challenge for Edward lay in trying to help Thomas find outlets for the commercial material he was reluctantly producing, while at the same time encouraging him to develop the distinctive talent which apparently could find expression only in writing that nobody wanted to buy. When in the spring of 1907 the publisher Hutchinson was considering asking Thomas to write a biography of his boyhood hero, the writer and naturalist Richard Jefferies, Edward put in a word on his behalf. Thomas was only grudgingly grateful: 'I am glad you could say what you did and thank you for it,' he told Edward, 'but I hope you were not moved in any way by thinking it would be good for my purse – I hardly think it would because I should have to drop some of my regular work and might not easily pick it up again.'[14] That the book might potentially bring Thomas's name to a wider reading public, thereby boosting his sales, was obviously desirable, but Edward's primary motive was based on his belief that Thomas's talents were ideally suited to the project. After a while Thomas overcame his reservations and turned to Edward for help in gaining access to Jefferies' widow and in tracking down relevant books and articles, one of which was Edward's own admiring piece on Jefferies in the *Academy* of 4 April 1903. As Thomas suspected, the book took what was for him a long time to write (a year) and as Edward suspected the affinities between biographer and subject allowed Thomas to give expression to his own voice, resulting in what Edward later described as 'one of the most perfect biographies in the language'.[15] 'In the first chapter,' Edward remarked, 'Thomas shows that he himself is a poet richly dowered with observation and imaginative insight into the great pageant of rural life under the open sky.' 'You have a paternal right to criticise my book,' Thomas told Edward, 'since very little but the expression is mine. I held the pen, but since you contradicted me about Whitman at The Cearne ... you have done the rest and I value your opinion more than anybody's because they are your ideas or the ramifications of them.'[16]

Edward wrote again, further congratulating Thomas on *Richard Jefferies* (1909); much as he liked the book, however, he felt that Thomas's writing was open to improvement, that he had still not fully emerged from the state of 'scholarly aestheticism' which had marred his earlier work. Part of the reason, Edward believed, lay in Thomas's personal reticence: his propensity to introspection resulted in writing that at times lacked spontaneity. 'You have been my chief guide to such knowledge as I have of the relationship between life and literature,' Thomas confessed to Edward. 'I shall not forget what you say about going forward still more into contact with the world at my gate and over the hills. You mean the world of men, I think. I should like to, equally as a man and a writer, but the ability grows slowly. I am still very much afraid of men and too easily repulsed from them into myself.'[17]

Thomas was far from a hermit, however. Towards noon on Tuesdays Edward would sit at his office desk, frequently glancing down Henrietta Street, eagerly anticipating his first glimpse of Thomas striding along in brown homespun and a tweed hat, having spent a dispiriting morning doing the rounds of newspaper and editors' offices. Upon his arrival the two men would decamp to the Mont Blanc for lunch, where they would be joined by the other regulars, who at that time included Stephen Reynolds. Reynolds, who came up from Devon, was sometimes accompanied by the fisherman Bob Woolley, whose cottage he shared, along with another Woolley brother. When at one of the lunches Reynolds had been holding forth interminably about the joys of domestic life amongst the fishing nets, Edward could bear it no longer: 'You live with two fishermen,' he told Reynolds, 'but some day a man will live with *three* fishermen, and what will you do then?'[18]

Fork in one hand, a book for review in the other, Edward was at his most expansive at these gatherings. Thomas said a great deal less, but when he did speak his comments were characterised by dry flashes of ironical insight which, according to Edward, 'added an indefinable salt to the talk'.[19] Edward tended to give his own acerbic wit free rein at the Mont Blanc, and those at the sharp end of it, like Reynolds, could be left smarting. The ex-tramp turned poet W. H. Davies, whom Thomas had introduced to Edward, recalls another instance; this time it was Thomas who was wounded by Edward's repartee. On hearing somebody ask for Thomas's address, Edward immediately flashed back: 'Every publisher in London has it.' Thomas, forced to pick up work anywhere and everywhere, was mortified. According to Davies, 'When Garnett ... saw the effect of his words, it was not long before he smoothed things over ... This little incident was soon forgotten, for Thomas knew that Garnett was a good friend – a man who sometimes said hard things to your face, but always said soft things behind your back.'[20] Just how good a friend Thomas considered Edward to be was made manifest in November 1909, when *The South Country* was published with a dedication 'To Edward Garnett'.

Although Thomas finished *Richard Jefferies* in the early summer of 1908, the book was not published until January 1909. In the meantime Edward was busy helping to place some of Thomas's sketches with various magazines. At the beginning of 1909 Thomas, so often driven in a negative sense, for six weeks found himself in a positive frenzy of creative energy, during which he wrote around twenty tales and sketches 'such as I have never attempted before'.[21] Unsure whether he was on 'a wise path – far less a profitable one', he immediately sent them to Edward – 'the only man I can turn to for an opinion'.[22]

One of the first pieces Thomas sent was 'The Attempt', which was eventually published in the *Nation* in November 1910 and reprinted in *Light and Twilight*, a collection of Thomas's short prose pieces published by Duckworth the following year. 'The Attempt', which is autobiographical, tells of a young man who late one afternoon leaves his wife and child and walks out into the country intending to shoot himself, but abandons the plan at the last moment. Edward had some pretty hard things to say about the sketch, describing it as 'intolerably affected' in places and chastising Thomas for the use of literary phrases that he maintained had the 'smell of the lamp' about them.[23] Thomas demurred, insisting that such expression came to him unbidden and that it was the 'simple and direct' phrases Edward sought which he had to wring out of himself.

On Sunday 1 August Edward went to stay with Thomas, who in December 1906 had moved to Ashford, near Petersfield. The pair talked until midnight and the following day made a short pilgrimage to Selborne, following in the footsteps of the eighteenth-century naturalist Gilbert White. Edward may have taken away a further batch of Thomas's sketches with him when he departed early on Tuesday morning, for just under a fortnight later Thomas received Edward's criticism of several pieces, including 'July', 'The Patriot', 'The Fountain', 'Winter Music' and 'The Castle of Cloud'. Some were too long, others overburdened with detail which caused the narrative to drag, while 'The Tower' was condemned as 'romantic' – 'I wish I knew what you meant'[24] Thomas complained – but nevertheless set about revising and cutting down. His reworking of the sketches was not in vain; Edward later listed 'The Attempt' as one amongst several by Thomas which 'vie in delicacy of perception and poetic insight with Turgenev's "A Sportsman's Sketches"'.[25] Thomas could have hoped for no higher praise from Edward than to be mentioned in the same breath as the Russian master.

The majority of Thomas's sketches were eventually published in various magazines and periodicals, with several finding their way into the *Nation*, including 'Olwen', in which a young Welsh girl plays with her sister-in-law's baby under the watchful eye of her lover. The day before the sketch appeared, Thomas wrote to Edward, anxious to let him know that it had been 'castrated without my knowledge and so I think spoilt ... The thing looks so stupid now that I must tell you, though for my purse's sake I suppose I must not complain to the Editor.'[26] The offending lines, which Thomas considered 'as chaste as The Daily News' ran as follows:

> Cheated of the smooth chin and the soft ears the child was still for a while, and so still and so silent it remained that it had been forgotten when suddenly the mother broke into a laugh and cried out:
> 'Well I never, Olwen! the impudence of the child! You will be suckling her next.'
> Olwen rose up undisturbed, smiling to herself and then glancing over at John, as she fastened two buttons below her neck.[27]

When 'Olwen' appeared in *Light and Twilight* the following year, Edward made sure the passage was reinstated, for by then he had become personally entangled in the snares of censorship.

Edward's previous forays into authorship had been marked by failure and disappointment, but shortly before meeting Thomas he decided to make a serious attempt to write for the stage. He may have turned to drama as one of the few remaining forms left to try – he had previously written a couple of children's plays for David and friends, which had been enthusiastically received by an audience at The Cearne that included George Bernard Shaw – but there may have been other motives too. In the opening years of the twentieth century, drawing-room drama was being replaced by the theatre of ideas. The inspiration had come from the Continent, particularly Ibsen. Edward had written about the Norwegian playwright in 1899, lamenting the fact that Ibsen's popularity was confined to a relatively small intellectual elite and condemning English insularity and English audiences' refusal to countenance productions that presented anything but a positive, morally 'healthy' solution to any problem. 'No school of young writers has been stimulated by [Ibsen's] work to try to create love for an intellectual drama,'[28] he complained, prematurely as it turned out.

A new band of playwrights was emerging whose primary objective was not merely to entertain their audience, but to make them think. Men like Shaw, Harley Granville-Barker and Galsworthy, whose first play *The Silver Box* was produced at the Court (later the Royal Court) in 1906, were determined that the plays they wrote should engage with contemporary life and raise social and moral issues which their predecessors had shied away from. The first decade of the twentieth century also saw the establishment of repertory theatre, which offered an opportunity to stage productions deemed too commercially risky for the large London playhouses. Chief among the risk-takers was Granville-Barker, who in 1904 had negotiated a deal with the leaseholder of the Court Theatre by which he and the theatrical manager John Vedrenne would produce repertory theatre in the evenings with some special matinee performances. Shaw was by far the greatest beneficiary of this arrangement, but works by progressive playwrights such as Galsworthy, John Masefield, St John Hankin, Elizabeth Robins, Ibsen and Maurice Maeterlinck were also staged over the next three years. Previously Granville-Barker had been involved with the Stage Society, an organisation with a private membership and strong Fabian connections, which on Sundays gave private performances of new, experimental plays, some of which had fallen foul of the Lord Chamberlain's office. These developments may well have encouraged Edward to try his hand, particularly as he heard that the Vedrenne-Barker company was actively looking for contemporary plays for the Court.

Edward's labours as a dramatist were made more agreeable through his sense of comradeship with Galsworthy, who started to write a play himself at the beginning of 1906 at Edward's suggestion. Each read and commented upon the other's script; Edward's effort was an Icelandic saga eventually called *The Feud*, Galsworthy's *The Silver Box*, in which two men from opposite ends of the social scale both steal items while drunk, but with contrasting consequences.

Edward's choice of subject may now seem strange, but the Icelandic sagas had been popularised by William Morris's translations in the 1870s, and Edward was highly enthusiastic about the dramatic potential of the sagas' powerful narratives and characterisation: 'The men are as hard as rock, and as slippery as seaweed,' he reported gleefully to Galsworthy.[29] As its title suggests, the action of *The Feud* revolves around two warring families, the Gudmunds and the Asbirnings, and the Gudmunds' desire to avenge the killing of their kinsmen by thralls in the service of the Asbirnings. The play makes much of the friction between Helga, a daughter of the house of Gudmund, and Bue, the eldest Asbirning son, and the sexual tension that underlies it. By the end of the play Helga's savage antagonism is overcome by the still more powerful attraction she feels for Bue. In an effort to reinforce the fact that the play is set in the thirteenth century, Edward interspersed the dialogue with 'thees' and 'thous' and various suitably ancient-sounding proverbs. This may make the play sound worse than it actually is: the scenes between Helga and Bue do relay the sexual attraction between them, and Edward manages to generate some suspense as the audience waits to hear the outcome of an offstage ambush.

Galsworthy wrote at length after reading the final two acts, offering some detailed advice and even rewriting the last two pages – 'Forgive the presumption.'[30] Edward, in the unaccustomed position of receiving criticism, seems largely to have ignored Galsworthy's suggestions and sent it off to Granville-Barker, who promptly rejected it.[31] Galsworthy proffered more guidance and tried to persuade Edward to change the end in order to make it less obviously sexually suggestive. 'You must realize that as it stands now you send the whole theatre away with their minds focused on copulation,' he explained. 'I like this myself – the majestic directness and simplicity fascinates. It is right and the proper dramatic end; but how many others will stand it?'[32]

Again, Edward took no notice of Galsworthy's advice to add 'a sudden inburst of thralls' in order to dilute the eroticism of the end, but by now his mind was not wholly concentrated on The Feud. He was finishing another play called The Breaking Point and it was this drama, rather than The Feud, that was to offend the delicate sensibilities of the Censor.

The subject of The Breaking Point was summarised by Edward in the preface he wrote to the play:

> A girl, Grace Elwood, has intimate relations with her lover, Sherrington, a man whose wife has previously left him. Her father, Dr Elwood, and her lover quarrel for control of her. The girl, fearing she is *enceinte*, cannot stand the strain, and succumbs.[33]

Edward's description is a model of circumspection and the play itself is hardly less reticent. The transgressing Grace 'succumbs' like so many of her Victorian predecessors by throwing herself in the river; the morality of The Breaking Point would appear to be unimpeachable, but that was not the opinion of George Alexander Redford, the official Examiner of Plays; when Frederic Harrison, who had accepted The Breaking Point for the Haymarket, applied for a licence, Mr Redford refused the application.

The Breaking Point is not a good play and the furore that ensued certainly did not reflect any feelings of outrage that a dramatic master-piece was being denied public performance. Redford initially contacted

Harrison privately, suggesting *The Breaking Point* be withdrawn; an enraged Edward wrote directly to Redford, demanding to know the reasons for his decision. He received a reply marked 'Private' in which Redford declined to discuss the matter – 'my official relations are only concerned with the Managers of Theatres' – and concluded that he could not 'suppose that [Mr Harrison] has any doubt as to the reason'.[34] Presumably Redford, a former bank manager, whose qualifications for his post appeared to rest on enthusiasm for amateur dramatics, felt *The Breaking Point* contravened the provisions of the 1834 Act for Regulating Theatres, which gave the Lord Chamberlain (and thereby his servant, the Examiner of Plays) power to forbid the acting of any drama he felt threatened the preservation of 'good Manners, Decorum, or the public Peace'. Redford's definition of 'good manners and decorum' was distinctly old-school Establishment: stage discussion of sex, politics and religion was out, plays such as Ibsen's *Ghosts* or Maeterlinck's *Monna Vanna* were beyond the pale, yet French farces and popular fare packed with double entendres were staged without a murmur of opposition. Redford's tactic of writing to Harrison rather than Edward was not unusual – when a dubious script landed on his desk or he heard a report that a play already in production might be 'indecent' he approached the theatre manager privately, expecting said manager to act like a 'gentleman' and withdraw the drama or remodel the offending scene or scenes. Edward however was not prepared to play Redford with a straight bat.

His response on learning that *The Breaking Point* had been censured was to publish the play with a preface in which he revealed the correspondence about it, all of which on Redford's side had been marked 'Private'. Duckworth was initially reluctant to publish – 'Damn all these worldly people,' Edward complained to Nellie. 'How they hang together! It's D's instinct to be "in" with the powers that be, and always to be on the side of the big battalions'[35] – but Duckworth relented when Edward confirmed that Frederic Harrison had given permission for the letters written to and by him about *The Breaking Point*, which Edward had included in the preface, to appear in print. The play, along with the preface and a 'Letter to the Censor', which carried Edward's name but had actually been written by William Archer with the help of Galsworthy, was published in October 1907. Also included as an appendix was a plea by Edward for the formation of a Society for the Defence of Intellectual Drama, 'to challenge authoritatively the Censor's vexatious and unintelligent verdicts'.[36] Taken together, the preface, Letter to the Censor, and Appendix constituted a powerful and in places vituperative attack on censorship in general and

Redford in particular. As it turned out, Edward's assault could not have been better timed, because just as *The Breaking Point* was being prepared for publication, Redford struck again.

His victim this time was Harley Granville-Barker. Granville-Barker's latest play, *Waste*, dealt with the subject of abortion and he was told by Redford that in order to obtain a licence he 'must be prepared to moderate and modify the extremely outspoken references to sexual relations'.[37] Granville-Barker refused. The banning of *Waste* and the publication of *The Breaking Point* proved to be a catalyst for action; Galsworthy had already sent copies of Edward's preface to William Archer, Cunninghame Graham, Gilbert Murray, George Bernard Shaw and H. G. Wells, amongst others, urging them to support Edward's call for a Society in Defence of Intellectual Drama, and now the Prime Minister Henry Campbell-Bannerman was petitioned to receive a deputation of dramatists in order to discuss the whole issue of censorship.

In the meantime, Galsworthy and William Archer drafted a letter to *The Times* calling for playwrights 'to be freed from the menace hanging over every dramatist of having his work and the proceeds of his work destroyed at a pen's stroke by the arbitrary action of a single official neither responsible to Parliament nor amenable to law'.[38] The letter was signed by seventy-one literary figures, including J. M. Barrie, Conrad, Hardy, Henry James, Somerset Maugham, Shaw, Edward Thomas, H. G. Wells, Yeats, and Edward himself. Archer planned a grand protest march from Trafalgar Square to Downing Street, to be headed by Shaw and the actor and playwright Arthur Wing Pinero walking arm in arm, followed by 'Garnett and Galsworthy, each bearing the pole of a red banner with the inscription "Down with the Censor!"',[39] with Yeats and Harrison behind them bearing an effigy of Redford.

The heart trouble that would kill him less than a year later spared Campbell-Bannerman this remarkable sight, and the agitating dramatists had to wait until February 1908, when a much reduced deputation, which did not include Edward, had an audience with the Home Secretary Herbert Gladstone. This had no immediate effect, but in 1909 a joint committee was established to look into the issue of censorship. Its recommendations effectively maintained the status quo; the one proposed change – that it should not be compulsory to submit a play for licence and not illegal to perform an unlicensed play – was never enforced. The protracted protests were not entirely a waste of time, however; Redford's appearance in front of the Committee revealed the extent of his foolishness and in 1911 he was in effect constructively dismissed. The debate about theatre censorship rumbled on and on, and it was not until the 1968 Theatres Act that the shadow of the censor was finally lifted from the British stage.

The Breaking Point occupied Edward a great deal in the latter half of 1907 and the spring of 1908. He talked, wrote about and sent it to almost everyone he knew: Thomas Hardy, Henry James, Cunninghame Graham, Shaw, Conrad, Edward Thomas and E. M. Forster all had the dubious pleasure of a copy landing on their doormat, forcing them to respond with varying degrees of diplomacy. Conrad was one of the first to read the play in November 1906 and immediately sent a long letter in which he abandoned his customary elaborate courtesy in favour of uncompromising truth-telling. His doubts and objections had 'rushed upon me, unexpected and anything but welcome. They have rushed upon me with such a force that I can not hold my tongue.'[40] According to Conrad, Sherrington and Grace are unbelievable as characters, the play is psychologically unconvincing and Grace's fate is obvious from the very start, making *The Breaking Point* not poignant, but harrowing. 'The effect is nightmarish,' Conrad contended. 'Whether you meant it to be so or not I don't know – but that's the effect.'[41] Years later David Garnett recalled how 'stung' Edward had been by these criticisms.[42] Henry James was typically circumlocutory and less openly brutal, telling Edward that he found the play 'in its gravity and intensity and general straightness and sincerity, a very interesting attempt to deal with a subject extracted, rather grimly bare, from the sombre truth of things'.[43] E. M. Forster's comment – 'I think it wonderful and unlike anything I have read before'[44] – was one of the kinder ones.

Banned from public performance, *The Breaking Point* was put on privately by the Stage Society at the Haymarket Theatre in April 1908. Rehearsals were fraught: Edward was unimpressed by the play's producer Lee Mathews and even more dissatisfied with Ethel McDowell, the actress first cast to play the part of Grace. Miss McDowell was ousted on the advice of George Bernard Shaw and replaced by Arminella Bruce-Joy, the daughter of the Irish sculptor Albert Bruce-Joy. Shaw warned Edward that Grace was not a part designed to appeal to an accomplished actress on account of the fact that 'there are only two scenes in which she has any sort of chance, and ... one of those ... is an exceedingly dangerous one, because the slightest slip on the part of the actress, or even a chance east wind putting the audience into a perverse humour, might make the lady's allusions to her condition provoke roars of laughter.'[45] The play provoked not roars of laughter but a critical pasting. Writing in the *New Age*, Leslie Haden-Guest had some sympathy for Miss Bruce-Joy, who 'did not do much with Grace, although that is not to be wondered at. If she had not so rigorously confined herself to expressing what the author wrote and had created the part anew for herself, she would have done both the play and herself a service.'[46]

Galsworthy was particularly anxious to console Edward; they had started to write for the stage at much the same time and Edward had harboured dreams of shared dramatic triumphs, but their careers as playwrights were taking very different trajectories. While Galsworthy was lapping up the plaudits for *The Silver Box*, Edward was facing up to further rejections of *The Feud* from theatre managers. Although Galsworthy did his best to lift Edward's spirits, pointing out that the lines in *The Silver Box* which provoked the most laughter from the audience were some suggested by Edward and therefore proof that he should continue writing a comedy he had started, in actual fact Galsworthy was inclined to take less notice of Edward's advice where playwriting was concerned. Wisely he ignored Edward's insistence that the Barthwick parents should share the same attitude about the events of the play, opting instead to draw out the differences between them: 'As to Mrs Barthwick, you don't seem familiar with the type,' Galsworthy complained, '– a fairly and increasingly common one in the upper-middle and upper class – ... I could give you several instances from my personal acquaintance.'[47] The embers of the old tensions about class still glowed.

Eventually *The Feud* was staged in April 1909 at the Gaiety Theatre in Manchester, which had recently been bought by the pioneering patron of repertory theatre Annie Horniman. The play was directed by Ben Iden Payne, a future Director of the Shakespeare Memorial Theatre at Stratford. Payne went through the play with some care, suggesting alterations: 'One of my chief difficulties is the puzzling way in which you have used the singular and plural in the second person,' he explained to Edward, 'I feel that you have some sort of system in this but for the life of me I cannot discover it.'[48]

In June *The Feud* was performed at the Coronet Theatre in Notting Hill Gate, used by the Gaiety Company as their base for a London season. Despite the best efforts of a cast which included Lewis Casson as Bue and Clarence Derwent, who played the part of Arnor, the play was mauled by the critics: 'To put it bluntly, the first three acts of Mr Garnett's play were tedious,' reported *The Times*'s reviewer, 'and even the more successful close was marred by occasional stretches of tedium, while the commonplace and crude dogged the heels of his choicest dialogue.'[49] Payne's wife Mona Limerick performed the role of Helga and, according to the same reviewer, she provided the one real point of interest in the evening, although whether she was 'accomplished and daring, or ... the mistress of a few telling, unusual mannerisms'[50] he could not quite decide. 'She has no tones in her voice between a strange, haunting, sometimes terrible monotone and a guttural scream, in which her words become inaudible,' he observed. The evening could not have been much fun for the audience, which included most of the members of the Garnett family and Edward and Helen Thomas. Thomas had initially been quite kind about the play when sending a copy of it to Gordon Bottomley, who was less than impressed. 'I daresay you are right about *The Feud*,' Thomas conceded,

> I am no critic. I saw a fine intention & a fine outline & words pass-able: add to this my knowledge of Garnett's character & singularity & you will see the way of my error ... In any case I should never have thought of saying it proved Garnett's powers. You have to see & hear him to know them & I am convinced he can never write anything worthy of them. He knows himself this weakness in literary expression & though he must feel my inferiority to him as a nature & a mind he says quite honestly with a smiling admiration that I have a natural talent for writing which he has not.[51]

Ironically, it was a play that Edward wrote not under his own name that was arguably his most successful. *Lords and Masters* by 'James Byrne' is a comedy about a wife who leaves her stolidly conventional husband for a lover, only to find that he has a mistress. Despite the lover's claim that the mistress, who is not his social equal, does not affect what he feels for the heroine, she walks out on the husband and the lover at the end of the play. Edward used a pseudonym as he was worried that Catherine, the principal character, would be identified by mutual friends. Edward sent the play to Conrad and Galsworthy, both of whom praised it. Iden Payne produced *Lords and Masters* at the Gaiety Theatre in December 1911. 'The audience was *extremely* puzzled,' Edward reported to Cunninghame Graham, 'quite taken aback, in fact, & not knowing *what* to think. "I call the whole thing very objectionable" said a Manchester man at the close. So we were all satisfied!'[52]

12

'Please make allowance for my point of view'

On 5 January 1907 Edward celebrated his fortieth birthday, 'Resigned – not really – but undergoing self-hypnosis to that effect.'[1] He may have smiled when conceding his lack of creative ability to Edward Thomas two years later, but the admission was painful and the resignation never quite complete.

The Breaking Point turned out to be an apt title; the furore surrounding the censorship of the play, the tensions during rehearsals and its poor critical reception took their toll on Edward, who, much to Constance's consternation, turned to bromide in order to sleep. His tolerance levels were low, particularly where poor manuscripts were concerned: 'Miss Nethersole must be told sternly that art is primarily a matter of *leaving out*, not of putting in,' he thundered at her agent J. B. Pinker. 'We do not want to find in a novel a confusion worse than life itself communicates.'[2] Most of Edward's friends rallied round, offering support with the anti-censorship campaign and consolation when the reviews of *The Breaking Point* appeared. There were exceptions, however. Stephen Reynolds denounced the play as brutal and explained that Sherrington's and Elwood's exchange about Grace while the girl herself was off-stage committing suicide 'offends my taste grievously'.[3] Reynolds's attitude towards the anti-censorship movement was at best lukewarm and he felt that this partly accounted for a propensity in Edward 'lately to sit on me unnecessarily much'.[4] There may well be an element of truth in this, but theirs was a combustible relationship in any case.

Edward met Reynolds in February 1906, probably at the Mont Blanc, where the then twenty-five year old was taken by Thomas Seccombe, advisor to the publisher Constable and ex-Assistant Editor of the *Dictionary of National Biography*. It was this job that had brought Seccombe into close contact with Richard Garnett, who introduced him to Edward.

Seccombe had for a time lectured in English at Owens College, part of Manchester University, where Reynolds was unenthusiastically studying chemistry. Always a voracious reader, Reynolds had attended a meeting of the Literary Society and heard Seccombe deliver a paper on *Romany Rye*; from then on the two men became firm friends and with Seccombe's encouragement Reynolds began to harbour aspirations of a literary career. In 1902 he left for Paris with the idea of trying to make a living as a writer. Dejected by his lack of success, he returned to England in 1903 and immediately suffered a nervous breakdown. When he first met Edward three years later he was only just recovering and possessed a greater pile of publishers' rejection slips than published material, but there was something interesting about the short, powerfully built young man with thick dark hair and grey eyes behind wire-framed glasses, especially when Reynolds overcame his initial shyness and began to talk. Articulate, and with some distinctly unorthodox ideas, Reynolds intrigued Edward, and when he heard that Reynolds had written several short stories and a half-finished novel he expressed a desire to see them. Reynolds issued an invitation to the little two-up, two-down terraced cottage where he lodged in Pans Lane, Devizes, promising to show Edward both his writing and the surrounding countryside.

Three weeks after the Mont Blanc lunch, Edward arrived for a long weekend. The two men spent their days tramping over Pewsey Downs; they must have presented a memorable sight to anyone who met them: the stocky Reynolds and the lanky Edward striding along, accompanied by Margot, Reynolds's brindle Great Dane, almost as tall as her master. After dinner in the evenings the pair talked, read – Edward had brought his manuscripts with him – and wrote letters. Reynolds soon began to reap the tangible and intangible benefits of Edward's friendship and interest. It was almost certainly through Edward that the *Nation* accepted a short story, 'Twinses' (previously rejected by the *Pall Mall Magazine*), and offered Reynolds some reviewing; and it was at the Mont Blanc that Reynolds met Edward Thomas, Conrad and Ford, valuable friendships all, although Reynolds's relationship with Ford was destined to turn sour. But perhaps the most important outcome of Edward's visit was the re-kindling of Reynolds's enthusiasm to take up his half-written novel, which had lain dormant since a bout of illness.

Strangely enough, Edward had had an unwitting hand in the genesis of the novel, which had been suggested to Reynolds by Seccombe, who in 1903 was walking from Westerham to The Cearne. As he passed Crockham Hill he suddenly wondered what would happen if the hill were to be magically transported to London. Later in the summer he was with Reynolds in Sidmouth and, as he glanced at High Peak, Seccombe was reminded of his earlier walk. 'Suppose a hill like that were suddenly to arise in London,' he said to Reynolds. 'What a disgusting scramble there would be for it, to make money out of it. Think of the newspapers and financial syndicates . . .'[5] The idea stayed with Reynolds, and over the next two years *The Holy Mountain* developed into a ferocious satire on local politics, the religious revival movement, empire and the popular press. When in 1907 Edward wrote to Reynolds's agent Pinker about the book, he described it as 'the strongest and most pungent satire that I have met for many years . . . the exposure of many aspects of modern humbug (in the religious world for example) is carried through with a deftness of touch that is just remarkable.'[6]

While Reynolds's arrows were aimed at what Edward considered thoroughly deserving targets the two men were in accord; however Edward had reservations about his new acquaintance: 'Reynolds is not a bad fellow, but no *softness* in him, no depth of emotion,' he complained to Nellie on an early occasion when Reynolds was staying at The Cearne. He found his guest 'hard and full of backbone of a kind – middle-class through and through; and in a very egoistic stage . . . I pitch into him – but it has, and can have no effect.'[7] Some of the hardness Edward detected may have been the result of Reynolds's determined suppression of his homosexuality: he found it almost impossible to express deep-seated emotion, but his not infrequent eruptions of verbal and physical violence – Margot was the victim of some severe beatings which Reynolds always immediately regretted – suggest that it was buried, rather than non-existent. Like Edward, Reynolds was fixed in his opinions and forceful in voicing them, but Reynolds's carapace was brittle: uncomfortable in his own class, he was acutely sensitive to any slight, perceived or otherwise, and behind the apparent egoism there lay a severe lack of self-confidence.

Part of Edward's irritation may have stemmed from political differences between himself and Reynolds. Reynolds met the fisherman Bob Woolley in 1903 and from that moment on was irresistibly drawn to the lives of the Woolley family and the Devon fishing community. In August 1906 Reynolds moved into a room in the Woolleys' cottage at Sidmouth, where more than ever he could appreciate the hardships involved in their struggle for survival and admire the qualities that made it possible. Reynolds was all for improving the lot of the working man, but he felt that Edward's brand of socialism would lead to rapid and damaging change to the fishermen's way of life: their material circumstances might improve, but the milieu

that produced the spiritual values Reynolds so admired would very probably perish. Politics was as likely to be the topic of discussion as literature
during the evenings when the two men lounged in the open-air porch at
The Cearne. Edward lost no opportunity to 'pitch in'; he found Reynolds's
obsession with the Sidmouth fishermen (which extended to an insistence
on wearing blue serge trousers, a guernsey and fishermen's boots, even
when in London) and his self-absorption extremely irksome at times.

Edward's irritation did not extend to the Woolleys themselves and they
immediately took to him when he stayed with Reynolds at Sidmouth
in September 1907. On a later visit, Edward described Bob Woolley
as 'Very warm, and soft-hearted and shrewd', adding, 'R[eynolds] is
certainly improved by his milieu: has not time to think about himself.'[8]
Nobody could dispute the positive effect the Woolleys had on Reynolds'
well-being, and like an excited child he felt the need to tell someone all
about the fishing trips, conversations with the locals and the joys of a
fishing-cottage kitchen: 'I'm collecting ideas – or rather impressions to
grow into ideas – at such a rate, that I must spout them to and share
them with somebody; and no one but you that I know is likely to see
what I'm getting at,'[9] he told Edward, who, seeing artistic potential
in the long letters Reynolds sent describing his experiences, assured
Reynolds they gave him pleasure and encouraged him to continue sending
them. Writing privately to Edward, rather than directly for publication
from the outset, gave Reynolds a freedom and spontaneity of expression
he might otherwise have struggled to find. In January 1907 he told Edward
that the *Daily Mail* had asked him to produce some sketches of fishing
life, but confessed that he was stumped as to how best to proceed with
them. By way of answer Edward returned two of the letters Reynolds
had sent him containing detailed descriptions of his life at Sidmouth.
Reynolds responded almost immediately, announcing that he had decided
to write a book about his experiences with the Devon fishermen that
would combine autobiography, fiction and the essay – 'autobiografiction'
as Reynolds had termed it in an essay in the *Speaker* in 1906.[10]

Reynolds changed real names and locations, but the book that became
A Poor Man's House is essentially an autobiographical account of his life
with the Woolleys, with a great majority of the material drawn from
his letters to Edward, some of it practically verbatim. The book takes
the form of a journal by an anonymous narrator; scattered amongst
the descriptions of people and incidents are socio-political lectures on
such subjects as cleanliness, class, and an exploration of the differences
between pluck and courage. It is a curious mélange and many readers

would agree with Roy Hattersley's opinion that 'A Poor Man's House is strongest when it chooses to reveal without attempting to instruct.'[11] Reynolds fretted over the form of the book for a considerable time; in February 1907 he was still thinking of presenting it as a series of letters and there is some suggestion that it was Edward who gave him the idea of the diary entries he eventually adopted. At this stage Reynolds was keen to include an explanatory preface and sent Edward two drafts of one. Edward saw the preface as Reynolds's egotism writ large and told him so in no uncertain terms. 'You hit hardish. But you're quite right,' Reynolds admitted, adding, 'I don't feel inclined to catch at your straw, that "youth is always egoistic".'[12]

By April 1907 Reynolds had written roughly 10,000 words, which he sent to Edward in the hope they were 'interesting' and 'picture-suggesting' – Reynolds was clearly another writer who had had the importance of 'picture-making' drummed into him by Edward – and assuring his mentor 'there's not now a morsel of egotism in it'.[13] He then spent six anxious days awaiting the verdict: to his immense relief it was favourable. Suitably encouraged, Reynolds continued with growing confidence prophesying that 'the book's going to be far better than any of my other attempts'.[14] However, he was still struggling to find a shape for the narrative, a problem relieved by Edward's 'splendid idea'[15] of writing a synopsis. Not all of his suggestions met with the same approval. At the end of June, Reynolds sent Edward another batch of manuscript, part of which contained a long lecture on cleanliness, a subject Reynolds believed to be intimately bound up with English snobbery. 'I've written a pretty vigorous, very scientific chapter on it which is going to stand whether it's liked or not,'[16] he warned Edward, who promptly advised him to leave it out. Reynolds's response was as vigorous as the offending chapter itself:

> I am determined not to leave [the chapter] out, for the simple reason that it is vitally important, in my thinking, to the book ... Good Lord, man, can't you see that I'm trying hard to put down some of the very essence of the best things I've seen in my life, and that I no more dare trifle with it for literary purposes than a deeply religious man dares trifle with what he holds sacred? Please make allowance for my point of view.[17]

Fearful that Edward might close his door on A Poor Man's House altogether, Reynolds ends the letter on a conciliatory note: 'And, above all, don't think I undervalue your advice and encouragement. I don't. It's very great. But ... when one is pretty deeply stirred, one has to go one's own way, which nobody else can quite see for one. 'Tisn't that I don't want your advice: don't think that.'[18] Edward's commitment to and belief in the power of literature resulted in opinions that were often vociferous and at times ferocious; he understood and indeed expected no less from his protégés. He would probably have been more annoyed and disappointed had Reynolds meekly conceded every criticism. As it was, *A Poor Man's House* was eventually published with a rewritten preface and a defiant chapter on cleanliness. At the beginning of September 1908 Reynolds sent the final proofs of the book to Edward: 'You won't like all of it,' Reynolds acknowledged, 'but I hope you'll think it justifies its existence.'[19] Six days later he wrote again, this time on a subject he had first broached in March:

> The dedication ... why, of course, to you along with Bob [Woolley]. Most of the thing came to you in letters, and but for you I shouldn't probably have started on the thing; and but for disagreeing with you I should have had no clear idea of what I was getting at; whereas I have a pretty clear idea – whether good or bad, the best or not, how am I to know? Besides, I *wanted* your name there – and that's the main thing. And 'tis an honour to have it there. Credit me with believing that for all my pigheadedness. And Bob is pleased it's there too. For they preserve, I think, a better recollection of you than of any of my friends.[20]

A Poor Man's House, dedicated 'To Bob and to Edward Garnett', was published on 21 October 1908 to widespread critical acclaim. Edward had hoped to review the book in the *Nation*, but lost out to the Liberal MP Charles Masterman, who a year later quoted extensively from *A Poor Man's House* in his magnum opus *The Condition of England* (1909). In his 1982 introduction to the book, Roy Hattersley maintains that Reynolds created 'an account of working-class life that remains a revelation seventy years after its original publication'.[21] *A Poor Man's House* made Reynolds's name; it also helped to end a long-running and at times bitter saga surrounding the publication of *The Holy Mountain*.

Reynolds sent *The Holy Mountain* to Constable in March 1907. Edward, who had praised the typescript loudly to those assembled at a Mont Blanc lunch that month, told Reynolds that if Constable didn't take it, he would strongly advise Duckworth to do so. *The Mountain* proved to be 'rather too full-blooded'[22] for Constable and duly arrived at Henrietta Street, where for some reason it landed on the desk of Stuart Reid, just about the dullest reader in the building, according to Edward. Despite Edward's enthusiastic advocacy of the book, Reid's negative opinion prevailed and Duckworth rejected it. Edward was furious and embarrassed; not only did he feel he had let Reynolds down and that Duckworth had passed up a genuinely fine novel, but his own judgement and authority within the firm had been openly undermined. Anxious to make amends and do everything he possibly could to ensure the matter ended happily for Reynolds, he did his utmost to persuade other publishers to take the book. When Reynolds went to J. B. Pinker's office to discuss a plan of action, his agent suggested that it 'might help' if Edward wrote a brief recommendation of the book he could show to publishers. Reynolds later related the rest of the dialogue to Edward:

S.R. With the literary ones. I don't think Garnett's good word would be an advantage with the purely commercial-minded ones. They'd say 'twouldn't pay, because Garnett has praised so many badly paying books.

Pinker (emphatically) If a publisher were to take Garnett's advice entirely, it would pay. The reason why it doesn't pay is because they only half take it, and try to compromise.[23]

It was in the piece Edward wrote in response to this request that he described The Holy Mountain as 'the strongest and most pungent satire that I have met for many years'. Aware that this very quality had scared off two publishing houses already, Edward shrewdly presented the book's potential to create controversy as a positive commercial advantage, pointing out that in the hands of 'an enterprising publisher'[24] The Holy Mountain would attract plenty of attention, provide excellent copy for reviewers and would probably be attacked, which could only be good for sales. When Grant Richards turned the manuscript down, Pinker suggested trying John Lane, who was known for taking on 'risky' books; the problem there, however, was that Lane abhorred all agents and so Pinker advised Reynolds to take the manuscript to Lane himself, concealing the fact of Pinker's involvement, a subterfuge Reynolds refused to countenance.

Things were getting serious: Reynolds's financial situation was such that he desperately needed to find a publisher for the book and the successful libel case brought by Lever Brothers against Lord Northcliffe's Associated Newspapers – one of Reynolds's prime targets in The Holy

Mountain – threatened to remove Northcliffe from the public stage and thus render Reynolds's satire obsolete. At this point Edward made good on his offer to take the book to his friend Sydney Pawling at Heinemann, a publisher who shared Lane's dislike of agents. Edward told Reynolds very firmly that now was not the time to pussyfoot around with scruples and that Reynolds must deal with Heinemann directly and not mention the Pinker connection.

All this coincided with the spat between Edward and Reynolds over the cleanliness chapter of *A Poor Man's House*, and Edward's command that Reynolds set aside his principles and personally negotiate with Heinemann met with the same furious and negative reaction. 'I'm afraid I'm constitutionally incapable of distinguishing between the times when "principle" may be raised and the times when it mayn't,' Reynolds wrote,

> And I don't intend to try ... If you object to this direct expression of what I mean, and want to throw me over for a blockheaded fool, I shall be sorry, very, but you must do it ... Your anxiety for the welfare of me and my MS has led you to ask me to do what I shall not believe you'd do yourself. I refuse absolutely to take any active steps towards playing a trick on any publisher to make him take my MS.[25]

Reynolds seems almost as affronted that Edward has failed to live up to Reynolds's vision of him as someone entirely governed by 'your faithfulness in literature itself'[26] as he is disappointed in Edward's assumption that he would be ready and willing to sacrifice his own principles in order to get *The Holy Mountain* published. When, on a previous occasion, Edward had told Reynolds what he would do in order to push the book if it were accepted the discussion left Reynolds feeling 'curiously chilled'.[27]

When Reynolds didn't hear from Edward for more than a month after his outburst about Heinemann, he was worried that it was his mentor who had turned frosty. In fact, Edward was awaiting Pawling's verdict on the manuscript; their opinions of it did not coincide: 'As regards the *Holy Mountain* MS,' wrote Pawling, 'I took it home to read, but I cannot agree with your view of it, as the taste of it seems to me execrable, and what cleverness there is in it is quite misspent.'[28] Despite this extremely unwelcome news, Reynolds professed himself 'Very, very glad to get your letter' when Edward wrote, relaying it. 'I wanted very badly to ... make plain ... how and why a youngster like me should sometimes take up a definite opposition to a critic like you,' Reynolds explained, going on to say that their disagreements over what constituted 'taste' (the current focus of Edward's criticism of what he had seen of *The Poor Man's House*) would never be resolved. 'If I can be told when I'm passing the limit – very good,' Reynolds conceded, 'I can then decide whether I wish to pass it or not, once I am informed where the limit lies.'[29]

Despite these ructions Edward was indefatigable in his efforts to secure the publication of *The Holy Mountain*, instructing Pinker to send it to E. V. Lucas – Methuen's reader – and to the publisher Werner Laurie, both of whom rejected it. Conscious of Reynolds's ever-worsening financial situation, Edward put in a good word for him with Rolfe Scott-James, literary editor of the *Daily News*, who provided Reynolds with an outlet for some of his sketches and regular reviewing. Reynolds was also revelling in the friendship of those he had met at Edward's Mont Blanc lunches – Conrad, W. H. Hudson and Edward Thomas. On 17 October Thomas and Reynolds accompanied Edward down to The Cearne, where they talked all day and finally turned in at half-past midnight. These relationships were extremely valuable to Reynolds at a time when publishers were slamming doors in his face and undermining his confidence. Edward's exertions on his behalf were taking place at the same time as the furore over *The Breaking Point*, and Edward could be excused for feeling aggrieved at Reynolds's refusal to give his whole-hearted backing to the censorship campaign.

In December 1907 Reynolds did what he had forsworn only five months' earlier and went to see John Lane himself. He could not have played it any better had Edward been at his elbow coaching him. Reynolds admitted that *The Holy Mountain* had been in the hands of an agent, but that nothing definite had yet transpired and so he was taking over the manuscript himself. 'My advice is to have nothing more to do with agents,' Lane responded warmly.[30] Reynolds explained that Lane had been recommended to him as an enterprising and courageous publisher who took on books others feared to touch; he mentioned his friendship with Edward and the new book he was writing, which he told Lane was set in Devon. His remarks proved remarkably fortuitous. Although Reynolds didn't know it, Lane was an extremely proud Devonian and he was feeling kindly disposed towards Edward, who had recently passed on a manuscript Lane was particularly pleased with. When Reynolds left Lane's office he was pretty certain that not only *A Poor Man's House* but also *The Holy Mountain* had at last found a berth. His confidence was not misplaced: Lane published both books in 1908 and 1909, respectively.

If Edward considered *The Holy Mountain* a finally extinct volcano he was wrong. Ford Madox Ford offered Reynolds £100 to serialise the novel in the *English Review* and the first instalment appeared in the April issue of 1909, alongside an essay by Edward on W. B. Yeats. When Reynolds, who was recovering from an operation and desperate for money, asked Ford for the first half of the payment, the reply came back that Reynolds had agreed that he would be paid only if the *Review* made a profit, which it had not. Reynolds, understandably furious, complained to Edward that he had been cheated out of his money.

Reynolds's accusation added another element to an already charged situation surrounding Ford, whose marriage and financial affairs were on the brink of collapse. Ford had gone round telling anyone who would listen that Arthur Marwood – a friend of Conrad and the man who had put money into the *English Review* – had attempted to seduce his estranged wife Elsie. This precipitated a serious breach in the friendship between Ford and Conrad, who was in a fragile mental state himself at the time. Other members of the Mont Blanc circle inevitably became drawn into the drama, and Edward's advice on the situation was sought by Perceval Gibbon, a Mont Blanc regular and friend to Ford and Conrad. 'I explained that Ford and Elsie were both children,' Edward reported to Nellie, 'that the only possible line was to bring Ford to apologise to Marlow [*sic*], and say he had been misled – which line Gibbon has decided to take ... Ford of course is idiotic in his behaviour – but never knows when to stop in his romantic pursuit of lies.'[31] Edward's earlier reference to a 'tragi-comedy' – and his inadvertent substitution of Marwood's surname for that of Conrad's fictional narrator Charles Marlow – suggests the manner in which he viewed the whole lurid business.

The Mont Blanc lunches generally facilitated fellowship and mutual help, but if some amongst the company fell out the ripples spread, and the atmosphere at the table could be tense, to say the least. When Reynolds came up to a Mont Blanc gathering in May he took offence that Edward failed to greet him 'alone of all the table-full' and then said Edward had accused him of sulking in a corner and refusing to join in the general talk. 'D'you suppose that facilitates gracious conversation?' Reynolds demanded testily. 'I don't. I thought you were offended over this damnable trouble with Hueffer [Ford].'[32]

This was hardly the case: Edward would remain on good terms with Reynolds for a further three years, although their relationship was cooling, but his lifelong friendship with Ford was deteriorating far more rapidly. Even without the Marwood furore, Ford's cavalier approach to business was causing serious financial problems at the *English Review* and creating severe tensions between Ford and the magazine's contributors, many of whom were personal friends of both Ford and Edward. If Edward was getting increasingly intolerant of Ford's 'Olympian manner',[33] Ford was distinctly nettled by Edward's propensity to say what he thought whatever the circumstances. 'I think I ought to tell you that I resent – and resent intensely – your telling people that I can't write,'[34] he fulminated in a letter to Edward. 'It does not matter before intimates but when it comes to a table full of comparative strangers I really think it is in distinctly bad taste.' (Matters of taste seem to have been something of a preoccupation amongst the Mont Blanc regulars around this time, vide Edward's spat with Reynolds on the subject.) As the letter goes on to reveal, the 'table full of comparative strangers' actually comprised 'two men whom I had invited to talk business with me' – a classic example of what Edward years later called Ford's 'gorgeous embroideries'[35] – but it also confirms just how edgy things were becoming between them.

In any case, Edward's mind at the time was preoccupied with a far more serious matter than friction between various members of the Mont Blanc crowd. His eldest sister May had come down with a severe bout of pneumonia from which she was not expected to recover. Although he had always had little time for May, there was a streak in Edward's character that Nellie once described as 'a faithfulness ... [that] gave him no joy, only a deep sense of duty',[36] and it was this, rather than any great affection, that led him to go and stay with May, who confounded all medical expectation by recovering just in time to witness her brother's entanglement in an episode that typified why May's prevailing attitude to Edward was so often one of disapproval.

At the beginning of June 1909 Constance went to dine in London with the journalist H. N. Brailsford and his wife Eva. There she met Alice Rothenstein, wife of the artist William, who, Constance later told Edward, 'seemed to derive much secret delight from meeting me at Hampstead'.[37] The reason soon became apparent. At the time of the dinner party Louise Bréal, a friend of the Garnetts and Nellie, had told a mutual friend of the Rothensteins that she was currently staying 'with the Garnetts at Limpsfield'. Clearly if Louisette, as she was familiarly known, was at The Cearne, then she was there alone with Edward. What made matters worse was that she was heavily pregnant at the time; the father was not her husband, Auguste Bréal, a French artist, but a Jewish doctor named Camille Wolf. As Constance pointed out to Edward, the underlying imputation of Alice Rothenstein's opening salvo – 'Isn't it perfectly *extraordinary* that she's going to have another baby but I daresay *you* weren't surprised – you know all about it' – was patent. That this exchange took place at the Brailsfords made it doubly embarrassing: Edward and Louise had history and the Brailsfords knew it.

Louise – described by her granddaughter as 'alternative in every way'[38] – knew the Garnetts through Nellie, who had met the Bréals when she was studying in Paris. By 1906 their marriage was in difficulties: Auguste was living in Spain with a mistress and Louise had fallen for Wolf. In December Edward wrote to her, assuring her of his and Nellie's sympathy and offering pearls of dubious wisdom: 'Remember men expect women to amuse them. If you insist in being tragically in earnest, or in tears, or suffering you will worry him [Wolf] ... Treat Auguste as a child, and don't take his moods too seriously ... Men are children.'[39] The letter ends with Edward inviting Louise to come to The Cearne by herself for a fortnight – 'And we will be gay.' It was signed 'your true friend', but the actual truth about their relationship is unclear.

It was August 1908 before Louise took up the invitation. Constance, on holiday in France with David, was dismayed to hear that Louise was at The Cearne in her absence. Later she discovered that the Brailsfords had visited The Cearne and met Louise there. 'I want you to understand that I have no *personal* feeling – I like Louisette and love the two children,' Constance wrote to Edward:

> But I should think it silly and undesirable for any young woman of our acquaintance ... to come to stay with you alone at the Cearne ... You know that Conrad, Hudson, Jack [Galsworthy] and Ada ... Duckworth etc etc – would all think it very strange and only to be accounted for in one way ... As for the ordinary run of people, well, you know that if Auguste were to take it into his head (and he really might take anything into his head) to divorce Louisette, the mere fact of her having stayed alone at the Cearne would be quite enough for any jury, French or English.[40]

What distressed Constance more than anything was the unnecessary loss of her dignity – 'for you really don't care for Louisette – and though her passion for Wolf seems always to have the curious effect of flinging her upon you, I assume that she hasn't a life and death sort of feeling for you either'.[41]

For Constance, the incident epitomised a pernicious element that was souring her relationship with Edward: 'You are always so sweet about wanting me to be happy and thinking I don't have a good time enough,' she explained:

It is so strange, for I am always feeling that you are destroying my good time! and it seems as if it would be so easy for you to be a little different – simply *not* to say and do things. It is such an extraordinary relief to escape to freedom, not to be afraid to speak for fear of being snubbed or of exciting 'vulgarity'. You told me that I 'make you vulgar' – and my only refuge from doing so is to try not to speak, try to be as absolutely blank and neutral as possible and I am getting to the point of feeling that my only safety is not to open my lips at all before strangers when you are present … After all, there is none living I care so much for, except David, and I know how much you care for my happiness … If only you could feel anxious I should be able to be myself, to express myself or even could simply realise that my dignity is part really of yours – that to put me out of countenance (to call me a 'boiled owl' for instance before the Lucases) is degrading us both. I want harmony – smoothness – I sometimes feel I would rather you hate me and treat me nicely and with respect – than be fond of me as you are and always be trying to wound me and make me ridiculous.[42]

Constance's deep sense of unhappiness is plain; the absence of Edward's side of the correspondence precludes a case for the defence: whether there was any cruel intent behind the remarks Constance found so wounding it is impossible to say, but what is clear is that although the arrangement with Nellie had brought some sort of equilibrium to the Garnett marriage, tensions remained – an indication, perhaps, that despite everything, both parties still had considerable emotional investment in it.

Nellie had written to her close friend Louise, telling her of Constance's feelings about her proposed solo visit, but Louise seems to have ignored the letter: what Nellie herself made of it all is unrecorded. This rather strange episode, which spun out over two years, certainly caused ructions, but the arrival of a letter in January 1910, addressed to Constance and marked 'Private', signalled the beginning of a far more serious row.

'I'm tired of books and MSS'

'The Prime Minister desires me to inform you that on his recommendation, the King has been pleased to award you a Civil List Pension of £70 per annum in consideration of the merits of your translations from the Russian.'[1] So began the letter that arrived at the Cearne at the beginning of January 1910. Up to that date, Constance had translated twenty volumes from the Russian, including most of Turgenev and the two great Tolstoy novels, *Anna Karenina* and *War and Peace*. She had yet to embark on Dostoevsky, the Russian author who arguably was to make the greatest impact on the literary world in Britain over the coming decade (*The Brothers Karamazov* appeared in 1912), but her contribution had already been such that the Prime Minister Herbert Asquith needed little persuasion that her work fulfilled the provisions of the 1837 Civil List Act, that such pensions should be awarded to those 'who by their performance of duties to the public, or by their useful discoveries in science and attainments in literature and the arts, have merited the gracious consideration of their sovereign and the gratitude of their country'.[2]

The whole process had been set in motion by one of the Garnetts' oldest friends, Ernest Radford. Both he and his wife Dollie were minor poets; Ernest had been involved with the Rhymers' Club and had organised the first three exhibitions of William Morris's Arts and Crafts movement. David Garnett describes him as a 'heavy, tired man, rather corpulent, going bald and with a noble forehead. Usually he seemed only half-awake, and most visitors must have thought him unconscious of the sparkling conversation and bursts of laughter going on all around him.'[3] Dollie was a complete contrast to her husband, being small, vivacious and possessed of what David Garnett calls a 'gay silliness [which] was one of her chief charms, as she was seldom *purely* silly: it was almost always mixed with so much fancy, such sudden spurts of imagination, and so qualified by little gusts of laughter at herself that one would have had to be a very hard-hearted and humourless person to resist her.'[4]

The Radfords were impecunious and very much aware that the Garnett finances were also frequently stretched, and this knowledge prompted Ernest to bestir himself sufficiently to draft a petition in support of a Civil List pension for Constance. He sent this to Galsworthy, who gave the project his wholehearted support; the successful petition soon boasted an impressive collection of signatories, including writers, editors, publishers, academics and politicians.

Constance was delighted; always much more conscious of their precarious financial situation than Edward, she calculated that the pension would almost exactly cover the cost of sending David to the Imperial College of Science, where he was planning to read Botany. Edward, on the other hand, was furious. He was instinctively and bitterly opposed to any honours or awards bestowed by the State and he was also convinced that he would be accused of living off his wife's money. As Constance pointed out, £70 a year was hardly enough to keep one person, let alone two, but Edward's anger made him unable to see the situation in anything but the most negative terms. There was what Constance described as a 'hideous scene'[5] at the Radfords', during which Edward was appallingly rude to Dollie; he then turned on Galsworthy, accusing him of lack of delicacy and disloyalty in not mentioning the petition to him. 'I feel greatly distressed about Jack [Galsworthy] and fear you have really wounded him,'[6] Constance chastised. 'Nothing could be more ungracious.' Galsworthy himself attempted to make Edward see sense: 'Surely you don't think any the worse of Hudson because he has [a pension],' he reasoned. 'It seems to me (but I daresay you will show me that I am quite wrong) that it cannot be right for you on a pure scruple of personal pride to stop what might be a substantial and deserved benefit to Constance.'[7] Edward's hot-headedness made him oblivious to Galsworthy's plea and he told Constance she must refuse the pension immediately. When she asked for time to consider her decision, Edward issued an ultimatum: him or the pension. Constance initially agreed to turn it down, but her resentment grew and she wrote to Edward, telling him that 'what might have been a source of great pride and satisfaction ... has all been the cause of some of the bitterest feelings I have ever had in my life'.[8] The situation brought back memories of the trouble that followed another of Edward's impulsive decisions – the hiring of Bill Hedgecock – when again Constance had been unable to withstand her husband's impetuosity and lived to regret it. 'I ought to have realised after these 20 years that you are always unreasonable on impulse and generous and clearheaded on second thoughts,' she continued, 'and I ought to have had the strength to hold out for time and independence of action. My weakness plays up to yours, unfortunately, if I had been a stronger character all these years, you too would have been wiser in some ways.'⁹

In the end it was David, showing a wisdom beyond his seventeen years, who was instrumental in resolving the crisis. He wrote an astute letter to Edward, emphasising their temperamental similarities, which he explained to his father made him aware that 'the continual remembrance of the possibility of having had [the pension] will cause [mother] greater misery and more futile regret, than the fact of her having it will cause you'.¹⁰ Edward was persuaded, withdrew his opposition and harmony was restored: 'Your warm sweet generous little letter is like yourself and it has healed the ache I had in my heart,'¹¹ Constance wrote to her husband, with no little generosity herself.

A few months after this crisis subsided, another one blew up. David, who had shown such maturity in helping to resolve the pension saga, now demonstrated that rashness he had identified as a trait he shared with Edward. In March 1909 he had met an Indian called Sukhasagan Dutt at the London Tutorial College, where they both were studying. Dutt introduced David to a couple of his friends, including Narajan Pal, the son of a minor leader of the Indian Nationalist movement. Dutt was also opposed to British rule in India and this political stance gained Pal and Dutt considerable status in David's eyes, support for political insurrection being something of a Garnett family tradition. One day, after having had tea with Constance at Grove Place, Dutt took David to a meeting at India House, a property on Cromwell Road in south-west London that accommodated around thirty Indian students and which was the London headquarters of the Indian Home Rule Society, an organisation founded in 1905 by Shyamji Krishna Varma. By 1909, the year in which David attended the meeting, India House was well known as a centre for Indian nationalism and had been under surveillance by both Scotland Yard and Indian intelligence for some time. It was here that David came across Vinayak Damodar Savarkar, who was giving a reading from his *History of the War of Indian Independence*, a propagandist account of the Indian Mutiny that was banned throughout the British Empire as soon as it was published.

David was entranced by the whole proceedings at India House and by Savarkar in particular, and so was more than a little worried for his new friends when the *Daily News* of 2 July 1909 reported that Sir Curzon Wyllie, one-time political aide-de-camp to the Secretary of State for India, had been assassinated at a soirée for Indian students at the Imperial Institute in London the previous evening. David recalled how Edward, who was well aware of David's friendship with the Indians, 'suddenly approached me, the newspaper in his hand, looking pale and shaken'.[12] He asked David if he knew the perpetrator of the crime, Madan Lal Dhingra, or anything about the assassination. 'It was obvious,' David later reflected, 'that Edward drew a very sharp distinction between Indian and Russian terrorists. Not that he was ever an advocate of violent measures.'[13] Although Dhingra had been present at the meeting David attended at India House, he could truthfully plead ignorance. Dhingra had been overpowered at the scene and was arrested, convicted and hanged on 17 August.

If Edward hoped that the incident would scare David into seeing less of his friends he was mistaken. The police rapidly closed India House and Savarkar and Dutt moved to a scruffy flat over an Indian restaurant in Red Lion Passage, Holborn. David arranged to have lunch at the restaurant five days a week and consequently saw a good deal more of Savarkar: 'I ... was more than ever struck by his extraordinary personal magnetism,' he recalled. 'There was an intensity of faith in the man and a curious single-minded recklessness which were deeply attractive to me.'[14]

London was becoming too dangerous for Savarkar, however; the police already suspected him of involvement in the assassination of Curzon Wyllie, and when the Indian police caught his brother concealing arms which Savarkar had sent out, he fled to Paris. He returned to England on 13 March 1910, was promptly arrested at Victoria Station and charged under the Fugitive Offenders Act with sedition and abetment of murder in India. Constance, who read a report of the arrest in the paper, immediately wrote to Edward in a state of great anxiety: 'If there is anyone you can go to, anything you can do, for God's sake do it,' she implored. 'You know what it will mean to David – at his sensitive age and with his tender nature one doesn't know what it might do for him – what it might drive him to.'[15]

Her remarks proved percipient: David regularly visited Savarkar in Brixton Prison. He was being held on remand while the authorities tried to come up with evidence that would enable them to extradite him to India, where it was likely that Savarkar would be condemned to a lifetime's imprisonment on the Andaman Islands. If he faced a similar charge in England, the sentence would be far less severe and both the British and the Indians were keen to see Savarkar locked up for as long as possible. In the meantime, he had to attend a remand hearing at Bow Street once a week, a trip he made by taxi, accompanied by one or sometimes two policemen.

A few weeks after Savarkar's arrest, the Indian authorities unearthed some speeches he had made while in India some years before and put these forward as grounds for extradition. With the prospect of his friend's removal looming, David decided to act. He hatched a plan whereby Savarkar would be rescued from the prison gates as he was leaving in the taxi en route to Bow Street. A car would arrive at the prison, supposedly carrying visitors, who would then overpower the guards; Savarkar would be whisked away in the ensuing melee, taken to the coast disguised in women's clothes and put on a boat to France. Clearly David needed help to effect this plan and at first thought he might recruit some London-based members of Sinn Féin. He consulted Florence Dryhurst, the Irish mother of Sylvia Lynd, whose husband Robert was the literary critic of the *Daily News* and a friend of the Garnetts. According to David, Florence's drawing room 'was often filled with Sinn Féiners, Egyptian Nationalists, Armenians, Georgians and Finns',[16] so she seemed an ideal ally and was keen to help.

Shortly afterwards he learned that there were Indians in Paris willing to rescue Savarkar, and so – spinning a tale to Edward and Constance about visiting his Aunt Lucy at Letchworth – David crossed the Channel and met up with a Tamil called Aiyar, whom he knew through his visit to India House. The day before he departed, he went to Florence Dryhurst's home and told her that he thought Sinn Féin sympathisers were unlikely to be sufficiently committed to helping an Indian and so was withdrawing his request. Just after he left, Mabel Hobson – the sister of one of David's best friends, Harold – arrived and Florence told her all about the plan. When Mabel relayed this to her parents, they let Constance know. Horrified and sick with worry, she got in touch with Edward, who immediately set off to Paris in pursuit, leaving a note for Nellie:

> I am on my way to Paris. D is there, engaged in a wild romantic scheme – which may have the most serious consequences. Luckily C discovered it this (Sunday) morning, and I go by the night mail to find him and bring him back. I have all details – and the poor boy is living in pure romantic cloudland: swept off his feet by his affection for S, and perhaps the tool of others.
>
> C is most ill. I left her absolutely a prey to nervous breakdown with fainting fits.[17]

Edward had hastily arranged to stay with Louise Bréal in Paris while he attempted to trace David. He found Aiyar at a hotel in the Rue La

Boétie (the details presumably supplied by Florence Dryhurst), but there was no sign of David, who had gone off to Le Havre in search of a boat in which he could bring back the Indians who were going to assist with springing Savarkar from Brixton Prison. 'I think I have succeeded in the object of my mission although I have not yet succeeded in getting hold of D,' he reported to Nellie. 'The whole episode is as wild as an Arabian Nights story with a most serious possible sequel – happily I think now averted.'[18] When David returned from Le Havre to Aiyar's hotel he was told Edward had arrived and was going to the French police. Aiyar later informed David that he had had 'an awful time. Your father's here and thinks I've kidnapped you.'[19]

Edward's appearance brought the whole plan to an abrupt end; David, furious that his father had interfered, nevertheless went round to Louise's, where he found Edward at breakfast, after which father and son caught the train to the French coast, neither speaking until they were nearly at Calais. There was a gale blowing on the Channel crossing and Edward was violently seasick, much to David's delight. The whole affair left David physically and emotionally exhausted, but he visited Savarkar in prison the next day and confessed the plot had failed. Savarkar was full of sympathy and assured David he had another escape plan worked out. This was true: when the ship taking him back to India reached Marseilles, Savarkar escaped out of a porthole and swam to shore, but was re-arrested by the British. A legal wrangle ensued between Britain and France, the French demanding, eventually in vain, that Savarkar should be returned to their jurisdiction. In 1911 a court in what was then Bombay sentenced him to fifty years' imprisonment on the Andaman Islands, but Savarkar was released under strict conditions in 1924 and finally granted full freedom in 1937. Eleven years later he was arrested in connection with the assassination of Mahatma Gandhi, but acquitted on lack of evidence. David never saw Savarkar again, nor had any communication with him after the visit to Brixton Prison on his return from France with his father.

'I hope very much that the *Daily News* suggestion of a Political amnesty in India will be the first act of the King's reign,'[20] Galsworthy wrote to Constance a couple of weeks before David's abortive excursion across the Channel, adding that the novel he was currently working on 'progresses in a way – forwards, backwards, sideways, and at times stationary.' This was *The Patrician*, and it was to create yet more tension in what was turning out to be a stormy year.

Although Galsworthy had been busy writing for the stage – by the end of 1910 he had written six plays, four of which, *The Silver Box, Joy,*

Strife and *Justice*, had been produced in London – he had also been working on novels. In November 1906 he sent Edward a manuscript he had taken just seven months to complete, with the warning 'I fear *The Country House* is inferior Dorset.'[21] Edward, however, loved what he saw, considering it 'a great advance, artistically'.[22] 'I feel this chiefly because the author is so much more in sympathy with his characters, so much fairer to them than to the people in *The Man of Property*,' he continued. 'There is no ethic at all; no *parti-pris* ... no *longeurs*.' The only major criticism Edward had concerned the end, where he felt Galsworthy was in danger of slipping back into sermonising. 'It should end with Mrs Pendyce's passing through the garden and that particularly happy touch of the Rector and Squire's appearance while talking, that's quite a touch of genius,' Edward advised. Galsworthy did as he was bidden; the passage Edward so admired reads as follows:

> Mrs Pendyce walked towards her garden. When she was near it, away to the right, she saw the Squire and Mr Barter. They were standing together looking at a tree and – symbol of a subservient under-world – the spaniel John was seated on his tail, and he, too was looking at the tree. The faces of the Rector and Mr Pendyce were turned up at the same angle, and different as those faces and figures were in their eternal rivalry of type, a sort of essential likeness struck her with a feeling of surprise. It was as though a single spirit seeking for a body had met with these two shapes, and becoming confused, decided to inhabit both.[23]

The Country House is a novel much preoccupied with definitions of 'Englishness'; Galsworthy satirises the narrow outlook of Horace Pendyce, his eldest son George and that of secondary characters like the Rev. Barter. As Edward enthused in his review of the novel in the *Nation*, 'The portraits of the well-meaning obstinate Squire, and of the sound and hearty Rector are intensely English in their insular provincialism';[24] that 'single spirit' which inhabits both men is just that inward-looking immutability Edward inveighed against in so many of his essays and reviews. In Galsworthy he felt he had an ally who could preach the same gospel. 'Write about the English,' Edward urged when he first met Galsworthy, 'for you've got it all inside you – all the keys that nobody turns in the locks.'[25]

In the summer of 1908 Edward went to stay with the Galsworthys in Devon. They had taken out a long lease on the guest wing of Wingstone, an old farmhouse at Manaton on the edge of Dartmoor and regularly retreated there. Ada, who much preferred Nellie to Constance, asked her to come down with Edward, but the invitation, though much appreciated, was declined, because Nellie had arranged to do some painting at Aldeburgh in Suffolk. Edward wrote to her every day, delighting in the landscape and the positive effect it was having on his hosts: 'Jack and Ada are at their best here,' he reported, 'not nervous, but quite restful & "home-like". Jack looks like a Devonshire squire.'[26] The afternoons were left free for walking, but all three wrote in the mornings – Edward mostly slaving over reviews, Ada typing in another room, while Galsworthy worked on his next novel, *Fraternity*, then entitled *The Shadows*. The weather turned wet, confining everyone indoors, and disagreements over the manuscript were further dampening the mood:

> Just had a tremendous conflict with Jack over a figure in his book – Mr Stone – who I think, pulls the whole novel to pieces – and is a burlesque figure destroying the illusion.
>
>   Jack, agitated and obstinate, sticks firmly, and nothing I can say has moved him. Ada, also agitated, sits in a window catching the echo of the conflict ... I think that we have now agreed to differ.[27]

Again, Edward was concerned that Galsworthy was in danger of overtly sermonising in the novel, and that Mr Stone – the retired professor who is writing an interminable book expounding his theory of 'Universal Brotherhood' – was little more than a grotesque. This was not the only area of contention; Edward also objected to the end of the novel, in which Galsworthy originally had one of the protagonists, Hilary Dallison, eloping with Ivy, the working-class girl who models for his artist wife. Edward felt the proposed ending was 'impossible'[28] and there was a forty-eight-hour stand-off at Manaton over the issue. Eventually Galsworthy succumbed and Hilary departs for France alone. 'In the hot blood of just finishing a book one is so apt to fight for everything one has done, and so apt to exaggerate the opposing mental attitude of the critic,'[29] he confessed, 'I have succeeded in eliminating most if not all of what you criticized as far as I have got ... and have hopes of getting it out all along.'

April 1910 found Galsworthy at Wingstone again, settling 'down to the drag of my novel ... which requires the heart hardened for the full stream, and the pull in'.[30] He sent the manuscript of *The Patricians*, as it was now called, to Edward at the end of August; the first line of the response warned of what was to follow: 'I'm not complimentary to *The Patricians*. I'm not going to be.'[31]

Edward's objections centred on the fact that he considered Galsworthy's depiction of the aristocrats who populate *The Patricians* to be implausible: ' ... *you don't know these people well enough* to produce an original and really convincing picture,'[32] he argued, going on to maintain that the novel was an inferior version of Galsworthy's earlier work – 'the same wine with another label'. *The Patricians* lacks those 'tiny touches' suggestive of an author's intimacy with his subject and Galsworthy is too deferential to the aristocracy as a class; as a result, the characterisation is brittle: 'Lord Dennis ... is handled with extraordinary gingerliness ... as though he might break into bits in the novelist's hands,'[33] Edward complains. The letter is brutally frank, and towards its end Edward seeks to explain himself:

> I don't suppose anybody but I would say this to you. Indeed I don't know why I say it, except that I write what I feel, on impulse, without bothering, ahead, about the effect or the result. I have told you always the effect of your work on me, and I simply continue to tell you.[34]

Yielding to impulse without considering the consequences: Edward may have recognised the truth of Constance's comments during the Civil List pension crisis nine months earlier, but he could not change his ways.

Galsworthy was far from crushed and accused Edward of missing the tone of the book. It was not in the satirical vein of his previous novels but had an altogether subtler aim: 'I wanted to go for the spirit behind the general spirit of things,'[35] he reasoned. It was Edward's failure to detect this shift of emphasis that had led to the criticism that there was 'an upward slant' in Galsworthy's attitude to his aristocratic characters. Galsworthy remained defiant about the novel: 'I can't alter it, for I don't *feel* your criticism, as I generally do,' he explained, 'but I'm grateful to you for writing what you felt, for it must have been very unpleasant.'[36] The letter ends with a plea not to mention 'this unfortunate book again'. Edward, however, could not let it go and wrote once more, asking Galsworthy to put the novel aside for two months as he felt he was too close to it and therefore unable to see its flaws, which he reiterated.

The dispute was rapidly taking a personal turn, the debate as much about perceived temperamental differences as aesthetic discord. When Galsworthy maintained that Edward's criticisms were based on his innate

hostility to the aristocracy as a class Edward hotly denied it, insisting that
'the only classes of people I do respect are: a) The free-spirited and consid-
erate aristocrat ... b) The hard-working doctor, etc [and] c) The carter,
woodman, navvy type of manual labourer.'[37] Once again he suggested
that in his desperation for balance in his presentation of the aristocracy
Galsworthy had sacrificed clarity of outline, and that although some scenes
had indeed achieved the beauty Galsworthy sought, 'taken and assimilated
along with all the passages I criticize in my Notes, they had much the same
effect as a beautiful seascape has on a man who feels squeamish on a boat'.[38]

Galsworthy pondered this letter for three days; his reply is curious in
that it opens and closes cordially, almost fondly, but in the middle section
the more he writes, the more Galsworthy is unable to suppress feelings
of resentment that have been festering for years.

Letters and manuscripts had been flying between London and Devon
during this time, not all concerning *The Patricians*. Edward was writing
another play, this time on the trial of Joan of Arc, and Galsworthy had
been reading it and making suggestions for improvements. The play
was not produced until 1931, but despite their differences over *The
Patricians* Edward told Galsworthy he wished to dedicate the play to
him. Galsworthy begins his letter confirming that it would be 'a great
honour and delight to have *Jeanne d'Arc* as my book',[39] and, after putting
forward a couple of ideas about possible cuts to the drama, he then
turns to *The Patricians*. What rankled Galsworthy more than anything
was Edward's suggestion that he didn't know the aristocratic class sufficiently well to draw convincing portraits of them and that those characters in his previous books Edward deemed successful were the result of
Galsworthy's intimate knowledge of the 'type'. Galsworthy draws up a
comprehensive list of these figures, most of which he claims were born
from fleeting encounters: 'Hussell Barter – half an hour's observation
in a train started him,' Galsworthy explains. The key to Galsworthy's
indignation lies in his remark that 'Because of my method I've always
been set down as a faithful recorder, but secretly I believe myself to be
an imaginative writer.'[40] The implicit distinction here is not altogether
dissimilar to that which Virginia Woolf makes in her now famous essay
'Modern Fiction', in which she labels Galsworthy, Arnold Bennett and
H. G. Wells 'materialists' whose close attention to the external detail of
life and lives results in a failure to capture what Woolf calls the 'unknown
and uncircumscribed spirit' that truly constitutes the essence of life. If
Woolf had joined Galsworthy in the railway carriage with the prototype
of the Rev. Barter, the resulting portrayals would have been very different.[41]

Galsworthy wished to be seen as more than a mere ponderous copyist, capable only of producing accurate but lifeless portraits of a milieu with which he was thoroughly familiar. After labouring the point about his successful characters rarely being actual faithful portraits, Galsworthy gives his pent-up resentments free rein:

Forgive this outpouring, dear boy, but I have always suffered a little from a sense of injustice at your hands – ever since I read an extract from your report on *Jocelyn (which should never have been sent to me)* to the effect that I should never be an artist but always look at life as from the windows of a Club. Well, book by book, I've always a little felt, that you *unconsciously* grudged having to recede from that position. That, with your strong, and in those days, still more set belief in your own insight (which is very great), you had summed me up and could not be wrong. I have always felt that I am deeper, more fluid, perhaps broader than you think. Being dumb, I've never said so – but perhaps you'll forgive me once in these ten years (and more) saying out my feeling. In fact I've always felt that I was contending with a *parti-pris*, perpetually confirmed in you, whenever we are together, by my slowness of tongue and manner. You say 'this book is not you', but this seems to suggest that you have fixed me as something special, definite, narrow. This is what I always feel in you. 'Jack is so-and-so, et voilà tout!' ... All this is in a sense most ungrateful, because I have always benefited enormously by your kindness, friendship, and criticism; and I know that when I come to work over [*sic*] I shall benefit here also.[42]

Further defence of *The Patricians* and refutation of Edward's criticisms followed, but Galsworthy ends, 'I'm not really as cantankerous as this letter makes out; and much more grateful'; he signs off, 'Yours affectionately'.

Edward's response opens with disarming charm: 'I'm very pleased with your letter. I think you prove your point against my *parti pris*, "and the sense of injustice at my hands." Damn you! Of course I'm unjust to you. Haven't you gone and done wonders, all along the line, in fiction and the drama, and left us gaping and scratching our heads.'[43] Edward freely admits that his initial opinion of Galsworthy 'was absurd and shallow', but protests, 'it's not in my nature to stick to a wrong estimate, or to believe in my original estimate. I'm much too *forgetful* and receptive to do that.' What are not up for retraction, however, are Edward's criticisms of the book, which he reiterates are made not from personal bias, but from deep reservations about the novel's artistic merits: 'I can only repeat that I was seriously upset at the thought of your publishing it, as it stands, and though it has many beauties, I felt that as your friend, I must use whatever influence I have on you,' Edward explains, ending the letter, 'Most affectionately'.

The personal breach seemed to have healed, but the dispute about the book rumbled on. Galsworthy seemed unable to forget Edward's charge that he wasn't really familiar with the class he was writing about and in November he proceeded to send Edward a list of 130 aristocrats he knew or had met. 'He must have felt fit to kill me,'[44] an amused Edward commented to Nellie. Ten days later, however, his mood had become considerably more depressed. Approving Galsworthy's decision to alter the title of the book from *The Patricians* to *The Patrician*, Edward continues:

> Alas! I'm glad indeed if my initial suggestions have helped my friends and acquaintances. I get very low sometimes as to the second-hand sort of existence that is implied in the game and its sequelae – even when I turn out by accident from an old box a testimony, etc., etc. – as I did the other day with a foreign letter of yours in 1905. How long ago it seems! We have both aged a good deal in those five years. However, a truce to these melancholy reflections. I'm tired of books and MSS – very tired – and I look forward in a few years to living on the seashore, with a little boat and a whitewashed cottage, on a pound or so a week.[45]

This admission that helping others amounted to a 'second-hand sort of existence' and resulted in feelings of depression is unique; Edward was forty-three when he wrote those words and they came towards the end of a difficult year that had started with the row over Constance's pension, continued with the anxiety of David's escapade with Savarkar, and was then followed by the quarrel with Galsworthy over *The Patrician*. Edward had stayed with Stephen Reynolds in Sidmouth for a couple of weeks at the end of September, and a year later Reynolds recalled the visit in one of a series of fictional articles he wrote featuring John Hannaford, a man who has retreated from literary London and taken a cottage in the fictional Nesscombe. Hannaford is visited by a critic, F. N. Jackson, whose views on the reading habits of the British public and the perils of an author achieving popular success sound remarkably like Edward's.

Jackson has 'brought down with him for the week-end a bundle of novels to review, and instead of reading them, to say nothing of writing about them, he sat all day long on the sunny beach in Nesscombe Cove, picking up pebbles and throwing them one after another into the water.'[46] It was the visit to Reynolds that Edward recalls in his melancholy remarks to Galsworthy, and Reynolds's re-creation of it suggests a desultory, disengaged figure, a far cry from the animated and passionately committed Edward who emerges from so many of the descriptions left by young writers who met him. 'I know you do waste your powers too much in the understanding and sympathy with the unworthy,' Galsworthy consoled. 'Waste is not the word, because it is so rare a gift to be able to do this. Still it's hard on you; especially when the recipient turns ungrateful like my cantankerous self.'[47]

Although the rancour is absent from the subsequent correspondence about *The Patrician*, Galsworthy was still defending the book right up to its publication in 1911. He re-wrote most of the passages queried by Edward, but never consulted him closely about his work again. The personal friendship between the two men endured, however, and in 1914 Galsworthy, perhaps recalling Edward's earlier dispirited letter, turned what was supposed to be a review of Edward's book on Tolstoy into an affectionate tribute to its author.

The value of a real critic is not to be measured by his actual writings, but by the force of his personality, persistently expressed in many ways that do not leap to the eye. There is a strange potency in that half-hidden figure, standing so firm on the base of an instinct and conviction which never swerves. It is a lighthouse hardly seen by the landsmen public, known only to us navigators of the shoals and cross-currents of fiction ...

To Edward Garnett, we owe a great debt, that perhaps cannot be paid. There are some men born to give out sympathy and help to others, and to forget themselves. They have reward, but it is seldom coined.

Truly, it is an odd comment upon the values of life, that, when a man is self-forgetful, when his love for what he does surpasses his love for himself, he is generally found to be more or less effaced. Here is one who has never beaten upon a tenpenny drum; how many are there, I wonder, who know his true worth![48]

Fishing out Lawrence

Galsworthy had been more than a little anxious as to Edward's reaction to the tribute, so Edward's response – 'I feel much as a grimy stoker must do when called suddenly from the hold and handed a medal on deck before the ship's company'[1] – came as a relief. Edward declared himself 'infinitely touched' by Galsworthy's gesture: 'You have always repaid, in so many ways, any spiritual obligations that my affection for you, your work, and what it stands for, may have seemed to lay you under – that I feel it is too bad for *you* to speak for the others who have kept silence,' he continued. On the odd occasion, Edward may have wished that some of the others *had* kept silent, and Galsworthy's remarks about the ingratitude of those who benefited from Edward's advice may have raised a sardonic smile when Edward read the piece by Stephen Reynolds in the *Westminster Gazette*.

This was the article in which Reynolds recalled the disconsolate Edward playing ducks and drakes on the beach at Sidmouth during his visit in 1910. The similarities between Edward and Reynolds's fictional critic F. N. Jackson were inescapable and Reynolds may well have quoted Edward practically verbatim when he has Jackson complain that 'English fiction is so horribly commonplace. Serious criticism is useless. Nobody takes any notice of it. I suppose our novelists are bound to write down to the stupidity of the public, unless their ambition is to starve.'[2] Hannaford, the Reynolds figure, issues a stinging riposte:

> You'd think a great deal better of them if they did starve, because you have a theory that if genius doesn't starve – well, it ought to. Otherwise you genius merchants couldn't go on feeling so superior to the poor stupid heedless public. I remember, when I was in London, that so long as a young author had no success whatever, you were all of you most kind to him and held him to be a budding genius; but directly his luck turned, you began to sneer at him,

because you assumed that in so far as his work became popular, it couldn't be good ... You are like the gardeners who take such pride in the vegetables of their own growing, that they don't like them eaten.[3]

Like most satire this is an exaggeration, but contains an element of truth. Writing to Edward in 1913, Galsworthy tells him that he had seen Conrad three weeks earlier and that 'we agreed it was natural you should take no real interest in our productions nowadays, because of our beastly success'. Galsworthy's reaction to Edward's withdrawal is, however, very different from Reynolds's: 'I don't say this in anything but admiration,' he continues, 'if you were not like that Literature would have been a big loser.'[4] Once a protégé overcame the resistance of muddle-headed critics and the obtuse public Edward considered his job done and moved on to preach his gospel elsewhere. That gospel never fundamentally altered, especially the verses on the essential philistinism of the middle classes.

'Full of notions for essays – the uses of history, poetry, criticism; perhaps a series. And "The Middle Classes and Literature" – suggested by an interesting though saddening talk with Garnett. He is a really admirable critic,'[5] noted E. M. Forster in a diary entry for March 1911. Forster's first novel, *Where Angels Fear to Tread*, was published in 1905 and enthusiastically reviewed by Edward in the *Speaker*.[6] The two men met shortly afterwards and were soon lunching together, an event Forster could find simultaneously stimulating and strenuous: 'Lunched with E. Garnett, and also made acquaintance of Clutton-Brock, Giblin, and a stare – at H. G. Wells who looks absolutely delightful,' he recorded in November 1905. 'Conversation witty and cultured but tiring.'[7] It was Forster's ability to catch 'the essential tone of the modern [middle-class] English mind so justly and finely,'[8] that delighted Edward, as did Forster's subtle irony, his refusal to be in thrall to the demands of a 'good plot' and his unbounded admiration for Russian writing. Forster was not reliant on Edward to the extent that some of his other protégés were – he was financially independent and had cultivated some influential friends during his years at Cambridge – but as Forster himself recalled, Edward 'picked up a book by an unknown writer, which, in his opinion, was promising ... forced an enthusiastic review into a magazine, and so gave me a chance of reaching a public.'[9]

Just before the publication of *Where Angels Fear to Tread* Edward read some short stories of Forster's for Duckworth and commended the way in which his 'neat satirical touches drive home the uncanny feeling that

our British everyday world is only the surface world of appearances'.[10]
Duckworth didn't take the stories, but Edward kept an eye on Forster
and in 1907 he reviewed his second novel, *The Longest Journey*, for the
Nation. Edward opens the review by quoting a passage from the novel
in which Agnes Elliott asks her husband Rickie, a writer: 'Couldn't you
make your stories more obvious? I don't see any harm in that. Uncle
Willie floundered hopelessly. I had to explain, and then he was delighted.'[11]
This, in Edward's opinion, was the likely reaction of the British reading
public to Forster's book and it was precisely that subtle, elusive quality
that made him consider *The Longest Journey* a 'brilliant novel'. 'All lies
in the telling,' Edward continues 'and how can the art of telling, this
network woven of a succession of tiny touches be brought home to Uncle
Willie!' Towards the end of the piece Edward insists that, 'A quiet hatred
of shams has inspired Mr Forster to one of the subtlest exposures of the
modern Pharisee that we can recall in fiction. Bit by bit he gently peels
off the respectable casings that enwrap his Philistines' souls.' Edward's
praise of *The Country House* by Galsworthy, which he had reviewed just
over a month earlier, had been fulsome, but even that was eclipsed by
Forster's stealthier assault on the towers of Philistia. Forster wrote to
Edward, telling him that the review had given him tremendous pleasure,
'for the Uncle Willies are encompassing me sorely', adding 'it is a great
encouragement that you think I've done it well.'[12]

If Edward passed public judgement on Forster's next novel, *A Room
With A View* (1908), he must have done so anonymously, but in 1910 he
was sent *Howards End* to review for the *Nation*. 'I'm in two minds about
Forster's book,' he told Nellie, 'I thought it *very* good when reading it
yesterday, but today it doesn't seem nearly so strong. It's a little *made-up*
I think – though all the parts are good and the thought and language
are true.'[13] After mulling it over for a day Edward passed his final verdict:
'Forster [is] very good – but his *ideas* are better than his art. I shall put
that in my review.'[14] Sure enough, when the notice appeared five days later
Edward suggested that Forster had 'sacrificed the inflexibility of artistic
truth to the exigencies of his philosophical moral ... The individuality of
each figure is made obedient to the convenience of the author's purpose.'[15]
He did, however, praise the acute analysis of the middle-class and the
novel's many 'fine, insidious strokes'. Forster responded immediately:
'With the possible exception of *The Times*, which avowedly omitted bad
points, your criticism is the only one that strikes me as just,'[16] he wrote.
'I only hope I may profit by it in the future, and a writer can't say more.

Though whether I can profit is another matter. It is devilish difficult to criticise society and also create human beings.'

Forster – who years later told David Garnett that his father had had a far greater influence on his writing than that of the Bloomsbury Group with whom he became closely identified – was one of a select band of authors Edward commended in a long article on the state of English fiction for the New York *Nation*. 'English Novels and English Life' appeared in March 1909; in it Edward surveys the contemporary literary landscape, explaining its evolving geography to the American reader and navigating that reader away from the well-worn but ultimately unrewarding paths of familiar and 'popular' literature. The title of the piece is important: Edward always had a strong belief that the word could change the world and that the link between literature and life was vitally important. He also felt that most Americans 'prefer to see us not as we are, but as we appear against the sentimental background of historical traditions'.[17] (The self-perception of the English was, of course, in Edward's opinion just as distorted in its own way.) For this reason, the first part of his article is as much an examination of the recent history and state of the nation as it is an overview of contemporary fiction. Victoria's reign had been a time of enormous economic, social and cultural change; however, according to Edward:

In spite of all the material benefits conferred, capitalism, commercialism, and industrialism combined have impressed on the bulk of our population a servitude to a narrow, petty, and mean town life that dwarfs and stunts the spirit. We are cramped, congested, and bound hand and foot by a network of 'vested interests'. Our middle class has entrenched itself in comfortable surroundings to enjoy the fruit of its own and other people's labor.[18]

The energy, optimism and expansiveness that characterised the mid-Victorian years have disappeared; gone too are the great novelists of that era: Thackeray, Dickens, Mrs Gaskell, George Eliot. 'What England needs today in her writers', Edward contends, 'is spiritual and mental audacity.' These are the qualities required to show the reader the world as it now is, however uncomfortable and unsettling that experience might be. Books that merely confirm existing and reassuring misperceptions are not worth the paper they are printed on, although all too often these are the volumes that sell in abundance.

The suburban middle class, according to Edward, 'suffers now most from the monotony and pettiness of its horizon, from its preoccupation with the small proprieties of social ritual and the keeping up of appearances, and from its lack of generous width and direct contact with first-hand realities.' This is the situation confronting the nation's writers and it is what makes the sharp, satirical criticism of men like Shaw, Belloc and Chesterton invaluable. However, it is Galsworthy, unique in writing from 'inside' his own class, who 'exposes better than any of our other novelists the practical outlook of the modern Englishman, the soft sentimental spot in his soul ... together with his amazing capacity for protecting himself from any inroad of disturbing ideas.' The American reader seeking to learn about the upper-middle classes and English 'good society' could do no better than study Galsworthy's *The Man of Property* (1906), *The Country House* (1907) and *Fraternity* (1909).

For unsentimental depictions of rural life that reader should reach for the books of Mary Mann, the Norfolk farmer's wife whose work shows 'a deep knowledge of human nature, a ruthless sincerity, and no little imaginative intensity'. Had Mann lived on the Continent, Edward argues, her reputation would be great; it is only her refusal to give the middle-class reading public what it wants – 'idealized ... pictures [that] please, amuse, or flatter its susceptibilities' – that has denied her talent proper recognition. So much for rural England, but what of the great manufacturing centres of the north, conspicuous by their absence from the pages of fiction since the death of Mrs Gaskell in Edward's opinion. Happily, two 'remarkable' novels have lately appeared to rectify the situation: Arnold Bennett's *Anna of the Five Towns* (1902) and *The Old Wives' Tale* (1908), books that Edward believes make Bennett 'the fairest critic and interpreter of the commercial classes'. Passing rapidly over those 'popular' writers who satisfy the majority of the undemanding public (his list includes Stanley Weyman, Arthur Conan Doyle and Anthony Hope) Edward draws attention to four authors 'who have something unique in their artistic gift, and a finer quality of mental outlook'. This august quartet comprises May Sinclair, the now widely forgotten Leonard Merrick, Evelyn Underhill (whose inclusion rested solely on *The Lost Word* [1907], the second of her three novels) and E. M. Forster. However, to Edward's mind there is only one novelist who has truly got to grips with the malaise afflicting English society – its lack of spiritual energy – and come up with an answer that embodies the necessary new social creed, and that is H. G. Wells. In *Kipps* (1905) and *Tono-Bungay* (1909) Wells has assailed 'with a cruel humour that is electrifying, the absurdity of

British shibboleths and conventions, and the haphazard irrationality of our social organization'.

Wells, Bennett and Galsworthy: the three writers Edward singles out for commendation are the selfsame trio that Virginia Woolf damns as 'materialists' in her now famous essay 'Modern Fiction' in which she argues that the old vestments of literary technique no longer adequately fit modern reality. On the face of it, this would seem to plant Edward firmly in the camp Woolf labelled 'Edwardian': writers whose focus is fixed on the external and who have little interest in the representation of the life of the mind. The final paragraph of Edward's essay, however, makes a crucial distinction; in it he regrets the fact that he has no space in which to discuss 'a little group of remarkable artists, of whom Joseph Conrad, Cunninghame Graham, W. H. Hudson, and Maurice Hewlett are the chief.' Edward commends the cleverness, audacity and subtlety of Wells, Bennett and Galsworthy, but his admiration of the latter is qualified by the remark that Wells is 'not a pure artist'. The exclusion of Bennett and Galsworthy from the elite group with which Edward ends his survey effectively denies them that elevated status too.

Until his article in the New York *Nation*, Edward had written very little that had appeared on the other side of the Atlantic, but his name was far from unknown in American literary circles. In 1911 he was asked to become the English representative of the *Century Magazine*, an illustrated monthly that had begun life thirty years earlier as the successor to *Scribner's Monthly*. Edward was tasked with finding material from established and promising writers that he considered would appeal to an American readership. Early on he made it very clear to the *Century*'s editor, Robert Underwood Johnson, that he was not prepared to be involved in financial negotiations between the magazine and its potential contributors or their agents, but viewed his role as that of literary advisor. Despite this, the subject of money was frequently a vexed issue, with agents looking for far more than the *Century* was prepared to pay. 'The American habit of waiting till a man has *already* "arrived" and then hastening up to secure him means that you are *already* too late – unless you are prepared to out bid everybody,'[19] Edward pointed out apropos Hilaire Belloc, who, he reminded Johnson, was now making three or four times the £600 a year he earned when Edward first knew him ten or so years earlier. In the same letter Edward rather loftily expressed his disappointment at the *Century*'s refusal to commission an article from Edward Thomas – 'as the standard of his writing is far above the bulk of your contributors; and I thought that you aim at mixing in papers of *high* quality among the more popular matter.'

Such discord over artistic merit and the taste of the *Century*'s readers was not altogether uncommon: 'I fear that all our best authors are "too" something or other for the needs of your public,' Edward complained, 'too "quiet", too "morbid", too "impressionistic"' etc'.[20] Johnson gave as good as he got, reminding Edward that the magazine sought work that had a broad popular appeal and intense human interest, and claiming that the principal fault of articles hailing from England was 'dilettantism'. Edward's response – 'I quite recognize that our writers do *not* combine artistic lightness and grace of treatment with a solid and comprehensive treatment of their subject. You must, I fear, accept the fact that E. V. Lucas, Belloc, Chesterton etc are each on his own temperamental basis, and that their literary value *lies* precisely in the expression of their individuality'[21] – comes close to casting aspersions on Johnson's powers of finer discrimination. In spite of his jaundiced view of the demands of the American market, Edward was assiduous in his efforts to find contributors for the *Century*. New and relatively unknown authors were of particular interest to him: problems over rates of pay were less likely and the magazine offered a great opportunity to promote deserving talent to a potentially huge readership. When Edward became the *Century*'s English representative in the summer of 1911 and was looking for suitable short stories he already had one such writer specifically in mind.

The train pulled into Oxted Station at just after half-past six on the evening of Friday 13 October 1911. Amongst those alighting was a young schoolmaster, who earlier that afternoon had dismissed his class of fifty – 'the boys are all right, only issued from God a good deal below sterling intelligence'[22] – with an even greater sigh of relief than usual. His discontent with teaching, which left him drained and had begun to take its toll on his health, meant that he habitually lived for the weekends, but the prospect of the next two days filled him with more than his customary sense of anticipation. This excitement may have blunted his fatigue: the weariness induced by the classroom had been exacerbated by working late into the night on some poems he planned to show Edward, whom he had met only once before in London. Exiting the station in the gathering darkness, he turned in the direction of Limpsfield and set out to walk the couple of miles to The Cearne. It was his first visit and he had to keep his wits about him: the house was isolated and not visible from the road. Trees thickened the darkness as the visitor followed a sharply sloping track; The Cearne stood beneath a steep, coppiced hill and it was not until he was nearly on top of it that he realised he had arrived. He made his way to the immensely solid oak front door and raised the knocker.

The guest Edward greeted was, at twenty-six, seventeen years his junior. Above average height, the young man was slight but wiry, with his hair, which had a definite reddish streak, parted to one side. He sported a rather scrubby moustache, but his eyes were his most arresting feature – blue and, according to David Garnett's later description, 'so alive, dancing with gaiety'.[23]

Edward's reputation as a discoverer of literary talent was by now established to the extent that any aspiring writer jumped at the chance of an introduction; but the young man's pleasure and excitement were not entirely unalloyed. He could see tricky times ahead, not with Edward, but his fiancée Louie, herself a schoolteacher in the Midlands. When he had written to her telling her about his first meeting with Edward in London he had been unable to suppress his enthusiasm: her response had been defensively scathing, referring to 'the great Garnett' and accusing her fiancé of being prepared to move heaven and earth in his 'madness' to meet him.[24] Her fears about Edward's influence cannot have been assuaged when she later received a parcel containing two plays the 'great' man had written, with the injunction, 'Don't show them to your people: it will be enough for them that The Breaking Point is censored, to make them look at me very much askance.'[25] A few months later she would have even greater cause to rue the day the man she loved moved into Edward's orbit, for when he appeared at the door of The Cearne that October night, Edward opened a whole new world to the young schoolmaster, David Herbert Lawrence.

When Lawrence came to report on his visit to his sceptical fiancée Louie Burrows, he began with something he thought she *would* approve of – the house:

[Garnett] has got one of these new, ancient cottages; called the Cearne. It is a house thirteen years old, but exactly, exactly like the 15th century: brick floored hall, bare wood staircase, deep ingle nook with a great log fire, and two tiny windows one on either side of the chimney: and beautiful old furniture – all in perfect taste. You would be moved to artistic rhapsodies, I think.[26]

Then came the awkward bit – the prevailing domestic arrangements in this rustic gem:

> Garnett was alone – He is about 42. [Actually Edward was 43.] He and his wife consent to live together or apart as it pleases them. At present Mrs Garnett with their son is living in their Hampstead flat. She comes down to the Cearne for week ends sometimes. Garnett generally stays one, or perhaps two days in the week, in London. But he prefers to live alone at the Cearne. But he is very fond of his wife also – only they are content to be a good deal apart.[27]

Try as he might to present the marital set-up as an ideal of connubial independence, Lawrence senses that Louie will disapprove, not just of Edward, but of his own desire to consort with such a man. 'We discussed books most furiously,' continues Lawrence, 'sitting drinking wine in the ingle nook, cosy and snug in the big, long room. We had a fine time, only he and I. He thinks my work is quite extra. So do I, of course. But Garnett rather flatters me. He praises me for my sensuous feeling in my writing.' It is an evocative picture, and one that offers a tantalising glimpse of Edward at work, eager to draw out the young author, and as excited at the prospect of adding another name to his already extensive list of literary 'finds' as his guest was at the chance of being added to that roll of honour. That their fireside conversation revolved around books is unsurprising. Edward would have been as interested in what Lawrence was reading as in what he was writing; he was acutely aware that reading is the lifeblood of any writer and was doubtless impressed with the young autodidact's already extensive literary knowledge, and highly gratified to discover that he was familiar with the works of Turgenev, Tolstoy and Chekhov. Lawrence was already indebted to the Garnetts for his literary education; one of the most prized possessions in the family house at Eastwood, Nottingham, was a set of bound, green books containing long extracts from famous authors. This was *The International Library of Famous Literature*, a twenty-volume anthology of passages from writers as diverse as Seneca and Swift, Tolstoy and Mrs Humphry Ward. They were published in 1899 and edited by Richard Garnett.

Edward's search for short stories for the *Century* had led him to contact Lawrence (probably on the recommendation of Ford Madox Hueffer) in August 1911, asking if he had anything suitable. Lawrence sent two stories, 'Intimacy' and 'Two Marriages' (subsequently rejected), with a letter telling Edward that 'if, anytime, you would give me a word of criticism on my MSS, I should go with surer feet'.[28] Edward's interest was aroused; enclosed with the returned manuscripts were helpful comments (he felt that 'Intimacy' dragged) and an invitation to lunch.

In one sense Edward and Lawrence had 'met' before, in the pages of the *English Review*. The third issue had carried some of Lawrence's verse and a long appreciation of the poetry of Charles Doughty by Edward. It was Jessie Chambers, Lawrence's first love and earliest literary mentor, who had sent some of his poems to Hueffer, who accepted them for the magazine and then agreed to read the manuscript of Lawrence's first novel, *The White Peacock*. Lawrence later recalled Hueffer's response, which he delivered 'in his queer voice when we were in an omnibus in London ... "It's got every fault that the English novel can have ... But" shouted Hueffer in the bus, "you've got GENIUS."'[29] However, when Lawrence showed Hueffer the manuscript of his second novel, then called *Nethermere*, he was in for a nasty shock. Hueffer pronounced it to be 'execrably bad art ... Also it is erotic, not that I, personally, mind that, but an erotic work *must* be good art, which this is not.'[30] Despite the fact that Heinemann had agreed to publish the novel, Hueffer's remarks preyed on Lawrence's mind and in February 1911 he wrote to the firm's reader, Frederick Atkinson, telling him that the book 'is execrable bad art: it has no idea of progressive action ... its purple patches glisten sicklily: it is, finally, pornographic. And for this last reason, I would wish to suppress the book ... I shall not publish it ever in its present state; and in any state, not for some years. This is not a whim, but a resolve.'[31]

Lawrence's fledgling career as a writer was at a crisis point in that autumn of 1911: besides his problems with the 'erotic' manuscript, he had failed to finish two versions of his 'colliery novel' (the eventual *Sons and Lovers*) and was unable to meet Martin Secker's request for a volume of short stories, because he had not written a sufficient number. Lawrence's woes were not purely professional: he was still haunted by the death of his mother the previous December and he was lonely, missing Eastwood and Jessie Chambers's support and encouragement of his writing. Furthermore, he was experiencing sexual frustration in his relationships with both Louie and Helen Corke, a teacher at another Croydon school. Small wonder that when he looked back at 1911 he remembered it as 'the sick year'.[32] Lawrence later recalled his predicament in a letter to his friend, the artist and illustrator Ernest Collings:

Ford Madox Hueffer discovered I was a genius – don't be alarmed, Hueffer would discover *anything* if he wanted to – published me

some verse and a story or two, sent me to Wm Heinemann with
the *White Peacock*, and left me to paddle my own canoe. I *very*
nearly wrecked it and did for myself. Edward Garnett, like a good
angel, fished me out.[33]

Edward's eagerness to throw Lawrence a lifeline was intensified by the
prospect of proving Hueffer's judgment of the 'erotic' manuscript wrong
(by 1911 their relationship had deteriorated markedly) and by the enticing
possibility of prising it out of the clutches of Heinemann, who of
course had sacked him ten years earlier. The very fact that the book
was deemed 'erotic' and thus liable to censorship made the challenge
altogether irresistible.

As that evening at The Cearne wore on, the talk and the wine –
recommended by Conrad as a potential cure for Edward's chronic
insomnia – flowed with increasing freedom. Edward was very much a
night bird, habitually growing more expansive as the hours advanced and
his agile wit became at its sharpest. He began to revel in the company of
the young Lawrence, later recalling the 'loveableness, cheekiness, intensity and pride' of his guest.[34] Scattered amongst gossip about Hueffer's
latest romantic and financial entanglements were nuggets of advice and
offers of help: Lawrence must make it his business to get known in the
literary world; Edward would introduce him to the editors of those magazines in which his work would be placed to best advantage; Lawrence
should get hold of some plays he had left with Hueffer – Edward held
out hopes of finding a publisher for them; and, most satisfying of all,
Edward wanted to read all Lawrence had written thus far: the verse, the
plays, *The White Peacock* and the manuscript of the 'erotic' novel, which
he commanded Lawrence to extract from Heinemann. Edward may not
have been the only one who found sleep elusive that night.

Daylight revealed the splendours of the Chart countryside. Lawrence
was enchanted: 'all the trees are quite fluffy and thick with yellow, like
fires among them,' he told Louie.[35] It is unlikely that Edward was able
to devote all his time to showing his guest the glories of the autumnal
woods, however: piles of manuscripts were waiting to be read and there
were reviews to be written too. It is tempting to speculate that this was
the first occasion on which Lawrence glimpsed Edward at his desk,
grappling to find the words that never came easily to him when he had
a pen, rather than a blue pencil, in his hand – later Lawrence would
recall that Edward 'ate his heart out trying to be a writer'.[36] Although
Lawrence returned to his lodgings in Croydon weighed down with copies

of *The Breaking Point* and *The Feud* he also carried with him the priceless assurance of Edward's interest in and commitment to his work, and the promise of another visit to The Cearne. Once again he was unable to temper his enthusiasm when writing to Louie, telling her he had had 'a ripping time at Garnetts' [*sic*].[37]

He was back again just over a month later, more discontented and frustrated with teaching than ever. In the interim Edward had 'bullyragged' the *Nation* into publishing some of Lawrence's verse – 'I am pleased to get a footing in the *Nation*. It is a sixpenny weekly, of very good standing,' he informed his sister Ada[38] – and he was sending Edward more poetry and short stories for scrutiny and advice. The accompanying letters reveal the rapid blossoming of their friendship: 'Dear Mr Garnett' swiftly becomes 'My dear Garnett'. True to his promise to get Lawrence's name known in the right circles, Edward invited Rolfe Scott-James, literary editor of the *Daily News*, down to Limpsfield to meet his newest protégé. The weather had turned wet and miserable and Lawrence got caught in the rain on his way from the station. Rather than change his wet clothes on arrival, he stood watching his host chop logs for the fire in the inglenook, around which Edward and his guests congregated that evening. It is almost certainly this particular occasion that Scott-James described over a quarter of a century later:

> Once, in the early days of Lawrence's authorship, he and I were week-end guests at the Cearne. We sat by the fire at night feasting on the genial eloquence of our host as he warmed to the theme of Lawrence's genius. 'Lawrence's genius, you see,' he would begin, and go on to explain just how, with that background, it lent itself to that fearless exposure of body and soul which was the reality of creative art. And Lawrence, at first shyly, but with growing confidence, began to see himself through Garnett's eyes and to relish the *rôle* of the distinctive 'genius' allotted to him. Garnett has been called the 'discoverer' of genius. He was more than that. He often evoked it, inspired it and moulded it in its early stages ...[39]

When Lawrence returned to Croydon, his landlord suspected a weekend of dissipation; his young lodger looked 'as if he was suffering from a frightful hangover'.[40] However, Lawrence was not feeling the after-effects of Edward's wine (although he might still have been drunk on his flattery); instead, he was hatching up a life-threatening bout of double pneumonia, the consequence of lingering in wet clothes on his arrival at The Cearne. That Lawrence was still unable to stand a week before Christmas gives some indication of the severity of the illness. The first person he asked to come and see him after the immediate crisis had passed was Edward. Lawrence had survived, but his doctor told him that if he returned to school he risked becoming consumptive. He never taught again. That weekend at The Cearne had effectively killed off the Croydon schoolmaster, but with Edward's help the professional writer was about to rise from those ashes.

'You are so russianised my dear'

If Edward did retreat to his desk during that first weekend when Lawrence went to The Cearne it may well have been to work on his review of Conrad's *Under Western Eyes* (1911), which appeared in the *Nation* the following Saturday. That review and a private letter Edward wrote to Conrad about the novel very nearly wrecked their friendship for good.

Edward's role in Conrad's career changed with the publication of *Lord Jim* in 1900; thereafter he no longer read Conrad's manuscripts nor offered private criticism of them. This did not reflect a diminution of their friendship or a lessening of Conrad's esteem for Edward's advice, but as Edward himself put it, 'with *The [sic] Heart of Darkness*, begun in December 1898, Conrad suddenly found the channel clear and forged ahead.'[1] With Conrad now more confident in his powers as a writer and more at home in the literary world, Edward turned his attentions to promoting Conrad's work and educating people as to how it should be read through his critical columns and reviews. The warning signs for Conrad were evident early on: Edward's appreciation in the *Academy* carried references to Conrad's 'Slavic' literary inheritance, and he continued in the same vein: *Heart of Darkness* was 'as enthralling as the pages of Dostievsky's *Crime and Punishment*',[2] while his review of *Nostromo* (1904) also drew comparisons with the great Russian novelists. Edward's insistence on Conrad's 'Slavic' virtues began to reach a crescendo in his piece on *The Secret Agent*, which appeared in the *Nation* of 28 September 1907:

It is good for us English to have Mr Conrad in our midst visualising for us aspects of life we are constitutionally unable to perceive, for by his astonishing mastery of our tongue he makes clear to his English audience those secrets of Slav thought and feeling which seem so strange and inaccessible in their native language ...

Mr Conrad ... is to us as a willing hostage we have taken from the Slav lands, in exchange for whom no ransom could outweigh the value of his insight and his artistic revelation of the world at our gates, by us so imperfectly apprehended.[3]

In case the reader had still not got the point, Edward ends the review insisting that Conrad's novel has 'the profound and ruthless sincerity of the great Slav writers'.

Conrad initially ignored the review's Slavic references, applauding instead Edward's astute insight that it is Verloc's mother-in-law who is the real heroine of the story. However, he failed to keep the lid on his simmering indignation three days later: 'I've been so cried up of late as a sort of freak, an amazing bloody foreigner writing in English,' he complained to Edward, '(every blessed review of S.A. [*The Secret Agent*] had it so – and even yours that anything I say will be discounted on that ground by the public.)'[4] Why Edward's emphasis on Conrad's 'foreign' qualities should come as a surprise to Conrad is difficult to fathom, given Edward's past track record, and the similarity of the reviews should not have come as a shock either – as early as 1902 Conrad admitted to Edward that when it came to criticism of his work 'the ruck takes its tone from you'.[5] Conrad's dismay that anything he says will be discounted by the public is a reference to the censorship campaign, which coincided with the tension over the *Secret Agent* review.

Edward asked Conrad to write a letter to the *Daily Mail*, protesting about the Censor of Plays. This Conrad did – his letter was so vituperative that Edward turned censor himself and cut two or three of the more extreme passages – but in a letter to Edward accompanying a draft of the *Daily Mail* missive, Conrad fired what was in effect a warning shot about Edward's perceived Russophilia. After claiming that Edward's own letter about censorship was not much to the point, Conrad continues:

You remember always that I am a Slav (it's your *idée fixe*) but you seem to forget that I am a Pole. You forget that we have been used to go to battle without illusions ... We have been 'going in' these last hundred years repeatedly, to be knocked on the head only – as was visible to any calm intellect. But you have been learning your history from Russians no doubt.[6]

Although Conrad tries to affect a light-hearted tone – 'Never mind. I won't say more or you'll call it a mutiny and shoot me with some nasty preface perhaps.' – the sarcasm is thinly disguised and the underlying exasperation clear to see. Edward either didn't see it or didn't want to.

Conrad's instinctive hatred of all things Russian is understandable. He was born in what is now Ukraine, but was then a region of Poland governed by the Russian Empire. Apollo Korzeniowski, Conrad's father, was a poet, playwright and translator, but he was principally famed as a political agitator. In 1861 Korzeniowski was charged with a range of 'unpatriotic crimes' by the Russian authorities. He and his co-accused wife Ewa were exiled to Vologda in the north-west of the Russian Empire, a common destination for dissidents, sometimes referred to as 'Siberia close to the capital'. Their four-year-old son accompanied them. Ewa's health rapidly deteriorated and she died in 1865 at the age of thirty-two; her husband outlived her by only four years. Russian-imposed exile had thus deprived the eleven-year-old Conrad of both his parents, their lives sacrificed for a cause he came increasingly to regard as noble, but ultimately self-destructive and hopeless.

Conrad always denied that he had ever spoken or understood Russian and he went out of his way to avoid meeting Russians. When in 1899 he was asked by Cunninghame Graham to join him on the platform of an anti-Tsarist meeting of pacifists organised by the Social Democratic Federation, the response was implacable: 'The platform! I pensez-Vous? Il y aura des Russes. Impossible.'[7] The only Russian writer Conrad rated was the Europeanised Turgenev, although he later admitted to a luke-warm admiration of Chekhov; the mere mention of Dostoevsky was guaranteed to send him into paroxysms of rage. Edward was aware of Conrad's history and his Russophobia, yet he continued to allude to his friend's 'Slavic' qualities and inheritance in his reviews. It was Conrad's unflinching scrutiny of man's moral and intellectual frailties and his exploration of the darker depths of psychology that Edward considered characteristically 'Slavic' – a word he and Conrad both inaccurately regarded as synonymous with 'Russian'. Edward's motives for harping on Conrad's 'slavonism', however, may have been commercial as well as aesthetic. Investing Conrad with an exotic, 'oriental' charisma was one way of marketing his work – and it should not be forgotten either that – with Constance producing a steady stream of translations – Edward had a personal stake in keeping Russian literature to the forefront of the public mind.

In 1908 Conrad published a collection of short stories, *A Set of Six*. Amongst the reviews was one by Robert Lynd, the Irish essayist and writer and future literary editor of the *Daily News*. The opening line – 'Mr Conrad, as everybody knows, is a Pole, who writes English by choice, as it were, rather than by nature'[8] – was not promising, but a good deal worse was to follow. Lynd goes on to compare Conrad unfavourably with Turgenev and suggests that he would have done better to have written the stories in Polish and then employed Constance as his translator (unaware or conveniently forgetting that she didn't know the language). Conrad exploded with fury: 'The ... Dly News genius claims that my novels would have been much better if translated by Mrs Garnett,' he fumes in a letter to Galsworthy. 'That's an idea. Shall I send her the clean type of Razumov [the preliminary title of *Under Western Eyes*]. But why complicate life to that extent? She ought to write them.'[9] There is a sense that his exasperation is directed as much against the Russophile Garnetts as it is against Lynd. The reference to 'Razumov' is significant; Conrad had been working on it throughout 1908 and at the end of July, the month before the furore over *A Set of Six*, Conrad told his agent J. B. Pinker that he was expecting Edward that evening 'to have a look at the MS of *Raz[umov]* as the subject interests him greatly'.[10] This is hardly surprising, given that *Under Western Eyes* is the story of a young Russian student, Kyrilo Razumov, who inadvertently becomes involved in Russian revolutionary politics: indeed, it has been convincingly argued that Conrad modelled several of the novel's characters on the Garnetts' émigré friends and Stepniak in particular.[11] Even though it was a further three years before *Under Western Eyes* was published, Edward may well have seen at an early stage that Conrad's portrait of Russian political exiles was likely to be anything but positive.

Conrad finally finished the first draft of *Under Western Eyes* at the end of January 1910 and immediately suffered a nervous breakdown, during which he conversed with characters in the novel in Polish and muttered the words of the service for burial at sea. He had been under tremendous pressure to finish the novel, which over the previous two years he had promised and repeatedly failed to deliver to the remarkably patient J. B. Pinker, to whom he owed large sums of money. On 27 January, three days before his complete collapse, Conrad had a furious row with Pinker in London. This led to an estrangement that lasted until the autumn of 1911, during which time Edward's brother Robert took over as Conrad's agent. The confrontation with Pinker may have triggered Conrad's subsequent prostration, but the signs of an impending crisis had been evident well before then and the psychological strain involved

Richard Garnett, Edward's
father, Keeper of Printed
Books at the British Museum,
prominent man of letters,
astrologer and lover of cats

Olivia ('Narney') Garnett.
Edward was very proud of his
mother's Anglo-Irish origins

Edward, aged eleven, 1879

Edward, the young cricketer, *c.* 1882

Olive Garnett, diarist and Edward's favourite sister

Arthur Garnett, Edward's younger brother. According to his niece, 'All the Garnetts had a talent for friendship, in Arthur it amounted to genius'

Edward by
the study fire
at The Cearne

The Cearne, near Limpsfield
in Kent. Edward and Constance
built the house in 1895

Constance and
David in the porch
at The Cearne

David and Edward (far left) and Nellie Heath (far right) with family friends

(*Left*) Nellie Heath, c. 1895
(*Above*) Edward in uniform, 1915

(*Top left*) Sergey and Fanny
Stepniak outside their cottage
in Limpsfield, 1895
(*Top right*) Ford Madox Ford
in 1915
(*Above*) Joseph Conrad in 1904
(*Left*) R. B. Cunninghame Graham
and his mother, Anne Bontine

(*Above*) John Galsworthy
(*Above right*) W. H. Hudson, c. 1905
(*Right*) Edward Thomas in 1900
(*Below right*) D. H. Lawrence in 1913
(*Below*) Stephen Reynolds and Margot in 1912

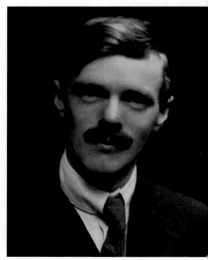

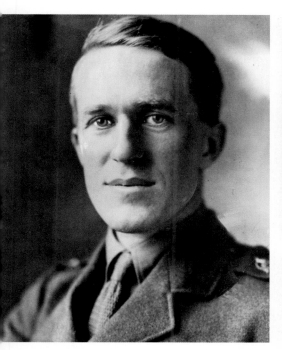

(*Above*) T. E. Lawrence in 1920
(*Above right*) Liam O'Flaherty in 1925
(*Right*) H. E. Bates, c. 1926
(*Below right*) Naomi Mitchison in 1925
(*Below*) Sean O'Faolain, c. 1930

Edward, David and the
young Richard at Hilton

Edward in later years

in confronting the novel's Russian subject matter should not be under-estimated. When Edward paid Conrad a visit in April 1910, possibly to help him cut the manuscript for magazine serialisation, he found his old friend still confined to bed.

The question remains as to why Conrad chose to write about Russia, given his painful family history and his consequent violent antagonism to all things Russian. One of several possibilities may be that he heard a good deal about the exploits of various Russian émigrés through Edward and that this offered the prospect of ready-made material for what he initially envisaged as a short story, to be completed swiftly and published in *A Set of Six*. What is not in question is Conrad's belief that he had captured 'the very essence of things Russian. Not the mere outward manners and customs but the Russian feeling and thought ... The subject has long haunted me. Now it must come out.'[12] This is quite an admission – of a great interest in and familiarity with the Russian psyche, something Conrad habitually fiercely denied, and the extent of the shadow that Russia cast over him. It came in a letter to J. B. Pinker, written at the beginning of 1908 when Conrad still conceived of 'Razumov' as a short story, but there is nothing to suggest that his opinion fundamentally altered as the manuscript grew and evolved into *Under Western Eyes*.

Edward was the obvious choice to review the novel for the *Nation* when it finally appeared in October 1911. As he read it his sense increased that Conrad had poured all his hatred of Russia and her people into *Under Western Eyes*. Although there were parts of the novel he admired, particularly the dramatic scenes, Edward felt that Conrad's portraits of the revolutionaries were animated by his personal rancour and that his use of irony, which had delighted Edward in earlier works, was employed as a blunt weapon of ridicule. '*Not* good: *not* Russian,'[13] he noted disap-provingly in his copy when he came to Sophia Antonovna's report of the letter she has received from St Petersburg; while the meeting between Razumov and Tekla drew the remark: 'A bitter comedy.' Victor Haldin's initial encounter with Razumov, during which he expounds at length on the 'Russian soul', presented Conrad with an irresistible opportunity to mock what he perceived to be the romanticised claptrap surrounding the 'Russian soul' then prevalent in England (a phenomenon from which Edward was not entirely free himself). Haldin's warning to Razumov – '... don't touch the soul. The Russian soul that lives in all of us. It has a future. It has a mission ...' – and similarly, 'don't you forget what's divine in the Russian soul – and that's resignation',[14] prompted a possibly discomforted Edward to comment: 'Haldin's talk not good.'

When it came to the actual *Nation* review, Edward expressed his judgements temperately, praising in particular Conrad's ability to evoke the dark atmosphere of the novel, the pictures of Natalia Haldin and her mother, and the last chapter in which Razumov confesses to Natalia that he has betrayed her brother to the authorities. Although he describes Conrad's sketches of the revolutionaries as 'corrosively bitter'[15] and refers to the potentially 'vindictive art' of the novel, Edward stops short of actually saying it is vindictive. He does not shy away from criticising Conrad's use of irony, indulging in a little of his own by way of riposte: of the fact that Haldin entrusts his life to a relative stranger, Edward sardonically observes – 'but he is a Russian, and after all–!' The review ends with the declaration that many of Conrad's pages 'may be placed by the side of notable passages in Turgenev and Dostoievsky, to both of which great masters Mr Conrad bears affinities and owes a debt'. Conrad would have been gratified by the comparison with Turgenev and steaming mad to have been mentioned in the same sentence as Dostoevsky.

His review was even-handed and has subsequently been praised for its acuity, but Edward was angered and upset by the book itself. The day before the *Nation* article appeared, he wrote to Conrad; unfortunately this letter is lost, but from Conrad's response it appears that in it Edward forcibly expressed his opinion that *Under Western Eyes* was a novel motivated by hatred. 'There's just about as much or as little *hatred* in this book as in the Outcast of the Islands for instance,' Conrad countered:

> Subjects lay [*sic*] about for anybody to pick-up. I have picked up this one. And that's all there is to it. I don't expect you will believe me. You are so russianised my dear that you don't know the truth when you see it – unless it smells of cabbage-soup when it at once secures your profoundest respect. I suppose one must make allowances for your position of Russian Embassador [*sic*] to the Republic of Letters.[16]

The letter is a sustained sarcastic onslaught, which ends with Conrad's acerbic reiteration, 'if hatred there were it would be too big a thing to be put into a 6/- novel. This too might have occurred to you, if you had condescended to look beyond the literary horizon where all things sacred and profane are turned into copy.' Years later Edward laconically referred to the letter as 'sharp',[17] but from thenceforth he cut the 'slavic' references from his articles until after Conrad's death, when they reappeared, suggesting their absence was prompted more by deference to his friend's sensibilities than any real change in Edward's own thinking.

Other reviewers found *Under Western Eyes* gloomy and 'foreign', as did Edward's latest protégé: 'Of course Conrad should always do the beautiful, magical atmospheres. What on earth turned him to Razumov,'[18] wondered D. H. Lawrence.

Lawrence's 'erotic' manuscript arrived back from Heinemann, while its author was recovering from his battle with pneumonia. Now provisionally titled *The Saga of Siegmund*, it was based on Helen Corke's written accounts of her traumatic relationship with her music teacher, Herbert Baldwin Macartney, a married man with whom she spent five days' holiday on the Isle of Wight. On their return, Macartney committed suicide. Buoyed by Edward's encouragement, Lawrence abandoned his resolve to suppress the book and instead set about revising it, using notes Edward had written on the back of the manuscript as reminders. Hueffer's comments were still preying on Lawrence's mind: 'Is Hueffer's opinion worth anything, do you think? Is the book *so* erotic?'[19] he asked Edward anxiously.

Edward's belief in the novel soon began to dispel the clouds cast by Hueffer, and as Lawrence re-wrote, his worries about eroticism evaporated: if anything, some of the recast passages in the novel are more explicit than they were in the original manuscript. This is certainly the case in Chapter 3. The first version reads:

> He covered her with his coats, and crushed her into his breast ...
> Now he strained her savagely to his breast, and she lay there hurt
> and stifled, but very willing <that> death should come that way,
> if it came at all. Siegmund remained perfectly still, his muscles set
> hard, holding Sieglinde. He was conscious of nothing ... It was
> just a burning bush, <flaming> (passionate) relief and joy flaming
> through their tissues.[20]

In the published text, Siegmund puts Helena (as she is now called) 'inside his overcoat':

> [S]he timidly slid her hands along his sides, pressing softly, to find
> the contours of his figure. Softly her hands crept over the silky
> back of his waistcoat, under his coats, and as they stirred, his blood
> flushed up, and up again, with fire, till all Siegmund was hot blood,
> and his breast was one great ache ...

His muscles set hard and unyielding; at that moment he was
a tense, vivid body of flesh, without a mind; his blood, alive and
conscious, running towards her.[21]

Freed from the fear of charges of 'eroticism', Lawrence began to develop
the distinctive language of his later novels; he was, of course, still an
apprentice, and some of Edward's criticisms were those he had oft
repeated to aspiring novices: don't overwrite, avoid laboured metaphors and too many adjectives, make sure dialogue sounds ordinary
and natural, condense and cut. Even after revision Lawrence confessed
that the novel was still 'too florid, too chargé', but adds, 'I must let it
stand.'[22] This was to be a characteristic reaction: once he had reached
a certain point with a book, Lawrence was always looking to move on
to the next project.

The Trespasser, as the novel was eventually called, was published
by Duckworth in May 1912 to reviews that were generally favourable,
although it raised moral outrage in some quarters. Edward tried his
best to put the novel in the path of those he thought would appreciate
it: 'If you can review The Trespasser by DHL do so, or speak to anyone
you know,'[23] he urged Walter de la Mare. 'It is a work of genius.' He
was not alone in his enthusiasm; Rebecca West, reviewing the novel in
the Freewoman, announced 'This book is magic.'[24] She wrote to Edward
shortly after her review appeared, asking him to intervene and send
her a volume of Strindberg's plays, recently published by Duckworth,
which were proving hard to get hold of. Evidently she felt flattery
would win the day: 'I understand you are the soul of Duckworth's,'[25]
she gushed, before informing him that she and Dora Marsden (the
editor of the Freewoman) had moved into 22 Grove Place, the flat
above the Garnetts' – 'so if you find the stairs blocked with vegetarians
and interpreters of sex you will understand'. Edward, no mean flirter
himself, responded by asking both ladies to drop in some time in the
future. 'It gives the editor and the assistant editor [of the Freewoman]
much pleasure to know that wisdom and learning are beneath their
feet,'[26] West responded.

Lawrence had formally resigned from teaching at the end of February
and the appearance of The Trespasser provided him with two essen-
tials: a £50 advance and that vital second novel. Money had been of
no little concern; Edward had loaned him seven guineas in December
and was amazed when Lawrence, always scrupulous in such matters,
paid him back.

Edward had been nurturing Lawrence very carefully, both mentally and physically. When Lawrence went to convalesce in Bournemouth, Edward sent a number of carefully chosen books, including W. H. Hudson's *Nature in Downland*, Turgenev's *Torrents of Spring*, a volume of short stories by Leonidas Andreyev and work by the Nottinghamshire regional writer James Prior Kirk. The selection may well reflect the direction Edward felt Lawrence's writing should take: English provincial subject matter, expressed in prose exhibiting those qualities Edward so admired in the Russians. When Lawrence left Bournemouth he came straight to The Cearne, from where he wrote boldly to Helen Corke, asking her to stay the night: 'You would not mind Garnett,' he told her. 'He is most beautifully free of the world's conventions.'[27] However, Miss Corke refused, horrified at the prospect of 'a casual introduction by night to the house of the unconventional Garnett'.[28] Despite the invitation, Lawrence was moving away from the world of his youth and women like Helen Corke and Louie Burrows. Edward was becoming increasingly important to him in a personal as well as a professional capacity – indeed the two roles were frequently conflated. On 4 February 1912, in what Louie afterwards called 'the dreadful Cearne letter',[29] Lawrence wrote to her, telling her that due to his precarious health, poor financial prospects and an illness which 'has changed me a good deal, has broken a good many of the old bonds that held me',[30] he was terminating their engagement. Three days later, still at The Cearne, he refused Louie's appeal simply to defer it.

Did Edward play any part in Lawrence's decision? Had the illness really changed him or was he increasingly convinced that a nice, conventional girl like Louie didn't quite fit the image of the 'distinctive genius' that Edward had allotted him? If Edward did offer counsel in affairs of the heart it wouldn't have been the first time, nor would it be the last. Certainly, Lawrence's sister Ada noticed a difference in him, as she explained in a consoling letter to his jilted fiancée: 'Its [*sic*] surprising how much changed Bert is since his illness, and changed for the worse too, I think,' she wrote. 'His flippant and really artificial manner gets on my nerves dreadfully.'[31] That manner is strikingly apparent in a letter Lawrence wrote to Edward describing a fraught trip to Nottingham Castle with Louie, where 'over tea and toast, [I] told her for the fourth time'.[32] Such a sentence as 'When she began to giggle, I asked her coolly for the joke: when she began to cry, I wanted a cup of tea' is too perfectly balanced to be anything other than the result of meticulous crafting. The whole account is a performance, the insouciance designed to create the impression of one sophisticated 'man of the world' writing to another.[33] Just over two months later Edward opened another of Lawrence's frequent letters, announcing amongst other things a forthcoming trip to London. The tone could not have been more different:

> Mrs Weekley will be in town also. She is ripping – she's the finest woman I've ever met – you must above all things meet her. Wife of one of my College professors ... she is the daughter of Baron von Richthofen, of the ancient and famous house of Richthofen – but she's splendid, she is really ... Mrs Weekley is perfectly unconventional ... I'll bet you've never met anybody like her, by a long chalk. You *must* see her next week. I wonder if she'd come to the Cearne, if you asked us. Oh but she is the woman of a lifetime.[34]

Edward may well have been amused to see how the measured cadences of the letter about the Nottingham expedition with Louie had been replaced by the breathless, scrambled sentences of this one. He would also have been more than intrigued at the prospect of meeting the woman who had effected such a transformation. The invitation to The Cearne was duly issued and on 27 April Lawrence and Frieda Weekley arrived.

Frieda was six years older than Lawrence and had been married to Ernest Weekley, Professor of Modern Languages at Nottingham University, for thirteen years; they had a son and two daughters, ranging in age from twelve to eight. Spontaneous, direct and extraordinarily attractive to men, Frieda had had several affairs before she met Lawrence. According to David Garnett, Frieda carried herself like the German aristocrat she was: 'Her head and the whole carriage of her body were noble,' he recalls. 'Her eyes were green, with a lot of tawny yellow in them, the nose straight. She looked one dead in the eyes, fearlessly judging one and, at that moment, she was extraordinarily like a lioness.'[35] Lawrence didn't stand a chance. When he and Frieda first met in Weekley's drawing room in early March 1912, the attraction was mutual and irresistible. Towards the end of April, however, Lawrence reported to Edward that things were 'getting difficult'.[36] 'Are you *quite* sure you would like her and me to come to your house?' he continued anxiously, seemingly forgetting that he was addressing the man 'beautifully free of the world's conventions'. The couple spent the weekend at The Cearne; Lawrence brought with him the manuscript of his 'colliery novel' *Paul Morel*, parts of which Edward may have read. If at times he wondered where his guests had disappeared to he would have discovered them beyond the beech hedge on the bluebell-covered bank below the orchard, Frieda sitting on a trestle with Lawrence on the ground at her side, a scene Lawrence recreates in his poem 'At the Cearne'.

No sooner had they left than a letter arrived from Lawrence asking Edward what he thought of Frieda: 'I'm afraid of you suddenly donning a cassock of a monk, and speaking out of the hood. Don't sound wise, and old, and – "When you've lived as long as I have" sort of thing.'[37] Edward, who viewed the situation with sardonic amusement, referred to Lawrence and Frieda 'making history',[38] and watched the rapidly unfolding events with more than a little relish. If he had known quite how much work Lawrence's and Frieda's history-making was about to create he may well have wished he had reached for the cassock after all – not that he was in any position to do so, as he was increasingly coming under the spell of a woman who was in her own way as magnetic a personality as Frieda Weekley.

Six-thirty on an evening in the middle of March and jostling pedestrians fill the streets round London's Leicester Square, some on their way home from work, others setting out to savour the delights of the capital's night-life. Standing at the entrance to the Tube station is a twenty-six-year-old Russian woman. Dark-haired, with a regular profile and rather inscrutable features, she is formidably intelligent, having arrived in London in 1906 to complete her studies at University College, London, from which she emerged with a first-class degree in Philosophy. Her mind is for the moment occupied with matters prosaic as she scrutinises the passers-by, until the familiar tall, long-striding figure appears from the direction of Garrick Street. After their initial greeting, the pair depart to a café for supper, followed by an evening at the theatre or music hall. 'I need the tonic,' Edward had written in a letter suggesting the rendezvous. 'It's good for me, you know, as well as for you. And you administer it so nicely too.'[39]

The dispenser of the elixir was Natalie Ertel, the elder daughter of the family that Constance and David had stayed with on their visit to Russia in 1904; and if there were questions as to what Constance and Nellie would have made of Natalie's evening out with Edward, the same could be said about the man she was shortly to marry. Natalie had gone to stay with the Rev. John Nightingale Duddington, his wife Elizabeth and daughter Iris very shortly after her arrival in England; having accepted the invitation from Duddington, a fellow Theosophist who had recently been appointed rector of Ayot St Lawrence. (The Duddingtons soon moved out of the newly built rectory to a more convenient house; the rectory was subsequently let to George Bernard Shaw and thereafter became famous as Shaw's Corner.) Ursula Cox, who lived in Russia and knew the Ertels very well, once told Constance that she had 'an unbounded admiration for Tata' [Natalie] and that when she spoke 'her magnetic personality mesmerizes me into doing anything that she tells me to, and what's more into feeling an intense desire to do it'.[40] Clearly she had just as powerful an effect on the Rev. Duddington. In 1907, around the time of her twenty-first birthday, Natalie wrote to her father telling him of their plans to live together. Duddington had to leave the church (he later became secretary and some-time curator of the Whitechapel Art Gallery) and in 1911 he divorced his wife, marrying Natalie a year later.

Constance was keen to return the hospitality she had received in Russia and to resume her friendship with Natasha, as the Garnetts always called Natalie. Eventually she would take over from Juliet Soskice (Ford's sister) as Constance's amanuensis. Both women had powerful intellects and shared a deep love of Russian literature, but their views on religion (Natalie was a devout Orthodox), politics and much else besides were poles apart. Despite this, Constance became extremely fond of Natalie, while Edward began to experience similar feelings to those of Constance years before when in the company of a charismatic Russian. Natalie for her part considered Edward 'an enchanting man',[41] later describing him as 'exceptionally fascinating ... kind, generous, and with an amazingly "light touch" – an ability to respond to the most unexpected situation lightly, wittily and cheerfully'.[42] Edward was rather more complex than Natalie indicates – she says nothing about the melancholic streak that ran through his character – but the enchantment increasingly became mutual.

At some point, although exactly when is unclear, they became lovers.[43] Edward's letters to Natalie are extremely cryptic and hers to him have not survived. This in itself is remarkable, as Edward was an assiduous preserver of letters; either he destroyed them because he was afraid they might be discovered by Constance or Nellie, or somebody else (possibly David) did so after his death. A reference in one of Edward's letters to them sitting 'on the Cearne gate in the moonlight and w[aking] up Connie in the year 1912'[44] suggests that by then the intimacy was growing and that in the spring and summer of that year it was not just Lawrence and Frieda who were enjoying the romantic landscape of The Cearne.

Less than a week after their own visit to Limpsfield, Lawrence and Frieda left the country. Lawrence had mentioned to Edward that Frieda was going to Germany for celebrations to mark her father's fifty years in the Prussian army and that he had decided to accompany her, as it would give them the opportunity of spending a week together. Initially both intended to return to England – contrary to popular legend, they did not elope – but Frieda had failed to carry out one vital part of the plan. In the letter asking Edward's opinion of Frieda, Lawrence had told him that she was going to inform her husband of their relationship that very day; Frieda, however, kept silent. Lawrence, by now in Germany and desperate to marry her and put an end to the 'subterfuge, lying, dirt, fear'[45] wrote to Weekley, telling him everything, thereby bringing a storm over their heads and exposing Frieda to the possibility of being sued for divorce and losing access to her children.

Lawrence and Frieda could almost hear the sound of slamming doors from across the North Sea; practically, the only one that stayed open was that of The Cearne. 'Frieda sort of clings to the idea of you, as the only man in England who would be a refuge,'[46] Lawrence told Edward, who was extremely busy at the time, finding outlets for Lawrence's stories and also preparing for the performance of one of his own plays, *The Spanish Lovers*, an adaptation of *La Celestina*, a novel composed entirely of dialogue by the fifteenth-century Spanish writer Fernando de Rojas. Ben Iden Payne and his wife Mona Limerick played the principal parts, but the drama, which was staged at the Little Theatre just off the Strand, was a critical and financial disaster: 'at the very worst I never reckoned on £3 and £4 houses as a possibility',[47] a worried Payne confessed to Edward, who had earlier tried to interest him in one of Lawrence's plays. The abysmal reception of *The Spanish Lovers* hit Edward hard: Lawrence sent his condolences from Bavaria, along with the news that he was sending 'the colliery novel' to Heinemann, adding 'it's rather great',[48] a view he repeated to the firm's reader Walter de la Mare in a letter informing him that the manuscript was on its way. Lawrence could, however, see possible trouble ahead, both over the loose form of the novel – 'It's not so strongly concentric as the fashionable folk under French influence – you see I suffered badly from Hueffer re Flaubert and perfection – want it'[49] – he explained, and on account of its length. Even at this early stage Lawrence was prepared for editorial intervention and offered to cut the childhood part if de la Mare wished. What he was not prepared for was outright rejection, which came in the form of a letter from Heinemann himself in which he criticised the manuscript for its lack of unity and the failure of the characters to engage the reader's sympathy. He concluded by telling Lawrence that 'its want of reticence makes it unfit, I fear, altogether for publication in England as things are'.[50]

'Duckworth tells me that Heinemann tells him that he (H) has returned Lawrence's new novel as far too indecent!'[51] Edward wrote to de la Mare on hearing the news. 'This sounds very queer to me – in fact absurd. To what address did the novel go back? I am anxious to get hold of it.' When he sent the address, de la Mare confirmed that Heinemann was fearful that the novel would be banned by the libraries and that even apart from this, he himself didn't 'feel that the book as a whole comes up to Lawrence's real mark. It seems to me to need pulling together: it is not of a piece. But the real theme of the story is not arrived at till half way through.' Despite these criticisms, de la Mare conceded: 'The best in it is of course extraordinarily good.'[52] The day after writing to de la Mare, Edward received a letter from a desperate and furious Lawrence in Germany. Weekley was demanding that his wife return to England; Frieda, torn apart after hearing how the children were missing her, had gone to stay with her sister, leaving Lawrence distraught and thinking about banging his head against a wall for relief. On top of all this he had just received the letter from Heinemann informing him of the rejection of *Paul Morel*. This brought forth a torrent of invective against the 'blasted, jelly-boned swines, the slimy, the belly-wringing invertebrates, the miserable sodding rotters, the flaming sods, the snivelling, dribbling, dithering palsied pulse-less lot that make up England today'.[53] Edward's letter, asking for the manuscript of *Paul Morel*, arrived almost immediately after Lawrence had poured out his woes. He sent the novel to Edward at once, with a note promising, 'Anything that wants altering I will do',[54] and at the time he wrote those words he probably meant what he said.

'My friend and protector in love and literature'

As Edward read *Paul Morel* he must have had a sense of déjà vu; many of the faults of *The Trespasser* were evident in the new manuscript. Once again Edward criticised Lawrence's recondite tendencies: '"one of Circe's erect swine" *no*', 'too literary'. He was also unconvinced by some of the dialogue: 'affected conversation rewrite'; 'all this talk doesn't ring true,' he notes.[1] *Paul Morel* (and *Sons and Lovers*, the novel it eventually became) is highly autobiographical; the Morel family and the events that take place are closely modelled on Lawrence's own experiences, and Edward accused him of failing to treat his material with the detachment of the deliberate artist. 'You are insensibly making Paul too much of a hero,' he complains, and 'This seems cheap: you identify your sympathies too much with Paul's wrath.'[2] The manuscript was back in Germany with Edward's notes less than three weeks after Lawrence had sent it. Lawrence responded enthusiastically and promised to 'slave like a Turk at the novel ... I begin in earnest tomorrow.'[3]

At the end of July David Garnett, by now studying botany at the Imperial College of Science, was in Munich attending some lectures. At Edward's suggestion he contacted Lawrence and went to stay with him and Frieda in Icking. 'He's awfully like you ... his walk, his touch of mischief and wickedness ... But he hasn't got your appetite for tragedy with the bleeding brow,'[4] Lawrence reported, before adding that he and Frieda had decided to walk away from their troubles over the Alps into Switzerland. At the end of the letter he casually mentions that he has decided to rewrite *Paul Morel* and that it will take him three months. As usual, money was a pressing problem and once again Lawrence looked to Edward for assistance in placing sketches and poetry: 'I *must* hear from you or of you,' he frets.[5]

Edward and Nellie had been on holiday in Wales, which explained his recent silence; he was also preoccupied with finding another London flat. Constance, who did most of the hunting, eventually recommended one very close to Grove Place: 4 Downshire Hill was a 'nice little old house'.[6] It had the advantage of being very quiet and very cheap (£42 10/- a year) and the disadvantage of being 'a bit grubby and dilapidated' and having a very small bathroom and kitchen. Constance was won over by the charm of the place and they took possession of it in September.

While Edward was on the move in London, Lawrence and Frieda were finally settling for a while near the shores of Lake Garda. Lawrence was immensely relieved when £50 arrived from Duckworth to ease his financial anxieties: 'It seems queer, that while I am straying about here, you are working like a fiend, and hampered with my stuff as well,' Lawrence remarks, before trying to persuade Edward to come out and stay for a while: 'I should love to talk to you – for hours and hours. I feel as if you were father and brother and all my relations to me – except wife,'[7] he confessed, promising that now his life was less itinerant he would really 'get at that novel'.

Only a few preparatory jottings of the notes Edward made survive, and little of what was Lawrence's third version of *Paul Morel* does either, but from the scraps of Edward's comments that remain and from the parts of the manuscript that Lawrence incorporated into what became *Sons and Lovers* it seems that he revised with Edward's notes at his elbow and his words ringing in his ears. When Edward came to the following passage, referring to Paul's assessment of his relationship with Miriam –

Now at last, since she denied that their love had ever been love at all, <at l> [*sic*] he was severed from her. She had spoken the historical phrase to him, as he to her when he said:
    'You are a nun.'
    He sat silent in bitterness. At last, the whole affair looked like a cynicism to him.[8]

– he underlined 'like a cynicism' and in his notes remarked 'like a cynicism *lurid*'.[9] Lawrence revised this to: 'He sat silent in bitterness. At last, the whole affair appeared in a cynical aspect to him.'[10] The rewritten phrase is less melodramatic and there is that sense of greater distance between the narrator and his subject that Edward had demanded. His influence may also be detected in the fact that the final manuscript contains several instances of Lawrence replacing authorial exposition with dramatic exchanges. A protracted analysis of the Morels' mutual irritability in Chapter 1 of the third draft is replaced in the manuscript by the scene in which Mrs Morel struggles with the boiling herb beer as Morel enters, drunk. Edward doubtless preached the same sermon he was to deliver to H. E. Bates ten years later: 'You've got to *visualise* and express the emotions by sharp *individual* details.'[11] The boiling cauldron does this to perfection. Lawrence rewrote rapidly; halfway through October Edward learned that he was three-fifths through the revision and wanted to change the title to *Sons and Lovers*, thus further diluting the earlier concentration on Paul. The new title also acknowledges William Morel's increased role in the novel and the incestuous element in Paul's relationship with his mother.

When the post brought an envelope addressed in Lawrence's hand, Edward could be sure that, whatever else, the contents would not be dull. The letter might detail news of the latest 'bowel-twisting'[12] missives from Weekley; agonised or amusing accounts of Lawrence's and Frieda's evolving relationship; or evocative descriptions of the landscape, people and customs of their latest surroundings. Literary business, of course, featured prominently – instructions and appeals about dealing with publishers, the selling and placement of sketches and the selection and ordering of a volume of poetry, which Duckworth published the following year under the title *Love Poems and Others*. Towards the end of November another letter bearing an Italian postmark arrived at The Cearne. As he scanned the opening lines, Edward realised that this was in a very different key:

> Your letter has just come. I hasten to tell you I sent the MS of the Paul Morel novel to Duckworth, registered, yesterday. And I want to defend it, quick. I wrote it again, pruning it and shaping it and filling it in. I tell you it has got form – *form*: haven't I made it patiently, out of sweat as well as blood.[13]

This was not a case of merely alerting Edward when to expect the novel: Lawrence is telling him how to read it. His anxious insistence that the novel had 'form' and his subsequent outline of its main theme and development owed much to the berating he had received from Hueffer about 'formlessness', which had clearly affected him profoundly. In her memoir, Helen Corke recalls Lawrence bringing her the novels of Flaubert and Maupassant to read: 'His talk was of literature for art's sake, of the essential of *form* in writing – it might have been a resumé of the lectures received from his mentor Ford Madox Hueffer.'[14] Heinemann's remarks explaining his rejection of *Paul Morel* may also have been echoing in Lawrence's mind. The vocabulary of the letter is calculated to convince Edward that this is a carefully crafted piece of work, shorn of superfluity. Lawrence was also worried that the 'naked scenes' in the novel weren't tame enough and told Edward that he could cut them if he wished. Yet for all his edgy defensiveness, Lawrence was convinced he had written a great book and that he wanted to dedicate it to Edward: 'To Edward Garnett, in Gratitude,' he suggested. 'But you can put it better.'[15]

Edward was far too independent a reader to be influenced by Lawrence's manifesto; he read the manuscript as soon as it arrived and it immediately became apparent that at close on 180,000 words the novel was too long for a 7/6- volume, which was usually around 120,000 words in length. After speaking to Gerald Duckworth, Edward wrote to Lawrence, relaying the excellent news that the publisher was prepared to pay a £100 advance, with a 15 per cent royalty on the first 2,500 copies and 17.5 per cent thereafter, and the considerably less welcome tidings that the manuscript would have to be cut and the scalpel would be in Edward's rather than Lawrence's hands. Lawrence would see the result of the surgery only when he was sent the proofs for correction. Two questions arise: were the cuts made purely on commercial grounds and did Edward decide he was going to make them without further reference to Lawrence unilaterally, or was he ordered to do so by Gerald Duckworth?

In the absence of Edward's side of the correspondence, it is impossible to arrive at definitive answers, but it is highly unlikely that he would have reduced the text by approximately a tenth on aesthetic grounds alone. The fact that there is a running word count on the edited manuscript further suggests that Edward was primarily motivated by the necessity to reduce the novel's length. Lawrence's peripatetic existence and the consequent risk of the manuscript getting delayed or lost may have persuaded Duckworth that it was far simpler and less time-consuming to get Edward to do the editing. Certainly, Lawrence's apology – 'I'm sorry I've let you in for such a job'[16] – suggests the decision was Duckworth's. Lawrence's reaction would have come as no surprise to Edward: 'I sit in sadness and grief after your letter. I daren't say anything. All right, take out what you think necessary ... but don't scold me too hard, it makes me wither up.'[17] Evidently Edward's letter had contained a 'wigging', but whether it was because Lawrence had failed to heed his mentor's aesthetic advice or that an overworked Edward was simply fed up at having to undertake a tricky editorial task it is impossible to say.

Reducing a manuscript by a tenth whilst preserving its fluency and coherence and without having to write bridging sections is not an easy job. Edward removed a total of 80 passages varying in length from 2 to 185 lines; most of the material he cut was from the first 11 chapters of the novel. Chapter 3, which describes the life of William Morel, is the most heavily edited. Edward deleted what he considered to be extraneous and repetitious dialogue, such as a conversation between William and his mother, which essentially repeats a scene in which a disapproving Mrs Morel interviews a girl who has called to see William, and the account of William's anger at his mother's action. Some of the material Edward eliminated resulted in situations becoming more implicit – 'showing' rather than 'telling'. An example of this occurs towards the end of Chapter 10, when Paul and Clara are discussing her treatment of Baxter Dawes. Edward cut thirteen lines of expository dialogue in which Paul suggests Clara 'broke [Dawes's] manliness' and accuses her of adopting a superior attitude towards Dawes and himself. The edited version is much more subtly suggestive:

' . . . But weren't you horrid with him? Didn't you do something that knocked him to pieces?'
  'What, pray?'
  'Make him feel as if he were nothing – *I* know,' Paul declared.[18]

Lawrence soon recovered his spirits: by the end of December he was writing gratefully to Edward: 'I'm glad to hear you like the novel better. I don't much mind what you squash out . . . I'm glad you'll let it be dedicated to you. I feel always so deep in your debt.'[19] Edward certainly was proud to have his name associated with *Sons and Lovers*: the day before it was published he wrote to de la Mare, perhaps a shade triumphantly, telling him: 'Lawrence rewrote his novel almost from beginning to end – and I think it is now quite as good as many of Hardy's.'[20]

Sons and Lovers, edited by Edward, was published on 29 May 1913 and for seventy-nine years this was the version available to readers. In 1992 Cambridge University Press published a text that restored the cuts made to the book, along with an introductory essay by Helen and Carl Baron in which they argue that Edward damaged Lawrence's novel. In another essay, Helen Baron goes so far as to describe the 1913 version as 'botched, censored, and butchered'.[21] The judgement seems harsh: an argument can be made that in fact Edward forced Lawrence to hone his narrative craft. For example, the passage when Miriam bends 'short-sightedly over [Paul's rose-design] drawings',[22] which Baron presents as an example of Edward's deleterious effect on the novel, is rather an excellent illustration of the positive effect his editing had on Lawrence's writing. Edward cut twenty lines of authorial exposition concerning the theory of gravitation, Miriam's compulsion to know what it is in the drawing that fascinates Paul, and the latter's feeling that he has to justify himself. When correcting the proofs Lawrence substituted the following line for the deleted passage: 'It irritated him that she peered so into everything that was his, searching him out.'[23] Those few words encapsulate Paul's resentment of what he perceives as Miriam's desire to possess him, the characteristic she shares with Mrs Morel. The juxtaposition of 'peering' with the reference to Miriam's short sight in the previous sentence also creates a richly suggestive allusion. As for censorship, predictably Edward exercised a very light hand; one passage he allowed to stand, in which Paul dons a pair of Clara's stockings, was later removed by somebody else at the publisher's, possibly Gerald Duckworth himself.

On 12 January 1913 Lawrence sent Edward a letter that sums up his attitude to Edward's editing and suggests that it actually liberated Lawrence creatively:

> The thought of you pedgilling away at the novel frets me. Why can't I do those things? – I can't. I could do hack work, to a certain amount. But apply my creative self where it doesn't want to be applied, makes me feel I should bust or go cracked. I *couldn't* have done any more at that novel – at least for six months. I must go on producing, producing, and the stuff must come more and more to shape each year. But trim and garnish my stuff I cannot – it *must* go.[24]

By assuming the responsibility of editing *Sons and Lovers* (and it is worth remembering that there is a real possibility the unedited novel might not have been published at all) Edward freed Lawrence and allowed him to follow that compulsive urge to 'go on producing'. As Lawrence put it in a letter to his friend Ernest Collings: 'I am a great admirer of my own stuff while it's new, but after a while I'm not so gone on it – like the true maternal instinct, that kicks off an offspring as soon as it can go on its own legs.'[25] There is a great sense that despite his initial dismay, in the end Lawrence was happy to move on and leave *Sons and Lovers* to 'go on its own legs' with Edward. Having corrected the first batch of proofs, Lawrence expressed his general satisfaction: 'It goes well, in print, don't you think? ... You did the pruning jolly well, and I am grateful. I hope you'll live a long time, to barber up my novels for me before they're published.'[26] Years later, when recalling his relationship with Edward, Lawrence declared, 'Garnett did a great deal for me ... He was a good friend and a fine editor.'[27] Words that hardly suggest he considered Edward had butchered his novel.

Lawrence reiterated his gratitude when he inscribed Edward's copy of Sons and Lovers, warmly acknowledging the support he had received during one of the most turbulent and momentous periods of his life: 'To my friend and protector in love and literature Edward Garnett from the Author.'[28] Edward's protection extended to defending Lawrence from attacks by other friends and family. 'It's not good enough to spend time and ink in describing the penultimate sensations and physical movements of people getting into a state of rut; we all know them too well,'[29] complained Galsworthy, while Hudson judged Sons and Lovers 'A very good book indeed except in that portion where he relapses into the old sty – the neck-sucking and wallowing in sweating flesh.'[30] Olive Garnett later declared that she couldn't read Lawrence's novels with pleasure and pronounced him 'a mixture of miner's boy and pagan fawn – impossible to live with; I think I sh[ou]ld have disliked him and his German wife very much ... What a gulf between him and Galsworthy! ... and both were your intimate friends!'[31]

As the tug of war between Frieda and Weekley over divorce and the future of their children intensified, Lawrence became increasingly reliant on his 'friend and protector' in England. At times Edward must have wondered exactly what he had taken on:

> Do you know a lawyer you could send us to about this matter of Frieda's ... Then there is the matter of Frieda's having any legal right to the children after the divorce. Do you know something about that? She ought, I suppose to be represented when the case comes on, and the request made for her share in the children? Can you tell me anything about it, and what to do?[32]

Edward recommended his brother Robert as Frieda's solicitor, while Arthur Garnett was detailed to investigate possible cottages the couple could rent on a proposed trip to England. Constance kept Lawrence's money in her own bank account and forwarded it as required; Edward's sister-in-law and nephew, Katharine and Douglas Clayton, typed manuscripts, while Edward himself continued to arrange Lawrence's literary business in England and sent out books, reviews and professional and personal advice. 'I should think you find me a bit of a burden on your hands,'[33] Lawrence admitted after revealing plans to travel to England and announcing, 'We shall come to the Cearne. It is the only place in England open to the pair of us.'

He and Frieda stayed with Constance and David in the third week of June; Edward was detained in London. Constance had been on tenterhooks, not because she expected Weekley to appear at any moment to try and shoot Lawrence, as Frieda predicted, but on account of the couple's volatile relationship. However, she was able to report to Edward that they had had 'a peaceful time. Lawrence is very sweet – he is a nice person in the house – and F[rieda] rather trying. She won't let things drop. L has been helping me by thinning the carrots.'[34] Constance, ever the peacemaker, was only too aware of Edward's penchant for mischiefmaking: 'L and F are in a peaceful and cheerful mood for the minute,' she warned, 'so don't upset them by talking of their mutual relations or they'll be at [it] hammer and tongs again.'[35]

Lawrence was right in conjecturing that Edward was finding sole and unpaid responsibility for his literary affairs increasingly onerous. In June 1913 he wrote to the agent J. B. Pinker, asking him if he would like to place 'some brilliant stories by Lawrence in America or elsewhere',[36] and followed this up a month later with a shrewd letter enclosing the story 'Honour and Arms' (later re-titled 'The Prussian Officer') and the promise of future riches: 'This study of German soldier life in my opinion is as good as Stephen Crane's best. In fact, Crane and Conrad are the only two writers to be named in conjunction with this remarkable piece of psychological genius. If you succeed with this there will be others to follow.'[37] Pinker took the bait.

Edward had had less luck earlier when he tried to persuade the Century's editor Robert Johnson of Lawrence's potential: 'I have now in my possession another remarkable story ... "The Right Thing to Do",' he wrote. 'I am convinced that Mr Lawrence has a distinguished future before him, but of course he may be too original for the big public's taste.'[38] Although he had been acting as the Century's English representative for only six months, Edward could already predict the likely response to work from writers he considered amongst England's best. He had persistently tried to get the American magazine to take some pieces by Edward Thomas, and Johnson had just as persistently resisted.

Edward had seen quite a bit of Thomas in the summer of 1911 and knew he was suffering particularly badly from tiredness and depression. At the beginning of the year Edward and Thomas had successfully campaigned for a Royal Literary Fund pension for the Welsh poet W. H. Davies, a noble effort, as Thomas himself was quite as financially harassed as Davies, and he longed for the time to write that Davies now enjoyed. In the early autumn Thomas mooted the idea of a sailing trip round the Mediterranean and writing a book or series of articles about it. Edward was enthusiastic, approached Duckworth and enlisted the help of one of the Mont Blanc regulars, Perceval Gibbon, who had been in the merchant navy. At the beginning of October Thomas pulled the plug on the scheme, telling Edward that he could not face the prospect of being 'thrown with new people'[39]; by the end of the month he was in the grip of a paralysing melancholy.

Edward once more came up with active advice. He regularly went to Wales on holiday with Nellie and told Thomas about Laugharne, the romantically situated old town on the Carmarthenshire coast (now best known for its associations with Dylan Thomas, who is buried there); by the beginning of November Thomas was installed in lodgings near the ferry. Edward had great belief in the restorative power of ancestral lands, but he also offered Thomas more practical balm and proposed sending him Sanatogen tonic wine and a camera. Thomas refused the Sanatogen, but was enthusiastic about the camera, which he felt would enable him to obtain 'vivid notes of places and [help] me to place articles and books'.[40] Cut off from London and 'immersed in [George] Borrow [the latest book he was writing] and my grievances',[41] Thomas asked Edward to look out for work for him and to rack his brains and tell Thomas 'of some celebrated monarch, poet, prostitute or other hero that I can write a book about. My own list includes none that publishers will look at.'[42] Edward, who had previously proposed in vain that Thomas write about Shakespeare's country, cajoled editors into sending him books to review, but his idea that Thomas stay at Laugharne may have been his most valuable suggestion. Just under a year later, Thomas told Edward that he had finished the first draft 'of a very loose fiction focussed on early memories of a remarkable Welsh household in London 20 years ago ... I wrote it to prove (to myself) that I could do something without being told to and on a fairly large scale.'[43] This was The Happy-Go-Lucky Morgans, a semi-autobiographical 'novel' (Thomas insisted that the book was more than a series of connected sketches) about a Welsh family living in Abercorran Street, Balham, the area of London a few streets north of where Thomas himself grew up. Before the Civil War, Laugharne was called Abercorran and Thomas drew on his time there when writing about the Welsh town to which the Morgans eventually return.

Thomas sent Edward the manuscript, worried that he had failed in his attempt to write something that was more than a collection of related essays. 'Is the thread too slender – too impudent?' he asked. 'Do you even perceive a thread?'[44] Edward liked the book, which was published by Duckworth in November 1913, praising its 'wistful, sensitive charm in atmosphere and characterization'.[45] His attention would have been caught by the chapter entitled 'Aurelius the Superfluous Man', with its allusion to Turgenev's *Diary of a Superfluous Man*, which Constance had translated in 1899. Thomas's definition of the 'superfluous' – 'those who cannot find society with which they are in some sort of harmony. The magic circle drawn round us all at birth surrounds these in such a way that it will never overlap, far less become concentric with the circles of any other in the whirling multitudes'[46] – may have given Edward pause to reflect the extent to which Thomas identified with the condition he describes. Edward's own aversion to the 'whirling multitudes' may have made him wonder if there wasn't a streak of superfluity in his make-up too. *The Happy-Go-Lucky Morgans* is free from the ornate, 'affected' prose that Edward detected in Thomas's earlier work; the whiff of the lamp does not linger. This didn't result in it selling any better than Thomas's previous non-commercial prose books, however. After correctly predicting that the public would not be in the least interested in it, W. H. Hudson told Edward: '[Thomas] is essentially a poet, one would say of the Celtic variety and this book shows it, I think more than any of the others.'[47] Hudson believed that Thomas should pluck up the courage 'to follow his own genius', but he was preaching to the converted: Edward had told Thomas he was a poet five years earlier. However, a further remark of Hudson's – 'You may say that no one can live by writing poetry' – suggests that if Edward was reticent in encouraging Thomas to follow the poetic path it was because he was acutely aware that Thomas's perilous financial situation had the potential to devastate his well-being. Yet despite its poor sales and structural shortcomings, *The Happy-Go-Lucky Morgans* was an important book for Thomas, marking a new direction in his writing.

In March 1913 Edward received a letter from Dillybrook Farm near Bath. Thomas was cycling from London to the Quantocks and writing an account of the journey for his latest book. 'I am ... using your camera freely and much more successfully,' he reports, 'and I hope to illustrate the book I am doing on my journey.'[48] *In Pursuit of Spring* was eventually published in April 1914, illustrated by Ernest Haslehurst. It was reviewed by Edward in the *Manchester Guardian*. The opening lines are as much an attempt to fix Thomas's evasive personality as they are a critique of the book:

> It was a happy thought of the publishers to send Mr Edward Thomas a-journeying from London to the Quantock Hills one Eastertide in search of spring, for Mr Thomas, with his elusive temperament, clear-eyed but delicately aloof, critically fastidious but sensitively creative, is well in keeping with the April weather. There is a coolness in his blood that suggests the fresh cold of a mountain brook, an instinct for guarding himself even when he is most receptive in spirit, that recall a spring wind tempering the noonday sun.[49]

According to Edward, Thomas has no peer when it comes to capturing the mutability of the weather. He quotes a passage from *In Pursuit of Spring* in which Thomas paints a picture of the countryside scoured by a north-east wind and the earth's subsequent transformation when that wind gives up its power to the south. 'This is the imagery of a poet,' Edward argues, 'and Mr Thomas shows a true poet's verbal mastery in catching the natural magic of open-air effects.' Nine months earlier Thomas had met the American poet Robert Frost at St George's Café in London; it was Frost who would conclusively persuade Thomas that his future as a writer lay in poetry rather than prose. Twelve days before Edward's review appeared, Thomas asked Frost 'whether you can imagine me taking to verse. If you can I might get over the feeling that it is impossible.'[50] Frost's encouragement of Thomas was crucial to his decision to try his hand at poetry, and at some point he suggested Thomas take paragraphs from books such as *In Pursuit of Spring* and experiment with recasting them in verse. Exactly when Frost mooted this idea is not clear, but Edward's review can only have given Thomas confidence to attempt it.

'The public have resisted me, but surely they cannot resist you when you make it plain that duty and pleasure both call them,' Thomas wrote in a letter thanking Edward for the review. 'At any rate I can't resist you. I *feel* tender and effusive tho my style isn't made that way, so I leave you the psychological task of imagining me in that state.'[51] Thomas had more

than one reason to feel particularly grateful to Edward, who had immediately responded to W. H. Davies's concerns about Thomas's financial
plight and endorsed Thomas's application to the Royal Literary Fund,
which granted him £150. In his supporting letter, Edward was at pains
to point out that in his opinion Thomas's temperament put him at a
disadvantage in the 'great competition ... for reviewing work [which]
tends to eliminate the shy and sensitive man'. If no financial assistance
was forthcoming, Edward added, he could only regard Thomas's future
'with grave apprehension'.[52] Those words, written in February 1914, might
also have described the outlook for an entire continent.

European conflict

The twelve months before the start of the conflict that would leave the world irrevocably altered were times of transition of a more personal kind for Edward, too. In the autumn of 1913 he and Constance were house-hunting in London again. This time it was Edward who found the ideal flat, 19 Pond Place, just off the Fulham Road. Close to South Kensington tube, the flat had three bedrooms, two sitting rooms, a 'decent' kitchen and 'lovely' bathroom. Constance agreed with Edward's opinion that it was 'the very place for us'.[1] Although the move was prompted by the need for David to be nearer Imperial College, the flat rapidly became Edward's principal residence and from now on when writers recalled their early meetings with him it would be the nervous ascent up the stairs to Pond Place that stuck in the memory, rather than the journey to the door of The Cearne.

Constance, who had sternly supervised the redecoration of their new quarters – '*No scrolls or flowers* on the papers'[2] – didn't spend long admiring the results. Sciatica always plagued her in the winter and in January she and Felix Volkhovsky's daughter Vera set out for Italy to take up an invitation from D. H. Lawrence and Frieda to stay with them at Lerici.

Even before *Sons and Lovers* was published, Lawrence was at work on his next novel and determined to break new ground with it. 'I shall not write in that style any more,' he informed Edward when his copy of *Sons and Lovers* arrived. 'It's the end of my youthful period.'[3] From some of the letters he had been receiving, Edward may well have detected signs of a nascent rebellion: that Lawrence felt that his progression as a writer involved not only embracing new ideas and directions, but actively shedding and disparaging anything and anyone he associated with his 'old' self. One such moment had come in February 1913 when Edward had returned three of Lawrence's plays with the disagreeable news that there was little chance of them finding a producer. Berating the 'bony, bloodless drama' of Shaw, Galsworthy and other 'rule and measure mathematical folk', Lawrence concludes:

> But you are of them and your sympathies are with your own generation, not with mine. I think it is inevitable. You are about the only man who is willing to let a new generation come in ... I don't want to write like Galsworthy, nor Ibsen, nor Strindberg, nor any of them, *not* even if I could. We have to hate our immediate predecessors, to get free from their authority.[4]

Edward had sent Lawrence a copy of Strindberg's *Miss Julie* and *There Are Crimes and Crimes*, recently published by Duckworth, and he was well aware of Edward's connection with Galsworthy and of his admiration for Ibsen. The intent to free himself, not just from his authorial predecessors but also perhaps subconsciously from Edward, the man who had shaped the writing Lawrence felt driven to discard, is evident.

A few days before *Sons and Lovers* was published, Edward received the first couple of hundred pages of Lawrence's new novel, *The Sisters* (an early version of what became *The Rainbow* and *Women in Love*), along with the prediction that 'you may dislike it – it hasn't got hard outlines'.[5] Three months earlier Lawrence had expressed his dissatisfaction with the technique of *Sons and Lovers* in strikingly similar terms, complaining that he 'hated the dodge of putting a thick black line round the figures to throw out the composition'.[6] The inference is that it is Edward, the lover of 'visualised realism', who is forcing the black pen into Lawrence's hand. Deep down, Lawrence knew the draft of *The Sisters* needed rewriting and confessed as much when Edward sent the anticipated unfavourable reaction to it. On 30 December 1913 he told Edward he would shortly be sending the new version, now called *The Wedding Ring*, and warning: 'It is *very* different from *Sons and Lovers*: written in another language almost. I shall be sorry if you don't like it, but am prepared. I shan't write in the same manner as *Sons and Lovers* again, I think: in that hard, violent style full of sensation and presentation. You must see what you think of the new style.'[7] Early in January the manuscript arrived, along with a note from a confident and defiant Lawrence informing Edward that although 'There may be some small weeding out to do – ... this will be the final form of the book ... My reputation is new-born and wants skilful handling, I think: but it is born.'[8]

Edward, unmoved by this announcement, told Lawrence that episodes in the novel were unconvincing, the character of Ella was incoherent and that the emotional and psychological elements would be better expressed through vivid episodes rather than abstract theorising. Lawrence protested once more that he was done with the 'scenic': 'I don't care much more about accumulating objects in the powerful light of emotion, and making a scene of them. I have to write differently,'⁹ he insisted.

Constance's proximity to Lawrence gave Edward a rare opportunity to discover how his letters about *The Wedding Ring* were being received first hand. She reported that Lawrence, who had been ill, looked 'hollow-eyed and thin',¹⁰ but that he had begun 'writing his novel again with great spirit. He told me of your letter and said you were quite right. He didn't seem downcast at all, but I fancy full of confidence that he could get it right.'¹¹ Edward's criticism of the manuscript was not confined to one letter, however; he wrote another (like all his letters to Lawrence it has not survived) in which he expressed his feelings about its failings in considerably stronger terms. It seems that he also pitched into Frieda, partly because he believed the continuing dramas about the divorce and the children were distracting Lawrence from his writing and partly because he felt that Lawrence was using his work as a way of theorising about his relationship with Frieda, to the detriment of his artistic integrity. 'I think it is rather nice of L and intelligent to accept your criticism as he does,' Frieda responded, 'because it is not easy to swallow criticism, but you need never be afraid and mind what you say, he would always much rather you said it! ... you are really the only man he has any opinion of – I do think you are good to him, only your second letter was too cross.'¹²

That second letter rankled Lawrence more than a little. When he sent Edward another instalment of *The Wedding Ring* towards the end of April it was accompanied by a long missive in which Lawrence continually refers back to it. Although Lawrence initially protests that Edward had insulted 'the thing I *wanted* to say: not me, nor what I had said, but that which I was trying to say, and had failed in',¹³ later in the letter he tells Edward, 'You had a right to go for my work, but in doing that, you must not make *me* cheap in your own eyes.' That very prickly subject – 'commonness' – lies at the heart of the matter. Only a fragment of the draft survives, but when Edward read a sentence such as 'He still had power over her: he was still Man to her,'¹⁴ he considered it belonged in the pages of a popular weekly magazine and condemned it as 'common'. Lawrence saw only a lack of patience and sympathy with what he was trying to do: 'you should understand, and help me to the new thing, not get angry and say it is *common*,' he complains, a little later adding, 'you should see the religious, earnest, suffering man in me first, and then the flippant or common things after.' Edward always admired Lawrence's energy and his intensity of feeling, but he was very much aware of the disparate and often conflicting elements in Lawrence's make-up, which he once identified as 'the poet, the artist, the preacher, the teacher and the *gamin*'.[15] When the preacher and teacher took over, Edward believed Lawrence became intoxicated by his own ideas and what he called 'wilfully one-eyed'.[16] Although Edward considered that the preacher is most in evidence in Lawrence's post-war writing, some of the letters he received in the first half of 1914 must have made him realise that Lawrence's feet were firmly planted on the pulpit steps.

Accounts from Duckworth had recently arrived in Italy, showing that the firm had lost money on *Sons and Lovers;* Lawrence felt bad about it and that he had let Edward down, but he was also upset by Edward's comment (probably in the infamous 'second letter') that Lawrence was at liberty to go to another publisher with his new novel: 'Do you mean you would perhaps be relieved if I went to another firm? Because if you did not mean that, wasn't it an unnecessary thing to say?'[17] Lawrence demands, sounding not unlike an aggrieved party in a marital argument. Edward was never shy of encouraging his protégés to seek a better deal at the expense of his own employer and he may have felt Duckworth hadn't done all he might to promote *Sons and Lovers*. Just over a fortnight later a contrite Lawrence confessed to Constance: 'I had bottled myself up with all kinds of steams, and I had to let it off. Now I am quite decent again, and hoping I haven't hurt anybody.'[18] But the genie had been let out of the bottle and the resentments expressed in the letter continued to ferment.

In the middle of May another letter arrived from Italy announcing that the novel was finished and would shortly be on its way to England. Lawrence had changed the title again, this time to *The Rainbow*, although this manuscript was not the version that would eventually be published under that name. Lawrence was keen to tell Edward that J. B. Pinker had offered £300 for the English volume rights and that two other interested parties had proposed the same sum; 'it is a pretty figure that my heart aches after,' Lawrence admitted. 'It is wearing to be always poor, when there is also Frieda. I suppose Duckworth can't afford big risks.'[19] If Lawrence thought the scent of competition might temper any criticism Edward had of the manuscript, he misjudged his man. Edward felt that the psychology was wrong and the characters inconsistent. He considered the novel to be 'shaky' and that it was only Lawrence's 'cleverness' (often a pejorative word in the Garnett vocabulary) that might just pull the thing through.

A week or so into June a letter arrived in Lawrence's hand, postmarked Tellaro. Edward began to read it: thanks for sending books, a promise to do as advised and tell Pinker nothing had been settled as far as the publisher of the new novel is concerned. So far so good. Then the bald statement: 'I don't agree with you about the Wedding Ring,' followed by a lecture on how the book should be read – 'I have a different attitude to my characters, and that necessitates a different attitude in you, which you are not as yet prepared to give.' A longish tirade about the Italian Futurist Marinetti and how he has made Lawrence think about ways to represent the 'physic – non-human in humanity'. Another admonishment: 'You mustn't look in my novel for the old stable ego of the character.' News followed that Lawrence and Frieda are about to leave Italy and a postscript asked for the letter to be kept and for the novel to be passed on to David: 'I want *him* to understand it.'[20]

This was the gist of a letter that was to become one of the most famous documents of literary Modernism. Edward's reaction to it can only be conjectured, but he may well have regarded it in a similar light to other tendentious pieces by Lawrence, such as the *Study of Thomas Hardy*, which he described as 'magnificent rant, most of it, but sown with pregnant things'.[21] The letter is simultaneously very personal – Lawrence pointedly criticises the Russian writers that Edward so admires for fitting their characters into a moral scheme which Lawrence insists is 'dull, old, dead', and the remarks about David suggest that the twenty-two year old son is now Lawrence's ideal reader and his forty-six year old father distinctly passé – but the passages in which Lawrence expounds on Marinetti and how his theories can open up new possibilities for the novelist are written as much for and to Lawrence himself (with one eye firmly on posterity) as they are addressed to Edward.

Lawrence and Frieda arrived in England on 24 June. Five days later he had a meeting with Gerald Duckworth at which Edward was not present:

'Well?' [said Duckworth as Lawrence entered his office.]
   'Pinker offers me the £300 from Methuen.'
   'He does?'
   'Yes'
   'Then,' [replied Duckworth,] as if nettled 'I'm afraid you'll have to accept it'.[22]

Lawrence relayed this conversation to Edward in a rather shamefaced letter. He explained that a few days after the encounter with Duckworth he had called to see Edward, who was out, and then 'I hung a few moments on the pavement outside, saying "Shall I go to Pinker?"'[23] A pressing lunch appointment, Frieda's disappointment at having no money and Duckworth's 'peremptory' tone at the earlier meeting decided him: 'So I went to Pinker and signed his agreement and took his cheque.' The fact that very shortly after arriving in England Lawrence had told a friend that he wanted to take Methuen's offer and that he was going to try and get the novel away from Duckworth suggests he didn't spend very long prevaricating on the pavement. That Duckworth didn't publish the novel that eventually became *The Rainbow* was in the end more on account of money than aesthetic discord between Lawrence and Edward. David Garnett later recalled that Duckworth refused to match Methuen's offer 'in spite of all Edward could do',[24] an indication that despite his criticisms, Edward had far from given up on Lawrence's novel. And though he was unimpressed when the substantially rewritten version was published in 1915 – later describing it as 'jumbled, inconclusive, faulty in planning, overheated in atmosphere'[25] – this did not stop him from springing to Lawrence's defence when the novel was suppressed soon after publication.

At the end of the letter explaining his defection to Methuen, Lawrence enquires rather timidly, 'Shall I see you at the Cearne –.'[26] Edward wasn't a man to bear a grudge and Lawrence and Frieda spent three days at Limpsfield discussing the volume of short stories Lawrence was giving to Duckworth as a sort of consolation prize. This was *The Prussian Officer and Other Stories*, which was published at the end of November 1914. All the stories with the exception of 'Daughters of the Vicar' had been published before, but Lawrence rewrote and revised them extensively, a task he had begun on his trip to England in 1913 and finished at breakneck speed a year later. Some of the revisions suggest that despite Lawrence's protestations, Edward's criticisms had hit home. When Lawrence rewrote 'The Thorn in the Flesh', for example, he made it more dramatic and pared down the language. Edward, with a shrewd eye on the market and the prevailing preoccupation with Germany, changed the title of the opening tale from 'Honour and Arms' to 'The Prussian Officer'. His decision to place the two stories of German military life first was in one sense a risky strategy, given the homosexual undercurrent of 'The Prussian Officer' and the eroticism of 'The Thorn in the Flesh'. When Lawrence learned that Edward was initially thinking of opening the collection with 'The Thorn in the Flesh' he was alarmed: 'I think you'd better read it through before you put it first,' he warned. 'We don't want them to sneeze at the first whiff.'[27] As for the change in title, Lawrence had no complaints when he mentioned it in a letter to Amy Lowell, but later flared up about it in a letter to Pinker, 'Garnett was a devil to call my book of stories *The Prussian Officer* – what Prussian Officer?'[28]

Edward's admiration for *The Prussian Officer* was unstinting: 'in each of the dozen tales,' he writes (in terms that sound positively Lawrentian), 'it is the same poetic realization of passion's smouldering force, of its fusion of aching pleasure and pain in the roots of sexual life, and the same twinness of senses and soul in the gathering and the breaking waves of surging emotion.'[29] *The Prussian Officer* achieves a perfect fusion of art and metaphysic, making it, in Edward's opinion, 'The purest expression of Lawrence's artistic genius.'[30]

By the autumn of 1914 Lawrence and Edward had practically ceased corresponding. There was no explosive quarrel, as happened at the end of many of Lawrence's friendships, but rather a tacit understanding on both sides that their relationship had run its course. Lawrence and Frieda married in July 1914; the wedding marked a new stage in his life. The initial traumas over Weekley and the children were behind them, their circle of friends was expanding rapidly, Lawrence's finances were (temporarily) better than they ever had been and his confidence in his own powers had never been higher. He no longer needed to depend on his 'friend and protector in love and literature' – indeed, he may well have come to resent that dependence. Yet Lawrence always retained an affection for his old mentor: 'I love your father,' he told David in April 1915. 'Though I don't see him, I do love him in my soul.'[31] By the time Lawrence wrote those words he realised that all chance of returning to Italy as planned was impossible; Edward, who had passed up Lawrence's repeated invitations to visit Lerici, would finally get out to Italy less than six months later, albeit under very different circumstances.

'The madness and wickedness is almost beyond one's powers of belief – but it really is true that all Europe – England, France, Germany, Austria, Russia are at war now,'[32] Constance wrote to Edward, who was on holiday in Ireland with Nellie when war was declared. People were buying up non-perishable provisions at the local store, Constance reported, adding that extreme frugality would have to be the order of the day and all luxuries, including Edward's tobacco, given up. Constance had already started to dig up some of the grass at The Cearne in order to grow extra turnips and potatoes: 'If we don't need them, lots of other people will. There is sure to be such terrible distress,'[33] she prophesied.

Edward was appalled and in black despair at the turn of events. His paci-fism put him at odds not only with his brother Robert and sister-in-law Mattie – 'you had better avoid discussing the war or politics at all with them',[34] counselled Constance – but also with some of his closest friends. 'You think it a "cursed war", I think it a blessed war,' wrote Hudson, going on to explain that he felt the bloodshed would 'purge us of our many hateful qualities'.[35] Others, like Cunninghame Graham, protested vigorously against the prospect of conflict, but once it commenced, he lent his support in the hope that the fighting would be brought to a swift resolution. Graham's mother, with whom Edward had always got on very well, upset him by 'as good as calling me a pro-German'.[36]

As the weeks passed Edward felt increasingly that he could no longer stand by, 'hearing day after day of these atrocious horrors, and of the frightful battles and yet doing nothing'.[37] In October he wrote to Louise Bréal, telling her that he and Nellie wanted to come out to France to see if they could be of any service. Edward's idea was to write some articles on events in France for the English press. 'It is not the military operations I wish to see,' he explained, 'but to write of the social evils and wickedness of War.'[38] They went to France in November and stayed with Louise at Les Mielles, near Cherbourg; Edward's articles did not materialise, but he and Nellie spent two months helping in the French hospital where Louise's lover Camille Wolf was chief medical officer. Despite the horror of some of the cases, tending the wounded lifted Edward's spirits and, according to Nellie, the visit broke 'the crushing gloom under which he lived'.[39] When they returned in December Edward immediately succumbed to a bad attack of flu, but was cheered and 'so touched'[40] by cards he received from some of the soldiers he had met in France.

The war was a contributory factor in Nellie's decision to go and live with Edward at Pond Place. She resolved to do so with some reluctance – 'I wish I need not,' she explained to Louise, 'but at such a time it seems absurd to be thinking of one's feelings of that kind and I feel to be with Edward as much as possible is the most important thing and that will be good.'[41] Nellie was forty-two at the time and she and Edward had been lovers for seventeen years; her reticence about the move was not on account of any diminution in her feelings for Edward – 'I love you more and more and more than ever,'[42] she wrote a couple of weeks after moving in – but perhaps stemmed from her aversion to anything that could conceivably be construed as pushing herself forward or staking some kind of claim. There was plenty of coming and going at Pond Place during this time. David was living there whilst conducting research, but he had plenty of free time and was frequently out on some excursion or other, while Edward, absorbed in work, spent three days and nights in London and four at The Cearne.

All three inhabitants of Pond Place were preoccupied with what they could do to help with the war effort in non-combatant roles. Nellie was working for a Quaker committee providing relief for 'enemy aliens' – 'shoals of poor governesses, servants etc ... the people are *so* tragic,'[43] she told Louise. Edward talked David out of his initial enthusiasm to enlist and at the end of June he decided to join the Friends War Victims Relief mission in France. The day before he left, David lunched with his father at a Soho restaurant (probably the Mont Blanc). Towards the end of the meal

Edward cleared his throat with what seemed a shade of embarrassment and said: 'Dear Boy, you are going abroad alone, for the first time ...' He paused and cocked a solemn eye at me and the thought flashed through my mind that he was going to touch on the moral dangers to which I might be exposed. It was incredible ... but his manner was decidedly odd. The pause lengthened interminably while he searched through several of his pockets without success. I had time to wonder what he was trying to find. Could it conceivably be some specific ... against venereal disease? ... At length he discovered what he was looking for ... 'You will be all alone ... the Quakers probably won't have one ... I think you may find this useful in France,' and his big, exquisitely shaped hand, with its tapered fingers, opened. On his palm was lying a pocket corkscrew.[44]

Edward himself had been taking an ambulance course, as he had decided he wanted to go out to the war as an orderly. He went to St Bartholomew's Hospital every day, helping to treat outpatients, but was as yet unsure whether, at the age of forty-seven, he would be considered too old to join an ambulance unit. Uncertainty seeped into every corner of life; publishing was for the moment relatively unaffected, but for how long it could remain so should the conflict drag on, nobody knew. Decisions about what to publish had to be made with an eye to the likely impact of the war, though, and it was partly this consideration that played on Edward's mind when he read a manuscript submitted by an Irish writer whose literary debut he had already noted: 'Mr Joyce published some very clever stories (with Maunsel) "Dubliners" in the summer,' Edward wrote, before turning his attention to the subject in hand – *A Portrait of the Artist as a Young Man*:

> In the MS now submitted he gives us reminiscences of his school-days[,] of his family life in Dublin and of his adolescence. It is all ably written and the picture is curious. But the style is too discursive and his point of view will be called 'a little sordid'. It isn't a book that would make a young man's reputation – it is too unconventional for our British public. And in War Time it has less chance than at any other.
> Decline with thanks.[45]

There is more than a suspicion here that Edward deplores the deficiencies of 'our British public' quite as much as the artistic shortcomings in Joyce's manuscript and he is certainly keenly aware that Joyce's uncompromising picture of Dublin life would not appeal at a time when the public was demanding light reading matter that would offer a temporary distraction from the realities of war.

This was not the only report he wrote on *A Portrait of the Artist*, however. There are two others: the first is a typescript, which is considerably more positive and leaves the door open for Duckworth to make an offer, should he be in the mood for speculation. In the opening paragraph Joyce receives the ultimate accolade from Edward – comparison with the Russians:

> Mr Joyce is to be reckoned with. You may dislike his work but you cannot ignore it. It is real, powerful subjective work, quite un-English. It is comparable more with the Russian writers than anything we know that has been written by any Englishman – or Irishman. He is not as fluent as our friend D. H. Lawrence and possibly he will never be prolific but it is sure, definite, confident writing, scholarly and full of insight and feeling.[46]

Edward praises the 'very deep and searching' analysis of the young Stephen Dedalus's sexual longings and experience, and the 'still more effective' presentation of his remorse and fear of damnation. However, *A Portrait of the Artist* 'is not a pleasant book. There is no beauty, no hint of anything joyous. It is drab and has the same effect on the reader as a short visit to Dublin has on the tourist. It is real, deals with normal people and presents them, even the most minor characters, swiftly and vividly.' Joyce's minute rendering of the salacious and on occasion blasphemous conversation between the students required toning down, but other than that Edward saw nothing objectionable in the manuscript. In conclusion, he puts the ball firmly in Gerald Duckworth's court:

> The question to decide is not whether this MS is worth accepting. Mr Joyce would do credit to any publisher's list. It is rather to what extent D and Co. care to speculate. Pinker doubtless will refuse anything less than £100 on account. It might be worth offering this with the proviso that the next two books could be had on the same terms. More than this is too big a risk as Mr Joyce may be some time in coming into his own.

This was still not the end of the matter. When Duckworth eventually decided to reject the novel, Pinker wrote and asked why. In response, Jonathan Cape, who was managing the firm while Gerald Duckworth was engaged with war duties, sent Pinker a '"copy" of a Reader's report'.[47] This has always been attributed to Edward, and he may indeed be the author, but there is room for doubt. The copy of the report Cape sent to Pinker is typed, but the original handwritten version is not in Edward's handwriting.[48] Cape does not mention Edward by name in his covering letter to Pinker, which is dated 26 January 1916, and by that time Edward was no longer employed at Duckworth's. Of course this does not necessarily mean that Edward did not write the report – he left the firm only the month before Cape's letter – and some of the phrases in the report – 'ably written', 'curious', 'too discursive', 'a little sordid', 'unconventional' are lifted straight from Edward's first judgement of the manuscript in autumn 1914. However, the fact of the handwriting remains and it is just possible that somebody else wrote the report that Cape sent to Pinker with Edward's first, much shorter version at his or her elbow.

Whoever the author, the report provoked a vitriolic response from Joyce's friend Ezra Pound, who had been campaigning to get *A Portrait of the Artist* published. Pound's opening salvo – 'I have read the effusion of Mr Duckworth's reader with no inconsiderable disgust. These vermin crawl over and be-slime our literature with their pulings, and nothing but the day of judgement can, I suppose, exterminate 'em'[49] – set the tone for what followed. While Pound reluctantly offered to approach Joyce 'if this louse will specify exactly what verbal changes he wants made', he refused to 'forward the insults of an imbecile to one of the very few men for whom I have the faintest respect'. After considerably more in the same vein Pound concludes, 'As for altering Joyce to suit Duckworth's readers [*sic*] – I would like trying to fit the Venus de Milo into a piss-pot. [*sic*] – a few changes required.'

Duckworth's reluctance to take on the novel was shared by many of his fellow publishers and it was not until 1917 that *A Portrait of the Artist* finally appeared in book form in England under the imprint of the Egoist Press, having been serialised by the *Egoist* magazine during 1914 and 1915. Ironically, in 1924 Jonathan Cape, who had by then set up his own firm and engaged Edward as his reader, bought the rights to Joyce's work (with the exception of *Ulysses*) from Harriet Weaver when she decided to wind up the Egoist Press.

One of the comments in the report that Pound singled out for particular invective was the reference to Joyce's manuscript as 'unconventional'. 'Hark to his puling squeak. [*sic*] too "unconventional",' Pound shrilly declaims. 'What in hell do we want but some change from the unbearable monotony of the weekly six shilling pears soap annual novel.' Edward would heartily agree with Pound's demand that literature constantly needed to be seeking new forms of expression, and had been promoting the work of two women who were starting out on just such a quest. When Virginia Woolf submitted her first novel, *The Voyage Out*, to her half-brother's firm, Edward wrote what Leonard Woolf described as 'an extremely appreciative report'[50] in support of it. Edward had also recommended that Duckworth publish Dorothy Richardson's *Pointed Roofs* (1915), the first of the series of thirteen volumes that make up *Pilgrimage*, which conveys the experiences and inner life of Miriam Henderson. Richardson was grateful to Edward, both for his 'illuminating guidance through the murkier depths of "Pilgrimage"',[51] as she put it in one of her rather arch letters to him, and for his reviews of the novels in the *Nation* in which he defended her against charges of formlessness. 'There are readers who will ask for "unity and design" in the plan of this book,' Edward conceded in his review of *The Tunnel* (1919),

> and those who complain that they don't find 'the reality which underlies the appearances'. But these readers must not ask Miriam to dive for their pearls, she is snatching at and bringing up the most wonderful things, by handfuls, just as they float and wave and interpenetrate in the flow and surge of old London's living tunnel.[52]

When he reviewed the next volume, *Interim*, a year later Edward again concentrated on Richardson's representation of the 'feminine multiple consciousness' and castigated those readers who demand 'clarity, construction, and form in every "picture"',[53] pointing out that it is not Richardson's intention to create 'pictures' but rather 'an acute registration of the fluid feminine perceptiveness' and that this requires a new method. 'Your article in *The Nation* ... set me in a glow,'[54] declared Richardson, who had suffered the complaints of the reviewer in the *London Mercury* that the novel was fragmentary and abnormal.

Edward's advocacy of writing that eschewed the conventional and his disparagement of those 'unsophisticated' readers insisting on traditional form might well have surprised D. H. Lawrence and Ezra Pound, although whether Pound would have retracted his demand that publishers' readers should be sent to the Serbian front in order 'to get some good out of the war'[55] is doubtful. Pound might have been gratified to learn that in August 1915 one of the dreaded breed was indeed on his way to the war; however, Edward was bound not for Serbia, but Italy.

'I want to tell you how much you have taught me'

In November 1914 Edward Thomas called in at Duckworth's looking for Edward, only to learn that he had gone to France. Thomas was doing a lot of searching just then – for work, which was in short supply, and for some sort of direction. 'I get scrappy work ... and plenty of time to write what I like and find I can write,'[1] he told Edward. Thomas was about to discover that what he wanted to write and was able to write was poetry.

At the end of the letter to Edward, Thomas asks if Hudson has passed on *North of Boston* (1914), a volume of poems by the American Robert Frost: 'I should be very glad if they pleased you.' Thomas's friendship with Frost had steadily deepened since their first meeting in October 1913; he had subsequently stayed several times with Frost and his family in Gloucestershire, walking the countryside with the American, absorbed in the discussion of verse. It was Frost who gave the final push and in Edward's words 'thrust Thomas out of the old nest of prose'.[2] In November 1914 Thomas began 'Up in the Wind', the first of 142 poems he would write in less than three years. He sent his verses to Frost and to Harold Monro, the proprietor of the Poetry Bookshop on Devonshire Street, London, and early in 1915 he also sent some to Edward, who later made unsuccessful attempts to persuade the *Nation* to take them. Edward's suggestion that Thomas alter 'Tears' so that the emphasis fell unequivocally on the British Grenadiers was made with one eye to the wartime market. Thomas rejected this idea, but agreed with the bulk of Edward's criticisms and was sufficiently encouraged to send nearly every poem he had written in the previous four months. 'I hope you will forgive me and survive the swamping,' he fretted. 'You cannot imagine how eagerly I have run up this byeway and how anxious I am to be sure it is not a cul de sac.'[3] Edward assured him the road ahead was clear and singled out 'Old Man', 'The Cuckoo' and 'Good-night' for high praise, but suggested that some of the poems suffered from 'dimness and lack of concreteness', and others (like 'The Signpost') were constructed on too petty an incident. Thomas expressed sorrow at Edward's judgement of 'The Signpost', but was particularly gratified that he found the poems *like me*. I had fears left I had got up in the air in this untried medium.'[4]

Edward's much later comment that Thomas 'directly attained an aerial element in which his isolated, brooding nature could shape in beauty, more subtly and more keenly than in prose, all that he felt or dreamed upon'[5] might have been written in response to that anxiety. Thomas did not escape criticism at the time, however; when Edward read 'Lob' in manuscript he felt it was 'a little breathless or rough'[6] and suggested planing what he considered to be irregular edges. 'I am doubtful about the chiselling ... you advise' countered Thomas:

> It would be the easiest thing in the world to clean it all up and trim it and have every line straightforward in sound and sense, but it would not really improve it. I think you read too much with the eye perhaps. If you *say* a couplet like
>
> > If they had mowed their dandelions and sold them fairly they could have afforded gold –
>
> I believe it is no longer awkward.[7]

Thomas's remark echoes his recent criticism of Walter Pater: 'His very words are to be seen, not read aloud; for if read aloud they betray their artificiality by a lack of natural expressive rhythm.'[8] Ironic then that it was Edward who had tried to break Thomas of his Paterian prose habits. Edward remained unconvinced by poems like 'Liberty', 'The Glory' and 'Parting' in which he felt Thomas's 'analytic musings' predominated detrimentally. 'Parting' was written in February 1915, when Thomas's fifteen-year-old son Mervyn left with the Frosts for America, a country that was increasingly occupying the thoughts of both Thomas and Edward.

As the war progressed, America offered one possible outlet for work that was becoming increasingly scarce in England, so Edward was pleased when Ellery Sedgwick, the editor of the *Atlantic Monthly*, asked him to write a piece on the current state and future prospects of writing on both sides of the Atlantic. 'Some Remarks on American and English Fiction' appeared in December 1914 and Edward took at face value Sedgwick's invitation 'to speak with candour'.[9] While the ordinary English novel 'is a mediocre affair' that represents middle-class limitations and demonstrates the tendency to shy away from bitter truths in preference for idealistic and sentimental solutions, it is, according to Edward, 'less vulgar, less false, less melodramatic' than it was a generation ago. The same cannot be said of America, where the intensification of the commercial imperative has resulted in a flood of inferior fiction and the work of truly talented writers like Sarah Orne Jewett, Edith Wharton, Frank Norris, Stephen Crane, Theodore Dreiser (whose *Sister Carrie* Edward recommended for publication in England) and Anne Douglas Sedgwick has been largely disregarded. In conclusion, Edward claims that 'the American novel fails by virtue of its idealistic bias and psychological timidity'. The commercial, ethical and sentimental ideals that make up American 'optimism' are antipathetic to the remorseless truth-telling that should be the instinct of every novelist. Nowhere is this more evident than in the 'conspiracy of silence in the American novel concerning the sexual passion', which Edward believes accounts for the 'alarming featurelessness of its portraits of women'. Whereas the English merely regard the artist with apathy, in America the attitude is positively hostile.

This onslaught did not go unanswered. 'The Dean of American Letters', W. D. Howells (whose novel *New Leaf Mills* Edward had singled out for commendation), used his editorial column in *Harper's Magazine* to praise 'the gentle intelligence'[10] of Edward's remarks, but then equally gently pointed out that 'it is chiefly from knowing the field better that we should claim to discover more wheat among the tares than he'. Small wonder then that when Edward told Edward Thomas that he was going to write a laudatory article on Robert Frost's *North of Boston* for the *Atlantic*, Thomas warned him that it might damage Frost 'if you rubbed the American noses in their own dirt'.[11] Frost arrived back in the States on 5 May 1915 and the following day went to see Ellery Sedgwick, who three years earlier told Frost there was 'no place in the *Atlantic Monthly* for your "vigorous verse"'.[12] Now, however, in recent receipt of a letter from Edward which expressed the view that 'since Whitman's death no American poet has appeared of *so unique a quality* as Mr Frost',[13] Sedgwick changed his mind, and 'Birches', 'The Road Not Taken' and 'The Sound of Trees' appeared alongside Edward's essay 'A New American Poet'.

It is Frost's creative originality that Edward considers one of his most valuable qualities, a style 'that obeys its own laws of grace and beauty and inner harmony'.[14] Frost's use of pauses and digressions, his 'crafty envisagement of his subject at fresh angles' and the fact that his dramatic dialogues are so close to everyday speech, sometimes resulting in apparently awkward scansion, may not please the reader looking for the conventionally 'poetical', but in Edward's opinion they make Frost 'a master of his exacting medium' – comments that suggest Edward was perhaps reading less 'with the eye' than formerly. He quotes at length from 'Home Burial' to illustrate how deceptive it is in its seeming simplicity and returns to the lines in which the grief-stricken mother addresses her husband and recalls watching him from a window as he digs a grave for their first child: 'Making the gravel leap and leap in air, / Leap up like that, like that, and land so lightly.' 'How exquisitely the strain of the mother's anguish is felt in that naked image,' Edward observes. 'It is indeed the perfection of poetic realism, both in observation and in deep insight into the heart.'

'What you say for me is bound to have a tremendous effect', wrote an appreciative Frost. 'I can see the impression you made by the way you came to judgement last winter on the novelists. We are all prepared to envy anyone you think well of.'[15] Further compliments from America came in a letter from the poet Sara Teasdale: 'Your wonderful appreciation in the *Atlantic Monthly* of Robert Frost's poetry has been the source of such deep and keen pleasure both to my husband and to me,' she told Edward. 'It is the first adequate thing that has been written on the work of this man who is coming surely into his own, thanks to you.'[16]

Edward Thomas applauded the article too, judging it to be 'absolutely right'.[17] Other matters were far from so clear-cut for Thomas, particularly where the war was concerned. He shared Edward's disgust for the jingoism of the popular press and both men refused to subscribe to the view that Germans were inherently less human than the British. Like Edward, Thomas was accused of being pro-German, in his case by his friend Ralph Hodgson. For some time Thomas had been contemplating the possibility of following Frost out to America, perhaps to set up a farm with his friend or to teach. Besieged by doubt, he wrote to Edward seeking his advice and asking if he thought there was any possibility of being granted a Civil List pension. 'Nobody would speak for me except you, I believe,' he explained, 'and I know very well that if you thought it reasonable and practicable you would.'[18]

Edward responded immediately. He promised to see what he could do about the pension and from Thomas's subsequent letters it appears that he urged him to go to America, but told Thomas that if he did so, he would need to be much more open to meeting people and be aware that his manner frequently appeared chilly to those with whom he was not intimate, something that would go down even less well in the States than it did at home. 'I can only say that at first sight you seem to wish me to try to turn over a new leaf and be some one else', Thomas countered. 'I can't help dreading people both in anticipation and when I am among them and my only way of holding my own is the instinctive one of turning on what you call coldness and a superior manner.'[19] The next day Thomas wrote again, reiterating that

> what you call superiority is only a self defence unconsciously adopted by the most faint-hearted humility – I believe. It goes on thickening into a callosity which only accident – being left to my own devices perhaps – can ever break through. I long for the accident but cannot myself arrange to produce it![20]

When Edward read the two four-line stanzas Thomas wrote by way of postscript, he was struck by the poignancy of Thomas's self-exculpation; he could also be left in little doubt as to the intensity of his friend's predicament:

> I built myself a house of glass
> It took me years to make it;
> And I was proud: but now alas!
> Would God some one would break it.
>
> But it looks too magnificent.
> No neighbour casts a stone
> From where he dwells, in tenement
> Or palace of glass, alone.[21]

Appropriately enough, on 4 July Thomas told Edward that he was likely to go to America; he had heard that if he was granted a Civil List pension it was unlikely to be more than £60, a sum 'that would barely detain me in England'.[22] Yet ten days later Thomas met Edward at St George's Café in St Martin's Lane and informed him that he had passed his army medical that morning; he had enlisted in the Artists Rifles. After all the indecision, in the end it was a choice Thomas felt impelled to make.

The war was catching up with Edward, too. At the end of July Constance reported to Natalie that he was shortly to depart for Italy as an orderly with the First British Ambulance Unit, organised by the Red Cross. The exact nature of his duties and whether or not he would be deployed at the Front was uncertain, but the prospect filled Constance with alarm, for 'apart from the danger of being shot, it would be so awful to have to pick up the wounded before they had been treated at all, and I am afraid it would be too great a strain for Edward. He is not accustomed to see much suffering and also, of course, he is not young or alert enough.'[23] Initially Edward, who had turned forty-seven in January, went to a training camp at Cookham in Berkshire, the home village of the artist Stanley Spencer (who would himself serve with an ambulance unit) in the grounds of a grandly crenellated mansion, Formosa Place. The unit was commanded by the historian G. M. Trevelyan and contained several figures from the world of literature and the arts, including Somerset Maugham (who ultimately went to France rather than Italy) and the artist (and surgeon) Henry Tonks, who taught at the Slade and ended the war as an official artist, accompanying John Singer Sargent on tours of the Western Front. Edward had a lot of time for Trevelyan, but little for the supercilious Tonks. 'What an old fraud Tonks is! with his Roman nose, and ashen face, and restless eye,' Edward complained to Nellie. 'He teaches us bandaging and is always pulling up A or B with "wrong"! . . . while I am very polite to him, I half wink at him, to say *"Tonks, I see through you."*'[24] On days when Trevelyan was absent, the camp was run by his adjutant, Philip Baker (later Baron Noel-Baker), described by Edward as 'one of those extremely brilliant and capable people'[25] – a perspicacious assessment of the future Nobel Peace Prize-winner, Labour MP and silver medallist over 1,500 metres at the Antwerp Olympics. Edward discovered he was fully occupied during the day with various classes, including Italian, which he struggled with, but he enjoyed the evenings: 'It is a *very* interesting and picturesque scene: all the men at night round the table in the marquee chatting and laughing' he told Nellie, 'Most of them are about 20–30 and only one or two older than me. The defect of the life is that one has no time to think, and no time to write. There is no interest in the War – intellectual interest I mean – and the newspapers may lie on the table scarcely opened.'[26]

Time would soon be in even shorter supply; on 22 August the unit embarked from Southampton on a crowded troop ship bound for Le Havre. From there the convoy of twenty-six cars and Buick ambulances began to wind its way south through France to Italy, travelling by day and pitching camp in the grounds of French farmhouses and occasionally a chateau. 'The people along the roads all through France have been most enthusiastic, all saluting or acclaiming our arrival,' Edward informed Constance. 'It has been a wonderful education seeing France in the day but the strain of camping is making me feel anxious as to whether I can keep up with the younger men.'[27] By the first week of September the unit was established in the two-hundred-year-old Villa Trento near the village of Dolegnano, a mile from the Austrian border. Shortly after his arrival, Edward wrote to Constance, describing the situation:

> I am sitting on a bank on a hillside which commands a beautiful view of the surrounding hills and mountains ... At my back is one of those whitewashed Italian farms, with brown tiled roofs, and little courtyard, all hung round with vines and at the side are barns & granaries ... A few miles off are the trenches and the boom of big guns sounds continually from the hills. But for that and for two or three observation balloons the country seems infinitely peaceful. All the futility and pathetic stupidity of war seems to be camouflaged by the smiling landscape.[28]

The first patients to appear were suspected typhoid cases, but the wounded arrived soon after. Edward was 'nervously wrung out' by the thirteen-hour days and as autumn advanced and news filtered through of preparations for big battles, he found himself nearer the scenes of the fighting:

> Yesterday I was on an excursion to the outpost and a shell exploded behind the car, but as you don't hear the droning sound of the shell coming (since it is drowned by the noise of the car) it doesn't affect the imagination like watching a shell burst on the road. Tolstoy's 'The Wood Felling' gives a very accurate idea of the impression and sensation when exposed to artillery fire.[29]

Tiredness was Edward's main cause for complaint; he enjoyed his work as a dresser, and got on well with the other medical staff. Letters bringing news from England were always a particular pleasure and like many others, Edward discovered that the separations and uncertainties of war made him reflect on relationships at home. 'I think of you always, dear little Puss, with deep and tender affection,' he declared to Constance. 'If I don't express it is because we have grown somewhat out of the habit and indeed you can read it between the lines of my letters, as I do between yours. Take care of yourself, dear one. You are a sort of guardian of David as well as his mother and have saved him so often by your love.'[30]

Constance was particularly worried by David's idea that he should leave France, where he was still working for the Friends War Victims

Relief mission, and join Edward in Italy as an ambulance driver. Two weeks of heavy rain had turned the Italian hill roads into liquid mud, making them even more hazardous and the ambulances returned to the Villa Trento plastered with the region's sticky white clay. The thought of David, who had little experience behind the wheel, negotiating such treacherous mountain roads in winter horrified Constance and she urged Edward to write and dissuade him. As it turned out, the job in France lasted longer than David anticipated and his mother's fears were put to rest.

Edward had nominally signed up for six months in Italy, but had been assured at the time that some men were returning to England in November and December and that this would be a possibility for him, too, if the Commandant agreed. It is not clear exactly why he made the decision to come back; the most likely explanation is that he found the work too physically demanding – the typhoid he had suffered nearly twenty years before had left him with varicose veins and prone to leg ulcers – but by the middle of November he was home again. Inside the box that Nellie had so carefully packed for the outward journey were diary notes Edward had made whilst at the Villa Trento: the day he had heard the big gun fired for the first time; the number of wounded admitted; brief descriptions of some of the men being treated. Shortly after his return to England, Edward turned these notes into two articles, 'The Battle-Fronts on the Isonzo: First Account by an English Witness' and 'Behind the Isonzo: In the English Hospital' for the *Manchester Guardian*. Edward was billed as 'the well-known man of letters [who] ranks amongst our first literary critics ... and is one of the very few Englishmen who have been privileged to see anything of the terrible fighting on the Austrian frontier'.[31] His first piece is a detailed description of the landscape of the region, emphasising how the conflict is being affected and to some extent dictated by the lie of the land. 'Behind the Isonzo' is very different; the focus is concentrated on the scenes outside the gates and within the walls of the Villa Trento. The human suffering that was being played out against the beauty – but implacable indifference – of nature was something that clearly struck Edward:

[I]nside the emptied lofty wards, reigns a feeling of suspended animation, of listless, expectant vacuity; one hears only the groans of poor Antonio, soldier of the 71st *fanteria*, with his shattered leg, calling 'Ah, Dio! Dio!', and the convalescents' feet shuffling in and out. From outside comes the shouting voices of peasants in the

maize field, from whose border one sees the deep blue slopes of
the rugged limestone hills, in the dazzling sunlight, and the great
mountainous wall of snowy Alpine crests, terrible in their beauty
and inaccessible purity.[32]

Consolation is nowhere to be found, and Edward returned more determined than ever to point out the 'frightful immorality'[33] of war. Over
the next couple of years he wrote a series of satires that appeared in
the *English Review*, the *Cambridge Magazine*, the *Nation* and the *Labour
Leader*; they were published as a volume in 1919 under the title *Papa's
War and Other Satires*. Edward's targets are far-ranging – the rulers of
the European powers, military chiefs, capitalism, politicians, diplomats,
the popular press – and the satire is sometimes not very subtle, but the
sketches gave him an outlet to express what he felt about the war. The
book was not widely reviewed; Edward told Walter de la Mare it had
been 'practically boycotted by the Press'.[34] Galsworthy admitted to being
swept along by one of the satires, 'A Week in Paris', while reading it,
but 'Afterwards, of course, one reverts to the old eternal question, given
the facts, what on earth else was there to do but become involved in
this ghastliness.'[35]

Edward returned from Italy to find things considerably altered. The
Mont Blanc crowd had dispersed: Edward Thomas was at Hare Hill
camp in Essex giving instruction in map reading. Absolved of many of
the responsibilities and choices he found burdensome, Thomas declared
that he had 'never been so well or so contented'.[36] Hudson was slowly
recovering from illness in Cornwall; Galsworthy was mostly in Devon,
writing essays putting forward the English view of the war to Americans;
Conrad, recently stricken by a particularly bad and prolonged attack
of gout, was anxiously following the progress of his eldest son Borys,
who had just joined the Army Service Corps, thanks to the influence of
Cunninghame Graham, who had returned to England from Uruguay in
May, where he had been procuring horses on behalf of the War Office to
be shipped out to the Western Front. Ford Madox Hueffer had changed
his surname to Ford by deed poll that July and at the age of forty-one
enlisted in the Welch Regiment. For D. H. Lawrence the year had been
nothing short of a nightmare. On the very day Edward was due back
in England a Bow Street magistrate had ordered the destruction of
all copies of *The Rainbow*, described by the prosecuting counsel as 'a
mass of obscenity of thought, idea and action throughout'.[37] Ill health,
poverty and a series of humiliating examinations for military service had

left Lawrence on the brink of despair. Nellie, too, had sometimes felt overwhelmed: her sister Margaret had been seriously ill; Nellie herself had been forced to take shelter from Zeppelin raids on more than one occasion and the relentless bad news from the Front was crushing. 'Oh this cruel, cruel war. Will it end before everyone is dead or their heart broken?' she wondered.[38] Constance battled on at The Cearne, growing as much produce as she could, economising wherever possible and worrying about how they would manage financially.

Her anxieties were intensified when a couple of weeks after Edward's return a letter arrived from Duckworth announcing that his job there no longer existed. Although the news did not altogether come as a shock – the outlook for publishing was growing increasingly uncertain and Edward's salary of £180 a year had been reduced to £120 by 1915 – it meant real difficulty in meeting the monthly bills. Galsworthy approached Alfred Knopf, who had just established his own publishing house in New York, on Edward's behalf, suggesting that he might read for the new firm, and telling Knopf that Edward had mentioned £100 a year as a possible salary. As the publisher intended initially to focus on European – and especially Russian – literature, such a job seemed tailor-made for Edward. However, Knopf eventually decided that the financial commitment and the difficulty of sending manuscripts abroad for reading made the project unviable, although, as Galsworthy related to Edward, '[Knopf] has no doubt you would be "a pleasure and a luxury".'[39] Edward's suggestion to Ellery Sedgwick that he review poetry for the *Atlantic Monthly* fell on deaf ears, too. There was no option but to pick up scraps of reading and reviewing work wherever possible, and Edward also put out feelers for a possible government job, with no result.

The beginning of 1916 brought yet another source of worry. At the end of January the Military Services Bill received royal assent. This called up all single men between the ages of eighteen and forty-one for military service. Edward escaped on grounds of age, but David, who would turn twenty-four in March, did not. David had returned from France in January: what he had witnessed there and the arguments of friends like Lytton Strachey, Clive Bell and Duncan Grant convinced him that if called upon to fight he would refuse to do so. Edward and Constance fully supported his decision, but the time inevitably came when he had to face a tribunal. Maynard Keynes advised him that he would stand a better chance if he was engaged in work classified as being of national importance, and so David and Duncan Grant moved to Suffolk, rented Wissett Lodge near Halesworth and set themselves up as fruit farmers. David discouraged his father from attending the tribunal, 'as it is increasing the agony for us both',⁴⁰ but when the case was dismissed and the appeal heard in Ipswich, Edward could no longer keep away. He told the Ipswich tribunal that David had been brought up by Constance in the four principles of Tolstoyism. 'They were much astonished but not unkind, and gave him "non-combatant" service with the right to appeal to the Central Tribunal,'⁴¹ Edward reported to Natalie. Much to everyone's relief the final appeal, which took place in July, was successful and David and Duncan Grant were given permission to work on the land.

There was no such resolution to the financial predicament, however; Edward had less than half his pre-war income and the cost of living had soared. Efforts to let the best rooms in Pond Place had come to nothing and by the autumn he and Nellie were seriously contemplating moving out of London and renting a cottage in the country. 'We both hate London very much and it makes [Edward] ill,' Nellie explained, 'but one of the chief things is the expense.'⁴² A week later she reported that Edward was 'horribly worried by work and the difficulty of making money. He finds it more and more harassing.'⁴³

Edward's frequent shortage of funds had always made him sympathetic to the gnawing financial anxiety that for many of his authors was a constant feature of literary life. The call-up to Italy had prevented him from properly pursuing the possibility of a Civil List pension for Edward Thomas, but in the spring of 1916 he and Walter de la Mare gave the matter serious attention, sending out letters to other writers asking them to lend their support to the application. In June Edward received a letter from Thomas informing him that their efforts had been rewarded and that he had been awarded a grant of £300. This was not the annual pension he had hoped for, but a one-off payment to assist him with his writing. An appreciative Thomas relayed the good news to Edward: 'Thank you for all you have done. The money will keep me going for quite a long time and enable me to do things for [his son] Mervyn which I couldn't have done without it.'⁴⁴ The two men had not met since Edward's return from Italy, and kept missing each other during Thomas's periods of leave, but in the autumn Edward was the admiring recipient of *Six Poems*, a privately printed edition of 100 copies issued under the pseudonym Edward Eastaway, the name Thomas used when writing verse. In October Thomas dispatched 'diverse pieces' to Edward for potential placement in the *Nation* with the instruction that they were to be submitted as being by Eastaway: he was still not yet confident enough publicly to declare himself a poet. By December 1916 Thomas had practically finished arranging a collection of his verse, *Poems*, for publication with Selwyn and Blount. He also learned that he was to be posted to 244 Siege Battery and that he would soon be bound for the Front. On 13 January he wrote to Edward, explaining that he had been unable to drop in that day to say goodbye; the letter ends:

In case I don't have another chance I want to tell you how much you have taught me (of what I *could* be taught) and how much I have enjoyed that and also many other things when I was not at school under you. Good luck to you and David.[45]

On 9 April, Easter Monday, the first day of the Battle of Arras, Thomas was shot through the chest by a 'pip-squeak', a 77mm shell.[46] When and how Edward learned the news is not clear: *The Times* reported the death on 14 April; the *Daily Chronicle*, the Garnetts' paper of choice, carried an obituary two days later. On 18 April Edward wrote to de la Mare: 'You have heard, I suppose, that poor Edward Thomas has been killed in France. I fancy that you and I were his best friends.'[47] Robert Frost, who might justifiably have contested that claim, told Edward that Thomas was 'the only brother I ever had'[48] and urged him to do everything he could for Thomas's poetry. However, Edward's immediate concern was for Thomas's wife and family. Less than three weeks after his friend's death, Edward wrote to the Royal Literary Fund in support of a grant for Helen Thomas, who shortly afterwards received £200.

Edward's appreciation of Thomas in the *Dial* appeared in February 1918, but he was well aware that Thomas's work could all too easily slip into neglect and obscurity as the years passed. Congratulating de la Mare on his preface to Thomas's *Collected Poems*, published in 1920, Edward emphasised the importance of such promotional pieces, 'for I feel that Thomas's fame hereafter is now trembling in the balance ... in default of that push, he may slide back into public forgetfulness and wait to be fished up again sixty years hence.'[49] The passage of time also caused Edward to reflect on Thomas's situation in the years when he was desperately seeking work from newspaper and magazine editors: 'ET was probably feeling bitterly isolated,' Edward confessed to de la Mare. 'I don't think I gauged the extent of this, myself, till later on.'[50] As the years passed Edward continued to proselytise on Thomas's behalf amongst his friends and the greater public: 'If you want to read some *very fine* poetry, order a copy of *Selected Poems of Edward Thomas* with an Introduction by myself. Gregynog Press,' he instructed Cunninghame

Graham in 1927. 'I regard Thomas as the finest poet of his generation. Only you must read, and reread. His method is so *subtly* beautiful that few people understand how great his achievement is.'[51] When the editors of the Dictionary of National Biography asked Helen Thomas whom she would recommend to write an essay on her husband she immediately approached Edward: 'There is no one who I feel is better qualified to fill this niche[?] in this National Institution and no one who I personally would better like to do this for Edward's memory,'[52] she wrote. But perhaps Thomas himself would have been most gratified by a remark Edward made in a letter to Robert P. Eckert, who had sent him the manuscript of his bibliography and biographical sketch of Thomas, with the proposed title 'Edward Thomas: Soldier-Poet'. Edward took issue with this, insisting it be changed to 'Poet-Soldier'. 'Thomas only became a soldier *by the call*,' he explained, 'but he was a Poet in his essence, his nature and genius.'[53]

Joining Cape

'Seriously my dear fellow it was comforting and warming to have you here, all to myself, and laugh, and ironise, and squabble with you as in the days when the wine was still red and women more than a mere memory of smouldering furies.'[1] As Edward mourned the death of one of his closest literary friends, he was rekindling his old intimacy with another. Joseph Conrad and Edward had always stayed in touch, but over the years both had been occupied with new projects and other friends and their meetings had become irregular. Conrad had finally found widespread fame and fortune with the publication of *Chance* in 1914 and three years later Edward asked him to contribute a preface to a book he was writing on Ivan Turgenev, the author he admired above all others. At first Conrad demurred, rather pointedly insisting that he didn't want to appear qualified to speak on things Russian and didn't know the language. He soon relented, however, the task made palatable by his admiration for Turgenev and the conviction that 'in truth Russia was for him no more than the canvas for the painter'.[2] The foreword appeared in the unusual form of a personal letter to Edward and the deprecating remarks Conrad makes about Dostoevsky in it may well be a none too subtle hint that their differences over Conrad's relationship with Russia had not entirely been forgotten.

Edward's book was based on the prefaces he had written for Constance's translations of the novels; it was the first full-length study of Turgenev in English and was generally well received. Reading the book gave one reviewer, T. S. Eliot, pause to ponder whether 'the method of Turgenev – this perfect proportion, this vigilant but never theoretic intelligence, this austere art of omission – is not that which in the end proves most satisfying to the civilized mind'.[3] *Turgenev* and the much briefer book Edward had written on Tolstoy in 1914 as part of Constable's Modern Biographies series confirmed his position as one of the foremost promoters of and commentators on Russian literature.

Not everyone was unreservedly enthusiastic, however: Hudson, never slow to speak his mind, criticised Edward for attacking those who acclaimed Tolstoy and Dostoevsky in order to depreciate Turgenev, whom Edward claimed to be superior in every way. 'No doubt he *was* a greater artist, but – and here's where our difference comes in – to be a great, an *exquisite*, artist is not the greatest thing,'[4] argued a somewhat tetchy Hudson. Edward's essay on American poets for the September 1917 issue of the *Atlantic Review*, in which he lauded Amy Lowell – 'Brilliant is the term for *Men, Women and Ghosts*'[5] – also came in for some stick. Hudson had previously expressed his low opinion of Lowell: 'as a "poet" she, is, to use an Americanism, "small potatoes",'[6] he grumbled, a description that Edward himself felt would better fit Ezra Pound, whose *Personae* he roundly condemned as 'a specimen of false poetic mosaic, pseudo mediaeval *tesserae* set in sticky modern cement that can never harden'.[7] 'His *Canzoni* may offer us technical feats,' Edward continues, 'but are they not bankrupt in feeling? Everything in Mr Pound's verse appears to us to be derived, or imitated, or cut out of old patterns.'

The remembrance of old patterns and an accompanying desire to return to them loomed large in the life of Conrad in the latter years of the war. He turned sixty in December 1917 and was increasingly subject to longer bouts of poor health. Jessie, too, was suffering – in 1904 she had had a serious fall which left her with chronic knee trouble and the Conrads spent the latter weeks of 1917 in London, as she prepared for the first of a series of major operations. Edward visited them there and brought with him the manuscript of Conrad's latest novel, *The Arrow of Gold*, which he had been reading at Conrad's request. Effectively, Edward was resuming the role he had played more than fifteen years earlier. One reason for this may have been that Conrad was returning to manuscripts he had abandoned during his time under Edward's tutelage. There are several similarities between *The Arrow of Gold* and *The Sisters* (the character of Rita, for instance, appears in both), which on Edward's advice Conrad had given up in 1896. Now Edward urged him to complete *The Arrow of Gold*, perhaps not one of his wiser bits of advice as it is generally ranked amongst Conrad's poorest efforts. Conrad also resurrected the manuscript of *The Rescue* (he had changed the title from *The Rescuer* in 1897), the novel that had been the cause of such trauma in the early years of his literary career. He put it to one side once more while writing *The Arrow of Gold*, but went back to it again in the second half of 1918, seeking Edward's advice, just as he had two decades earlier. Both men found themselves considerably affected by the rekindling of the close relationship: 'I missed you immensely my dear old friend during all these days,' wrote Conrad.

> The resumption of our intercourse has been very precious to me. It was a great and comforting experience to have your ever trusted and uncompromising soul come forward again from the unforgotten past and look closely at my work with the old old wonderful insight, with unimpaired wisdom and in unalterable friendship.[8]

For Edward, taking up the threads again brought with it the realisation 'that we are nearer to one another in our sere and yellow leaf even than in our summer days'.[9] 'Hang it all!' he confessed a couple of years later, 'I *am* deeply attached to you, and on the threshold of this 1920 I reaffirm it in the presence of the Fates. Our courses may be erratic, but our orbits intersect in affection.'[10]

The Rescue was being serialised in *Land and Water* magazine, prior to publication in book form. Edward read the serial parts as they appeared and marked up any passages that struck him as weak. (Unfortunately, the copies of the magazine he annotated appear to have been lost.) His letters about *The Rescue* show a remarkable similarity to those written twenty-three years earlier to a despairing Conrad in Brittany. There is the familiar diplomacy – 'This is a note devoted to the Achilles heel – you understand'[11] – the advice to cut – 'You will see from my notes in the margins that I suggest little but *excisions*,'[12] and the unfailing encouragement: 'What I specially admire is the *breadth* of the whole canvas.'[13] However, Edward also expressed concern at the handling of dialogue; to his own surprise the flaws he detects are those of which Conrad was guilty at the beginning of his career:

> You have, here, a habit of saying too much, of letting the characters express themselves too fully. It[']s as though you were beating out their consciousness for them into words ... It[']s remarkable how much firmer and more suggestive the expression is if you merely cut out two or three lines, a line here, or a line there.[14]

Reading the novel in instalments made Edward doubt his own judgement: 'I have rarely felt so uncertain about a work of art,'[15] he confessed. 'What confuses me is that looking back on the story, all of the detail seems in place, but *at the time of reading* ... I was continually being a little surprised and questioning.'[16] Conrad – now occupying an elevated literary status he could only have dreamed about when Edward last criticised *The Rescue* – was nonetheless warmly appreciative of this most recent critique: 'I don't think there is a single remark You make that I don't understand both in the letter and in the spirit,'[17] he conceded, and later told Edward, 'I think that every mark of your pen has been attended to.'[18]

Early on in their correspondence about *The Rescue* Edward apologised for not responding sooner to the instalments he had received. 'I ... have been buried under fresh cartloads of MSS dumped on me by Lane',[19] he explained. In November 1917, after almost two years of piecemeal employment, Edward got a job reading for John Lane at The Bodley Head. The pay of two and a half guineas a week was considerably less than the £180 a year he had been getting from Duckworth before the war and Lane had no compunction about setting his new employee to work – fourteen months after he started at the Vigo Street office Edward calculated that he was reading between 400 and 500 manuscripts a year. This would be a good number even under normal circumstances, but the situation in which Edward found himself was far from that. On 18 April 1918 Parliament passed the Military Service Act (No. 2), which raised the age of exemption from military service to fifty-one. Edward, who had celebrated his fiftieth birthday that January, was now placed in an extremely difficult position: 'As you know I have no earthly objection to killing the responsible people who engineered the war or who are prolonging it,' he explained to Conrad, 'but I refuse absolutely to do military service for objects I do not believe in – such as the conscription of Ireland, the break-up of Austria, the recovery of Alsace-Lorraine, or other such objects (open or secret) of our ruling caste!'[20]

His options were severely limited: pleading conscience would, as Edward put it, 'relegate me to the land, to Dartmoor or any other job fixed upon as sufficiently unpleasant by officials'.[21] The only other possibility was getting a civilian government post. Eventually Edward landed a job at the Ministry of Fisheries. 'I am to work in a small attic at the top of [a] building in Parliament Street 4 days a week from 10 to 5 at a modest remuneration,'[22] he reported to Natalie. For six months Edward juggled the demands of publishing and Parliament Street, but when peace was finally declared he was released from his duties with the Fisheries at the end of December.

All in all, Edward's circle had survived the war reasonably unscathed, although of course there had been casualties: Edward Thomas lay in Agny Military Cemetery and David Rice, who had worked with Edward at Fisher Unwin and was one of his close friends, lost his son Felix in 1917.

Edward's nephew Felix Mahomed had been killed in the Royal Flying Corps and Borys Conrad had been gassed and severely shell-shocked, but was alive. However, the old Mont Blanc brigade was further reduced only three months after the armistice. In February 1919 Stephen Reynolds became a victim of the Spanish flu pandemic: he died on Valentine's Day at the age of thirty-seven. 'I felt very bad about Stephen Reynolds' premature death,' Hudson wrote to Edward on hearing the news. 'He had done good work, but it was nothing to what he had it in him to do.'[23]

Constance remained at The Cearne during the war, occupied with her translations of Dostoevsky and Chekhov and making sure the garden produced as much food as possible. She and Edward effectively lived separate lives: Constance in Kent and Edward and Nellie at Pond Place. However, Edward and Nellie came down to The Cearne most weekends, a routine that continued for the rest of Edward's life. During the ensuing years Edward never stopped worrying about his wife's often frail health and her ability to cope at The Cearne. 'I feel that what you say about Mother's necessity for rest & doing much less is true and imperative,' he told David. 'She has achieved so much by herself.'[24]

David had seen out the war working on the land; despite his scientific training he was increasingly drawn to a career in literature and in 1919 published a novel about a cocaine addict, *Dope-Darling*, under the pseudonym Leda Burke. He described it to his father as a 'sevenpenny shocker', and assured him it was written only with the view of getting a bit of money. 'Please don't think I am going to the bad,' he begged Edward. 'This has absolutely no pretensions to any merit.'[25] When in 1920 David and his friend Francis Birrell opened a bookshop at 19 Taviton Street, London, several of Edward's authors lent their support to the venture.

While the immediate post-war years offered David exciting new opportunities, for Edward they were proving to be depressing times. He suffered various niggling health problems, including rheumatism and a series of varicose ulcers that prevented him from taking exercise. Things weren't much better on the work front, either; John Lane now took little personal interest in the company and Edward was becoming irked at the volume of manuscripts he was expected to read for what he considered to be a poor salary. His interest was therefore aroused when at the beginning of January 1921 he received a letter from Jonathan Cape, his old colleague at Duckworth. 'I have started to publish on my own account,' wrote Cape, 'and hope if you are ever in the neighbourhood you will come in and see me.'[26] Cape's promise that he hoped 'to keep to a respectable standard and will not fight shy of new authors' was sufficiently enticing to get Edward through the door of Cape's recently acquired premises at 11 Gower Street.

Herbert Jonathan Cape was forty-one when he established the new firm with his partner George Wren Howard, who was fourteen years his junior. Howard, a shy and fearsomely self-disciplined only child, borrowed the £5,000 from his parents that made the venture possible. Cape contributed slightly more of the finance and was accordingly the senior partner. He had joined Duckworth in 1904 as a salesman, was promoted to manager in 1911 and ran the business when Gerald Duckworth was summoned to war duties. When Duckworth returned, Cape signed up to the Royal Army Ordnance Corps; he was demobilised in 1919 and rejoined Duckworth, only to find that his prospects there were limited. Gerald Duckworth had never considered Cape, the son of a builder's clerk, to be his social equal and it was clear that the door to a directorship would remain firmly closed. Cape resigned, and went to work for the Medici Society and it was here that he met Howard. Cape quickly recognised that Howard possessed considerable skill in book design and production and that he had a fine business brain. Both men grew increasingly frustrated with the frailties in the management of the Medici and in the summer of 1920 took the decision to set up on their own. Their talents were well matched: Cape, tall, broad and handsome, was prodigiously hard-working, shrewd and knew the market in which he wished to operate extremely well. Howard, a man of slight build and almost obsessively tidy habits, was accomplished in the technical aspects of publishing. What they lacked was someone steeped in literature, someone who could nose out fresh talent and enable the new company to assemble a distinctive and distinguished list. Cape knew what Edward had achieved at Duckworth's – who better fitted the bill?

Edward received Cape's approach with a mixture of caution and curiosity. He feared the outlook for publishers old and new was not very promising, but was tempted by the possibility of joining a firm that might be receptive to his ideas and suggestions, which would make a welcome change from the prevailing situation with Lane. On 18 January he went to see Cape and afterwards wrote to him, agreeing to Cape's proposal to pay 5 per cent commission on sales of all books published on Edward's initiative. However, Edward needed the assurance of a guaranteed level of income and so asked for a minimum of £39 a quarter on account; he also offered to report on all manuscripts Cape sent to him for an additional £13 a quarter. Hearing that Cape was shortly going to the States prompted Edward to add that the financial arrangement he was suggesting

> would probably be to your advantage, as to take one aspect alone, you should bring back with you from America a number of offers of the work of authors whose *future* it is most important for you to gauge correctly. I have myself some definite suggestions to make about American works, and I consider it most important for you to establish contacts and to procure and study very carefully announcements and advance sheets well ahead. Briefly, if you meet my modest requirements, I should be prepared to throw myself into the interests of your firm and try and extend its activities quickly in various quarters. At the same time I realize that your capital does not give you much scope for experiments.[27]

It was a nicely calculated letter, suggesting the possibility of grand horizons ahead, whilst acknowledging the new firm's financial limitations. After talking things over, Cape and Howard offered Edward a salary of £200 a year, rather than a commission on books sold. When Cape suggested Edward come into Gower Street for one day a week and that a room should be set aside for him, Edward immediately informed him that he had an aversion to offices. The proposal was modified, almost certainly reluctantly on Cape's part, so that Edward was tied only to a weekly conference from noon to 3 p.m. on Wednesdays at which they would discuss the manuscripts he had reported on. This would be the only time he would have to be present at Gower Street. This concession made Cape's offer attractive, but the deciding factor was the prospect of exercising real influence over decisions as to what got published. As Edward himself later put it, Cape's 'greatest gift was that he knew nothing about books and admitted it. He looked around him for the best reader he could find, chose me, and followed me blind.'[28]

Having accepted Cape's offer, Edward quickly fell into a regular way of working. He insisted on reading every manuscript that was submitted, initially running his eye over a few pages to discover whether or not it was worth putting aside for the weekly parcel that was sent to Pond Place for closer scrutiny. On average the package contained eight to ten manuscripts, which Edward usually reported on at the next Wednesday meeting. He continued to read for Lane for well over a year after he joined Cape. As he always considered his first duty to be to the author rather than whoever might be employing him, potential conflict of interest probably didn't even cross his mind. The two jobs did leave him exhausted, though; Nellie reported to Louise Bréal that he 'was working just now against time for two publishers and is pretty worried'.[29]

Less than a month later, Nellie was writing to Louise again with happier news. David had just announced his engagement to Rachel Marshall, an illustrator who was working as assistant to the editor of the *Burlington Magazine*. Edward and Constance had seen very little of Ray, as she was known, before the announcement: Constance had met her just once and at first wished David had chosen someone she knew better. Ray was very shy and in consequence said little – David later described her as 'the most silent woman I have ever known'[30] – but as Constance's relationship with her developed, she came to love her daughter-in-law. Edward was the sole person amongst family and friends who welcomed the marriage unreservedly from the start and immediately discerned Ray's qualities and her vulnerabilities. According to David, Edward 'was intuitively aware that Ray could not stand up for herself and he never teased her. She, on her side, became devoted to him.'[31]

Edward felt protective towards Ray, just as he did towards his authors, for whom he was more than willing to take up cudgels against his employer, as Cape very soon found out. If Edward discovered that a contract did not correspond with his idea of what had been agreed, and that a writer stood to lose by it, he lost no time in telling Cape so. 'In future it will be well to keep a note of terms suggested in conversation,' he insisted rather tetchily in one such instance. 'And I should prefer not to offer you books by my friends than to have any dispute about the terms.'[32] In 1922 he found himself in the unusual position of having to conduct negotiations on his own account, as Cape had agreed to publish the book of criticism many of Edward's friends had long urged him to write.

Friday Nights brought together essays Edward had written over more than twenty years. In his preface, he explains the genesis of the book's title and the rationale lying behind it:

> The following papers ... were written mainly in years gone by on favourite authors whose sails were either flapping in the uncertain breezes of public esteem, or had borne their craft on far reaches athwart the popular tide. The writer had a habit of saying to himself on Friday nights, after he had returned to his cottage from town, 'let me write something on this or that author, from this aspect

or from that angle.' And lying in his porch he would reach for paper and ink and jot down on the fly leaf of a book some notes of 'appreciations'.[33]

The literary line-up of *Friday Nights* reflects Edward's cosmopolitan and eclectic tastes – there are representatives from America, Australia, England, Germany Norway and Russia – and includes pieces on some of the writers whose careers he had personally guided and promoted: Hudson, Doughty, Conrad, Lawson, Crane and Lawrence. Seven of the eighteen essays are on American authors, which suggests both Edward's belief in the potential of some of the emerging writers across the Atlantic and the strategic importance of introducing them to the British public in view of Cape's trips to the States in search of talent to publish back in England. The fact that *Friday Nights* was to appear in America under the Knopf imprint doubtless had some bearing on Edward's decisions when he drew up the contents list too.

On finishing the book, the reader could be in no doubt as to some of the qualities Edward sought and admired in a writer: the ability to suggest the intangible from the palpable; a willingness to shake the reader out of his or her settled perceptions, and the facility to make a small, apparently insignificant detail reveal the depths of a situation. The aptitude to draw nature not merely as a savage or picturesque backdrop, secondary to human will, but as integral to life and yet indifferent to it, so indicating the vast forces at play in the universe and placing man and his affairs in their true perspective is something Edward also prizes highly, as are 'veracity', originality and an unflinching readiness to show people what they are. The last two characteristics in particular are, in Edward's opinion, precisely those that will immediately snuff out any hope of a writer winning acclaim or popularity.

It almost goes without saying that the pages of *Friday Nights* contain sustained attacks on what Edward sees as the obstacles confronting the advancement of the literary cause in Britain: commercialism, the insularity of the English, their demand that literature should merely endorse prevailing social norms and conformities, the expectation of 'healthy optimism' and a happy ending, and the indifference, bordering on contempt for writers as a class, who, Edward argues, are 'kept ... as a sect of *dilettanti*, apart, ministering to scholarly aestheticism or drawing room culture, and are disregarded in the central stir and heat of worldly activities'.[34]

The book ends with 'The Contemporary Critic', the essay in which Edward had set out his critical credo two decades earlier. However, he also takes the opportunity to express his thoughts on the subject elsewhere: in 'American Criticism and Fiction' he defines what he sees as the role and responsibilities of the critic and the part he or she plays in the relationship between writer and public:

> It is really on the catholicity of taste and mental responsiveness of [the critic] that the public reception of works of cultivated talent depends. They form an indispensable bridge between the talent and the public at large, and on their measure of insight and sincerity it rests whether a man of original genius can fight his way through to favouring recognition.[35]

Fittingly though, it is in his essay on Conrad that Edward states what was in effect the guiding principle of his entire working life: 'The born artist must be true to his own vision; the born critic to those of other men.'[36] Putting the book together reminded Edward just how hard he had to labour when it came to writing: 'Most of [*Friday Nights*] was written in the sweat of agony,' he told David, 'so take that as a finger post to your own work – that one can only hammer out anything decent with sweat and agony. That's specially true of *criticism* however – it is hell to *define*.'[37]

Friday Nights was published to mixed notices. The reviewer in the *Observer* complained about Edward's 'very uninspiring style',[38] claimed that he discussed Chekhov 'with enthusiasm rather than understanding', and that he overrated Hudson, Richard Jefferies and Sarah Orne Jewett. Hugh l'Anson Fausset in the *Times Literary Supplement* was much kinder, and called the book 'a stirring argument alike against physical complacency and spiritual hopelessness',[39] while John Middleton Murry used his review in the *Nation and Athenaeum* to laud Edward as the 'most single-minded, the most austerely devoted, and the most influential critic of modern English literature'.[40] Galsworthy's review for the *New York Times* was predictably favourable, although he did wonder whether Edward's 'horror of the commonplace' led him into 'sheer worship of the unconventional' and to 'praise as a living masterpiece what is really lifeless, however strange'.[41] A veiled reference, perhaps, to Edward's enthusiasm for the work of D. H. Lawrence, which Galsworthy was a very long way from sharing. Lawrence would have his own say about Galsworthy in a stinging essay of 1927 that brought Edward to the defence of his old friend.

Edward's jaundiced view of his fellow literary journalists was confirmed by the reception of *Friday Nights*. 'No one has seen the *intention* of my book,'[42] he grumbled to de la Mare, and went on to condemn the reviewers for dismissing writers whose work they had not even read, thereby missing the whole purpose of the essays, which was to get people to do just that.

W. H. Hudson, who could be one of Edward's fiercest critics, wrote to him at the end of July, endorsing Murry's eulogistic review of *Friday Nights*. It was the last letter Edward received from him. On 18 August, a fortnight after his eighty-first birthday, Hudson died in his sleep from heart failure. 'Hudson's death is a heavy blow,' Edward told Conrad. 'I loved him as a unique and precious personality, much as I love you … One feels that the shadows are stretching and stealing round.'[43] Hudson was buried in Broadwater Cemetery at Worthing, the place where Richard Jefferies, the subject of another of Edward's admiring essays in *Friday Nights*, also lies. Hudson left his entire estate to the Royal Society for the Protection of Birds, with the exception of small bequests to those who had looked after him and £100 each to his three closest friends: Edward, the writer Morley Roberts and Linda Gardner, with whom Hudson had secretly conducted an affair for many years.

'Alas, dear Hudson!' Edward adds in a postscript to a letter to de la Mare written shortly after hearing the news of his death. This letter was again about *Friday Nights*, which de la Mare had just reviewed in the *Saturday Westminster*, but its tone was altogether different from Edward's earlier missive. Despite the loss of Hudson, Edward was excited as only he could be when he had come across a new discovery. 'I've read a tremendous, a staggering book lately,' he enthused. 'I doubt if we shall see it published for many years. It's simply Truth itself and acts like an explosive shell on one. He's a most amazing man.'[44] The amazing man was T. E. Lawrence, the staggering book *Seven Pillars of Wisdom*.

'A tremendous, a staggering book'

RAF Miranshah Fort, Waziristan, India, ten miles from the Afghan border. Ringed by 'low bare porcelain-coloured hills, with chipped edges and a broken-bottle skyline',[1] the place is just about as remote an outpost as it is possible to imagine. On 20 November 1928 a parcel arrives from London, addressed to AC1 Shaw, the commanding officer's orderly room clerk. The package contains a book, *Letters from Conrad*, edited and with an introduction by Edward Garnett. In lulls between his duties Shaw skimmed the pages and later that day wrote to Edward:

> I was (again) suddenly overwhelmed with contrition. There you were, bringing another great writer to birth; easing him, and encouraging him, and confirming him. I tell you, I recognised every tone and inflection of it. Conrad responded and became a splendid writer ...
>
> You did your best with me, wasting on me the critical talent that evoked the artist in so many other would-be writers ...
>
> If there'd been a spark in the smoke heap your fanning would have blazed the mass: and it didn't. I'm honestly sorry for having failed you.[2]

George Bernard Shaw's wife Charlotte also received a letter written on the same date, in which AC1 Shaw mentions the current mission to destroy local villages in an effort to bring the population to heel. 'My sympathies, in such shows,' he explains,

> are always with the weaker side. That's partly, perhaps, why I was able to help the Arabs whole-heartedly. (Was it whole-hearted? Perhaps: but often I think that it's only in trying to write that my whole heart has ever been engaged: and then not for very long).[3]

These two letters hint at the complexities and contradictions that characterise Edward's relationship with Shaw, the name under which T. E. Lawrence had been living since February 1923. *Revolt in the Desert*, a substantially abridged version of *Seven Pillars of Wisdom*, had been published to critical acclaim and tremendous sales in 1927; in conventional terms Lawrence could hardly call himself a literary failure: but of course there was nothing even remotely conventional about T. E. Lawrence, which was one of the reasons Edward admired him so much. Another reason can be found in the letter to Charlotte Shaw. Lawrence's propensity to side with the underdog was also something he shared with Edward, whose own quick sympathy rapidly discerned Lawrence's desire to achieve literary greatness, as well as the conflicting impulses within Lawrence that would make his literary career such a tortuous affair. Edward, who dealt with several Irish writers in his career, once complained to Benjamin W. Huebsch of the Viking Press that he found them to be 'like eels, [they] twist through your fingers'.⁴ In many ways the Anglo-Irish T. E. Lawrence was the slipperiest of them all.

It was Charles Doughty's *Travels in Arabia Deserta* (1888) that brought Edward and Lawrence together. Both had unbounded enthusiasm for the book: Edward had abridged it for Duckworth under the title *Wanderings in Arabia* in 1908 and Lawrence had long been trying to persuade various publishers to reprint the complete text. In July 1920 the Medici Society showed interest in doing so. Jonathan Cape was still working at the Medici at the time, but thinking of setting up on his own. He remembered the book from his Duckworth days and held it in high regard. Somehow he managed to persuade Philip Lee Warner of the Medici to make it a joint imprint. The reprint, which was issued in 1921, was to be a limited edition of 500 copies, published at the exorbitantly high price of nine guineas, with an introduction by Lawrence – undoubtedly a real selling point. Edward, according to his own account, told Cape very firmly 'you must publish the book in full. You will lose money on it, but it will make your name ... [Cape] spent all his capital on that first book. And it made his name.'⁵

By 1921 T. E. Lawrence certainly didn't need anybody to make *his* name. Thanks in large part to the efforts of the American journalist Lowell Thomas, who in 1919 had given a spectacularly successful series of illustrated lectures about Lawrence and the Arab Revolt, Lawrence was, to use that hackneyed phrase, a legend in his own lifetime. Edward's innate scepticism and his hostility to the whole concept of 'heroism' should surely have made him immediately suspicious of Lawrence, but Lawrence was a maverick, a charmer (if he chose to be) and a mass of contradictions. Edward, who was himself once described by Constance as 'a bundle of paradoxes whom *no one* can possibly understand',[6] found it an irresistible combination. The admiration was far from one-sided; in 1927 Lawrence told Edward that 'in the distant future, if the distant F[uture] deigns to consider my insignificance, I shall be appraised rather as a man of letters than as a man of action.'[7] Lawrence valued literature extremely highly and had no small ambitions for his own writing. He numbered several literary figures amongst his friends – Doughty, Shaw, E. M. Forster, Siegfried Sassoon, Robert Graves – and he would have known Edward by reputation before he met him. Lawrence himself may well have been more than a little flattered at Edward's reaction to and interest in his literary efforts.

Seven Pillars of Wisdom, that 'astounding' work, already had a complicated history before Edward became engaged 'in a frantic struggle to master [it]'[8] during August 1922. In 1919 Lawrence began drafting the book, which describes his experiences as a liaison officer during the Arab Revolt of 1916–18. He was not far off completing it when the manuscript was stolen at Reading railway station – Lawrence inadvertently left it in the station café when changing trains and it was never recovered. He had already thrown away many of the notes he had used and so when in December 1919 he started the book again, he had to do so from memory. Astonishingly, he wrote 400,000 words in three months, living on the top floor of a house in Barton Street, Westminster and deliberately depriving himself of food, sleep and heat in the belief that this sharpened his creative faculties. In August he started abridging the text in order to produce a book for the American market. The motive behind this was purely financial, but it became clear that the project would not raise the capital he needed. For this, and other never entirely explained reasons, Lawrence abruptly abandoned it. Believing the second version of *Seven Pillars* to be careless in style and 'hopelessly bad as a text',[9] Lawrence wrote a third, 'composed with great care' in 1921 and 1922, after which he burned all but one page of Text II. At the beginning of 1922 he began to send batches of the book as it now stood to the *Oxford Times* for typesetting, having discovered that doing so would not cost much more than having the manuscript typed, and that the printers would be able to run off a very limited number of copies on a proofing press. Lawrence ordered eight copies of what has become known as the 'Oxford Edition' of *Seven Pillars*; the whole process of writing the book had been nightmarish and in the latter stages had come close to driving Lawrence from his right mind. Some of the reason for this was the sheer physical and mental exhaustion involved in writing and revising the text, but no small part of it also lay in the fact that in the book Lawrence had confronted and described some of the most traumatic episodes in his life, not least allegedly being raped and savagely beaten at Deraa. He had not spared himself in recounting other profoundly disturbing events, too: his execution of one of his own followers in order to prevent a blood feud and shooting his badly wounded servant Othman ('Farraj' in *Seven Pillars*), to whom he was very close, so as not to leave him at the mercy of the Turks. Little wonder then that as Edward turned the pages of the 330,000-word manuscript, 'astounding' and 'staggering' were descriptions that kept floating into his mind.

Evidently Edward felt favoured when Lawrence asked him if he would read the manuscript: 'That was the "honour" I spoke of that was coming,'[10] he explained to Natalie, before asking her not 'to mention the Lawrence affair to anyone as it is strictly *private*'. Edward was in the privileged position of being one of only two people who had read the book. Eric Kennington, the artist and sculptor, was the other and Lawrence sent a copy to George Bernard Shaw very shortly afterwards. This was no pre-publication exercise, however; Lawrence wanted his book read, but strictly only by those to whom he chose to give it, those whose judgement in his mind counted for something: the thought of *Seven Pillars* being in the public domain filled him with horror: 'please don't consider the point of publication,' he told Edward. 'That never came into my mind when writing it: indeed I don't know for whom I wrote it, unless it was for myself ... I cannot imagine showing it except to a few minds (like yours) already prejudged to kindness.'[11] Yet in the same letter Lawrence thanks Edward for the pencilled notes he has sent on the text he has read thus far and the next day again expresses his gratitude for the trouble Edward is taking, telling him that it will make the book 'pages better than it was', while at the same time urging him 'to let the matter drop'.[12] Lawrence informed Edward that he had received an offer of £7,000 for an abridged version of the book and confessed that it might be 'rather fun' to have a go at reducing the current 140 chapters down to forty: 'However I've said "nothing doing". I'd rather sink with all hands than build a raft out of the wreck.'[13]

Edward could be forgiven for being frustrated; he was convinced the book was extraordinary – it had left him feeling quite shaken – and he could see that with some judicious editing it could be made even better.

He may also have suspected that if he could persuade Lawrence to publish some form of *Seven Pillars* it would encourage him to further writing, as well as providing him with financial security. However, Lawrence only harped on at what he perceived to be the book's failures and refused to commit himself to publication, although he was soon admitting that Edward's praise had made him dream again of 'publishing a little, and so getting cash in hand'.[14]

In telling Edward about the offer for an abridgement Lawrence had opened a minute crack in the door: Edward determined to prise it fully open. At this stage Cape knew nothing about the book and when Edward offered to shorten the text himself he did so in an entirely private capacity. He doubtless hoped that the job he had done on Doughty's *Arabia Deserta* would persuade Lawrence to agree. If Cape could eventually get the book, so much the better, but Edward's motives were literary, not financial. He believed *Seven Pillars* to be an extraordinarily important work and that Lawrence must somehow be persuaded to publish it in some form or other. Lawrence finally agreed to Edward's proposal for an abridgement, albeit not without reservations: 'It's very good of you, amongst all your work, to think of attempting it for me', he wrote, 'and you will think me very ungrateful if after all I say "No" ... I hope I won't, but things are variable, and myself most of all: and I must have the deciding word over my own writing while I'm alive.'[15] Edward had been warned.

The task in hand was of a completely different order from the one Edward had faced when he got out the blue pencil on behalf of the other Lawrence ten years earlier. Edward was to reduce the Oxford text to 150,000 words. This involved shedding more than half of it, after which Lawrence was to cut it still further. Out went any passages that did not advance the narrative of the war or slowed it down, which meant deleting Books VIII and IX and substantial sections of other Books too; this telescoped the action into a quick-fire series of dramatic events. Unnecessary descriptive passages were also targeted, but Edward did not change Lawrence's words; instead he noted parts of the text he felt could be improved upon. He made the abridgement in five weeks, completing it 'in ten days' active work'[16] while laid up with phlebitis.

Lawrence's mind was by no means focused entirely on *Seven Pillars* that summer, however. At the beginning of the year he had decided secretly to enlist in the ranks of the Royal Air Force, then in its early days. His reasons for doing so were multiple, complex and probably not entirely clear even to himself. What was apparent is that Lawrence wished to leave the Colonial Office where he had been serving as an advisor on Arab Affairs; he had no ambition to follow a conventional career, was determined to escape the fame that had recently descended upon him and – most intriguingly from Edward's point of view – he wanted to write a book about the new Air Force from inside the ranks. After much negotiation and no little trouble Lawrence was enlisted as 352087 a/c John Hume Ross on 30 August at the RAF recruiting office at 4 Henrietta Street, London, next door to Edward's old stamping ground at Duckworth's. He was then sent to the RAF training depot at Uxbridge.

The news of Lawrence's decision must surely have come as an unwelcome shock to Edward. Although Lawrence claimed that it was partly prompted by his desire to write about the RAF from within, Edward strongly suspected that in reality Lawrence's new career would leave him little time to write. By now, though, he knew his man well enough to realise that there was no point in trying to dissuade him; Lawrence was ungovernable and you simply had to work with whatever situation he chose to create. Nevertheless, this did not stop Edward from telling Lawrence how he viewed the situation, both about *Seven Pillars* and the new RAF recruit's literary future:

The first abridged book if it comes off, must be edited for *artistic* reasons. But I want you to understand my desire for you and my view of you. Why I want you to write, and why you must write later on is this: I will put it objectively.

Supposing you heard a new composer, and recognized at once in the fibres of the work that he was doing something nobody had done before, a new approach, and a new combination of things in him. I feel somehow that your analysis of life may carry us *further*: there's a quality in your brain that suggests a new apprehension of things, or rather a very *special* apprehension of things that will be lost to us if you don't communicate it to us. And you can only do that through writing: by the S.P. [*Seven Pillars*] and by things to come.

Well, *that's* your work, this *special apprehension* of things. I didn't criticise your going into the R.A.F.C. for I felt you are a law to yourself and you might extract from *that* just what you were needing. And I can quite *see* 'your study of men in the ranks of the RAF'. I can *feel* it, for I have had myself glimpses of that *sort* of world on that level. So anything you store up in your brain, any fresh contact may yield that *new apprehension of things* of which I speak.

> But manual work will tire you out too much for you to write. I
> think you will want more and more 'an empty room' and 'a solitary
> bed' to express yourself.[17]

Edward countered Lawrence's expressed fear of giving himself away in
Seven Pillars and his conviction that parts of the book were sentimental
by reminding him that he needed to consider *Seven Pillars* '*as art*', not
as historical record or autobiography. 'If it's *essential* truth, it's great
art,' Edward insisted. 'It conquers: it leaves everybody dumb: it replaces
everything. Its *it*.' It was this quality that had 'acted like an explosive
shell' when he first read the text. 'It's *all* there,' Edward told Lawrence,
'except the relations of your inner world to it, the expression of which
is to *harmonize* the whole, and make it greater than it is.'[18] The historically minded Lawrence, however, felt the book had to be anchored in
fact and saw such personal expression purely in terms of self-exposure
and not merely as faulty technique.

Edward was convinced he could help Lawrence and tell him 'where
you need to be *more* of an artist'. What he meant by this can be seen in
the letter he wrote when he had finished the abridgement and had met
Lawrence to discuss it. In it, he talks about the necessity of 'the *fusion*
of the characteristic elements in the creative imagination' and cites as an
example Lawrence's writing about Rum, a place described several times
in *Seven Pillars*. On each occasion the reader is taken back to it, Lawrence
needs to evoke former impressions with some '*poetic fresh detail* ... i.e. if
you had seen a bird winging his way against a cliff; or heard the scream
of some animal; or were oppressed by the stillness at night, or gave us
a feeling of the night wind in the cave – etc. etc. the picture would be
living again,'[19] Edward explains.

'Garnett's reduction is in my hands and is a good one,' Lawrence told
his friend D. G. Hogarth, then keeper of the Ashmolean Museum, 'but
it's a bowdlerising of the story and the motives of it, and would give the
public a false impression. I don't like doing that. It's a favourable false
impression, you see.'[20] However, when Lawrence returned the manuscript
to Edward with his own additional excisions, it was Edward who felt
'sulky, *very*',[21] and he could justifiably argue that if there was bowdleri-
sation then he was not the guilty party. He had already been alarmed
when he heard about some of Lawrence's proposed cuts, and counselled
him against taking out the more playful episodes, citing the moment in
the battle for Akaba 'where your camel fell and you lay still, chanting
those abominable Kipling verses. The picture is so fresh and full of sap

... Don't take the curl out of the hair!'[22] Now Lawrence had removed anything else that was remotely controversial or self-revelatory, including the death of Farraj and the camel charge (Lawrence had already taken out the incident at Deraa which had greatly impressed Edward earlier). 'At present I feel sulky at your suppression of the *best* personal passages,' Edward complained. '"I *gave you up* Deraa," I say, reproachfully like a sobbing woman, and now you take Farraj's death from me!' Although the tone of the letter is bantering, exasperation bubbles beneath the surface:

> I'm not sure that you *can* delete Farraj. You don't seem to see that you are only thinking of *yourself* in preserving intact and secret these moments. What a world it would be if all the great writers had suddenly shied off 'wearing their hearts upon their sleeves'.[23]

This gets to the crux of the difference between them. For all his literary ambition, Lawrence could not entirely subscribe to Edward's view that great art requires the abandonment of self, that it must be forged in the crucible of personal experience and then transmuted into something universal.

Edward now mentioned the abridgement to Jonathan Cape, who was keen to publish it and started discussions about a possible contract. Lawrence, meanwhile, told George Bernard Shaw that Edward had abridged the book. Shaw's response was initially encouraging, but he then decided to do his utmost to prevent Cape getting *Seven Pillars*. His tactic was to persuade Lawrence, whom he had met only once, that the book should be published unabridged in several volumes. Shaw also intimated – quite unfairly – that Cape was not to be trusted. Lawrence responded by telling Shaw firmly that Cape, 'a new publisher of the respectable sort ... is first in the running ... Garnett reads for Cape, and liked parts of the book: so that Cape has a special wish for it.'[24]

All this was happening just as a storm was breaking over Lawrence's head. On 27 and 28 December the *Daily Express* carried banner headlines revealing that Lawrence, the 'Uncrowned King' of Arabia, was serving in the ranks of the RAF under an assumed name. The *Daily Chronicle*, meanwhile, ran an article stating that Cape was likely to publish a book by Lawrence on the Arab Revolt. This stirred Shaw – who had not yet received Lawrence's letter telling him that Cape was almost certainly getting *Seven Pillars* – into writing another even more impassioned missive in which he argued the book must be published unabridged, as no publisher would ever consider taking it on in the future if the abridgment appeared first. Shaw even offered to lend Lawrence money to repay any advance he had already received from Cape. Shaw's motives in all of this seem very strange, but it is highly likely that his wife Charlotte was spurring him on. When Cape took over another publisher, A. C. Fifield, in 1921, one of the titles he inherited was Charlotte's *Knowledge is the Door* (1914). The book, which meant an awful lot to Charlotte, was not to Cape's taste and, much to her chagrin, he made little or no effort to sell it. This may account for at least some of the Shaws' animosity.

Events were turning sour for Lawrence, however: the *Daily Express* exposé horrified his masters in the RAF and they were fast coming to the conclusion that he could no longer remain in the force. Although Lawrence had seen the money he would make from the abridgement of *Seven Pillars* as a means of leaving the ranks and allowing him to follow his long-cherished dream of establishing his own private printing press, the RAF now appeared a refuge from the glare of unwelcome publicity. As he later explained to Cape, publishing anything about the Arab Revolt at this juncture would catapult him into the spotlight still further and make it impossible for him to remain in the Air Force. There had always been a residuum of doubt in Lawrence's mind about an abridgement; this – his new-found desire to remain in the RAF and the letters from Shaw, one of the biggest living literary names – decided him. After talking the matter over with his agent Raymond Savage on 1 January 1923, Lawrence wrote to Cape announcing that he was not proceeding with the abridgement: at this stage he offered no explanation as to why. Cape understandably was furious, although partially mollified when six days later Lawrence explained the situation regarding the RAF. Edward received a brief note, informing him that Lawrence had decided to 'cancel that blessed thing, and to carry on here as I am. It feels the lesser evil, but the whole business is a disgusting mess.'[25] Shaw's meddling had backfired spectacularly: it seemed that there would be no *Seven Pillars*, abridged or otherwise, for the foreseeable future and henceforth Edward 'would never cease growling over [Lawrence] wasting his creative talent in RAF drill and clerking and petty duties'.[26]

Edward's abridgement remained valuable to Lawrence, however; it formed part of the security he put up to the bank to finance the Subscribers' Edition in 1923 and it served a similar purpose in 1925, when Lawrence sold the rights to a new abridgement that, at the time, didn't actually exist. Had he failed to meet that contract, the publisher would have been at liberty to publish Edward's text. That Lawrence felt bad about how things had turned out is evident from a letter he wrote to Cape in which he asked him, 'Would you give Garnett the cut-down copy of the thing? [*Seven Pillars*] It was his work, and very well done, and he spent much vain time upon it, and I feel guilty in his sight.'[27]

Amidst Edward's disappointment surrounding *Seven Pillars of Wisdom* there was some happy news. On 8 January Ray gave birth to her first child, a boy named Richard. His arrival was not the only cause for celebration; in the autumn of 1922 David published his second book, *Lady into Fox*, an enigmatic tale about a young woman who turns into a vixen. Edward had read and liked the book in manuscript and had helped David find material about the life and habits of foxes. *Lady into Fox* won the James Tait Black Memorial Prize for 1922 and the Hawthornden Prize a year later. It was the first book David had published under his own name and immediately brought him the literary success for which his father had long striven in vain; if there was a slight twinge of jealousy, Edward gave no sign of it. David looked set to join the emerging new generation of novelists, one of whose stars had glittered all too briefly: 'I was much concerned at the news of your wife's death,' Edward wrote to Katherine Mansfield's widower, John Middleton Murry. 'One grows resigned to the gradual blotting out of the talents of one's own generation. But her genius stood out so finely in the younger generation's record; that one feels keenly the gap.'[28]

The deaths of Edward Thomas, Stephen Reynolds and W. H. Hudson had already thinned the ranks of those writers with whom Edward had been associated earlier in his career and news of Conrad suggested the shadows were also drawing in at Oswalds, the house the novelist was now living in near Canterbury. In September 1923 Jessie reported to Edward that Conrad was in poor health 'and in consequence not less irritable',[29] and at the beginning of December she wrote again, confessing that she felt very anxious about Conrad's continual gout and that the doctor had said his heart was 'distinctly rocky'.[30] This, coupled with a letter dictated by Conrad on the same day expressing a desire to see Edward 'As soon as you like' and ending 'it won't be really safe for me to come up to town for quite a long time'[31] set the alarm bells ringing at Pond Place. Edward responded immediately and begged Conrad to put himself in the hands of Sir Robert Jones, Jessie's orthopaedic surgeon and a family friend. 'You can't go on like this,' he insisted. 'Don[']t you understand that the gouty poison in the body will do for your heart or your kidneys soon.'[32] Conrad's reply – 'Of course it will do me in the end – but one must go sometime'[33] – was hardly reassuring.

Conrad's purpose in writing to Edward had been not to spread panic about the state of his health, but to thank him for his criticism of *The Rover*, the last novel Conrad would finish, which was published in England in December 1923. Finally, Conrad seemed to have conquered what Edward always considered his Achilles' heel, the construction of dialogue: 'You seem to me to handle conversations with greater certainty and ease than in the old days. The talk in "The Rover" is extremely good, with no awkwardness,'[34] he noted, before slipping in a typically diplomatic criticism, which in this case centred on the figure of Scevola, who Edward did not consider a fully rounded character. Conrad's response was equally characteristic in its effusiveness and self-deprecation, but he was almost certainly speaking from the heart when he told Edward 'the belief in the absolute unflawed honesty of your judgment has been one of the mainstays of my literary life.'[35]

The two men had been in contact earlier in the year about another of their long departed friends. Thomas Beer, an American writer, had been to see Edward in connection with his forthcoming biography of Stephen Crane. Edward had effected an introduction to Conrad and was pleased when he subsequently agreed to provide a preface to Beer's book. Conrad used the introduction to pay public tribute to his early mentor, describing Edward as 'the articulate literary conscience at our elbow' and his 1898 *Academy* article on Crane as 'masterly'.[36] As the years passed inexorably, taking his old friends with them, Edward gradually began to assume the role of 'keeper of the flame', defending and promoting posthumous reputations. When there was a knock at the door of 19 Pond Place, Edward was quite likely to find a young writer clutching a notebook and pencil, seeking him out not for advice on their own manuscript, but rather as the sage repository of information and memories of the authors whose careers he had moulded.

Not long after Hudson's death Edward re-read the letters he had received from him over the preceding two decades. In 1923 *Letters from W. H. Hudson*, edited and with an introduction by Edward, became one of the early productions of the Nonesuch Press, which David had recently set up with Francis Meynell and his wife Vera. Edward told Galsworthy that the letters 'convey [Hudson's] personality in a remarkable way', adding, 'Old Huddy is amusingly down on me in many passages: a bit of a sham fight goes on mixed in with the realities.'[37] Edmund Gosse, who reviewed the book in the *Sunday Times*, disagreed, and judged it to be a 'partial disappointment'.[38] Gosse and Edward had never hit it off and Gosse complains that because Edward has little interest in natural history (which was quite untrue), but 'a strange passion for third-rate novels by nobodies' the letters are much too full of remarks about 'ephemeral and even worthless novels'. Gosse detected something 'sophisticated and angular about the moral temperament of Mr Garnett ... [that] clearly oppress[es] Hudson a little'. Whereas Hudson's delightful humour prevents him from taking life too seriously, 'his friend seems to be one of those people who cannot refrain from fiercely seeing good in Boers and Irish rebels, and Germans, and even Bolshevists, where no doubt it may be found, but is hardly worth looking for.' Gosse could turn remarkably feline when the mood struck.

'I read a very scurrilous attack on you in the *Sunday Times* by a man called Gosse. It pained me very much. It is terrible that such creatures should be able to get into print in an English newspaper, especially with the name of Gosse.'[39] This vigorous defence came from the pen of Edward's latest protégé – who just happened to be an Irish rebel himself.

'The dear friend of all my writing life'

'I have bought chops and peas and potatoes for Blood Brother and must begin cooking after posting this,' wrote Edward to Nellie before being interrupted by a knock at the door of Pond Place. 'Oh damn it!' Edward continues in his letter. 'Here's O'Flaherty! I thought I said *seven* and he has turned up at six.'[1] The next day Edward sent a report on the evening with his premature guest:

> I was rather cross with Blood Brother yesterday. I thought him too Irish, and a bit too conceited and couldn't get quite into touch. But this morning we hit it off very well and I thought him 'rather a dear'![2]

Edward had spent the previous eight months getting 'into touch' with Liam O'Flaherty, whom he had first met at Cape's offices in January 1923. The twenty-six-year-old Irishman who showed up for the meeting was a bit less dishevelled and a great deal less despondent than he had been a few days earlier, when he had appeared at Gower Street unannounced and demanded the return of the manuscript of a novel he had submitted for consideration. Penniless and exhausted, he had decided to stow away on a ship bound for New York and wanted to take the manuscript with him. Much to O'Flaherty's surprise and to his considerable consternation he was conducted to Jonathan Cape's own room, where he was convinced he would be confronted with a detective, who would arrest him on account of his Irish Republican activities. Instead, he was received by Cape 'as an important personage'[3] and read a letter from Edward advising the acceptance of his manuscript, not because it would sell, but because Edward discerned a promising writer.

Elated as always at the prospect of a new discovery, Edward was probably nearly as excited as O'Flaherty when they met soon afterwards. The young Irishman was quite a striking presence: good looking, with what H. E. Bates later called 'fierce ... unstable'[4] blue eyes, O'Flaherty was garrulous, erratic and temperamental. Over the ensuing months Edward learned much about him and his extraordinary life. By the time he wrote to Nellie about O'Flaherty's visit to Pond Place, Edward was beginning to sum him up:

> I'm very fond of him. I realize that he is a post-war type, hardened and made anarchic by the war.[5]

The anarchic streak Edward recognised in O'Flaherty had certainly been exacerbated by his experiences serving in the Irish Guards during the First World War, but it was apparent well before then. By the time he was twenty O'Flaherty had spurned the soutane and the tenets of Thomism, thereby disappointing both the visiting priest who had mapped out a clerical career for the boy and his lecturers at University College Dublin, who could only look on in horror as he threw out his books on Classics and St Thomas Aquinas in favour of those by Karl Marx. Having abandoned his university education, O'Flaherty enlisted in the British Army under his mother's maiden name and adopted the anglicised version of his forename. It was as William (Bill) Ganley that he entered the Irish Guards in February 1916.

One night in September 1917 O'Flaherty was in Belgium working in the transport unit on the road from Boesinghe to the front line when a shell exploded in the hole near a railway track where he was sheltering. O'Flaherty suffered a head wound and severe shellshock. Diagnosed with 'melancholia acuta' in May 1918 O'Flaherty was invalided out of the army. He suffered periodic bouts of depression for the rest of his life.

O'Flaherty was released into the care of his father with a small pension and few prospects. In August 1918, the month he turned twenty-two, he 'set out to conquer the world'.[6] He arrived in London and took a series of short-lived jobs, including hotel portering and working as a clerk. As soon as O'Flaherty discovered he loathed fixed hours and routine, he walked out of the office and went off to sea. By the time Edward met him O'Flaherty had been to North and South America, Canada, Italy, Turkey, Greece and many points in between. According to the far from reliable O'Flaherty, the number of countries he had visited was exceeded only by the variety of jobs he had undertaken during his travels: ordinary seaman, lumberjack, copper miner, carpenter, docker, pastry cook – he had tried them all and more besides. The one thing that had stayed constant during this time was his admiration for Marx. In December 1921 O'Flaherty returned to Ireland to co-found the Irish Communist Party and the following month attempted a revolution of his own when, along with a couple of hundred unemployed men, he seized part of the Rotunda building in Dublin. *The Times* reported that 'a large red flag floats from one of the windows of the seized building'.[7] The rebellion ended somewhat ignominiously after only four days when the authorities threatened to storm the Rotunda and the would-be revolutionaries left by a side door. O'Flaherty fled to Cork, but was back in Dublin six months later, this time as a member of the Irish Citizen Army, fighting on the Republican side in the Irish Civil War. By early July the government had gained the upper hand in Dublin and O'Flaherty had to take off again, this time to Liverpool from whence he made his way to London. Several of Edward's protégés over the years had led colourful lives, but O'Flaherty was certainly one of the brighter hued amongst them.

O'Flaherty had been a storyteller even as a boy and now he decided to try and earn a living by his pen. In January 1923 the *New Leader* published 'The Sniper', a short story by O'Flaherty set during the Irish Civil War. Edward read it and was impressed, just as he was when the manuscript of O'Flaherty's novel arrived at Cape's office. This was *Thy Neighbour's Wife*, a tale of conflict between religion and love, set in the Aran Islands. By April O'Flaherty had embarked on his next novel, *The Black Soul*, and was sending Edward regular reports on its progress.

When an envelope arrived addressed in O'Flaherty's changeable hand, Edward could be sure the contents would be entertaining. O'Flaherty was nothing if not mercurial and his letters extravagantly reflect the full range of his moods, from high exuberance – 'I feel like seducing a Pope's daughter, I am that full of life'[8] – to the depths of despair – 'I am in a very low condition here and absolutely friendless – everybody has turned against me. I have no money.'[9] Edward responded to that particular lament by sending £10 and a volume of Rabelais. The letters were quite as likely to contain details of O'Flaherty's turbulent love life as news of his latest literary efforts: Edward dispensed advice freely on both. O'Flaherty received a steady stream of books from Pond Place, carefully selected by Edward as exemplars to be followed. Conrad, Hudson and George Borrow found their way on to the Irishman's bookshelves, as did Turgenev and Chekhov, whose use of the small detail O'Flaherty regarded as a minor miracle:

What struck me in ... 'Peasants' was the marvellous power that Tchekov had in giving us reams of the peasants' history and outlook in life and habits, by the mere statement, 'their shoulders knocked together as they walked.' Damn it, I think that there is more poetry and literature in a slight action of that kind than in violent dialogue or clever portraiture, from a long distance. I can't do it myself so I know.[10]

As far as Edward was concerned this was a lesson well learned; he also swiftly discerned that O'Flaherty's forte lay not in writing page-turning accounts of violence and high drama but in descriptions of the things he knew best – the Irish landscape and the creatures that inhabited it, hence the gifts of Hudson's and Borrow's books. It also soon became apparent to Edward that O'Flaherty was a particularly talented writer of short stories and sketches, and he began a concerted campaign to bring O'Flaherty's name to the attention of the editors of those periodicals and newspapers where his work was likely to get noticed. This Edward called 'securing': before long Desmond MacCarthy, the literary editor of the *New Statesman*, had been 'secured' and Edward had sold some of O'Flaherty's sketches to the *Manchester Guardian*. Middleton Murry, the editor of the *Adelphi*, was not persuaded, however. 'I don't think there's much doubt [O'Flaherty] is a writer,' he told Edward, 'though I don't believe he's as good as you think he is.'[11] If it was important that O'Flaherty's sketches got placed in order to establish his name, financially it was imperative. Writing was O'Flaherty's sole source of income (other than his small army pension) and funds were often in short supply. Edward not infrequently loaned him money, in addition to getting him a bike, sending him to a dentist and providing the wherewithal for a set of false teeth. He also persuaded Jonathan Cape to subsidise O'Flaherty: 'I can see your hand in this as in everything else,' O'Flaherty remarked to Edward. 'How can I thank you, my friend?'[12]

In March 1924 O'Flaherty went back to Ireland; returning to his familiar element was something that Edward believed could only benefit O'Flaherty's writing and initially the move seemed to have worked: O'Flaherty was stimulated and in good spirits, although he complained that he missed not being able to see Edward when he wanted to. He was eagerly awaiting the appearance of his second novel, *The Black Soul*, which he dedicated to Edward. O'Flaherty had had a real struggle writing the book, which, like *Thy Neighbour's Wife*, is set in the Aran Islands.

Edward made him re-draft parts of it several times over, chastising him for lack of style and trying to help him with the end of the novel and with dialogue, which gave him particular difficulties. As Edward later explained to H. E. Bates, 'The old father [in the novel] was a frightful hard nut to crack and to my horror he suddenly put *me*, in an idealized form, into the figure!!! I had a great scene with him and made him rewrite that part, and he did so and put his own father in my place which saved the book.'[13] O'Flaherty was ill during some of the time he was wrestling with *The Black Soul* and on one occasion Edward had to put him to bed with brandy. That O'Flaherty modelled the old father on Edward says much about how he viewed their relationship, subconsciously or otherwise, and about the extent of his dependence.

Letters from Ireland arrived at Pond Place in rapid succession, many asking Edward's advice about sketches and where to place them. By now O'Flaherty had written a sufficient number to put together a collection; he admitted to Edward that the move back to Ireland had put him 'in closer touch with life and [I] am writing with greater discrimination'.[14] However, Ireland had its drawbacks, too:

> For me life is very lonely here without you. It seems nobody else is in any way deeply interesting. You see one has a devilish hero worship for a man one allows to throw one's manuscript in the fire. During the past month when I was in agonies trying to find the right way out for my novel, I said to myself: 'Now, if Edward Garnett were here he would tell me in half an hour what I should do and the way would be clear.'[15]

By the end of June O'Flaherty was back in England, staying at a farm near Tring with Margaret (Topsy) Curtis, the wife of a Professor of History at Trinity College Dublin. O'Flaherty had met Topsy, who was also a writer, at George Russell's house in March and less than a month later he wrote to Edward with the news that he had 'secured the wife of Professor Curtis, which is, of course, the most important conquest!'[16] Edward, by now long accustomed to such embroilments amongst his protégés, regarded this one with amusement and was soon on excellent terms with Topsy.

News from another writer's wife was less welcome: in June Edward received a letter from Jessie Conrad telling him that Conrad had been laid up for some time with a bad cough and congestion. Edward went down to Oswalds to see his old friend. He found him fatigued and when it came to saying goodnight 'something moved me ... to put his hand to my lips. He then embraced me with a long and silent pressure.'[17] Just as Edward was about to leave the next morning, Conrad snatched a copy of a Polish translation of *Almayer's Folly* from a shelf, wrote an inscription, and handed it to Edward. The fact that the book was a Polish translation may have been a final thrust at Edward's fixation about Conrad's 'Slavic' origins and influences, but the inscription was a fitting tribute to a thirty-year friendship:

> To Edward Garnett. The first reader of *Almayer's Folly* in the year 1894 and ever since the dear friend of all my writing life, never failing in encouragement – and inspiring criticism. With love Joseph Conrad[18]

The valedictory tone may well have caused Edward some disquiet and on 3 August came the news he had been half-expecting: Conrad had died early that morning from a heart attack at the age of sixty-six. Edward was one of the official mourners at the funeral, which took place at St Thomas's Church, Canterbury, amidst the crowds and flags of Cricket Week. Cunninghame Graham was also at the graveside: 'You helped Conrad greatly,' he told Edward shortly afterwards, 'and I am sure he was grateful to you. You may have been young ... but I do know you were full of enthusiasm and that is the quality that moves more mountains than Faith has ever stirred.'[19] Later, Walter de la Mare wondered 'if JC would have gone on writing if it hadn't been for you ... [W]hat your help meant to him, and to so many other writers, when it was most needed, is past measuring. For after all,' de la Mare continues, 'these things were not done on behalf of the silly old public, but for friendship's sake.'[20]

Conrad's death inevitably caused those who had known him to reflect on former days, and less than four months after the funeral Ford Madox Ford published his own memoir of his erstwhile collaborator. *Joseph Conrad: A Personal Remembrance* is characteristically Fordian, both in the evocative impression it creates of its subject and in Ford's disregard for factual accuracy. As Edward read the book he grew increasingly exasperated. Ford's account of his friendship with Conrad and their collaboration played fast and loose with the truth and was to Edward's mind a sickening mixture of romantic exaggeration, fiction and self-aggrandisement. An unsuspecting reader could only conclude that Conrad owed much of his technical development to Ford, who assumes for himself a central place in Conrad's life in the early nineteen hundreds, relegating others amongst Conrad's circle, Edward included, very much to the shadows. Edward had been going through Conrad's letters to him with an idea of publishing them; now he rubbed his hands with glee at the thought of one in particular getting into the public domain and blasting apart Ford's spurious claims. For the moment, however, Edward had to content himself with a preliminary attempt to set the record straight when he reviewed Ford's memoir for the *Nation*.

In his preface to *Joseph Conrad*, Ford contends that the book is constructed 'exactly along the lines laid down by us both [i.e. Ford and Conrad] for the novel which is biography, and for the biography which is a novel'. Edward would have none of it:

> To accept a fiction-biography would be to invite the three-card trick from every ingenious manipulator. In the magic name of 'impressionism' a man can magnify, distort, or suppress facts and aspects to his own glorification, he can dye everything with his own hues and belittle others, and then, on being brought to book, he can turn round reprovingly and protest, 'But this is a work of art!'[21]

He then goes on to enumerate several examples of where Ford twists or ignores facts and pointedly mentions that it was he who introduced Ford to Conrad in the first place and that he had 'known Mr Ford as a lad of eighteen and sponsored his early works'. The review concludes with the dark observation that the publication of Conrad's letters will 'throw interesting light on various statements ... and separate the wheat from the chaff. That there is genuine wheat in this book I should be the last man to deny,' Edward continues, 'but if Mr Ford throws on others the task of winnowing it, well, it is – his misfortune.'

'But *nothing* would have affected Ford,' Edward wrote to his sister Olive, who had seen a lot of Ford when they were both younger. 'I used to come down on his gorgeous embroideries in the early days – with the result that he shunned me, and as he never could stand criticism our relations practically ceased before the war.'[22] Edward's review of Ford's book would obviously do nothing to restore them and two months later he wrote another piece about it, this time in the *Weekly Westminster*. Although he comments that 'acute things and flashes of true discernment are sandwiched with Munchausen-like anecdotes and childish conceit',[23] this piece is actually less astringent than the *Nation* review and the focus is different. Edward concentrates his fire on Ford's account of Conrad's literary methods and the crucial role Ford claims for himself in their development. When Edward comments that 'It is natural for the planets that circle round the sun each to believe that his orbit is of particular importance,' he perhaps touches upon one of the most important factors underlying his relations with Ford.

Besides being a prolific and successful writer, Ford also was a considerable talent-spotter, particularly during his years as editor of the *English Review*. He and Edward moved in the same circles and a competitive edge may well have developed when it came to literary prospecting and guiding emerging writers' careers. Ford and Edward agreed that the home-grown novel was in need of rejuvenation, but differed as to where aspiring writers should look to find it. Ford's gods were French – Flaubert and Maupassant – Edward's Russian, and in particular Turgenev (admittedly the most Europeanised of the Russian writers). According to Ford, he and Conrad had long discussions about the techniques of novel writing in which French writers were consistently held up as the ideal. He had already ridiculed Edward's devotion to the Russians in a *roman à clef* he had written in 1911 under the pseudonym Daniel Chaucer. Edward features in *The Simple Life Limited* as Mr Parmont, the cynical critic, who, according to the narrator, claims that 'It was only Russians who could write because they hadn't any conventions, they went straight to life, they went straight to nature.'[24] A couple of pages later the narrator observes that 'Russia had played during all Mr Parmont's life since he had left school the part of a tremendous ground bass, rising occasionally to an uproar that drowned the noise of all the other advanced movements in Europe.'[25]

There may be a germ of truth in Ford's satire, and he was clearly irritated by Edward's insistence that the Russians were the guides to literary greatness rather than his own beloved Flaubert and Maupassant. The individual foibles that in Ford's and Edward's early youth had been the subject of jokes and teasing had developed into running sores between them and they grew increasingly intolerant of each other at a personal level, but the spat over Ford's memoir went deeper than petty jealousy as to who was better friends with Conrad. Rumbling beneath the surface was the question of who exerted the greater literary influence, not just over Conrad, but in the wider world of early twentieth-century letters.

Edward retained considerable respect for Ford's literary judgement, however. In 1927 Cape published *The Left Bank*, a collection of short stories by Jean Rhys, who had been mentored by Ford, with whom she had had a turbulent relationship. Ford wrote a long and rather rambling introduction to the book, which was well received but sold relatively poorly. When Edward read the manuscript of Rhys's first novel *Quartet* (at that stage alternatively titled *The Samaritans*) he was impressed and strongly advised Cape to publish it.

Rhys wrote *Quartet* in the bitter aftermath of her affair with Ford, who appears thinly disguised as 'Mr Heidler' in the book. It is not a flattering portrait and Rhys always maintained that Cape's refusal to publish was on account of his fear of being sued for libel. The commercial failure of *The Left Bank* may also have had quite a bit to do with Cape's decision. An infuriated Edward advised Rhys to send the manuscript to Chatto & Windus and he himself wrote to Charles Prentice at Chatto, pointing out that Rhys was in his opinion 'a born writer & in "The Samaritans" she has developed a situation, taken from life in Paris, with grand skill'.[26] Much to Rhys's delight, Chatto accepted the book. 'Thank you very, very much for speaking to them, and for all your kindness to me,' she wrote to Edward, later thanking him again 'for all your dearness to me' and confessing that she had been 'horribly depressed & discouraged about my writing & now I have some hope of doing something good – better.'[27] Chatto had suggested that Edward write an introduction to *Quartet*,[28] but Edward declined the invitation, aware that Heidler was based on 'a well known figure in literary circles'.[29] His refusal was probably based on a determination to avoid any further entanglement with Ford, rather than any desire to spare Ford's feelings, for by then their relationship had deteriorated still further.

At around this time – four years after Ford's book on Conrad had appeared – Edward published Conrad's letters to him, including one that Conrad had written in 1900 at the time he was collaborating with Ford on *The Inheritors*:

> I set myself to look upon the thing as a sort of skit upon the political (?!) novel, fools of the Morley Roberts sort do write ... And poor H[ueffer] was dead in earnest! Oh Lord. How he worked! There is not a chapter I haven't made him write twice – most of them three times over
>
> ... H has been as patient as no angel had ever been. I've been fiendish. I've been rude to him; if I've not called him names I've *implied* in my remarks and in the course of our discussions the most opprobrious epithets. He wouldn't recognize them. 'Pon my word it was touching ...
>
> You'll have to burn this letter – but I shall say no more. Some day we shall meet and then –![30]

A more different view of the collaboration from Ford's account in *Joseph Conrad* is difficult to imagine. Here it is Conrad, the master craftsman, standing over Ford, the rather inept literary apprentice. There was no one more adept than Conrad at adapting his tone according to his correspondent, and doubtless he knew Edward would appreciate this scathingly humorous description, especially as he had not been keen on the idea of the collaboration in the first place, believing Ford's and Conrad's talents to be ill-suited to such a venture. *The Inheritors* had been written for the marketplace and Edward, despite his reservations – but very much mindful of Conrad's empty purse – had persuaded Heinemann, his employer at the time, to accept it.

It was George T. Keating, an American collector of all things Conradian who sent Ford a copy of Edward's book with the offending letter clearly marked, just in case Ford missed it. Ford wrote to Edward the same day, pointedly marking the letter 'Private and not for publication in *perpetuity*'.[31] In it, he expresses sorrow that Edward has published the letter, not because of Conrad's sarcasms against Ford, to which he professes to be 'fairly indifferent', but because he maintains that doing so 'much discredits the memory of that unfortunate man', who according to Ford was at that time 'living in my house and I was letting my own family go short in order to keep him and I was giving my whole time to giving him moral support and to putting his affairs in order – and to writing his books.' Edward probably snorted derisively at that, marking it down as characteristic exaggeration. Throughout a lengthy letter, Ford attempts to seize the moral high ground. Edward had sold his collection of Conrad and Hudson manuscripts and letters in New York less than a fortnight earlier. Lot 187 comprised 'An interesting letter about Hueffer's collaboration with Conrad in the writing of "The Inheritors"'[32] with the most scathing sentences quoted in the catalogue for all to see. Ford, unaware the sale had already taken place, rather loftily commented that 'For myself I have never sold and never will sell anything of Conrad's', and he asked Edward to withdraw the letter from the sale, even offering to buy it himself. Ford goes on to pour out a litany of perceived wrongs perpetrated against himself and Conrad by all and sundry, including that, according to Conrad, Edward had got his knife terribly into Ford. Towards the end of the letter he announces to Edward that 'as we never did agree about anything in literature I see no possibility of our now doing so' – which suggests the antagonisms were both literary and personal. If Edward did respond, the letter has been lost, and so Ford's is the last word on the complex relationship between the two men that had started in the drawing rooms of Ford Madox Brown and William Rossetti in the 1880s.

The dispute over *Joseph Conrad* sealed the inexorable decline in the friendship between Edward and Ford, but theirs was not the only relationship under strain around this time. At some point, possibly towards the end of the war, Nellie found out about Edward and Natalie Duddington. Writing more than twenty years after Edward's death, Nellie recalled that when she 'suddenly realised that his love was divided the shock was terrible and the agony then, was often unbearable'.[33] Unanswered questions gnawed away in Nellie's mind for years, but she seems to have given voice to very few of them, afraid of giving pain and expressing jealousy. 'A sort of silence seemed to have settled on us both[,] broken by the practical details of *life*, by details of the world outside, by the expression of *words* of love – a silence about all that seemed so vital, that he seemed so unwilling to speak of and I so incapable of doing so,'[34] she wrote. There are hints of Nellie's unhappiness in some of her letters to Louise Bréal: 'Life here at Pond Place is pretty much as you already know it,' she explained in March 1924. 'I do not think it's a very good way of living – but it has its advantages.'[35]

Nellie later confessed that she thought of leaving several times, but her love for Edward and her conviction that if she did he would come and force her to return, because 'he would have felt it was impossible to let me feel myself isolated and cut off, after all we had had together,'[36] prevented her from doing so. Outwardly things continued as before – regular holidays to their favourite spots at St David's in Wales and to the West Country; weekends at The Cearne or at the caravan they now had on a meadow at Hankley Farm, Elstead, Surrey; the weekdays spent at Pond Place – but 'the sickening doubt'[37] was for a long time never far from Nellie's mind.

Edward, too, was discontented, although his malaise was not on account of his relationship with Nellie. 'It's so annoying not being able to work consecutively at anything,' he complained. 'I plunge into other people's worlds every day, and have no continuity of my own.'[38] This rare reference to the self-sacrifice involved in mentoring the careers of others was prompted by Edward's frustration at his lack of progress on *Barbara's Case*, a stage comedy he was writing that eventually came to nought. He had little opportunity to work on it during the autumn of 1924, which was particularly busy, and by the time of his fifty-seventh birthday in January the combination of overwork, increasing weight and chronic circulatory problems was taking its toll. Climbing stairs made

Edward breathless and varicose ulcers were affecting his mobility. 'The doctor tells me my arteries are not in a good state,' he reported to David, 'but that if I give up smoking and take iodine they should get better.'[39] Stopping smoking proved to be beyond Edward's powers – some of his later protégés always associated him with the lingering aroma of herbal cigarettes – and in October 1925 he consulted a heart specialist, who told him not to overdo things physically and to avoid worry – easier said than done, particularly when you were dealing with characters like Liam O'Flaherty and T. E. Lawrence.

Threats and tensions

The beginning of 1925 brought a rush of letters from Ireland, some from O'Flaherty himself, the majority from Topsy Curtis. Cape was bringing out *The Informer*, O'Flaherty's second novel about an Irish revolutionary who betrays one of his comrades, later in the year. The book, a thriller that owed no small debt to Dostoevsky, was certainly not the sort of thing Edward had urged O'Flaherty to write: *Spring Sowing*, a collection of short stories published by Cape in the latter half of 1924 and containing such sketches as 'The Cow's Death', 'His First Flight' and 'The Rockfish', was to Edward's mind a far superior work.

O'Flaherty had fallen ill while he was finishing *The Informer*, his poor state not helped by shortage of money and the peripatetic existence that resulted. Edward made various suggestions as to additional sources of income, including the newly formed Irish Boundary Commission, all of which were peremptorily dismissed by O'Flaherty: 'as far as the Irish Boundary is concerned I don't see any chance,' he retorted, adding that what he had seen of Fleet Street had convinced him that he 'would rather live starving than push myself into an early grave at that line of work'.[1] There was little Edward could do in the face of such recalcitrance and by January 1925 O'Flaherty was back in Ireland, in the grip of a complete breakdown, suffering terrible nightmares and racked by serious kidney trouble. Edward sent money, books and moral support; 'I don't know what I have done to deserve all this consideration from you,' O'Flaherty wrote at the end of January. 'I know I have been a dreadful worry and nuisance to you since I met you, but the more I worry you and the more trouble I cause you, the more you exert yourself on my behalf ... I do verily believe I was done for this time, had you not come to my assistance ... the consciousness that you were abroad, working ceaselessly for me, came like a great cool healing draught.'[2]

O'Flaherty's increasingly serious financial predicament prompted Edward to lobby the Royal Literary Fund to give O'Flaherty a grant.

Edward's old friend E. V. Lucas was recruited to the cause, although when he heard that O'Flaherty had been in trouble with the Catholic Church, he warned Edward 'there may be opposition ... The members of the Committee are very staid people, at least when they sit round the table.'³ Lucas himself sent £5 for O'Flaherty, and Galsworthy also sent money. 'I think you're a brick to back your friend so staunchly,'⁴ he told Edward. In February the Royal Literary Fund agreed to give O'Flaherty a £200 grant. 'Now everything is rosy and the heart sings and the mind dreams of conquests, of beautiful rhythms and splendid epics,'⁵ purred the grateful recipient, who in March moved to Kilmacanogue in Co. Wicklow, to a house which, according to O'Flaherty, was 'so ugly that it hurts to approach it'.⁶ Edward and Nellie saw this architectural blot in May when they visited O'Flaherty and Topsy, who reported that the two men 'argued day and night as usual'.⁷

While in Dublin Edward met Sean O'Casey, who made a deep impression on him: '*Juno and the Paycock* is a fine – a very fine thing – a real work of art,' Edward told Natalie. 'How delightful it is to listen to genius.'⁸ Edward always loved going to Ireland, but this trip in particular emphasised his feelings of dislocation. 'Its [*sic*] rather sad to be a hybrid,' he confessed. 'I realized that I might have found a place in Dublin if I had been brought up in Ireland and that London was always the wrong place for me – quite wrong.'⁹ To David he complained that he was 'a "bad fit" in England[,] a monument put up in the wrong place, conscious of its inappropriate position!'¹⁰ Temperamentally, he declared he felt much closer to the Irish than the English – 'so heavy and matter of fact in comparison'.¹¹ Edward was not alone in pondering how different his life might have been had he been based across the Irish Sea: 'If you had lived in Ireland instead of living in England you would have become the father of Irish literature, instead of waiting till your death in England to get due recognition of your genius,' wrote O'Flaherty. 'I say damn the English bourgeoisie!'¹²

Almost as soon as Edward got back, a crisis blew up involving another Anglo-Irish 'hybrid'. T. E. Lawrence's suppression of Edward's abridgement of *Seven Pillars of Wisdom* had not prevented him from being kicked out of the Air Force at the end of January 1923. A month later he had enlisted in the Tank Corps under another pseudonym, T. E. Shaw. The work was undemanding, but Lawrence disliked his new situation and fell into spells of deep depression. 'The irk [*sic*] to write is burned away, and I read less and less ... music all gone, painting now indifferent, conversation nil,'¹³ he reported despondently in August. In the same letter he told Edward he was short of money and toying with the idea of publishing the abridgement after all, but by the end of the year he had decided to issue a privately printed subscribers' edition of *Seven Pillars*, unabridged but revised. Lawrence worked on the revision throughout 1924 and 1925, his mood growing ever blacker: 'I'm sick just at present – in mind and body – and hate myself and all the circumstances of life,'[14] he revealed to Edward. By 1925 the production costs of *Seven Pillars* were such that Lawrence informed Edward that he was 'flirt[ing] again with the idea of an abridgement, for profit' and approached Cape about it. 'Roughly it would be the abridgement which you made: translated into the revised text,'[15] Lawrence explained. Cape, who showed remarkable patience given Lawrence's history of vacillation about *Seven Pillars* in all its projected forms, offered him £3,000 for the shortened text.

However, by now Lawrence's mind was focused on only one thing: his desire to rejoin the air force had become all-consuming. 'I can't get the longing for it out of my mind for an hour,'[16] he told John Buchan. Lawrence's hopes were raised in the spring, but in May he learned that his application had failed. The news sent him into a tailspin of despair and on 13 June he wrote to Edward, enclosing the revised Book VI of *Seven Pillars*. When Edward read Lawrence's protestations – 'What muck, irredeemable, irremediable, the whole thing is! ... There isn't a scribbler in Fleet Street who wouldn't have got more fire and colour into every paragraph'[17] – he may initially have marked them down as characteristic self-deprecation. Then came the news that Samuel Hoare, the Secretary of State for Air, had refused to entertain the idea of Lawrence's re-entry into the Air Force: 'That, and the closer acquaintance with the *Seven Pillars* ... have together convinced me that I'm no bloody good on earth,' Lawrence confessed to Edward. 'So I'm going to quit: but in my usual comic fashion I'm going to finish the reprint and square up with Cape before I hop it! There is nothing like deliberation, order and regularity in these things. I shall bequeath you my notes on life in the recruits camp of the RAF. They will disappoint you.'[18]

This may have been an attempt by Lawrence to galvanise his friends into sustained lobbying on his behalf as much as a genuine threat of suicide, but Edward was taking no chances. He wrote immediately to George Bernard Shaw, asking for help. Shaw sent the letter to the Prime Minister Stanley Baldwin, warning of an appalling scandal should Lawrence be true to his word. Baldwin took note and, at a meeting on 1 July, Lawrence learned he had got his way and could rejoin the air force after all. A couple of weeks later he confessed that he owed Edward two letters, implicitly of thanks, the first for a Greek gem Edward had sent him, the second 'for the RAF'.[19]

Meanwhile, various parts of the revised *Seven Pillars* arrived at Pond Place for scrutiny. The book was becoming a test of endurance for both writer and reader, as Lawrence admitted: 'Twice you have read the thing: once you have abridged it. I've read it twenty times, written it five times. Will there never be an end for either of us?'[20]

Edward's patience with Lawrence may have been inexhaustible, but Jonathan Cape's forbearance of Edward's maverick working methods was about to run out. Cape was growing increasingly irked at how little time Edward spent in the office, not to mention his habit of acidly pointing out clauses in contracts which he considered detrimental to an author's interests. When Cape wrote suggesting a new arrangement and mentioning his disquiet about his reader's infrequent attendance at Bedford Square, a furious Edward retorted that it was clear Cape wished to reduce him to a packer's or a typist's salary. This prompted Cape to consult Wren Howard; their discontent was expressed in no uncertain terms: 'the present arrangement does not suit us and we want either to mend it or end it,'[21] announced Cape at the beginning of a long letter. He went on to deplore Edward's 'complete detachment' – a consequence of his all too brief appearances in the office – and complained that his reader had 'very little knowledge of what we are doing; what sort of organization we have built up; or of the volume and nature of the business we are handling'.[22] 'You speak of being the "literary conscience" of the firm,' Cape continues, 'but this literary conscience has been in the keeping of others besides yourself – to a larger extent than you realize.' All the hopes Cape had fostered – of Edward taking an increasing interest in the company's activities, of his introducing authors other than those who submitted manuscripts directly, and that he 'would be the active agent and advocate of the firm in preference to all others' – had been largely disappointed. Scrutiny of the profit and loss columns for those books published on Edward's advice proved 'a depressing business' and Cape considered some amongst his recommendations to have been 'highly dangerous and calculated to give us a reputation for publishing erotic books'.[23] (Sherwood Anderson's *Many Marriages* is mentioned as one such example.) 'That we have had other advice to supplement yours is perhaps news to you,' Cape adds pointedly. The letter ends with what was effectively an ultimatum: if he wished to continue to draw a salary, Edward had to undertake to be in the office for at least two hours on Tuesdays and Fridays and more frequently if occasion demanded; otherwise Cape would institute a fresh agreement and merely pay Edward a fee for each manuscript he read.

How this went down at Pond Place can only be imagined – no response has survived – and whether Edward appeared at Bedford Square on Tuesday mornings and Friday afternoons as Cape commanded is also a matter for conjecture. However, Edward remained with Cape in salaried employment for a further twelve years, so some sort of compromise must have been reached. Despite the 'depressing' balance sheets, Cape had tremendous respect for Edward's judgement, and Edward had to acknowledge, however grudgingly, that Cape was an astute businessman who knew his trade. Some of Cape's remarks – particularly his accusation that Edward did little in the way of seeing and meeting existing and prospective authors – seem unfair, but Cape's conviction that Edward's allegiance to the firm was less than wholehearted was well-founded: if Edward thought an author could get a better deal or a greater opportunity with a rival publishing house, he didn't hesitate to say so. Edward also had other irons in the fire – in April he had been appointed English representative of the newly established Viking Press in New York. Viking's declared intention to 'publish a strictly limited list of good nonfiction … and distinguished fiction with some claim to permanent importance rather than ephemeral popular interests'[24] would have appealed to Edward – but he could not afford to dismiss Cape's comments out of hand.

Had Cape ever been invited to Pond Place one evening, the scene before him might have made him revise his remarks about Edward's alleged failure to cultivate authors. There, in the long sitting room facing the street would be Edward, reclining on his wicker chaise longue, holding court to one or more of the upcoming generation of writers. The surroundings were hardly plush – the floor uncarpeted, books, manuscripts, letters and notes scattered everywhere – but it was a place of powerful presences. Autographed portraits of Hudson, Conrad, Galsworthy, Crane and W. H. Davies stood on the mantelpiece or hung on the walls alongside many other pictures, some of which were by Nellie. One of the numerous bookcases held Edward's collection of signed first editions; on a table sat a chessboard, a gramophone by His Master's Voice and a stack of records, chiefly of Bach, Mozart and Beethoven.

The young writers who gathered at Pond Place mostly remember Edward recumbent on the chaise longue, a glass of wine at his elbow, or in another characteristic posture, standing with one leg thrust forward, his right hand aloft in a curious gesture, looking at the ground, musing. Amongst those who might be in attendance were O'Flaherty, excitable, loquacious, liable to recite 'flowing nonsense from some as yet unwritten book about "women pressin' their thoighs into the warm flanks of the horses",'[25] and two young men dissimilar in practically every respect except their year of birth, 1905.

One had just arrived in London from his home town in Northamptonshire. A grammar school boy, with a 'long lean face and look of dyspeptic dreaminess',[26] he had already worked as a reporter on the local paper and as a warehouse clerk. During the evenings at Pond Place he said little, but listened intently. The other, described by Evelyn Waugh as 'lean, dark, singular',[27] had recently gone up to Magdalen College, Oxford, having completed his schooling at Eton. Although the more gregarious and socially confident of the two, he was still subject to bouts of acute shyness. His first visit to Pond Place had been marked by a moment of acute discomfort when Edward pointed to a photograph of a bas-relief of Leda and the Swan hanging on the wall of a dingy corridor. The subject was treated with considerable indecency: 'What do you think of this?' Edward had demanded 'with great malice'. 'Oh, very amusing!' came the flustered response, at which Edward snorted disapproval and his young guest all but fled.[28] Edward may have been playfully testing the mettle of this prospective new protégé, but the real examination of both these twenty-year-olds had already taken place: he had read their work, which like their backgrounds and temperaments could not have been more different. Edward delighted in both as personalities and as writers – he could scent promise in H. E. Bates and Henry Green.

Green, whose real name was Yorke, was a perfect example of Edward's steadfast refusal to comply with Jonathan Cape's insistence that he should promote the company interest above all else. None of Green's books would be published by Cape; the two that appeared in Edward's lifetime, *Blindness* (1926) and *Living* (1929), did so under the J. M. Dent imprint. Edward first heard of Green when he received a letter from Guy Pocock of Dent's, asking him to read *Blindness*, which was then titled *Young and Old*, in manuscript. Green had started the novel in 1924, when he was in his final year at Eton and although in June 1925 a completed manuscript had gone first to Chatto (who turned it down) and then to Dent, Green was not entirely satisfied with it and accepted the publisher's verdict that the novel required revision.

As he read the manuscript detailing the life of John Haye, a boy who is blinded in an accident on a train on his way home from boarding school, Edward's interest in it and in its youthful author grew. Even at this early stage in his career Green had a distinctive, experimental voice,

and originality always scored highly with Edward, who also admired the
novel's allusive quality and Green's portrait of the boy's step-mother.
He wrote to Pocock, advising acceptance, suggesting alterations and
expressing a desire to meet Green, who promptly received an invitation
to tea at Pond Place. 'You went at the appointed time and rang the bell,'
Green later recalled. 'You were just confronted by a huge old man, his
buttons undone all over the place, who stared you down with pale eyes
behind deep spectacles and whose white hair was combed over his forehead in a fringe – a pale-faced, menacing, wordless object, immeasurably
tall.'[29] However, once Edward (who in point of fact was only fifty-seven
at the time) regained the chaise longue

> ... it was all different. He began with the most delicious praise. He
> had not only read your work, the stuttering work, but he had seen
> in it more, far more, than in your dreams you had dared to claim.
> Better still he had an intense curiosity about you, which is perhaps
> of even greater importance to young writers ... Like a St Bernard
> he could smell out the half-frozen body which, if encouraged, might
> yet be able to wrestle with words. The bottle of brandy round his
> neck was flattery, and at the next meeting with him it was blame.
> Afterwards he bullied you with a mixture of blame-flattery, nearly
> always to your good.[30]

Green was particularly concerned about the last chapter of *Blindness*,
in which John Haye meditates on his condition while walking round
London. Edward urged him to rewrite it, and less than three weeks later
Green sent a new version, this time with Hayes confined to a drawing
room, his thoughts prompted by the sounds and scents of the house
and surrounding streets. This Edward considered excellent: 'You have ...
done, what Tchekov said should be done i.e. suggested what went before
in the end,'[31] he told Green, who even so never felt entirely happy with
the novel's conclusion. Although Edward admired Green's work, he was
not averse to pointing out faults and warning Green against repeating
them in the future. 'I think you run on too long ... the great art is to
put things without *any inessential* details, and to cut out every word that
is not necessary. Most novels perish through *prolixity*.'[32]

A few months after *Blindness* was published, Green left Oxford without
taking his degree. He then entered his father's engineering works in
Birmingham, not at junior managerial level, as might be expected of the
owner's son, but as a lowly operative on the factory floor. This decision

was not primarily political – Green's reaction to the General Strike the previous year had been one of laconic amusement, tinged with guilt when he thought about his own inherited wealth – but taken very much with an eye to his writing. 'My address may surprise you,' he confessed to Edward in a letter from the Farringdon Works, almost a year after starting there, 'but for 12 months I worked at Oxford on sketches for a novel of "working class" life and when these had matured so to speak I persuaded my father to let me come here to do manual labour ... and 20,000 words is the miserable result.'[33] Edward applauded Green's 'pluck in becoming a moulder' and assured him that the experience of the past year would not go to waste, but he warned that writing out of your own class was 'damned difficult' and reminded Green 'the British public *hates* books about the labouring classes'.[34] In the meantime he recommended that Green read *The Ragged Trousered Philanthropists*, a novel by the house painter Robert Tressell that attacked the capitalist system. Edward always found Green's references to the rest of the Yorke clan vastly entertaining, and what he really wanted him to do was turn his attention to that 'perfectly gorgeous material' and write a family novel. 'If you are not *too* intellectual in your fiction you might do A1 work,'[35] Edward concluded. Green followed the advice and started a story about a high society girl which he hoped he might make into a novel,[36] but reading the manuscript aloud to Edward induced nothing but a 'rising sense of despair'[37] and he was never able to finish it.

While Green chose to return to the Midlands in the belief that it would improve his writing, H. E. Bates was convinced that if he stayed in Rushden his literary future was doomed. 'I'm dying of solitary confinement I shouldn't wonder. God knows how people keep alive here ... I can't write, I can't read or think,'[38] he complained to Edward, who as usual had sent volumes of exemplary authors – Turgenev, Conrad, Chekhov and Crane. He had been delighted to discover that Bates was already familiar with most of these names when they first met at the Etoile restaurant in January 1926. Bates had been summoned to London following Cape's acceptance of his first novel, *The Two Sisters*. After a meeting with the partners, the gauche twenty-year-old was taken to lunch in Charlotte Street, at which point

there came into the restaurant a semi-patriarchal, semi-diabolical figure in a floppy cloak-like overcoat, a grey scarf wound round his neck like a python, and a preposterously small felt hat. He had grey hair, grey jowl-like cheeks that quivered ponderously like the gills of

an ancient turkey, and he appeared to have lost himself completely
…. His thick-lensed glasses gave him an appearance that was in that
moment, and remained for me for a long time afterwards, quite
frightening. He staggered about for some moments like a great bear
unable to recall the steps of a dance he had just begun, and then
hung up his coat, hat, scarf and walking-stick on the hat-stand. He
then smoothed his hair with his hands, gave several painful snorts
of breath through his mouth as if the whole procedure had winded
him completely, and advanced towards us.

I stood up, hypnotized and terrified by this enormous and grizzly
figure, and as I shook hands there was in the air a faint smell of
herbal cigarettes and a weird glint of myopic eyes.

'Mr Edward Garnett,' someone said, and I could have fainted.[39]

Bates's fear of Edward lasted some considerable time. Expressions of
dread frequently accompanied manuscripts sent to Pond Place and in 1927
Bates openly confessed that he had been 'absolutely afraid'[40] of Edward
for more than a year. This was not simply a strategy to diffuse anticipated criticism: Edward's comments could be lacerating. In September
1927 Bates sent him the manuscript of a novel, *The Voyagers*, only to be
told that it was written in 'that *hollow sounding*, repetitive style, *like a*
muffled echo of Conrad, *with* a lot of clichés'.[41] 'You keep *commenting*
and *explaining* and *repeating* things,' continued an exasperated Edward.
'You make Ellen's brown skirt and Ellen's staring eye, for example, do
treble the amount of work they ought to do towards the end'.[42] Twenty-
three years later, Bates described this chastisement as 'purifying', but
his immediate response was that the letter had 'skinned [his] soul'[43] and
to wonder if he should give up altogether. Over time Bates came to
realise that Edward's bursts of irritation soon evaporated: a week after
his eruption over *The Voyagers* Edward assured Bates that he had 'as a
matter of fact, great confidence in your creative power; it is your power
of criticizing your work that is incomplete *as with most authors*'.[44]

This Edward certainly felt to be true of the combustible O'Flaherty.
Towards the end of 1925 the Irishman sent Edward material for a volume
of short stories, including 'The Tent', which O'Flaherty insisted should
be the title story. Edward considered it 'faked – and inferior to the
others',[45] and left O'Flaherty in no doubt as to his feelings. However,
O'Flaherty got his way, partly because Jonathan Cape himself intervened
after O'Flaherty wrote to him, effectively threatening to sell his work to
another publisher if the price was right. Fearful that a rival firm might

reap the benefits of the talent Edward had been nurturing, Cape told him that he felt 'the only thing to do is to let [O'Flaherty] have his own way', adding rather shamefacedly 'you may think I should have taken a stronger stand.'[46] O'Flaherty himself pleaded with Edward: 'Now that the whole business of *The Tent* is settled let us in the name of God resume amicable relations. Not that my feelings towards you have not been all this time those of the deepest love, but I have felt that you are vexed with me, and in fact rather violent.'[47] Bates would have recognised that sentiment and also O'Flaherty's sense of relief when he received a letter from Edward. 'I have been so violently oppressed for the past month by your quarrel with me,' confessed O'Flaherty, who attributed his conduct to a conviction that the book would sell better with 'The Tent' as the title story. 'And please don't make any resignation of your position as literary uncle,' he continued, 'for no matter if you never read another word of mine ... I will always write now as if you were about to read it – Topsy and you. For I always believe that you care for me myself, apart from my work, and that is what pleases me and makes me feel tender towards you.'[48] O'Flaherty's plea suggests that Edward may have openly pondered the possibility of withdrawing his help, but the concil-iatory letter worked, and in April O'Flaherty's 'literary uncle' agreed to be godfather to his newly arrived daughter Pegeen.

Courting controversy

'What fun it must be for you being godfather to such a lot of us!'[1] wrote another of Edward's recent authors, Naomi Mitchison. In 1923 Cape accepted her first novel *The Conquered*, which is set during the Gallic Wars. When Mitchison came to Bedford Square to discuss the book, Edward was expecting a middle-aged, rather dowdy historian. He was agreeably surprised to find himself in the company of a very attractive, fashionable twenty-six-year-old, sporting a multi-coloured leather cloche hat with a tassel. The only thing Edward didn't like about Mitchison's novel was its original title, *Headlong Westering*. Mitchison, overjoyed at the prospect of being published, readily agreed to change it. However, as time went on she became considerably less compliant and Edward found himself acting as an unwilling buffer between an author determined not to pussyfoot around such subjects as rape and homosexuality and a publisher equally resolved to observe what Mitchison rather scathingly called 'the decencies'.[2] 'I shouldn't worry over the absence of two or three words,' Edward counselled when Mitchison complained her work had been censored:

> Mr Cape showed me the passage and asked my advice – and I suggested this slight alteration. A great many people are not in our happy position of taking sexual facts simply and naturally and they might raise an outcry which would be annoying. It is impossible for me to pose as arbitrator. I think the passage beautiful myself – but I don't think a little cutting or two or three changes of words would affect its beauty.[3]

Edward admired Mitchison's feistiness, and was quite prepared to back her against his employer if he believed Cape was being unnecessarily prudish. 'I stuck up for the "poor bloody tarts" ... but Cape is a puritan and he said it would cost you and him a couple of hundred readers!' he explained when Cape objected to a poem Mitchison had written for *Black Sparta*. 'In future you should take a stronger line and tell him that you insist on the inclusion of a piece. Don't bow your neck in the House of Rimmon.'[4] When Edward read Mitchison's *Barbarian Stories*, which Cape published in 1929, he sensed trouble ahead:

> If Cape worries you about changing passages in 'Barbarian Stories' I should simply refuse – except in the matter of two or three isolated words. I am suspected of being on the side of Licence against the Law and Commerce and so I have no influence to help you but only to harm you by espousing your side. I simply advise you to stick to your guns.[5]

Mitchison valued Edward's support tremendously and she loved his tea-time visits to River Court, her substantial Georgian house on Chiswick Mall, where he talked 'always helpfully and with an undertone of – not flirtation, but the warm relationship between male and female which can be very valuable to both'.[6]

Edward's determination that Mitchison should resist any attempt to alter parts of *Barbarian Stories* was stiffened by his involvement with another female writer whose work had recently fallen foul of the law. *Sleeveless Errand* was the first novel by Norah James, who managed Cape's advertising department. Edward had recommended the book to Eric Partridge of the Scholartis Press, who had published it. The book contained strong language and dwelt on some of the seedier aspects of London's nightlife. This was enough to stir the Home Secretary William Joynson-Hicks (popularly known as 'Jix') into action. He demanded the seizure of all copies of the novel before it went on sale and it was banned by order of the Bow Street magistrate on 4 March 1929. The trial prosecutor, Percival Clarke, claimed that the story was told in the form of 'conversations by persons entirely devoid of decency and morality ... who not only tolerated but even advocated adultery and promiscuous fornication. Filthy language and indecent situations appeared to be the keynote of the book.' Despite the defence lawyer's contention that the novel had had 'an extraordinarily good report upon it by a very well known reader', the magistrate sided with the prosecution. He was certain that *Sleeveless Errand* 'would suggest to the minds of the young of either sex, or even to persons of more advanced years, thoughts of a most impure character'.[7] The trial was reported in the continental version of the *Daily Mail*, which also mentioned that Edward had recommended the novel to Eric Partridge in the first place. The Paris-based publisher Jack Kahane read the article and, knowing 'the flawlessness of Edward Garnett's discrimination',[8] he immediately contacted Partridge. A little over a month later the book was published by his Obelisk Press 'and selling like mitigated wildfire at a hundred francs a copy'.[9] It carried a preface by Edward, who fulminates against the follies of censorship and cites *Sleeveless Errand* as 'a perfect example of official blundering'.[10] For those officials involved in the novel's suppression he had nothing but contempt: 'How British in its mixture of moral righteousness and official Pecksniffery. And that is why *Sleeveless Errand*, banished from Albion's virtuous shores, appears in a new edition across the Channel.'[11]

A week after the *Sleeveless Errand* trial, another crisis blew up when the printer of H. E. Bates's second novel *Catherine Foster* declared the book indecent. 'It really amounts to that on the page about the girl's seduction he [the printer] has had the cheek to write cryptically "*Very warm*",'[12] explained a furious Bates to Edward. '[Wren] Howard wishes me to amend this error. I have refused, saying that the passage needs no toning down because the tones are low and quiet enough already. An enormous fear of Jix seems to have bitten everyone, and Howard talks already of "banning".'[13] Bates may well have been unaware of the English laws of libel, which made the printer of a libel subject to prosecution as well as the author and publisher. However, he must have realised that anyone involved with Cape would be particularly sensitive to any suspicion of literary 'indecency' in the wake of the *Sleeveless Errand* trial. Furthermore, it was less than six months since Cape had lost the case brought against Radclyffe Hall's lesbian novel *The Well of Loneliness*. If there was a fear of 'Jix' at Bedford Square, it was hardly surprising. Wren Howard agreed to Bates's proposition that Edward should have the final say about the disputed passage, and as only minor alterations were required, Edward counselled pragmatism and Bates accepted the revisions.

The fracas over the publication of *Catherine Foster* was the final hurdle for a book that had given Bates considerable trouble to write. After the appearance of *The Two Sisters* he brought out a collection of short stories, *Day's End*, published by Cape in 1928. Much as he admired the book, Edward told Bates that his future 'in the public's and the publishers' eyes depends as to whether you can produce a strong novel: they don't count "sketches" or short stories'.[14] Bates had been toiling away for eight months at a novel he intended to call *The Voyagers* and in August 1927, with considerable trepidation, he sent 130,000 words to Edward.

It took Edward a day and a half to read the manuscript: his response was blistering. When Bates re-read the letter more than thirty years later 'I marvel that I survived ... It blasted me; it skinned my soul; it seemed momentarily to sever every hope I had.'[15] Edward began by telling Bates the novel was unpublishable and that he should have sent it to him when he had written a third of it and thus saved himself much time and trouble. In paragraph after paragraph Edward castigates Bates for committing pretty much every sin a writer is capable of: cliché, repetition, weak and unrealistic characterisation, explanation – the list goes on – Bates didn't really need to read much past the fourth paragraph:

> ... you've written it in the facile, flowing, over-expressive, half-faked style, gliding over the difficulties, not facing the real labour of *realistic* painting. All that I've condemned in your *bad* sketches – the generalities, the vague cynicism, the washy repetitions and the lack of *firm outlines* and *exact touches* – You've written it, I repeat, in the bad Batesian facile manner that you can turn on like a tap to cover up deficiencies.[16]

Somehow Bates recovered – at least Edward offered a chink of light when he urged him: 'Don't despair. You have a *facile demon* in you, who gets hold of the reins as well as the real artist who retreats into the background.'

Less than four months later, Bates sent the first chapter of *Catherine Foster*, which to his immense relief met with Edward's approval. In June Edward went to Cork on holiday and read the latest instalments of the manuscript there: he was not wholly impressed. He felt there was a 'certain vagueness' in the portrait of Catherine and that Bates had failed to address or develop the relationship between the two brothers who vie for her affections. Here Edward made a suggestion: that Bates write a scene in which Catherine plays the piano to both men. The prosaic brother, Charles, insists that Catherine plays a 'pom-pomming' air performed by a band at the circus they have just returned from, while Andrew, the more romantic (although unreliable) sibling is entranced by the Chopin that follows. The brief episode succinctly illustrates the gulf between the brothers. Edward also criticised Bates's dialogue: '"[D]renched in dew" – too literary for talk,' he admonishes, and suggests Bates try 'The grass is frightfully wet' as an alternative. Edward concluded the letter with a finely calculated challenge: 'Of course if you cannot bring off their [the brothers'] development the story must remain as it is with a paring down of various passages.'[17] Bates knew he needed a second novel and took up the gauntlet: 'As to the idea of cutting it down to a long-short story I don't want that ... So I shall begin the development at once.'[18] Bates slogged away for the next four months, rewriting sections of the novel and sounding out Edward with his ideas: 'If you're a little tired with all this I'm sorry,' he explained, 'but only to tell someone of the structure of the thing helps, as you know.'[19] Finally, on 5 November 1928 he despatched the finished manuscript to Edward: 'You will let me know what your opinion is? You know I have been desperately anxious and careful about it all. And I haven't a cent ...'[20]

Edward was never entirely convinced by *Catherine Foster*. While he admired certain things in it – the 'seduction' scene the printer so objected to, and the episode in which Catherine and her husband visit the terminally ill clerk, Hands – Edward felt Bates had still not fleshed out the relations between characters sufficiently and that the story was told too much through Catherine's consciousness, resulting in 'a certain monotony'. Edward considered the novel to be 'quite artistic' and 'beautifully written', but that it had 'very definite limits'.[21] Luckily for Bates, Wren Howard admired *Catherine Foster* and promised a much needed advance and publication the following February. Bates's sense of relief was palpable, as was his gratitude for all Edward had done. 'I have a great wish ... to dedicate a piece of work to you, who have been literary father to me,' he declared. 'So if you have any objections, moral, intellectual, spiritual or otherwise against my dedicating *Catherine Foster* to you, in the simplest kind of formula, minus all the horrible trappings, would you say, would you enumerate them?'[22] Edward gladly accepted 'as a real proof of our continued confidence in one another, not to speak of more intimate feelings'.[23]

'I've read Bates' book about the seduction of a wife ... It's like trying to get a full stomach out of meringues,'[24] complained T. E. Lawrence to Edward. Life had altered considerably for Lawrence by the time he read Bates's novel in 1929: his posting to India had ended and he had come back to RAF Cattewater near Plymouth, published two versions of *Seven Pillars of Wisdom* and written up the notes on RAF life he had promised Edward in 1925. Lawrence finally brought out the subscribers' edition of *Seven Pillars* at the end of 1926. Finding subscribers had been something of a struggle initially and so Edward wrote to J. G. Wilson, the manager of the Bumpus bookshop in London, asking him to promote the book privately to his wealthier customers. Twenty new subscribers quickly emerged, relieving fears that the highly priced edition would be unviable.

'Yes, you immensely strengthened and perfected the *Seven Pillars* by your continuous work on it,'[25] Edward confirmed:

There is no doubt at all that the *S Pillars* now is a 'master-piece' ...

I have criticised you severely in the past for your self-conscious-ness, for your hiding of your own emotions, for your subtle evasions and omissions, – and for the elaborate tricks you play and for the *Peccavi* thrown at us in the abrupt section 'Myself'.

I take this back, in recognising that you are built that way, and that the whole character of the book reflects and is governed by the law of your own character. One can't quarrel with the individuality that has made the *SP* what it is – a masterpiece of narrative.

Despite Edward's apparent retraction of his former criticisms, he still felt frustrated by Lawrence. 'You are a born writer,' he told him, 'fearfully handicapped by fixed ideas and all sorts of complexes, which the great achievement of the *S Pillars* should have dissipated.' This was said with the aim of getting Lawrence to write another book 'from the personal side, dictated by the unofficial you – a book of episodes, like beads on a string. Say episodes from your life as an archaeologist, of your pre-war life in Syria, your fruitless journey to Syria during the war – etc.' At the end of this long letter Edward once more exhorted Lawrence: 'there is a deeper self in you as yet unexpressed ... Rabelais, Sterne, Walt Whitman, Herman Melville, Dostoevsky, Turgenev, Dante and all the great spirits ... don't hesitate about expressing themselves frankly. Your "six years" has produced a masterpiece – so don't make bones about expressing yourself in future.'[26]

That the subscribers' edition of *Seven Pillars* would be read by so few – 'rich men ... *never* let their books be read for fear of spoiling their "condition"'[27] – vexed Edward considerably. Only around 200 copies of the sumptuously produced book were published at 30 guineas each.[28] Each was uniquely bound; Edward subscribed to one (at considerable expense – at today's values 30 guineas is well over £1,500) and so, when Lawrence presented him with another, Edward gave it, at Lawrence's suggestion, to David. The lavishness of the book's production had landed Lawrence in debt and so he set about producing a popular abridgement himself in the hope that it would alleviate his financial predicament. Lawrence worked from the subscribers' edition, rather than the 1922 Oxford text, as Edward had done. The resulting book, *Revolt in the Desert*, differs significantly from Edward's abridgement. It was an immediate bestseller and Cape's profits for 1927 rose from around £2,000 to nearly £28,000. Edward's salary was increased to £400 a year and he was given 500 shares in the company. Indirect compensation perhaps for the time and trouble he had taken with the 1922 abridgement. Meanwhile, Lawrence chiselled away at the 'Uxbridge notes' about his life in the Air Force that he had promised Edward in 1922: 'I think the job may be worth its trouble,'[29] Lawrence reported in September 1927. In the same letter he refers to life itself as 'the job' and adds that the thought that it 'will end some-where, may end soon, is an abiding comfort to 99% of the people over thirty'. This, according to Lawrence, meant that sorrowing too much over others' deaths 'is to contradict ourselves'. In his idiosyncratic way, Lawrence was offering Edward some form of consolation for a tragedy that had struck a month earlier.

Nearly every year Edward's older brother Robert and his family left London during the summer and spent time at their house in Morcombelake near Bridport in Dorset. Arthur, the youngest brother, had joined them in August and one Friday morning he and Robert discussed the prospect of swimming, something all the Garnett brothers loved. Robert was reluctant, as he thought the sea was too rough, but Arthur persuaded him it would be safe as long as they went in only as far as the surf. They went down to the beach at about 11 a.m.: Robert set off first, but was soon drawn over a dip in the beach to deep water. He managed to swim back to shore and began to dress, not unduly worried that there was no sign of Arthur, who was a very strong swimmer. Robert imag-ined his brother had gone further up the coast to find a better landing place. He went to the water's edge and looked in vain for Arthur, but was relieved to see a figure walking down the beach: it turned out to be a fisherman. Robert then began to get seriously alarmed and went to a nearby farm for help. The people there alerted the fishermen, one of whom spied someone in the sea. Arthur's body eventually washed up on the beach and just over five hours after he went missing he was pronounced dead by police who attended the scene. He was forty-six and had spent much of his working life in horticulture, first in the Curator's office in Kew and then fruit farming in Tasmania and England. His obituary in Gardening Illustrated spoke of someone who 'held original views and did not measure success from a monetary point of view',[30] words that could equally have described Edward. Arthur was greatly mourned by all who knew and loved him for his charm and humour: 'I know you realise what it has meant to Edward,'[31] wrote Nellie to Louise

Bréal, while Constance confessed to Natalie Duddington that she felt 'as though a great piece of life had been cut out'.[32]

Edward and Nellie went to Cornwall on holiday immediately after Arthur's funeral. They returned to find a letter from an author asking permission to quote Edward's approving comments in the prospectus for a novel he had read in proof 'about an otter and its wanderings in Devon and the sea-coast'.[33]

'Do you know the work of Henry Williamson?' John Galsworthy had written to Edward in November 1926. 'It's uneven but at its best extraordinarily good ... I told him to send you proof of the new book. If you like it give him a word of encouragement. He can see and he can write.'[34] A month later Williamson contacted Edward, sending him not the proofs of *Tarka the Otter*, but a copy of *The Old Stag*. Edward was impressed with Williamson's writing and soon discovered they shared a love of Richard Jefferies, whose books had inspired Williamson to follow a literary career. Edward liked and understood Williamson, who could be awkward and difficult, describing him as 'a nice chap ... I fancy the War strained his nervous system dangerously.'[35] Edward's dealings with another war-damaged character, O'Flaherty, may have enhanced his sympathy for Williamson. When Williamson once bemoaned that he grew up 'in an uncultured atmosphere'[36] Edward responded: 'All you tell me about yourself & your education, & your struggle are very interesting. But without that struggle you would not be so original now. You've fought for what is worth getting.'[37] Nevertheless, Edward was well aware of Williamson's weaknesses: 'His fault was always intense preoc-cupation with his affairs, his books etc,'[38] Edward observed, on another occasion commenting that Williamson had appeared in London 'looking a bit wild and still concentrating on himself'.[39] For his part, Williamson saw his friendship with Edward as something of an achievement in itself, confirmation that he had arrived as a writer: 'I saw your review of Roy Campbell's *Terrapin*,' he told Edward, 'and I remember thinking "Ah, I wonder if I will *ever* be known to these people – Garnetts, Galsworthys, Hardys, that stratum".'[40]

Edward read the proofs of *Tarka the Otter*, which was published by Putnam, at the beginning of April 1927. 'I should value a frank opinion on *Tarka* if you should care to give it,' Williamson had written. 'If you think *Tarka* false and humanised, you will be right, I expect. I don't know what otters think or feel: I do believe they are nearer to us than is usually conceded.'[41] Edward loved the book and dismissed Williamson's misgivings, describing it as 'a regular epic'. 'You handle the narrative as though you had been a young otter yourself in a previous incarnation,'[42] he told Williamson. Edward's review for the *Manchester Guardian* was no less fulsome: 'In *Tarka* Mr. Henry Williamson has written an extraordinarily full and fascinating narrative of the life of a family of otters,' he wrote, and went on to praise Williamson's depiction of the surrounding countryside and its inhabitants as 'remarkable'.[43] He urged Arnold Bennett to take up the novel, describing it as 'extraordinarily fine' and 'beautifully written'.[44] A copy was dispatched to T. E. Lawrence in Karachi, who sent Edward a highly detailed criticism of the book in the mistaken belief it was Williamson's first novel. Edward passed Lawrence's comments to Williamson, instigating a mainly epistolary friendship between the two men that lasted until Lawrence's death.

Tarka the Otter won the Hawthornden Prize for 1927. Edward's reaction was laconic: 'I think the Hawthornden Prize has rather gone to Williamson's head. But he may calm down presently.'[45] Meanwhile, Williamson was working on *The Pathway*, the final novel in a series of four based on his early life. It was a book written in fits and starts, but by April 1928 it was ready for Edward's scrutiny. Edward read it over two days and swiftly dispatched his verdict: 'Its [*sic*] a very fine thing up to a point. It begins well, & goes on well, but slowly *a looseness & over talkativeness & overwordiness* develops & takes off not a little from what should be *a book of the first class*.'[46] While Edward saw great potential in the novel, he disapproved of the ending and felt that the speeches of Willie Maddison, the protagonist, were too obviously propaganda and that it appeared Williamson had brought them in from another source, which was true: Williamson confessed he had taken them from earlier letters he had written. 'But the idea of *deliberately* working in "propaganda speeches" from those undelivered letters! what [*sic*] *do* you expect can come from such barbarity?'[47] thundered Edward. He suggested that Williamson severely prune Parts III and IV of the novel and that the reader be given different perspectives of Maddison through other characters' eyes: 'such criticisms would have given the story a *more all-round and powerful effect*,'[48] he pointed out. Williamson was grateful for the advice, but unenthused at the prospect of having to do what he described as 'ant work'[49] on the book. 'It is all very depressing for me at the moment,' Williamson confessed, 'but I know my powers of recovery, and shall some time fall on it.'[50] He rallied reasonably quickly and the novel was published six months later. 'Garnett will like its ending now,' Williamson told Jonathan Cape, 'a rearrangement, and a filling in; it is a perfect climax.'[51] However, Edward was not entirely persuaded by the book as a whole when he reviewed it for *Now and Then*: 'One cannot sufficiently praise the truthfulness and naturalness of the novel,' he declared, but he still found it 'too full, too copious in flow, too rich in detail'.[52]

Williamson wrote prodigiously following the publication of *Tarka the Otter* and inevitably this began to take its toll on him. On Midsummer's Day 1929 he composed a despondent letter to Edward, questioning whether he could write at all and confessing to a creative block. 'The night was on me, is on me, & now I can't write,' he lamented. 'I'm forcing myself to do so, but you will say "Mere Journalism" in your report to Cape on the Village Book, & you'll be right. It is flat, dreadful.'[53] The letter was waiting for Edward when he returned from a short holiday in France and he lost no time in sending words of reassurance: '*I am a firm believer in you as a writer. You have rare powers of observation, individuality, keen insight & great expressiveness,*' Edward insisted; 'You are probably fatigued by doing too much & by mental restlessness. *All* writers have the black mood when nothing comes but weary commonplaces ... But next week or even next day the creative impulse may suddenly get possession of you – as was Conrad's case.'[54]

The relationship between Edward and Williamson was not without its tensions however: 'I hope to God you don't still think I meant what I said in fun when I was tugging your ears like a puppy in play,' Williamson fretted in the Midsummer Day's letter. 'It was a terrible blow when you said you thought I was serious about hurting you ... Even now, my jaw's askew.'[55] Had Edward been alive in 1963, it would have been difficult for him to be anything other than hurt by the fictional portrait Williamson paints of him in *The Power of the Dead* in which Edward features as Edward Cornelian, a self-opinionated, overpowering literary critic who drinks too much and delights in minutely picking the protagonist's novel to pieces. At one point in *The Power of the Dead* Cornelian is upset when Phillip Maddison, the Williamson figure, likens writers to clean-run salmon in the estuary and the critic to a lamprey that fastens on to the salmon and sucks its life away; he also accuses critics of having correspondence with authors with the aim of selling the letters for considerable sums after the writer's death. Cornelian is offended by both jibes, detecting 'an undercurrent of dislike in all your remarks to me'.[56] Williamson may well have made these comments to Edward in real life – the sale of Conrad's and Hudson's letters in New York had made him a fair amount of money – and then felt compelled to apologise. Another of Williamson's supporters, Galsworthy, receives similar treatment in *The Power of the Dead*: by 1963 much had changed for Williamson, personally and professionally, and if the novel is anything to go by it seems that he looked back on those connected with his earlier days as a writer with less than affection.

Williamson's apparent antipathy towards Edward may have something to do with a row he had with David Garnett after Edward's death. In 1938 David edited a collection of T. E. Lawrence's letters and included some from Williamson, who sent his letters from Lawrence to David. The package also contained an appraisal of *Lady Chatterley's Lover* by D. H. Lawrence. This had been written by Williamson, whose handwriting was remarkably similar to that of T. E. Lawrence. Williamson later said that he had sent it to David entirely by mistake, but by then the letter had been published as being written by T. E. Lawrence and with David's remark that it was the astutest judgement of *Lady Chatterley* that he had ever read. When the true author was revealed, David was furious and Williamson apologised, but the incident may well have poisoned his attitude to the Garnett family as a whole.

When Putnam, the publisher of *Tarka* suggested to Williamson that he seek T. E. Lawrence's permission to reproduce the letter he had written to Williamson containing his minutely detailed criticism of the book, Williamson turned to Edward for advice. His response – 'Lawrence is very eccentric, both hating and courting publicity'[57] – reflected Edward's experience of Lawrence over the years, not least with the 'Uxbridge notes' about his life in the air force. Lawrence sent *The Mint* to Edward in March 1928 and asked him to show it to nobody but David and Jonathan Cape. He hoped Cape would refuse the book, but that offering it to him would fulfil a clause in his contract for *Revolt in the Desert* that stipulated that Lawrence would give Cape an option on the next thing he wrote. Two days later Lawrence wrote to Sir Hugh Trenchard, Chief of the Air Staff, informing him of the existence of *The Mint* and that it had been sent to Edward, 'whose name you probably know as a critic of genius'.[58] Trenchard didn't give a straw about Edward's genius: the prospect of Lawrence's book reaching the general public appalled him. He sought the advice of Edward Marsh, who, besides being Winston Churchill's private secretary was also well known in literary circles through his editorship of *Georgian Poetry*. Marsh arranged a lunch with Edward and Trenchard at which Edward agreed to send Trenchard a copy of *The Mint* when the manuscript had been typed up. 'I said of course that *The Mint* would not harm the Air Force,' Edward explained to Lawrence, 'but *he* said he was the Air Force, and the Air Force was him and that many powerful enemies were plotting its disruption etc etc.'[59]

In the face of both Lawrence's and Trenchard's implacable opposition to publication, Edward could only conclude that *The Mint* was destined to remain hidden from the public until such time that either Lawrence or Trenchard died. This Edward found immensely frustrating as the manuscript had impressed him mightily: 'Well, you've gone and done it this time!' he told Lawrence, 'and knocked all your feeble pretences of not being a writer, etc etc into final smithereens.'[60] According to Edward, *The Mint* was a classic 'for there's not a word too much. It's elastic, sinewy, terse: and spirit and matter are the inside-out of its technique, perfectly harmonious throughout, inseparable, as in all first rate stuff.'[61] Edward particularly admired 'The Funeral' chapter, which details the morning the men heard of the death of Queen Alexandra. 'A man who can write "Funeral" – can write anything – whenever he pleases:–,' Edward told Lawrence. 'He's only got to write tersely of what he *sees* and *feels* and there it is. I told you, how many times? before.'[62] Edward signed off the letter 'your exultant and "told you so" critic', but while Lawrence was gratified by the praise, he remained adamant that the book was not to be published for another two decades until 1950. Refuting Edward's claim that he had put much of himself into it, Lawrence insisted '*The Mint* gives nothing of myself away: personally, I shouldn't mind its appearing tomorrow: but the other fellows wouldn't understand how I'd come to betray them: and Trenchard would not have it. It would hurt him: and I value his regard beyond that of most men.'[63] Edward was convinced that Lawrence would eventually publish *The Mint*: 'He will forget all this in three years or earlier,' he predicted to David. 'But as he is in this Tolstoyan mood you'd better *not* show your typescript about but sit still and await developments.'[64]

Edward misjudged Lawrence's determination to stick to his decision: but when *The Mint* was finally published in 1955, twenty years after Lawrence's death, it carried the inscription he had written inside the front cover of the bound book:

TO
EDWARD GARNETT
You dreamed I came one night with this book
Crying, 'Here's a masterpiece. Burn it.'
Well – *as you please*[65]

24

Shadows lengthen

While Edward vainly battled to persuade T. E. Lawrence of the merits of publishing his account of life within the ranks of the air force, Henry Green continued working with the men in his father's plumbing and brewery works in Birmingham. At the end of each day he spent a couple of hours on his 'factory novel'. 'The book being about intrigue with so many characters I've had to write it in paragraphs,'[1] he explained to Edward, 'each paragraph quite distinct from the one before and the one after it, and usually no longer than 500 words ... No descriptions at all, nearly all conversation.' When Edward read *Living* in November 1928, he pronounced it '*very* clever'[2]. 'Clever' was always a slightly pejorative word in the Garnett vocabulary, as Green knew only too well: 'It was a blow to me that you should think it clever,'[3] he confessed. For his part, Edward admitted that he had found the style 'difficult and a trifle affected'.[4] 'You have accomplished a feat in carrying *Living* through,' Edward conceded, 'and so far as it goes it's admirably true. Only just as there is more in the upper class life than your "interlude" [*sic*] convey so there is more in the working class life than the "conversations" express.'[5] There are very few articles in *Living* and, as Green had warned, little description. Edward wanted more 'snapshots': descriptive passages that he felt would help the reader visualise the environment. This Green resisted, ostensibly on the grounds that it would 'hang the whole thing up' and delay publication. Despite his reservations, Edward put in a word for *Living* with Dent, who promised what Green described as 'really very good terms for it'. 'I must take this opportunity of thanking you again,' Green wrote. 'I never dare to your face. But all through *Living* I kept half an eye on 19 Pond Place.'[6]

Reviews of *Living* were mixed. Some critics thought the book affected; a proportion applauded Green's experimentation, while others were simply bemused by it. Writing in the *Observer*, Gerald Gould complained that Green had rendered the novel 'unreadable by a style of infinite perversity, which simply distracts one all the time from the thing to be said. In particular, what has the definite article done to him? It could do so much *for* him!'⁷ Edward was greatly amused: 'I saw that Gerald Gould was scandalised by *Living* and your little tricks with the definite article,' he remarked to Green. 'Poor mutt! Well you are punished for not making it easier to start with[,] i.e. inserting those descriptive bits.'⁸ After the publication of *Living* Green became immersed in other areas of his life and it was ten years before he produced another novel, *Party Going*. Edward got Natalie's sister Lola Ertel to type up the manuscript, which Edward described as 'sparkling',⁹ but he died before it was published in 1939. Years later Green told David Garnett, 'I loved your father ... I owe far more to him than to anyone else. He had an attitude towards novels and how to write them, from which stems almost any original idea that I have gained.'¹⁰

'What an emotional life you lead with your young authors,' David wrote to his father in 1926. 'I am glad that Cape doesn't publish my books or perhaps you and I would have to correspond through him, if I refused to rewrite.'¹¹ By 1926 David had published four novels; his latest, *The Sailor's Return*, had been the cause of disagreement between father and son. Edward was as forthright in his criticism of David's work as he was of those of his other protégés and he did not hide his dismay on discovering that *The Sailor's Return* was influenced by George Moore. David was sorry his father disapproved, but he was convinced that 'each generation must expect to be scorned by the generation that went before it'.¹² Edward objected again when he saw traces of Moore in David's next novel *Go She Must!* (1927), but he was aware that his words might be a source of further irritation: 'Don't forget when I criticize you that I was the first man to be enthusiastic over *Lady into Fox* and to take you in my arms with delight,' Edward reminded his son. 'I know what a frightful tussle all writing is.'¹³

Despite the odd tense exchange about David's novels, theirs was a close relationship and if Edward was at all jealous that his son had succeeded creatively where he himself had tussled to no avail, he did not show it. Many of Edward's authors were friends of David's and as the years went by their mutual respect for each other's literary talents and achievements grew. They were of course bound together by far more than books: Edward's second grandson, William, was born in 1925 and he and David shared their worries about Constance, whose health was a frequent concern, as was her refusal to contemplate giving up living alone at The Cearne. Edward always had a strong sense of familial duty: he donated his share of Arthur's estate to his unmarried sister Olive, and when David's wife Ray needed somebody to talk to, it was Edward she sought out. Since their marriage in 1921 David and Ray had both had affairs, but in 1928 David met Norah McGuinness, an artist who was married to the poet Geoffrey Phibbs (also known as Taylor). David became obsessed with Norah, much to Ray's misery. 'I am very unhappy and I think if I could talk to someone about it I might discover what I am really feeling,'[14] she told Edward, whose sympathetic and non-judgemental response provided some temporary relief. Edward's position as one of Ray's confidants could have affected his relationship with his son, but David knew his father well enough to realise that Edward's kindness to Ray was typical of the way he responded to anyone he saw in distress and it was not a question of him taking his daughter-in-law's side. The relationship between David and Norah continued, with Ray growing ever more wretched: 'I am in a desperate state and feel like smashing up everything,' she confessed to Edward after he had been to see her. 'That is why I think you should take back the £50 [which Edward had given her to go on holiday] as I shall not spend it on what it is meant for.'[15] If this was not enough, in the spring of 1929 Ray was diagnosed with breast cancer and had to undergo debilitating radium treatment. In April she wrote to Edward with the good news that her surgeon had told her the lumps were disappearing. Edward, of course, was delighted; he had been to see Ray in the nursing home when she had been diagnosed. 'She is admirably calm and brave – but the shock of the discovery ... is upon all of us,'[16] he had reported in a letter to a young writer he had recently taken up.

Harold Alfred Manhood had come to Edward's attention when Andrew Dakers, a literary agent and publisher, sent Cape a selection of his stories, some of which had appeared in *John O'London's Weekly*. After looking over a couple of pages, Edward was inclined not to continue: the rather lush romanticism went against his literary creed. Yet something about the stories drew him back and he found himself compelled to finish them. In the end Edward was 'mesmerize[d]'[17] by what he read and immediately sent Manhood a volume of Dostoevsky and an invitation to tea at Pond Place. There he discovered more about the twenty-four year old, the son of a carpenter, who was living in Walthamstow and had been a City clerk for seven years. Two years previously Manhood had thrown up his job in order to write the sixteen stories that made up his first collection, *Nightseed* (1928). He was now living in straitened circumstances and could no longer afford to write full-time. Hearing this, Edward managed to persuade Cape and the Viking Press to subsidise Manhood for two years in order to allow him to go on writing. Much as he admired Manhood's work, Edward could see that some of the stories were flawed. He considered that 'Little Peter the Great' should be taken out of the volume as it contained a profusion of detail, and he asked Manhood to revise the end of 'The Hero', which he believed exceeded the bounds of probability. Enclosed with the letter about 'The Hero' was a volume of Chekhov: 'I want you to read Gusev ...,' Edward commanded. 'Take it away and meditate on it. It's great art: its "point" is the breadth of life and nature.'[18] Manhood initially resisted Edward's criticism of 'The Hero', but very soon confessed that he realised he was right all along: 'I'll think more in future and work better,' he promised. 'You see till now, no one has taken a *craftsman's* interest in my stuff – I've become a little slack – an intermittent feeling of "O, what a clever young pup I am!" – You have jerked my mind back to the straight.'[19] As *Nightseed* neared publication, Edward's fear that the reviewers might not share his opinion of Manhood's work grew and he issued a frank warning:

A devil, a mean devil is in man's [*sic*] hearts, who loves to depreciate, find the weaknesses and disparage. You will find most reviewers try and get even with an author by putting his faults or blemishes *first*, and directing attention away from his positive achievement and his originality. I'll wager you will suffer heavily from mediocre reviewers who all suffer secretly from "an inferiority complex". They may even kill your career as an author.[20]

Edward's suspicions were right: the early reviews were negative. Unwilling to leave Manhood undefended at the mercy of his critics, Edward wrote to Arnold Bennett, knowing that a public endorsement from him would silence the detractors and boost sales of *Nightseed*. After telling Bennett about Manhood and his work, Edward went on to explain that

the reviewers of the modern young highbrow type are staring super-ciliously at the book and saying "This isn't the way to write!" ... Whereas to anyone with instinct the vitality and force of the man's vision show that he has *genius, real genius*. You can't admit Keats and *Endymion* with all its lush extravagance, and damn Manhood for the same qualities. And the reviewers are going to kill him and send him back to the City – "Go back to your gallipots" – if somebody doesn't lend a powerful hand ... Look carefully at *Nightseed* and see if what I say isn't true.[21]

Manhood, meanwhile, was thoroughly depressed by the reviews; Edward immediately sought to reassure him, telling him that *Nightseed* would appeal to a wide readership – Cape's typist had been unable to put it down – and exhorting Manhood to '*stick to it*: ... put your back into it ... put your outstretched thumb to your nose and make "a long nose" at the reviewers. It all depends on your guts and sticking power.'[22]

Bennett came up trumps. 'Praised be God for the enclosed by EB [*sic*] which will make all the difference to the public's interest in your work,' wrote an exultant Edward when he sent Bennett's review to Manhood. 'Agents and publishers will *now* be tenderly enquiring about your health and Cape will have a flow of "orders" for *Nightseed*. You have turned the corner!'[23] Sales of the book did indeed increase and the subsidy from Cape and Viking allowed Manhood to achieve his ambition to escape Walthamstow for a while and find a more congenial place to work in the countryside he loved. He rented rooms near Bridgwater in Somerset and then in Sennen in Cornwall, from whence he regularly dispatched packages to 19 Pond Place. These were just as likely to contain eggs, rabbits, duck, apples, grey mullet and various other produce from land and sea as they were manuscripts. Edward, however, was worried by Manhood's retreat to the countryside: although he was now living amongst the rural communities he wrote about, Edward could see that Manhood was becoming steadily more and more isolated. Thanks to Edward's introduction, Manhood did make contact with Henry Williamson in Devon and met some of Edward's other younger protégés when he came up to London, but he confessed to Edward that he felt lonely and especially lacked female company. Back in Cornwall, Manhood sent the opening pages of a projected novel – *The Bald Women* – to Pond Place and triggered not only a slashing critique of his writing, but also a disquisition on the perils of men without women.

Edward's initial letter ran to nine pages, in which he tore *The Bald Women* into tiny shreds. 'Your village and villagers have no semblance of existence,' Edward complained. 'One can't *locate* them in any country, or even in fairyland, nowhere but in your brain.'[24] According to Edward, Manhood had spent the previous nine months getting further away from reality in his writing, and when Edward had talked to him about this when they had gone walking, he had elicited no response 'except a doubtful grunt'. 'A picture of a commonplace bedroom can be as beautifully "done" in words as in a master's drawing,' Edward explained. 'The writer's eye and mind single out those objects that express a thing's or place's or man's *character*: and record them with delicate phrases, and powerful or beautiful touches (of language or paint).' He commanded Manhood to abandon the 'conglomerate, fabricated, unreal world' of *The Bald Women* and 'face reality'. Why Manhood was withdrawing into an over fanciful imagination was a mystery to Edward. 'Is it the sexual damming up?' he asked. 'If so you *must* let yourself go …. I wouldn't say this but for your own allusions to it, three months back.' Edward signs off the letter with an apology for his bluntness, adding 'I shall end by taking a sledgehammer to you.'[25] Manhood responded immediately: 'All too true,' he conceded. 'I have scrapped the "BW". I'm a bloody fool, tormented by a miserable, sordid devil – a kind of madness when the brain turns from all reality lest it further excite the body – a hellish business and it's against my nature to pick up casually with a girl … I write pretty fantastic rubbish to keep sane.'[26] Edward replied at once, insisting that the current state of affairs could not continue: 'You are practically living the life of a young Catholic priest, cut off from women,' he maintained. 'Your future, your art, your livelihood are all concerned.'[27] He urged Manhood to return to London, and offered to introduce him to three or four girls 'worth meeting'. In the meantime Edward advised a diet of milk, bread, vegetables and green salad in an effort to cool the blood. Manhood, however, remained meat-eating in Cornwall.

Edward's demolition of *The Bald Women* left Manhood with nothing to show Cape or Viking, both of whom were, as Edward put it, 'expecting you to lay an egg fairly soon'.[28] Manhood set to work on a novel in March 1929 and sent the first chapter to Edward, who found it 'hopelessly congested'.[29] All went quiet for the next few months, but at the beginning of November, after some vigorous prodding from Edward, Manhood sent the chapters he had been working on. These met with approval, although to Edward's mind Manhood had not entirely shaken off his previous faults: 'You have still got the *rags and tatters* of a *false* romanticism hanging round your neck,' Edward wrote, 'and it is very curious to see how you keep harking back (like a dog to his vomit!) to the bastard romantic style. Even so late as page 97 you relapse, as though you had a recurring spell of malaria.'[30]

Gay Agony tells the tale of Micah, a young engineer who is sent to an isolated valley to oversee the construction of the sluice gates of a dam. He falls foul of Shaphan, the overseer, a bully and inveterate womaniser. Micah is injured in an 'accident' rigged by Shaphan and recuperates at an inn run by Drusilla, an alluring but scheming widow. The two men vie for Drusilla's affections and Micah eventually succumbs to her charms. This leads to a denouement that is both shocking and violent. There is abundant description of local communities and customs, some of which incurred Edward's displeasure; he came down particularly hard on some of the words Manhood put into the mouths of his rural characters. 'It's really extraordinary that a man who can write pages 72–99 [which Edward had praised] doesn't see that Old Zacky couldn't possibly say these carefully turned, intellectually-wrought, artificially-constituted, *planned* sentences,' he told Manhood.

> Equally *bad* is the speech [beginning] 'I'll make a' – [up to] 'mother'. He might *think* this, or bits of this – but the line *'as if t'was a marriage bed and carefulness heeds an uncommon thirst'* is destructive of the whole illusion of the scene's reality. You *must* get it into your head that if you make a rustic talk sententious, intellectual, artificial stuff … [such] as: 'carefulness *heeds an uncommon thirst'* you are flatly preferring fireworks to reality – and damning truth.[31]

When the later chapters came Edward's way, he was concerned that Manhood had overdone what Edward called 'the sex-lust atmosphere'[32] and that some of the description would lead to the book being banned, besides offending from an aesthetic point of view. 'Copulative act' was condemned as 'too *medical* and heavy' and Edward told Manhood that he would not have made 'Shaphan's gelded state *absolute* – but something ominously *suggested*, deliciously suspicious and indecisive. You see you get much more out of a state which everybody's curiosity can question, pity, sneer at and dispute over than by flinging the bold brutal *fact* in our faces,' he continued.

Gay Agony, which is dedicated to Edward, was published in 1930 to generally good reviews. Edward then tried to persuade Manhood to write a novel based on his own life, but without success. In 1931 Manhood bought four acres in Henfield, Sussex and lived there in a converted railway carriage; he published three more collections of short stories with Cape during Edward's lifetime. At times Edward felt Manhood's writing had progressed – 'Your style has improved a great deal, being more natural and easy and broad in effect and less brain-spun and twisted than in your early stories,' he told him, after reading 'Three Nails'[33] – but at others he saw the old faults repeated: 'You are too mannered and artificial for the highbrows and too *difficult* and eccentric for the Philistine public,' Edward remonstrated, 'you are no nearer to nature than you were when you published the first volume. You have learned nothing except the description of landscape – and the fine shades of feeling and of character don't enter into your scheme.'[34] Nevertheless, Manhood enjoyed something of a reputation as a short story writer in his lifetime, although his name is now forgotten and few of his books remain in print. In 1953, dismayed by the paucity of the payments he received for his writing, he gave up altogether and spent the years until his death in 1991 brewing cider in Henfield.

Several of Edward's letters to Manhood contain references to his own bouts of illness and the effects of the passing years. Edward had bad attacks of bronchitis in 1928 and 1929 that laid him up for weeks, and the varicose veins in his legs – a legacy of the typhoid he suffered in 1896 – grew increasingly troublesome. 'Age exposes all the chinks in one's armour,' he lamented to Manhood. 'I used to be a strong swimmer in stormy seas: but now I daren't enter on account of my heart.'[35]

It wasn't only physical decline that reminded Edward of time's onward march. In March 1930 he heard that D. H. Lawrence had died of tuberculosis in Vence. Lawrence had had practically no contact with Edward for years, but he never forgot his old mentor. When *Lady Chatterley's Lover* was published privately in 1928 Lawrence enquired if Edward would like a copy: 'Let me know will you,' he asked David. 'In my early days your father said to me "I should welcome a description of the whole act" – which has stayed in my mind till I wrote this book ... I always look on the Cearne as my jumping-off point into the world *and* your father as my first backer.'[36] Lawrence inscribed the copy 'To Edward Garnett who sowed the first seed of this book, years ago, at the Cearne – and may not like the full fruit.'[37]

Lawrence knew his man. H. E. Bates recalls that when he asked Edward his opinion of the novel 'He gave me one of those characteristic ironical leers of his from behind flashing spectacles, and said: "It's the last pressing of the grapes before the end."'[38] Shortly after Lawrence's death, Edward received a letter from Frieda in response to his note of condolence in which she wrote: 'We neither of us forgot, ever what you meant to us in our first being together or what you meant to Lawrence as the midwife of his genius!'[39]

'When you get past sixty the horizons change with surprising swiftness,' observed Edward, who turned sixty-two in 1930. 'Old landmarks and old faces disappear, new problems loom up and the perspective you knew assumes fantastic shapes.'[40] In the summer of 1932 two more links with the past were severed. First, Edward lost one of his oldest friends, David Rice, whom he had known since his days at Fisher Unwin. Then, very shortly afterwards, Edward's elder brother Robert died. Although the siblings were poles apart temperamentally, and their views rarely coincided, they became closer during Robert's final months. The brothers had also been in contact the previous year about a play Edward had written in 1911. He had shown *The Trial of Jeanne d'Arc* to Conrad and D. H. Lawrence amongst others, both of whom had criticised it. The general consensus was that the scenes were static and lacked variation and progression and several managers rejected it. However, parts of the play were performed on 26 October 1913 at the Ethical Church in Bayswater, with Edith Evans rather improbably playing the Bishop of Beauvais. Edward sent *Jeanne d'Arc* out again in 1923, but as George Bernard Shaw had just announced that he had finished *St Joan*, nobody was interested in taking on another play about the same subject. Shaw was a source of frustration once more in 1931, as he had chosen the same actress as Edward – Jean Forbes-Robertson – to play the title role in a Gala performance of *St Joan* in aid of RADA. This delayed the staging of *The Trial of Jeanne d'Arc*, which was finally performed at the Arts Theatre, Great Newport Street, in May, with Forbes-Robertson as Joan. Inevitably, unfavourable comparisons were made with Shaw's play and, although some of Edward's friends loyally attended and said they had enjoyed it, David Garnett's comment that 'the fault of concentration and lack of counter-plot made the performance emotionally exhausting'[41] would probably have been endorsed by most of the audience.

Amongst the playgoers was John Galsworthy, who had valiantly given Edward a long, detailed and very astute criticism of *Jeanne d'Arc* in 1910. They had always remained in touch and when Edward sent Galsworthy *West Country and Other Verses* to sign in 1929, it triggered fond memories of the trips they had taken in that part of the world and of the past they shared: 'It reminds me of all your unceasing benevolence towards my early efforts,' Galsworthy wrote. 'And so I sign it, dear Edward, after all these years, with the gratitude of your faithful and affectionate friend.'[42] In 1932 Galsworthy was awarded the Nobel Prize for Literature, but by then he had a brain tumour and was too ill to attend the ceremony. He died of a stroke on the last day of January 1933. A year later Edward published some of their correspondence in *Letters from John Galsworthy 1900–1932*, despite having reservations about its merit: 'Galsworthy, unlike D. H. Lawrence, was not a good letter writer as he didn't like to give himself away,'[43] he confessed to his sister Olive; and to Herbert Faulkner West, the American critic and author, Edward admitted that 'G[alsworthy]'s letters are not particularly interesting except when he is defending parts of *The Man of Property* and *The Patrician* against my strictures.'[44]

Edward was responding to a letter from Faulkner West congratulating him on a volume of short stories Cape had recently published. Edward had selected the contents and written an introduction. *Capajon* (the title taken from Cape's telegraphic address) was made up of fifty-three stories by twenty-four authors, all of whom had been published by Cape. A few, like Henry Lawson and Sarah Orne Jewett, were old favourites of Edward, but the majority were from the younger generation, including Bates, Manhood, O'Flaherty, and A. E. Coppard. Given Edward's cosmopolitan tastes it was unsurprising that half the authors were not English – Ernest Hemingway, Sherwood Anderson and Giovanni Verga were all represented, and there were several stories by Irish writers, including 'The Dead' by James Joyce, described by Edward as 'a masterpiece'.[45] The ten female contributors came from all over the world and included Katherine Susannah Prichard (Australia), Kay Boyle and Dorothy Canfield [Fisher] (America), Pauline Smith (South Africa) and the Finnish author Aino Kallas. The last five stories in the volume are by Malachi Whitaker, 'the Bradford Chekhov', whose initially fragile self-confidence Edward had nurtured. Naomi Mitchison features twice with 'The Lamb Misused' and 'A Matter of No Importance', but by the time *Capajon* was published in 1933 her relationship with Edward was about to end.

Mitchison had been working on a novel, *We Have Been Warned,* based on her recent visit to the Soviet Union and asked Edward if he would look at it. She had already told him that the book was 'very difficult' and 'very different'[46] from the historical fiction she had written, and as he read it Edward could see why he had been warned. He had backed Mitchison stoutly when Cape had previously fretted about perceived indecency, but he felt the manuscript was impossible as it stood. Not only did he find parts of it poorly written – 'There's no *illusion* of reality,' he complained, chiding Mitchison for 'such a lot of woolly thought stuff' and 'smeary jam-like symbolistic literary stuff'[47] – but the sexual explicitness, especially the descriptions of contraception, would lead to the book being banned. 'I suggest you simply ... make Idris Pritchard try to rape Dione,' Edward counselled, 'and then you get rid of the "rubber" business which I also think is impossible. And I'm not generally squeamish.'[48] On the final page of a long letter Edward sums up his feelings about the manuscript: 'The general effect of the novel is that of a piece *of machinery in which the screws are wearing looser and looser* – and though it's still holding together, it's functioning badly.' Mitchison was unbowed: 'I'm sorry you don't like the book,' she wrote, 'but I was afraid you wouldn't. Perhaps it's inevitable. I'll consider your criticisms, but in general I'm afraid I can't accept them. You see, I'm more sure about this book than I've ever been about any of the other books.'[49] She was adamant the contraception scene was necessary and tried to bring the shutters down on any further argument:

> But a lot of what you don't like is stuff that I've worked over a lot, read aloud and so on; I know it's not what it ought to be on a lot of grounds, but I *must* finally go my own way. I'm awfully sorry because, as you know, I've always taken your criticism before and always believed in it. You are my literary godfather. But I've got to do this on my own. After all, I'm thirty-six, and I must be able to judge for myself.[50]

Edward didn't give up easily: throughout the summer and early autumn letters went back and forth, lists of page numbers with suggested alterations from him, followed by further, often incredulous queries from Mitchison asking what exactly it was he objected to. Eventually, Cape himself got involved and demanded extensive alterations. Mitchison refused to make them and looked for another publisher. Victor Gollancz and John Lane both refused *We Have Been Warned*, fearful of the consequences should they publish it. Constable brought the book out in 1935, but annoyed Mitchison by querying passages once it was in page proof. Long afterwards, Mitchison confessed that she had been 'very miserable' about the whole situation, 'especially about the hurt to my long friendship with Edward Garnett'.[51] At the time, she hoped that Edward realised that her quarrel with him was intended to be only temporary. 'I still feel bad about it,'[52] she confessed nearly forty years later.

'For Edward Garnett, Best of Friends'

In August 1926 an envelope with an Irish postmark arrived at Pond Place. Edward was half-expecting a letter from Liam O'Flaherty, who had recently visited London, but the postmark was Cork, not Enniskerry, and the address was not in O'Flaherty's hand. Unbeknownst to Edward, O'Flaherty and his wife had spent a week in Cork, where they had met a young writer called Sean O'Faolain. O'Faolain had mentioned that he would welcome criticism of some stories he had written; O'Flaherty told him how helpful Edward had been and urged him to send a couple to Pond Place. Enclosed with the letter were 'The Bombshop' and 'Under the Roof'. Edward was impressed and offered an invitation to visit London, but by then O'Faolain had left on a trip to Belgium and there was no time to arrange anything before he departed to America to take up a Commonwealth Fund Fellowship at Harvard.

Although O'Faolain's early life had not been as turbulent and dramatic as O'Flaherty's, it was far from colourless. Born John Francis Whelan on 22 February 1900 in Cork, O'Faolain was the son of a constable in the Royal Irish Constabulary. Up until the age of sixteen O'Faolain was tremendously proud of being a citizen in a country that belonged to the British Empire: the 1916 Easter Rising changed that outlook dramatically. Within two years Jacky Whelan, the anglophile enthusiast of empire, was no more: in his place was Sean O'Faolain, the Irish-speaking Republican member of the Irish Volunteers. He served the next six years as a rank-and-filer in the Volunteers and the Irish Republican Army, performing a series of 'undemanding if essential jobs',[1] including a stint as a bomb-maker, and ended up as Publicity Director for the IRA in Dublin. However, O'Faolain's Republican experiences left him disillusioned and in 1924 he enrolled for a Master's degree at University College Cork, after which he took up the Fellowship at Harvard. Academic life frustrated O'Faolain, who found that concentrated study left him little time to write. He sought O'Flaherty's advice and received an uncompromising reply: staying in academe would destroy him as a writer, Edward had told O'Flaherty that he thought O'Faolain 'had genius' and was 'deeply impressed'.[2] O'Flaherty urged him to abandon Harvard and take up the pen full time. Despite this report, O'Faolain stayed in America: in 1927 his girlfriend Eileen Gould arrived from Ireland; they married the following year and O'Faolain gained his degree. However, his academic achievement was not the high point of O'Faolain's year: that distinction was reserved for a letter he received following the publication of his short story 'Fugue' in *Hound and Horn*:

> I at once sent off the September issue, containing my story, out of the blue, to Edward Garnett, the most remarkable and influential publisher's reader of his time in England ... He wrote back those joyous words that every young writer dreams wildly of hearing some day from some reader of Garnett's calibre: 'You are a writer.' He also asked me to send him everything else I wrote and to call on him if I ever came to London. That letter alone would have made this year a complete success.[3]

Edward's praise went some way to helping O'Faolain out of a dilemma: whether 'to write and starve, or to be a professor and live (and chance the writing)'. Worried by his responsibilities as a husband – 'I dislike the assumptive pride that does not consider others. I am afraid I am born to be a nice, bothered, troubled person rather than a Protean outpourer of beauty' – O'Faolain nevertheless ends a letter to Edward by declaring 'I have at last decided not to sell myself to any job. I am a literary man and *not* a scholar, which is a great decision for me to make.'[4] Four months later the O'Faolains were back in Ireland, but like so many of his countrymen O'Faolain felt that he had to distance himself from his homeland in order to write about it: 'I wish to cut Ireland off as thoroughly as I can before I have to return to it,' he told Edward. 'I want to return a disinterested stranger.'[5] In the autumn he and Eileen moved to Richmond and O'Faolain took up a post as lecturer in English at St Mary's Training College, Strawberry Hill. One of his first calls was on Edward, 'who straightway became our best and dearest friend in London'.[6]

O'Faolain's rented Richmond apartment was not far from the house where Charles Stewart Parnell used to visit Katherine O'Shea and it was O'Faolain's play about Parnell, *The Red Petticoat*, that was the subject of his early London correspondence with Edward, who had serious misgivings about the play. O'Faolain's declaration that he must '*cut* and make more terse those long confabulations, eliminate sentimentality and rhetoric, search after more subtlety'[7] gives some indication of the thrust of Edward's objections. Edward also felt that O'Faolain's view of Parnell was misconceived: his reasoning rankled O'Faolain more than a little:

> But you owe me an apology – if I read your letter aright. *I* 'look at P through the eyes of a peasant'? *I* and *peasant* in the one sentence!! My God, am I a peasant? Do I look like a peasant, think or talk like one? I should drown myself to think so! I beg of you to understand that my father and mother tore the soil with their hands but I have torn myself out of their blighted, blinded, uncivilised, intolerant, shutminded tradition at no small cost to my nature and my immortal soul and will not be spoken of in the same breath with that loath-some tradition. Have I not warned you I am an Anglo-Irishman now? I believe you said it to hurt my feelings!![8]

The exclamation marks may suggest an element of jocularity, but this was a subject about which O'Faolain was acutely sensitive – he was nothing if not determined to escape the ingrained prejudices and conventions of his upbringing and forge his own identity: when he called himself an 'Anglo-Irishman' he was claiming kinship with the *cultural* traditions of writers like George Moore, W. B. Yeats and Æ (George Russell). The generation that followed those writers – O'Flaherty, O'Faolain, Frank O'Connor – were Catholics who had direct or indirect links to peasantry and that may have been exactly what commended them to Edward, who felt they brought a new voice and perspective to Irish writing.

O'Faolain abandoned *The Red Petticoat* and started work on a volume of short stories, composing some when free of his teaching duties and rewriting others he had by him. If the original versions that appeared in various journals are compared with those in his first short story collection *Midsummer Night Madness* (1932), it is noticeable that O'Faolain recasts the original material in more dramatic form and tones down some of the metaphors. Mrs Dale, the old woman in 'The Bombshop', was originally described as having a mouth 'like a little pale daisy pursed in the centre of her grey face, and then who could tell whether it was merriness or bitterness that made her stare at you so? To look at the daisy – a hard brain, this: to look at the eyes – a great-hearted woman.'⁹ In the *Midsummer Night Madness* version of the story we are told that Mrs Dale:

> ... was a wonderful old woman; even Sean and Caesar, rough fellows as they were, could find no other word for her but that, and as she peered down at them, with child-soft eyes and inclined brow, unbuttoning her little mouth, that was wrinkled like cloth, into a smooth gentle smile they would wink at her or smile foolishly, not knowing whether to believe those open mother's eyes or her torture-tightened lips.¹⁰

Few of Edward's letters to O'Faolain survive, but given his insistence that other writers dispense with lush metaphors and strive for greater emotional and technical detachment, it is not unreasonable to suppose that O'Faolain benefited from similar counsel. At the last minute he added another story to the volume, 'The Patriot', which he sent to Edward for approval. 'Thanks for reading it,' O'Faolain writes

> and thanks a thousand times for all the encouragement you have given me. You don't know what it means to be able to say – I hope E.G. will like this, to have an audience before one's mind which is discriminating, ready to praise and blame with justice. You are a brick, a Godsend ... You are Cape's *soul*. And all the frigid 'thoroughly enjoyed' etceteras of the usual reader are not worth a puff of a ram's horn beside one hearty 'Good!' from you.¹¹

Whenever he could, O'Faolain joined Edward for lunch or dinner, often at a Russian restaurant on Harrington Road or at the Commercio in Soho. O'Faolain recalls that Edward 'always had somebody interesting to meet us at these places, but never a lion, always a cub, somebody young like myself, at the beginning of his career, like H. E. Bates, or Malachi Whitaker, or H. A. Manhood'.¹² This fits the pattern of Edward's career, as soon as one of his cubs began to resemble a literary lion he withdrew; partly, perhaps, from the knowledge that the young lion regards himself as king of all he surveys and has neither need nor desire for guidance, and partly also because he always found the cub a much more interesting and exciting animal in any case.

O'Faolain was finding teaching increasingly tiresome and longed to devote more time to his writing. The Viking Press had agreed to subsidise O'Faolain and Edward set about convincing Wren Howard, Jonathan

Cape's partner, that Cape should do the same. 'I think very highly of the quality of O'Faolain's work,' Edward explained. 'He is the most talented Irish writer in sight and much more *of an artist* than O'Flaherty ... The Viking Press will pay him 200£ for the next two years and I should think if Cape offered him about the same it would be a fair speculation.'[13] Edward also mentioned two projects that were of considerable importance to O'Faolain's immediate future: his desire to return to Ireland and Edward's own plan to write a foreword to *Midsummer Night Madness* 'attacking the Irish for not backing up their own writers'. Little did Edward realise that these plans were to prove to be incompatible.

O'Faolain had for some time had his eye on the vacant chair of English at University College Cork and in the spring of 1931 he started traipsing into remote corners of Ireland in an effort to persuade the members of the governing body to lend him their electoral support. Edward was worried that the rigours of an academic post would leave O'Faolain little time to write and so he may have felt a certain relief when he lost the election; O'Faolain, however, was bitterly disappointed at the result. 'I groan to see my life stretching out in a succession of years of barren experience,' he complained despondently to Edward. 'I sit like a seed that someone has cast on stony ground and the rain never falls and nothing happens!'[14] Edward's response may have been brisker and less sympathetic than O'Faolain hoped, because it provoked a stinging riposte:

> Your reference to my negative nature gave me a jolt ... You have talked like an [*sic*] University professor who thinks he knows every-thing. And though you know much more about men than an University professor you do not know everything. If thats [*sic*] all the help you can give a man on his way through a bitch of a world you should be content to shut up. Do you think you have helped any? ... You surely have heard that young men take themselves seriously – and most seriously when their egos are out of order? You will allow me to tell you to go to hell? Consider it said.[15]

Edward was used to dealing with volatile characters – D. H. Lawrence and O'Flaherty could be highly combustible when the mood took them – but this letter is one of the most forthright he ever received from a protégé. It probably didn't worry Edward unduly, though – he could be pretty forthright himself – and he certainly wasn't prepared to mince his words when he sat down to draft his foreword to *Midsummer Night Madness*.

Writing as 'an Anglo-Irishman and a London publisher's advisor who has always taken an interest in Irish authors and Irish literature',[16] Edward lambasts Ireland and the Irish, claiming the country to be the most culturally backward in Europe and her people the 'most indifferent to literature and art, and least aware of critical standards'. 'Any nation,' he continues, 'that takes so little interest in its own writers and leaves them dependent on English attention and English alms is culturally speaking contemptible and not worth the snuff of a candle.' Strong stuff indeed, but Edward then turned both barrels on the Church:

> Ireland is a Catholic country and is directed by the most intolerant and retrograde body of priests in Europe. Look at their mediaeval fear of sex, their spiritual negativeness, their edicts against the works of 'intellectuals' such as Aldous Huxley. How, it may be asked, can literature flourish in such a sterile atmosphere? It is true that in the last two generations nearly every Irishman of talent whether it be George Moore, Oscar Wilde and Bernard Shaw yesterday, or James Joyce and Liam O'Flaherty to-day, has had to emigrate to find a welcome outside his own land.

Having vented his spleen, Edward goes on to praise O'Faolain's rendering of 'the Irish sensitiveness to place and emotional mood, in a style free and flowing, punctuated by passages of that brutal frankness which is the conscience of the younger generation'. The caustic note, however, is resumed at the end: '[O'Faolain] has passed some years in America, he lives by teaching English literature to English elementary school teachers. He has a play on Parnell in MS. He lives in London. How typical!'

Initially O'Faolain professed himself to be 'as proud as Punch' with the foreword. 'I have intimated that I am quite happy to hear you slang the priests who deserve it,' he told Edward. 'I might here say that it will probably be resented bitterly, and be remembered for me if ever I try for a job from the RCs. But a writer must be true to himself at all costs.'[17] However, five months later O'Faolain decided that the potential costs of Edward's hard-hitting remarks were just too high. He showed the foreword to Father Joseph Leonard, vice-principal of St Mary's, who, O'Faolain hastily assured Edward, was a broad-minded, literary man. Father Joseph left O'Faolain in no doubt that Edward's attack would scupper any chance of a teaching job in Ireland, which in itself might mean he could not afford to return there at all. Although O'Faolain told Edward he was happy to let the foreword stand, he was clearly worried about it, as he attached 'a *suggestion* – humbly offered – as to a way of making the *same charges* generically ... without giving any class a *personal* swipe'.[18] Edward had no wish to jeopardise O'Faolain's chances of going back to Ireland, and so agreed to modify the foreword. This he did by turning his potentially inflammatory statements into a challenge: he dares his targets to prove his accusations wrong, citing the publication of *Midsummer Night Madness* as an 'opportunity ... to rebut the charges of apathy and indifference shown to Irish authors at home'.[19] Edward knew only too well that the foreword would ensure the book was discussed and would get O'Faolain's name in the public eye. 'I am posting you this complete copy of *Midsummer Night Madness and Other Stories*,' he told Wren Howard, 'together with the Foreword I propose to print attacking the Irish etc, in the hope of raising a shindig over the book.'[20] It did that all right: *Midsummer Night Madness* was banned in Ireland on the grounds of 'being in general tendency indecent'.[21] Outwardly O'Faolain laughed at the news, but he later confessed that 'in my heart I felt infuriated and humiliated'.[22]

Midsummer Night Madness received favourable reviews in Britain and established O'Faolain's name, although the book's sales were unremarkable. Edward's foreword did not escape attention: the reviewer in the *Bookman* described it as a 'tactless diatribe against the Irish people',[23] while John Chamberlain in the *New York Times* claimed that it was 'suffused with a brilliantly caustic bitterness toward the Irish'.[24] Liam O'Flaherty was prompted to contact Edward again after a gap of four years: 'I am writing to you after reading your introduction to S. O'Faolain's book,' he wrote. 'I think your foreword is great, but ... O'Faolain has little in him except a great deal of imitative cunning. Your introduction is so much stronger than he is.'[25] Although Edward had helped O'Flaherty with *Mr Gilhooley* (1926) and *The Assassin* (1928), their association had effectively come to an end when O'Flaherty fell out with Cape, and there is little doubt that O'Flaherty was jealous of O'Faolain's critical success. When Eileen O'Faolain expressed to Edward her surprise at the critics' positive reaction to *Midsummer Night Madness* and reminded him that he had said critics couldn't recognise a good book when they saw it, Edward growled back: 'It was too damn good – even for *them*.'[26]

During the summer of 1931 O'Faolain took up a novel he had begun to write in 1927, when he was still in America. Now, heartened by Edward's support and encouragement, he made swift progress. *A Nest of Simple Folk* spans the years from 1854 to 1916 and tells the story of three generations of the O'Donnell family, charting their migration from the countryside to the city and their involvement with the nationalist movement. When Edward read it, he told O'Faolain to cut prolixity and add strong scenes. O'Faolain found writing scenes difficult and cutting even harder: 'I know it should be cut but where I don't know,' he confessed. 'I hope in Christus that you know. Do be a Herod and massacre all my innocents that you want to ... I have a hell of a lot to learn.'[27] Edward thought the manuscript was not a rounded whole and the city scenes, where O'Faolain was not writing from his own experience, 'anaemic'. More revision was required: 'I feel like a prisoner who has been awaiting release for a year of days and is caught as he leaves the jail gate and flung back on the treadmill again,'[28] O'Faolain complained. Eventually he had had enough and decided to publish *A Nest of Simple Folk* as it stood. When Edward demurred, O'Faolain rose up spiritedly:

> I feel like saying Damn strong scenes! ... I finished with wild scenes in *Midsummer Night Madness*. I wanted calm and dust and the pollen of the bogflowers on my boots and the streaks of dew through it. This is a bloody great book. Hurrah! I read it again all over and loved it. I don't care whether it's art or not. It's TRUE ... Christus! What more can one ask?[29]

Yet in the very next paragraph O'Faolain conceded the wisdom of Edward's advice – 'But You [sic] are quite right about country scenes deepening it and your excisions are nearly almost wise and right. Out they go. Heaven bless you.'

Privately, both men vented their frustrations with each other: O'Faolain told Cape that the novel was much better than Edward realised, while Edward agreed with his fellow Anglo-Irishman T. E. Lawrence that the Irish were

> disappointing men ... 'They go so far magnificently and cease to grow. They bring forth more promise and less fruition than the rest of the English world massed against them'.
>
> They have no sense of architecture and they wont [sic] take enough pains *to be* artists. O'Faolain has just written a novel, for example, 'A Nest of Simple Folk' which starts off magnificently and then declines into a mere chronicle of family life in Limerick and Cork. It's unusual, and real and has much quality: but compared

with what it ought to be and might have been, it's a damned piece of Irish evasiveness.[30]

It was around this time that Edward received a novel in manuscript from another Irish writer that he condemned not for its evasiveness, but because he considered it 'a slavish, and rather incoherent imitation of Joyce, most eccentric in language and full of disgustingly affected passages'.[31] This was Samuel Beckett's first novel *Dream of Fair to Middling Women*. While Edward conceded that Beckett 'probably is a clever fellow', he advised Cape not to touch it with a barge pole. As it turned out no other publisher would either; the novel finally appeared in 1992, sixty years after Beckett wrote it and three years after his death.

O'Faolain finished *A Nest of Simple Folk* on his return to Ireland in 1933, when Edward finally persuaded Cape to follow the Viking Press and subsidise him for two years. Under the agreement, O'Faolain was to get £12 a month, the amount to be set against royalties on *Midsummer Night Madness* and any future work. Until he secured this agreement O'Faolain was reluctant to take his chance back in Ireland. His daughter Julia was born in 1932 and parenthood brought added financial responsibility. However, by June 1933 the O'Faolains had saved a couple of hundred pounds and 'with Edward's warmest blessings and direst forebodings [on account of the banning of *Midsummer Night Madness*], we set off for Ireland and the Life of a Man of Letters'.[32] They rented Killough House in Co. Wicklow, fifteen miles from Dublin. O'Faolain turned one of the upstairs rooms into a study, complete with a photograph of Edward. 'Theres [*sic*] your thoughtful eyes looking at me reproachfully from your picture in my room and its as bad as double-conscience,'[33] he told his mentor. Edward wasted no time in checking up on his protégé. A month after the move, he descended. His reaction is best left to O'Faolain:

> That July, Edward visited us to see how we were faring, looked about him at my ménage, threw up his hands and cried: 'You are lost!'
> His reasons for this dismal prophecy were threefold.
> 'You are living,' he growled 'like a lord! You have a car! Your wife has a French maid! And you are living in a mansion! You will either never write a line, or you will become a hack!'[34]

There was more than a little exaggeration in Edward's assessment – the maid was on a short visit and the 'mansion' somewhat ramshackle – however, 'Edward glared about him, took it all in, and disapproved.' This

was not on account of any Puritan streak, but rather because Edward felt
such a standard of living would either distract O'Faolain from writing
altogether or force him into hack journalism in order to maintain it.
Despite his apparent horror at O'Faolain's lifestyle – and surely to some
extent his tongue was in his cheek – Edward and Nellie made several
trips to Ireland to see O'Faolain, whose 'pet image' of Edward comes
from one such visit:

> One day we paused at Oliver St John Gogarty's hotel in Renvyle,
> near which there is a lovely deserted beach with the Atlantic waves
> always rolling in on its pallid sand. There we bathed, he in his bare
> pelt. He had always reminded me of 'old Silenus lolling in the
> sunshine', large, big of belly, soft of eye, now dreamy, now belli-
> cose, now ironical, now mocking, sunk in an armchair or bowed
> over a restaurant table, his white locks tousled, his herbal cigarettes
> dropping ash all over the place. That day he just lay down naked on
> the sands and luxuriously let the waves roll and rock his big belly
> and bottom to and fro, a blissful pagan child of the waves and the
> skies. He was in this sense one of the most romantically tempered
> men I have ever met; a happy – I stress the word – lover of the
> body and of nature, in no least way a *malade* of romanticism . . .[35]

O'Faolain's other recollections of Edward in Ireland are equally affectionate: a half-tipsy Edward and an equally inebriated Irish farmer in a
salmon-pink creel cart on their way to inspect the 'serpents' in the latter's
well; and Edward's early morning encounter with a handsome young
woman – 'Like a fairy woman coming to me out of the morning mist!' –
swinging a chamber pot![36] David, who observed his father and O'Faolain
together in Ireland, felt that Sean and Eileen might have found Edward a
handful: 'Ireland brought out the Paddy in him,'[37] David observes. It may
also have stimulated the combative side in Edward, as it was in Ireland
that he and O'Faolain had the 'great set-to'[38] about the novel that was
to end their relationship.

O'Faolain anticipated a fight over the novel that was to become *Bird
Alone* from the start. 'I have well begun the novel now,' he told Edward.
'You won't like it because I am breaking away in it from psychology-
as-it-is known.'[39] From his letter, it was clear that O'Faolain's mood
was darkening – the initial enthusiasm at being back in Ireland was
wearing off; he was feeling isolated and chafing against the monotony
of his domestic existence: 'If only I could get out from under the gentle

eagle-eye of Eileen and with some fellow like Eric [Linklater] be shook to bits by a chorusgirl from the Kit-Cat, it would do me as much good as a doze [*sic*] of Epsom Salts.'[40] Perhaps it was these feelings of isolation that drove O'Faolain within himself and led him to write a novel that was highly subjective. The first 20,000 words arrived at Pond Place with a warning: 'I send you now not a pleasure, but a task – that of reading what cannot please you.'[41] He was not wrong.

Edward's main objection to the novel was that O'Faolain had tried to mix an almost Dickensian realism with Joycean subjectivity and this did not work. He also accused O'Faolain of repeating situations – the relationship between Corney, the protagonist of *Bird Alone*, and his grandfather is very similar to that between two characters in *A Nest of Simple Folk*. O'Faolain flared up at this and denied it, adding that repetition was 'the great quality of your Englishman. Like Bates he will keep on saying the same tune all over again ... O'Flaherty is a sad example. He has just repeated himself, ad nauseam, nothing to say and same technique.'[42] It is a barbed retort; the reference to Edward's other protégés give it a very personal edge, as does the pointed comment about 'your Englishman'. As Edward read the letter, he might well have been taken back to his quarrel with D. H. Lawrence over *The Rainbow*: the argument that 'each generation finds its own idea of what is true and real' would have sounded very familiar. O'Faolain wanted to depict his characters subjectively, whereas Edward believed that it was the small outer detail that gave the clue to character. Edward wasn't against what O'Faolain termed 'subjective' novels – he had been enthusiastic about Virginia Woolf's *The Voyage Out* and had supported Dorothy Richardson, for example – but he felt that O'Faolain's attempt at writing in that vein simply wasn't very good. O'Faolain might have fancied himself as a radical pioneer, but in truth he was never a formal innovator like Lawrence or Joyce. Edward praised the novel's ending, but the differences between the two men proved irreconcilable as O'Faolain later recalled:

> [Edward] told me I should see myself as the Balzac of Ireland (no less) and, to shorten many heated arguments on his side, met obstinately and rather coldly on my side, he demanded that I rewrite the whole story on solid Balzacian lines or scrap it entirely. I refused to alter a line; he washed his hands of me; and we were both wrong.[43]

O'Faolain had very little contact with Edward after their dispute. 'I had by then left London,' O'Faolain later explained, 'though I doubt if we would have met very often even if I had stayed on – he tired of his ducklings as soon as he had launched them.'[44] Garnett's experience with O'Faolain left him feeling disappointed and frustrated, as he made clear to Benjamin Huebsch: 'The Irish are the most disappointing of races – and individually like eels and twist through your fingers. They are damned perverse.'[45]

Despite their differences O'Faolain continued to regard Edward with admiration and affection: 'I will always revere him for his boundless generosity of mind and his gallant independence of the world,'[46] he writes in his autobiography *Vive moi!* (1964). Maurice Harmon, O'Faolain's biographer and a personal friend, states unequivocally that 'the relationship with Garnett was the most important in Sean's entire literary life.'[47]

Less than a year after the row over *Bird Alone*, Edward was dead. O'Faolain's next book was a volume of short stories entitled *A Purse of Coppers* (1937), which O'Faolain declared to be

FOR
EDWARD GARNETT,
BEST OF FRIENDS
This handful of modest life out of Ireland – much rubbed,
perhaps even with the superscription defaced by time and
compression. You have wished me more passionate and heroic,
and I have said, 'What can a writer do but gather up the coins and
make his own fumbling effort to say to what Caesar each belongs?'
If there is some lovely figure here, blotted by time, and maligned
by me, you, in Avalon, will know how much I am astray.
Alas, that, for once, we cannot contradict each other.[48]

'Mentor, pater in literis, et al'

'I hope you have found something worth reading, of late, and that your encouragement to those eager yet uncertain in letters is still demanded. You have been such a centre for so long. If only I had done you credit!'[1] These were the last words T. E. Lawrence wrote to Edward in November 1934. Edward's encouragement was indeed still in demand: H. E. Bates and the other 'cubs' of his generation continued to seek his advice and Edward was about to take an active interest in the work of Geraint Goodwin, a young Welsh author. He was also sought out by those wishing to write about the likes of Conrad, D. H. Lawrence and Edward Thomas, whose reputations he had done so much to make.

In 1936 the American author Robert P. Eckert contacted Edward about a book he was writing on Thomas. Edward congratulated him for writing about Thomas 'with such conscientious care, good taste and also exactitude'.[2] When he read Jessie Conrad's second memoir of her husband, *Joseph Conrad and his Circle* (1935), he had felt the exact opposite. Jessie's portrait of her husband is not exactly flattering: Conrad is irascible, selfish and spends quite a lot of the book gout-ridden and muttering 'damn' with a thick Polish accent. Edward was appalled. He wrote a scathing review for the *London Mercury* in which he contends that 'All the fine shades of [Conrad's] character have disappeared from his wife's portrait of him, because she herself had no fine shades of understanding to match them.'[3] Caustic as the review is, it is mild compared with the letter he wrote Jessie. 'I think it is the most detestable book ever written by a wife about her husband,' he tells her. 'You have exposed Conrad and yourself to ridicule by your petty vindictiveness ... Your insensitiveness and lack of sympathy are in evidence on nearly every page.' He ends the letter: 'In publishing this detestable book you have betrayed Conrad's trust in you. I judge that no friend of his will wish to see you again.'[4] Jessie's reply is rather magnificent: 'I hope for the sake of your reputation as a cultured man of letters and as a "gentleman" the tone of your contribution to the L[ondon] M[ercury] may be a trifle more moderate in tone and expression,'⁵ she countered, and continues:

> There is not a single word in my book that belittles my husband. I may not be capable – as you say – of appreciating or even understanding his genius, but you may remember one point I make in the 'detestable book' which is that to live in this world one talented partner is enough, the other must be more commonplace and ordinary. I have claimed that distinction for myself.

Edward continued to fume about the book: 'Jessie ought to have been the manageress of a fourth rate Hotel or a House for Barmaids,' he told Cunninghame Graham, 'I knew that from the first and Conrad having no knowledge of the social shades in Englishwomen and wanting a Housekeeper has had to pay, at last, for his experiment.'⁶ Ironically, the foreignness that Edward considered one of Conrad's greatest assets as a writer was now suggested to be the underlying cause of his being held up to personal ridicule.

Edward was genuinely fearful that Jessie's book might lessen the esteem in which Conrad was held, but in general he was no mere respecter of reputations, of either the living or the dead. After D. H. Lawrence's death Edward was asked to edit his posthumous papers. He started the task, but realised that it was much bigger than he anticipated and so got the American bibliographer Edward D. McDonald to take over the editing and bibliographic work. Edward agreed to write an introduction to the book, which he had tentatively called *The Last Cargo*. This he also found hard: 'Everything about DHL and his genius is in a sense clear,' he explained to McDonald, 'but it is difficult to *analyse* its kaleidoscopic character.'⁷ Edward nevertheless rose to the challenge, pointing out that the volume displayed Lawrence 'at his best and his worst, i.e. as poet and artist, and as argumentative preacher'.⁸ Lawrence's fearlessness in taking on 'the Old British Goliath, the Philistine giant who had maimed or mutilated so many writers in the 19th century' comes in for high praise, and Edward delights in many of the contents, drawing attention to Lawrence's extraordinary sensibility to the atmosphere of place and his genius for describing the natural world. However, some of the pieces come in for sharp criticism: the *Study of Thomas Hardy* is dismissed as 'magnificent rant, most of it'; Lawrence is described as 'unfair and one-eyed' in his attack on Galsworthy; and Edward declares that in order to get through *Women in Love* one requires 'great determination and a keen diagnostic interest'. Edward himself felt the introduction 'gives a clue to DHL's complex mentality and holds the balance fair between his contradictory impulses',[9] but Harold K. Guinzberg of the Viking Press and Alexander Frere-Reeves of Heinemann, who were jointly publishing the book, disagreed. Guinzberg conceded that Edward had written 'an admirable essay' on Lawrence's work, but he believed that 'in its honesty it necessarily belittles a large part of the contents of this volume'[10] and cancelled the introduction. Edward understood the reasons for the decision, but turned down the suggestion that he should act as co-editor with McDonald. He resigned from the whole project. McDonald was dismayed, but wrote appreciatively about Edward's contribution in his own introduction to *Phoenix* (1936), as the book was eventually called. When Edward reviewed it, he used much of the cancelled introduction, albeit in a slightly shorter and milder form, and paid public tribute to McDonald's 'devoted labours, wide knowledge and research'.[11]

Just at the time when *The Last Cargo* was rekindling memories of D. H. Lawrence, Edward received news that another protean Lawrence, T. E., was in a coma; he had been thrown from his motorbike, while attempting to avoid two boys on bicycles on his way back to his cottage from Bovington Camp. 'I am afraid you are terribly anxious about Shaw [Lawrence],' wrote David. 'I saw the stop-press in the *Daily Mail* yesterday.'[12] Lawrence died from his injuries six days later. Edward contributed a long essay for *T. E. Lawrence by His Friends* (1937) in which he relates the history of *Seven Pillars of Wisdom* and *The Mint* and discusses Lawrence's capacity as a critic: 'of the authors I have known,' writes Edward, 'TE possessed, I think, the most responsive and the widest critical taste. He combined the true scholar's sense of literary values with the unconventional judgment of a man of culture who tests books by life.'[13]

Less than a year after Lawrence's death, Edward was writing another article in memory of a great friend and man of action. Robert Bontine Cunninghame Graham died in Buenos Aires on 20 March 1936. A fortnight before his death, Cunninghame Graham dictated a letter to Edward from his bed, telling him about his visit to W. H. Hudson's birthplace: 'I never was more impressed by anything [than] when I sat writing in that little room and thought that from such unlikely surroundings so great a genius had arisen. That nothing should be wanting, there was a chestnut horse tied to one of the posts of the house, as it were, waiting for Hudson.'[14] It was apt that Cunninghame Graham's last letter to Edward raised the spirit of Hudson, who had meant so much to them both, as man and writer.

Edward was not one to dwell on the ghosts of the past, however. Nothing excited him more than discovering a new talent and he was convinced that Geraint Goodwin had the potential to become a unique voice in Anglo-Welsh literature. Goodwin was born in 1903 in Llanllwchaearn, Montgomeryshire. He came to London in 1923 to work for a publicity and news agency, but soon joined Allied Newspapers and became a successful reporter, mainly for the *Daily Sketch*. Goodwin had contracted tuberculosis in 1929: it would kill him twelve years later at the age of thirty-eight. By the time Edward met him, he had published two books and had more or less decided to pack in journalism in order to write full time. His first novel, *Call Back Yesterday*, published by Cape in 1935, was autobiographical, but, according to his wife Rhoda, Goodwin 'had still not found himself'.[15] Diffidently, Goodwin showed Edward some short stories with a Welsh background; Edward was broadly impressed, although he pointed out passages he thought diffuse and suggested that some of the dialogue was too flowery. The criticism inspired Goodwin: '[A]lthough I have had lots of encouragement before, it all seemed to be wrong – it never reached me if you understand. Yours has,'[16] he explained. In the summer of 1935 Goodwin and his wife moved from London to a farm in Dagnell, and Goodwin planned to write a novel. 'Better a few strongly or deeply drawn characters, clashing, than too many figures,'[17] Edward advised. Goodwin wrote more than 20,000 words, but when Edward criticised the manuscript adversely he abandoned it. 'I felt very happy that you had come down where you had and still more so that you headed me off where you did,'[18] he confessed. 'I am sure – ten times sure – that your gospel (write of what you know) is the only one.' Goodwin mentioned going back to work on some sketches, but Edward may well have warned him, as he had Bates, that publishers found short story collections hard to sell, because Goodwin started another novel shortly after scrapping his previous attempt. This was based on an extended idea Edward had suggested to him which used some of the characters from the abandoned draft. At the beginning of 1936 Goodwin sent Edward 58,000 words of the new novel. '*I congratulate you*,' Edward replied. 'I think (with one or two reservations) that you have written a fine original thing ... All the characterisation is good ... All the nature pieces are real nature ... and the atmosphere is true and haunting.'[19] The only criticism Edward had was that the chapters did not flow into one another, but 'suggest[ed] sketches brought together'. He also advocated the addition of a few more 'strong scenes'. Goodwin, a less confident and less combative character than O'Faolain, did not demur. 'For to be quite

frank there is very little credit to me in the whole thing,' he confessed
to Edward. 'Item – you gave me the plot: item – you sketch it out: item
– you tell me what to do and what not to do ... And but for you God
only knows what a mess I might have got into.'[20]

Edward loved *The Heyday in the Blood* (1936), which was dedicated to
him. The novel received good reviews. Goodwin was now being spoken
of in the same breath as D. H. Lawrence and Thomas Hardy: *'Your course
is perfectly clear now,'* Edward wrote, 'what you have got to do is *be the*
Welsh novelist – recorder and narrator of the *popular* Welsh life – *as you
know it* and as you get to know it in a larger and widening circle.'[21] When
Goodwin suggested bringing out a volume of short stories, Edward
agreed, but trotted out his oft-repeated warning that short stories *'never*
increase a writer's reputation except with the judicious few. They are just
accepted and the author is patted on the back ... and the reviewers wait
for the new novel.'[22] When Goodwin showed Edward the stories, however,
he was impressed: 'Cape is just sending to press a vol. of short stories
by [Goodwin],' he told Huebsch of the Viking Press, *'all* good ... He
certainly *is* a writer: he has the pithy phrase and real emotional force.'[23]
Edward had suggested the title of the volume, *The White Farm and Other
Stories*, which was published in 1937. When Viking asked Goodwin for
some biographical details, he told Edward that he wrote the following:
'Goodwin was still trying to find himself when he came under the most
important influence of his life. This was Edward Garnett.'[24]

Goodwin was not alone in realising the significance of Edward's
contribution to contemporary literature. In January 1936 Manchester
University offered Edward an honorary doctorate; the letter went to
The Cearne, where Constance opened it. She was convinced Edward
would refuse the honour and asked David to beg him not to. Nothing
would induce Edward to accept. David wrote several times in an attempt
to persuade his father, in the end telling him, 'My concern is that it
can only be interpreted as the ungracious action of a churl who thinks
what is offered is not good enough for him.'[25] The letter distressed
Edward: 'Could anyone be less "academic" than myself? Less suited to
be Doctor Garnett?' he asked David. 'Why force me into an academic
style and robes that I do not feel at ease in? For what reason?' The
episode uncovered fundamental differences between father and son, as
the end of Edward's letter makes clear:

By your 'Lady into Fox' you jumped right into a large circle of
literary friends: but I have always been 'an outsider': outside *all*

coteries and collections of people, I prefer to be plain Edward Garnett, and why you should not understand this and not let me remain freely and simply myself discloses a rift in spirit between us.[26]

David was never going to win that particular battle. In a letter to Baker Fairley, who had also hoped to persuade Edward to accept the doctorate, Edward explained that he was declining the honour 'on the grounds that I regard myself as an outsider, a solitary person, unacademic in essence and unfitted to be Dr Garnett ... I may add that a few months ago I refused the Birthday Honour that has I see, been conferred on Dr Dover Wilson – because for me a writer loses part of his independence when he is honoured by the Government.'[27] This was a reference to Edward having declined a Companionship of Honour. When he had received a letter from Stanley Baldwin's office informing him that the Prime Minister proposed to submit his name to the king for a CH, Edward had been baffled and annoyed.

Edward's longevity in the publishing business was clearly one factor that made him a candidate for public honour. He had been reading manuscripts for nearly half a century and his eyes were starting to trouble him. 'I get slower in my work now,'[28] he confessed to Manhood in 1935. Since the beginning of the thirties, Edward had been joined as reader by Hamish Miles, a scholarly writer and translator with whom Edward got on very well. In general he was more comfortable in the company of the younger members of Cape's staff like Miles, Hamish Hamilton and Rupert Hart-Davis, but for all that he might grumble about Jonathan Cape himself, Edward was happy working for the company and was accorded a significant degree of autonomy and considerable influence over Cape's list.

Towards the end of 1936, Edward wrote to Cape:

While I feel quite up to my usual work now, I have reached an age when a yearly agreement gives me no assurance for the future. I feel that my judgement about an MS's possibilities is as good as ever; but each added year makes one's anticipations physically more and more grey. The firm of Cape I take it is in a solidly prosperous position, and you might like to show practically your appreciation of my literary advice in the past by adding a clause to the agreement for 1937 guaranteeing me while I am living, and perhaps expanding, my (nominal) share in the business.[29]

Edward was still attending regular Wednesday luncheons with Cape at the Etoile restaurant in Charlotte Street and he was there as usual on 17 February 1937. Two days later, he rose to dress, but complained to Nellie of a terrible pain. After about five minutes he became unconscious and when the doctor came half an hour later he was dead. He was sixty-nine and had suffered a cerebral haemorrhage.

★

Edward was cremated on 23 February at Golders Green. David arranged the funeral; he acted according to what he believed Edward would have wanted: there was no religious service, no music and no speeches. Constance and Nellie did not attend – according to Richard Garnett neither felt up to going[30] – and so, in the words of H. E. Bates 'it was a following of very young men who stood to pay homage to him that day – H. A. Manhood, Geraint Goodwin, Arthur Calder-Marshall, Rupert Hart-Davis, Hamish Miles and myself. All of us, but myself I think most of all, owed him much; all of us had delighted in him.'[31] Looking back years later, Calder-Marshall recalled that:

> Edward's was the only cremation which has ever struck me as dramatically first class. None of that slow descent into the basement, to be burnt hours later. The coffin rolled majestically to the left and doors opened revealed [sic] a Biblical 'burning fiery furnace' and then closed like a dragon's jaws. What an exit!
>
> Rupert [Hart-Davis] (who of course sported a topper) had kept up a cheerful line on the way out but was grave on the way back, if that is not a mixture of metaphors.
>
> Bates was deeply moved. EG meant a very great deal to him. Mentor, pater in literis, et al.[32]

Edward's estate totalled £11,500. He left his chattels to Constance and David and the caravan he had owned for several years to Nellie, who also received Edward's record collection and £1,100. Small monetary bequests were made to Edward's sister Olive and his two nieces. Constance received the rest of the money in trust until her death, after which it went to David and then to Edward's grandsons, Richard and William. Nellie moved out of Pond Place shortly after Edward's death into a small flat in north London. Edward's grandson Richard recalls that Nellie 'drew closer to the remaining Garnetts, especially to Constance, and became an extra grandmother to William and me'.[33] Constance remained at The Cearne until her death in 1946.

David and Constance received numerous letters of condolence, including one from Ramsay MacDonald, who recalled their very early days in the East End. Geraint Goodwin told Constance that to him Edward 'was a sort of talisman – to everything that was true and of good report'.[34] Writing in the *Spectator*, Rolfe Scott-James described how Edward 'went on reacting to the last to the impressions which new literature can afford – bold and cross as an old lion defending its lair, but without losing the affection of those for whom he cared';[35] while Hamish Miles argued that Edward should be remembered 'as a unique personality in the literary life of England during at least two generations, and as a man with an exacting but singularly charming and animating faculty for friendship'.[36]

Jonathan Cape paid Edward fulsome tribute in the in-house journal *Now and Then*. Describing him as 'keeper of the firm's literary conscience', Cape insisted that Edward's 'power to assimilate and assess literary work was amazing. There was never any flagging in his interest, or his search for fresh talent. He was always a keen prospector.' Cape ends the piece: 'We can count Edward Garnett as one of the main contributors to our present position in the publishing world. May his spirit never be troubled by any sins of commission or omission on the part of those who have to wear his mantle!'[37]

In 1931 Edward had published four of his plays in one volume. It was reviewed by E. M. Forster, who focused not so much on the book as its author. 'Mr Edward Garnett occupies a unique position in the literary history of our age,' he wrote. 'He has done more than any living writer to discover and encourage the genius of other writers, and he has done it without any desire for personal prestige.' Towards the end of the piece Forster remarks:

> Mr Garnett always has been a little unfortunate. He has never pushed into the front row of the dress circle or joined a really slap-up club. When he reaches heaven he is sure to be told that the best seats have all been booked, and he will learn the news with infinite relief.[38]

The last word should perhaps be left to T. E. Lawrence, who, in the final letter he ever wrote to Edward, summed up his qualities and his legacy admirably:

I am inclined to think that in time your own writing will be put second, by judges, to the writing of which you have been the cause in others. 'School of Edward Garnett' might be the classification of English literature across a quarter of a century – or indeed for more than thirty years. I think that it is an unparalleled achievement for a person whose critical writing is less than his creative writing. Your criticisms have always gone personally from you to the artist, instead of being exhibition pieces to catch the public eye on the way. Astonishing, as I said![39]

Acknowledgements

I am greatly indebted to the late Richard Garnett for his unfailing help and support. He and his wife Jane showed me great kindness and wonderful hospitality on my trips to Hilton Hall: I am only sorry that the book was not finished in time for him to read it. I am very grateful to Richard's son Oliver for granting me permission to quote from the published and unpublished writing of Edward Garnett, Dr Richard Garnett, Ray Garnett and Richard Garnett. Oliver also kindly allowed me to reproduce photographs from the various Garnett family albums at Northwestern University.

Caroline White of Tabb House has given me tremendous support and encouragement throughout and has kindly granted me permission to reproduce the material from Olive Garnett and Nellie Heath.

Barry Johnson, editor of Olive Garnett's diaries, could not have been more helpful; not only has he passed on valuable information, but he has also accompanied me on various trips to places associated with the Garnetts. His friendship and encouragement, along with that of the late Robert Gomme, have helped to make writing the book a real pleasure.

I would like to thank Sebastian Garrett for his interest in the book, for sharing his memories of his grandmother, Natalie Duddington and for permission to quote from her letters.

Thanks to Martin and Katharine Brunt for their hospitality and for giving me information about Louise Bréal and Nellie Heath's friends in France.

Many people have kindly answered my queries about specific authors; in particular I am grateful to Jeremy Wilson, who read and commented on extracts from the sections on T. E. Lawrence; it goes without saying that any mistakes that remain are entirely my own. I would also like to thank Victoria Wicks and Anne Williamson for all their help with H.E. Bates and Henry Williamson respectively. Thanks also to Sarah Baxter, Laurence Davies, Paul Eggert, Sue Fox, Andrew Harrison, Matthew Hollis, Wilhelm Meusburger, Jean Moorcroft Wilson, Robert Nantes, Victor Sage, Christopher Scoble and John Stape.

Sarah Knights, biographer of David Garnett, generously passed on valuable information throughout my research and accompanied me on a trip to The Cearne, for which many thanks. I would also like to thank Mr and Mrs Kirkwood for their kind hospitality when I visited The Cearne and for all the information they gave me about the house.

This book started life in a very different form as a PhD thesis supervised (until her death) by Lorna Sage; I will always be tremendously grateful for the support, encouragement and inspiration she gave me. I was fortunate that Richard Holmes agreed to become my supervisor after Lorna died and I would like to thank him for his stimulating conversations about Garnett in particular and writing in general. Max Saunders, my secondary supervisor, was extremely generous in sharing his wide knowledge of the period and especially his expertise about Ford Madox Ford and his circle.

I am most grateful to the Royal Society of Literature and the Jerwood Charitable Foundation for an RSL Jerwood Award for Non-Fiction in 2011. The proposal for the book was joint winner of the 2006 Biographers' Club Prize (now the Tony Lothian Prize) and this early support was much appreciated. I would also like to thank the London Library for granting me Carlyle Membership and the Arts and Humanities Research Council for a PhD scholarship.

My agent Caroline Dawnay has been extraordinarily patient and under-standing throughout the very long time it has taken me to write this book: I am extremely grateful to her for keeping the faith and for giving me such stalwart support.

I am so privileged to have had Dan Franklin as my editor at Jonathan Cape. I would also like to thank my wonderful desk editor, Ana Fletcher, who has been a pleasure to work with. Ian Pindar did a great job on the copy editing and thanks also to Douglas Matthews for the index. At Farrar, Straus & Giroux I would like to thank Jonathan Galassi for the confidence he has shown in the book, and my editor Ileene Smith and her editorial assistant Jackson Howard for all the help they have given me.

I am grateful to the following for granting permission to quote from published and unpublished work: Extracts from *Edward Garnett* by H.E. Bates and Extracts from unpublished letters from H.E. Bates to Edward Garnett at Harry Ransom Center, University of Texas at Austin reprinted by permission of Pollinger Limited (www.pollingerltd.com) on behalf of the Estate of H. E. Bates; Dr Quentin Bone (Gertrude Bone); Letter from Arthur Calder-Marshall to David Garnett © The Estate of Arthur Calder-Marshall. Reproduced with the kind permission of Johnson & Alcock Ltd.; The Trustees of the Joseph Conrad Estate; Letters from R. B. Cunninghame Graham © The Estate of R. B. Cunninghame Graham. Reproduced with the kind permission of Johnson & Alcock Ltd.; Extracts from the letters of C M Doughty by Permission of the Master and Fellows of Gonville and Caius College, Cambridge; Faber & Faber (T. S. Eliot); David Higham Associates on behalf of the Ford Madox Ford Estate; The Provost and Scholars of King's College, Cambridge and The Society of Authors as the E.M. Forster Estate; United Agents LLP on behalf of the Executor of the Estate of Constance Garnett; United Agents LLP on behalf of the Executor of the Estate of David Garnett; Sebastian Yorke (Henry Green); The Society of Authors as the Literary Representatives of the Estate of W. H. Hudson; Bay James, (Henry James); Extracts from the *Letters of D H Lawrence*, and the manuscripts of *The Trespasser* and *Sons and Lovers* by D. H. Lawrence reprinted by permission of Pollinger Limited (www .pollingerltd.com) on behalf of the Estate of Frieda Lawrence Ravagli; Letter by Frieda Lawrence in *The Letters of D H Lawrence* (Vol. 2) p. 151 reprinted by permission of Pollinger Limited (www.pollingerltd.com) on behalf of the Estate of Frieda Lawrence Ravagli; Extract from letter from Frieda Lawrence to Edward Garnett (not dated) thanking Garnett for his note of condolence after D H Lawrence's death quoted in *The Garnett Family* reprinted by permission of Pollinger Limited (www.pollinger.com) on behalf of the Estate of Frieda Lawrence Ravagli; Letters from T.E. Lawrence are quoted by permission of the Seven Pillars of Wisdom Trust; The Society of Authors as the Literary Representatives of H. A. Manhood; The Society of Authors as the Literary Representatives of John Middleton Murry; *The Bombshop* by Sean O'Faolain, published by Dial Magazine, 1927; *Midsummer Night Madness & Other Stories* by Sean O'Faolain, published by Cape, 1932; Unpublished Letters 1929–1933 by Sean O'Faolain; Dedication to *A Purse of Coppers* by Sean O'Faolain, published by Cape, 1937; *Vive Moi!* By Sean O'Faolain. Published by Sinclair-Stevenson, 1993 all Copyright © Sean O'Faolain. Reproduced by permission of the author's estate c/o Rogers, Coleridge & White Ltd., 20 Powis Mews, London W11 1JN; Letters to Edward Garnett from *The Letters of Liam O'Flaherty* by Liam O'Flaherty reprinted by permission of Peters Fraser & Dunlop (www.petersfraserdunlop.com) on behalf of the Estate of Liam O'Flaherty; Ezra Pound, from New Directions Pub. acting as agent, copyright © 2017 by Mary de Rachewiltz and the Estate of Omar S. Pound. Reprinted by permission of New Directions Publishing Corp.; The Marsh Agency Ltd., on behalf of the Estate of Dorothy Richardson; The Society of Authors, on behalf of the Bernard Shaw Estate; Extract from *Background with Chorus* by Frank Swinnerton reprinted by permission of Peters Fraser & Dunlop (www.petersfraserdunlop.com) on behalf of the Estate of Frank Swinnerton; Mrs Rosemary Vellender (Edward Thomas); United Agents LLP on behalf of the Literary Executors of the Estate of H G Wells; Extract from unpublished letters by Rebecca West to Edward Garnett reprinted by permission of Peters Fraser & Dunop (www.petersfraserdunlop.com) on behalf of the Estate of Rebecca West; Mrs Anne Williamson (Henry Williamson); United Agents LLP on behalf of Catriona Yeats, (W.B. Yeats).

Every effort has been made to identify and trace copyright holders. However if I have inadvertently omitted any please contact the publishers who will be pleased to rectify the omission in any future editions.

I have received great help from various libraries and archives. The bulk of the Garnett papers are in the Charles Deering McCormack Library of Special Collections, Northwestern University, the Harry Ransom Center, University of Texas at Austin and the Berg Collection, New York Public Library. The staff of these libraries have handled my numerous requests with great courtesy and efficiency and have given me tremendous assistance. I would like to thank Scott Kraft, Nick Munagian and especially Sigrid S Pohl Perry at Northwestern, Pat Fox at the Ransom Center and Isaac Gewirtz, Anne Garner and Anna Culbertson at the Berg Collection.

I would like to acknowledge my gratitude to the following institutions for granting me access to their collections and answering my queries: Beinecke Rare Book and Manuscript Library; The Bancroft Rare Book and Manuscript Library, University of California; The Bodleian Library, Oxford (Colin Harris); British Library Department of Manuscripts; Rare Book and Manuscript Library, Columbia University Libraries; Rauner Special Collections, Dartmouth College Library; Eton College Library; Heritage Collections, University of Exeter (Christine Faunch), Gloucestershire County Archives; The Hugh Walpole Collection, King's School, Canterbury; The Houghton Library; The Lilly Library, National Library of Scotland (Sheila Mackenzie); National Library of Wales (Martin Robson-Riley); Rare Book & Manuscript Library, University of Pennsylvania Libraries; The John Rylands University Library; Rosenbach Museum & Library.

It only remains for me to thank friends and colleagues who have supported me throughout, particularly Kathryn Hughes, who I have turned to innumerable times and who has always offered tremendous help, advice and encouragement. I would like to thank my colleagues at the University of East Anglia and all the students I have taught on the MA in Biography and Creative Non-Fiction for stimulating and thought-provoking discussions. To Rachel Baker, Susan Burton, Kate Drayton, Bernard Heine, Marjory Howie, Harriet Sharp and Ian Thomson thanks for your friendship, encouragement and support, which has kept me going through the trickiest patches of writing this book.

Finally, thanks to my husband James for his unfailing love and support which has sustained me in so many ways.

Picture credits

The majority of the photographs of Edward Garnett, his family and friends included in this book can be found in the archive at Northwestern University, and have been reproduced with the kind permission of Oliver Garnett. All other image credits are given below.

The Cearne © Gerald Duckworth & Co. Ltd

Ford Madox Ford © Getty: The LIFE Images Collection

Joseph Conrad © Getty: George C. Beresford / Stringer

W. H. Hudson © Chronicle / Alamy Stock Photo

Edward Thomas © Getty: Hulton Deutsch / Contributor

Stephen Reynolds, from the *Letters of Stephen Reynolds*, ed. Harold Wright (Hogarth, 1923)

T. E. Lawrence © Getty: Illustrated London News / Stringer

Liam O'Flaherty © Getty: The LIFE Images Collection

H. E. Bates © Yvonne Gregory / Performing Arts Images

Naomi Mitchison © Getty: Evening Standard / Stringer

Sean O'Faolain © National Portrait Gallery, London

Notes

List of abbreviations

Berg = The Berg Collection of English and American Literature, The New York Public Library, Astor, Lenox and Tilden Foundations.

BL = British Library.

Bodleian = Bodleian Library, Special Collections, University of Oxford.

Dartmouth =Rauner Special Collections Library, Dartmouth College, USA.

Eton = College Archives, Eton College.

Houghton = Houghton Library, Harvard University, USA.

HRC = Harry Ransom Center, The University of Texas at Austin, USA.

Lilly Library = The Lilly Library, Indiana University, Bloomington, Indiana, USA.

Northwestern = Garnett Family Papers, The Charles Deering McCormick Library of Special Collections, Northwestern University, Evanston, Illinois, USA.

Reading = Reading University, Special Collections, Archive of Jonathan Cape Limited.

Rylands = The John Rylands Library, University of Manchester.

A note on sources

For the convenience of the reader, where letters have appeared in published form the published – rather than the archival – source has been cited.

Olive Garnett's diary has been edited and published in two volumes by Barry C. Johnson. This is the source given for those extracts that appear in *Tea and Anarchy!* and *Olive & Stepniak*. For unpublished extracts the reader is referred to the archival source.

Chapter 1

1. Edward Garnett, draft Cearne time capsule (Northwestern).
2. Constance Garnett to Dr Richard Garnett, 1 September 1895 (Northwestern).
3. David Garnett, 'A Whole Hive of Genius', *Saturday Review of Literature*, 1 October 1932, p. 1.
4. Osbert Sitwell, *The Scarlet Tree* (London: Macmillan & Co. (1946), p. 223. Quoted in *Tea and Anarchy! The Bloomsbury Diary of Olive Garnett 1890–1893*, ed. Barry C. Johnson (London: Bartletts Press, 1989), p. 23.
5. Olive Garnett to David Garnett, 29 March 1951 (Northwestern).
6. Olive Garnett to David Garnett, 8 October 1937 (Northwestern).
7. Obituary, *Speaker*, 21 April 1906, p. 60, quoted in Carolyn G. Heilbrun, *The Garnett Family* (London: George Allen & Unwin, 1961), p. 45.
8. Obituary, *Bookman*, June 1906, p. 93, quoted in Heilbrun, *The Garnett Family*, p. 41.
9. Olive Garnett, 'Anecdotes of my father's childhood' (Northwestern), p. 7.
10. David Garnett, *The Golden Echo* (1953) (London: Chatto & Windus, 1970), p. 3.
11. Dr Richard Garnett to William John Garnett, 15 May 1862, quoted in Barbara McCrimmon, *Richard Garnett: The Scholar as Librarian* (Chicago: American Library Association, 1989), p. 44.
12. Olive Garnett, 'Anecdotes of my father's childhood' (Northwestern), p. 7.
13. Arundell Esdaile, *The British Museum Library: A Short History and Survey* (London: Allen & Unwin, 1946), p. 367, quoted in Johnson, *Tea and Anarchy!*, p. 5.
14. Anne Lee-Michell, 'A Bloomsbury Girlhood' (Caroline White), p. 6.
15. Edward Garnett to John Galsworthy, 'Thursday night' [speculatively dated 23 February 1907 in another hand] (Eton).
16. Edward Garnett to John Galsworthy, 28 February 1907 (Eton).
17. Edward Garnett to Nellie Heath, 'Sunday evening' (Northwestern).
18. Olive Garnett to David Garnett, 8 October 1937 (Northwestern).
19. 'The Gunpowder Explosion', *The Times*, 5 October 1874, p. 8.
20. 'The Cats' Newspaper' (Northwestern).

21. Ibid.

22. Ibid.

23. Thomas Hinde, *Carpenter's Children: The Story of the City of London School* (London: James & James, 1995), p. 55.

24. City of London School magazine, Vol. 8, No. 52, October 1884.

25. Constance Garnett, memoir (Northwestern).

26. David Garnett, *The Golden Echo*, pp. 35–6.

27. Olive Garnett to David Garnett, 8 October 1937 (Northwestern).

Chapter 2

1. If Constance is correct in stating that Edward was eighteen at the time, then this initial meeting must have taken place in 1886.

2. Constance Garnett, memoir (Northwestern).

3. Ibid.

4. Ibid.

5. Nellie Heath notes (Caroline White).

6. Ibid.

7. Constance Garnett, memoir (Northwestern).

8. Ibid.

9. Ibid.

10. Ibid.

11. Ibid.

12. Ibid.

13. Ibid.

14. Ibid.

15. Frank Swinnerton, *Background with Chorus: A Footnote to Changes in English Literary Fashion between 1901 and 1917* (London: Hutchinson, 1956), p. 110.

16. R. H. Horne, *Exposition of the False Medium and Barriers Excluding Men of Genius from the Public* (1833), quoted in Royal A. Gettmann, *A Victorian Publisher: A Study of the Bentley Papers* (Cambridge: Cambridge University Press, 1960), p. 263.

17. Ibid.

18. Marie Corelli, *The Sorrows of Satan* (1895), quoted in Philip Waller, *Writers, Readers and Reputations: Literary Life in Britain 1870–1918* (Oxford: Oxford University Press, 2006), p. 775, n.42.

19. Swinnerton, *Background with Chorus*, p. 115.

20. Philip Unwin, *The Publishing Unwins* (London: Heinemann, 1972), p. 38.

21. Ibid., p. 46.

22. Ibid. pp. 41, 47.

23. Stanley Unwin, *The Truth About a Publisher: An Autobiographical Record* (London: Allen & Unwin, 1960), p. 97.

24. David Garnett, *The Familiar Faces* (London: Chatto & Windus, 1962), p. 101.

25. Richard Garnett, *Constance Garnett: A Heroic Life* (London: Sinclair-Stevenson, 1991), p. 54.

26. Edward Garnett, *The Paradox Club* (London: T. F. Unwin, 1888), p. 47.

27. Ibid., p. 151.

28. W. Wallace, review of Edward Garnett, *The Paradox Club*, *Academy* XXXIV (1888), p. 132.

29. Edward Garnett, *The Paradox Club*, p. 207.

30. Constance Garnett, memoir (Northwestern).

31. Review of Edward Garnett, *Light and Shadow*, *Athenaeum*, No. 3243 (1889), pp. 851–2.

32. John Galsworthy to Edward Garnett, 25 February 1902, quoted in Edward Garnett (ed.), *Letters from John Galsworthy 1900–1932* (London: Jonathan Cape, 1934), pp. 33–4.

33. Edward Garnett to Dr Richard Garnett, 14 September 1889 (Northwestern).

34. Edward Garnett to Dr Richard Garnett, 12 July 1890 (Northwestern).

35. H. G. Wells to Edward Garnett, 19 November 1903, in *The Correspondence of H. G. Wells* (Vol. 1), ed. David C. Smith (London: Pickering & Chatto, 1998), p. 439.

36. Edward Garnett to Dr Richard Garnett, 14 September 1889 (Northwestern).

37. Constance Garnett to David Garnett (Eton). The letter is Constance's hand, but as if from Edward. Undated, but the reference to David's trip to Germany suggests it was written in 1910.

38. Richard Garnett, *Constance Garnett*, pp. 65–6.

39. Speedwell Massingham, memoir, 'Rosemary for Remembrance' (Northwestern).

40. Edward Garnett, reader's report, 14 March 1895 (Berg).

41. Ibid., 4 January 1898.

42. Ibid., 19 January 1899.

43. Ibid., 27 October 1898.

44. Ibid., undated.

45. Ibid., 5 June 1895.

46. Ibid., 16 June 1898.

47. Ibid.

48. T. Fisher Unwin, 'My first success', *Mainly About People* 24 (616), 2 April 1910, pp. 438–9, quoted in George Jefferson, 'The Pseudonym Library', *The Private Library* (4th Series), 1:1 (Spring 1988), pp. 13–26.
49. Edward Garnett, reader's report, 23 August 1897 (Berg).
50. Ford Madox Ford, *Return to Yesterday: Reminiscences 1894–1914* (1931), ed. Bill Hutchings (Manchester: Carcanet, 1999), p. 102.
51. Ibid.
52. Edward Garnett, reader's report, undated (Berg).
53. Edward Garnett to Dr Richard Garnett, 22 December 1890 (Northwestern).
54. Ibid.
55. Roy Foster, *W. B. Yeats: A Life*, I: *The Apprentice Mage 1865–1914* (Oxford: Oxford University Press, 1997), p. 107.
56. *In Excited Reverie: A Centenary Tribute to William Butler Yeats 1865–1939*, ed. A. Norman Jeffares (New York: St Martin's Press, 1965), p. 1.
57. See Victoria Glendinning, *Elizabeth Bowen: Portrait of a Writer* (London: Weidenfeld & Nicolson, 1977), p. 11.
58. Edward Garnett to David Garnett, 25 June 1925 (Northwestern).
59. Edward Garnett to Nellie Heath, 4 December 1898 (Northwestern).
60. W. B. Yeats to John O'Leary, 'after 17 February 1892', *The Collected Letters of W. B. Yeats*, Vol. 1: 1865–95, ed. John Kelly (Oxford: Clarendon Press, 1985), p. 285.
61. Roy Foster, *W. B. Yeats*, p. 118.
62. W. B. Yeats to Edward Garnett, *c.* 9 November 1892, *The Collected Letters of W.B. Yeats*, Vol. 1, pp. 329–30.
63. Edward Garnett to W. B. Yeats, 18 November 1892, *Letters to W. B. Yeats*, ed. Richard J. Finneran, George Mills Harper and William M. Murphy (London: Macmillan, 1977), pp. 6–8.
64. Edward Garnett to W. B. Yeats, quoted in J. Hone, *W. B. Yeats 1865–1939* (London: Macmillan & Co., 1942), p. 98.
65. Edward Garnett, reader's report, 6 December 1896 (Berg).
66. Edward Garnett, 'Books Too Little Known: The Cuchullin Saga', *Academy and Literature*, 14 February 1903, pp. 156–8.
67. Eleanor Hull to Edward Garnett, 4 February 1903 (Northwestern).
68. Edward Garnett, 'The Work of W. B. Yeats', *English Review*, Vol. 2, 1909, pp. 148–52.

Chapter 3

1. Olive Garnett, diary, 4 November 1891, Johnson, *Tea and Anarchy!*, p. 52.

2. Constance Garnett, memoir (Northwestern).

3. Ibid.

4. Edward Garnett to Dr Richard Garnett, 10 March 1891 (Northwestern).

5. Constance Garnett to Dr Richard Garnett, 10 March 1891 (Northwestern).

6. Constance Garnett to Dr Richard Garnett, 18 September 1891 (Northwestern).

7. Olive Garnett, diary, 12 November 1891, Johnson, *Tea and Anarchy!*, p. 53.

8. Olive Garnett to Dr Richard Garnett, 17 November 1891, ibid., p. 55.

9. Constance Garnett to Edward Garnett, 6 February 1892 (Northwestern).

10. Constance Garnett, memoir (Northwestern).

11. Ibid.

12. Constance Garnett to Edward Garnett, 'Thursday, 6 o'clock' [1892] (Northwestern).

13. Ibid.

14. Constance Garnett, memoir (Northwestern).

15. Constance Garnett to Edward Garnett, '11 o'clock, Thursday' [1892] (Northwestern).

16. Constance Garnett, memoir (Northwestern).

17. Yvonne Kapp, *Eleanor Marx* (London: Lawrence & Wishart, 1972), Vol. 1, Appendix 5.

18. George Bernard Shaw, 'A Word About Stepniak', *To-Morrow* 1 (January-June 1896), pp. 99–107.

19. Olive Garnett, diary, 16 December 1893 (Caroline White).

20. Constance Garnett, 'Tribute to Stepniak', unpublished (Northwestern).

21. Constance Garnett, memoir (Northwestern).

22. E. F. S. Pigott, Examiner of Plays for the Lord Chamberlain, testimony to the Select Committee on Theatres 1892, quoted by Samuel Hynes, *The Edwardian Turn of Mind* (1968) (London: Pimlico, 1991), p. 308.

23. Matthew Arnold, 'Count Leo Tolstoi', *Fortnightly Review*, December 1887, reprinted in Arnold, *Essays in Criticism*, 2nd Series (London: Macmillan, 1888), p. 254.

24. [Edward Garnett], 'The Russian Novel', review of Charles Edward Turner, *The Modern Novelists of Russia*, *Speaker*, 1 March 1890, p. 241. The article is unsigned, but can be attributed to Garnett from notes in Constance Garnett's notebook. See Richard Garnett, *Constance Garnett*, p. 373, n.51.

25. Edward Garnett, Preface to Ivan Turgenev, *The Jew and Other Stories*, trans. Constance Garnett (London: Heinemann, 1900), p. ix.

26. Edward Garnett to R. B. Cunninghame Graham, 15 August 1913 (National Library of Scotland).

27. John Garrard (ed.), *The Russian Novel from Pushkin to Pasternak* (New Haven: Yale University Press, 1983), pp. 15–16.

28. Olive Garnett, diary, 28 December 1892, quoted in Johnson, *Tea and Anarchy!*, p. 140.

29. David Garnett, 'Burst Balloons', unpublished TS (Northwestern).

30. David Garnett, 'Brief Memoir of Constance Garnett', quoted in Richard Garnett, *Constance Garnett*, p. 87.

31. David Garnett, *The Golden Echo*, p. 48.

32. Margaret Pease, *Richard Heath: 1831–1912*, privately printed booklet (Letchworth: Garden City Press, 1922), pp. 27, 25.

33. Rayne Nickalls, 'The Time is Past and Gone', unpublished memoir, p. 202 (Caroline White).

34. David Garnett, *The Golden Echo*, p. 50.

35. Nellie Heath, notes (Caroline White).

36. Ibid.

37. The letter refers to Stephen Crane's short story 'Pace of Youth', which appeared in various American newspapers in 1895 and was included in *The Open Boat and Other Stories*, published in Britain by Heinemann in 1898. Edward wrote an appreciation of Crane's work for the *Academy* in December 1898 and these facts strongly suggest that the letter to Nellie was written around that time.

38. Edward Garnett to Nellie Heath, 'Sunday' [1898?] (Northwestern).

39. Ibid.

40. Edward Garnett to Dr Richard Garnett, 19 January 1893 (Northwestern).

41. *Brighton Examiner*, 24 January 1893, quoted in Richard Garnett, *Constance Garnett*, p. 94.

42. Edward Garnett to Dr Richard Garnett, 20 January 1893 (Northwestern).

43. Edward Garnett, Introduction to *Letters from Joseph Conrad 1895–1924*, ed. Edward Garnett (London: Nonesuch Press, 1928), p. xix.

44. Ibid.

45. Edward Garnett to Dr Richard Garnett, 20 January 1893 [misdated 1892 by Edward] (Northwestern).

46. David Garnett, *The Golden Echo*, p. 14.

47. Olive Garnett, diary, 16 May 1893.

48. Ibid.
49. Constance Garnett to Edward Garnett, 6 July [1893] (Northwestern).
50. Olive Garnett, diary, 29 July 1893, Johnson, *Tea and Anarchy!*, p. 220.
51. Ibid.
52. Olive Garnett, diary, 1 August 1893.
53. Ibid.
54. Edward Garnett to Dr Richard Garnett, March 8, 1891 (Northwestern).
55. Ibid.
56. Rayne Nickalls, memoir (Caroline White), pp. 3–4.
57. Olive Garnett, diary, 1 August 1893.
58. Constance Garnett to Fanny Stepniak [1893] (Central State Archive of Literature and Art, Moscow), quoted in Richard Garnett, *Constance Garnett*, p. 109.
59. Olive Garnett, diary, 7 December 1893.
60. David Garnett, *The Golden Echo*, p. 11.
61. 'Ivanoff' (P. I. Rachkovsky), 'Anarchists: Their Methods and Organisation', *New Review*, No. 56 (January 1894), pp. 1–16, quoted in *Olive & Stepniak: The Bloomsbury Diary of Olive Garnett 1893–1895*, ed. Barry C. Johnson (Birmingham: Bartletts, 1993), pp. 1–2.
62. 'Z', 'Anarchists II', quoted in Johnson, *Olive & Stepniak*, p. 4.
63. Olive Garnett, diary, 24 February 1893.
64. Ibid., 30 December 1893.
65. Ibid., 31 December 1893.
66. Ibid.

Chapter 4
1. Constance Garnett to Edward Garnett, 5 January 1894 (Northwestern).
2. Ibid.
3. Constance Garnett to Edward Garnett, 7 January 1894 (Northwestern).
4. Ibid.
5. Constance Garnett to Edward Garnett, 'Sunday evening' [11 February 1894] (Northwestern).
6. Constance Garnett, memoir (Northwestern).
7. Dr Richard Garnett to William Michael Rossetti, 5 March 1894 (University of British Colombia Library), quoted in McCrimmon, *Richard Garnett*, p. 126.
8. Olive Garnett, diary, 25 February 1894.
9. Ibid., 24 March 1894.
10. Ibid., 2 March 1894.
11. Advertising leaflet (Northwestern).

12. Olive Garnett, diary, 28 February 1894.

13. Ibid., 14 March 1894.

14. Ibid.

15. Ibid., 20 March 1894.

16. Edward Garnett to Nellie Heath, undated other than 'Sunday evening' (Northwestern).

17. Ibid. The Whitman quote is from the poem 'From Pent-up Aching Rivers' (1860) in *Leaves of Grass* (1855–91).

18. Edward Garnett to Nellie Heath, incomplete and undated letter (Northwestern).

19. Olive Garnett, diary, 'Tuesday 9th' [actually Tuesday, 10 April] 1894.

20. Ibid., 'Saturday, Sunday, Monday', 31 March and 1 and 2 April 1894.

21. Ibid., 'Thursday, Friday, Saturday', 19, 20 and 21 April 1894.

22. Ibid., 23 April 1894.

23. Ibid., 14 July 1894.

24. Swinnerton, *Background with Chorus*, p. 32.

25. Ford Madox Ford, quoted in Max Saunders, *Ford Madox Ford: A Dual Life*, Vol. 1: *The World before the War* (Oxford: Oxford University Press, 1996), p. 118.

26. Edward Garnett to Dr Richard Garnett, 11 January 1891 (Northwestern).

27. Ernest Rhys, review of Edward Garnett, *An Imaged World*, *Academy*, 27 October 1894, p. 325.

28. Ibid.

29. Edward Garnett, *An Imaged World* (London: Dent, 1894), pp. 54–5.

30. [W. B. Yeats], review of Edward Garnett, *An Imaged World*, *Speaker*, 8 September 1894, pp. 273–4.

31. Henry Norman (?), review of Edward Garnett, *An Imaged World*, *Daily Chronicle*, 13 July 1894, p. 8.

32. Review of Edward Garnett, *An Imaged World*, *New York Critic*, 8 December 1894.

33. Review of Edward Garnett, *An Imaged World*, *Boston Literary World*, 29 December 1894.

34. Constance Garnett to Dr Richard Garnett, 18 June 1894 (Northwestern).

35. Olive Garnett, diary, 10 November 1894.

36. Constance Garnett to Edward Garnett, 12 August 1894 (Northwestern).

37. See Richard Garnett, *Constance Garnett*, p. 143.

38. Edward Garnett, *Turgenev: A Study*, Foreword by Joseph Conrad (London: W. Collins, Sons & Co., 1917), p. 136.

39. Garnett, Preface to Ivan Turgenev, *The Jew and Other Stories*, p. xiv.

40. Arnold Bennett to Edward Garnett, 14 February 1897 (HRC).
41. Arnold Bennett, 'Some Adventures Among Russian Fiction', *The Soul of Russia*, ed. Winifred Stephens (London: Macmillan, 1916), pp. 84–8, p. 86.
42. Edward Garnett to Dr Richard Garnett, 19 July 1890 (Northwestern).
43. Constance Garnett to Dr Richard Garnett, 15 January 1890 (Northwestern).
44. Olive Garnett, diary, 14 November 1894.
45. Ibid.
46. Ibid., 20 November 1894 [misdated 19 November by the diarist].
47. Ford Madox Ford to Edward Garnett, 'Blomfield, Bonnington, Hythe, Kent', undated (HRC).
48. Olive Garnett, diary, 28 September 1895.
49. Ibid., 17 November 1894.
50. Ford Madox Ford to Edward Garnett, undated (HRC).
51. W. H. Chesson, 'The Discovery of Joseph Conrad', *To-day*, Vol. 5 (June 1919), p. 152, reprinted in Martin Ray (ed.), *Joseph Conrad: Interviews and Recollections* (Basingstoke: Macmillan, 1990), p. 83.
52. Edward Garnett, Introduction to *Letters from Joseph Conrad*, p. vi.
53. Ibid., p. vii.
54. Ibid., p. xi.
55. Ibid., p. vii.
56. Ibid.
57. Ibid, pp. vii–viii.
58. Ibid. p. viii.
59. Ibid.
60. Gertrude Bone account enclosed in undated letter to Edward Garnett (HRC).
61. Edward Garnett, Introduction to *Letters from Joseph Conrad*, p. ix.
62. Ibid., pp. xi–xii.
63. Ibid., p. xiii.
64. Richard Garnett, *Constance Garnett*, p. 50.
65. Edward Garnett, Introduction to *Letters from Joseph Conrad*, p. xiv.

Chapter 5

1. David Garnett, *The Golden Echo*, p. 51.
2. Ibid., pp. 17–18.
3. Olive Garnett, diary, 28 January 1895.
4. Ibid.
5. Ibid., 20 May 1895.

6. Ibid., 15 March 1895.
7. Joseph Conrad to Edward Garnett, 12 May 1895, *The Collected Letters of Joseph Conrad*, Vol. 1, ed. Frederick R. Karl and Laurence Davies (Cambridge: Cambridge University Press, 1983), p. 216. All letters from Conrad will be taken from the Cambridge volumes and hereafter will be cited *CLJC* with the volume number.
8. Edward Garnett, reader's report, undated (Berg).
9. Joseph Conrad to Edward Garnett, 8 March 1895, *CLJC* (Vol.1), p. 203.
10. Edward Garnett, Introduction to *Letters from Joseph Conrad*, p. xiii.
11. Ibid., p. xii.
12. Joseph Conrad to Edward Garnett, 24 September 1895, *CLJC* (Vol. 1), p. 246.
13. Ibid.
14. Ibid.
15. Edward Garnett, Introduction to *Letters from Joseph Conrad*, p. xxv.
16. Nellie Heath to Edward Garnett, 'Saturday night' (Northwestern).
17. George Bernard Shaw to Ellen Terry, 15 October 1896, quoted in *Ellen Terry and Bernard Shaw: A Correspondence*, ed. Christopher St John (London: Constable & Co., 1931), p. 103.
18. Matthew Sturgis, *Walter Sickert: A Life* (London: Harper Perennial, 2005), p. 242.
19. Olive Garnett, diary, 18 November 1895.
20. Ibid.
21. Quoted in Johnson, *Olive & Stepniak*, p. 235. The account of the inquest was compiled from the *Acton and Chiswick Gazette* (28 December 1895) and the *Chiswick Times* (3 January 1896).
22. Olive Garnett, diary, 1 November, 1892.
23. Johnson, *Olive & Stepniak*, p. 236.
24. Olive Garnett, diary, 23 May 1895.
25. Johnson, *Olive & Stepniak*, p. 237.
26. Ibid., p. 238.
27. David Garnett, *The Golden Echo*, p. 20.
28. Anne Lee-Michell, 'A Bloomsbury Girlhood' (HRC), quoted in Johnson, *Olive & Stepniak*, p. 242.
29. Richard Garnett, *Constance Garnett*, p. 155.
30. Ibid.
31. Speedwell Massingham, unpublished memoir, 'Rosemary for Remembrance' (Northwestern).
32. Jessie Conrad, *Joseph Conrad and His Circle* (London: Jarrolds, 1935), p. 15.

33. Edward Garnett, Introduction to *Letters from Joseph Conrad*, p. xxii.

34. Joseph Conrad to Edward Garnett, 23/24 March 1896, *CLJC* (Vol. 1), p. 267.

35. Ford Madox Ford, Introduction to Joseph Conrad, *The Sisters*, ed. Urgo Mursia (Milan: Urgo Mursia & Co., 1968), p. 25. The original manuscript has been lost.

36. Joseph Conrad, *The Sisters*, reprinted in Samuel Hynes (ed.), *Joseph Conrad: The Informer and Other Stories*, Vol. 2 (London: William Pickering, 1992), p. 286.

37. Joseph Conrad to Edward Garnett, 23/24 March 1896, *CLJC* (Vol. 1), p. 268.

38. Ibid.

39. Ford, Introduction to *The Sisters*, p. 12.

40. Joseph Conrad to Edward Garnett, 23/24 March 1896, *CLJC* (Vol. 1), p. 268.

41. Joseph Conrad to Edward Garnett, 13 April 1896, *CLJC* (Vol. 1), p. 273.

42. Constance Garnett to Narney Garnett, 8 April 1896 (Northwestern).

43. Constance Garnett to Dr Richard Garnett, 'Saturday morning' [postmarked 4 April 1896] (Northwestern).

44. Constance Garnett to Narney Garnett, 10 April 1896 (Northwestern).

45. Constance Garnett to Dr Richard Garnett, 27 April 1896 (Northwestern).

46. Olive Garnett to Dr Richard Garnett, 5 May 1896 (Northwestern).

47. Edward Garnett to Narney Garnett, 'Tuesday' [2 or 9 June] 1896 (Northwestern).

48. Constance Garnett to Dr Richard Garnett, 27 April 1896 (Northwestern).

49. Edward Garnett to Joseph Conrad, 26 May 1896, quoted in *A Portrait in Letters: Correspondence to and about Conrad, Conradian,* Vol. 19, Nos. 1 and 2, 1995, p. 22.

50. Joseph Conrad, 'The Rescuer', British Library, Ashley MSS, 4787, 1. Conrad completely altered the opening of the novel when he revised it in 1916.

51. Joseph Conrad to Edward Garnett, 2 June 1896, *CLJC* (Vol. 1), p. 284.

52. Conrad, 'The Rescuer' MSS, p. 17.

53. Edward Garnett, 'Tolstoy and Turgenieff', *Anglo-Saxon Review* 6, September 1900, pp. 150–165, p. 159.

54. Olive Garnett, diary, 4 November 1894.

55. Conrad, 'The Rescuer' MSS, p. 15.

56. Edward Garnett to Joseph Conrad, 26 May 1896, quoted in *A Portrait in Letters*, p. 22.

57. Joseph Conrad to Edward Garnett, 2 June 1896, *CLJC* (Vol. 1), p. 284.

58. Joseph Conrad to Edward Garnett, 10 June 1896, ibid., p. 287.

59. Edward Garnett to Joseph Conrad, 17 June 1896, quoted in *A Portrait in Letters*, pp. 25–6.

60. Joseph Conrad to Edward Garnett, 10 June 1896, *CLJC* (Vol. 1), p. 287.

61. Joseph Conrad to Edward Garnett, 19 June 1896, ibid., p. 288.

62. Letter from Edward Garnett, quoted by Joseph Conrad, Joseph Conrad to Edward Garnett, 22 July 1896, *CLJC* (Vol. 1), p. 291.

63. Joseph Conrad to Edward Garnett, 14 August 1896, *CLJC* (Vol. 1), p. 300.

64. Joseph Conrad to Edward Garnett, 5 August 1896, ibid., pp. 295–7.

65. Edward Garnett, Introduction to *Letters from Joseph Conrad*, p. xxiii.

66. Joseph Conrad to Edward Garnett, end of September 1896, *CLJC* (Vol. 1), p. 305.

67. Nellie Heath, notebook (Caroline White).

68. Nellie Heath to Edward Garnett, 9 August 1896 (Northwestern).

69. Nellie Heath to Edward Garnett, 8 June 1896 (Northwestern).

70. Nellie Heath to Edward Garnett, 26 September 1896 (Northwestern).

71. Joseph Conrad to Edward Garnett, 16 October 1896, *CLJC* (Vol. 1), p. 307.

Chapter 6

1. David Garnett, *The Golden Echo*, p. 22.

2. Joseph Conrad to Edward Garnett, 16 October 1896, *CLJC* (Vol. 1), p. 306.

3. Joseph Conrad to Edward Garnett, 6 November 1896, ibid., p. 313. Edward advised Conrad to reject Smith Elder's eventual proposal.

4. Joseph Conrad to John Quinn, 8 December 1912, *CLJC* (Vol. 5), p. 145.

5. Joseph Conrad to Edward Garnett, 25 October 1896, *CLJC* (Vol. 1), p. 310. Conrad insists that he 'must enshrine my old chums in a decent edifice'.

6. Edward Garnett, Introduction to *Letters from Joseph Conrad*, p. xxvii.

7. Joseph Conrad to Edward Garnett, 19 December 1896, *CLJC* (Vol. 1), p. 323.

8. Joseph Conrad, *The Nigger of the 'Narcissus'* MS (Rosenbach Museum & Library), p. 57.

9. Edward Garnett, *Turgenev*, p. 64.

10. Joseph Conrad, *The Nigger of the 'Narcissus'* MS, p. 176.

11. Joseph Conrad to Narney Garnett, 4 November 1897, inscribed copyright copy of *The Nigger of the 'Narcissus'*, held at Colgate University Library. Inscription reproduced in *CLJC* (Vol. 1), p. 403.

12. See, for example, Peter D. McDonald, *British Literary Culture and Publishing Practice 1880–1914* (Cambridge: Cambridge University Press, 1997) and Todd G. Willey, 'The Conquest of the Commodore: Conrad's Rigging of "The Nigger" for the Henley Regatta', *Conradiana* 17:3, 1985, pp. 163–82.

13. Edward Garnett, 'Conrad's Place in English Literature', *Conrad's Prefaces to His Works*, with a biographical note on his father by David Garnett (London: Dent, 1937; reprinted New York: Haskell House, 1971), p. 10.

14. Quoted by Joseph Conrad in his Note to the Collected Edition of *The Nigger of the 'Narcissus'*. Also quoted in *CLJC* (Vol. 1), p. 320, n.3.

15. Joseph Conrad to Edward Garnett, 25 November 1896, *CLJC* (Vol. 1), p. 320.

16. Joseph Conrad to Edward Garnett, 24 August 1897, ibid., p. 375.

17. David Garnett, *The Flowers of the Forest* (London: Chatto & Windus, 1955), p. 155.

18. Joseph Conrad, Preface to *The Nigger of the 'Narcissus'* (1897) (London: Penguin, 1988), p. xlviii.

19. Joseph Conrad to Edward Garnett, 27 September 1897, *CLJC* (Vol. 1), p. 385.

20. Edward Garnett, reader's report, 27 February 1897 (Berg).

21. Edward Garnett, reader's report, 8 January 1898 (Berg).

22. Edward Garnett, reader's report, 25 January 1897 (Berg).

23. Edward Garnett, reader's report, 20 July 1896 (Berg).

24. Somerset Maugham, *The Partial View* (London: Heinemann, 1954), p. 95.

25. Edward Garnett, reader's report, 13 January 1898 (Berg).

26. Edward Garnett, reader's report, 18 January 1899 (Berg).

27. Edward Garnett, reader's report, 5 March 1902, Duckworth, Box 1, Vol. 1 (Berg).

28. Joseph Conrad to Edward Garnett, 11 October 1897, *CLJC* (Vol. 1), p. 395.

29. Margaret Hartley married Charles Burton eight months after Eustace's death. In Edward's notes on Hartley there is a reference to 'Burton. Scene with his [i.e. Hartley's] enemy'. Edward Garnett notes on Eustace Hartley (Northwestern).

30. Narney Garnett to Olive Garnett, Good Friday, 16 April 1897 (Northwestern).

31. Edward Garnett, notes on Eustace Hartley (Northwestern).

32. Constance Garnett to Dr Richard Garnett, 28 June 1897 (Northwestern).

33. David Garnett, *The Golden Echo*, p. 32.

34. Ibid.

35. Fanny Stepniak to Olive Garnett, 15 November 1897 (Northwestern). Crane had indeed brought twin brothers out of Greece with him. However, only one, Adoni Ptolemy – described by one of Crane's biographers as a 'butler in shirtsleeves' – was employed at Ravensbrook. The other brother had been left in Paris, because Crane had insufficient funds to bring both Ptolemys to England. R. W. Stallman, *Stephen Crane* (New York: G. Brazillier, 1968).

36. [Edward Garnett], 'Stephen Crane', *Academy*, 9 June 1900, p. 491.

37. Ford Madox Ford, *Thus to Revisit: Some Reminiscences* (1921) (Manchester: Carcanet Press, 1999), p. 47.

38. 'Stephen Crane' in Edward Garnett, *Friday Nights: Literary Criticism and Appreciations* (London: Cape, 1922), p. 203.

39. Crane to James Gibbons Huneker, Dec [?] 1897, *Stephen Crane Letters*, ed. R. W. Stallman and Lillian Gilkes (London: Peter Owen, 1960), p. 160.

40. 'Stephen Crane' in Edward Garnett, *Friday Nights*, p. 203.

41. Joseph Conrad to Stephen Crane, 1 December 1897, *CLJC* (Vol. 1), p. 415.

42. Joseph Conrad to Edward Garnett, 5 December 1897, *CLJC* (Vol. 1), p. 416.

43. 'Stephen Crane' in Edward Garnett, *Friday Nights*, p. 202.

44. Ibid.

45. Quoted in Lillian Gilkes, *Cora Crane: A Biography of Mrs Stephen Crane* (London: Neville Spearman, 1962), p. 129.

46. Edward Garnett to Cora Crane, 13 March 1898 (Columbia University Rare Book and Manuscript Library).

47. Joseph Conrad, Introduction to Thomas Beer, *Stephen Crane* (London: William Heinemann, 1924), p. 25.

48. Stallman, *Stephen Crane*, p. 443.

49. Edward Garnett, 'Stephen Crane: An Appreciation', *Academy*, 17 December 1898, pp. 483–4.

50. Ibid., p. 484.

51. Edward Garnett to Nellie Heath, '7 o'clock', January [?] 1899 (Northwestern).

52. Cora Crane to Edward Garnett, [first week of January, 1899], *Stephen Crane Letters*, p. 203.

53. Cora Crane to Edward Garnett, first week of January 1899, ibid., p. 202.

54. Cora Crane to Edward Garnett, 19 January 1899, ibid., p. 206.

55. Stephen Crane to Sanford Bennett, 14 May 1900, ibid., p. 284.

56. 'Stephen Crane' in Edward Garnett, *Friday Nights*, p. 202.

57. [Edward Garnett], 'Stephen Crane, *Academy*, 9 June 1900, p. 491.

58. Ibid.

59. Edward Garnett to H. E. Bates, 2 February 1927 (HRC).

60. 'Some Remarks on English and American Fiction' in Edward Garnett, *Friday Nights*, pp. 248–9.

61. Constance Garnett to Dr Richard Garnett, 4 March 1898 (Northwestern).

62. Fanny Stepniak to Olive Garnett, 3 March 1898 (Northwestern).

63. Edward Garnett, Foreword to *Thirty Paintings by E. M. Heath* (London: Cape, 1935).

64. Edward Garnett, Introduction to *Letters from Joseph Conrad*, p. xvii.

65. David Garnett, *The Golden Echo*, p. 45.

66. Constance Garnett to Olive Garnett, 7 September 1898 (Caroline White).

67. Joseph Conrad to Edward Garnett, [7 June 1898], *CLJC* (Vol. 2), p. 66. The novel was eventually serialised more than twenty years later in 1919 and appeared in book form in 1920.

68. Edward Garnett, Introduction to *Letters from Joseph Conrad*, p. xxv.

69. Ibid., xii.

70. Edward Garnett to Nellie Heath, 'Friday' (Northwestern). In a letter to R. B. Cunninghame Graham of 22 May 1898 Edward mentions 'a very good analysis of the Polish spirit in Lister's *Life of Chopin*' which 'hits off all Conrad's characteristics in a remarkable degree' (National Library of Scotland). It is highly likely that the letters are very close in date.

Chapter 7

1. Nellie Heath to Edward Garnett, undated other than 'Sunday' (Northwestern).

2. Edward Garnett to Nellie Heath, 'Genoa, seven o'clock, Saturday' [April/May 1898] (Northwestern).

3. Edward Garnett to Nellie Heath, 'Friday night' [1899?] (Northwestern).

4. Edward Garnett to Nellie Heath, 'The Cearne, Sunday night' (Northwestern).

5. Edward Garnett to Nellie Heath, undated and incomplete letter (Northwestern).

6. Edward Garnett to Nellie Heath, 'Monday' (Northwestern).

7. Edward Garnett to Nellie Heath, 'Monday' (Northwestern).

8. Edward Garnett to Nellie Heath, 'The Cearne, Monday' (Northwestern).

9. Edward Garnett to Nellie Heath, 'Wednesday' [April 1898] (Northwestern).

10. Edward Garnett to Dr Richard Garnett, 12 April 1898 (HRC).

11. Edward Garnett to Nellie Heath, 'Tuesday evening, 9 o'clock' (Northwestern).

12. Edward Garnett, prospectus for The Overseas Library, reprinted in Vol. 8 of the Library, John Gaggin, *Among the Man–Eaters* (London: Unwin, 1900).

13. Edward Garnett to R. B. Cunninghame Graham, 16 May 1898 (HRC).

14. Joseph Conrad to R. B. Cunninghame Graham, 17 May 1898, *CLJC* (Vol. 2), p. 61.

15. Ford Madox Ford, *Thus to Revisit: Some Reminiscences*, p. 35.

16. Anne Taylor, *The People's Laird: A Life of Robert Bontine Cunninghame Graham* (Easingwold: The Tobias Press, 2005), p. 92.

17. Quoted in Cedric Watts and Laurence Davies, *Cunninghame Graham: A Critical Biography* (Cambridge: Cambridge University Press, 1979), p. 86.

18. Ibid., p. 30.

19. Ibid., p. 35.

20. Edward Garnett, Introduction to *Thirty Tales & Sketches* by R. B. Cunninghame Graham (London: Duckworth, 1929), p. ix.

21. Edward Garnett to R. B. Cunninghame Graham, 27 January 1905 (National Library of Scotland).

22. R. B. Cunninghame Graham to Edward Garnett, 13 December 1902 (HRC).

23. Edward Garnett to R. B. Cunninghame Graham, 26 January 1899 (National Library of Scotland).

24. Edward Garnett to R. B. Cunninghame Graham, 22 May 1898 (National Library of Scotland).

25. R. B. Cunninghame Graham to Edward Garnett, 18 May 1898 (HRC).

26. Edward Garnett, Introduction to R. B. Cunninghame Graham, *Mogreb-el-Acksa* (Evanston: Northwestern University Press, 1997), p. xii. The Introduction was originally printed in the American edition of 1930.

27. Ibid., p. xi.

28. Edward Garnett to R. B. Cunninghame Graham, 23 June 1898 (National Library of Scotland).

29. David Garnett, *The Golden Echo*, p. 69.

30. Edward Garnett to R. B. Cunninghame Graham, 16 May 1898 (HRC).

31. Edward Garnett to R. B. Cunninghame Graham, 30 June 1898 (National Library of Scotland).

32. R. B. Cunninghame Graham to Edward Garnett, 6 August 1898 (HRC).

33. Edward Garnett to R. B. Cunninghame Graham, 31 July 1898 (National Library of Scotland).

34. R. B. Cunninghame Graham to Edward Garnett, 7 July 1898 (HRC).

35. Edward Garnett to R. B. Cunninghame Graham, 31 July 1898 (National Library of Scotland).

36. Edward Garnett to R. B. Cunninghame Graham, 23 June 1898 (National Library of Scotland).

37. Edward Garnett to R. B. Cunninghame Graham, 4 October 1900 (HRC).

38. R. B. Cunninghame Graham to Edward Garnett, 6 October 1900 (HRC).

39. Ibid.

40. R. B. Cunninghame Graham to Edward Garnett, 26 December 1905 (HRC).

41. Edward Garnett to R. B. Cunninghame Graham, 28 December 1905 (National Library of Scotland).

42. R. B. Cunninghame Graham to Edward Garnett, 9 January 1906 (HRC).

43. R. B. Cunninghame Graham to Edward Garnett, 20 September 1931 (HRC).

44. Edward Garnett to R. B. Cunninghame Graham, 4 July 1898 (National Library of Scotland).

45. Ibid.

46. Edward Garnett to R. B. Cunninghame Graham, 11 July 1898 (National Library of Scotland).

47. Ibid.

48. Edward Garnett to R. B. Cunninghame Graham, 4 July 1898 (National Library of Scotland).

49. Joseph Conrad to Edward Garnett, 13 January 1899, *CLJC* (Vol. 2), p. 152.

50. Edward Garnett, 'Mr Joseph Conrad', *Academy*, 15 October 1898, pp. 82–3. The article is unsigned.

51. Joseph Conrad, Preface to *The Nigger of the 'Narcissus'*, p. lxix.

52. Quoted in Frederick R. Karl, *Joseph Conrad: The Three Lives* (London: Faber, 1979), p. 22.

53. Joseph Conrad to Edward Garnett, 12 October 1898, *CLJC* (Vol. 2), pp. 102–3.

54. Peter Clayton, account of Grace's Cottage, in the possession of Chris Varcoe.

55. Edward Garnett, 'A New Study of Conrad', review of Edward Crankshaw, *Joseph Conrad: Some Aspects of the Art of the Novel*, London *Mercury*, Vol. XXXIV (1936), pp. 67–9.

56. Joseph Conrad to Edward Garnett, 7 November 1898, *CLJC* (Vol. 2), p. 115.

57. Edward Garnett, 'A New Study of Conrad'.

Chapter 8

1. Rayne Nickalls, 'The Time is Past and Gone', unpublished autobiography (Caroline White), p. 2.

2. Olive Garnett, diary, 'Monday 27th' [March], 1899.

3. Edward Garnett to Nellie Heath, 22 March 1899 (Northwestern).

4. Edward Garnett to Nellie Heath, undated, incomplete letter (Northwestern).

5. David Garnett, *The Golden Echo*, p. 55.

6. Ibid., p. 61.

7. Edward Garnett to Nellie Heath, 'Friday' (Northwestern).

8. Edward Garnett to John Galsworthy, 21 September 1910, in H. V. Marrot, *The Life and Letters of John Galsworthy* (London: Heinemann, 1935), p. 298.

9. Edward Garnett, *Letters from Joseph Conrad*, p. 155, footnote 2.

10. Constance Garnett to Dr Richard Garnett, 26 December 1899 (Northwestern).

11. 'Ibsen and the English' (1899) reprinted in Edward Garnett, *Friday Nights* (London: Cape, 1922), p. 79.

12. Ibid., pp. 77–8.

13. Edward Garnett to Nellie Heath, 'Sunday night' [1899] (Northwestern).
14. Edward Garnett to Nellie Heath, '4 o'clock, Wednesday' [1902?] (Northwestern).
15. Olive Garnett to David Garnett, 8 October 1937 (Northwestern).
16. David Garnett, *The Golden Echo*, p. 66.
17. Constance Garnett to Dr Richard Garnett, 5 July 1900 (Northwestern).
18. David Garnett, *The Golden Echo*, p. 68.
19. Ibid., p. 71.
20. Edward Garnett, Introduction to *Letters from John Galsworthy*, p. 5.
21. Quoted in Marrot, *The Life and Letters of John Galsworthy*, p. 88.
22. Edward Garnett, Introduction to *Letters from John Galsworthy*, p. 5
23. Arthur Waugh, 'John Galsworthy as Novelist', *Bookman*, March 1933, p. 485, quoted in James Gindin, *John Galsworthy's Life and Art: An Alien's Fortress* (Basingstoke: Macmillan, 1987), p. 45.
24. Edward Garnett to Nellie Heath, 'Monday' [24 September 1900] (Northwestern).
25. Edward Garnett to Nellie Heath, 'Saturday' [29? September 1900] (Northwestern).
26. Edward Garnett to John Galsworthy, 25 September 1900, *Letters from John Galsworthy*, p. 19.
27. Edward Garnett to John Galsworthy, 19 October 1900, ibid., p. 21.
28. Edward Garnett to John Galsworthy, 3 April 1901, ibid., p. 27.
29. Edward Garnett to John Galsworthy, 21 April 1901, ibid., p. 28.
30. Edward Garnett to R. B. Cunninghame Graham, 9 February 1901 (National Library of Scotland).
31. David Garnett, *The Golden Echo*, p. 73.
32. Ibid.
33. Edward Garnett to Dr Richard Garnett, 3 February 1901 (Northwestern).
34. H. N. Cappe to Edward Garnett, 21 April 1901 (Northwestern).
35. William Hedgecock to Edward Garnett, 10 July 1901 (Northwestern).
36. William Hedgecock to Edward Garnett, 12 February 1904 (Northwestern).
37. Edward Garnett to Dr Richard Garnett, 5 July 1901 (Northewestern).
38. William Heinemann to Edward Garnett, 2 July 1901 (Northwestern).
39. Edward Garnett to Dr Richard Garnett, 5 July 1901 (Northwestern).
40. Ibid.
41. Ibid.
42. Ibid.
43. William Heinemann to Edward Garnett, 2 July 1901 (Northwestern).

Chapter 9

1. Edward Garnett, Introduction to *Letters from W. H. Hudson 1901–1922* (New York: E. P. Dutton & Company, 1923), p. 3.

2. Ibid.

3. Edward Garnett to R. B. Cunninghame Graham, 28 August 1928 (National Library of Scotland).

4. W. H. Hudson's work and memory is very much kept alive by the Royal Society for the Protection of Birds, of whose work he was an ardent supporter and to whom he left by far the greatest part of his estate.

5. Ford Madox Ford, *Mightier than the Sword* (London: George Allen and Unwin Ltd, 1938), p. 67.

6. Edward Garnett, Introduction to *Letters from W. H. Hudson*, p. 5.

7. W. H. Hudson to Edward Garnett, 26 February 1920, *Letters from W. H. Hudson*, p. 267.

8. W. H. Hudson to Edward Garnett, June 12 [1915], *Letters from W. H. Hudson*, p. 203.

9. R. H. Mottram, *For Some We Loved: An Intimate Portrait of Ada and John Galsworthy* (London: Hutchinson, 1956), p. 30.

10. Edward Garnett, Introduction to *Letters from W. H. Hudson*, p. 4.

11. Constance Garnett to Dr Richard Garnett, 30 August 1901 (Northwestern).

12. Joseph Conrad to Edward Garnett, Wednesday [7?] August 1901, *CLJC* (Vol. 2), p. 352.

13. William Blackwood to Joseph Conrad, 17 September 1901, *Joseph Conrad: Letters to William Blackwood and David S. Meldrum*, ed. William Blackburn (Durham, N.C.: Duke University Press, 1958), p. 134.

14. Joseph Conrad to William Blackwood, 3 August 1901, *CLJC* (Vol. 2), p. 350.

15. Dr Richard Garnett to Edward Garnett, 29 September 1901 (Northwestern).

16. Edward Garnett, 'The Contemporary Critic', *Monthly Review*, Vol. 5, December 1901, pp. 92–109, p. 97.

17. Ibid., p. 96.

18. Ibid. p. 97.

19. Ibid., p. 105.

20. Ibid., p. 108.

21. W. H. Hudson to Edward Garnett, 29 December 1901, *Letters from W. H. Hudson*, p. 21.

22. Andrew Lang, 'At the Sign of the Ship', *Longman's Magazine* XXXIX, January 1902, pp. 279–83, p. 280.
23. Edward Garnett, 'The Contemporary Critic', p. 101.
24. Lang, 'At the Sign of the Ship', p. 281.
25. Ibid., p. 282.
26. Ibid., p. 283.
27. Constance Garnett to Dr Richard Garnett, 4 October 1901 (Northwestern).
28. Virginia Woolf, diary, 18 March 1918, *The Diary of Virginia Woolf 1915–1919*, ed. Anne Olivier Bell (London: Hogarth Press, 1977), Vol. 1, p. 129.
29. Edward Garnett to Allan Monkhouse, 28 June 1912 (Rylands).
30. Anthony Powell, *To Keep the Ball Rolling: The Memoirs of Anthony Powell*, Vol. 2: *Messengers of Day* (London: Heinemann, 1978), p. 6.
31. Edward Garnett, reader's report, undated [1907?] (Berg).
32. Edward Garnett, reader's report, undated [1915] (Berg).
33. Edward Garnett, reader's report, undated [1907] (Berg).
34. Edward Garnett, reader's report, undated [1905] (Berg).
35. Edward Garnett, reader's report, 4 November 1903 (Berg).
36. Edward Garnett, reader's report, undated [1902?] (Berg).
37. Swinnerton, *Background with Chorus*, p. 128.
38. Edward Garnett, reader's report, undated [1906] (Berg).
39. 'Notes', *Times Literary Supplement*, 14 February 1902, p. 38.
40. Edward Garnett to Nellie Heath, 6 March 1902 (Northwestern).
41. Edward Garnett to May Sinclair, 16 March 1902 (Kislak Center for Special Collections, Rare Books and Manuscripts, University of Pennsylvania Libraries).
42. May Sinclair to Edward Garnett, 20 March 1902 (HRC).
43. Edward Garnett to May Sinclair, 16 March 1902 (Kislak Center, University of Pennsylvania Libraries).
44. May Sinclair to Edward Garnett, 20 March 1902 (HRC).
45. [Edward Garnett], 'Two Novels', review of George Gissing, *Veranilda* and May Sinclair, *The Divine Fire*, *Speaker*, 22 October 1904, pp. 88–9.
46. Edward Garnett to Arnold Bennett, 6 March 1902 (The King's School, Canterbury).
47. Edward Garnett, reader's report, 29 October 1902 (Berg).
48. Edward Garnett to Arnold Bennett, 26 February 1902 (The King's School, Canterbury).
49. Ibid.

50. Arnold Bennett to Edward Garnett, 10 March 1902 (HRC). When Bennett adapted *Anna of the Five Towns* for the stage in 1907 – the play was called *Cupid and Commonsense* – he did change the ending, with Willie returning from Canada, wealthy and brash and accompanied by a similarly bumptious wife.

51. [Edward Garnett], 'The Novel of the Week', review of Arnold Bennett, *The Grim Smile of the Five Towns*, *Nation*, 22 June 1907, p. 642.

52. Ibid.

53. Edward Garnett, notes on 'Suggestions for the Over Seas Library', 14 May 1898 (Berg).

54. Edward Garnett to Nellie Heath, 'Friday Night' [March 1902] (Northwestern).

55. David Garnett to John Barnes, 21 October 1976, quoted in Barnes, 'Edward Garnett and Australian Literature', *Quadrant*, June 1984, pp. 38–43.

56. Edward Garnett to Nellie Heath, 'Friday Night' [March 1902] (Northwestern).

57. Edward Garnett, 'An Appreciation', *Academy and Literature*, 8 March 1902, pp. 250–251.

58. Edward Garnett, reader's report, 29 July 1902 (Berg).

59. Edward Garnett to Nellie Heath, 'Saturday' [July or early August 1906] (Northwestern).

60. Edward Garnett, review of Barbara Baynton, *Human Toll*, *Bookman*, March 1907, pp. 264–265.

61. Edward Garnett, *The Art of Winnifred Matthews* (London: Duckworth & Co., 1902), p. 1.

62. Edward Garnett to Narney Garnett, postmarked 22 May 1900 (Northwestern).

63. Edward Garnett to Nellie Heath, 'Sunday night' [21 June 1903] (Northwestern).

64. Olive Garnett, diary, 23 June 1903.

65. Olive Garnett, diary, 24 June 1903.

66. Edward Garnett to Nellie Heath, 'Wednesday' [1903] (Northwestern).

67. Sarah Orne Jewett to Edward Garnett 13 October [1903] (HRC).

68. Edward Garnett, undated reader's report for Unwin (Berg).

69. Edward Garnett, 'Books Too Little Known: Miss Sarah Orne Jewett's Tales', *Academy*, 11 July 1903, pp. 40–41.

70. Sarah Orne Jewett to Edward Garnett, 10 March 1904 (HRC).

Chapter 10

1. David Garnett, *The Golden Echo*, pp. 64–5.
2. Constance Garnett to Edward Garnett, undated, but from the contents probably May or June 1899 (Northwestern).
3. [Edward Garnett], 'As Subtle as Life', review of Henry James, *The Awkward Age, Outlook*, 10 June 1899, p. 620.
4. Henry James to Ford Madox Ford, 9 July, 1899, quoted in George Monteiro, '"There *Is* a Figure in the Carpet": James, Hueffer and Garnett', *Nineteenth-Century Literature*, 51:2 (September 1996): pp. 225–32, p. 225.
5. Henry James, Preface to *The Awkward Age*, ed. Ronald Blythe (London: Penguin, 1987), p. 15.
6. [Edward Garnett], 'Some Significant Books of the Year', *Academy*, 6 December 1902, pp. 629–31, p. 629. Edward can be identified as the author through notes he made for the review (Northwestern).
7. Edward Garnett to Allan Monkhouse, 16 July 1918 (Rylands).
8. Edward Garnett, 'Mr Henry James's Art', review of Henry James, *The Ambassadors, Speaker*, 14 November 1903, pp. 146–7. Edward would not be alone in privately thinking James a bit of an old woman – he was referred to as 'Henrietta' by W. E. Henley and his circle.
9. [Edward Garnett], 'Russian Realism', review of Maurice Baring, *Landmarks in Russian Literature, Nation*, 2 April 1910, pp. 25–6, p. 25.
10. Edward Garnett, Preface to Ivan Turgenev, *A Desperate Character*, trans. Constance Garnett (London: Heinemann, 1899), p. viii.
11. Constance Garnett to Edward Garnett, 'Wednesday' [18 May 1904] (Northwestern).
12. Constance Garnett to Edward Garnett, May 28 [Russian dating; English dating 10 June] 1904 (Northwestern).
13. Ibid.
14. Constance Garnett to Edward Garnett, 9 July 1904 (Eton).
15. David Garnett, *The Golden Echo*, p. 78.
16. Constance Garnett to Edward Garnett, 13 July 1904 (Northwestern).
17. Edward Garnett, Introduction to *Letters from John Galsworthy*, p. 11.
18. Edward Garnett to John Galsworthy, 3 November 1902, *Letters from John Galsworthy*, p. 43.
19. Edward Garnett to John Galsworthy, 25 March 1903 (Eton).
20. Edward Garnett, reader's report, undated [19 May 1903] (Berg). (Datable from letter Garnett sent to John Galsworthy, 20 May 1903.)
21. John Galsworthy to Edward Garnett, 'Sunday' [May 1903], *Letters from John Galsworthy*, p. 50.

22. John Galsworthy to Edward Garnett, 1 February 1905, *Letters from John Galsworthy*, p. 57.

23. Edward Garnett to Nellie Heath, 'Monday' [February 1905] (Northwestern).

24. Ada Galsworthy to Frances Mottram, 29 October 1905, quoted in James Gindin, *John Galsworthy's Life and Art*, p. 145.

25. Edward Garnett to John Galsworthy, 27 May 1905, *Letters from John Galsworthy*, p. 68.

26. Ibid.

27. Edward Garnett, Introduction to *Letters from Joseph Conrad*, p. vii.

28. Edward Garnett to John Galsworthy, 7 June 1905, *Letters from John Galsworthy*, p. 81.

29. John Galsworthy to Constance Garnett, 14 June 1905, ibid., p. 87.

30. John Galsworthy to Edward Garnett, 26 June 1905, ibid., p. 92.

31. John Galsworthy to Constance Garnett, 14 June 1905, ibid., p. 87.

32. Edward Garnett to Nellie Heath, 'Monday morning' [Summer 1905] (Northwestern).

33. Edward Garnett to John Galsworthy, 12 July 1905 (Eton).

34. Edward Garnett to Nellie Heath, undated [1906/7] (Northwestern).

35. Edward Garnett to Nellie Heath, 'Tuesday, 5.30' (Northwestern).

36. H. W. Massingham to Edward Garnett, undated (HRC).

37. H. W. Massingham to Edward Garnett, undated (HRC).

38. Edward Garnett, 'Books Too Little Known – Mr C. M. Doughty's *Arabia Deserta*', *Academy*, 24 January 1903, p. 86.

39. R. B. Cunninghame Graham to Edward Garnett, 18 February 1900 (HRC).

40. C. M. Doughty to Edward Garnett, 21 December 1905, typed copy of letter (Northwestern).

41. C. M. Doughty to Edward Garnett, 8 April [1906] (Northwestern).

42. 'Mr C. M. Doughty' in Edward Garnett, *Friday Nights*, p. 120.

43. C. M. Doughty to Edward Garnett, 'Sunday' [May 1906] (Northwestern).

44. Edward Garnett to Nellie Heath, '1.30, Thursday' [12 April 1906] (Northwestern).

45. McCrimmon, *Richard Garnett*, p. 157.

46. Olive Garnett, diary, 24 April 1906.

47. Olive Garnett, diary, 25 May 1906 [misdated Friday 26th].

48. Constance Garnett to Edward Garnett, 'Friday' [1906] (Eton).

49. Edward Garnett, 'Notes on the Correspondence 1903–1906 by E.G.', 26 October 1906 (Northwestern).

50. [Edward Thomas], 'Something New', review of [Richard Garnett], *De Flagello Myrteo*, *Daily Chronicle*, 15 July 1905.

Chapter 11

1. Edward Garnett, 'Some Letters of Edward Thomas', *Athenaeum*, 16 April 1920, pp. 501–3, p. 501.
2. Ibid.
3. Edward Thomas to Gordon Bottomley, 15 March 1909, *Letters from Edward Thomas to Gordon Bottomley*, ed. R. George Thomas (London: Oxford University Press, 1968), p. 181.
4. Edward Garnett, 'Edward Thomas', *Oxford Dictionary of National Biography*.
5. Edward Garnett, 'Some Letters of Edward Thomas', p. 501.
6. Edward Garnett, 'Edward Thomas', *Dial*, 14 February 1918, pp. 135–7, p. 135.
7. Edward Garnett, 'Some Letters of Edward Thomas', p. 502
8. Edward Garnett, Introduction to Edward Thomas, *Selected Poems of Edward Thomas* (Newtown: Gregynog Press, 1927).
9. Edward Thomas to Gordon Bottomley, 17 March 1904, *Letters to Gordon Bottomley*, p. 53.
10. Edward Garnett, 'W. H. Hudson: An Appreciation', *Academy*, 21 June 1902, pp. 632–4, p. 633.
11. Edward Thomas to Gordon Bottomley, 19 September 1905, *Letters to Gordon Bottomley*, p. 94.
12. Liam O'Flaherty to Edward Garnett, [? May 1924], *The Letters of Liam O'Flaherty*, ed. A. A. Kelly (Dublin: Wolfhound Press, 1996), p.91.
13. Edward Thomas to Gordon Bottomley, 7 February 1908, *Letters to Gordon Bottomley*, p. 156.
14. Edward Thomas to Edward Garnett, 19 April 1907 (HRC).
15. Edward Garnett, 'Edward Thomas', *Dial*, p. 135.
16. Edward Thomas to Edward Garnett, 10 February 1909, 'Some Letters of Edward Thomas', p. 502.
17. Edward Thomas to Edward Garnett, 13 February 1909, ibid., p. 503.
18. W. H. Davies, *Later Days* (London: Jonathan Cape, 1925), p. 37.
19. Edward Garnett, 'Some Letters of Edward Thomas', p. 502.
20. Davies, *Later Days*, p. 49.
21. Edward Thomas to Edward Garnett, 11 February 1909, 'Some Letters of Edward Thomas', p. 503.
22. Ibid.

23. Edward Thomas to Edward Garnett, 'Friday' [March 1909], ibid., p. 503.

24. Edward Thomas to Edward Garnett, 15 August 1909, ibid., p. 503.

25. Edward Garnett, 'Edward Thomas', *Dial*, p. 137.

26. Edward Thomas to Edward Garnett, 20 May 1910 (HRC).

27. Ibid.

28. 'Ibsen and the English' (1899), *Friday Nights*, p. 71.

29. Edward Garnett to John Galsworthy, 15 May 1905 (Eton).

30. John Galsworthy to Edward Garnett, 6 January 1906, *Letters from John Galsworthy*, p. 102.

31. Barker himself may not have actually read the play. The rejection letter, which is typed but lacks Barker's signature, is dated 6 February 1906. There is, however, a further letter from Barker, written in April, in which he apologises for the delay over the play – the verdict remains the same. One of Barker's main objections is that Bue's appearance is too long delayed.

32. John Galsworthy to Edward Garnett, 22 February 1906, *Letters from John Galsworthy*, p. 109.

33. Edward Garnett, Preface to *A Censored Play: The Breaking Point* (London: Duckworth & Co., 1907), p. x.

34. G. A. Redford to Edward Garnett, 5 July 1907, quoted in 'A Letter to the Censor', ibid., pp. xii–xiii.

35. Edward Garnett to Nellie Heath, 6 August 1907 (Northwestern).

36. Edward Garnett, Appendix to 'A Society for the Defence of Intellectual Drama', *The Breaking Point*, p. xix.

37. G. A. Redford, 'Report from the Joint Select Committee of the House of Lords and the House of Commons on the Stage Plays (Censorship)', *Reports from Committees*, 1909, Vol. 3, para. 1232, quoted in Samuel Hynes, *The Edwardian Turn of Mind*, p. 222.

38. 'The Censorship of Plays', *The Times*, 29 October 1907, p. 15.

39. William Archer to Lady Mary Murray, 1 November 1907, quoted in Peter Whitebrooke, *William Archer: A Life* (London: Methuen, 1993), p. 268.

40. Joseph Conrad to Edward Garnett, [17 November 1906], *CLJC* (Vol. 3), pp, 375–80, p. 379.

41. Ibid., p. 376.

42. David Garnett in conversation with George Jefferson, 7 December 1969, reproduced in George Jefferson, *Edward Garnett and the Literature of the Twentieth Century* (unpublished PhD thesis), University of Leeds, 1974, p. 298. Hereafter cited as Jefferson thesis.

43. Henry James to Edward Garnett, 23 March 1908. This letter is pasted into a copy of *The Breaking Point* (Northwestern).

44. E. M. Forster to Edward Garnett, 28 October 1907, cited in Introduction to Edward Garnett, *The Trial of Jeanne d'Arc and Other Plays* (New York: Viking Press Inc., 1931), p. 10.

45. George Bernard Shaw to Edward Garnett, 14 March 1908 (Northwestern).

46. Leslie Haden-Guest, 'Drama: The Breaking Point', *New Age*, Vol. 2, No. 25, 18 April 1908, pp. 497–8, p. 498.

47. John Galsworthy to Edward Garnett, 10 March 1906, *Letters from John Galsworthy*, p. 114.

48. Ben Iden Payne to Edward Garnett, 4 February 1909 (Northwestern).

49. 'The Feud', *The Times*, 12 June 1909, p. 11.

50. Ibid.

51. Edward Thomas to Gordon Bottomley, 1 September 1909, *Letters to Gordon Bottomley*, p. 190.

52. Edward Garnett to R. B. Cunninghame Graham, 27 December 1911 (National Library of Scotland).

Chapter 12

1. Stephen Reynolds to Edward Garnett, 7 January 1907, *Letters of Stephen Reynolds*, ed. Harold Wright (London: Hogarth, 1923), p. 65. Reynolds is quoting from a letter he received from Edward.

2. Edward Garnett to J. B. Pinker, 4 March 1908 (Berg).

3. Stephen Reynolds to Edward Garnett, 9 October 1907 (HRC).

4. Stephen Reynolds to Edward Garnett, 27 March 1908 (HRC).

5. Quoted in Christopher Scoble, *Fisherman's Friend: A Life of Stephen Reynolds* (Tiverton: Halsgrove, 2000), p. 86.

6. Edward Garnett to J. B. Pinker, 16 July 1907 (Northwestern).

7. Edward Garnett to Nellie Heath, 'Sunday' [July 1906] (Northwestern).

8. Edward Garnett to Nellie Heath, 'Sidmouth' [September 1910] (Northwestern).

9. Stephen Reynolds to Edward Garnett, 17 September 1906, *Letters of Stephen Reynolds*, p. 32.

10. Stephen Reynolds, 'Autobiografiction', *Speaker*, 6 October 1906 pp. 28–9. Reynolds's essay forms a central component of recent critical study, see in particular Max Saunders, *Self-Impression: Life Writing, Autobiografiction and the Forms of Modern Literature* (Oxford: Oxford University Press, 2010).

11. Roy Hattersley, Introduction to Stephen Reynolds, *A Poor Man's House* (Oxford: Oxford University Press, 1982), p. viii.

12. Stephen Reynolds to Edward Garnett, 27 February 1907 (HRC).

13. Stephen Reynolds to Edward Garnett, [12 April 1907] (HRC).

14. Stephen Reynolds to Edward Garnett, 14 June 1907 (HRC).

15. Ibid.

16. Stephen Reynolds to Edward Garnett, 25 June 1907 (HRC).

17. Stephen Reynolds to Edward Garnett, 21 July 1907 (HRC).

18. Ibid.

19. Stephen Reynolds to Edward Garnett, 1 September 1908 (HRC).

20. Stephen Reynolds to Edward Garnett, 7 September 1908 (HRC).

21. Roy Hattersley, Introduction to Reynolds, *A Poor Man's House*, p. viii.

22. Stephen Reynolds to Edward Garnett, 10 April 1907 (HRC).

23. Stephen Reynolds to Edward Garnett, 12 July 1907 (HRC).

24. Edward Garnett, 'The Holy Mountain by Stephen Reynolds', enclosed with letter to J. B. Pinker, 16 July 1907 (Northwestern).

25. Stephen Reynolds to Edward Garnett, 24 July 1907 (HRC).

26. Stephen Reynolds to Edward Garnett, 2 June 1907 (HRC).

27. Ibid.

28. Sydney Pawling to Edward Garnett, 14 August 1907, quoted in Wright, p. 97.

29. Stephen Reynolds to Edward Garnett, 25 August 1907 (HRC).

30. Reynolds recounted his interview with Lane in a letter to J. B. Pinker [6 December 1907], quoted in Scoble, *Fisherman's Friend*, p. 196.

31. Edward Garnett to Nellie Heath, '5 o'clock', from the references in the letter to May Hall's illness this letter can be dated May 1909 (Northwestern).

32. Stephen Reynolds to Edward Garnett, 17 May 1909 (HRC).

33. In a letter to Edward, Ford protests that he can't help 'my Olympian manner' – a description he may well be quoting from a previous letter from Edward. Ford Madox Ford to Edward Garnett, [December 1908?] (HRC).

34. Ford Madox Ford to Edward Garnett, [?1909] (HRC).

35. Edward Garnett to Olive Garnett, 9 December 1924 (HRC).

36. Nellie Heath, notebook (Caroline White).

37. Constance Garnett to Edward Garnett, 'Sunday' [6 June 1909] (Eton).

38. Katharine Brunt interview with the author, 7 March 2008.

39. Edward Garnett to Louise Bréal, 1 December 1906 (Martin Brunt).

40. Constance Garnett to Edward Garnett, 16 August 1908 (Eton).

41. Constance Garnett to Edward Garnett, 'Tuesday' [25? August 1908] (Eton).

42. Ibid.

Chapter 13

1. Quoted in Constance Garnett to Edward Garnett, undated [January 1910] (Eton).

2. Civil List Act, 1837, c.2.

3. David Garnett, *The Golden Echo*, p. 124.

4. Ibid.

5. Constance Garnett to Edward Garnett, 'Wednesday' [5 January 1910] (Eton).

6. Constance Garnett to Edward Garnett, 'Thursday' [6 January 1910] (Eton).

7. John Galsworthy to Edward Garnett, [January 1910]. The original of this letter appears to be lost, but it is quoted in George Jefferson, *Edward Garnett: A Life in Literature* (London: Cape, 1982), pp. 167–8.

8. Constance Garnett to Edward Garnett, undated [probably 7 January 1910] (Eton).

9. Ibid.

10. David Garnett to Edward Garnett, undated [January 1910] (Northwestern).

11. Constance Garnett to Edward Garnett, 'Monday' [10 January 1910] (Eton).

12. David Garnett, *The Golden Echo*, p. 147.

13. Ibid.

14. Ibid., p. 149.

15. Constance Garnett to Edward Garnett, envelope postmarked 15 March 1910 (Eton).

16. David Garnett, *The Golden Echo*, p. 119.

17. Edward Garnett to Nellie Heath, 'London, 8 o'clock' [29 May 1910], (Northwestern).

18. Edward Garnett to Nellie Heath, 30 May 1910 (Northwestern).

19. David Garnett, *The Golden Echo*, p. 158.

20. John Galsworthy to Constance Garnett, 12 May 1910, *Letters from John Galsworthy*, p. 179.

21. John Galsworthy to Edward Garnett, 3 November 1906, ibid., p. 126.

22. Edward Garnett to John Galsworthy, 4 November, 1906, ibid., p. 127.

23. John Galsworthy, *The Country House* (London: William Heinemann, 1907), p. 295.

24. [Edward Garnett], 'The Novel of the Week', *Nation*, 2 March 1907, pp. 19–20.

25. Edward Garnett to John Galsworthy, 13 January 1910, *Letters from John Galsworthy*, p. 175.

26. Edward Garnett to Nellie Heath, 'Friday' [July? 1908] (Northwestern).

27. Edward Garnett to Nellie Heath, 'Wednesday' [July? 1908] (Northwestern).

28. Edward Garnett, Introduction to *Letters from John Galsworthy*, p. 13.

29. John Galsworthy to Edward Garnett, 14 October 1908, ibid., p. 168.

30. John Galsworthy to Edward Garnett, 24 April 1910, ibid., p. 177.

31. Edward Garnett to John Galsworthy, undated [early September 1910], H. V. Marrot, *The Life and Letters of John Galsworthy*, p. 288.

32. Ibid.

33. Ibid., p. 289.

34. Ibid.

35. John Galsworthy to Edward Garnett, undated [September 1910], *Letters from John Galsworthy*, p. 181.

36. John Galsworthy to Edward Garnett, undated [September 1910], ibid., p. 182.

37. Edward Garnett to John Galsworthy, 15 September 1910, Marrot, *The Life and Letters of John Galsworthy*, pp. 293–4.

38. Ibid., p. 294.

39. John Galsworthy to Edward Garnett, 18 September 1910, *Letters from John Galsworthy*, p. 189.

40. Ibid., p. 190.

41. Woolf does indeed imagine sharing a railway journey with Galsworthy, Bennett and Wells in another of her celebrated essays 'Mr Bennett and Mrs Brown' in which she discusses the differences between the 'Edwardian' and the 'Georgian' approaches to the drawing of character in fiction. Galsworthy falls firmly into the Edwardian camp. 'Mr Bennett and Mrs Brown' (1923) and 'Modern Fiction' (1925), the other essay in which Woolf criticises Galsworthy, are reprinted in Virginia Woolf, *Selected Essays* (Oxford: Oxford World's Classics, 2008).

42. John Galsworthy to Edward Garnett, 18 September 1910, *Letters from John Galsworthy*, pp. 191–2.

43. Edward Garnett to John Galsworthy, 21 September 1910, Marrot, *The Life and Letters of John Galsworthy*, p. 298.

44. Edward Garnett to Nellie Heath, 6 November 1910 (Northwestern).

45. Edward Garnett to John Galsworthy, 16 November 1910, Marrot, *The Life and Letters of John Galsworthy*, pp. 304–5.

46. Stephen Reynolds, 'The Commonplace', *Westminster Gazette*, 17 June 1911, quoted in Scoble, *Fisherman's Friend*, p. 402.

47. John Galsworthy to Edward Garnett, 13 November 1910, *Letters from John Galsworthy*, p. 199.

48. John Galsworthy, 'Edward Garnett: An Appreciation', review of Edward Garnett, *Tolstoy, Westminster Gazette*, 27 March 1914.

Chapter 14

1. Edward Garnett to John Galsworthy, 28 March 1914, *Letters from John Galsworthy*, p. 215.

2. Stephen Reynolds, 'The Commonplace', *Westminster Gazette*, 17 June 1911, quoted in Scoble, *Fisherman's Friend*, p. 402.

3. Ibid., p. 403.

4. John Galsworthy to Edward Garnett, 18 August 1913, *Letters from John Galsworthy*, pp. 210–11.

5. E. M. Forster, entry for 13 March 1911 in 'The Locked Diary', *The Journals and Diaries of E. M. Forster* Vol. 1, ed. Philip Gardner (London: Pickering & Chatto, 2011), p. 24. In his notes, the editor suggests Forster is talking about David Garnett, but as David was only nineteen at the time and had yet to embark upon a literary career, the Garnett in question is clearly Edward.

6. Some commentators have attributed the review of the novel in the *Spectator* to Edward; however, he didn't write for the magazine. The *Speaker* was Edward's regular reviewing platform at the time and the tone of the *Speaker* piece is distinctly Garnettian. The review appears in the edition of 28 October 1905, p. 90.

7. E. M. Forster, Notebook Journal, 22 November 1905, *The Journals and Diaries of E. M. Forster* (Vol. 1), p. 140.

8. [Edward Garnett], 'Fiction', review of E. M. Forster, *Where Angels Fear to Tread, Speaker,* 28 October 1905, p. 90.

9. E. M. Forster, 'The Man Behind the Scenes', *News Chronicle*, 30 November 1931, p. 4.

10. Edward Garnett, reader's report on E. M. Forster, 'Tales', 18 October 1905 (Berg).

11. [Edward Garnett], 'The Novel of the Week', *Nation*, 27 April 1907, pp. 357–8, p. 357.

12. E. M. Forster to Edward Garnett, 5 May 1907 (HRC).

13. Edward Garnett to Nellie Heath, 6 November 1910 (Northwestern).

14. Edward Garnett to Nellie Heath, 7 November 1910 (Northwestern).

15. [Edward Garnett], 'Villadom', *Nation*, 12 November 1910, pp. 282–4, p. 284.

16. E. M. Forster to Edward Garnett, 12 December 1910 (HRC). Forster dated the letter 12 November in error.

17. Edward Garnett, 'English Novels and English Life', *Nation* (New York), Vol. 88, No. 2281, 18 March 1909, pp. 272–5, p. 274.

18. Ibid., pp. 274–5.

19. Edward Garnett to Robert Underwood Johnson, 11 October 1911 (New York Public Library).

20. Edward Garnett to Robert Underwood Johnson, 8 November 1911 (New York Public Library).

21. Edward Garnett to Robert Underwood Johnson, 29 November 1911 (New York Public Library).

22. D. H. Lawrence to Louie Burrows, 11 September 1911, *The Letters of D. H. Lawrence*, Vol. 1, ed. James T. Boulton (Cambridge: Cambridge University Press, 1979), p. 302. All letters from D. H. Lawrence will be taken from *The Letters of D. H. Lawrence* and will be cited as *LDHL* followed by the volume number.

23. David Garnett, *Great Friends* (London: Macmillan, 1979), p. 76.

24. See D. H. Lawrence's letter to Louie Burrows of 25 September 1911 – 'Why should Garnett see us flitting, by the way – ? and he's not great, and I should certainly tell him myself that he'd have to invite me other days than Tuesdays or Wednesdays, if I were mad on seeing him.' *LDHL* (Vol. 1), p. 305.

25. D. H. Lawrence to Louie Burrows, 10 November 1911, ibid., p. 325.

26. D. H. Lawrence to Louie Burrows, 16 October 1911, ibid., p. 314.

27. Ibid., pp. 314–315.

28. D. H. Lawrence to Edward Garnett, 10 September 1911, ibid., p. 301.

29. D. H. Lawrence, 'Autobiographical sketch', *Phoenix: The Posthumous Papers of D. H. Lawrence* (1936), ed. Edward D. McDonald (London: Heinemann, 1970), pp. 593–4.

30. D. H. Lawrence to Edward Garnett, 18 December 1911, *LDHL* (Vol. 1), p. 339. Lawrence puts Hueffer's comments in quotation marks and so presumably is quoting from the letter Hueffer sent him in early September 1910, which he refers to having received in a letter to Louie Burrows of that date.

31. D. H. Lawrence to Frederick Atkinson, 11 February 1911, *LDHL* (Vol. 1), p. 229.
32. D. H. Lawrence, Preface to *Love Poems*, reprinted in *Phoenix*, p. 253.
33. D. H. Lawrence to Ernest Collings, 14 November 1912, *LDHL* (Vol. 1), p. 471.
34. Edward Garnett, Introduction to D. H. Lawrence, *A Collier's Friday Night* (London: Martin Secker, 1934), p. vii.
35. D. H. Lawrence to Louie Burrows, 16 October 1911, *LDHL* (Vol. 1), p. 315.
36. Edward Nehls (ed.), *D. H. Lawrence: A Composite Biography* (Madison: University of Wisconsin Press, 1958), Vol. 2, p. 413.
37. D. H. Lawrence to Louie Burrows, 16 October 1911, *LDHL* (Vol. 1), p. 316.
38. D. H. Lawrence to Ada Lawrence, 8 November 1911, ibid., p. 324.
39. Rolfe Scott-James, 'Edward Garnett', *Spectator*, 26 February 1937, p. 362.
40. Quoted in John Worthen, *D. H. Lawrence: The Early Years* (Cambridge: Cambridge University Press, 1991), p. 322.

Chapter 15

1. Edward Garnett, Introduction to *Letters from Joseph Conrad*, p. vi.
2. [Edward Garnett], 'Mr Conrad's New Book', review of Joseph Conrad, *Youth: A Narrative and Two Other Stories*, *Academy*, 6 December 1902, pp. 606–7.
3. [Edward Garnett], 'The Novel of the Week', review of Joseph Conrad, *The Secret Agent*, *Nation*, 28 September 1907, p. 1096.
4. Conrad to Edward Garnett, [4 October 1907], *CLJC* (Vol. 3), p. 488.
5. Conrad to Edward Garnett, 22 December 1902, *CLJC* (Vol. 2), p. 468.
6. Conrad to Edward Garnett, 8 October 1907, *CLJC* (Vol. 3), p. 492.
7. Conrad to R. B. Cunninghame Graham, 8 February 1899, *CLJC* (Vol. 2), p. 158.
8. Robert Lynd, review of Joseph Conrad, *A Set of Six*, *Daily News*, 10 August, 1908, p. 3, reprinted in *Conrad: The Critical Heritage*, ed. Norman Sherry (London: Routledge and Kegan Paul, 1973), pp. 210–11.
9. Conrad to John Galsworthy, 23 August 1908, *CLJC* (Vol. 4), p. 110.
10. Conrad to J. B. Pinker, 28? July 1908, *CLJC* (Vol. 4), p. 97.
11. Thomas Moser, 'An English Context for Conrad's Russian Characters: Sergey Stepniak and the Diary of Olive Garnett', *Journal of Modern Literature*, 11 (1984), pp. 3–44.

12. Conrad to J. B. Pinker, 7 January 1908, *CLJC* (Vol. 4), p. 14.

13. Edward Garnett's annotated copy of the novel is now in the Philadelphia Free Library. See David Leon Higdon, 'Edward Garnett's copy of *Under Western Eyes*', *Conradian*, Vol. 10 (1985), pp. 139–43.

14. Joseph Conrad, *Under Western Eyes* (London: Methuen & Co., 1911) pp. 20, 21.

15. [Edward Garnett], 'Mr Conrad's New Novel', *Nation*, 21 October 1911, pp. 141–2.

16. Conrad to Edward Garnett, 20 October 1911, *CLJC* (Vol. 4), p. 488.

17. Edward Garnett to Olive Garnett, 9 December 1924, included in Appendix G of 'A Bloomsbury Girlhood', ed. Mrs Anne Lee-Michell, (Caroline White).

18. D. H. Lawrence to Edward Garnett, 30 October 1912, *LDHL* (Vol. 1), p. 467.

19. D. H. Lawrence to Edward Garnett, 18 December 1911, ibid., p. 339.

20. D. H. Lawrence, *The Trespasser*, ed. Elizabeth Mansfield (Cambridge: Cambridge University Press, 1981), p. 35. A deleted reading is in pointed brackets and an addition is shown in parenthesis.

21. Lawrence, *The Trespasser*, p. 63.

22. D. H. Lawrence to Edward Garnett, 29 January 1912, *LDHL* (Vol. 1), p. 358.

23. Edward Garnett to Walter de la Mare, 5 June 1912 (Bodleian).

24. Rebecca West, 'Spinsters and Art', *Freewoman* (Vol. 2, No: 34), 11 July 1912, p. 147.

25. Rebecca West to Edward Garnett, undated [July 1912] (HRC).

26. Rebecca West to Edward Garnett, undated [July?] 1912 (HRC).

27. D. H. Lawrence to Helen Corke, 5 February 1912, *LDHL* (Vol. 1), p. 362.

28. Helen Corke, *In Our Infancy: An Autobiography* (Cambridge: Cambridge University Press, 1975), p. 215.

29. Worthen, *D. H. Lawrence: The Early Years*, p. 337.

30. D. H. Lawrence to Louie Burrows, 4 February 1912, *LDHL* (Vol. 1), p. 361.

31. Ada Lawrence to Louie Burrows, 16 February 1912, ibid., p. 361, n.2.

32. D. H. Lawrence to Edward Garnett, 12 February 1912, ibid., pp. 365–6.

33. Louie only read what must have been a devastating letter when it was published fifty years later. She noted the inaccuracies in the margin of her copy of Lawrence's letters. (According to her, she did *not* cry.) Worthen, *D. H. Lawrence: The Early Years*, p. 338.

34. D. H. Lawrence to Edward Garnett, 17 April 1912, *LDHL* (Vol. 1), pp. 384–5.

35. David Garnett, *The Golden Echo*, p. 243.

36. D. H. Lawrence to Edward Garnett, 23 April, 1912, *LDHL* (Vol. 1), p. 386.

37. D. H. Lawrence to Edward Garnett, 29 April 1912, ibid., p. 388.

38. D. H. Lawrence to Frieda Weekley, 2 May 1912, ibid., p. 390.

39. Edward Garnett to Natalie Ertel [Duddington], 11 March 1912 (Sebastian Garrett).

40. Ursula Cox to Constance Garnett, incomplete and undated (Eton).

41. Natalie Duddington to Augusta Tovey, 30 December 1959 (Sebastian Garrett).

42. Natalie Duddington to Augusta Tovey, 5 February 1960 (Sebastian Garrett).

43. Natalie confirmed this to her daughter much later in life.

44. Edward Garnett to Natalie Duddington, 11 August 1916 (Sebastian Garrett).

45. D. H. Lawrence to Frieda Weekley, [7 May 1912], *LDHL* (Vol. 1), p. 393.

46. D. H. Lawrence to Edward Garnett, 21 May 1912, ibid., p. 410.

47. Ben Iden Payne to Edward Garnett, 26 May 1912 (Northwestern).

48. D. H. Lawrence to Edward Garnett, 2 June 1912, *LDHL* (Vol. 1), p. 415.

49. D. H. Lawrence to Walter de la Mare, 10 June 1912, ibid., p. 417.

50. William Heinemann to D. H. Lawrence, 1 July 1912, ibid., p. 421, n.4

51. Edward Garnett to Walter de la Mare, 2 July 1912 (Bodleian).

52. Walter de la Mare to Edward Garnett, undated (HRC).

53. D. H. Lawrence to Edward Garnett, 3 July 1912, *LDHL* (Vol. 1), p. 422.

54. D. H. Lawrence to Edward Garnett, 'Thursday' [4 July 1912], ibid., p. 423.

Chapter 16

1. Introduction to D. H. Lawrence, *Sons and Lovers*, ed. Helen and Carl Baron (Cambridge: Cambridge University Press, 1992), pp. xl–xli.

2. Ibid., pp. xl–xli.

3. D. H. Lawrence to Edward Garnett, [22 July 1912], *LDHL* (Vol. 1), p. 427.

4. D. H. Lawrence to Edward Garnett, 4 August 1912, ibid., p. 429.

5. D. H. Lawrence to Edward Garnett, 13 August 1912, ibid., p. 434.

6. Constance Garnett to Edward Garnett, 9 September 1912 (Eton).

7. D. H. Lawrence to Edward Garnett, 7 September 1912, *LDHL* (Vol. 1), p. 448.

8. Lawrence, *Sons and Lovers*, explanatory note, 341:28, p. 565.

9. Introduction to Lawrence, *Sons and Lovers*, p. xli.

10. Lawrence, *Sons and Lovers*, p. 341.

11. Edward Garnett to H. E. Bates, 19 July 1926 (HRC).

12. D. H. Lawrence to Edward Garnett, 3 October 1912, *LDHL* (Vol. 1), p. 457.

13. D. H. Lawrence to Edward Garnett, 19 November 1912, ibid., p. 476.

14. Corke, *In Our Infancy*, p. 201.

15. D. H. Lawrence to Edward Garnett, 19 November 1912, *LDHL* (Vol. 1), p. 477.

16. D. H. Lawrence to Edward Garnett, [1 December 1912], ibid., p. 481.

17. Ibid.

18. Lawrence, *Sons and Lovers*, p. 320. Edward cut the thirteen lines following 'What, pray?'.

19. D. H. Lawrence to Edward Garnett, 29 December 1912, *LDHL* (Vol. 1), p. 496.

20. Edward Garnett to Walter De La Mare, 28 May 1913 (Bodleian).

21. Helen Baron, 'Some Theoretical Issues Raised by Editing *Sons and Lovers*', in *Editing D. H. Lawrence: New Versions of a Modern Author*, ed. Charles L. Ross and Dennis Jackson (Ann Arbor, Mich.: University of Michigan Press, 1995), pp. 59–77, p. 76.

22. Lawrence, *Sons and Lovers*, p. 240.

23. The variant is given in the textual apparatus and is mentioned in the explanatory notes, p. 548. It appears in versions of the novel edited by Edward Garnett.

24. D. H. Lawrence to Edward Garnett, 12 January 1913, *LDHL* (Vol. 1), p. 500.

25. D. H. Lawrence to Ernest Collings, 4 December 1912, ibid., pp. 491–2.

26. D. H. Lawrence to Edward Garnett, 18 February 1913, ibid., p. 517.

27. Nehls, *D. H. Lawrence: A Composite Biography* (Vol. 2), p. 413.

28. Heilbrun, *The Garnett Family*, p. 149, n.3.

29. John Galsworthy to Edward Garnett, 13 April 1914, *Letters from John Galsworthy*, p. 218.

30. W. H. Hudson to Edward Garnett, 2 November 1913, *Letters from W. H. Hudson*, p. 181.

31. Olive Garnett to Edward Garnett, 25 April 1933 (Northwestern).

32. D. H. Lawrence to Edward Garnett, 18 February 1913, *LDHL* (Vol. 1), pp. 516–7.

33. D. H. Lawrence to Edward Garnett, 1 February 1913, ibid., p. 511.

34. Constance Garnett to Edward Garnett, 'Monday' [23 June 1913] (Eton).

35. Constance Garnett to Edward Garnett, undated [June 1913] (Eton).

36. Edward Garnett to J. B. Pinker, 24 June 1913 (Berg).

37. Edward Garnett to J. B. Pinker, 23 July 1913 (Berg).

38. Edward Garnett to Robert Johnson, 10 January 1912 (New York Public Library). 'The Right Thing to Do' is an early version of 'Shades of Spring'.

39. Edward Thomas to Edward Garnett, 4 October 1911 (HRC).

40. Edward Thomas to Edward Garnett, 'Sunday' [October/November? 1911], *Edward Thomas Fellowship Newsletter*, No. 52 (August 2004), p. 13.

41. Edward Thomas to Edward Garnett, 2 December 1911 (HRC).

42. Edward Thomas to Edward Garnett, 13 December 1911 (HRC).

43. Edward Thomas to Edward Garnett, 25 November 1912 (HRC).

44. Edward Thomas to Edward Garnett, 6 February 1913 (HRC).

45. Edward Garnett, 'Some Letters of Edward Thomas', *Athenaeum*, 23 April, 1920, p. 534.

46. Edward Thomas, *The Happy-Go-Lucky Morgans*, in *Prose Writings: A Selected Edition* Vol. 1: *Autobiographies*, ed. Guy Cuthbertson (Oxford: Oxford University Press, 2011), p. 39.

47. W. H. Hudson to Edward Garnett, 29 December [1913], *Letters from W. H. Hudson*, p. 185.

48. Edward Thomas to Edward Garnett, 24 March 1913 (HRC).

49. Edward Garnett, 'Mr Thomas's Pilgrimage', *Manchester Guardian*, 1 June 1914, p. 4.

50. Edward Thomas to Robert Frost, 19 May 1914, quoted in Matthew Hollis, *Now All Roads Lead to France* (London: Faber & Faber 2011), p. 134.

51. Edward Thomas to Edward Garnett, undated [Summer 1914] (HRC).

52. Edward Garnett to The Committee, Royal Literary Fund, 12 February 1914 (BL).

Chapter 17

1. Constance Garnett to Edward Garnett, 9 September 1913 (Eton).
2. Ibid.
3. D. H. Lawrence to Edward Garnett, 19 May 1913, *LDHL* (Vol. 1), p. 551.
4. D. H. Lawrence to Edward Garnett, 1 February 1913, ibid., p. 509.
5. D. H. Lawrence to Edward Garnett, 2? May 1913, ibid., p. 546.
6. D. H. Lawrence to Edward Garnett, 3 March 1913, ibid., p. 522.
7. D. H. Lawrence to Edward Garnett, 30 December 1913, *LDHL* (Vol. 2), p. 132.
8. D. H. Lawrence to Edward Garnett, 6 January 1914, ibid., pp. 134–5.
9. D. H. Lawrence to Edward Garnett, 29 January 1914, ibid., p. 143.
10. Constance Garnett to David Garnett, 31 January 1914 (Eton).
11. Constance Garnett to Edward Garnett, 31 January 1914 (Eton).
12. Frieda Lawrence to Edward Garnett, March? 1914, *LDHL* (Vol. 2), p. 151.
13. D. H. Lawrence to Edward Garnett, 22 April 1914, ibid., p. 164.
14. This fragment and one from the first version of 'The Sisters' are appendices in D. H. Lawrence, *The Rainbow*, ed. Mark Kinkead-Weekes (Cambridge: Cambridge University Press, 1989), p. 479. In his biography of D. H. Lawrence, Kinkead-Weekes speculates that Edward never saw the surviving fragment; however, as he argues, much of the tone and direction of the rest of the manuscript can be gauged from what survives. See Mark Kinkead-Weekes, *D. H. Lawrence: Triumph to Exile 1912–1922* (Cambridge: Cambridge University Press, 1996), p. 110.
15. Edward Garnett, typescript of a cancelled Introduction to *Phoenix* (HRC).
16. Ibid.
17. D. H. Lawrence to Edward Garnett, 22 April 1914, *LDHL* (Vol. 2), p. 165.
18. D. H. Lawrence to Constance Garnett, 6 May 1914, ibid., p. 167.
19. D. H. Lawrence to Edward Garnett [16 May 1914], ibid., p. 174.
20. D. H. Lawrence to Edward Garnett, 5 June 1914, ibid. pp. 182–4.
21. Edward Garnett, typescript, cancelled Introduction to *Phoenix*.
22. D. H. Lawrence to Edward Garnett, 1 July 1914, *LDHL* (Vol. 2), p. 189.
23. Ibid.
24. David Garnett, *The Golden Echo*, p. 264.

25. Garnett made these comments on *The Rainbow* in his 10 December 1920 review of D. H. Lawrence, *The Lost Girl*, reprinted in *D. H. Lawrence: Critical Assessments*, p. 84.

26. D. H. Lawrence to Edward Garnett, 1 July 1914, *LDHL* (Vol. 2), p. 189.

27. D. H. Lawrence to Edward Garnett, 17 July 1914, ibid., pp. 198–9.

28. D. H. Lawrence to J. B. Pinker, 5 December 1914, ibid., p. 241.

29. 'Mr D. H. Lawrence and the Moralists' in Edward Garnett, *Friday Nights*, pp. 156–7.

30. Edward Garnett, 'D. H. Lawrence: His Posthumous Papers', review of *Phoenix*, *London Mercury*, Vol. XXXV (1936), pp. 152–60, 155–6.

31. D. H. Lawrence to David Garnett, 19 April 1915, *LDHL* (Vol. 2), p. 321.

32. Constance Garnett to Edward Garnett, 5 August 1914 (Eton).

33. Constance Garnett to Edward Garnett, 'Sunday' (Eton).

34. Constance Garnett to Edward Garnett, 'Monday' (Eton).

35. W. H. Hudson to Edward Garnett, 10 February 1915, *Letters from W. H. Hudson*, pp. 201–2.

36. Edward Garnett to Nellie Heath, 'Tuesday' (Northwestern).

37. Edward Garnett to Louise Bréal, 4 October 1914 (Martin Brunt).

38. Ibid.

39. Nellie Heath to Louise Bréal, 5 December 1914 (Martin Brunt).

40. Nellie Heath to Louise Bréal, 21 December 1914 (Martin Brunt).

41. Ibid.

42. Nellie Heath to Edward Garnett, 'Sat. morning' [23 January 1915] (Northwestern).

43. Nellie Heath to Louise Bréal, 18 January 1915 (Martin Brunt).

44. David Garnett, *The Flowers of the Forest*, p. 59.

45. Edward Garnett, Duckworth reader's report, undated (Berg).

46. Edward Garnett, Duckworth reader's report, TS, undated (Northwestern).

47. Jonathan Cape to J. B. Pinker, 26 January 1916, *Letters of James Joyce* Vol. 2, ed. Richard Ellmann (London: Faber, 1966), p. 371.

48. The handwritten report is in the Berg Collection.

49. Ezra Pound to J. B. Pinker, 30 January 1916, *Letters of James Joyce* Vol. 2, p. 372.

50. Leonard Woolf, *Beginning Again: An Autobiography of the Years 1911–1918* (London: Hogarth Press, 1964), p. 87.

51. Dorothy Richardson to Edward Garnett [Spring 1915] (HRC).

52. [Edward Garnett], 'The Tunnel', *Nation*, 8 March 1919, p. 682.

53. [Edward Garnett], 'Miriam's Chronicle', *Nation*, 31 January 1920, pp. 613–4.

54. Dorothy Richardson to Edward Garnett, 7 February 1920 (HRC).

55. Ezra Pound to J. B. Pinker, 30 January 1916, *Letters of James Joyce* Vol. 2, p. 372.

Chapter 18

1. Edward Thomas to Edward Garnett, 24 October 1914 (HRC).

2. Edward Garnett, Introduction to Edward Thomas, *Selected Poems*.

3. Edward Thomas to Edward Garnett, 13 March 1915 (HRC).

4. Edward Thomas to Edward Garnett, 17 March 1915 (HRC).

5. Edward Garnett, Introduction to Edward Thomas, *Selected Poems*.

6. Ibid.

7. Edward Thomas to Edward Garnett, 'Monday' [April 1915] (HRC). Thomas later changed 'mowed' to 'reaped'.

8. Edward Thomas, *Walter Pater: A Critical Study* (London: Martin Secker, 1913), p. 104.

9. 'Some Remarks on American and English Fiction', *Atlantic Monthly*, December 1914, pp. 747–56, reprinted in Edward Garnett, *Friday Nights*, pp. 245–71, page references taken from *Friday Nights*.

10. William Dean Howells, 'Editor's Easy Chair', *Harper's Magazine*, Vol. CXXX, April 1915, pp. 796–9.

11. Edward Thomas to Edward Garnett, 17 March 1915, quoted in Garnett's Introduction to Edward Thomas, *Selected Poems*. Thomas's remark was edited out of the letter when it was reproduced in the *Athenaeum*.

12. Quoted in Peter Davison, 'Robert Frost in *Atlantic Monthly*: The First Three Poems and One that Got Away', April 1996,www.theatlantic. com/past/unbound/poetry/frost/frostint.htm.

13. Ibid.

14. 'Robert Frost's *North of Boston*' (originally published as 'A New American Poet' in *Atlantic Monthly*, August 1915, pp. 214–21), reprinted in Edward Garnett, *Friday Nights*, pp. 221–42, p. 224.

15. Robert Frost to Edward Garnett, 12 June 1915 (HRC).

16. Sarah Teasdale to Edward Garnett, 29 October 1915 (Northwestern).

17. Edward Thomas to Edward Garnett, 'Monday', [April 1915] (HRC).

18. Edward Thomas to Edward Garnett, 20 June 1915 (HRC).

19. Edward Thomas to Edward Garnett, 24 June 1915 (HRC).

20. Edward Thomas to Edward Garnett, 25 June 1915 (HRC).

21. The punctuation in the published poem 'I built myself a house of glass' differs slightly from that in the letter, which is the version given here.

22. Edward Thomas to Edward Garnett, 4 July 1915 (HRC).

23. Constance Garnett to Natalie Duddington, 27 July 1915 (Sebastian Garrett).

24. Edward Garnett to Nellie Heath, 'Tuesday' [August 1915] (Northwestern).

25. Edward Garnett to Constance Garnett, 'Saturday' [August 1915] (Northwestern).

26. Edward Garnett to Nellie Heath, 'Saturday' [August 1915] (Northwestern).

27. Edward Garnett to Constance Garnett, 'Sunday' [August 1915] (Northwestern).

28. Edward Garnett to Constance Garnett, 5 September 1915 (Northwestern).

29. Edward Garnett to Constance Garnett, 13 and 14 October 1915 (Northwestern).

30. Edward Garnett to Constance Garnett, 27 September 1915 (Northwestern).

31. Edward Garnett, 'The Battle-Fronts on the Isonzo', *Manchester Guardian*, 10 January 1916, p. 8.

32. Edward Garnett, 'Behind the Isonzo', *Manchester Guardian*, 14 January 1916, p. 12.

33. Edward Garnett to Allan Monkhouse, 21 January 1916 (Rylands).

34. Edward Garnett to Walter de la Mare, 28 March 1919 (Bodleian).

35. John Galsworthy to Edward Garnett, 19 July 1917, *Letters from John Galsworthy*, p. 228.

36. Edward Thomas to Edward Garnett 14 December 1915 (HRC).

37. 'The Rainbow: Destruction of a Novel Ordered', *The Times*, 15 November 1915, p. 3.

38. Nellie Heath to Edward Garnett, 27 October 1915 (Northwestern).

39. John Galsworthy to Edward Garnett, 15 February 1916, *Letters from John Galsworthy*, p. 222.

40. David Garnett to Edward Garnett, 1 May [1916] (HRC).

41. Edward Garnett to Natalie Duddington, 'Saturday' [20 or 27? May 1916] (Sebastian Garrett).

42. Nellie Heath to Louise Bréal, 27 September 1916 (Martin Brunt).

43. Nellie Heath to Louise Bréal, 4 October 1916 (Martin Brunt). (This is a continuation of the letter of 27 September.)

44. Edward Thomas to Edward Garnett, 9 June 1916 (HRC).

45. Edward Thomas to Edward Garnett, 13 January 1917 (HRC).

46. Until recently, Helen Thomas's account of Edward's death – that he was killed by the concussive force of a shell exploding close by, his body unmarked – has remained unchallenged. However, Jean Moorcroft Wilson convincingly argues that the incident with the shell happened the day before Thomas's death and that letters written by officers serving with Thomas leave little doubt that he was directly hit by a shell. Jean Moorcroft Wilson: *Edward Thomas: From Adlestrop to Arras* (London: Bloomsbury, 2015), pp. 412–13.

47. Edward Garnett to Walter de la Mare, 18 April 1917 (Bodleian).

48. Robert Frost to Edward Garnett, 29 April 1917 (HRC).

49. Edward Garnett to Walter de la Mare, undated [1920] (Bodleian).

50. Edward Garnett to Walter de la Mare, 29 April [1920] (Bodleian).

51. Edward Garnett to R. B. Cunninghame Graham, 9 August 1927 (HRC).

52. Helen Thomas to Edward Garnett, undated (HRC).

53. Edward Garnett to Robert Paul Eckert, 24 November 1936 (Bodleian). The title of the published book was *Edward Thomas: A Biography and a Bibliography* (London: J. M. Dent & Sons, 1937).

Chapter 19

1. Joseph Conrad to Edward Garnett, 'Friday' [11 May 1917], *CLJC* (Vol. 6), p. 90.

2. Joseph Conrad to Edward Garnett, undated [late April 1917], ibid., pp. 78–9.

3. T. S. Eliot, 'Turgenev', *Egoist*, December 1917, p. 167.

4. W. H. Hudson to Edward Garnett, 25 November [1917], *Letters from W. H. Hudson*, p. 241.

5. 'Critical Notes on American Poets', *Atlantic Monthly*, September 1917, pp. 366–73, reprinted in Edward Garnett, *Friday Nights*, pp. 311–331, p. 322.

6. W. H. Hudson to Edward Garnett, [May 1917], *Letters from W. H. Hudson*, p. 233.

7. 'Critical Notes on American Poets' in Edward Garnett, *Friday Nights*, p. 314.

8. Joseph Conrad to Edward Garnett, 22 December 1918, *CLJC* (Vol. 6), p. 335.

9. Edward Garnett to Joseph Conrad, 13 October 1919, *A Portrait in Letters*, p. 142.

10. Edward Garnett to Joseph Conrad, 3 January 1920, ibid., p. 150.
11. Edward Garnett to Joseph Conrad, 25 September, 1919, ibid., p. 140.
12. Ibid.
13. Edward Garnett to Joseph Conrad, 4 June 1919, ibid., p. 138.
14. Edward Garnett to Joseph Conrad, 25 September, 1919, ibid., p. 140.
15. Edward Garnett to Joseph Conrad, 4 June 1914, ibid., p. 138.
16. Ibid.
17. Joseph Conrad to Edward Garnett, 24 [or 25 or 26] September 1919, *CLJC* (Vol. 6), p. 493.
18. Joseph Conrad to Edward Garnett, 4 April 1920, *CLJC* (Vol. 7), p. 69.
19. Edward Garnett to Joseph Conrad, 4 June 1919, *A Portrait in Letters*, p. 138.
20. Edward Garnett to Joseph Conrad, 13 May 1918, ibid., p. 129.
21. Ibid.
22. Edward Garnett to Natalie Duddington, 21 June 1918 (Sebastian Garrett).
23. W. H. Hudson to Edward Garnett, 2 March 1919, *Letters from W. H. Hudson*, pp. 257, 258.
24. Edward Garnett to David Garnett, 'Tuesday night' [23 May 1922] (Northwestern).
25. David Garnett to Edward Garnett, undated (HRC).
26. Jonathan Cape to Edward Garnett, 10 January 1921 (Reading).
27. Edward Garnett to Jonathan Cape, 18 January 1921 (Reading).
28. Edward Garnett quoted in Sean O'Faolain, *Vive moi! An Autobiography* (London: Rupert-Hart Davis, 1965), revised edition, ed. Julia O'Faolain (London: Sinclair-Stevenson, 1993), p. 254.
29. Nellie Heath to Louise Bréal, 23 February 1921 (Martin Brunt).
30. David Garnett, *The Flowers of the Forest*, p. 230.
31. Ibid., p. 233.
32. Edward Garnett to Jonathan Cape, 19 July 1921 (Reading).
33. Preface to Edward Garnett, *Friday Nights*.
34. 'Mr D. H. Lawrence and the Moralists' in Edward Garnett, *Friday Nights*, pp. 145–60, p. 149.
35. 'American Criticism and Fiction', ibid., p. 278.
36. 'Mr Joseph Conrad', ibid., p. 99.
37. Edward Garnett to David Garnett, 'Tuesday night' [23 May 1922] (Northwestern).
38. 'Modern Values', *Observer*, 25 June 1922, p. 4.

39. Hugh l'Anson Fausset, 'Tracts for the Times', *Times Literary Supplement*, 29 June 1922, p. 424.

40. John Middleton Murry, 'Edward Garnett', *Nation and Athenaeum*, 22 July 1922, pp. 568–9.

41. John Galsworthy, 'English View of American Letters', *New York Times*, 14 May 1922, pp. 3 and 27.

42. Edward Garnett to Walter de la Mare, 28 August 1922 (Bodleian).

43. Edward Garnett to Joseph Conrad, 21 August 1922, *A Portrait in Letters*, p. 194.

44. Edward Garnett to Walter de la Mare, 28 August 1922 (Bodleian).

Chapter 20

1. T. E. Lawrence to H. S. Ede, 30 June 1928, *The Letters of T. E. Lawrence*, ed. David Garnett (London: Cape, 1938), p. 614.

2. T. E. Lawrence to Edward Garnett, 20 November, 1928, *T. E. Lawrence: Correspondence with Edward and David Garnett* (Vol. VII of *T. E. Lawrence Letters*), ed. Jeremy and Nicole Wilson (Salisbury: Castle Hill Press, 2016), pp. 183–4. All future references to this correspondence will be cited as *TEL/Gar. Corr.*

3. T. E. Lawrence to Charlotte Shaw, 20 November 1928, *The Letters of T. E. Lawrence*, ed. Malcolm Brown (London: Dent, 1988), p. 390.

4. Edward Garnett to Benjamin Huebsch, 17 April 1936 (Jefferson thesis).

5. O'Faolain, *Vive moi!*, p. 254.

6. Olive Garnett, diary, 30 December 1893.

7. T. E. Lawrence to Edward Garnett, 23 December 1927, *TEL/Gar. Corr.* p. 114.

8. Edward Garnett to Natalie Duddington, 26 August 1922 (Sebastian Garrett).

9. Details from 'Some Notes on the Writing of the *Seven Pillars of Wisdom* by T. E. Shaw' are included in A. W. Lawrence's Preface to the book. See *Seven Pillars of Wisdom*, Subscriber's Edition (1926) (London: Penguin, 2000), p. 16.

10. Edward Garnett to Natalie Duddington, 26 August 1922 (Sebastian Garrett).

11. T. E. Lawrence to Edward Garnett, 22 August 1922, *TEL/Gar. Corr.* p. 5.

12. T. E. Lawrence to Edward Garnett, 23 August 1922, *TEL/Gar. Corr.* p. 7.

13. T. E. Lawrence to Edward Garnett, 'Monday' [21 August 1922], *TEL/ Gar. Corr.* p.4.

14. T. E. Lawrence to Edward Garnett, 26 August 1922, *TEL/Gar. Corr.* p. 9.

15. T. E. Lawrence to Edward Garnett, 7 September 1922, *TEL/Gar. Corr.* p.13.

16. Edward Garnett, 'Bibliographical note' to his abridgement of *Seven Pillars of Wisdom* (Houghton).

17. Edward Garnett to T. E. Lawrence, 9 September 1922, *TEL/Gar. Corr.* p. 15.

18. Ibid.

19. Edward Garnett to T. E. Lawrence, 16 October 1922, *TEL/Gar. Corr.* p. 20.

20. T. E. Lawrence to D. G. Hogarth, 19 October 1922, *The Letters of T. E. Lawrence*, (ed. David Garnett) p. 374.

21. Edward Garnett to T. E. Lawrence, undated [*c.* 21 November 1922], *TEL/Gar. Corr.* p. 31.

22. Edward Garnett to T. E. Lawrence, 16 October 1922, *TEL/Gar. Corr.* p. 20. The verses Garnett to refers to – 'For, Lord, I was free of all Thy flowers, but I chose the world's sad roses / And that is why my feet are torn and mine eyes are blind with sweat' – are actually from 'Impenitent Ultima' by Ernest Dowson. Eric Kennington supplied a delightful comic drawing of this incident.

23. Edward Garnett to T. E. Lawrence, undated [*c.* 21 November 1922], *TEL/Gar. Corr.* p. 32.

24. T. E. Lawrence to George Bernard Shaw, 27 December 1922, *The Letters of T. E. Lawrence*, (ed. David Garnett) p. 391.

25. T. E. Lawrence to Edward Garnett, 7 January 1923, *TEL/Gar. Corr.* p. 41.

26. Edward Garnett, 'T. E. Lawrence as Author and Critic', MS (Northwestern). Published as 'T. E. As Author and Critic' in *T. E. Lawrence by his Friends*, ed. A. W. Lawrence (1937) (London: Cape, 1954), pp. 287–293.

27. T. E. Lawrence to Jonathan Cape, 23 March 1923, *The Letters of T. E. Lawrence*, (ed. David Garnett) p. 404. Edward left the copy to his grandson Richard in his will.

28. Edward Garnett to John Middleton Murry, 20 January 1923 (Berg).

29. Jessie Conrad to Edward Garnett, 21 September 1923 (HRC).

30. Jessie Conrad to Edward Garnett, 4 December 1923 (HRC).

31. Joseph Conrad to Edward Garnett, 4 December 1923, *CLJC* (Vol. 8), p. 239.

32. Edward Garnett to Joseph Conrad, 5 December 1923, *A Portrait in Letters*, p. 227.

33. Joseph Conrad to Edward Garnett, 11 December 1923, *CLJC* (Vol. 8), p. 246.

34. Edward Garnett to Joseph Conrad, 2 December 1923, *A Portrait in Letters*, p. 225.

35. Joseph Conrad to Edward Garnett, 4 December 1923, *CLJC* (Vol. 8), p. 237.

36. Joseph Conrad, 'Stephen Crane: A Preface to Thomas Beer's *Stephen Crane*' in Joseph Conrad, *Last Essays* (London: J. M. Dent, 1926), reprinted 1963, pp. 110, 111. Beer's book is now considered highly controversial; in the late 1980s Stanley Wertheim and Paul Sorrentino, the editors of a new edition of Crane's correspondence, discovered that Beer had invented letters and events and altered the chronology of Crane's life.

37. Edward Garnett to John Galsworthy, 25 September 1923 (Lilly Library).

38. Edmund Gosse, 'Hudson's Letters', *Sunday Times*, 23 December 1923, p. 5.

39. Liam O'Flaherty to Edward Garnett, 24 December 1923, *The Letters of Liam O'Flaherty*, p. 63.

Chapter 21

1. Edward Garnett to Nellie Heath, 'Thursday' [23 August 1923] (Northwestern).

2. Edward Garnett to Nellie Heath, 'Friday, 3 o'clock' [24 August 1923] (Northwestern).

3. Liam O'Flaherty, *Shame the Devil* (1934) (Dublin: Wolfhound Press, 1981), p. 42.

4. H. E. Bates, *Edward Garnett* (London: Max Parrish, 1950), p. 47.

5. Edward Garnett to Nellie Heath, 'Friday, 3 o'clock' [24 August 1923] (Northwestern).

6. Liam O'Flaherty, autobiographical note in E. J. O'Brien (ed.), *Best Short Stories of 1926*, quoted in *The Letters of Liam O'Flaherty*, p. 8.

7. 'For the Free State: Southern Unionists' Policy; Post Office Taken Over', *The Times*, 20 January 1922, p. 12.

8. Liam O'Flaherty to Edward Garnett, 'Tuesday' [?] 26 June 1923, ibid., p. 27.

9. Liam O'Flaherty to Edward Garnett, undated [early January 1925], ibid., p. 111.

10. Liam O'Flaherty to Edward Garnett, 28 November 1923, ibid., p. 59.

11. John Middleton Murry to Edward Garnett, undated [August?] 1923 (HRC).

12. Liam O'Flaherty to Edward Garnett, undated [? April 1924], *The Letters of Liam O'Flaherty*, p. 88.

13. Edward Garnett to H. E. Bates, 26 February 1927 (HRC).

14. Liam O'Flaherty to Edward Garnett, undated [? May, 1924], *The Letters of Liam O'Flaherty*, p. 91.

15. Ibid.

16. Liam O'Flaherty to Edward Garnett, 3 April 1924, ibid., p. 81.

17. Edward Garnett, Introduction to *Letters from Joseph Conrad*, p. xxxiii.

18. Reproduced in Bates, *Edward Garnett*, p. 27.

19. R. B. Cunninghame Graham to Edward Garnett, 18 August 1924 (HRC).

20. Walter de la Mare to Edward Garnett, 12 June 1928 (HRC).

21. Edward Garnett, 'Romantic Biography', *Nation and Athenaeum*, 6 December 1924, p. 366.

22. Edward Garnett to Olive Garnett, 9 December 1924 (HRC).

23. Edward Garnett, 'Instructive and Amusing', *Weekly Westminster*, 14 February 1925, p. 473.

24. Daniel Chaucer [Ford Madox Ford], *The Simple Life Limited* (London: John Lane, 1911), p. 204.

25. Ibid., p. 206.

26. Edward Garnett to Charles Prentice, 1 May 1928 (Reading).

27. Jean Rhys to Edward Garnett, undated [1928] (Northwestern).

28. The novel appeared under the title *Postures* when it was originally published by Chatto. It was published in America as *Quartet*, the title which was later universally adopted.

29. Edward Garnett to Charles Prentice, 1 May 1928 (Reading).

30. Joseph Conrad to Edward Garnett, 26 March 1900, *CLJC* (Vol. 2), p. 257.

31. Ford Madox Ford to Edward Garnett, 5 May 1928 (Northwestern).

32. *The Historic Edward Garnett Conrad-Hudson Collection* (New York City: Catalogue of the American Art Association, Inc., 1928), p. 36.

33. Nellie Heath, notebook entry, 5 January 1960 (Caroline White).

34. Nellie Heath, notebook entry, 'Autumn 1939' [this date has been crossed out] (Caroline White).
35. Nellie Heath to Louise Bréal, 9 March 1924 (Martin Brunt).
36. Nellie Heath, notebook entry, 28 May 1955 (Caroline White).
37. Nellie Heath, notebook, 20 April [no year] (Caroline White).
38. Edward Garnett to Mrs Cyril Bruyn Andrews, 24 July 1924 (Northwestern).
39. Edward Garnett to David Garnett, 14 February 1925 (Northwestern).

Chapter 22

1. Liam O'Flaherty to Edward Garnett, 26 September 1924, *The Letters of Liam O'Flaherty*, p. 104.
2. Liam O'Flaherty to Edward Garnett, 29 January 1925, ibid., p. 113.
3. E. V. Lucas to Edward Garnett, 15 January 1925 (HRC).
4. John Galsworthy to Edward Garnett, 19 January 1925 (HRC).
5. Liam O'Flaherty to Edward Garnett, 12 February 1925, *The Letters of Liam O'Flaherty*, p. 115.
6. Liam O'Flaherty to Edward Garnett, 8 March 1925, ibid., p. 118.
7. Margaret Curtis to Violet and Theodore Powys, undated, ibid., p. 120, n.1.
8. Edward Garnett to Natalie Duddington, 'Tuesday' [2 June 1925] (Sebastian Garrett).
9. Ibid.
10. Edward Garnett to David Garnett, 25 June 1925 (Northwestern).
11. Edward Garnett to Natalie Duddington, 'Thursday' [4 June 1925] (Sebastian Garrett).
12. Liam O'Flaherty to Edward Garnett, 1 November 1926, *The Letters of Liam O'Flaherty*, p. 166.
13. T. E. Lawrence to Edward Garnett, 23 August 1923, *TEL/Gar. Corr.* p. 47.
14. T. E. Lawrence to Edward Garnett, 'Sunday' [*c.* 18 May 1924], ibid., p. 54.
15. T. E. Lawrence to Edward Garnett, 9 April 1925, ibid., p. 67.
16. T. E. Lawrence to John Buchan, 19 May 1925, *The Letters of T. E. Lawrence*, ed. David Garnett, p. 475.
17. T. E. Lawrence to Edward Garnett, 13 June 1925, *TEL/Gar. Corr.* p. 68.
18. Ibid.

19. T. E. Lawrence to Edward Garnett, 17 July 1925, ibid., p. 71.

20. T. E. Lawrence to Edward Garnett, 21 June 1925, ibid., p. 70.

21. Jonathan Cape to Edward Garnett, 2 November 1925, quoted in Michael Howard, *Jonathan Cape: Publisher* (London: Cape, 1971), p. 37.

22. Jonathan Cape to Edward Garnett, 2 November 1925, ibid., p. 37.

23. Jonathan Cape to Edward Garnett, 2 November 1925, ibid., pp. 37 and 38.

24. Quoted on Penguin USA website: www.us.penguingroup.com/static/pages/publishers/adult/viking.html.

25. Bates, *Edward Garnett*, p. 47.

26. Ibid., p. 10.

27. Evelyn Waugh, *A Little Learning: An Autobiography* (London: Chapman & Hall, 1964), p. 213.

28. 'Edward Garnett' in Henry Green, *Surviving: The Uncollected Writings of Henry Green*, ed. Matthew Yorke (1992) (London: Harvill, 1993), p. 134.

29. Ibid.

30. Ibid.

31. Edward Garnett to Henry Green, 26 December 1925 (Sebastian Yorke).

32. Edward Garnett to Henry Green, 28 March 1926 (Sebastian Yorke).

33. Henry Green to Edward Garnett, 22 November 1927 (Northwestern).

34. Edward Garnett to Henry Green, 24 November 1927 (Sebastian Yorke).

35. Edward Garnett to Henry Green, 1 December 1927 (Sebastian Yorke).

36. Eventually this was published as 'Mood' in Green, *Surviving*, pp. 28–47.

37. Green, *Surviving*, p. 257.

38. H. E. Bates to Edward Garnett, 19 March 1926 (HRC).

39. Bates, *Edward Garnett*, p. 13.

40. H. E. Bates to Edward Garnett, undated, but 1927 because Bates refers to being twenty-two years old (HRC).

41. Edward Garnett to H. E. Bates, 5 September 1927, quoted in Bates, *Edward Garnett*, p. 54.

42. Edward Garnett to H. E. Bates, 5 September 1927, ibid., pp. 57–8.

43. Ibid., p. 53.

44. Edward Garnett to H. E. Bates, 12 September 1927, ibid., pp. 60–61.

45. Edward Garnett to Naomi Mitchison, 29 June 1926 (National Library of Scotland).

46. Jonathan Cape to Edward Garnett, 21 January 1926, quoted in Jefferson, *Edward Garnett*, pp. 216–7.

47. Liam O'Flaherty to Edward Garnett, 18 January 1926, *The Letters of Liam O'Flaherty*, p. 138.

48. Liam O'Flaherty to Edward Garnett, 24 January 1926, ibid., pp. 139–40.

Chapter 23

1. Naomi Mitchison to Edward Garnett, 2 July? 1926 (Northwestern).

2. Naomi Mitchison to Edward Garnett, 12 March 1928 (Northwestern).

3. Edward Garnett to Naomi Mitchison, 27 August 1925 (National Library of Scotland).

4. Edward Garnett to Naomi Mitchison, 12 March 1928 (National Library of Scotland).

5. Edward Garnett to Naomi Mitchison, 21 March 1929 (National Library of Scotland).

6. Naomi Mitchison, *You May Well Ask: A Memoir 1920–1940* (London: Gollancz, 1979), p. 172.

7. 'Seized Novel Condemned', *The Times*, 5 March 1929, p. 13.

8. Jack Kahane, *Memoirs of a Booklegger* (London: Michael Joseph, 1939), p. 223.

9. Ibid.

10. Edward Garnett, Preface to Norah James, *Sleeveless Errand: A Novel* (Paris: Henry Babou & Jack Kahane, 1929).

11. Ibid.

12. H. E. Bates to Edward Garnett, 12 March 1929 (HRC).

13. Ibid.

14. Edward Garnett to H. E. Bates, 5 July 1928 (HRC).

15. Bates, *Edward Garnett*, p. 53.

16. Edward Garnett to H. E. Bates, 5 September 1927, reproduced in Bates, *Edward Garnett*, pp. 54–9.

17. Edward Garnett to H. E. Bates, 5 July 1928 (HRC).

18. H. E. Bates to Edward Garnett, 6 July 1928 (HRC).

19. H. E. Bates to Edward Garnett, 31 July 1928 (HRC).

20. H. E. Bates to Edward Garnett, 5 November 1928 (HRC).

21. Edward Garnett to H. E. Bates, 11 November 1928 (HRC).

22. H. E. Bates to Edward Garnett, 27 November 1928 (HRC).

23. Edward Garnett to H. E. Bates, 5 December 1928 (HRC).

24. T. E. Lawrence to Edward Garnett, 26 June 1929, *TEL/Gar. Corr.* p. 204.

25. Edward Garnett to T. E. Lawrence, 18 July 1927, ibid., pp. 87–90.
26. Ibid.
27. Ibid.
28. There were only 170 copies of the 'complete' book – Lawrence produced 32 others that were lacking some of the colour plates.
29. Lawrence to Edward Garnett, 22 September 1927, *TEL/Gar. Corr.* pp. 94–95.
30. 'Obituary – Arthur Garnett', *Gardening Illustrated*, 20 August 1927.
31. Nellie Heath to Louise Bréal, 24 August 1927 (Martin Brunt).
32. Constance Garnett to Natalie Duddington, 29 August 1927 (Northwestern).
33. Henry Williamson to Edward Garnett, 31 December 1926 (Northwestern).
34. John Galsworthy to Edward Garnett, 29 November 1926, *Letters from John Galsworthy*, p. 243.
35. Edward Garnett to H. A. Manhood, 26 July 1928 (BL).
36. Henry Williamson to Edward Garnett, 11 April 1927 (Northwestern).
37. Edward Garnett to Henry Williamson, 20 April 1927 (Special Collections, University of Exeter).
38. Edward Garnett to H. A. Manhood, 26 July 1928 (BL).
39. Edward Garnett to H. A. Manhood, 23 November 1928 (BL).
40. Henry Williamson to Edward Garnett, 11 April 1927 (Northwestern). Edward had reviewed Roy Campbell's *The Flaming Terrapin* in the *Nation* on 7 June 1924, describing Campbell's 'fresh and triumphant' poetic imagination. Edward had advised Campbell about the poem when the South African was in London.
41. Henry Williamson to Edward Garnett, 30 March 1927 (Northwestern).
42. Edward Garnett to Henry Williamson, 5 April 1927 (Special Collections, University of Exeter).
43. Edward Garnett, review of Henry Williamson, *Tarka the Otter*, *Manchester Guardian*, 6 December 1927, p. 9.
44. Edward Garnett to Arnold Bennett, 3 October 1927 (King's School, Canterbury).
45. Edward Garnett to H. A. Manhood, 26 July 1928 (BL).
46. Edward Garnett to Henry Williamson, 7 May 1928 (Special Collections, University of Exeter).
47. Edward Garnett to Henry Williamson, 10 May 1928 (Special Collections, University of Exeter).

48. Edward Garnett to Henry Williamson, 1928, p. 3 of a letter, the rest of which has been lost (Northwestern).

49. Henry Williamson to Edward Garnett, 8 May 1928 (Northwestern).

50. Ibid.

51. Henry Williamson to Jonathan Cape, undated (Northwestern).

52. Edward Garnett, review of Henry Williamson, *The Pathway, Now and Then*, undated, reproduced on Henry Williamson Society website: http://www.henrywilliamson.co.uk/bibliography/a-lifes-work/the-pathway#crit.

53. Henry Williamson to Edward Garnett, Midsummer Day 1929 (Northwestern).

54. Edward Garnett to Henry Williamson, 27 June 1929 (Special Collections, University of Exeter).

55. Henry Williamson to Edward Garnett, Midsummer Day 1929 (Northwestern).

56. Henry Williamson, *The Power of the Dead* (London: Macdonald, 1963), p. 309.

57. Edward Garnett to Henry Williamson, 30 June 1928 (Northwestern).

58. T. E. Lawrence to Hugh Trenchard, 17 March 1928, *The Letters of T. E. Lawrence*, (ed. Malcolm Brown) pp. 368–70.

59. Edward Garnett to T. E. Lawrence, 3 May 1928, *TEL/Gar. Corr.* p. 164.

60. Edward Garnett to T. E. Lawrence, 22 April 1928, ibid., p. 154.

61. Ibid.

62. Ibid.

63. T. E. Lawrence to Edward Garnett, 17 May 1928, ibid., p. 166.

64. Edward Garnett to David Garnett, 25 May 1928 (Northwestern).

65. Jeremy Wilson points out that Lawrence inscribed the inside of the front cover of the manuscript when he presented it to Edward, and that the inscription was subsequently and erroneously taken to be a dedication – a mistake that has been perpetuated in several published editions.

Chapter 24

1. Henry Green to Edward Garnett, 2 December 1927 (Northwestern).

2. Edward Garnett to Henry Green, 26 November 1928 (Sebastian Yorke).

3. Henry Green to Edward Garnett, undated (HRC).

4. Edward Garnett to Henry Green, 26 November 1928 (Sebastian Yorke).

5. Ibid.
6. Henry Green to Edward Garnett, 5 January 1929 (Northwestern).
7. Gerald Gould, review of Henry Green, *Living, Observer*, 28 April 1929, p. 8.
8. Edward Garnett to Henry Green, 7 May 1929 (Sebastian Yorke).
9. Edward Garnett to Lola Ertel, 3 April 1936 (Sebastian Garrett).
10. Henry Green, quoted in a letter from David Garnett to Mina Curtiss, 27 June 1950 (Berg).
11. David Garnett to Edward Garnett, 6 April 1926 (Northwestern).
12. David Garnett to Edward Garnett, undated [April 1925] (Northwestern).
13. Edward Garnett to David Garnett, 20 October 1926 (Northwestern).
14. Ray Garnett to Edward Garnett, 6 September 1928 (Northwestern).
15. Ray Garnett to Edward Garnett, undated [11 February?] 1929 (Northwestern).
16. Edward Garnett to H. A. Manhood, 3 March 1929 (BL).
17. Edward Garnett to H. A. Manhood, 5 March 1928 (BL).
18. Edward Garnett to H. A. Manhood, 22 March 1928 (BL).
19. H. A. Manhood to Edward Garnett, 23 March 1928 (Northwestern).
20. Edward Garnett to H. A. Manhood, 29 June 1928 (BL).
21. Edward Garnett to Arnold Bennett, 5 July 1928 (King's School, Canterbury).
22. Edward Garnett to H. A. Manhood, 20 July 1928 (BL).
23. Edward Garnett to H. A. Manhood, 26 July 1928 (BL).
24. Edward Garnett to H. A. Manhood, 29 November 1928 (BL).
25. Ibid.
26. H. A. Manhood to Edward Garnett, 'Friday', 29 November 1928 (Northwestern).
27. Edward Garnett to H. A. Manhood, 30 November 1928 (BL).
28. Edward Garnett to H. A. Manhood, 7 December 1928 (BL).
29. Edward Garnett to H. A. Manhood, 5 March 1929 (BL).
30. Edward Garnett to H. A. Manhood, 4 November 1929 (BL).
31. Edward Garnett to H. A. Manhood, [2] January 1930 (BL).
32. Edward Garnett to H. A. Manhood, 22 February 1930 (BL).
33. Edward Garnett to H. A. Manhood, 24 November 1933 (BL).
34. Edward Garnett to H. A. Manhood, 15 March 1934 (BL).
35. Edward Garnett to H. A. Manhood, April 1928 (BL).
36. D. H. Lawrence to David Garnett, 24 August 1928, *LDHL* (Vol. 6), p. 520.
37. Quoted in Heilbrun, *The Garnett Family*, p. 161.

38. Bates, *Edward Garnett*, p. 80.
39. Frieda Lawrence to Edward Garnett, undated, quoted in Heilbrun, *The Garnett Family*, p. 161.
40. Edward Garnett to Herbert Faulkner West, 13 July 1932 (Dartmouth).
41. David Garnett, *The Golden Echo*, p. 135.
42. John Galsworthy to Edward Garnett, 11 December 1929, *Letters from John Galsworthy*, p. 147.
43. Edward Garnett to Olive Garnett, 25 August 1934 (Northwestern).
44. Edward Garnett to Herbert Faulkner West, 20 August 1933 (Dartmouth).
45. Edward Garnett, Introduction to *Capajon: Fifty-four Short Stories* (London: Jonathan Cape, 1933).
46. Naomi Mitchison to Edward Garnett, undated [postmarked 11 March 1933] (HRC).
47. Edward Garnett to Naomi Mitchison, 2 April 1933 (Jefferson thesis).
48. Edward Garnett to Naomi Mitchison, 1st June 1933 (Jefferson thesis).
49. Naomi Mitchison to Edward Garnett, 'Friday' [1933] (HRC).
50. Ibid.
51. Mitchison, *You May Well Ask*, p. 176.
52. Naomi Mitchison to George Jefferson, 6 January 1972, quoted in Jefferson, *Edward Garnett*, p. 259.

Chapter 25

1. O'Faolain, *Vive moi!* (London: Sinclair-Stevenson, 1993), p. 137.
2. Liam O'Flaherty to O'Faolain, undated, quoted in Maurice Harmon, *Sean O'Faolain: A Life* (London: Constable, 1994), p. 75.
3. O'Faolain, *Vive moi!*, p. 247.
4. Sean O'Faolain to Edward Garnett, 4 February 1929 (HRC).
5. Sean O'Faolain to Edward Garnett, 2 April 1929 (HRC).
6. O'Faolain, *Vive moi!*, p. 252.
7. Sean O'Faolain to Edward Garnett, undated (HRC). The letterhead is 51 Queen's Road, the Richmond apartment O'Faolain lived in from September 1929 to June 1930.
8. Sean O'Faolain to Edward Garnett, undated (HRC). This letter is the first exchange on *The Red Petticoat*.
9. Sean O'Faolain, 'The Bombshop', *Dial* 83 (March 1927), p. 197.
10. Sean O'Faolain, 'The Bombshop' in *Midsummer Night Madness and Other Stories* (London: Jonathan Cape, 1932), p. 184.
11. Sean O'Faolain to Edward Garnett, undated [27 October 1931] (HRC).
12. O'Faolain, *Vive moi!*, p. 253.

13. Edward Garnett to Wren Howard, 24 January 1931 (Cape Archive, Reading University).

14. Sean O'Faolain to Edward Garnett, 'Saturday' (HRC).

15. Sean O'Faolain to Edward Garnett, undated (HRC).

16. Edward Garnett, typewritten draft of Foreword to *Midsummer Night Madness* (Northwestern).

17. Sean O'Faolain to Edward Garnett, undated [probably August 1931] (HRC).

18. Sean O'Faolain to Edward Garnett, 1 December 1931 (HRC).

19. Edward Garnett, Foreword to *Midsummer Night Madness*, pp. 13–14.

20. Edward Garnett to Wren Howard, July 1931 (Cape archive, University of Reading).

21. Quoted in Harmon, *Sean O'Faolain*, p. 98.

22. O'Faolain, *Vive moi!*, p. 267.

23. *Bookman* LXXXII, April–September 1932, quoted in Harmon, p. 88.

24. *New York Times*, 27 March 1932.

25. Liam O'Flaherty to Edward Garnett, 29 February 1932, *The Letters of Liam O'Flaherty*, p. 256.

26. O'Faolain, *Vive moi!*, p. 267.

27. Sean O'Faolain to Edward Garnett, 'Wednesday' (May 1933) (HRC).

28. Sean O'Faolain to Edward Garnett, undated (May 1933) (HRC).

29. Sean O'Faolain to Edward Garnett, undated (1933) (HRC).

30. Edward Garnett to T. E. Lawrence, undated [mid-August 1933], *TEL/Gar. Corr.* p. 234.

31. Edward Garnett to Jonathan Cape, 13 August 1933 (Cape archive, University of Reading).

32. O'Faolain, *Vive moi!*, p. 171.

33. Sean O'Faolain to Edward Garnett, undated (HRC).

34. O'Faolain, *Vive moi!*, p. 270.

35. Ibid., p. 252.

36. Ibid., pp. 255–6.

37. David Garnett, *The Familiar Faces*, p. 171.

38. Edward Garnett to Benjamin Huebsch, 17 April 1936, Jefferson thesis, p. 483.

39. Sean O'Faolain to Edward Garnett, undated (HRC).

40. Ibid.

41. Ibid.

42. Sean O'Faolain to Edward Garnett, undated (HRC).

43. O'Faolain, *Vive moi!*, p. 258.

44. Ibid., p. 260.

45. Edward Garnett to Benjamin Huebsch, 17 April 1936, Jefferson thesis, p. 483.

46. O'Faolain, *Vive moi!*, p. 260.

47. Harmon, *Sean O'Faolain*, p. 89.

48. Dedication to Sean O'Faolain, *A Purse of Coppers* (London: Jonathan Cape, 1937).

Chapter 26

1. T. E. Lawrence to Edward Garnett, 26 November 1934, *TEL/Gar. Corr.* p. 250.

2. Edward Garnett to Robert P. Eckert, 24 November 1936 (Bodleian).

3. Edward Garnett, 'Joseph Conrad and His Wife', *London Mercury*, August 1935, pp. 385–7.

4. Edward Garnett to Jessie Conrad, 11 July 1935, reprinted in *A Portrait in Letters*, p. 256.

5. Jessie Conrad to Edward Garnett, 14 July 1935, ibid., p. 257.

6. Edward Garnett to R. B. Cunninghame Graham, 20 August 1935 (National Library of Scotland).

7. Edward Garnett to Edward McDonald, 25 October 1935 (HRC).

8. Edward Garnett, TS Introduction to *The Last Cargo* (HRC).

9. Edward Garnett to Harold K. Guinzberg, 6 August 1935 (Jefferson thesis), p. 469.

10. Harold K. Guinzberg to Edward Garnett, 5 February 1936 (Jefferson thesis), p. 479.

11. Edward Garnett, 'D. H. Lawrence: His Posthumous Papers', *London Mercury* XXXV, pp. 152–60.

12. David Garnett to Edward Garnett, 17 May 1935 (Northwestern).

13. Edward Garnett, 'T. E. Lawrence as Author and Critic', *T. E. Lawrence by His Friends*, pp. 287–93, p. 290.

14. R. B. Cunninghame Graham to Edward Garnett, 6 March 1936 (HRC).

15. Rhoda Goodwin, 'The Geraint Goodwin–Edward Garnett Letters', (Part 1), *Anglo-Welsh Review*, 22:48 (1973), pp. 10–23.

16. Geraint Goodwin to Edward Garnett, 3 June 1935 (HRC).

17. Edward Garnett to Geraint Goodwin, 12 September 1935, 'The Goodwin–Garnett Letters', *Anglo-Welsh Review*, p. 16.

18. Geraint Goodwin to Edward Garnett, 7 November 1935 (HRC).

19. Edward Garnett to Geraint Goodwin, 2 February 1936, 'The Goodwin–Garnett Letters' Part 2, *Anglo-Welsh Review*, 22:49 (1973), pp. 119–48, p. 123.

20. Geraint Goodwin to Edward Garnett, 3 February 1936 (HRC).

21. Edward Garnett to Geraint Goodwin, 24 March 1936, 'The Goodwin–Garnett Letters', *Anglo-Welsh Review*, pp. 129–30.

22. Edward Garnett to Geraint Goodwin, 19 August 1936, ibid., p. 136.

23. Edward Garnett to Benjamin Huebsch, 5 November 1936 (Jefferson thesis), p. 488.

24. Geraint Goodwin to Edward Garnett, 1 January 1937 (HRC).

25. David Garnett to Edward Garnett, 30 January 1936 (Northwestern).

26. Edward Garnett to David Garnett, 31 January 1936 (Northwestern).

27. Edward Garnett to Baker Fairley, 30 January 1936, quoted in Jefferson, *Edward Garnett*, p. 282.

28. Edward Garnett to H. A. Manhood, 17 October 1935 (BL).

29. Quoted in Howard, *Jonathan Cape: Publisher*, p. 167.

30. Richard Garnett, *Constance Garnett: A Heroic Life*, p. 347.

31. Bates, *Edward Garnett*, p. 82.

32. Arthur Calder-Marshall to Richard Garnett, 12 January 1990 (Northwestern).

33. Richard Garnett, *Constance Garnett*, p. 347.

34. Geraint Goodwin to Constance Garnett, 12 March 1937, 'Goodwin–Garnett Letters' *Anglo-Welsh Review*, p. 148.

35. R. A. Scott-James, 'Edward Garnett', *Spectator*, 26 February 1937, p. 362.

36. Hamish Miles, 'Edward Garnett', *New Statesman and Nation*, 27 February 1937, p. 327.

37. Quoted in Jefferson, *Edward Garnett*, pp. 284–5.

38. E. M. Forster, 'The Man Behind the Scenes', *News Chronicle*, 30 November 1931, p. 4.

39. T. E. Lawrence to Edward Garnett, 26 November 1934, *TEL/Gar. Corr.* p.249.

Bibliography

Manuscript sources

Joseph Conrad, MS of *The Nigger of the 'Narcisuss'* (Rosenbach Museum & Library).

Joseph Conrad, MS of 'The Rescuer' (Ashley MSS 4787) (BL).

Constance Garnett, unpublished memoir (Northwestern).

David Garnett, 'Burst Balloons', unpublished TS (Northwestern).

David Garnett, 'Brief Memoir of Constance Garnett' (Northwestern).

Edward Garnett, Reader's Reports for T. F. Unwin (Berg).

Edward Garnett, Reader's Reports for Duckworth (Berg).

Olive Garnett, 'Anecdotes of my Father's Childhood' (Northwestern).

Olive Garnett, diary (Caroline White).

Nellie Heath, notes and notebook (Caroline White).

Anne Lee-Michell, 'A Bloomsbury Girlhood' (Caroline White).

Speedwell Massingham, memoir, 'Rosemary for Remembrance' (Northwestern).

Rayne Nickells, unpublished memoir, 'The Time is Past and Gone' (Caroline White).

Works by Edward Garnett

The Paradox Club (London: T. F. Unwin, 1888).

Light and Shadow (London: T. F. Unwin, 1889).

An Imaged World (London: Dent, 1894).

The Art of Winnifred Matthews (London: Duckworth & Co., 1902).

A Censored Play: The Breaking Point (London: Duckworth & Co., 1907).

Hogarth (London: Duckworth, 1910).

Tolstoy (London: Constable, 1914).

Turgenev: A Study, Foreword by Joseph Conrad (London: W. Collins, Sons & Co., 1917).

Papa's War and Other Satires (London: Allen & Unwin, 1919).

Friday Nights: Literary Criticisms and Appreciations (London: Cape, 1922).

The Trial of Jeanne d'Arc and Other Plays. Comprises *The Trial of Jeanne d'Arc* (1912), *The Feud* (1909), *The Breaking Point* (1907), *Lords and Masters* (1911), Foreword by John Galsworthy (New York: Viking Press, 1931).

Prefaces, forewords and works edited by Edward Garnett cited in the text

Preface to Ivan Turgenev, *A Desperate Character*, trans. Constance Garnett (London: Heinemann, 1899).

Preface to Ivan Turgenev, *The Jew and Other Stories*, trans. Constance Garnett (London: Heinemann, 1900).

Editor, *Letters from W. H. Hudson 1901–1922* (New York: E. P. Dutton & Company, 1923).

Introduction to Edward Thomas, *Selected Poems* (Newtown: Gregynog Press, 1927).

Editor, *Letters from Joseph Conrad 1895–1924* (London: Nonesuch Press, 1928).

Introduction to *Thirty Tales & Sketches* by R. B. Cunninghame Graham (London: Duckworth, 1929).

Preface to Norah James, *Sleeveless Errand: A Novel* (Paris: Henry Babou & Jack Kahane, 1929).

Introduction to R. B. Cunninghame Graham, *Mogreb-el-Acksa* (first published with Garnett's introduction 1930) (Evanston: Northwestern University Press, 1997).

Foreword to Sean O'Faolain, *Midsummer Night Madness and Other Stories* (London: Jonathan Cape, 1932).

Introduction to *Capajon: Fifty-four Short Stories* (London: Jonathan Cape, 1933).

Editor, *Letters from John Galsworthy 1900–1932* (London: Jonathan Cape, 1934).

Introduction to D. H. Lawrence, *A Collier's Friday Night* (London: Martin Secker, 1934).

Foreword to *Thirty Paintings by E. M. Heath* (London: Cape, 1935).

'Conrad's Place in English Literature', *Conrad's Prefaces to His Works*, with a biographical note on his father by David Garnett (London: Dent, 1937; reprinted New York: Haskell House, 1971).

Articles by Edward Garnett cited in the text

'Mr Stephen Crane: An Appreciation', *Academy*, 17 December 1898, pp. 483–4.

'Tolstoy and Turgenieff', *Anglo-Saxon Review* 6, September 1900, pp. 150–165.

'The Contemporary Critic', *Monthly Review*, Vol. 5, December 1901, pp. 92–109.

'W. H. Hudson: An Appreciation', *Academy*, 21 June 1902, pp. 632–4.

'Books Too Little Known – Mr C. M. Doughty's *Arabia Deserta*', Academy, 24 January 1903, pp. 86–7.

'Books Too Little Known: The Cuchullin Saga', *Academy and Literature*, 14 February 1903, pp. 156–8.

'Books Too Little Known: Miss Sarah Orne Jewett's Tales', Academy, 11 July 1903, pp. 40–41.

'Mr Henry James's Art', review of Henry James, *The Ambassadors*, *Speaker*, 14 November 1903, pp. 146–7.

Review of Barbara Boynton, *Human Toll*, *Bookman*, March 1907, pp. 264–265.

'English Novels and English Life', *Nation* (New York), Vol. 88, No. 2281, 18 March 1909, pp. 272–5.

'The Work of W. B. Yeats', *English Review*, Vol. 2, 1909, pp. 148–52.

'Mr Thomas's Pilgrimage', review of Edward Thomas, *In Pursuit of Spring*, *Manchester Guardian*, 1 June 1914, p. 4.

'A New American Poet', *Atlantic Monthly*, August 1915, pp. 214–21.

'The Battle-Fronts on the Isonzo', *Manchester Guardian*, 10 January 1916, p. 8.

'Behind the Isonzo', *Manchester Guardian*, 14 January 1916, p. 12.

'Critical Notes on American Poets', *Atlantic Monthly*, September 1917, pp. 366–73.

'Edward Thomas', *Dial*, 14 February 1918, pp. 135–7.

'Some Letters of Edward Thomas', *Athenaeum*, 16 April 1920, pp. 501–3.

Romantic Biography', review of Ford Madox Ford, *Joseph Conrad: A Personal Remembrance*, *Nation and Athenaeum*, 6 December 1924, pp. 366–8.

'Instructive and Amusing', review of Ford Madox Ford, *Joseph Conrad: A Personal Remembrance*, *Weekly Westminster*, 14 February 1925, p. 473.

'An Otter's Epic', review of Henry Williamson, *Tarka the Otter*, Manchester Guardian, 6 December 1927, p. 9.

Review of Henry Williamson, *The Pathway, Now and Then*, undated, reproduced on Henry Williamson Society website: http://www.henry-williamson.co.uk/bibliography/a-lifes-work/the-pathway#crit

'Joseph Conrad and His Wife', review of Jessie Conrad, *Joseph Conrad and His Circle*, London Mercury, August 1935, pp. 385–7.

'A New Study of Conrad', review of Edward Crankshaw, *Joseph Conrad: Some Aspects of the Art of the Novel*, London Mercury, Vol. XXXIV (1936), pp. 67–9.

'D. H. Lawrence: His Posthumous Papers', review of *Phoenix*, London Mercury, Vol. XXXV (1936), pp. 152–60.

'Thomas, Philip Edward 1878-1917', *Oxford Dictionary of National Biography 1912–1921*, ed. H. W. C. Davies and J. Weaver (Oxford: Oxford University Press, 1927).

Unsigned articles by Edward Garnett cited in the text

'The Russian Novel', review of Charles Edward Turner, *The Modern Novelists of Russia*, *Speaker*, 1 March 1890, p. 241.

'Mr Joseph Conrad', *Academy*, 15 October 1898, pp. 82–3.

'As Subtle as Life', review of Henry James, *The Awkward Age*, *Outlook*, 10 June 1899, p. 620.

'Stephen Crane', *Academy*, 9 June 1900, p. 491.

'Mr Conrad's New Book', review of Joseph Conrad, *Youth: A Narrative and Two Other Stories*, *Academy*, 6 December 1902, pp. 606–7.

'Some Significant Books of the Year', *Academy*, 6 December 1902, pp. 629–31.

'Two Novels', review of George Gissing, *Veranilda* and May Sinclair, *The Divine Fire*, *Speaker*, 22 October 1904, pp. 88–9.

'The Novel of the Week', review of John Galsworthy, *The Country House*, *Nation*, 2 March 1907, pp. 19–20.

'The Novel of the Week', review of E. M. Forster, *The Longest Journey*, *Nation*, 27 April 1907, pp. 357–8.

'The Novel of the Week', review of Arnold Bennett, *The Grim Smile of the Five Towns*, *Nation*, 22 June 1907, p. 642.

'The Novel of the Week', review of Joseph Conrad, *The Secret Agent*, *Nation*, 28 September 1907, p. 1096.

'Russian Realism', review of Maurice Baring, *Landmarks in Russian Literature*, *Nation*, 2 April 1910, pp. 25–6.

'Villadom', review of E. M. Forster, *Howards End*, *Nation*, 12 November 1910, pp. 282–4.

'Mr Conrad's New Novel', review of Joseph Conrad, *Under Western Eyes*, *Nation*, 21 October 1911, pp. 141–2.

'The Tunnel', review of Dorothy Richardson, *The Tunnel*, *Nation*, 8 March 1919, p. 682.

'Miriam's Chronicle', review of Dorothy Richardson, *Interim*, *Nation*, 31 January 1920, pp. 613–4.

Other works cited in the text

l'Anson Fausset, Hugh, 'Tracts for the Times', *Times Literary Supplement*, 29 June 1922, p. 424.

Arnold, Matthew, 'Count Leo Tolstoi', *Fortnightly Review*, December 1887, reprinted in Arnold, *Essays in Criticism*, 2nd Series (London: Macmillan, 1888).

Barnes, John, 'Edward Garnett and Australian Literature', *Quadrant*, June 1984, pp. 38–43.

Baron, Helen, 'Some Theoretical Issues Raised by Editing *Sons and Lovers*', in *Editing D. H. Lawrence: New Versions of a Modern Author*, ed. Charles L. Ross and Dennis Jackson (Ann Arbor, Mich:, University of Michigan Press, 1995), pp. 59–77.

Bates, H. E., *Catherine Foster* (1929) (London: Severn House Publishers Ltd., 1988).

Bates, H. E., *Edward Garnett* (London: Max Parrish, 1950).

Bates, H. E., *The Ripening World: A Writer's Autobiography containing The Blossoming World and The World in Ripeness* (London: Robinson Publishing, 1987).

Beer, Thomas, Introduction by Joseph Conrad, *Stephen Crane* (London: William Heinemann, 1924).

Blackburn, William (ed.), *Joseph Conrad: Letters to William Blackwood and David S. Meldrum* (Durham, N.C.: Duke University Press, 1958).

Brown, Malcolm (ed.), *The Letters of T. E. Lawrence* (London: Dent, 1988).

Boulton, James T. (ed.), *The Letters of D. H. Lawrence*, Vol. 1 (Cambridge: Cambridge University Press 1979).

Boulton, James T., Boulton, Margaret H, Lacy, Gerald M. (eds.), *The Letters of D. H. Lawrence*, Vol. 6 (Cambridge: Cambridge University Press, 1991).

Chaucer, Daniel [Ford Madox Ford]. *The Simple Life Limited* (London: John Lane, 1911).

Conrad, Jessie, *Joseph Conrad and His Circle* (London: Jarrolds, 1935).

Conrad, Joseph, *Almayer's Folly* (1895) (Cambridge: Cambridge University Press, 1994).

Conrad, Joseph, *An Outcast of the Islands* (1896) (London: Penguin, 1975).

Conrad, Joseph, *The Nigger of the 'Narcissus'* (1897) (London: Penguin, 1988).

Conrad, Joseph & Ford, Ford Madox,*The Inheritors* (1901) (Liverpool: University of Liverpool Press, 1999).

Conrad, Joseph, *Under Western Eyes* (London: Methuen & Co., 1911).

Conrad, Joseph, *The Rescue* (1920) (London: Penguin 1996).

Conrad, Joseph, *Joseph Conrad: The Informer and Other Stories*, ed. Samuel Hynes, Vol. 2 (London: William Pickering, 1992).

Conrad, Joseph, *Last Essays* (London: J. M. Dent, 1926) reprinted 1963.

Corke, Helen, *In Our Infancy: An Autobiography* (Cambridge: Cambridge University Press, 1975).

Davies, W. H., *Later Days* (London: Jonathan Cape, 1925).

Davis, Kenneth W. and Rude, Donald W., 'The Transmission of the Text of *The Nigger of the 'Narcissus'*', *Conradiana* 5:2 (1973), pp. 20–45.

Davison, Peter, 'Robert Frost in *Atlantic Monthly*: The First Three Poems and One that Got Away', April 1996, www.theatlantic.com/past/unbound/poetry/frost/frostint.htm.

Eckert, Robert Paul, *Edward Thomas: A Biography and a Bibliography* (London: J. M. Dent & Sons, 1937).

Eliot, T. S., 'Turgenev', review of Edward Garnett, *Turgenev, Egoist*, December 1917, p. 167.

Ellis, David and De Zordo, Ornella (eds.), *D. H. Lawrence: Critical Assessments* (Vol. 1), (Robertsbridge: Helm Information, 1992).

Ellmann, Richard, (ed.), *Letters of James Joyce* Vol. 2 (London: Faber, 1966).

Esdaile, Arundel, *The British Museum Library: A Short History and Survey* (London: George Allen & Unwin, 1946).

Finneran, Richard J., Mills Harper, George and Murphy, William M. (eds.), *Letters to W. B. Yeats* (London: Macmillan, 1977).

Ford, Ford Madox, *Return to Yesterday: Reminiscences 1894–1914* (1931), ed. Bill Hutchings (Manchester: Carcanet, 1999).

Ford, Ford Madox, *Thus to Revisit* (1921) (Manchester: Carcanet Press, 1999).

Ford, Ford Madox, *Mightier than the Sword* (London: George Allen and Unwin Ltd., 1938).

Ford, Ford Madox, Introduction to Joseph Conrad, *The Sisters*, ed. Urgo Mursia (Milan: Urgo Mursia & Co., 1968).

Forster, E. M., *The Journals and Diaries of E. M. Forster* Vol. 1, ed. Philip Gardner (London: Pickering & Chatto, 2011).

Forster, E. M., 'The Man Behind the Scenes', *News Chronicle*, 30 November 1931, p. 4.

Foster, Roy, *W. B. Yeats: A Life*, I: *The Apprentice Mage 1865–1914* (Oxford: Oxford University Press, 1997).

Galsworthy, John, *The Country House* (London: William Heinemann, 1907).

Galsworthy, John, 'Edward Garnett: An Appreciation', review of Edward Garnett, *Tolstoy, Westminster Gazette*, 27 March 1914.

Galsworthy, John, 'English View of American Letters', *New York Times*, 14 May, 1922, pp. 3 and 27.

Garnett, David (ed.), *The Letters of T. E. Lawrence* (London: Cape, 1938).

Garnett, David, *The Golden Echo* (1953) (London: Chatto & Windus, 1970).

Garnett David, *The Flowers of the Forest* (London: Chatto & Windus, 1955).

Garnett, David, *The Familiar Faces* (London: Chatto & Windus, 1962).

Garnett, David, *Great Friends* (London: Macmillan,1979).

Garnett, David, 'A Whole Hive of Genius', *Saturday Review of Literature*, 1 October 1932, p. 1.

Garnett, Richard, *Constance Garnett: A Heroic Life* (London: Sinclair-Stevenson, 1991).

Garrard, John (ed.), *The Russian Novel from Pushkin to Pasternak* (New Haven: Yale University Press, 1993).

Gettmann, Royal A., *A Victorian Publisher: A Study of the Bentley Papers* (Cambridge: Cambridge University Press, 1960).

Gilkes, Lillian, *Cora Crane: A Biography of Mrs Stephen Crane* (London: Neville Spearman, 1962).

Gindin, James, *John Galsworthy's Life and Art: An Alien's Fortress* (Basingstoke: Macmillan, 1987).

Glendinning, Victoria, *Elizabeth Bowen: Portrait of a Writer* (London: Weidenfeld & Nicolson, 1977).

Goodwin, Rhoda, 'The Geraint Goodwin–Edward Garnett Letters', *Anglo-Welsh Review* (1973) (Part 1), 22:48, pp. 10–23; (Part 2) 22:49, pp. 119–148.

Gould, Gerald, review of Henry Green, *Living*, *Observer*, 28 April 1929, p. 8.

Green, Henry, *Surviving: The Uncollected Writings of Henry Green* (1992), ed. Matthew Yorke (London: Harvill 1993).

Haden-Guest, Leslie, 'Drama: The Breaking Point', *New Age*, Vol. 2, No. 25, 18 April 1908, pp. 497–8.

Harmon, Maurice, *Sean O'Faolain: A Life* (London: Constable, 1994).

Heilbrun, Carolyn G., *The Garnett Family* (London: George Allen & Unwin, 1961).

Higdon, David Leon, 'Edward Garnett's copy of *Under Western Eyes*', *Conradian*, Vol. 10 (1985), pp. 139–43.

Hinde, Thomas, *Carpenter's Children: The Story of the City of London School* (London: James & James 1995).

Hollis, Matthew, *Now All Roads Lead to France: The Last Years of Edward Thomas* (London: Faber & Faber, 2011).

Hone, J., *W. B. Yeats 1865–1939* (London: Macmillan & Co., 1942).

Howard, Michael S., *Jonathan Cape: Publisher* (London: Cape, 1971).

Howells, William Dean, 'Editor's Easy Chair', *Harper's Magazine*, Vol. CXXX, April 1915, pp. 796–9.

Hynes, Samuel, *The Edwardian Turn of Mind* (1968) (London: Pimlico, 1991).

James, Henry, *The Awkward Age* (1899) (London: Penguin, 1987).

Jefferson, George, *Edward Garnett and the Literature of the Twentieth Century* (unpublished PhD thesis), University of Leeds, 1974.

Jefferson, George, *Edward Garnett: A Life in Literature* (London: Cape, 1982).

Jefferson, George, 'The Pseudonym Library', *The Private Library* (4th Series), 1:1 (Spring 1988), pp. 13–26.

Johnson, Barry C., (ed.) *Tea and Anarchy! The Bloomsbury Diary of Olive Garnett 1890–1893* (London: Bartletts Press, 1989).

Johnson, Barry C. (ed.), *Olive & Stepniak: The Bloomsbury Diary of Olive Garnett 1893–1895* (Birmingham: Bartletts Press, 1993).

Kapp, Yvonne, *Eleanor Marx* (London: Lawrence & Wishart, 1972).

Kahane, Jack, *Memoirs of a Booklegger* (London: Michael Joseph, 1939).

Karl, Frederick J., *Joseph Conrad: The Three Lives* (London: Faber, 1979).

Karl, Frederick R., Davies, Laurence, Knowles, Owen, Moore, Gene M. and Stape, J. H. (eds.), *The Collected Letters of Joseph Conrad*, Vols. 1–9 (Cambridge: Cambridge University Press, 1983–2007).

Kelly, A. A. (ed.), *The Letters of Liam O'Flaherty* (Dublin: Wolfhound Press, 1996).

Kelly, John, (ed.), *The Collected Letters of W. B. Yeats*, Vol. 1: 1865–95 (Oxford: Clarendon Press, 1985).

Kinkead-Weekes, Mark, *D. H. Lawrence: Triumph to Exile 1912–1922* (Cambridge: Cambridge University Press, 1996).

Lang, Andrew, 'At the Sign of the Ship', *Longman's Magazine* XXXIX, January 1902, pp. 279–83.

Lawrence, A. W. (ed.), *T. E. Lawrence by his Friends* (1937) (London: Cape, 1954).

Lawrence, D. H., *The Trespasser* (1912), ed. Elizabeth Mansfield (Cambridge: Cambridge University Press, 1981).

Lawrence, D. H., *Sons and Lovers* (1913), ed. Helen and Carl Baron (Cambridge: Cambridge University Press, 1992).

Lawrence, D. H., *The Prussian Officer* (1914), ed. John Worthen (Cambridge: Cambridge University Press 1983).

Lawrence, D. H., *The Rainbow* (1915), ed. Mark Kinkead-Weekes (Cambridge: Cambridge University Press, 1989).

Lawrence, T. E., *Seven Pillars of Wisdom* (The 'Oxford' Text), (2 Vols) ed. J. and N. Wilson (revised edition) (Salisbury: Castle Hill Press, 2014).

Lawrence, T. E., *Seven Pillars of Wisdom* (1926) (London: Penguin Classics, 2000).

Lawrence, T. E., *The Mint* (1955) (London: Jonathan Cape 1988).

Lynd, Robert, review of Joseph Conrad, *A Set of Six*, *Daily News*, 10 August, 1908, p. 3.

Manhood, H. A., *Gay Agony* (London: Jonathan Cape, 1930).

Marrot, H. V., *The Life and Letters of John Galsworthy* (London: Heinemann, 1935).

Maugham, Somerset, *The Partial View* (London: Heinemann, 1954).

McCrimmon, Barbara, *Richard Garnett: The Scholar as Librarian* (Chicago: American Library Association, 1989).

McDonald, Edward D., *Phoenix: The Posthumous Papers of D. H. Lawrence* (1936) (London: Heinemann, 1970).

McDonald, Peter D., *British Literary Culture and Publishing Practice 1880–1914* (Cambridge: Cambridge University Press 1997).

Middleton Murry, John, 'Edward Garnett', *Nation and Athenaeum*, 22 July 1922, pp. 568–9.

Miles, Hamish, 'Edward Garnett', *New Statesman and Nation*, 27 February 1937, p. 327.

Mitchison, Naomi, *You May Well Ask: A Memoir 1920–1940* (London: Gollancz, 1979).

Monteiro, George, '"There *Is* A Figure in the Carpet": James, Ford and Garnett', *Nineteenth-Century Literature*, 51:2 (September 1996): pp. 225–32.

Moorcroft Wilson, Jean, *Edward Thomas: From Adlestrop to Arras* (London: Bloomsbury, 2015).

Moser, Thomas C., 'An English Context for Conrad's Russian Characters: Sergey Stepniak and the Diary of Olive Garnett', *Journal of Modern Literature*, 11 (1984), pp. 3–44.

Mottram, R. H., *For Some We Loved: An Intimate Portrait of Ada and John Galsworthy* (London: Hutchinson, 1956).

Nehls, Edward, (ed.), *D. H. Lawrence: A Composite Biography* (3 vols.) (Madison: University of Wisconsin Press, 1958).

Norman, Henry (?), review of Edward Garnett, *An Imaged World*, *Daily Chronicle*, 13 July 1894, p. 8.

Norman Jeffares, A. (ed.), *In Excited Reverie: A Centenary Tribute to William Butler Yeats 1865–1939* (New York: St Martin's Press, 1965).

O'Faolain, Sean, 'The Bombshop', *Dial* 83 (March 1927).

O'Faolain, Sean, *Midsummer Night Madness and Other Stories* (1932) (London: Penguin, 1982).

O'Faolain, Sean, *A Nest of Simple Folk* (London: Jonathan Cape, 1933).

O'Faolain, Sean, *A Purse of Coppers* (London: Jonathan Cape, 1937).

O'Faolain, Sean, *Vive moi! An Autobiography*, (London: Rupert Hart-Davis, 1965), revised edition, ed. Julia O'Faolain (London: Sinclair-Stevenson, 1993).

O'Flaherty, Liam, *Shame the Devil* (1934) (Dublin: Wolfhound Press, 1981).

Pease, Margaret, *Richard Heath: 1831–1912*, privately printed booklet (Letchworth: Garden City Press, 1922).

Powell, Anthony, *To Keep the Ball Rolling: The Memoirs of Anthony Powell*, Vol. 2: *Messengers of Day* (London: Heinemann, 1978).

Ray, Martin (ed.), *Joseph Conrad: Interviews and Recollections* (Basingstoke: Macmillan, 1990).

Reynolds, Stephen, *A Poor Man's House* (1908), Introduction by Roy Hattersley (Oxford: Oxford University Press, 1982).

Reynolds, Stephen, 'Autobiografiction', *Speaker*, 6 October 1906, pp. 28–9.

Reynolds, Stephen, 'The Commonplace', *Westminster Gazette*, 17 June 1911.

Rhys, Ernest, review of Edward Garnett, *An Imaged World, Academy*, 27 October 1894, p. 325.

Saunders, Max, *Ford Madox Ford: A Dual Life*, Vol. 1: *The World before the War* (Oxford: Oxford University Press, 1996).

Saunders, Max, *Self-Impression: Life Writing, Autobiografiction and the Forms of Modern Literature* (Oxford: Oxford University Press, 2010).

Schorer, Mark, (ed.), *Sons and Lovers: A Facsimile of the Manuscript* (Berkeley: University of California Press, 1977).

Scoble, Christopher, *Fisherman's Friend: A Life of Stephen Reynolds* (Tiverton: Halsgrove, 2000).

Scott-James, Rolfe, 'Edward Garnett', *Spectator*, 26 February 1937, p. 362.

Shaw, George Bernard, 'A Word About Stepniak', *To-Morrow* 1 (January–June 1896), pp. 99–107.

Sherry, Norman (ed.), *Conrad: The Critical Heritage* (London: Routledge & Kegan Paul, 1973).

Sitwell, Osbert, *The Scarlet Tree* (London: Macmillan & Co.).

Smith, David C. (ed.), *The Correspondence of H. G. Wells* (Vol. 1) (London: Pickering & Chatto, 1998).

Stallman, R. W., *Stephen Crane* (New York: G. Brazillier, 1968).

Stallman, R. W. and Gilkes, Lillian (eds.), *Stephen Crane Letters*, (London: Peter Owen, 1960).

Stape, J. H. and Knowles, Owen (eds.), *A Portrait in Letters: Correspondence to and about Conrad, Conradian*, Vol. 19, Nos. 1 and 2, 1995.

Stephens, Winifred (ed.), *The Soul of Russia* (London: Macmillan, 1916).

St John, Christopher (ed.), *Ellen Shaw and Bernard Shaw: A Correspondence* (London: Constable & Co., 1931).

St John, John, *William Heinemann: A Century of Publishing 1890–1990* (London: Heinemann, 1990).

Sturgis, Matthew, *Walter Sickert: A Life* (London: Harper Perennial, 2005).

Swinnerton, Frank, *Background with Chorus: A Footnote to Changes in English Literary Fashion between 1901 and 1917* (London: Hutchison, 1956).

Taylor, Anne, *The People's Laird: A Life of Robert Bontine Cunninghame Graham* (Easingwold: The Tobias Press, 2005).

Thomas, Edward, *The Happy-Go-Lucky Morgans* (1913), in *Prose Writings: A Selected Edition* Vol. 1: *Autobiographies*, ed. Guy Cuthbertson (Oxford: Oxford University Press, 2011).

Thomas, Edward, *Walter Pater: A Critical Study* (London: Martin Secker, 1913).

[Thomas, Edward], 'Something New', review of [Richard Garnett], *De Flagello Myrteo, Daily Chronicle*, 15 July 1905.

Thomas, R. George (ed.), *Letters from Edward Thomas to Gordon Bottomley* (London: Oxford University Press, 1968).

[Unsigned], Review of Edward Garnett, *Light and Shadow, Athenaeum*, No. 3243 (1889), pp. 851–2.

[Unsigned], Review of Edward Garnett, *An Imaged World, New York Critic*, 8 December 1894.

[Unsigned], Review of Edward Garnett, *An Imaged World, Boston Literary World*, 29 December 1894.

Unwin, Philip, *The Publishing Unwins* (London: Heinemann, 1972).

Unwin, Stanley, *The Truth About a Publisher: An Autobiographical Record* (London: Allen & Unwin, 1960).

Wallace, W., review of Edward Garnett, *The Paradox Club, Academy* XXXIV (1888), p. 132.

Waller, Philip, *Writers, Readers and Reputations: Literary Life in Britain 1870–1918* (Oxford: Oxford University Press, 2006).

Watts, Cedric and Davies, Laurence (eds.), *Cunninghame Graham: A Critical Biography* (Cambridge: Cambridge University Press, 1979).

Watts, Cedric, 'Edward Garnett's Influence on Conrad', *Conradian* 21:2 (1996), pp. 70–91.

Waugh, Evelyn, *A Little Learning: An Autobiography* (London: Chapman & Hall, 1964).

West, Rebecca, 'Spinsters and Art', *Freewoman* (Vol. 2, No. 34), 11 July 1912, p. 147.

Whitebrooke, Peter, *William Archer: A Life* (London: Methuen, 1993).

Willey, Todd G., 'The Conquest of the Commodore: Conrad's Rigging of "The Nigger" for the Henley Regatta', *Conradiana* 17:3, 1985, pp. 163–82.

Williamson, Henry, *The Power of the Dead* (London: Macdonald, 1963).

Wilson, Jeremy and Wilson, Nicole, *T. E. Lawrence: Correspondence with Edward and David Garnett* (T. E. Lawrence *Letters*, Volume VII) (Salisbury, Castle Hill Press, 2016).

Woolf, Leonard, *Beginning Again: An Autobiography of the Years 1911–1918* (London: Hogarth Press, 1964).

Woolf, Virginia, *The Diary of Virginia Woolf 1915–1919*, ed. Anne Olivier Bell (London: Hogarth Press, 1977).

Woolf, Virginia, *Selected Essays* (Oxford: Oxford World's Classics, 2008).

Worthen, John, *D. H. Lawrence: The Early Years* (Cambridge: Cambridge University Press, 1991).

Wright, Harold (ed.), *Letters of Stephen Reynolds* (London: Hogarth, 1923).

[Yeats, W. B.], review of Edward Garnett, *An Imaged World*, *Speaker*, 8 September 1894, pp. 273–4.

Zytaruk, George J. and Boulton, James T. (eds.), *The Letters of D. H. Lawrence*, Vol. 2 (Cambridge: Cambridge University Press, 1981).

Index